BURYING CAESAR

BURYING CAESAR

CHURCHILL, CHAMBERLAIN AND THE
BATTLE FOR THE TORY PARTY

GRAHAM STEWART

$40.00 hc

1/2001

The Overlook

Press

First published in Great Britain in 1999
by Weidenfeld & Nicolson

© 1999 Graham Stewart

A CIP catalogue record for this book is available from the British Library.

ISBN 0 297 81831 7

Typeset by Deltatype Ltd, Birkenhead, Merseyside

Printed and bound in Great Britain by
Butler & Tanner Ltd, Frome and London

Weidenfeld & Nicolson
The Orion Publishing Group Ltd
Orion House
5 Upper Saint Martin's Lane
London, WC2H 9EA

For my Mother and Father

CONTENTS

ACKNOWLEDGEMENTS

We usually read about <u>history in the 1930s</u> either from the perspective of the '<u>appeasers</u>' in government, or the '<u>anti-appeasers</u>' excluded from it. Writing a book about Churchill *and* Chamberlain therefore provides something much more rare, the opportunity to view the events and unenviable choices of that decade from both sides of the debate.

<u>Primary sources</u> are the foundation of this book. I would like to thank the staff and archivists of Churchill College, Cambridge, the Bodleian Library, Oxford and the university libraries of Birmingham and Cambridge. Extracts from Churchill's papers are reproduced with the permission of Curtis Brown Ltd, London, on behalf of the Estate of Sir Winston S. Churchill (copyright Winston S. Churchill). The archives of Sir Austen and Neville Chamberlain are quoted with the permission of the Special Collections department of the University of Birmingham and Cabinet Papers with the permission of Crown copyright. I should also like to thank the Amery Estate and Lord Kelvedon for allowing me to quote from the diaries of Leo Amery and Sir Henry Channon.

I have greatly benefited from the <u>published work</u> of a number of distinguished historians whose contributions have influenced me, especially Paul Addison, John Charmley, Maurice Cowling, David Dilks, Sir Robert Rhodes James, Alastair Parker and, of course, Sir Martin Gilbert. I should like to thank Lord Blake for his kind assistance and Lord Deedes for his illuminating recollections. I owe a particular debt to <u>Peter Clarke</u> who first suggested that I should take a look at the Churchill archives. As the supervisor of my <u>doctoral thesis</u> he helped to guide me through four formative years at Cambridge. Since moving to Kent, my 'mentor' has been the Rt. Hon. Alan Clark. He has provided much trenchant political insight and a quite extraordinary amount of hospitality. Many friends deserve to be cited, but Jean-Marc Ciancimino and Simon Cave stand out for their generosity and unfailing sense of humour. Simon kindly read through the text in its entirety, enhancing it considerably.

Amongst those directly responsible for ensuring that this book has seen the light of day, I would like to thank Andrew Roberts for first suggesting that it was publishable and my agent, Georgina Capel, whose infectious enthusiasm ensured that this prophecy came to pass. Alexandra Ranson and Celia Levitt made countless improvements to the text. For his continual support and advice I must especially thank my editor, Toby Mundy.

This book is dedicated to my parents. Their love and encouragement have been the bedrock of my life.

GRAHAM STEWART
Saltwood, Kent
March 1999

INTRODUCTION

I

How do politicians attain what they most desire – power? They are expected to attack the policies of their opponents, but surpassing rivals in their own party can prove no less a battle. Cabinet ministers nearing the top of the 'greasy pole' may find themselves forced to defend their position by tactics very different to those deployed by ambitious backbenchers outside the party leader's noose of patronage. The careers of Neville Chamberlain and Winston Churchill during the 1930s illustrate how two politicians at opposite ends of the same political pole responded to this challenge at a particularly vital moment in history.

'I come to bury Caesar, not to praise him,' Mark Antony famously declares in Shakespeare's great drama about the conflicts of duty and ambition. More than half a century after Churchill's confrontation with Chamberlain, historians have still not been able to agree on the wording of either politician's epitaph. Reputations are a matter of interpretation. Both men have been served by fine biographers as well as by hagiographers and iconoclasts with an interest in the dark art of grave defacement. This book is not a work of straight biography. Rather, its task is to seek a better understanding of both Churchill and Chamberlain in relation to their political environment. In studying the campaigns and compromises at the heart of their struggle, we gain a picture which resembles Rab Butler's description of politics as the 'art of the possible'. Acknowledging the constraints of 'time and chance' is to accept the reality that there is no such thing as absolute power.

In his book, *The Impact of Labour*, the historian Maurice Cowling writes about the study of 'high politics': 'it is necessary to understand the details of political manoeuvre in order to highlight the relationship between situational necessity and the intentions of politicians. In this respect one has to convey the involvement in the compulsions and uncertainties of the system which was characteristic of the whole of a politician's public life.' According to this view, biography only conveys one aspect of a politician's life and work. It can give the impression that connections between different situations are simpler than is actually the case. Cowling has argued that far from being linear:

> The system was a circular relationship: a shift in one element changed the position of all others in relation to the rest. The reactions of politicians were developed in full awareness of the relationship and in conscious knowledge of the need to move whenever it moved. Without understanding the perpetual nature of these motions, one can convey neither the powerlessness nor the impact of individual politicians nor understand the extent to which they were moved by antipathy towards their rivals.[1]

Put another way, understanding a political career purely through biography is like watching the actions of a footballer without following the simultaneous movements of the other players on the pitch.

Players, of course, move not only in relation to one another but in anticipation of where the ball is likely to land next. Exponents of 'chaos theory' have tried to suggest the limitations inherent in viewing events as a series of linear connections. Whether we study the international money markets, the weather or the daily vicissitudes of life, the frequency with which unforeseen events throw expectations suddenly off course is all too clear. In this respect, politics is no exception. The machinery of government is intended to ensure that the policy initiative stays with the Cabinet. However circumstance may dictate otherwise. Reaction to a particular event is not necessarily in keeping with adherence to a general principle. One badly handled incident can threaten the complete reversal of grand strategy itself. Governments are sometimes better at defeating long and persistent campaigns of criticism (which they can see coming and plan against) than dealing with abrupt convulsions which catch them off guard. Cabinet ministers in the 1930s faced difficulties stemming from the unexpected consequences of particular events such as the world financial crash and suspension of the gold standard in 1931, the controversies over the Unemployment Assistance Boards and the Hoare–Laval Pact of 1935, the National Defence Contribution of 1937 and, most importantly of all, Hitler's behaviour from 1938 onwards. The German *Führer*'s failure to react in the rational manner expected of him by Chamberlain ensured that many MPs who had always agreed with the intellectual case for appeasement and who had expressed no previous wish to 'die for Danzig' found themselves barracking their leader to issue and then honour Britain's guarantee to Poland.

Such unpredictable behaviour undermines the case for the historical determinism that has plagued our understanding of the period. To return to the footballing metaphor, a side that has for a long period enjoyed a territorial advantage is often tempted to over-concentrate its players in an attack for what the run of play suggests will be an imminent goal. Such confidence can soon come crashing down when the bounce of the casually mis-hit ball presents the beleaguered opposition with an open field in which to charge to the other end and boot the ball into a virtually undefended goal. Politicians, like football player–managers, try to work out a strategy for keeping possession of the ball and scoring as many times as possible, but no tactic can take account of the unexpected bounce and the lucky break.

II

This book examines politics in the 1930s when Britain was led by a coalition government in which the Conservative Party was the dominant force. For the coalition to survive, the exercise of power necessitated the pursuit of policies that were acceptable not only to the minority partners in the alliance but also to the Tory majority as well. The compromises that this involved suited Ramsay MacDonald and Stanley Baldwin who, as political moderates, were not naturally at one with the more partisan elements within their respective parties. One of the themes recurring through much of this study is the ability of the leadership to circumvent criticism within the party by appealing to the bipartisan advantages of coalition rather than of sectional party government. Baldwin had to lay his political life on the line to defend his cross-party pact against those who felt that the Conservative Party was not making enough of the whip-hand it held over a coalition that could not survive without it. As we shall see, some Tories felt that the party might even be better served without the excess baggage of a 'National' coalition at all. Until 1935, this debate was at the centre of the conflict within government and the Tory Party over the fate of free trade and reform of the Indian Raj.

By the time Neville Chamberlain became Prime Minister in May 1937, successful leadership was beginning to require a different balancing act. The distinctive nature of the minority coalition parties within the 'National' coalition had been largely submerged into a greater Conservative hegemony. This, together with the demands for rearmament and debate over appeasement, shifted Chamberlain's attention from maintaining the harmony of the groups included within the government to dealing with the hostile attacks of those outside it. When in 1939, events blew to pieces the assumptions upon which he had acted, his own position was at last threatened. The following year the parliamentary minority (on both sides of the Commons) opposing him became too large to sustain his claim to political legitimacy during a time of consolidated national endeavour. Ironically, it was a previous sceptic of the 'National

Government' and its works, Winston Churchill, who became the chief beneficiary of its logic.

This book sets itself the task of comparing two different approaches by two different men seeking to be Prime Minister. Perhaps inevitably, given Churchill's extraordinary personality, Chamberlain is the shaded background against which Churchill dazzles. Nonetheless, the attempt has been made to do justice to both. For most of the 1930s, they pursued their ambition without personal rancour. Churchill did not mount a sustained attack upon Chamberlain or his policies until 1938. Whilst Chamberlain disagreed with Churchill's revolt over India from 1929 until 1935, he played relatively little part in countering the campaign. Churchill's crusade for rearmament rarely singled out as the prime culprit the Chancellor of the Exchequer from 1931 to 1937, Chamberlain, despite the role of the Treasury in resisting large increases in defence expenditure. Furthermore, whilst rejecting what he saw as Churchill's alarmism, Chamberlain shared his favouritism towards the RAF over the other armed services in rearmament priorities.

What follows is a study in ambition and power. It has been written as two separate but related books bound together in one volume. The first book is as much about the politics of the early 1930s as it is a study of Churchill and Chamberlain. It deals primarily with the issues in domestic politics created by economic crisis and it analyses how the subsequent political settlement proved strong enough to resist Churchill's assaults on the issue of Indian reform. Having established the framework in which the political debate took place, the second book follows the current of a flowing stream, taking the reader through the desperate events that drifted the country from peace, across the rocks and into the rapids of total war. It is in this period that Churchill and Chamberlain fought each other on the issue of appeasement. It is a well-known story, but its complexities continue to entice research and sharply contrasting interpretation. Although the style and pace in these two books is different, one is intended to reinforce the other. In doing so, the aim is to further our understanding of the drift towards war, with a depth unavailable to conventional studies that focus more narrowly on foreign policy and appeasement.

It may be helpful to provide a brief route-map to what follows. Chapter 1 discusses the legacy bequeathed to Churchill and Chamberlain by their two famous fathers, both of whom had set out to dominate the politics of late Victorian Britain. It shows how the period was marked by the retention of power by the parliamentary party over its constituency footsoldiers. Yet it also recounts the salutary tale of how the Conservative Party leader, Neville Chamberlain's brother Austen, could be forced out by his fellow MPs for persisting with a coalition government in which most of his own parliamentary party had lost confidence. This event, the Carlton Club meeting of 1922, was to inspire and haunt Tory politicians in the 1930s. Chapters 2 and 3 chronicle the internecine warfare that broke out in the Conservative Party after it fell from power in 1929 and the extraordinary crisis that returned it to office with a seemingly invincible majority only two years later. This was the period in which Churchill's prospects of slipping effortlessly into the party leadership were dashed and Chamberlain emerged as the most likely successor to Stanley Baldwin. Chapter 4 examines Chamberlain's record at the Treasury during the lean years of the early thirties. The next three chapters look at how Churchill tried to break the decision-making power of the Cabinet by a concerted campaign from the backbenches, first on the issue of India and subsequently in his campaign for air rearmament. It is here that the balance of power within the Conservative Party is weighed and some historically 'revisionist' contentions made both about the India rebellion and its unforeseen contribution towards encouraging rearmament – the subject of Chapter 8. Book Two examines how the darkening picture in Europe shaped the destiny of Churchill and Chamberlain. Chapters 9 and 10 demonstrate the fracture within the Conservative Party over ditching 'collective security' as a policy and take a fresh look at Churchill's machinations over the abdication crisis. Chapter 11 follows Chamberlain from his arrival at 10 Downing Street to his triumphant return from Munich. Chapter 12 examines Churchill's revolt against appeasement and Chapter 13 takes the story to the outbreak of war on 3 September 1939. The final chapter assesses how well Churchill and Chamberlain worked together in the War Cabinet, ending with Churchill's call to the Palace. The epilogue examines their subsequent relationship, ties together the themes of the book and leaves the scene at Westminster Abbey, with the interment of Chamberlain's ashes amidst the ruins of his life's work.

BOOK ONE

One

ANCESTRAL VOICES:
1880–1929

I

Westminster rises from the banks of the Thames, a palace housing no enduring dynasty. The Nehru/Gandhi family in India, the Bhuttos in Pakistan and the Kennedys in the United States have not found an equivalent in Britain's post-war politics. This is surprising. Even in the last decade of the twentieth century, there have been several MPs whose fathers or grandfathers had sat in the House of Commons before them. A few could trace family involvement back into the seventeenth or eighteenth centuries. Meanwhile, the endurance of the House of Lords in the fifty years since the Second World War guaranteed the continuing involvement of the hereditary peerage in the legislative process. Between 1994–97 the Conservative peers were led by Viscount Cranborne, the fourth generation of the Cecil family to have done so in the twentieth century alone; a family that had been holding the highest offices of state since the reign of the first Elizabeth. But these facts should not distract us from two fundamental truths: not since a Cecil in 1903 – Lord Salisbury – has Britain's Prime Minister sat in the Lords; and not since the 1950s have two successive generations of the same family held one of the four highest offices whilst sitting in the Commons.[1]

For some, inheritance has cast a long shadow. At a time in the 1990s when the Italian politician, Alessandra Mussolini, sought to capitalize upon being the granddaughter of Il Duce, the career of Winston Churchill (junior) was quietly drawing to its close, virtually unnoticed, on the green leather backbenches of the Commons chamber. Neither he nor his father Randolph (junior) before him had risen far in the profession indelibly associated with their surname. It was a name not borne by those members of the family who proved more successful.[2]

This picture hangs in stark contrast to the scene framed by the advent of mass democracy and the intrusion of total war. Between 1886 and 1940, two Churchills and three Chamberlains attempted to serve their country as Prime Minister, two of them eventually achieving the feat. On the way, four of them served as Chancellor of the Exchequer and three of them were to be leaders of the Conservative Party. One picked up a Nobel Prize for Peace, and another a Nobel Prize for Literature.[3] One of them remains a source of intense historical and political controversy, whereas another has been hailed as the man of the century. British politics in the last quarter of the nineteenth century and the first half of the twentieth were fundamentally shaped by the rival dynasties of the Churchill and Chamberlain families, in a way that has had no equal in Britain since the war.

It was during the early 1880s that the Churchill and Chamberlain clans became unmistakable features on the political landscape of Westminster. Lord Randolph Churchill was emerging as the brilliant *enfant terrible* of a Conservative Party demoralized both by electoral defeat and the death of its great counter-tenor, Benjamin Disraeli, Earl of Beaconsfield. Meanwhile, William Ewart Gladstone's leadership of the Liberal Party appeared to be threatened by Joseph Chamberlain, a radical Birmingham MP. Both challengers saw their chance to be Prime Minister. Neither lived long enough to see their respective sons achieve the office in their place. Politics in the age of Lord Randolph Churchill and Joseph Chamberlain were shaped by the triumph of the party leadership over its extra-parliamentary caucus and by the process in which groups of Liberals detached themselves from their traditional moorings in order to broaden the national basis of the Conservative Party and widen its appeal accordingly. Tactical and strategic lessons were to be learned from this process as from the rise and fall of the fathers of Winston Churchill and Neville Chamberlain. Which son learned or ignored which lesson from the politics of his father's career helped to determine the course of the 1930s.

II

Lord Randolph Churchill was the third son of the Duke of Marlborough. Joseph Chamberlain was a Midlands screw manufacturer whose nonconformist father had started out in the former family business of making boots. Yet if the Chamberlains lacked the Establishment background and connections of Lord Randolph, the Churchills had done their utmost to imprison themselves in a gilded cage. A tendency towards disreputable behaviour had condemned serveral Churchills to the fate that can befall those who consort within too narrow an elite – ostracism when events take a turn for the worse. Lord Randolph spectacularly gave a helping hand to the process in 1876 when, in order to cover for his brother who had compromised Lady Aylesford, he appeared prepared to expose the Prince of Wales's adultery with her as well. It was less than surprising that the Conservative leadership, and Lord Salisbury in particular, retained serious misgivings about the erratic Churchills. These reservations were matched by those of Liberal grandees towards the upstart in their own ranks, Joseph Chamberlain. Faced with this blockade of suspicion, both Lord Randolph and 'Radical Joe' explored unorthodox routes to attain power in their parties. In doing so, they pursued similar strategies.

The Reform Acts of 1867 and 1884 had greatly increased the size of the electorate, transforming Britain into a mass – if not yet universal – male democracy. This had impressed upon the Liberal and Conservative parties the need to organize a proper framework of constituency associations dedicated to coordinating and stimulating support from the new voters. The problem for any master who becomes over-dependent on his servant is that the latter will realize the fact. Consequently, parliamentarians feared the possibility of the new constituency associations attempting to flex their muscles. Particularly worrying in this respect was the prospect that the party workers might seek to challenge the prerogative of the party leadership to determine policy. A development of this kind would inevitably be unwelcome to constitutionalists nurtured on the tradition most famously articulated by Edmund Burke that a politician was a representative, responsible to his constituents for exercising his own considered diagnosis rather than being merely his constituents' delegatory mouthpiece. Politics in Burke's time had been characterized by shifting factions. By the late nineteenth century the profession had solidified into a more rigid party system in which the executive leadership sought to monopolise the exercise of good judgement. The leadership were united in seeking to prevent their respective constituency associations – the caucus – from dictating their priorities. The arrival in the government of Joseph Chamberlain, champion of caucus involvement, brought the matter to a head.

Forming his second Liberal administration in 1880, Gladstone appointed Chamberlain to the Cabinet as President of the Board of Trade. His background and progressive views ensured that Chamberlain felt himself closer to the concerns of the Liberal Party caucus than to those of the parliamentary leadership in an organization described by one historian as 'like a people's crusade at the bottom and like a gentlemen's club at the top'.[4] Surveying the vista from that small and crowded summit, the remaining whig families grouped around the heir to the Duke of Devonshire, the Marquess of Hartington. They had been joined by recruits to the Liberal intelligentsia of which, for all his rather Tory High Anglicanism, Gladstone was so impressively a part. It was scarcely surprising that this party leadership had suspicions about the personal motives of the outsider Chamberlain in championing caucus concerns. It did not seem accidental that the caucus's primary organization, the National Liberal Federation, was based in Chamberlain's own municipal grand duchy of Birmingham. His hold over the city that he had served as an active and forward-looking Lord Mayor appeared total. The Liberal hierarchy were understandably troubled by his attempts to exert his authority from a territorial domain of this kind. It was even more disturbing that his determination to advance the cause of caucus participation in Liberal policy had as its goal turning the party upside down by taking the existing flow of policy formation from leadership to parliamentary party to extra-parliamentary caucus and reversing it. This threatened to transform the Liberal Party into a radical movement with which Chamberlain's own radical ideas were in tune. In 1885 he took it upon himself to launch his own 'unauthorized programme' of policies without seeking the sanction of the leadership.

The Liberal hierarchy had more to fear than merely the future of their own ascendancy over the party. Believing the caucus to be disproportionately under the influence of lay preachers, teetotallers and the other worthy wagon followers of local Liberal politics, they feared that a caucus-led Liberal Party was also an unelectable one. What could not be denied was that the parliamentary party was increasingly reliant upon its constituency workers to consolidate its hold with the electorate and that Chamberlain personally was a man of proven ability and a dangerous enemy. Suddenly in 1886 events conspired to alter the whole picture drastically. Gladstone committed himself to Irish home rule. Appalled, a third of the parliamentary Liberal Party split away. Into this new rebel camp, radicals under Chamberlain and traditional whigs under the Marquess of Hartington unexpectedly found themselves pitched up in the same tent. With the Gladstone Government unpopular and the Liberal Party so publicly divided, the Conservatives gained ground in the general election of that year. The result was the formation of a Tory Government dependent for its majority upon the support of the anti-home-rule rebel whig and radical 'Liberal Unionists' who constituted a force of seventy-eight MPs in the new Parliament. Lord Salisbury assumed the Premiership. Lord Randolph Churchill became Chancellor of the Exchequer; at thirty-seven he was the youngest to do so since William Pitt in 1782.

During the same period in which Gladstone's Government had come under strain, the Conservatives had experienced the mixed blessings of their own 'Radical Joe' in the guise of Lord Randolph. Demoralized in the Commons under the weak front-bench command of Sir Stafford Northcote, Tories at first delighted in the political satire performed by Lord Randolph and his small but dramatically irreverent group of 'Fourth Party' Conservatives. The result, as Lord Randolph intended, was that

Northcote became as much the casualty as Gladstone the target of their japes and jeers. Churchill had proceeded to launch a crusade for 'Tory Democracy', promoting the cause of the party's main caucus organization, the National Union of Conservative Associations. His stated aim was to promote a redistribution of power similar to that attempted by Chamberlain in the Liberal Party. By mixing this process up in the mystical language of Disraeli, Churchill gave to a radical notion the prescriptive credentials needed to convert Tory hearts and minds. Although the reality was somewhat different, in 1884 he appeared to believe that his popularity had been proven. Making an issue of the campaign for greater caucus autonomy, he resigned the chairmanship of the National Union and was promptly re-elected. It was not a stunt that he should have repeated too frequently. Only four months into his tenure as Chancellor of the Exchequer, he suddenly offered to resign, ostensibly over the increase in the armed forces budget but banking on the belief that his indispensability made the resignation's acceptance impossible. Salisbury instead recognized a bluff when he saw it, promptly called it and let him go. If Churchill had expected Joe Chamberlain and the Liberal Unionists to break off their parley with the Salisbury administration in order to march to his aid, then the calculation misfired horribly. When none of the reinforcements came, Churchill, outgunned, was with seeming ease manoeuvred out of contention for the leadership. His place at the Treasury was filled by Goschen, the first Liberal Unionist to accept office in a Conservative Government.*

Until the schism created by Gladstone's promotion of Irish home rule, Churchill had been locked in an intense rivalry with Chamberlain. In October 1884 Churchill's attempt to address a mass rally of Birmingham Conservatives at Aston Park had ended in chaos when the gathering was mobbed by marauding Liberals. His belief that the ugly scenes had been deliberately orchestrated by the Liberal caucus had encouraged a subsequently chilly atmosphere between him and Chamberlain. This only strengthened Churchill's determination to take on the Liberal machine on its home ground and in the 1885 general election he had stood against John Bright in Birmingham Central. Along with all the other Conservative candidates fighting Birmingham seats, Churchill lost and subsequently had to make do with a seat representing South Paddington instead. However, it was not long before events were to make him reasess his

---

* From this period onwards the Conservative Party was more commonly known as 'Unionist', a title that only began to die out after 1921 (and much later in Scotland). Since 1912, the official title of the party has been 'Conservative and Unionist' and in the interest of conformity, the terms 'Conservative' and 'Tory' are used throughout this text.

relationship with Chamberlain and the Birmingham Liberals. The evolution of the anti-home-rule Liberals into an independent Liberal Unionist Party raised the possibility of a realignment in British politics. Churchill believed he could work with the new group, the ultimate goal being to create a progressive centre party. He certainly shared their concerns over Ireland; his response to Gladstone's declaration for home rule had been to turn up in Belfast and opine that 'Ulster will fight and Ulster will be right'. In the run up to the 1886 general election, he had written to Chamberlain promising to deliver the support of the Tories in Birmingham: 'We shall give all our support to the Liberal-Unionists, asking for no return, making no boast nor taunt. I will engage that all your Unionist candidates have the full support of our party.'[5]

Churchill was anticipating a new alignment ahead of the pace of events. Chamberlain had by no means given up on the prospect of returning to a post-Gladstone Liberal Party, but understandably he wanted to spread his liabilities. He therefore encouraged Churchill to believe a new centre party possible, reminding him, as if it were necessary to do so, that 'you and I are equally adrift from the old organisations'.[6] On 1 January 1887, Churchill welcomed in the new year for the Conservative Chief Whip by informing him that he regarded himself as a free agent who could join any political grouping committed to realizing his (rather ill-defined) objectives. The difficulty was that whilst the Liberal Unionists were, by their numbers alone, an inescapable presence in British politics, Churchill, like Oscar Wilde, had nothing to declare but his own genius. His personal unpredictability combined with the disintegration of his own power base were hardly appreciating assets in which to invest political capital. This was especially evident to the whigs, without whose support a new centre party would lack gravitas.

For Liberal Unionists of a more whiggish disposition like Hartington, an emerging accommodation with Lord Salisbury's Conservative Party appeared to be an easier and more established course. There was little ideologically to separate whig grandees from their Tory counterparts, as those who had already made the journey could testify. Support for Salisbury's leadership therefore appeared to be a relatively safe route towards preserving the traditional union of Britain and Ireland without promoting the new and destabilizing forces for whom radical politicians in the Churchill mould postured as foster-parents. After all, the Anglo-Irish Union was hardly going to be served by attempting to break up the Conservative Party, which was the greatest force for its maintenance in the country. Conscious of Hartington's scepticism, during the summer of 1887 Chamberlain too conceded that forming a new party with Churchill did not make sense. His personal relationship with the Tory rebel deteriorated accordingly.

The decision of the Liberal Unionists to reject membership of a new political party and instead to bolster the Conservatives in a national alliance ensured that the grievous split in the Liberal Party of the previous year failed to develop into the destruction of the existing party system. Whilst there were now four main parties, they were divided into two alliance groups (Conservatives with the Liberal Unionists versus Liberals with the Irish Nationalists) thus preserving the essence of the two-party system in Britain. The other impetus for this Tory/Liberal Unionist alignment came from Lord Salisbury's Conservative administration itself. Its pursuit of a moderately reformist domestic policy was certainly acceptable as far as the whigs in the Liberal Unionist faction were concerned. Compared to that of the whigs, Chamberlain's flirtation with the Conservative Government was more hesitant. Given the rhetoric of class war that he had employed before the split over Irish home rule, this was hardly surprising. However, having lost control of the National Liberal Federation, there was no point in his returning to a Liberal Party that offered him no opportunity for advancement. Gladstone continued to defy the ageing process and to keep home rule at the forefront of the Liberal agenda. All prospect of a centre party gone, Chamberlain had no real option other than to move further into the Conservative embrace. In December 1891, he assumed the leadership of the Liberal Unionists in the Commons. By 1894 he was publicly describing himself as a Unionist, an epithet greater than the sum of its Conservative and Liberal parts.[7] The following year he accepted office in Salisbury's Government. In choosing the Colonial Office rather than a domestic portfolio, he demonstrated that he was committed to the imperial vision shared by most Conservatives. The trouble was to come later.

During the 1890s, fears receded that the caucus would gain the upper hand over parliamentary politics. Gladstone still had trouble from his Party Conference, as the list of pledges and grievances it attempted to foist upon him at Newcastle in 1891 demonstrated, but structurally, the leadership managed to stay in the saddle even if its style was badly jolted. The self-destruction of Lord Randolph Churchill removed any lingering fear of caucus dictation in the Conservative Party. In any case, during the 1880s he had articulated caucus concerns that went far beyond what most of the National Union – quietly satisfied by an 1884 measure of appeasement by Salisbury – apparently wanted for themselves. In contrast to the National Liberal Federation, there was not within the Tory caucus the same degree of interest in radical policies and conflict with the parliamentary leadership. It is hard, therefore, to envisage how Churchill's National Union was ever going to challenge the party hierarchy on the sort of ideological divisions of which Chamberlain had formally been such an exponent in the pre-1886 Liberal Party. To Churchill, 'Tory Democracy' whilst embodying the maxim 'trust the people' was also about opportunism, and especially his own. There had already been signs that had he reached the top, he would have quickly lost interest in being told what to do by those he snubbed for being brewers and booksellers. As we shall see in the chapters ahead, the victory of parliamentary government over delegatory caucus in the Conservative Party was to have important repercussions for those politicians who attempted to use the constituency party against Chamberlain's elder son, Austen, over Ireland in 1921 or, on the side of Churchill's son, Winston, over India between 1933 and 1935.

In the last fifteen years of the nineteenth century the Conservative Party recovered its composure and its direction, leaving behind it the uneasy period that it had experienced during the early 1880s. Far from leading a breakaway from a sectional Tory Party to create a truly national centre party, Lord Randolph Churchill had instead been forced to watch on the sidelines whilst Salisbury, Hartington and Chamberlain gradually moulded the Conservative Party into that very national alliance instead. This was the same process that was to be conducted by Stanley Baldwin and Ramsay MacDonald after 1931, and with a similar result in excluding Winston Churchill from office. However, events which were unexpectedly to resurrect Winston Churchill's career never came to the aid of his father. As a result, Lord Randolph was left stranded, condemned to obliterate his talents and his liver in a haze of alcoholic excess which even before his early death in 1895 had reduced him to becoming 'the chief mourner at his own protracted funeral'.[8] His attempts to maintain his profile in Westminster only heightened his public humiliation. In the House of Commons, many former colleagues even denied him the courtesy of staying to listen to his speeches. In 1891 he confided pitifully to his wife: 'I expect I have made great mistakes; but there has been no consideration, no indulgence, no memory of gratitude – nothing but spite, malice and abuse. I am quite tired and dead-sick of it all, and will not continue political life any longer.'[9] Winston Churchill later recalled how the verbatim press reports of his father's speeches 'dropped from three columns to two columns and then to one and a half. On one occasion *The Times* mentioned that the hall was not filled.' Sensing his father's growing infirmity, the younger Churchill yearned to be fighting alongside him in Parliament where Chamberlain's eldest son Austen and Gladstone's son Herbert had already followed their fathers.

With Lord Randolph's death in 1895, Winston later lamented that 'all my dreams of comradeship with him, of entering Parliament at his side and in his support, were ended. There remained for me only to pursue his aims and vindicate his memory.'[10]

Winston Churchill became more fully aware of the extent of the Tories' disregard and dislike for his father when he began writing his biography. By the time the work was completed in 1906, he had deserted his father's party altogether. But to Lord Randolph himself, Winston retained throughout his life an unfailing loyalty that far outweighed the desultory affection he had received in return. Amongst those of his father's generation whom he sought out to help him get to know the distant figure he so much revered was Joseph Chamberlain. The time and consideration that 'Old Joe' extended to him, left him deeply impressed. Instead of cold-shouldering a young pup who had recently crossed the floor and become a precocious political opponent, the old statesman showed him the greatest sympathy and charm, sitting up late with him, recalling the fights of yesteryear with a bottle of 1834 port until two in the morning.[11] These remembrances contrasted markedly with the way in which Winston Churchill thought the Conservative leadership had shunned his father, particularly during his all too public disintegration. On an evening during the Battle of Britain in September 1940, Churchill, by then Prime Minister, was seated having dinner. Sullen and uncommunicative, he appeared at this grave moment in the country's fortunes to be understand-ably preoccupied in thought. Turning to Lord Salisbury who was also at the table he suddenly announced: 'I always consider that your grandfather treated my father disgracefully.'[12]

Winston Churchill had always made a point of marking the anniversary of his father's death. Having slipped into a coma, he died on the morning of 24 January 1965, exactly seventy years after that event.

III

Winston Churchill's attempt to find a political legacy in his father's declaration for 'Tory Democracy' inevitably fell upon stony ground. Few could discern in the career of Lord Randolph any message beyond a salutary lesson in self-destruction. In contrast, Joseph Chamberlain's contribution to the Conservative Party was to be of vital significance and was to be every bit as tied up with Churchill's fortunes as it was with the next generation of the Chamberlain family, Austen and Neville.

Joseph Chamberlain's imperialist objectives at the Colonial Office had coincided with conflict with the Boers. The resulting outbreak of hostilities in South Africa, soon nicknamed 'Joe's War', had unforeseen consequences for the future of British politics. One of those caught up in the war was the young Churchill. Considered an academic failure at Harrow, he had sought out adventure and joined the 4th Hussars. Against the Dervish tribesmen at the battle of Omdurman in 1898, he had ridden with the 21st Lancers in the last great cavalry charge of the British Army. Employed in the unlikely combination of journalist-in-arms, he was subsequently sent off to cover the war in South Africa where, under fire, he was captured by the Boers. Churchill hid for several days at the bottom of a mine shaft before being smuggled out in a goods train, and the *Boy's Own* nature of his dramatic escape caught the popular imagination, catapulted him into the public eye and helped win him a Conservative parliamentary seat in Oldham. In the longer term, however, the war's legacy was to put Churchill on the wrong side of his party. The need to fund the huge cost of the military expedition, combined with the incompetence and inefficiency that the Boer War revealed (not only about the army but about the wider British economy and society), encouraged Chamberlain and others to think afresh. If the existing orthodoxy had come under such strain tackling a ragbag of *voortrekkers*, it certainly promised to constrain Britain from taking on new obligations at home and abroad. The way out of this cul-de-sac, Chamberlain now announced, was tariff reform.

Tariff reform involved moving towards a tariff-free common market between Britain and her dominions but at the cost of abandoning free trade with traditional foreign competitors. Politically, it was the bomb that had always threatened to explode in the Conservative Party's face as a consequence of getting too close to the independently minded Joseph Chamberlain. When in May 1903 he launched his crusade for this new departure, typically in his own backyard of Birmingham, the master of surprises was promoting a new 'unauthorized programme' of unsolicited advice for the Conservatives to update that with which he had once tried to shackle the Liberals in 1885.

For many, free trade had become the totem of Victorian Britain, synonymous with her claim to being the workshop of the world. From a purely political perspective at least, there was much to be said in favour of leaving the issue well alone. Ingrained in the mind of any Tory with even the barest historical consciousness was the story of Sir Robert Peel's attempt in the 1840s to convert the party from protectionism to free trade. The resulting internecine division proved to be the precursor to the Conservatives' exclusion from power for the best part of the following thirty years. During that period in the wilderness, they had successfully struggled to make the necessary accommodation with the principles of free trade. The prospect of the whole issue now being reopened was the very last thing that the party leadership needed. This was especially the case since the issue would split the Conservatives but unite the Liberals.

On the other hand the Conservative and Unionist alliance had to be seen to have a purpose beyond preventing Irish home rule, especially given its success in keeping the measure off the statute books. Chamberlain's ideas on tariff reform filled the Unionists' policy vacuum. The crusade started on a restricted platform designed for limited purposes. However, once its bandwagon started to roll, it found itself picking up various additions (welcome or otherwise) with the effect that it ended up resembling a whole-hog protectionist programme promising the curative properties of a universal panacea. The prospects of increasing the budget for social reform whilst at the same time paying for the upkeep of an empire had always been restricted by the perceived unwillingness of the taxpayer to pick up the bill. Diverting the burden of revenue collection from income tax to foreign import levy thereby avoided the sort of fiscal redistribution of wealth that would have infuriated Conservatives and the middle class. Furthermore and most crucially of all, by binding the British Empire together into a common market, tariff reform could prove a step on the road to Chamberlain's dream of imperial federation. However, there was a fundamental flaw to the scheme's attractiveness. Import levies on non-imperial foreign produce threatened to increase the cost of basic foodstuffs, and in particular bread. This suggested to its detractors that these tariffs would reap a dubious electoral harvest in which the cost of social reform would fall primarily on necessities bought by the working class. This point was not lost on the Liberal Party which rallied so well to the orthodoxy of free trade and its role in keeping down the cost of living that the traditional Liberal parlour game of internal feuding was momentarily put aside.

Chamberlain's attempt to hijack the Conservative Party with his new progressive protectionist brand of Unionism immediately established a wide following, but it did not capture party policy outright nor did it sweep all MPs before it. Some of the whigs who had resisted his radical notions in the pre-1886 Liberal Party were now amongst those who tried to prevent his new radical ideas reaching fruition in the Conservative fold. The Duke of Devonshire (as Hartington had become), leader of the Liberal Unionists in the Lords, was a staunch free trader. Amongst the Tory MPs who felt likewise was the bumptious young member for Oldham, Winston Churchill. This was despite the fact that his father had included protectionist 'fair trade' sentiment in his campaign for 'Tory Democracy'. Then, its hour had not yet come. Arthur Balfour, who had succeeded his uncle, Lord Salisbury, as Prime Minister, attempted to hold a median position between Chamberlain's scheme and the outright free traders by favouring a moderate extension of tariffs against foreign competition as a means of negotiation for fairer trade all round. Balfour's caution satisfied neither camp and led to the Cabinet resignations of both Chamberlain and Devonshire. Already lacking Tory partisan spirit even before the tariff crisis exploded, Winston Churchill meanwhile hoped that he would find a future in a government to defend free trade headed by the Duke of Devonshire and Lord Rosebery. Rosebery, who had been Liberal Prime Minister from 1894 to 1895, was now touting himself as a figure of cross-party unity and was revered in the young Churchill's eyes for being one of his father's admirers. Yet just as Lord Randolph's proposed centre party of 1887 had proved superfluous to the greater guns already firing away in the defence of the Union, so there was no call for a new free trade party when the Liberal Party was already rallying successfully to that cause. In 1904, Churchill followed the logic of this reality and crossed the floor.

Churchill's former colleagues now loathed him. This was despite the fact that his actions were prompted by the campaign launched by Joseph Chamberlain, another turncoat whose switching sides the Conservatives had been happy enough to celebrate. The difference was that Chamberlain had proved his worth and had the intellectual depth for his policy swings to carry conviction. In contrast, many saw in the precocity of the 29-year-old Churchill the machinations of opportunism that they had long identified with his late father. When in March 1904 Churchill rose in the Commons to deliver his first major speech from the Liberal benches, the Prime Minister and his colleagues, together with most of the Conservative backbench, walked out.

Churchill had what proved to be the first, if not the last, laugh over his former colleagues when the Conservatives lost the 1906 general election by a landslide. Their cause had not been helped by Chamberlain's initiative which was so easily labelled 'stomach taxes' by its opponents. It had divided the Tories and united the Liberals. Yet once the smoke of battle had cleared, the Conservative forces found to be still standing represented a marked swing towards the protectionist wing of the party. Chamberlain had a sizeable following amongst these forces. Indeed, whilst professing loyalty to Balfour, he had been well placed to take control of the party organization when a sudden stroke transformed him into an invalid and removed him from the political stage. Like Lord Randolph Churchill, Chamberlain now had to watch from the sidelines as physical disability accompanied exclusion from the march of public events, becoming equally and frustratingly reliant on the care and hopes of his politically motivated family around him. But for Chamberlain, the physical debilitation cut down the man but did not strangle the policy.

His strident brand of radical unionism inspired the right wing to steer the party from Balfour's essentially moderate and reactive conservatism towards a proactive alternative to the social interventionism of what was now being labelled 'New Liberalism'. The Chamberlainite prescription was given fresh momentum when the Liberals, having denied themselves the use of tariff levies, had to pay for their increased spending plans by raising direct taxation. Following the controversy over Lloyd George's 1909 Budget, the Tories rose to the challenge to fight the Liberals, squeezing their parliamentary majority in the two general elections of the following year on a 'peers versus people' platform. At first sight their siding with the peers demonstrated a unique occasion when a party's chief electoral gambit was to back a group in society who could not vote. It certainly did not hang easily with the 'Radical Joe' of olden time who had lambasted the class that 'toil not, neither do they spin'. But the Tories' combativeness owed much to Chamberlain's former self-confidence. The Conservative alliance with Liberal Unionism had been built upon a common resistance to Irish home rule. Only by preserving the legislative veto powers of the House of Lords could the measure be prevented from reaching the statute books. Serving as the Liberals' Home Secretary and subsequently First Lord of the Admiralty, Winston Churchill's role in both the constitutional crisis and home rule debate further marked him out as a hate figure for Unionists. For the moment, however, and enjoying rapid promotion in office, he appeared to be on the winning side. The Lords lost their absolute veto powers in 1911 and, despite the threat of civil war from loyalists, the Liberals had also put Irish home rule on to the statute book when its enactment was postponed for the duration (then thought to be only a matter of months) of the First World War.

Whilst Churchill bobbed upon the high tide of personal ambition, Joseph Chamberlain's legacy was driven on in turn by his two sons. The younger of the two, Neville, carried forward his father's work in Birmingham municipal affairs. But it was the elder son, Austen, who was groomed for the greatness that had only narrowly escaped his charismatic father. Following a suitable education at Cambridge and the sub-parliamentary playpen of its Union, his career had proceeded with all the outward signs (perhaps too much of the outward signs) of effortless superiority. He had been elected as a Liberal Unionist MP at the age of twenty-nine for a Worcestershire constituency close to the family's Birmingham heartland. Before the great defeat of 1906 he had served as Balfour's Chancellor of the Exchequer. In 1911, the cautious and philosophical Balfour, under pressure, gave up the leadership. He was succeeded by Andrew Bonar Law, a teetotal, chain-smoking, Scots-Canadian devotee of the chessboard; the only man to have combined the unique double act of leader of the Conservative Party and Member of Parliament for Glasgow Central. Nonetheless, Austen Chamberlain's failure to lead the Unionist alliance and complete his stricken father's unfinished business at Westminster at this juncture by no means ruled him out of succeeding in the future. In 1912, when the Conservative and Liberal Unionist parties were formally merged, the continued profile of those like Austen Chamberlain and Lord Lansdowne, the party leader in the Lords, were evidence of the ongoing strength of input from the old Liberal Unionist remnant in what was now officially called the 'Conservative and Unionist Party'. Whatever old animosities they had formally stirred up against the aristocracy, the Chamberlains were now entrenched occupants of the political Establishment. They had even developed hereditary traits of their own. Already of similiar physical appearance to his father, Austen took devotion to the point of mimicry, adopting the same modes of dress right down to wearing a monocle in his eye and an orchid in his buttonhole.

The net result of twenty years of dynastic crossfire in British politics had manifested itself in the sons of Lord Randolph Churchill and Joseph Chamberlain sitting on opposite benches not only to each other but also to those which their illustrious fathers themselves had first occupied. This was the Parliament that in 1908 welcomed the new member for the Bewdley division of Worcestershire, a 41-year-old of no particular distinction who with similar hereditary logic had been nominated to succeed to the constituency on the death of its previous occupant, his father. In the next six years the new member only spoke in the Commons five times but he was to beat the more precocious Churchills and Chamberlains to the Premiership. His name was Stanley Baldwin.

IV

When in August 1914 the Liberal Government declared war on Germany, the Conservatives promised general support from the opposition benches. The case for an immediate coalition was not overwhelming, especially if the conflict was going to be over by Christmas. Indeed, there had been a fear that Tory inclusion in the government would drive the radical Liberals into opposing the war. Asquith, the Prime Minister, in any case regarded it as by no means essential to join forces with Conservative politicians whom he had always held in little regard and for whom the unprecedented bitterness of the previous five years in Parliament had only further poisoned relations. But it proved not to be a short war and consequently in May 1915, over the heads of the Conservative and Liberal parliamentary parties, a coalition was finally created. In the new

Cabinet, the Liberals not only retained a clear majority but continued to occupy all of the key offices necessary to the conduct of the war. Asquith conceded one of Bonar Law's main demands, however: the removal of Churchill from the Admiralty. Churchill's sustained unpopularity with his Tory former colleagues had reached breaking point when the opening up of a new front in the Dardenelles, of which he had been a prime advocate, ended in the military fiasco of the Gallipoli landings. Like that of his father, his political career now seemed prematurely cut down in its prime. Deeply unhappy, Churchill returned to his first career, donned the uniform of the Royal Scots Fusiliers and went off to serve in the trenches. He was, it seemed, going to do the decent thing.

Asquith's personal conduct, in particular his aloofness and intransigence in the face of clearly necessary changes in the institutional mechanisms through which the war was being prosecuted, did as much to undermine his position as any policy or reversal on the battlefield. Conservatives were particularly resentful that he continued to project himself as primarily a Liberal Party leader. This contrasted with Lloyd George. The Welsh radical, scourge of the landed aristocracy and proponent of progressive income taxes, had been greatly feared by Conservatives before the outbreak of war. Yet in politics, a short memory is often expedient. Had not Joseph Chamberlain, now so great a figure in tender Unionist memory, been seen at one time as such a dangerous foe when he articulated some of the prejudices developed by Lloyd George? As with the late 'Radical Joe' (he had finally died in 1914), so Tories who had previously regarded Lloyd George as a disagreeably extreme figure in domestic affairs now saw in him the dynamism and determination needed to win the war, qualities so lacking in Asquith. Lloyd George, meanwhile, was by no means the coy and unsuspecting recipient of these affections. In contrast to the Prime Minister, he now projected himself as a figure above party considerations and a source of national unity. Given the Tory detestation of Churchill (who returned to Westminster from active service in May 1916) he was the obvious man of action from the Liberal Party who could, at the same time, gain a sufficient measure of cross-party support to oust Asquith. With resignations and threats of counter-resignations pilling up, the crisis came in December 1916. Displaying signs of being on the verge of a mental breakdown, Asquith resigned. He may have intended this to be a temporary measure from which he would bounce back, but more likely his resignation was an act of recognition that the situation had slipped out of his control. Supported by Bonar Law, Lloyd George became Prime Minister, endowed with semi-dictatorial powers to win the war. These events were to find their parallel in 1940 between Neville Chamberlain and Winston Churchill.

In <u>December 1918,</u> with the Kaiser defeated, the Liberal and Conservative supporters of the Lloyd George coalition were overwhelmingly returned to power in the famous '<u>coupon' general election.</u> Earlier in the year, exploration of possible options for fusing the supporters of the coalition into a new national centre party had foundered. One of the reasons for this was the apprehension of many of its Liberal supporters who feared that joining a new party would make irrevocable the split between them and the section of the Liberal Party that remained loyal to Asquith. In fact, it was to be the deposed Premier's refusal to accept the olive branches of office (the Lord Chancellorship) proffered to him in September that ensured that the Liberals would be divided between Independent Liberals led by Asquith on the opposition benches and National Liberals led by Lloyd George on the government benches. The effects of having <u>two rival Liberal factions</u> with two different leaders had proved damaging enough after the split of 1886. The opening of this fresh division at a time when the <u>Labour Party</u> was beginning to present a significant challenge was a blow from which the fortunes of the parliamentary Liberal Party never recovered.

There were sound reasons for <u>Conservatives</u> to support the new Lloyd George coalition government into peacetime. In the first place, on their own the Tories had lost the previous three general elections in a row and such a legacy naturally made many of them favourably disposed towards coasting into office on the coat-tails of the popular war leader. Universal male suffrage and the granting of the vote to all women over thirty was also thought to create a fresh uncertainty as to how the electorate would act and this helped arguments favouring a broad-based appeal. Furthermore, the continuing rise of the <u>Labour</u> Movement and the spread of <u>industrial unrest</u> between 1919 and 1921 encouraged the jumpy to fear the <u>prospect of a Bolshevik challenge.</u> With Soviet Russia undermined by internal strife and civil war, <u>Churchill,</u> who as a Liberal supporter of Lloyd George was now Secretary of State for War, <u>kept himself busy spreading world counter-revolution</u> via military expeditions against the Reds on their home soil. <u>Strident opposition to socialism</u> had become central to his stated political objectives, even if it took some time for the Tory right wing to appreciate his help in the matter.

Senior Conservative figures including Balfour – whose career was enjoying an Indian summer in ongoing high office – and Austen Chamberlain, once again Chancellor of the Exchequer, now looked more seriously at a 'fusion' of the Conservative Party with those pro-Lloyd George Liberal MPs who took the coalition Whip. In this, Balfour and Chamberlain had the enthusiastic support of the Lord Chancellor, Lord

Birkenhead, and, from amongst the Liberal ministers, his friend, Churchill. This was not surprising. Seeking a way out of the constitutional crisis
of 1909–11, these men had been involved in supposedly secret negotiations with the then Liberal Chancellor of the Exchequer, none other than
Lloyd George himself, to see whether a moderate coalition could be
created to avoid the looming degeneration of honest party conflict over
the House of Lords and Irish questions. The talks had broken down then
but the idea took on a new momentum in the aftermath of the First World
War in the face of the rising challenge from the Labour Movement.
During 1919 and 1920 even the naturally reluctant Conservative leader,
Bonar Law, allowed himself to be involved in the discussions designed to
bring about 'fusion'. In March 1920, however, the whole concept had to
be put on ice when the coalition Liberals made clear to Lloyd George their
opposition to the scheme. Even those who shared the new emphasis
against socialism still did not want to find themselves irrevocably outside
the organization and structure of the Liberal Party. Nor could they all
guarantee that their local association would follow them into a new party.
Therefore, they preferred to look to reuniting with Asquith's Independent
Liberals in the long term. Clinging to the 'Liberal' tag with all the
traditions and historic associations that it involved seemed much safer
than joining an ill-defined new party.

This effective veto on immediate fusion did not necessarily rule it out in
the future, but (as far as Conservative commitment to the project was
concerned) the opportunity was never to present itself so favourably
again. Despite representing almost three-quarters of the coalition's
numbers in the Commons, the Conservatives only scraped the barest of
majorities in seats around the Cabinet table. This was not a happy state of
affairs for pushy Tories, eagerly seeking promotion. Furthermore,
opposition to the compromises necessitated by coalition, having previously been the marching tune of the instinctively fractious right wing, was
beginning to be whistled throughout the rest of the Tory ranks.

In March 1921, ill-health forced Bonar Law to retire from the
Conservative Party leadership in the Commons. Austen Chamberlain's
moment had come. Having initially been washed up on the Conservative
shores, refugees adrift on the political tide, the Chamberlain dynasty had
at last taken charge of the island. But for all the outward physical
manifestations of cloning between father and son, Austen proved
temperamentally different to 'Radical Joe'. His father's personal dynamism and originality of mind had cut across the normal boundaries of
party politics, but regardless of his essential divisiveness, he had always
presented himself as a partisan fighter. Austen exuded the confidence of a
man of government, not the raw enthusiasm of a party champion.

Seemingly burdened by a desire to prove himself the responsible statesman, he too readily appeared the willing accomplice of less scrupulous politicians like Lloyd George and Churchill. This lack of partisan fight from their party's new leader intensified the Tory right's fears for the safeguarding of their interests.

These fears were not baseless. Chamberlain made no secret of his belief in the principle of 'fusion' as a goal. To him, it was an extension of the process that had brought Liberal families like his own into the Conservative Party in the first place, enhancing its claim to be the natural party of orderly government and leaving its opponents looking increasingly fractious and extreme. In fact, the moment had already passed for merging the Conservative and coalition Liberal parties. Amongst Tories there was a returning self-confidence, fuelled by the belief that they could win elections in their own right. Given his duplicitous past, it was not unreasonable for Lloyd George's motives to be questioned by those who had spent all their life in the Tory fold. As one Liberal MP noted in his diary, Lloyd George's purpose was 'to split the Tory Party and to use a general election for the purpose of wiping out the Diehards as a Parliamentary force' after which he could be master of his own party.[13] The fracture of the Liberal Party – although as much Asquith's fault – provided Tories with a vision of what Lloyd George's scheming could do to a great political party.

Whatever the possible future of a 'fused' centre party, the Tory right wing – known as the diehards – already had reason enough to loathe the coalition as it stood. The degeneration into violence that accompanied the rise of Sinn Fein over the more moderate Irish Nationalists had proceeded to throw the whole process into chaos. In contrast to their support for the great Unionist cause championed by his father, the diehards saw Austen Chamberlain's role alongside Lloyd George in negotiating with Sinn Fein as a deep betrayal. That he was joined in this act by Lord Birkenhead, who had previously been one of the most gung-ho Unionists in Westminster, and by Churchill, whose father had played the Orange card, further confirmed fears about the sort of company the Conservative leader was keeping. Given that home rule had already been conceded in 1914, the treaty negotiated in December 1921, which rescued six of the counties of Ulster from the new Irish Free State, actually salvaged something for the Unionist cause and addressed Lord Randolph Churchill's concerns about the rights of Ulster. Nevertheless, the leaders of the greatest empire in the world which had seen off the most formidable power in continental Europe, were now within three years of that victory inviting into Downing Street, for face-to-face arbitration, a band of Celtic terrorists whom only weeks before they had been trying to arrest.

Inevitably, denunciations of the leadership's role in appeasing Michael Collins and his IRA colleagues flowed freely. Heated exchanges took place both on the floor of the Commons and at the Conservative Party Conference which was in that year rather inconveniently held in the sectarian citadel of Liverpool. Overcoming opposition of this kind only encouraged Austen Chamberlain's view that the party should prolong the life of the coalition and that it should fight the next general election still combined on that basis. In other words, he drew precisely the wrong conclusion.

In February 1922, the Tory diehard, Colonel John Gretton, led a delegation of thirty-five MPs to tell Chamberlain that it was time to reclaim the Conservative Party's independence. Lacking the duplicitous ability to give such factions the impression that he was really on their side but that the time was not yet ripe, Chamberlain displayed an honesty that was fatally commendable. He began instead voicing publicly his obvious intentions by regarding 'Unionist and National Liberals as, under present circumstances, two wings of one great constitutional and progressive party'.[14] Days after Chamberlain had articulated this view, 200 members of his party convened to discuss the prospect of a new centre party and promptly demonstrated their lack of enthusiasm for the project. Lord Salisbury, son of the former Tory Prime Minister, launched an appeal for an anti-coalition 'Conservative and Unionist Movement' which raised a £22,000 fighting fund from the right-wing daily, the *Morning Post*. Meanwhile, Conservative junior ministers, regarding their career prospects as hindered by the need to find key portfolios for coalition Liberals in the Cabinet, also began to demonstrate schismatic intentions. Despite the mounting evidence that the Conservative backbench wanted to end the coalition, Chamberlain supported the Cabinet decision of 10 October to spring a general election on the country flying the coalition colours. This was to take the prerogatives of leadership beyond what the led would tolerate. Outrage ensued and the forthcoming Party Conference was expected to be raucously outspoken against prolonging the coalition into a fresh Parliament. Chamberlain now sought a clear mandate from his parliamentary party in the Commons in order to head off any such demonstration. He therefore opted to put his case to a vote of his party's MPs who would, in effect, decide the coalition's future.

With the requisite loyalty from colleagues, Chamberlain's gamble might have paid off. In different circumstances, it did when John Major briefly resigned the party leadership in 1995 to lance the boil of mounting criticism. Major, however, had kept the support of the party machine and of almost all his senior colleagues when he placed his job on the line. Unfortunately for Austen Chamberlain, his own Party Chairman, Sir

George Younger, went behind his back and was amongst those who persuaded Bonar Law to come out of retirement in order to oppose the continuation of the coalition. Younger's intrigue was all the more remarkable given that he was supposedly at the disposal of the existing leader. The Foreign Secretary, Lord Curzon, also now took this opportunity to turn against the coalition in which he held office, and wrote his letter of resignation to the Prime Minister. On 18 October, the day before MPs were due to meet in the Carlton Club to cast their votes, Bonar Law told Chamberlain that he was heading towards making his decision and that it would be against the continuation of the coalition. The rebels, who previously lacked a credible alternative leader of their own, now found their chances of ending the alliance were greatly strengthened by Bonar Law's return to the fray.

The following morning Austen Chamberlain faced his party, supported by members of his government including Balfour, the most recent Conservative Prime Minister. Despite being the largest party in the Commons since 1918, the Tory Party had last held absolute power seventeen years before when Balfour had presided over its electoral decapitation. MPs who had acclaimed Chamberlain as their leader only the previous year now believed he was trying to dragoon them into fighting yet another general election on a coalition basis without their consent. Captain Ernest Pretyman, the same MP who had proposed Chamberlain for the leadership eighteen months previously, now proposed the motion that would end it. Such is the movable feast of political loyalties. On top of this, the President of the Board of Trade, Stanley Baldwin, suddenly found his voice and spoke out against his own government. In a well-received speech, he condemned the coalition, and Lloyd George in particular; the Prime Minister's influence as a 'dynamic force' was 'a terrible thing' that would end up destroying the Conservative Party as it had the Liberals. Since Baldwin had sat passively throughout Lloyd George's Cabinet meetings for over a year without evidently raising so much as a squeak of serious complaint, this was proof indeed of the old adage that still waters run deep. Nevertheless, his view was echoed by Bonar Law, who made clear that if Chamberlain insisted on ignoring the will of most of his party, then there would result 'a repetition of what happened after Peel passed the Corn Bill. The body that is cast off will slowly become the Conservative Party, but it will take a generation before it gets back to the influence which the Party ought to have.'[15]

The margin of the resulting vote against Chamberlain, 187 to 87, was decisive. In the afternoon, Lloyd George resigned as Prime Minister and the coalition government came to an end. With Chamberlain standing down, Bonar Law was re-elected as party leader and accepted King George V's commission to form a purely Conservative administration. When with considerable irony Baldwin himself was later to be found after 1931 relying on the case for coalition government to get his policies accepted, those on the Tory right were aware of the precedent of 1922 and drew up their plans against him accordingly. It was to be a yet greater irony that they would run this campaign to return government to Tory men with Tory measures with the support of Winston Churchill. What the 1922 Carlton Club revolt demonstrated clearly was that the theoretical power of the leader to determine party policy was unworkable unless he commanded the support, or at least the acquiescence, of the majority of his party and had no serious rival who commanded greater adherence. Austen Chamberlain had overlooked the power of the backbencher every bit as much as had Asquith in December 1916. In the chapters to follow, it will be seen how Winston Churchill was to hope that Stanley Baldwin and Neville Chamberlain were making the same mistake in the 1930s. The arithmetic represented in this equation between the leader's intentions and his followers' tolerance was to determine who led the party in the years that led up to the great denouement of 1940.

V

Had it been a military exercise, the Carlton Club revolt would have resembled renegades on the General Staff joining their foot-soldiers in order to shoot their commanding officers. It achieved what the young Adolf Hitler merely attempted in his *putsch* two years later in Munich. In Germany, the revolt took the form of a violent and unconstitutional insurrection in a vulgar beer cellar led by an undersized ex-corporal with hate in his eyes. The revolt in England took on a much more agreeable form, wholly constitutionally, in the hushed decorum of a London gentlemen's club, virtually without so much as the returning of a incorrectly folded newspaper to the members' smoking-room desk. Hitler's intent in Munich was to replace parliamentary party democracy, whereas the revolt in Pall Mall* represented an ongoing faith in the workings of that style of democracy – and was indeed one of its highest expressions. However, the clubland insurrection achieved the goal that in 1924 was still to elude Hitler: it purged a whole generation of leaders and their protégés in one stroke. Indeed, the Carlton Club *putsch* has been described as having marked out the political battle-lines that lasted into

---

* The Carlton Club was originally in Pall Mall until, taking a direct hit from the *Luftwaffe*, it moved to its current site on St James's Street.

the Second World War.[16] Cleared away were the coalitionist 'old guard' who had presided over the winning of the First World War and the switching of the Irish question seemingly from British to Irish politics.

The list of casualties and walking wounded was headed by Austen Chamberlain, who lost the party leadership. Lord Birkenhead, once the brilliant young rising star of the party, was now seen as an unprincipled opportunist. The Chancellor of the Exchequer, Sir Robert Horne, began to look to the City for his remuneration. It could now be hoped that Lloyd George and Winston Churchill would fade away with the fractured Liberal Party fortunes they represented. Taking their place in power was a new ascendancy of men such as Stanley Baldwin, Samuel Hoare and, extraordinarily, Austen Chamberlain's younger brother, Neville. This was the generation that was later to mastermind the years of appeasement.

Whilst Bonar Law had allowed himself to be put at the head of the revolt, the Carlton Club debacle came as a huge shot in the arm to the previously unassuming Stanley Baldwin, whose personal attack on Lloyd George had attracted considerable approval. He had served as Financial Secretary to the Treasury and President of the Board of Trade, but, no less importantly, he had been Bonar Law's parliamentary private secretary (PPS) between 1916 and 1917. On arriving in Downing Street, Law made Baldwin his next-door neighbour. Yet as Chancellor of the Exchequer, Baldwin was not to prove an unqualified success. His negotiation of the war debt problem left Britain for some of the period making larger repayments to her erstwhile ally, the United States, than Germany was making in actual cash transfers as part of her reparations to her erstwhile enemies. Bonar Law considered the deal so bad that he took the bizarre step of writing an anonymous letter criticizing his own Chancellor's deal in *The Times*. However, a pedestrian performance in one office is not necessarily an irrevocable barrier to gaining the very highest party rank. None of the party's three successive leaders in the last quarter of the twentieth century (Margaret Thatcher, John Major, William Hague) reached the top primarily on the strength of recognized concrete achievements at the government ministries from which they were plucked. Baldwin was an earlier example of this phenomenon and when in May 1923 Bonar Law had to retire once again through ill-health, he succeeded him as leader and Prime Minister. In doing so, he stepped over the more obvious candidate for the role, Lord Curzon, the Foreign Secretary and former Viceroy of India, whose talents were more ostentatiously on public display. Baldwin's improbable path to power had been created by the exile of so many senior figures who had gone down with the coalition, while Curzon, the one remaining rival, was – on top of being disadvantaged by a peerage – self-evidently over-conscious of his suitability for the post. Baldwin thus became leader without many of his Tory colleagues knowing very much about him. All that could honestly be said was that, in contrast to Lloyd George and some of his acolytes, the new leader was neither brazenly dishonest, drunk, corrupt, nor some kind of sexual decathlete.

VI

Austen Chamberlain had suffered from the oppressive expectation of success burdened upon him as the son of the great political dynamo of late Victorian Britain. Winston Churchill, too, had seen his card marked early as the charismatic overhasty son of the charismatic overhasty father. Yet all this time and for the most part unobserved from Westminster, Neville Chamberlain had been developing his talents. Whilst family connections would always have prevented him from playing the role he had desired at the Carlton Club, Austen Chamberlain's untheatrical younger half-brother now emerged as a chief beneficiary of the *putsch*. Educated at Rugby School, Neville was, like Austen, given the first footing on the Establishment ladder that his father had missed, an advantage dimmed by the fact that he had endured a miserable adolescence there. Austen had been sent on from the Midlands' foremost public school to Trinity College, Cambridge – the powerhouse that provided three of the Conservative Party's four leaders in the first quarter of the twentieth century. Neville, however, was not shown such Augustan favours. His educational progress terminated with a degree from a Birmingham college in metallurgy, making him the only graduate of an English institution of higher education other than Oxford or Cambridge to become Prime Minister.[17] Although he failed to show much academic inclination, it was hoped that he was capable of displaying the sort of business acumen that had been one of the family's chief characteristics. At first perseverance triumphed over perspicacity. Sent out to the Bahamas at the age of twenty-one as a plantationist, he tried to grow sisal on the island of Andros. But for all his hard work, young Neville was no new Cecil Rhodes. The sisal refused to grow and after spending six years and a minor fortune, in 1897 he had to return home. He had failed at the first attempt to become the successful transubstantiation of the imperial vision evangelized by the then Colonial Secretary, his father.

Returning from the Bahamas, Neville Chamberlain brought his experiences as a white settler back to the more familiar home colony of Birmingham. During the next twenty years he carved out a successful business career, becoming Chairman of a company that made ships' berths. Active in the work of the health and educational institutions of the

great industrial city, his involvement in town planning led to his election
to the City Council in 1911, the year of his marriage at the late age of
forty-two. In 1915 he became Lord Mayor, a post that had been held by
five of his uncles, ten of his relations and, most famously and importantly
of all, by his father. This sort of cliquish family monopoly of office rather
belied 'Radical Joe's' former rantings against inherited power. There, in a
place that vied with Glasgow as the second city of the empire, Neville's
advance might have peaked. After all, his achievement was already
considerable. He was custodian of the family's first realm in the industrial
heart of the empire whilst his brother Austen continued his work in the
imperial political epicentre at Westminster. Together, they presided over
their father's two domains like Roman emperors of the East and West.
Neville's work in Birmingham during the First World War was to
encourage the supercilious jibe that he had proved 'a not bad Lord Mayor
in a lean year'. Yet the quality of his administration had proved sufficient
to be brought to the attention of the then new Prime Minister, Lloyd
George, who with only the briefest of interviews appointed him Director
of the Government's National Service department.

The work of the National Service department represented a last attempt
to coordinate the voluntary substitution of those from the less essential to
the more essential industries so that a greater number of potential soldiers
could be made available for service. The appointment was of a piece with
Lloyd George's tendency to advance business experts into positions
within the administration but in Neville's case it was not a success. Even
after he had supposedly settled in, a fellow minister thought that he
seemed 'not to know even now what he is going to do and does not
appear to have the remotest notion as to how he is going to do it'.[18] This
was not all, or even primarily, his own fault. He was being asked at no
notice to work a system that had been hastily cobbled together without a
proper job description or a seat in Parliament. Almost inevitably, he
found himself in conflict with the Ministry of Labour. Worse, he got no
support from Lloyd George who had some amateur notions about
phrenology and had quickly taken a dislike to 'that pin-head'.[19] The Prime
Minister even replaced the National Service department's parliamentary
secretary without consulting Chamberlain. This act prompted a wounded
Chamberlain to write to Lloyd George accusing him of perpetrating 'an
exhibition of discourtesy so extraordinary that I have difficulty in
believing it to be unintentional. I accepted office at your urgent request
with great reluctance. I have done my best in very difficult circumstances,
with very little support. If your disregard of me yesterday signifies your
want of confidence in me, the sooner I know it the better.'[20] This was
tough talking and Lloyd George found himself apologizing for what he

maintained was a mix-up. Nonetheless a <u>mutual loathing</u> had developed between the two men. The department's progress was extremely disappointing and Lloyd George with his 'almost animal aversion from a sick member of the herd'[21] made no attempt to offer the beleaguered Chamberlain any help. Eight months after agreeing to take up the job, Chamberlain <u>resigned</u>.

Neville Chamberlain displayed the same tenacity in the face of his poor performance in national government that he had shown in the face of repeatedly failing sisal crops in the Bahamas. Instead of failure encouraging him to give up or pursue a different course, it encouraged him to try again all the harder. It was this stubborn trait of character, perhaps encouraged by his knowledge that many dismissed him as the 'also ran' of the family, that led him to the otherwise curious deduction that having failed in government he should enter politics. With geographical unadventurousness he duly became the member for Birmingham Ladywood. At first, it was not clear what future lay for him in this course especially since his half-brother's coalition administration under Lloyd George appeared strong enough to cope without him. Regardless of that fact, Chamberlain felt compelled to play a role in public service particularly whilst the war continued, even though he felt that his future was uncertain. He confided in his diary his fear that 'my career is broken. How can a man of nearly 50, entering the House with this stigma upon him, hope to achieve anything? The fate I foresee is that after mooning about for a year or two I shall find myself making no progress.'[22]

These fears were to be short-lived. Fortuitously, the unenviable divided loyalties placed upon him by his views on Lloyd George combined with a reluctance to oppose his brother Austen were alleviated by his absence abroad when the coalition was ousted at the Carlton Club meeting. Although no particular enthusiast for the replacement regime, the <u>lasting loathing for Lloyd George</u> that he had developed during his period at National Service jettisoned him into influential company amongst the 1922 insurrectionists. As a consequence, starting off as Postmaster-General, he was soon appointed Minister for Health (the portfolio covering local government) and, in quick succession, Chancellor of the Exchequer. This was a speed of advancement already known only to Baldwin himself. Neville Chamberlain may have entered politics twenty-six years after his brother, and eighteen years after Winston Churchill, but the insurrection of 1922 that had seemingly ended their right to rule now gave him the opportunity to overtake them both on the route to the Premiership. Despite his occasional denials that this was his intended destination, he now began demonstrating the ministerial credentials that would give him poll position in the race.

VII

Three-party politics encouraged the period of political instability that followed the break-up of the Conservative–Lloyd George Liberal coalition. General elections were held in 1922, 1923 and 1924. Only months after succeeding Bonar Law as Conservative Prime Minister, Stanley Baldwin squandered his sizeable majority in going to the polls in 1923. By fighting the election on a platform favouring protectionism against foreign imports he predictably left his party open to the familiar charge of supporting policies that would drive up the cost of basic commodities, especially foodstuffs. Indeed, with equal predictability, Baldwin's call for protectionism had the same consequence as that of Joseph Chamberlain in 1903. It did the seemingly impossible and reunited the Liberal Party. The result was a hung Parliament with, for the first time, Labour as the largest party and the Conservatives in second place. In holding the balance of power, the Liberals (over which the septuagenarian Asquith was still paramount leader, despite the brooding presence of Lloyd George over his shoulder) opted to allow Labour to form its first administration. This decision was the final straw in convincing the vehemently anti-socialist Churchill that his future lay outside Liberal ranks. Under the Premiership of its leader, Ramsay MacDonald, the new Labour Government survived at the mercy of Liberal forbearance for less than ten months before crumbling in October 1924. It was routed by the Conservatives in the subsequent general election.

In winning an overwhelming majority in October 1924, Baldwin's electoral gamble of the previous year had paid off – although since he had not expected defeat in 1923 it was doubtful how much credit he could take for the foresight. By championing tariff reform in the 1923 election he had, against his expectations, done his party no favours at the polls but had at least gone some way towards reuniting the Tory part of the ex-coalition element behind him in the campaign. With victory in 1924, the ex-coalitionists stayed with him whilst, in order to reassure the electorate, he dropped any commitment to whole-hog protectionism. This self-denying ordinance made sense to the party from an electoral standpoint but annoyed some of its more imperialist theoreticians like the MP for Birmingham Sparkbrook, Leopold Amery. Diminutive in size and immense in mental strength, Amery, a Fellow of All Soul's and a Harrow contemporary of Churchill, became Colonial Secretary in the new administration, combining it the following year with the freshly created Cabinet post of Dominions Secretary. The straitjacket of free trade similarly held no appeal for Neville Chamberlain, loyal to the family gospel. He declined Baldwin's seemingly half-hearted offer of the Chancellorship of the Exchequer in favour of the more lowly Ministry of

Health where he felt he could perform more usefully. In place of Neville Chamberlain as Chancellor, Baldwin decided to appoint an alternative candidate for the post, Winston Churchill.

By any measure, Churchill's appointment was extraordinary. It took him as much by surprise as it shocked many of his colleagues. Walter Bridgeman, Leo Amery and Neville Chamberlain were amongst those prominent figures in the party who showed the least delight in welcoming him back into the fold.[23] He had gone down with the coalition still a Liberal. Twenty years previously he had walked out of the Conservative Party over its appeasement of Joseph Chamberlain's tariff crusade. Now he wanted to rejoin, seeing the party as the only bulwark against socialism and, worse, revolution. Furthermore, he hoped other Liberals would do likewise and ally with the Conservatives in the fight against the menace of the Labour Movement. Thus Churchill's defection was the latest example of a half-century of migration from Liberalism by those seeking to defend their interests in the one party they thought strong and determined enough to do so, be it resistance to Irish home rule or defence of the rights of property. Typically, Churchill wrapped this direction in more hyperbolic terms, writing of his support for 'a broad rallying ground for those forces which work for the greatness of Britain, and the Conservative Party have an imperial duty to perform in this respect far superior to ordinary Party lobbies'.[24]

Churchill's logic was irrefutable, but to many his desire to be rescued by a Tory lifeboat from the capsized twin-hulk of the Liberal catamaran was typical of his unprincipled habit of exspousing any cause which furthered his own career. He was unperturbed by this resentment. Standing as an Independent, he proved his worth by coming within forty-three votes of beating the Conservative candidate in a by-election for the Abbey division of Westminster. This was the prelude to his formal readoption by the party of his father and having secured the Epping constituency as a 'Constitutionalist' for the October 1924 general election, he officially rejoined the Conservative Party. Originally, he had hoped to play the role of a latter-day Joe Chamberlain by bringing a Liberal dissident group with him into alliance with the Conservatives. The success of his candidacy at Epping and the national destruction of the Liberal Party on election day (it was reduced to forty MPs) meant that with no followers to bring with him, he was clearly better off joining the Tory Party properly. What, therefore, was in Baldwin's mind when he appointed him Chancellor? In contrast to the overwhelming sympathies of Tory MPs, Churchill's commitment was still to the principles of free trade even if he was prepared to see them frayed at the edges. By sending him to the Treasury, Baldwin was at least making it clear that he would not renege on his pledge, following the 1923 defeat, not to force through tariff reform when the party was re-elected to office. Furthermore, given the damage a resurgent Liberal force could be in three-party politics, Baldwin was determined to squeeze it out of the main electoral contest. Subsequently he was keen to attract Liberal refugees to the Conservative fold on essentially Tory terms. This was in contrast to Austen Chamberlain's strategy which worked on the assumption that a Liberal–Conservative 'centre party' was the only way of fighting the impact of Labour. For this reason, the offer of the Treasury to Churchill was of a piece with Baldwin's previous (and unsuccessful) offer of the Treasury to another displaced Liberal statesman, Reginald McKenna, in 1923.

Although he forlornly hoped Sir Robert Horne would be invited back to the Treasury, Austen Chamberlain had warned Baldwin that Churchill would be 'leading a Tory rump in six months' time' if he was left out of office.[25] Doubtless, spending more time in the dinner-table company of her husband than in that of his multitudinous enemies, Churchill's wife, Clementine, encouraged her husband to believe that his return to the governing party 'endangered' Baldwin's leadership, especially with support from his friend and old accomplice in the coalition, Lord Birkenhead, whom he 'would bring back . . . as a possible Leader'.[26] Baldwin knew he needed to keep an eye on his new ministers, but having just won a resounding victory at the polls he had no reason to anticipate fatal consequences from a stab in the back. Churchill was a man not merely of great ability but also of enormous parliamentary and administrative experience. Tellingly, the other figure of experience Baldwin could call on, Austen Chamberlain, was given the prestigious post of Foreign Secretary. Most of the other Tory ex-coalitionists were brought back in a variety of other positions. This, of course, was a recovery of some of their former glory but, with Baldwin now firmly in the driving seat, not of their patronage nor, consequently, of their power. The 'new guard' were still very much in control.

VIII

Churchill's mother had kept Lord Randolph's robes as Chancellor neatly preserved ready for her son to unpack and 'the one-sheet summary in his father's writing of the Budget which Lord Randolph never introduced'[27] was in his pocket when he arrived on his first day at the Treasury. With Baldwin's support, Churchill hoped to fund better pensions and a fresh housing programme as part of the post-war reconstruction. The general feeling that Lloyd George had failed to deliver his pledge to 'build homes fit for heroes' animated the continuing desire to construct a better society from the mud of Flanders. This was an emotion that would help the 1945 landslide of Clement Attlee's Labour Government in its promise to win the peace after yet another great war. However, already bankrupt before it began, Attlee's Government had to contend with the draining expense of defence commitments, the like of which did not seem necessary in the mid-1920s in the absence of a serious threat from a hostile power. Working on the ongoing assumption that there would not be another major war for at least the next ten years, Churchill therefore intended to fund a whole series of social reforms *and* cut taxation. In order to achieve this, he adopted the policy of his father at the Treasury and proposed cutbacks in the Royal Navy. The cuts had the support of most of the Cabinet but mounting acrimony, especially the threatened resignation of Walter Bridgeman, the First Lord of the Admiralty and his Board, led Baldwin to encourage Churchill to accept a compromise. In other spheres, the Chancellor pursued orthodoxy, and his decision to return Britain to the gold standard, the effects of which will be discussed in Chapter 3, was widely regarded within his party as sound wisdom and a sign that, after the disasters of the Great War, normality had been regained. Upon this basis, he slowly began to regain credibility in Tory circles.

Meanwhile, having declined the Treasury, Neville Chamberlain was excelling at the Ministry of Health, his administrative talents at last realized when concentrated upon a field in which he had personal experience. Under his guidance, the confused and complicated patchwork of local government was entirely rationalized by 1929 with a command-ing sweep which – put to a different goal – would have been the envy of any totalitarian central planner. In tandem with Churchill at the Exchequer, Chamberlain drew up extensions to Lloyd George's pre-war insurance schemes to include widows and orphans. His mastery of detail, and the manner in which he paraded it, was, according to taste, valuable or insufferable. Inevitably he resented the way in which he thought Churchill received too much credit for what had been his own work on the social reforms of the period. He nonetheless had to concede that this was partly because Churchill was a brilliant orator who could capture the imagination of his audience on the subject, whereas he himself had no such command and had, consequently, to hope that God was in the detail.[28]

Neville Chamberlain may have had cause for jealousy at the way in which so much of his own work was attributed to the sweeping vision of the Chancellor. However, it was this very dichotomy in their make-up that made the partnership a fruitful one for the government. Churchill was five years younger than Chamberlain but in terms of government experience was far his superior. What Chamberlain really resented was the fact that whilst he had first-hand experience of the workings of local government and the provision of social services, Churchill dared to argue with him despite having no practical knowledge whatsoever. Compared to many of his Cabinet colleagues, Chamberlain had grounds for feeling that he had a better knowledge of working-class conditions and aspirations. It would perhaps have been more accurate to say that his talent was not in understanding the outlook of the less fortunate so much as in assuming responsibility for measures aimed at making their lives more endurable and enjoyable. He had a Victorian belief in the value of 'improvement' and saw it as his mission in public life to spread it as far and wide as possible.

As Paul Addison's study on the subject makes clear, Churchill was genuinely sympathetic to those less fortunate than himself. In particular 'his sympathies extended to the struggle of the "small man" – the shop-keeper, the tradesman and the clerk. It was the upper middle classes, secure in leafy suburbs, who puzzled him: the business leaders, professionals and Hampstead intellectuals.'[29] Nonetheless, he had limited knowledge of what working-class life was really like. He was personally incapable of undertaking some of the most trivial of daily chores. He travelled on the London Underground only once. Even this excursion went wrong. With childlike incompetence he proved unable to work out how to alight from the Circle Line and had to be rescued from the carriage having already done a number of complete circuits in it.[30] Yet if he was an aristocrat, then he was certainly no idle one. He had to work for his living and for much of the 1930s was never far from bankruptcy. Indeed his capacity for hard work was extraordinary and drove to distraction many of those in his staff who believed in the merits of a good night's sleep. Furthermore, whilst he may not have known what it was actually like to live in slum tenements or to dig coal from the bottom of a mine, Churchill had *volunteered* to brave the hardships of army life and the horrors of the Flanders trenches – including thirty-six dangerous reconnaissance missions into no man's land.[31] There he was prepared to place himself in danger alongside his fellow men, winning the respect of those with whom he soldiered. This was a valuable experience which Baldwin and Chamberlain had missed, being too old to fight.

Churchill was a paternalist. This led him to advocate Liberal imperialist sentiments for social reform. In this sense, he shared with Chamberlain a common vision. But, whilst Chamberlain was associated with his father's campaign for creating an imperial market, Churchill was still attached to international free trade, believing that it allowed the working class to afford more of life's basic necessities. He could allow himself poetic allusions to the England of the cottage home but, like Chamberlain, his view of Britain was essentially industrial and urban. With this homage towards the first industrial nation, came his belief in capitalism as the motor of competition and thus of progress. Socialist notions of regulation and standardization conflicted with his admiration for the strivings of the individual. As a result, his paternalism was far removed from what he took to be left-wing attempts to level down. His sense of history, and in particular his belief in the majestic pageantry of British progress, was punctuated by stories of Francis Drake and Clive of India. He believed in a Britain fit for adventurers.[32] To his admirers, Churchill was the living embodiment of this spirit. To his detractors, he displayed the downside of this trait – a penchant for recklessness.

The recklessness was evident in some of the friends with whom he surrounded himself. In the political field, his greatest companion was Lord Birkenhead, the clever and sparkling former Lord Chancellor who, in the language of the day, regularly 'dined well'. It is hard to imagine Neville Chamberlain ever quite looking forward to unhooking his stiff collar over port and cigars with a colleague of this kind. Indeed, unlike Churchill whose drinking habits have become legendary (if occasionally exaggerated), Chamberlain was not a socially outgoing figure. He reserved his emotions primarily for his family. He preferred not to dine out because, as he once told Lady Stanhope, 'I always have so much work to do in the evening.'[33] Churchill was never so fastidious about separating work from pleasure. Chamberlain's favourite pastimes centred around fishing and nature watching. Churchill derived strange and unlikely therapy from bricklaying. This, together with painting excursions and redesigning Chartwell, his country house in Kent, helped to fight off his periods of 'black dog' depression. Chamberlain was also interested in painting, but not as a practitioner, and his artistic tastes in general were noticeably conventional. Whilst he confessed to enjoying the occasional trip to the cinema, it is hard to imagine what kind of a conversation he could have attempted with a Hollywood legend had the opportunity presented itself. During the course of his life Churchill, by contrast, was more than happy to invite the likes of Charlie Chaplin, Laurence Olivier and Vivien Leigh to Chartwell for the weekend (although he was less than overjoyed with the prospect of the popular comedian, Vic Oliver, as his son-in-law). He even had an unsuccessful stab at writing a film script for Alexander Korda on the life of King George V. His daughter, Sarah, became an actress. It was in writing, however, that Churchill's spare time was most profitably spent. Although he employed a team of assistants, his output was every bit as remarkable as his literary style. The command of the English language with which he was to rally the country in 1940 was already long evident in his books and newspaper articles.

Chamberlain was sure of his judgement to an extent that led him to preclude alternative evidence. Ultimately, this was to prove extremely unfortunate. Churchill meanwhile often behaved in a manner that suggested that he thought that everything revolved around himself. After the publication of the first volume of Churchill's study of the First World War, Balfour reportedly made the priceless observation: 'I hear that Winston has written a big book about himself and called it *The World Crisis*.'[34] Chamberlain believed that he had detected a self-important trait in Churchill long before he had even known him or was involved in national politics. In 1907, the *Birmingham Daily Post* recorded the young Neville in partisan mood speaking of Churchill, then the Liberal parliamentary Under-Secretary for the colonies: 'the Colonial Office was represented in the House of Commons by a bumptious youth (laughter) who thought he could harangue those great self-governing states as if they were a parcel of schoolboys and he, forsooth, their schoolmaster. (Applause.) The sooner ... Mr Winston Churchill was sent as an Ambassador to Timbuctoo the better it would be for the country and the Empire. (Applause).'[35] Really this was a back-handed compliment to Churchill since no other personality then occupying such a junior position would be expected to play such a part on the world stage nor consequently have merited such oratorical attention. Nevertheless, whilst many future occasions must have given Chamberlain pause to reflect that his early summation of Churchill had been apposite, he had to admit to Baldwin in 1925 that the great survivor had proved to be a bonus to the government. 'I like him. I like his humour and his vitality. I like his courage,' and yet, conceded Chamberlain, 'there is somehow a great gulf fixed between him and me which I don't think I shall ever cross.'[36]

IX

The effects of the return to the gold standard were to be broadly deflationary and unemployment never fell below 10 per cent of the insured workforce during the life of the 1924–9 Baldwin Government (although this depressing figure was nonetheless a considerable improvement on the jobless figures immediately before and after Churchill's tenure at the Treasury). Despite his orthodoxy, Churchill continued to preside over budget deficits, sweetened by some creative accountancy. It was the failure of his economic policies to lessen unemployment at a time when wide-scale protective tariffs were still proscribed both by his own outlook and by Baldwin's pre-election promises that necessitated the exploration for a new initiative. Prompted and advised by the young MP for the unemployment black spot of Stockton, Harold Macmillan, the

Chancellor hit upon the idea of lifting the burden of local government rates from industry and agriculture and making up the resulting shortfall by block grants from central government raised through new taxes on petrol. Given his opposition to the role of indirect taxes in increasing the price of commodities, Churchill's source of revenue raising was surprising, even if petrol was still claimed to be a luxury. However, this was not the point upon which he ran into trouble in the Cabinet.

To Chamberlain, Churchill's proposals were an enormous nuisance landing just in time to disturb his own Ministry of Health's carefully worked out proposals for local government and poor law reform. Increasing central government's role in local authority funding reduced the latter's accountability, a process enhanced if local businesses no longer had to pay local rates and subsequently lost interest in the efficient execution of town hall housekeeping. Yet the validity of these points did not counter the need for a radical new initiative and Churchill's was virtually the only one on offer. Outside the failure to reduce unemployment, the government had by most yardsticks been a successful one, but with a general election due in 1929, it needed to be seen to be still capable of promoting fresh ideas to cure the country's ills. Without 'de-rating' (as the new policy was known), it was looking decidedly short of them. Yet much of what Churchill proposed was not practical politics and involved further spending cuts. To the cautious, there simply was not time before going to the polls to indulge this latest adventure. Now drawing on a familiar theme, Chamberlain noted that Churchill was the opposite to himself since 'it is comic how he flounders directly we get to the difficult details. His part is to brush in broad splashes of paint with highlights and deep shadows. Accuracy of drawing is beyond his ken.'[37] The resulting clash almost brought Chamberlain's resignation from the government. This was only avoided by Baldwin's mediation in persuading Churchill to compromise on the details of the scheme. However, the Prime Minister's passing on to Chamberlain what Churchill had said about him behind his back over the episode pointed to Baldwin's preferences amongst his colleagues.[38]

Although mentally and physically exhausted during the mid-term of his office, by 1927 Baldwin appeared to desire at least one further term as Prime Minister. For the most part, he enjoyed good relations with Churchill during this period, the Chancellor proving genuinely loyal to the man who had not only resurrected his political career but provided him with one of the highest offices in the land. Nevertheless, in conversation with Chamberlain, Baldwin thought that Churchill would not be the next leader since 'his candidature would split the Party from top to bottom'. Chamberlain himself, or the Attorney-General, Douglas

Hogg, seemed to Baldwin more likely successors.[39] No enormous importance should be attached to the fact that Baldwin told Chamberlain that he had a great future ahead of him. He was hardly likely to encourage his Minister of Health to continue performing good deeds for the administration by telling him that he would never progress beyond the role of hewer of wood and drawer of water. It was other considerations that gave meaning to Baldwin's prophecy. Neither Chamberlain nor Hogg could in 1927 be said to have been inspiring leaders in waiting. Yet to some extent this worked in their favour since they were nonetheless sound men not likely to be given to acts of momentous political folly. The reverse was the case for Churchill. Chamberlain conceded that Churchill was 'a brilliant creature . . . but not for all the joys of Paradise would I be a member of his staff! Mercurial! A much abused word, but it is the literal description of his temperament.'[40] Writing to his friend the Viceroy of India, who was not (then) considered to be running in the party leadership stakes, the Prime Minister summed up his Chancellor's chances of the succession with a ring of genuine objectivity. Churchill, Baldwin thought, was popular amongst Tory MPs who 'love listening to him in the House, look on his as a star turn and settle down in the stalls with anticipatory grins. But for the leadership, they would turn him down every time.'[41] Chamberlain thought that Hogg's elevation to a peerage as Lord Hailsham when he became Lord Chancellor the following year ended his chances of the leadership, an assumption that the recipient at first shared.[42] As we shall see, Hogg's peerage dimmed, but by no means removed, his prospect of succeeding Baldwin. Nonetheless, Churchill's odds were still strong enough to worry both Chamberlain and the (by then) ennobled Lord Hailsham.

Whilst Churchill liked to imagine that he was part of a government committed to enacting the 'Tory Democracy' of his father and of Disraeli, his own political behaviour straddled normal political classifications. His work with Chamberlain on social legislation, together with his cultivation of some of the younger MPs, increased his appeal to Conservative backbenchers on the left wing of the party. Meanwhile, his bullish behaviour during the General Strike of 1926, in which, as generalissimo of the government's information organ, the *British Gazette*, he was seen to epitomize the administration's victorious no-surrender attitude, displayed the sort of macho behaviour that appealed to the party's right wing. He gained further plaudits from these diehards for his uncompromising line against Egyptian nationalism and his advocacy of breaking off diplomatic relations with the Soviet Union. However, for so long as they differed on the historic debate between free trade and tariff reform, it was hard to see how he was ever going to emerge as the right wing's long-term hope for the future leadership. Many were critical of his resistance to backsliding on the commitment not to start imposing fresh protective tariffs to support ailing British industries. Caucus activists at the Party Conference were particularly condemnatory of him in this respect and the protectionist Empire Industries Association could count 200 Conservative MPs amongst its members. However, once he had conceded that an inquiry should be made into what was euphemistically called the 'safeguarding' of the iron and steel industries, it was an issue on which the Chancellor fully enjoyed the Prime Minister's support.

The nature of where the Prime Minister's personal preferences lay was further opened out in March 1929 when he considered reshuffling his Cabinet before the election. Baldwin appeared to want Chamberlain to take Churchill's place at the Treasury but by May Chamberlain thought that the Prime Minister intended to send him to the Colonial Office, a volte-face to which he was by no means hostile.[43] This opened up the possibility that Baldwin wanted Churchill to stay on as Chancellor into the next government. This was a frightening prospect to protectionists like Leo Amery who lobbied Baldwin to remove the free trader, Churchill, from control of the economy. Amery thought that Churchill's 'fine sense of the historic sweep and diversified drama of the world's affairs' might be suited to running the Committee of Imperial Defence or to directing foreign policy which he would make 'much more interesting'.[44] However, Baldwin, who wanted anything but an 'interesting' foreign policy, was thought to 'dread to find himself waking up at nights with a cold sweat at the thought of Winston's indiscretions'.[45] It might be added that if Churchill had been given the Foreign Office, having previously been Home Secretary and Chancellor of the Exchequer, his Prime Ministerial credentials would have been further boosted. Instead, Baldwin considered moving his Chancellor to the India Office, a demotion sweetened by the anticipation that it would become an active portfolio in the next government where much fresh legislation was anticipated. The Prime Minister was soon disabused of the notion that Churchill was the man for the job by the Indian Viceroy himself, Lord Irwin, who accurately predicted that Churchill was not sufficiently in sympathy with Indian aspirations.[46] The reshuffle never came, and Baldwin went into a general election, still undecided as to who should be given which portfolio or indeed whether Churchill, described even by the Labour Party's Chancellor in waiting, Philip Snowden, as the government's 'one remaining asset',[47] should be moved from the Treasury at all.

Six months before the final date by which he could call an election, Baldwin went to the polls, at the head of a campaign resplendently (if a little self-consciously) advertised by a large photograph of himself above the message 'Safety First' – a slogan borrowed from a road safety campaign. Victory was anticipated but by no means guaranteed. Would Churchill's 'de-rating' policy produce electoral dividends as he promised? With the failure to curb unemployment, would a rejuvenated Liberal Party back under the leadership of Lloyd George regain ground with its pledge to tackle the jobless queues by measures of demand management? Already the largest opposition party, could the Labour Party make a breakthrough? As the possibilities presented themselves, the Tory politicians made their own personal calculations as to how the results would affect themselves. Neville Chamberlain thought that a spell in opposition would strengthen Churchill's claim to the leadership since whereas his 'half-baked ideas' would not need to be put to the test, his 'wonderful debating and oratorical gifts would have full play'.[48] On the night of 30 May 1929, the first results started coming out of the tape machine installed in 10 Downing Street.

Two

CIVIL WAR INSIDE
THE CONSERVATIVE PARTY

I

The scene in 10 Downing Street on election night 1929 was painted in his
diary by Thomas Jones, the Deputy Secretary to the Cabinet: at one desk
'sat the PM with narrow slips of paper on which he inscribed the three
lists as they arrived'. At the desk of Baldwin's private secretary

> sat Winston doing similar lists in red ink, sipping whisky and soda, getting
> redder and redder, rising and going out often to glare at the machine himself,
> hunching his shoulders, bowing his head like a bull about to charge. As Labour
> gain after Labour gain was announced, Winston became more and more
> flushed with anger, left his seat and confronted the machine in the passage;
> with his shoulders hunched he glared at the figures, tore the sheets and
> behaved as though if any more Labour gains came along he would smash the
> whole apparatus. His ejaculations to the surrounding staff were quite
> unprintable.[1]

Once the tally had been completed, the final result proclaimed the return
of 287 Labour MPs, 260 Conservatives and 59 Liberals. It was a hung
Parliament. Dashed were any hopes that a period of stable administrations with workable majorities would continue. With the clock turned
back to the situation created by the 1923 election, it was once again the
Liberals who held the balance of power.

Baldwin was presented with two options. He could cling on to power
by concluding an anti-socialist alliance with the Liberals in order to
exclude Labour. Alternatively, he could distance himself from the Liberal
Party in the hope that they would be increasingly viewed as an
obstruction to British politics, capable only of propping up Labour
administrations. His views were influenced by personal considerations.
On the one hand, he respected the Labour leader, Ramsay MacDonald,
for his attempt to maintain his party as a moderate constitutional force
wholly distanced from the more ideological socialist incarnations on the
European continent. On the other, Baldwin's loathing of Lloyd George
had reached the extent to which he found it necessary to deface pictures

of the Welshman in his photograph collection, ensuring his devilish
resemblance to 'The Goat' nickname to which he was subjected. Baldwin
had been propelled along the Prime Ministerial road by his prominent
role in the denunciation of Lloyd George at the Carlton Club and as the
historian Paul Addison has observed, it seemed 'to have been one of his
primary aims after 1922 to prevent the most able and inventive politician
of the age from ever again holding office'.[2] Thomas Jones, who in his
secretarial capacity served both MacDonald and Baldwin, believed that
the Labour and Conservative leaders both got on together, 'because they
both hate and fear Ll.G. He is rarely for long out of their minds. The
speeches they make, the times they make them, especially when the House
is sitting, are largely determined in relation to the movements of Ll.G.
known or guessed.'[3]

In part, MacDonald and Baldwin's antipathy towards the Liberal
leader was motivated by fear of his talents and resourcefulness. Lloyd
George was certainly calculating beyond the call of British politics. As a
man who had usurped his own party leader as Prime Minister, he was
hardly likely to be the sort of role model that the Tory and Labour leaders
wanted to hold up to their colleagues as a fine example of the craft of
statesmanship. Yet a sense of insecurity was not the only emotion that
Lloyd George provoked in his rival leaders. The Liberal leader was
corrupt. That his secretary was also his mistress was bad enough,
although he was hardly the first or the last politician to find solace in a
woman more clever and attractive than his own wife. His tenure as Prime
Minister, despite its contribution towards beating Britain's deadliest foe
for a hundred years, was marred by his endowing preferment and
honours on those prepared to pay for them, and especially on those who
funded his own personal political coffers. Again, it called for selective
interpretations, on what counted as public service and what as self-
seeking ingratiation. Both Baldwin and MacDonald, after all, sat at the
top of what were well-oiled and funded parties in comparison to the
organization that Lloyd George had tried to raise in a hurry from scratch.
Nevertheless, the brazen manner in which Lloyd George operated his cash
for honours activities and, in particular, the unsavoury characters with
whom it brought him into contact, were unworthy of one who held the
highest office. It was a character attribute that did as much, and perhaps
more, than any one individual policy misjudgement to prevent him from
ever holding office again.

Baldwin was a politician who exuded a commonsense scepticism about
the value of politics. To one as unideological as the Conservative leader, it
was personal character that mattered most in the occupation of
government, a point he hammered home on what sometimes seemed like

every available speaking engagement. This was a time when many on the right wing of the Tory Party regarded trades unions as organizations through which Bolshevism might spread in Britain. In contrast, Baldwin admired the values and integrity of many of his opponents in the Labour Movement, even if he thought their policies wrong-headed and ultimately divisive. Baldwin tried to foster this non-partisan spirit amongst his colleagues; he once warned Neville Chamberlain that he was giving the impression at the dispatch box that he looked down upon the Labour members as if they were dirt. The attempt was unsuccessful. Chamberlain commented to his sister in one of the sanctimonious observations to which he was prone, that 'the fact of the matter is that intellectually, with a few exceptions, they are dirt.'[4]

After the cautionary lesson of the 1923 election, Baldwin's desire to move with, rather than shape, popular opinion led the Tory Party's more ideological thinkers to the brink of despair: there was some truth in a 1930 description of him as the 'Minister for Public Opinion'. This was not just the cynical desire to win elections that it was later painted. Rather it came from the reactionary fear that despite their innate common sense, the new mass electorate had inherited 'a political status in advance of their cultural status' that could lead them to be duped by political snake-oil sellers of the Lloyd George variety. This was not an argument against democracy, a process that Baldwin, imbued with the whig interpretation of history, acclaimed as part of the uniqueness of British progress. Rather, Baldwin believed that democracy should be fortified by the discerning judgement that dynamic politicians were incapable of sustaining. Furthermore, to the Conservative leader, discerning judgement meant the established Treasury orthodoxy of balanced budgets and the avoidance of superficial quick 'fix-its'. The latter method of grubbing for votes he considered prejudicial to the survival of democracy, given the bitter harvest he thought that it would reap when the promised goods were not delivered. The 'Safety First' election strategy stood in stark contrast to Lloyd George's sweeping 'We Can Conquer Unemployment' manifesto.[5] Lloyd George promised to build roads. Baldwin reminded voters of the speed limit.

In at least one respect, there was an important similarity of outlook between Baldwin and Churchill. They both emphasized the importance of personal character in politics. The difference was that dynamism, imagination and initiative, the very attributes that Baldwin feared, were exactly the marks of character that won Churchill's admiration – especially whenever he came into contact with Lloyd George, or looked in the mirror. This was a difference that was to foster Baldwin's underlying suspicion about Churchill. Yet if Baldwin doubted Churchill's faculties of judgement, he never quite extinguished a bemused regard for him. Baldwin never doubted that Churchill was personally a honourable man, devoid of corruption or scandal and, in contrast to the likes of Lloyd George or Birkenhead, always a fitting member of any 'Cabinet of faithful husbands'. Indeed, as we shall see, despite the irritation that Churchill was to cause both Baldwin and Neville Chamberlain in the years ahead, they did not personally make scurrilous assaults on his moral integrity, nor he on theirs.

Churchill took Baldwin's conception of the importance of character in politics and applied it not merely to the present, but also to the past. He shared Baldwin's whig conception of Britain's role as the light of world progress. This inheritance was made all the greater in Churchill's eyes not least because his ancestors had played a glittering part in the process. John Churchill, first Duke of Marlborough, had exemplified the proud and confident spirit of the new Britain that emerged from the Glorious Revolution of 1688 by masterminding the country's first sustained series of important victories on European soil since Agincourt. Likewise Churchill viewed his own father, Lord Randolph, complete with his rhetoric for 'Tory Democracy', as the dazzling manifestation of the growth of reform and parliamentary government in Britain. Churchill did his best to ensure that this interpretation became widely accepted by completing a two-volume biography of his father in 1906 and a four-volume life of the first Duke of Marlborough in 1938. These were epic works in the rich genre of historical narrative. Inevitably they associated the author with the subject in the public mind. By the time the last volume of the Marlborough biography arrived in the bookshops, the European countenance was beginning to darken to the possibility of war, and Churchill was projecting himself as the fusion of his two illustrious forebears – a great parliamentarian leading a modern democracy to military victory against a continental power dangerously seeking European hegemony.[6]

To speak of both Baldwin and Churchill as worshippers at the whig temple of British greatness needs the qualification that they both seemed to fear that the tradition had been broken in the twentieth century. Never previously squeamish in the face of battle (of which he had seen more than his fair share), Churchill's faith in scientific progress was shattered by the catastrophe of the Great War. The guns of August 1914 had not only blown away the lives of a generation but had smashed the liberal certainties upon which his faith in the inevitability of progress had depended.[7] Unlike Churchill, Baldwin had not witnessed the slaughter on the western front at first hand but he was deeply affected by it nonetheless. This emotion – perhaps even this sense of guilt – manifested itself in his anonymous donation of much of his personal wealth, accumulated through his family's ironworks, to help pay off the National Debt with which the war had lumbered its survivors. Commentators have sneered at the way in which Baldwin reacted to the realities of inter-war Britain by making so many speeches on the pre-industrial rural idyll, about which he memorably commented that as far as he was concerned, 'England is the country and the country is England' before rhapsodizing about the 'tinkle of the hammer on the anvil' and 'the sight of a plough team coming over the brow of a hill'.[8] Critics of Britain's industrial performance have linked this sort of escapism from the reality of an urban nation to the consequence of economic decline[9] – although the post-1945 worship of the bulldozer and all things modern did not noticeably improve Britain's industrial standing relative to her competitors. In fact, Baldwin's rural mysticism, so far removed from the source of his own family's wealth, served a positive need in the years following the Great War's destruction of much that was comforting and familiar. His words came as a reassurance that despite the carnage of war, something had yet been salvaged of the old values, sights and sounds, and that there was more to treasure than merely a land left to mourn its lost content. Baldwin gave voice to the popular yearning that, after the deluge, there was still hope.

Inclined towards the preservation of stability as the fundamental goal of office, Baldwin was now to find himself at odds with the profound effect that electoral defeat had on the Conservative Party. The loss of office was to liberate the party from the caution that it had inherited as part of the discipline of government. In part, this was because protectionists felt free to argue that if the party could lose an election without any significant tariff programme, then why should it not risk fighting on such a platform in the future? Alternative policies, like Churchill's de-rating scheme, were argued to have contributed to the defeat. Furthermore, the fall of seats increased the proportion of committed wholehearted protectionists amongst those Tory MPs returned to Parliament from just under a half to two-thirds. A more homogenous Conservative Party composed on this basis promised to be zealously in favour of protectionism. This would isolate completely those like Churchill whose instincts were still essentially for free trade. Given this equation, it is little wonder that the ex-Chancellor favoured an anti-socialist alliance with the Liberals, whose ideological commitment to free trade would prevent the Conservatives from consummating their protectionist infatuation. Concomitantly, this would secure his own position in a Conservative Government cooperating with the free traders. Here, Churchill's strategy was concerned with more than the exigencies of his own career. The

Labour Party, particularly under its new Chancellor, the neo-Gladstonian Philip Snowden, shared the Liberals' commitment to free trade. This was not surprising given the perceived hostility of the working class towards protectionist tariffs that promised to raise the price of their basic food necessities. On the morrow of the 1929 election defeat, Churchill wrote to Baldwin warning that a protectionist Tory Party would ensure 'one result – very likely final for our life time, namely a Lib–Lab block in some form or another and a Conservative Right hopelessly excluded from Power'. Raising the spectre of internecine warfare to a sceptical Neville Chamberlain, Churchill warned that a more protectionist Tory Party would ensure that a fifth of the Conservative Party and its popular vote would be 'split off'.[10] No less ominous to Baldwin and Chamberlain for being unstated was the potential threat that Churchill would make a nuisance of himself by leading the schism. Politics, it seemed, could revert to the uncertainties and upsets of the loose-anchored statesmen that had marked out the age of Joseph Chamberlain and Lord Randolph Churchill.

Churchill was not alone in seeking rapprochement with Lloyd George. Austen Chamberlain, prepared to put his protectionist leanings to one side, spoke in a shadow cabinet meeting on 11 July arguing for an approach to the Liberals with fusion as the ultimate goal. Baldwin had to tread carefully, since if he mishandled the situation, then the danger appeared to be that the old coalitionist element might regroup in order to reverse the verdict of the 1922 Carlton Club *putsch*. Baldwin allowed Churchill to keep private channels open with Lloyd George, a device that kept the leader personally out of danger if and when the scheme backfired.

The Liberals had fought the 1929 election committed to an interventionist programme, *We Can Conquer Unemployment*, which owed much to the thinking of the economist John Maynard Keynes and called for far greater state interference in the workings of the economy than was advocated by the Labour leadership of MacDonald and Snowden. In fact, the main effect of Lloyd George's declaration in favour of financing investment through running up budget deficits was that Labour (and those similarly minded in the Conservative Party) scored out their own proposals in this direction so that they could point the finger of irresponsibility at him. Whilst Labour were the more obvious party for the Liberals to maintain in power, especially if the socialists could be convinced that their goals were compatible with Lloyd George's progressive tendencies, the Liberal leader nonetheless claimed to be prepared to drop the adoption of his economic programme as the price for alliance with the Conservatives. Churchill reported this breakthrough to his colleagues in the shadow cabinet, suggesting that the Liberals would ditch

Labour and put in power the Conservatives in return for the introduction of electoral reform. A fresh general election would then be called and, with the alternative vote system replacing that of 'first-past-the-post', the Liberals could be expected to make substantial gains under the new system. However, the likely outcome of this state of affairs promised continual coalition government with the free trading Liberal Party permanently calling the shots as the central power-broking force. This naturally was unappealing to the protectionist majority amongst the Tories.[11] As we shall see, when the barriers of Lloyd George and free trade ideology were removed from the equation in 1931, Neville Chamberlain would prove more than willing to negotiate an alliance with Liberals marshalled by the more compliant and less overtly duplicitous Sir John Simon. The previous generation of Conservative leaders had, after all, been prepared to do a deal with Chamberlain's father, a Liberal radical, when it was clear that he would drop the more discordant aspects of his outlook in a common defence of the issues that they agreed were of more fundamental importance.

Before the 1929 election, Lloyd George had put to both Churchill and Sir Robert Horne options for cooperation if a hung Parliament was to be returned. It was nonetheless an eventuality that Churchill hoped to avoid. In his last days as Chancellor, he deliberately went out of his way to make the Tories' economic manifesto commitments jar with the Liberals as much as possible. He regarded Lloyd George's loan-financed employment schemes to be a waste of money which, without an inflationary expansion of credit, would only crowd out more profitable private investment. Indeed, Churchill was at the forefront of the 'Safety First' campaign. He helped block the right wing's imperially dressed copy of Keynesian investment, 'Empire Development', arguing that the Tories 'should not try to compete with L.G., ... but take our stand on sound finance'.[12] Reporting on a dinner conversation he had had with Churchill, Lord Beaverbrook, the intrigue-addicted owner of the *Daily Express*, recorded that whatever the talk in favour of a Liberal–Conservative coalition, Churchill thought that, although the Tories' faith in Baldwin had evaporated, he personally 'had no intention whatever of allying himself with Lloyd George, although rumours to this effect in Conservative circles have been doing him a great deal of harm'.[13] His behaviour on election night could not leave even the most suspicious mind in any doubt that what he wanted was the return of a Conservative Government with a working majority. It was Neville Chamberlain who noted in his diary two years later that Lloyd George could be surprisingly reticent about discussing inter-party deals: 'he had done so before with Winston but

Winston had told S.B.* and S.B. had told Ramsay† which was very embarrassing to him'.[14] Churchill, therefore, was not at this stage negotiating behind his leader's back. Indeed, if there was any double dealing at work, then it revolved around what the leader of the Conservative Party was doing in warning the leader of the Labour Party about manoeuvres to oust his government.

II

With Lloyd George unable to offer terms acceptable to the Tories, it looked increasingly likely that the Conservatives would have to dig in for a prolonged siege of the minority Labour Government. Given his hesitancy to involve himself in personalized attacks on the Labour ministers, Baldwin's credentials to wage an effective war from the opposition benches was open to question. As Neville Chamberlain had anticipated, the situation therefore provided Churchill with his chance to demonstrate the partisan powers of debate at his command. Churchill's experience of being out of government from 1929 has been interpreted by historians as the period in which he adopted right-wing views against reform in the British Empire whilst most of those on the Conservative front bench – and Baldwin in particular – were moving towards a looser control of imperial domains. These views isolated Churchill both from his party's reformist leaders and from the younger generation of 'progressives' on the backbenches. Indeed, Churchill himself later came to share some of this analysis, writing after the Second World War that his leader's failure to mount a sustained attack on the Labour Government's relaxation of British authority in Egypt and its recall of the imperialist-minded High Commissioner in Cairo, Lord Lloyd, was the beginning of his 'divergence from Mr Baldwin'.[15] However, at the time, Lloyd's dismissal did not provide the fertile ground for creating trouble that Churchill had hoped. His blundering interjection in the debate in the House of Commons on the issue was widely regarded as a misjudgement by gloating rivals for the leadership. Chief amongst this group was Neville Chamberlain, who noted with scarcely suppressed glee that the intervention had made Churchill 'look exceedingly foolish'.[16]

In the debates over constitutional reform in Egypt, Churchill laid down the doctrine that was to guide his reactionary view on reform elsewhere in the empire: 'Once we lose confidence in our mission in the East, once we repudiate our responsibilities to foreigners and minorities, once we feel ourselves unable calmly and fearlessly to discharge our duties to vast

* Stanley Baldwin.
† Ramsay MacDonald.

helpless populations, then our presence in those countries will be stripped of every moral sanction, and resting only upon selfish interests or military requirements, it will be a presence which cannot long endure.'[17] As a Liberal, in both the Asquith and the Lloyd George governments, Churchill had established his credentials on the side of the progressive reformers of the British Empire. When in 1919, British-led troops had opened fire on unarmed demonstrators at Amritsar in the Punjab, Churchill had been amongst those politicians shocked by the crime that had left 379 dead and more than 1200 injured. Tory diehards, on the other hand, had viewed the commanding officer, Brigadier General Dyer, as the hero of the hour, maintaining that his action had restored order to an increasingly lawless part of India. In a fine speech to the Commons, Churchill had deplored this attitude, declaring that

> Governments who have seized upon power by violence and by usurpation have often resorted to terrorism in their desperate efforts to keep what they have stolen, but the august and venerable structure of the British Empire, where lawful authority descends from hand to hand and generation after generation, does not need such aid. Such ideas are absolutely foreign to the British way of doing things . . . our reign in India or anywhere else has never stood on the basis of physical force alone, and it would be fatal to the British Empire if we were to try to base ourselves only upon it.[18]

In all, 129 diehards had defied the party whip and voted against the government's condemnation of Dyer's action. In contrast, the Conservatives' moderates, men like Baldwin, Austen and Neville Chamberlain and the Tory MP Edward Wood (the future Viceroy, Lord Irwin and later still, Foreign Secretary as Lord Halifax), had had no hesitation in siding with Churchill and the front bench on the issue. Dyer was dismissed from the army.

Churchill's association with Lord Lloyd in 1929 combined with his unending admiration for the right-wing former Secretary of State for India, Lord Birkenhead, suggest that his liberal sentiments had been wearing thin for some time before he began to make 'diehard' pronouncements on imperial matters in public. This seems to have been the reality even if, as is made clear by the two quotations above on his stances on Egypt in 1929 and the Punjab in 1919–20, there was a consistency in his belief that the empire had to be about more than merely the imposition of order by any means necessary. The occasion of Lloyd's dismissal marked the commencement of Churchill's campaign to appeal to the right wing of the Conservative Party. The evidence suggests that the political strategy underpinning such imperialist outbursts was also directed with an eye to alliance with Lloyd George.

In October 1929, Baldwin gave his backing to the policy of the Labour Government as proclaimed by the Indian Viceroy, Lord Irwin, that 'dominion status' should be the goal of Britain's gradual relinquishment of the government of India. Extraordinarily, Baldwin defended himself against the outrage this caused within his party by claiming that, being out of the country at the time, he had supported the Irwin Declaration on the misunderstanding that it would have his shadow cabinet's support.[19] Churchill, who had been annoyed during the Lloyd debate that the Liberals had been 'sourly impartial',[20] saw a greater opportunity over the controversy surrounding this new Indian imbroglio. He was encouraged by the fact that Lloyd George (influenced by the hostile sentiments of the former Liberal Viceroy of India, Lord Reading) appeared as if he too would oppose Indian reform based on Irwin's agenda.[21] Even Irwin himself heard that the Liberal leader wanted 'to make trouble and to attract Diehards to his Imperial flag'.[22] Whilst on a lecture tour of the USA and Canada, Churchill received a letter from Lloyd George warning him that the new Labour Government was receiving a favourable press and that without a Tory–Liberal combination, Labour would be in office for another seven years. Lloyd George expressed the hope that the two of them might 'interchange views' on his return and unify against the Coal Bill.[23] Baldwin's disastrous mishandling of the Irwin Declaration now promised richer pickings. Churchill raced back across the Atlantic to attend the ensuing debate.

Amongst the senior Tories who shared Churchill's misgivings about supporting the process of Indian home rule were Lord Birkenhead, Sir Austen Chamberlain and Sir Laming Worthington-Evans. These men were all ministers and prominent supporters of the old Lloyd George coalition government. Controversy over Indian home rule promised, therefore, not merely to bond old Tory diehards together against the common progressive front shared by Ramsay MacDonald and Stanley Baldwin, but, more unexpectedly, to realign the Tory right wing behind the 'old gang' coalitionists whom they had voted out in 1922.

The debate in the Commons over the Irwin Declaration confirmed the suspicions of the Conservative Party Chairman, J.C.C. Davidson, that the old gang of 1922 were plotting to get their own back on the Baldwin ascendancy which had replaced them:

> For days it has been obvious that the arch-tactician, the 'Goat'* was setting the trap which would have resulted, if we had walked into it, in complete disaster to the Party. He had wanted to put down a Motion of Censure on the

* Lloyd George.

Government, but Stanley* had put his foot down and said that under no circumstances would he have a discussion on India founded on a Vote of Censure. The 'Goat' had made his speech without any reference to India but solely in order to get in a right and a left. With his right barrel he hoped to wing the socialist government, and with his left to kill S.B. and split the Tory Party . . . If there had been a Division . . . S.B. and probably two-thirds of the Party would have brigaded with the Socialists in one lobby, and the 'Goat' and his colleagues in the Coalition, and the Diehards and all S.B.'s personal enemies would have trooped into the other. And the fools never saw it, and even some of our leaders like Neville† hadn't twigged the situation.[24]

Davidson, it must be said, was an obsessive when it came to real or imagined plots by the old coalitionists to undermine the Baldwin supremacy. Beyond the principled influence of Lord Reading on the issue, Lloyd George was as much indulging in short-term mischief-making as anything else. The idea that the Liberal Party was going to forward the colours of imperial reaction not just on a set of particular details but on principle really would have pointed to a Barnum and Bailey world. However, the threat that Lloyd George posed was real insofar as there were clearly many Tories ready to fall in with him as a price worth paying to oust the Labour Government on a censure motion. Had Baldwin not managed to thwart the censure motion, it 'would have meant', in the eyes of one of his supporters, 'a stormy party meeting and Baldwin's resignation'. It did not go unnoticed that 'as soon as Lloyd George got up Winston and Worthington-Evans on each side of him leant forward and punctuated every sentence with emphatic "Hear hears!"'[25] The 'old coalition element', as Samuel Hoare (one of Baldwin's chief supporters on Indian home rule) referred to them, were sitting side by side in the chamber for the occasion. 'Throughout the debate', recorded Hoare ominously, 'Winston was almost demented with fury and since the debate has scarcely spoken to anyone.'[26]

During 1930, the prospect of Lloyd George fighting on the same side as the Tory right-wing 'diehards' and the former members of his coalition diminished. Whilst Baldwin was secure as leader, there was no prospect of his doing a deal with the Liberal leader. The appropriate action therefore was for Lloyd George to ensure the continuation of the Labour Government. At the same time this decision, coupled with the effects of a mounting economic recession, further encouraged Tories to place protectionism as the top political priority above that of saving India for the empire. In consequence, it is hard to see who amongst the Tories was

---

* Stanley Baldwin.

† Neville Chamberlain.

seriously going to support any kind of Churchill–Lloyd George coalition
even if one had been on offer. The situation was no different for the
Liberals, most of whom had no wish to be part of a coalition leaning
towards protectionism (at least in 1930) and who had been, in Clement
Attlee's tart observation, only temporarily reunited by a common distrust
of their leader.[27]

III

The policy that made a Tory rapprochement with other parties most
difficult was the issue that had never been far from the centre of
Conservative debate since it was launched by Joseph Chamberlain in
1903. Protectionist tariffs against foreign imports had three main
commendations. They were a means of raising revenue without increasing
recourse to progressive income and other direct taxes. Second, they were a
means of reducing imports, especially at a time when countries like
Germany and the USA had erected tariffs against British trade. British
production would therefore receive a boost in satisfying demand in the
domestic market which – according to progressive economists – suffered
from under-investment. Third, by conceding free trade to the countries of
the British Empire, a common market would be created that would assist
the political and economic cooperation of the white Dominions whilst
raising united tariff barriers to curtail trade with the rest of the world.
Imperialists hoped that this common market would inevitably move its
members further towards shared interests and, as a result, lead towards
the building up of the empire into a political federal union with Britain at
its heart.

Against the arguments of the economic imperialists, the mid-nine-
teenth-century wisdom of classical liberalism could be fielded. Protecting
the domestic market by discouraging competition encouraged industrial
inefficiency, removed marginal advantage and thereby brought about
economically disabling higher costs for both the British consumer and
producer. Protectionism, therefore, would lead to an economy trampled
down by uninnovative dinosaurs. Furthermore, the centrepiece of the
Tory protectionists' vision, empire free trade (otherwise known as
imperial preference), was unobtainable without the consent of the
imperial Dominions. For the most part these emerging nations (Canada,
South Africa, Australia, New Zealand) were not anxious to have their
fledgling industries opened up to better-established British competition
any more than they wanted their own sovereign powers reabsorbed by
London. The siren voices now pointed to the 1929 defeat as evidence that
the Tories could lose elections without a protectionist commitment.

Furthermore, the main charge was still irrefutable that the Tories had never won an election on a pro-protection platform. The 'dear food' card had always been played with success by their opponents in the pro-free trade Labour and Liberal parties. By necessitating duties on foreign wheat, empire free trade failed to answer this charge, since wheat from the Dominions was still above the floor of the world market price.

Despite these observations, Conservative MPs elected to the 1929 Parliament were overwhelmingly enthusiastic for increasing the scope of protection. Many of the remaining free traders in the party were marginalized – their main appearances in the popular press reduced to occasional photographs of them arriving or leaving church at each other's funerals. Churchill was the only Tory front-line contender in the Commons still wedded to the principles of free trade. During 1930 even he had to shift his ground on the conviction that he mourned was 'the only one which is left to him'.[28] Although rising unemployment promised to tarnish the free trade case, Baldwin remained cautious. To win a future general election, the Conservatives would have to win back conceded constituencies in the North of England and because of their higher concentration of working-class votes, this was where it was felt food taxes held least appeal. Yet if Baldwin wanted to stall the enthusiasm of the protectionist zealots around him, then keeping Churchill as a human shield – an excuse to hide behind the failure to move more swiftly towards food taxes, thereby deflecting criticism of the party leader – proved a more far-sighted strategy. Keeping Churchill on board also prevented him from finding an excuse to cross the floor back to Lloyd George. Baldwin's front bench was short of good orators and, for all his hazardous eccentricities, Churchill was still the star performer.

Baldwin's cautious policy centred upon the extension of protectionist measures to help threatened core industries but did not go as far as a whole-hog imperial policy embracing import tariffs on basic foods. The device of assisting the staple industries, known as 'safeguarding', was acceptable even to Churchill who had permitted its mild extension during his period at the Exchequer as a way of fending off more damaging wide-ranging initiatives. That the Conservative Party was in 1930 committed to distorting the market to thwart free trade and prop up 'lame ducks' indicates not only the difference in industrial policy between the party of Baldwin and that of Thatcher and Major, but also shows how far Baldwin's party had moved from that of its architect, Sir Robert Peel, whose government committed Britain to the process of creating free trade in the 1840s. However, in 1930, as at so many other times, the party was accurately reflecting the views of large sections of business as expressed through its interest groups and in the City itself.[29] This did not lead to the adoption of corporatist politics – indeed, tariffs were a way of safeguarding industry without direct state planning in business strategy. They were a manifestation of the priority that the Tories appeared to be giving to the demands of the producer above the interests of the consumer. Furthermore, 'safeguarding' may have involved interfering in the market but that market had already been severely dislocated. Most of Britain's foreign competitors were taking advantage of her free trading policy in order to dump their products – products that were in turn produced behind a tariff barrier to keep British exports out of their markets. Unemployment rose from over one million in 1929 to two and a half million by the end of 1930. Baldwin's attempts to retard the pace of the protectionist ideologues in his party were therefore hampered by a worsening economic recession and the belief amongst so many sections of business and his party that free trade was not working. The launch of a concerted press campaign in favour of all-out tariffs against the rest of the world, combined with empire free trade, now threatened to divide Baldwin from the rest of his party.

The campaign was spearheaded by the rival press barons, Lord Rothermere, owner of the *Daily Mail*, and Lord Beaverbrook, owner of the *Daily Express*. The two were divided by a circulation war but united in a personal detestation of Baldwin. As an émigré Canadian, Beaverbrook was particularly interested in encouraging imperial solidarity and pushed for empire free trade far harder than did many of his compatriots back in Canada. Rothermere was on the authoritarian wing of the political right, his loathing of weak leadership from whatever quarter a somewhat unhealthy inclination in the decade of dictatorship. In a bizarre distraction that gave him considerable satisfaction, Rothermere's interest in righting the supposed wrongs of the post-war territorial settlement in eastern Europe encouraged a campaign in Hungary to offer him the throne (in the end he made do with a few public places being renamed after him and an agreeable official visit lined with cheering peasants chanting 'Long live the Lord!)'[30] To Rothermere Baldwin was 'a completely incompetent person who, by the accident of post-war politics, flunked his way into high office'.[31] In view of the sort of leader that Rothermere admired, Baldwin's rambling style might well have been a small mercy for which to be thankful. For his part, the Conservative leader regarded Beaverbrook and Rothermere in the same nocturnal light as Lloyd George, their characters confirming everything he had always thought about the importance of personal integrity in political life.

A press campaign was one thing, but when Beaverbrook and Rothermere joined forces to fund and promote their own party to put up candidates against Conservatives at by-elections the position became much more serious. Success for the press barons' 'Empire Crusade' and 'United Empire' parties in splitting the Tory vote to the advantage of Labour inevitably alarmed Conservative MPs whose natural inclinations were in any case for the imperialist vision advocated by Beaverbrook. It was therefore increasingly difficult for Baldwin to articulate woolly views on protectionism indefinitely. This suited Chamberlain who wanted a more vigorous statement of policy on the subject but it did not please Churchill who suggested that the Tories should deliberately face the press barons head-on in a choreographed mini-general election in four test case by-elections. This was regarded by one prominent Tory ex-minister and advocate of protectionism, Leo Amery, as extraordinarily foolish. In his view the 'immense importance even in the eyes of our own members and candidates, of not quarrelling with the press' spoke volumes for where he envisaged the sympathies of the party's foot-soldiers lay.[32] He was far from alone in this interpretation. The sense that the Conservatives were on the run – not least from their natural supporters – was echoed by the Party Chairman who feared that the confrontation proposed by Churchill would 'be disastrous to the Party and might break it up altogether'.[33]

The press barons' campaign at first paralysed the naturally lethargic Baldwin, a man who, even by his own admission, was 'not one of the world's workers'.[34] In marked contrast, Neville Chamberlain was far more active in responding to the vigorous challenge posed by the 'Empire Crusade' movement. Chamberlain thought Beaverbrook's policy impractical and obsolete, but he recognized the press lords' capacity for mischief. In any case he thought the party should extricate itself from the tight pledges against tariff reform in which Baldwin seemed content to keep it bound. It was Chamberlain who took the initiative in trying to broker a deal with Beaverbrook, marginalizing Churchill whose free trade history made him unsuitable for the task. This was significant since the former Chancellor and ongoing Chairman of the party's Finance Committee was technically still the figure expected to undertake the spade work of economic policy. By the time Chamberlain departed for a three-month holiday to East Africa that kept him out of the country until March 1930, he had got as far as an understanding, if not an agreement, with Beaverbrook.

Days before Chamberlain's return, Beaverbrook briefly halted his campaign when Baldwin agreed to his suggestion that if the Tories were re-elected, they would hold a referendum on enforcing food taxes. However, as evinced from Churchill's enthusiasm for the proposal,[35] it soon became clear that the referendum was a device aimed to put off the issue and remove it from party politics in the meantime. Hostilities soon resumed. Rothermere appeared to be more interested in the blood sport of hunting Baldwin than in attaining realizable objectives, whilst Beaver-brook inevitably saw through the attempt, in his words, to turn an Empire Crusade spear into a Conservative Party shield.[36]

Chamberlain wanted a 'free hand' policy whereby a future Conservative Government could, subject to parliamentary approval, negotiate any appropriate deal with the Dominions, declaring void the party's previously made restrictive pledges on fiscal policy. In this way, he hoped that Beaverbrook's opposition could be bought off without the party having to anchor itself to the unrealizable goal of empire free trade. By proposing a negotiating position that delayed having to declare a fixed position, Chamberlain could also hope that his scheme would avoid too close a scrutiny during the heat of a general election campaign.

By May 1930, the Conservatives were racked with self-doubt. With the re-emergence of Beaverbrook's Empire Crusade, Baldwin found a scapegoat by accepting the resignation of his loyal friend, J.C.C. Davidson, as Party Chairman. With few takers for this thankless task, Neville Chamberlain reluctantly agreed to assume the position. Meanwhile, Baldwin was humiliated when a Conservative constituency association refused to let him address a meeting at Crystal Palace unless it was chaired by Beaverbrook. Since Beaverbrook was fielding candidates against those of the Conservative Party this was an extraordinary affront (although Beaverbrook somehow managed to retain his membership of the party). In June, Conservative MPs gathered in Caxton Hall to decide the fate of the referendum policy and, consequently, the authority of Baldwin. With the usual pleas for unity at a time when a general election might not be far off, the party leadership's victory by 150 to 80 was decidedly outside the margin of comfort. Far from settling the matter, the issue of Baldwin's ability to command allegiance was now open to question. With Conservative Party policy the prerogative of the leader, the obvious evidence that so many Tory MPs did not like the policy threatened to spell doom for Baldwin. Chamberlain was already in effect contradicting him by forgetting about the referendum pledge and speaking publicly once again of a 'free hand' policy to discuss future wheat quotas and an emergency 10 per cent tariff on non-empire imports. Echoing his father, Chamberlain admitted that this was an 'unauthorized programme' of his own. Well-received, it was intended to bounce Baldwin into action. In scenes to be repeated in the mid-1990s by John Major's attempt to avoid his government having to declare whether or not it proposed to abolish sterling in favour of the Euro, different Conservatives all appeared to be contradicting each other, and doing so in public as a way of trying to force the hand of the leader to declare where party policy lay.

Chamberlain had made his play for replacing the referendum pledge for the 'free hand' during Baldwin's annual sojourn in Aix-les-Bains. When the leader at last returned, Chamberlain argued the wisdom of the proposed change. Baldwin referred the issue to his colleagues on the front bench. Whilst they were considering it in October, the Canadian Prime Minister played into Chamberlain's hands at the Imperial Conference in London by declaring Beaverbrook's empire free trade objective to be 'neither desirable nor possible'.[37] When the Labour Government rejected Canada's suggested alternative of reciprocal preferences, Chamberlain seized the initiative and rushed Baldwin into announcing Conservative support for the Canadian proposals as the basis for future tariff policy. With this announcement, Chamberlain's 'free hand' tactic replaced the referendum pledge as party policy. The decision had rested with Baldwin, but there was no doubt who had been its main architect and proponent. Chamberlain had moved his party back on to the perimeters of the agenda laid out by his father twenty-seven years previously. In bolstering the Tories' sense of purpose, he threatened to marginalize Churchill.

The new policy had as its first step a preferential 10 per cent duty on non-empire goods. This implied a tax on meat, which Churchill had set his hand against. Chamberlain was aghast to witness his rival's failure to be manoeuvred off the party's front bench during a meeting of senior colleagues to discuss the policy. Churchill said that he would have to go: '(he even took the opportunity of bidding us all a sort of formal farewell) that for a time no one found anything to say. Probably the majority felt that if he really meant to go it would be hailed with delight by the party generally. At last Austen* spoke up and begged him not to take a course which would so seriously injure the cause. Winston started to reply but broke off apparently overcome with emotion and we separated.'[38] Preparing to part company with the party leadership, Churchill allowed himself to be dissuaded by an emollient letter from Baldwin and by the relatively little fuss which the proposed adoption of meat tariffs created in the media. Even Chamberlain, with measured insincerity,[39] urged him against 'any irrevocable step'.[40] Instead, Churchill played for time, not wishing to go out on a policy for which he had no backing in the party and hoping that the Dominions might not in the end prove to be 'willing to offer any new entry into their markets for our manufactures which would justify such drastic measures'.[41]

Yet as efforts were renewed to further the constitutional reform in India, Churchill found himself at the apex of a number of alliances. He had joined the Indian Empire Society, a pressure group designed to thwart home rule in the subcontinent and, whilst alienated by Lloyd George's

* Sir Austen Chamberlain.

increasingly interventionist economic views, he was still captivated by the Liberal leader and the prospects of political realignment.[42] Writing to Baldwin, Churchill stated that he now cared more about India than anything else.[43] He reiterated this view to Beaverbrook, reflecting on the battles of the First World War and commenting that 'when I think of the way in which we poured out blood and money to take Contalmaison or to hold Ypres, I cannot understand why it is we should now throw away our conquests and our inheritance with both hands, through sheer helplessness and pusillanimity'.[44] Churchill's reluctance to concede to protectionism distanced him from much of the Tory right wing, many of whom were 'diehards' against Indian reform. In part because of this, he still harboured the fantasy that he and Beaverbrook could 'gather the Liberals to us' in defence of the Raj.[45] His conniving with Beaverbrook at this moment was no less extraordinary, considering the damage the press baron's campaign for tariffs was doing to his position on the Conservative front bench.[46]

Churchill's attempt to augment his position came at a time when Baldwin's own future was becoming yet more doubtful, despite the success of the change in policy over tariff reform. Rumours were circulating that over forty Conservative MPs were demanding the leader's resignation.[47] When seventeen of them called for a meeting of MPs, Baldwin decided to ask for a personal vote of confidence. By putting his leadership on the line, he was forcing his opponents to declare themselves openly rather than waiting for them to dispose of him quietly at the moment of their choosing. John Major was later to employ this device when his leadership was questioned in 1995. Baldwin could not take anything for granted since many of the Tories' senior figures were amongst those most uneasy about his grip on events. Were it not for the 'revolting' prospect of handing over a victory to the press plutocrats, Austen Chamberlain was toying with getting Walter Bridgeman to suggest to Baldwin that it was time that, like Captain Oates in the Antarctic, he performed for his party an act of courageous self-sacrifice.[48] Yet, of the senior figures in the party, only Lord Derby stated publicly that it was time for Baldwin to go. Even he characteristically changed his tune when it became clear that Baldwin was not going to do so.[49]

Despite being the potential prime beneficiary of the leader's demise, it was the new Party Chairman, Neville Chamberlain, who selflessly did his best to ensure a victory for Baldwin by drafting the resolution of support for his leadership. He also made sure that peers and as yet unelected parliamentary candidates as well as MPs would be eligible to vote. It could be assumed that these additional voters would swamp the more right-wing southern English-orientated block of MPs.[50] As before, the meeting was held in Caxton Hall, but this time on the day of the South Paddington by-election. An effective speech from Baldwin was backed up by support on the platform from Lord Hailsham. Confidence in Baldwin was retained by 462 votes to 116. News of the 'Empire Crusade' by-election victory over the Conservative candidate arrived after the meeting had broken up.

IV

Baldwin's problems were far from at an end. Although Churchill toed the line by speaking out against the press lords 'who on the morrow of our defeat will sail away on some new adventure of their own', he too was now embarking on his own odyssey against Baldwin's broad acceptance of the Labour Government's policy for India. On this issue, Rothermere was promising Churchill support.[51] The nature of the proposed Indian reforms will be discussed in Chapter 5, but at this stage, with a constitutional convention – the Round Table Conference – meeting in London attended by Indian as well as British delegates, the process of imperial abdication appeared to diehards to be already under way. Civil order in India had been undermined by the concerted campaign of the nationalists to disregard British authority and boycott her interests. The crunch came on 22 January 1931 when the Viceroy, Lord Irwin, released leaders of the Indian pro-home rule Congress Party from gaol. Contrary to British hopes, the freed Congress leaders failed to suspend their campaign of civil disobedience. Having in 1896 gazed down upon India from his mount in the 4th Hussars, Churchill decided he could take no more.

The prospect of food taxes had brought Churchill close to breaking from party policy but he had certainly not wanted to resign from the front bench on the issue. As we have seen, he underwent several political contortions in order to avoid doing so. India was different and, judged by the rumblings in the party, it seemed possible that (unlike tariff policy) it was an issue upon which Churchill's views were supported by much of the parliamentary party. Furthermore, with the death of Lord Birkenhead in September 1930, Churchill had clearly become the foremost diehard opponent of Indian reform. Accustomed to overcoming the less adept speeches of the traditional right wing on the subject, the Labour front bench would now have a formidable cross-examiner. Consequently, a real attempt to spike Churchill's guns was made at the outset of the adjournment debate on India by the Prime Minister, Ramsay MacDonald. He reminded the Commons of the new convert to diehardism's personal

involvement in the previous extension of Indian democracy (the Montagu–Chelmsford reforms) back in 1919 when he was a member of the
coalition government.

If past inconsistencies had troubled Churchill, then he would have
achieved little in politics. His fighting contribution to the Indian debate
focused upon a mixture of asserting Britain's right to rule along the lines
he had set out in the debates over Egypt in 1929 and how, if that right
was surrendered, the Muslims and Untouchables would be at the mercy of
an intolerant 'Hindu-raj'. This terrible day of reckoning coincided with
the build-up for his peroration: 'The great liner is sinking in a calm sea.
One bulkhead after another gives way; one compartment after another is
bilged; the list increases; she is sinking; but the captain and the officers
and the crew are all in the saloon dancing to the jazz band. But wait till
the passengers find out what is their position.'[52] Speaking off the cuff,
Baldwin rose to respond to his colleague, claiming that he would not have
spoken had it not been for Churchill's performance, which had been
delivered like King George III losing the American colonies but 'endowed
with the tongue of Edmund Burke'. Baldwin's more temperate response
centred less upon the right form of government for India as upon the
niceties of not polarizing Westminster politics over Indian home rule as
had Irish home rule before the war. This was typical of Baldwin's
consensus approach to government in contrast to the sort of ideological
conflict upon which Churchill thrived. Had Baldwin left it at that,
retaining his customary vagueness, matters may not have come to a head
at that moment. However, he went further still, declaring that if his party
was returned at the next election, it would 'have only one duty, and that
one duty is to try to implement so far as we can what has been done in the
[Round Table] Conference . . . I should consider it my duty, so far as I
was able if I were leading the party still, to use every effort in my power to
bring about that federal constitution.'[53]

This sentiment was delivered at a time when unemployment and
government spending were spiralling upwards at home and shouts in the
party for full-blooded protectionism were becoming deafening. Into this
atmosphere, Baldwin seemed to be suggesting that a future Conservative
Government's primary commitment should be to support the Labour
Party's policy in giving more power to Indians halfway across the world.
Referring to his future leadership of the party as an 'if' was a particularly
dangerous admission of vulnerability when there were so many Tory MPs
who needed no encouragement in contemplating life without him.
Baldwin seemed to be almost willing a contest. In making his stand on the
issue of Indian reform, he appeared to have chosen poor ground upon
which to fight.

Churchill's resignation from the Conservative Business Committee came the day after his speech in the Commons over India. Historians are generally in agreement that this action marked the irrevocable breach between him and the Tory front bench. Yet this view is an overstatement. The Business Committee was not, as is usually presumed,[54] a full shadow cabinet in the modern sense of the term. In fact, the real shadow cabinet had not convened since the Irwin Declaration controversy in 1929.[55] In contrast, the Business Committee was a relatively low-key affair established only in March 1930, whose existence was unknown even to prominent Conservative ex-ministers like Leo Amery.[56] Indeed, given the committee's proceedings, 'resignation' was rather a strong term and significantly, Churchill spoke instead in less exacting language: that he 'ought not any longer to attend' its meetings.[57] Continued membership would certainly not guarantee senior Cabinet office in the next administration – indeed most members were not found places in the National Government that was to emerge.[58] As will be argued in the next chapter, Churchill's exclusion from the Cabinets of August and November 1931 had little to do with his decision in January 1931.

The real importance of Churchill's resignation from the Business Committee was that, seemingly without Baldwin's knowledge, he proceeded to highlight the breach by letting the resignation correspondence be published in the press. Neville Chamberlain thought this was done deliberately as a means of giving maximum publicity to Churchill's forthcoming Indian Empire Society rally in Manchester which would be 'damaging to S.B.'s position'.[59] Yet Churchill chose not to cut himself off from the front bench entirely. 'Shadow' posts did not exist in the rigid form they were to take later in the century but in holding on to his position as the Conservative Chairman of the Finance Committee, Churchill retained the right to be considered as effectively the Opposition's main spokesman on economic affairs.[60]

If he wanted to be leader, Churchill had to walk a tightrope. On the one hand he had to set out his stall; he had to demonstrate why his approach was preferable to that of the existing leader. However, it was no less important that he was not seen to be too disloyal. An attempt to attack Baldwin that weakened the public standing of the party would not be looked upon with favour. Since there were no formal rules to steer the process in which a Conservative leader could be supplanted (leadership elections were not instituted until 1965), precedent was the only guide. There had never been a contest that had taken the form of an open campaign. In 1911, the last time in which the leadership changed hands whilst the party was in opposition, the two contenders, Austen Chamberlain and Walter Long, had both agreed to stand down in favour of Bonar

Law, the compromise candidate, rather than risk differences being aired in a campaign for support. Even the Carlton Club revolt of 1922, when the party was in power but the leader was not Prime Minister, did not decide who would become the next leader. The situation then was only settled when the King concluded that Bonar Law was the man best able to form a new government and, consequently, asked him to become Prime Minister. Before accepting, Law asked for, and received, an unopposed vote in his favour from the parliamentary party. In the circumstances this was a fait accompli. When, the following year, the King had to select a new Prime Minister, neither of the likely contenders, Baldwin and Curzon, ran a public campaign to drum up parliamentary support for their cause. In 1931, on the other hand, the party was in opposition, so the King would not be involved in the selection process. However, the party's senior figures – whom Iain Macleod was later to call the 'magic circle' – would still play a key role in creating the right atmosphere for their preferred choice to 'emerge'. This was bad news for Churchill.

If the Tory grandees had improbably been somehow impressed by Churchill's unifying credentials, then they would have been cautious on personal grounds. The senior Tories who remained the most openly sceptical of Baldwin's India policy were Austen Chamberlain and Lords Salisbury and Hailsham. In the event of Baldwin's resignation, Chamberlain wanted his brother Neville to become leader.[61] Salisbury generally agreed with Churchill's stance in opposition to both food taxes and Indian reform but the two of them were not personally intimate. Although Hailsham was similarly unenthusiastic about Irwin's actions in India,[62] he was of the view that Churchill would be a disastrous leader of the Conservative Party. Furthermore, by sabotaging Churchill's chances, Hailsham could not but be aware that his own claim was enhanced. He was a credible candidate of the centre-right and had almost refused the Lord Chancellorship in 1928 because he feared that its removal of him to the House of Lords would ensure a twin handicap of reducing his own chances of becoming party leader, thereby helping Churchill's prospects.[63] Although in 1931 Churchill tried, unsuccessfully, to persuade him 'to speak out like a man' against Irwin's policy in India,[64] Hailsham decided that his own interests were best served by a more publicly temperate approach to the issue. Resigning from the Business Committee did not make much difference to Churchill's leadership chances since none of those likely to be instrumental in the succession would have conspired on his behalf anyway. If he was to win, he would have to emerge as the popular challenger, buoyed by a groundswell of opinion from the backbenches.

Alternative options for the leadership were canvassed. Sir Robert

Horne's name was mentioned. His distance from the recent responsibility of office was argued either to be in his favour, or against it, according to taste. However, as the party's leader in the House of Lords, Hailsham had a stronger claim. The legacy of the nineteenth century had been maintained in that the Tories had no single leader when in opposition; rather they had a leader in the Commons and a leader in the Lords. Upon the Conservatives winning a general election, the monarch, acting on 'magic circle' advice, would select as Prime Minister whichever of the two leaders could best be presumed to command more effectively the support of the larger section of the parliamentary party. Once appointed Prime Minister, the agreed choice would then become leader of the Conservative Party. The advent of universal suffrage and, concomitantly, the 1911 Parliament Act which clipped the power of the peers, augured in favour of the leader in the Commons being chosen in preference to the leader in the Lords. This did not make a choice from the peerage impossible. Curzon's peerage may have been a consideration in the King's decision to pass over him in favour of Baldwin in 1923, but it was not the only, nor perhaps the main, reason. Nor, as we shall see, was membership of the House of Lords the main cause for Lord Halifax (as the former Viceroy, Lord Irwin became in 1934) not becoming Prime Minister in 1940.[65]

As the Tories' leader in the Lords, Hailsham's claim for the future leadership of the party was already staked out. When Sir Robert Horne failed to show sufficient hunger for the post, this left Churchill and Neville Chamberlain to fight it out for the leadership in the Commons. Churchill's seniority and experience were countered by Chamberlain's claims; the latter had fewer detractors (and party unity was seen as an important sine qua non) and, unlike Churchill, he was more supportive of the majority view in favour of protection. In contrast to Churchill, he had been a consistent member of the Conservative Party. Indeed, with the latitude that knowledge of his ultimate success was to provide him, Churchill was later to write in 1948 that after ceasing to be Chancellor in 1929 he had 'no great influence with the Conservatives [because his qualified] Free Trade outlook . . . ran counter to the deep-seated desires of the Tory Party. The Exchequer is not an office which confers popularity upon its holder.'[66] There was little prospect of Chamberlain bowing out of the contest in the interests of party unity as his brother had done in 1911, since it was unlikely that he could have been convinced that the party could unite behind Churchill. If the latter was prepared to be awkward, then the two would have to break precedent and battle it out for the support of the parliamentary party. The leadership of a Conservative–Lloyd George alliance in which Neville Chamberlain would refuse to serve had been Churchill's best hope. There now appeared little prospect of such a combination being formed. The Carlton Club *putsch* of 1922 had demonstrated the muscle that the parliamentary party could bring to bear on the official leadership. The Caxton Hall meeting of October 1930 had also broken the tradition of the leader's fate being effectively decided by a small clique behind closed doors. With Baldwin's grip visibly weakening, there was still everything to play for. Baldwin's reported belief that Churchill had 'severed himself from the Party' was about to prove singularly premature.[67]

V

The day after his resignation from the Business Committee, Churchill was back in the Commons delivering a lengthy speech against the second reading of the government's Trades Disputes Bill. Having fun at the Labour leader's expense by making him out to be cowering behind Lloyd George, Churchill jibed that MacDonald reminded him of the malleable 'boneless wonder' circus act that his parents had forbidden him to see as a child. The performance was well received; one spectator, Harold Nicolson, thought it 'the wittiest speech of his life' and one that left most of the chamber 'chuckling'.[68] These sentiments were shared by a worried Neville Chamberlain, who thought the speech had 'raised his prestige to a higher level than ever'.[69] Warming to his new theme, on 30 January 1931 Churchill addressed an overflowing Manchester Free Trade Hall in an open meeting organized by the India Empire Society. All of a sudden it was Churchill who seemed unbreakable, bouncing back, once again, from having been written off as a spent force.

The real fight, however, was not in preaching to the converted in Manchester, but in raising the revolt in the parliamentary Conservative Party. Having failed to win over Baldwin's Business Committee, the party's India Committee was Churchill's next target. The committee, now meeting weekly, had by 1931 almost a hundred backbench MPs and peers as regular participants[70] although it was open to any Conservative politician to attend and take part. Despite skilful assurances that there was nothing to worry about from the party's India spokesman, Sir Samuel Hoare, many of its members had been nervous about Conservative goals at the Round Table Conference. Although Baldwin 'ambled along' to the committee's meeting on 9 February, his lukewarm reception contrasted with the voluble support for Lords Winterton and Lloyd, both of whom condemned appeasing the Indian nationalists. Whilst the India Committee Chairman, John Wardlaw-Milne, was essentially a party loyalist, the diehards were 'obviously very much in the majority' and succeeding in turning it into their 'policy soviet'.[71] Churchill subsequently felt that he performed well to a sympathetic gathering of the party caucus's Central Council on 24 February:[72] his first real attempt to strike at the party at the non-parliamentary level. Rothermere's unimpartial *Daily Mail*, reporting the 'prolonged and enthusiastic ovation' that Churchill received from the Central Council, waxed lyrical that 'every day at home the influence of Mr Winston Churchill upon public opinion grows stronger . . . He is showing the true qualities of Leadership which are most urgently required . . . He is the most discussed man in politics to-day.'[73] This eulogy would make it hard for Churchill to deny that he was not in cahoots with the press lords' campaign to dictate the future of the Tory leadership.

The support for Churchill and the diehards from the Beaverbrook and Rothermere press and the dependably imperialist *Morning Post* was balanced by hostility from other areas of the media. The Board of Governors of the BBC rejected Churchill's application to broadcast his views on one of their eight proposed radio programmes on India. Sir John Reith condescendingly told him that as the broadcasts were to be 'informative with a view to giving listeners an appreciation of the problems involved' it would not be suitable for him to be given 'facilities to broadcast your own views'. As Reith made clear, this was on the advice of such impartial arbiters of information as the party Whips and the India Office.[74] On top of this, Baldwin also had the unswerving and influential support of *The Times*. The editor, Geoffrey Dawson, was an ally who occasionally helped him with ideas for his speeches.[75] The more the *Daily Mail* moved diehard news towards the heart of its news coverage, the more Dawson deliberately moved such activities to the small print at the back of *The Times*.[76] When Baldwin made his famous comment about press barons having 'power without responsibility' he was being conveniently selective. In fact, during the inter-war period the Conservative Party contemplated taking over, directly and indirectly, controlling stakes in media organizations in order to promote 'subtly propagandist' material itself.[77] A median position meanwhile was adopted by the *Daily Telegraph*. The paper condemned Irwin's appeasement of Gandhi but felt that Churchill's views were 'unhelpful'. For the *Telegraph*, an attempt to make a bigger split on the issue of India, which it thought Churchill 'would deplore', was a 'mischievous' device of the Beaverbrook and Rothermere press.[78] Interestingly the *Telegraph*'s 'Peterborough' columnist summed up the speculation about Churchill's position: 'Whether Mr Churchill would . . . be prepared to accept any office inferior to that of Chancellor of the Exchequer, for which presumably Mr Neville Chamberlain is destined, are possibly more legitimate subjects for speculation . . . I cannot think that Mr Churchill has any intention either to withdraw from active politics or to fight under any other banner. That he has been pressed to do so, as has Sir Robert Horne also, is obvious.'[79]

The haemorrhage in support for Baldwin did not necessarily translate into personal endorsement for Churchill. The India diehards and the Beaverbrook/Rothermere Empire Crusaders were separate and uncoordinated bodies.[80] Regarding the Caxton Hall result as merely a temporary setback in his campaign for empire free trade, Beaverbrook resented the fact that Rothermere gave the Indian issue primacy.[81] Yet they were both happy to unite in the overriding objective of the removal of Baldwin. In any case, the failure formally to fuse the three main right-wing organizations (the India Empire Society, the Empire Crusade and the United Empire Party) did not necessarily hinder their mission to force Baldwin's resignation. There is no reason to believe that a single thrust would have been more effective than the chosen three-pronged attack. Furthermore, the existence of the India Empire Society (which purported to be cross-party) acted as a more respectable forum for those who might be sympathetic to Beaverbrook's and Rothermere's goals but who would recoil from public association with an organization directly controlled by the two main press plutocrats. The policy directives masterminded by Neville Chamberlain in October 1930 had greatly undermined the will of dissident Tory MPs to encourage the Empire Crusade, but the issue had now moved beyond policy alone. To the rebels, the crisis of early 1931 also raised the issue of whether the party could win a future general election with the reposeful Stanley Baldwin at its head.[82]

Writing from his Monte Carlo winter retreat, Rothermere encouraged Churchill to forget about appeasing his 'old colleagues'. Since a general election might still be over a year away he should 'make the most of this breathing space'. The Rothermere press had been instructed to provide him with as much publicity as he wanted, though to Churchill's annoyance this worked more at the editorial level than in the coverage of his speeches which he asserted were 'the only weapon I have for fighting this battle'.[83] Whilst Rothermere purred felinely to his new friend that he would become Prime Minister as long as he went 'unswervingly forward',[84] Churchill urged caution, arguing that before long 'we must look for a party meeting not upon the question of the leadership which should most carefully be excluded from our discussions, but upon the question of the policy in India. It is too early to do more than contemplate this.'[85]

The crisis came sooner than Churchill imagined. The death of Sir Laming Worthington-Evans meant that a by-election was due in Westminster St George's, one of the safest seats in the country. Poised to receive what was essentially a job for life, the Conservative candidate,

J.T.C. Moore-Brabazon, announced that he was standing down since he could not speak in favour of Baldwin's leadership when challenged. Had it been the action of a fifth-rate candidate in a no-hope seat, the matter might have received little attention, but Moore-Brabazon was a former junior minister who, with Harold Macmillan, ran the Conservative Candidates' Association. This opened the floodgates. Baldwin was even subjected to pro-Churchill mutterings in his own Bewdley constituency association.[86] Meanwhile, a dire prognosis came from the party's London Whip, Earl Howe, who told Amery that Beaverbrook's campaign and the 'tremendous strength of the anti-Baldwin feeling everywhere' meant that the Tories stood to lose every seat in London.[87] Howe was not the only man who wanted the Party Chairman to organize a deputation to tell Baldwin it was time to go. Neville Chamberlain received with 'reluctance'[88] a memorandum from the party's Chief Agent, Robert Topping, on 25 February 1931 claiming that despite there being little support for Beaverbrook, the popular feeling was that the party could not win a general election with Baldwin as its leader. Topping suggested that

> Many of our supporters are worried about the question of India. They lean much more towards the views of Mr Churchill than to those expressed by Mr Baldwin in the House of Commons, but they would be very perturbed at the possibility of any change of leadership taking place as a result of the differences between those two statesman. They would prefer, I believe, that if a new leader is to be chosen, he should be elected on broad policy and not on any one single issue.

Whilst Topping was claiming that Churchill would not be the choice of those wanting a change at the top, there was nonetheless amongst this group a 'grave apprehension [that] a sudden development might bring about a change which would not eventually prove advantageous to the Party'. Neville Chamberlain summarized Topping's memorandum to read that 'there was a serious danger that Churchill should seize the leadership himself if something was not done quickly.'[89]

That events during 'the last few days'[90] were moving in Churchill's favour was not in doubt. Yet he was not the choice of the Tory front bench nor was he, according to Topping, that of the constituency associations. This left the backbench MPs as the unknown quantity. One possibility is that Chamberlain was trying to get Baldwin to stand down swiftly by raising the chimera of a Churchill victory if the leader attempted to protract the crisis by trying to cling on to office. This scenario would give only the supposedly sound men of the front bench time to organize the succession so that a relatively trouble-free changeover to Hailsham, or Chamberlain himself, could be effected. This does suggest a serious panic about Churchill's growing popularity amongst backbench Tory MPs who, it was feared, might yet throw their weight behind him. Amery, on the other hand, whilst doubting that 'the rest of us can hold [Baldwin] up much longer', felt that it was 'only the absence of an obvious successor and the dislike of being coerced by the Press [that] has prevented things from collapsing before now'.[91]

Determined to bring matters to a head, Chamberlain received, separately, the views of his senior colleagues. All advised him to show Topping's letter to Baldwin. All, save for Walter Bridgeman, believed that this action would instigate his resignation. Chamberlain also thought that Baldwin could not 'survive' and, not wanting to 'miss the bus' as his half-brother Austen feared he might by delaying the fateful interview, he was himself ready to replace Baldwin. He was acutely aware, however, that as Party Chairman he could not be seen to be knifing Baldwin for personal advantage. The advice of so many key colleagues therefore worked in his favour in this respect.[92]

Neville Chamberlain recorded in his diary a conversation that his colleague, Philip Cunliffe-Lister (the future Lord Swinton), claimed to have had with Sir Robert Horne. When pushed for an answer, Horne had said that he would, regrettably, have to do his duty and accept the party leadership if it was forced upon him. This was a further twist in the possibilities opened up by a sudden vacancy at the top. When Horne had enquired about Churchill's prospects, Cunliffe-Lister had claimed that there was no chance of his capturing the leadership since 'he would have very few votes in the House of Commons, still fewer if it were known that he wanted to leave us over food taxes.'[93] Cunliffe-Lister was not alone in insisting that Churchill had almost no support amongst Tory backbenchers,[94] which makes the stated fears to the contrary of Topping and Chamberlain all the more intriguing. Either one or the other was mistaken or Cunliffe-Lister was trying to discourage Horne from germinating the idea that his old colleague Churchill had a real prospect. Talking down Churchill's prospects might help to nip in the bud any possible Churchill–Horne arrangement of mutual support which, for all Cunliffe-Lister knew, might have been in the making between two former colleagues of the Lloyd George coalition government. Horne was a seasoned enough politician to know that in the bluff and counter-bluff world of internecine Tory Party self-advancement, whatever he said in private might be repeated to the Party Chairman (which indeed it was). Likewise for all Cunliffe-Lister knew, any loose talk to Horne might well be telephoned straight back to Churchill. Whatever he thought about the privacy of political conversations, Cunliffe-Lister then determined to twist the knife one turn further by assuring Horne that even if Churchill gained backbench support, 'most of his colleagues including himself, [Neville Chamberlain] and Hailsham and the younger men such as Oliver Stanley would refuse to serve under him'. Horne then said that this ruled out Churchill's prospects and agreed with Cunliffe-Lister's advocacy of a 'Hailsham, Chamberlain combination. That both of [them] were so loyal to the party that each [would] willingly serve under the other.'

In Baldwin's temporary absence in 1928, Hailsham had been acting Premier. At that time, Chamberlain had been terrified that Churchill and his friend at the India Office, Lord Birkenhead, would rather support Hailsham (then in the Commons as Sir Douglas Hogg) than himself in a future leadership contest, and he had approached Hogg to declare his disinclination to 'see W. Churchill Prime Minister'.[95] Little had changed in the intervening period and in private conversation, Hailsham and Chamberlain both assured each other that, like Horne, they too had no wish to be leader, but if the party should desire it then, *regretfully*, they would have to do their duty. Either way, they should work together.[96] On the surface, this appeared to settle the matter, but only if the key players were as good as their word – and their resolve. Here was a potential difficulty. After all, the cabal by senior Tory figures to unite in favour of Rab Butler and against Alec Douglas-Home's attempt to form a government collapsed in 1963 when it came to the crunch. Similarly, some of the most senior politicians in the Edwardian Liberal Party had met at Sir Edward Grey's Scottish fishing lodge in 1905, and made a private compact that none of them would join a Cabinet formed by Sir Henry Campbell-Bannerman unless he was removed to the House of Lords. Their little coterie quickly collapsed when the new Prime Minister, Campbell-Bannerman, successfully picked off one conspirator at a time and dangled office before them. There was, therefore, always going to be the possibility that when seriously offered office, one of the leadership contenders would give in to temptation.

Even if Baldwin was going to be removed, the leadership was certainly not going to fall to Churchill without a struggle. The terms of the 'Delhi Pact' reached between Irwin and Gandhi were read out to the Commons on 5 March: the release of Indian agitators from gaol in return for an end to civil disobedience and the boycott of British goods. Even this glimmer of hope was short-lived and within a couple of days Amery was less sure that 'the Party [was] likely to listen to reason on India from S.B.'[97] Both Chamberlain and Sam Hoare felt that Baldwin's case was still irretrievable and that he should resign before the crisis turned into a catastrophe.[98] However, Hailsham now seemed to be against the emerging consensus amongst the members of the Business Committee that Baldwin should be told to resign before the Westminster St George's by-election had been

fought. Hailsham's fear that the party might be viewed as pandering to
the press barons, so soon after he had publicly criticized Beaverbrook,
aroused Amery's suspicions: 'I was surprised to find that he thought even
Winston might be accepted. I do not know whether [Hailsham] regards
himself as a possible leader and feels that his chances would be prejudiced
if the situation arose too soon after describing Beaverbrook as a "mad
dog".'[99] Whether the ensuing debate in the Commons, in which Baldwin
got the better of Churchill, significantly altered the balance of forces in the
Conservative Party is unclear.[100] The main combatants' punditry as to
whom amongst them could command support seemed to alter by the hour
as the volatile political climate changed around them.

Chamberlain showed Baldwin most of Topping's memorandum on 1
March. For a moment, Baldwin decided it was time to go. *The Times*
prepared for publication a suitable political obituary. Yet the coming
Westminster St George's by-election convinced Baldwin that he should
not go down without the one last fight for which it provided an
opportunity. The by-election proved to be the press barons' final throw
and Baldwin's comment about them seeking 'power without responsibility, the prerogative of the harlot throughout the ages'[101] – hit home (even
if it allegedly lost him the harlot vote). It was not the failure of the Indian
diehards and the press barons to merge into one united anti-Baldwin
foe,[102] but, on the contrary, rather their obvious association that helped to
save the Conservative leader. The press barons' intervention the previous
month at the East Islington by-election had split the Tory vote, handing
over the seat to Labour in the process. This was a clear warning to natural
Tories that the press campaign was more divisive than constructive. This
made Baldwin's decision to turn St George's effectively into a referendum
on press arrogance all the more clever. Whilst he was willing to resign at
the private request of his front-bench colleagues, he was not going to do
so in an act of public humiliation before a couple of over-mighty press
plutocrats. It was the advice of his wife, as well as that of Chamberlain's
predecessor as Party Chairman, J.C.C. Davidson, and Walter Bridgeman,
to stand himself against the press barons' candidate in St George's which
prevented his immediate resignation. By the time he had been dissuaded
from this bizarre option, there was no point in his resigning before the
result of the by-election was known. In this way it ironically proved to be
the tactics of the press barons in putting up their 'Independent
Conservative' candidate in St George's that gave Baldwin a lifeline for his
leadership.

Alfred Duff Cooper's 5710-vote victory flying the official Conservative
colours in St George's transformed the situation overnight. Besides the
press barons, Churchill and the diehards were the immediate losers. The

proposed great rally of the India Empire Society at the Albert Hall had been moved forward a month on Rothermere's advice to 18 March[103] before the announcement of Sir Laming Worthington-Evans' death on 14 February and the resultant calling of the St George's by-election. Therefore, whilst it may not have looked that way to detractors, the timing of the Albert Hall rally, on the eve of poll, was entirely accidental. It was the failure to reschedule the meeting to a less subversive moment for the Conservative Party, combined with the Rothermere press's banner headline insistence that 'GANDHI IS WATCHING ST GEORGE'S',[104] that suggested that the press barons and the India diehards were all part of the same meretricious conspiracy. This point was emphasized by the fact that six Tory MPs resident in the constituency refused to sign a letter of support for Duff Cooper and a further one actually wrote in favour of the press barons' candidate.[105] Churchill at least had the sense to have it insisted that his platform appearance at the Albert Hall in condemnation of the forthcoming Gandhi-Raj had nothing to do with the St George's by-election[106] but the implication was clearly there. The pages of the *Daily Mail* associated the activities of Churchill and the Indian Empire Society with the campaign in St George's, presenting the India debate in the headlines as the 'BALDWIN–CHURCHILL INDIA DUEL'.[107]

If this was Churchill's first great chance for the leadership, then it was missed. His performance was made to look all the more treacherous since with Duff Cooper's victory he appeared to be part of the sniping losing faction in the struggle for party mastery. Baldwin was convinced that Hailsham had been plotting his overthrow too, but his hostility towards Neville Chamberlain who had, in fact, behaved to his leader as loyally as any man in his position could be expected to do, was short lived. Chamberlain's resignation from the party chairmanship was the prelude to his formal emergence as the Chancellor-in-waiting. This fact was confirmed in April, when Churchill grudgingly resigned from the chairmanship of the Finance Committee leaving Chamberlain to spearhead the attack on the coming Budget. Chamberlain's status as Baldwin's effective deputy was enhanced by his successful bringing to heel of the Beaverbrook campaign on favourable terms to the Tories (peace at the price of a minor extension of the 'free hand' throughout all areas of agriculture) at the end of March, which Beaverbrook had agreed to, having taken Churchill's advice on the matter.[108] Meanwhile, this cessation of hostilities and the St George's by-election victory gave Baldwin a temporary reprieve, even if he was still very much on parole.[109] His period in purgatory did not last long, rescued by the collapse of the Labour Government and the extraordinary events of August 1931, which led to his rehabilitation as a man seen to be putting the country before party advantage. These developments were to stack the cards firmly in Baldwin's favour, ensuring that by failing to take control of party policy on India in early 1931, Churchill would find a future attempt all the more difficult. To succeed, he would have to challenge the whole machinery of leadership itself.

Three

ALL CENTRE AND NO CIRCUMFERENCE: THE NATIONAL GOVERNMENT

I

When it came to personal animosity and political intrigue, Conservatives found their match in the Liberal Party. The old worries about Lloyd George's scruples had never entirely disappeared. Concerns of this kind might have been suppressed if the Liberals had been gaining ground against their opponents, but there was little evidence of it. Indeed, the crisis that gripped them was worse than that afflicting the Tories. Conservative MPs were seeking to determine their party's policy by squabbling over who should be at the helm. This was natural in a party which made a virtue out of ceding the power of policy articulation to its leader. The prize was to capture the controls of the party and its organization intact. In contrast, Liberal infighting had reached a point whereby the question had bypassed the issue of who should be leader and was concerned with whether there could remain a single Liberal Party to lead. Groups of its MPs were effectively forming into sub-parties, some of the most important gathering round the political custodian of the Asquithian mausoleum, Sir John Simon. In a party of only fifty-nine MPs, there seemed to be a startlingly high ratio of Chiefs to Indians.

Far from taking advantage of the dissent within the two main opposition parties, personal rivalries and conflicting viewpoints were also threatening to splinter the Labour Government. The word 'betrayal', to be found inscribed on the heart of so many Labour administrations, was already on the lips of the disaffected. For socialist ideologues, inherent contradictions in capitalism would inevitably bring about its downfall. They were naturally reluctant to be the party to prop it up at a time when it appeared to be struggling. However, this was neither the view of the party leader nor of the majority of Labour MPs. Ramsay MacDonald's primary concerns in government were the protection of the victims of unemployment from the worst ravages of destitution and a general, if imprecise, desire to better the lot of the working man. As the historian Martin Pugh has written, MacDonald's brand of socialism was 'as much spiritual as political'. He believed that socialism, which he did not expect to see in his lifetime, would emerge not from the collapse of capitalism but rather 'it would grow from the steady evolution, even success, of the system'.[1] He shared much of Baldwin's preference for personal character over ideological zeal. He shied away from the sort of reflationary strategies proposed by Lloyd George. Fundamentally, his internationalist outlook was suited to the liberalism of free trade rather than an introverted socialism in one country. This was reflected in his appointment of the essentially Gladstonian Philip Snowden to the Treasury.

The downturn in the world economy conspired to deny the Prime Minister the security he sought for the less wealthy and the Chancellor of the Exchequer his balanced budget. The official figures alone touched on the misery of the rising dole queues: 1.15 million in July 1929; 2 million the following July; and 2.7 million in July 1931.[2] The problem was not all of the administration's own making. A third of government spending was taken up in repaying debt charges accumulated by the First World War. These had increased the National Debt twelve times over. This alone would have been an enormous burden, but the cost of unemployment had risen out of control as well. In consequence, the government had to borrow in order to meet claims far in excess of the limits of the existing unemployment insurance scheme. By January 1931, the deficit in government revenue had nearly doubled its 1928 level. In 1928 the cost to the state of unemployment insurance had been £11.75 million and the following year when Labour took office the figure had risen to £19.4 million. What now caused further alarm was that by the beginning of 1931 estimates suggested that the figure would reach £37 million in that financial year alone and over £50 million in the following year.[3]

Sterling was once again a commodity-based currency – its price fixed in terms of gold. The post-war fall in prices had increased the burden of debts fixed in gold. Countries like France had greatly reduced the gold value of the franc when readopting the gold standard but on her own re-entry Britain had maintained her pre-war parity of £1 equalling $4.86. The decision had been taken by Churchill at the Exchequer in 1925. It was soon to come to haunt him. In fact, at the time, the principle of returning to the gold standard had the support not merely of the City, the Treasury and the Bank of England, but of the main party leaders as well (even if they chose to find quarrels over the small print of the policy). Even the economist John Maynard Keynes, whilst regarding the rate of re-entry to be an overvaluation, did not dispute in principle the concept of Britain's return to the gold standard.

Conventional wisdom now points to the errors of Britain's return in 1925 to the gold standard at its pre-war rate. But the decision has to be viewed in the light of the time in which it was made. It was seen to facilitate Britain's role at the centre of a system underpinning the international trade upon which she was dependent. The example of countries which had not shown tight monetary control was a warning against generating inflationary money in the 1920s, as the unhappy experience of Weimar Germany demonstrated. Indeed, the hyperinflation which destabilized the German economy encouraged the alternative of a 'sound money' policy in London. In September 1931 (ironically only ten days before Britain abandoned the gold standard) the Chancellor, Philip Snowden, had defended its maintenance:

> London has established itself in its pre-eminent position because all over the world British currency has been regarded as being as good as gold. . . . A paper currency which has not an adequate backing in gold loses its value, because those to whom it is tendered have no assurance that it has a stable value. The result is that its value falls and the paper pound becomes worth much less, or, as has happened in many Continental countries in recent years, hardly worth the value of the paper on which it is printed.[4]

It was the circumstances of the decade that tarnished what was a considerable achievement in returning sterling to its pre-war parity – a rate which at the time of sterling's re-entry on to the gold standard was certainly considered sustainable by the markets. Unfortunately, the accumulation of three-quarters of the world's gold supply by the central banks of France and the United States increased gold scarcity and thereby drove up its price and that of sterling with it. The combination of falling prices at home and an overvalued currency set the British trade balance sharply into deficit as imports outstripped exports.[5] Industrialists were further worried that whilst most foreign competitors discriminated against British exports through tariffs, Britain had imposed little in the way of retaliation.

Committed to the gold standard, the Labour Government still intended to avoid the sort of loan-financed 'stunt' promised by Lloyd George. However, by October 1930, public work schemes worth £140 million had been approved.[6] This was not enough for Oswald Mosley who had resigned from his junior post in the government in May when his proposals for the planning of trade and industry together with a credit-driven expansion programme were rejected by the Cabinet. They were subsequently, if more narrowly, defeated at the Labour Party Conference. Mosley promised positive action to tackle unemployment but his maverick temperament, summed up in the pithy epithet 'Vote Labour, sleep Tory', was unappealing to most of the massed ranks of the parliamentary Labour Party. They were suspicious of his wealth and the fact that he had started his parliamentary career as a Conservative.

However interested in winning over the floating voter, Labour MPs remained suspicious of the floating politician. They voted 292 to 29 against his proposals. When in December he launched his own manifesto, only seventeen backed it. Mosley calculated from this rebuff that he was better being master of his own fate. In February 1931 he founded his own 'New Party' with the help of four MPs (one of whom was his wife, Lord Curzon's daughter) and was expelled from the Labour Party. It was to MacDonald's advantage that Mosley, thwarted at the first assault, allowed himself to be manoeuvred out of the massed ranks of the Labour Movement and into the no man's land of fringe politics.

The launch of the interventionist 'New Party' appealed only to the misfits of the Tory and socialist folds. Left-wing Conservatives like Harold Macmillan and Bob Boothby shared Mosley's obsession with the removal of the existing generation of tired established politicians and their replacement by the young men with new ideas – themselves for example. It has been noted that factionalism within the parliamentary Conservative Party did not manifest itself in the form of desertion from its ranks, but several of these younger Tory MPs gave the prospect some thought. Dissatisfied with a party which appeared to be offering them an insufficiently quick route to promotion, they contemplated moving over to a centre party with Lloyd George,[7] or to Mosley's New Party itself.[8] However, with Mosley still a democrat fighting within the constitutional structure of parliamentary democracy, few were prepared to join his group until it had shown its worth in electoral combat.

Whatever their views on Mosley's extreme form of protectionism and his claim that he could reduce income tax, most of the wiser Tories had no doubt where his interventionist schemes would lead. In consequence, retrenchment – the tightening of the government spending belt – re-emerged as a core Conservative electoral policy. This widened the breach between Mosley, Lloyd George and the young turks like Harold Macmillan on the one hand and the rest of the political establishment on the other. The rediscovery of thrift as a political weapon appealed to all the factions within the Conservative Party save the young progressives, and it was the platform from which both Neville Chamberlain and Winston Churchill savaged the Labour Government in the finance debates during the winter and spring of 1931. It also appealed to a large section of the Liberal Party, for whom the recession had proved a sobering experience, diluting their enthusiasm for the interventionist spirit of their increasingly nominal leader, Lloyd George, and driving them back to the traditional classical liberal nostrum of the balanced budget. With this in mind, they supported the appointment of the May Committee to investigate ways of cutting public spending. Whilst tariffs versus free trade remained a point of departure between the Tories and most Liberals, the shared values of retrenchment undermined the ability of the minority Labour administration to continue. As this realignment gathered momentum, Lloyd George and Mosley found themselves stranded, summed up in Churchill's jibe that the difference was that whilst the former had said that 'we' could conquer unemployment, the latter had said, typically, that it could be done by the first-person singular, but that both positions added up to the same miscalculation.[9] Churchill had himself attracted enough suspicion as it was by flitting from Conservative to Liberal and back. Mosley's own political hopscotch had led him from Conservative to Labour and into the chilly uncertainties of independence. None of this augured well for his commitment to team spirit. His desire to stand aside rather than play by the rules and the marginalization that this brought, was to be a warning to those politicians who thought they could free themselves of restraint and compromise by operating outside the conventional party game. The career of Lord Randolph Churchill should have provided Mosley with a warning from history.

In contrast to Mosley, Winston Churchill appreciated that politicians had few prospects outside membership of one of the three main parties. Chamberlain was now indelibly seen as part of the natural front-bench establishment for which soundness and aloofness from faction were the prerequisites of continued patronage. For Churchill, the strategy was now to take control of a faction within the Tory Party and in so doing make himself an indispensable figure. Despite his desire to stay in step with the Conservatives' economic policies, he had realized that his own chances of office in the near future were diminished by his opposition to the policies of all the main parties on Indian constitutional reform. As early as February 1931 he had made clear to his constituency in Epping that although he would be a 'loyal member of the Conservative Party' on other issues, his intention to fight the reform proposals for India meant that he would 'not be able to serve in any Administration' upon whose Indian policy he 'was not reassured'.[10] A month later he reiterated this view, claiming that he had 'cheerfully and gladly put out of my mind all idea of public office'. He did not regard this as a futile self-sacrifice, however, since as India would become 'the culminating issue in British politics' during 'the next two to three years' he would shortly receive the powerful ally of 'The March Of Events'.[11]

In the meantime, Churchill found the calls for government spending cuts a convenient way for him to accept his party's tariff commitments. In his liberated and often whimsical speech in the 1931 Budget debate he noted Snowden's confession that 'the limits of direct taxation ha[d] been reached'. He therefore associated himself with Chamberlain's view that the 'compulsive need for revenue must bring the tariff' to generate it. This would help 'in welding together the production and consumption of our Empire'.[12] In this acrobatic backflip he managed to support the legacy of Liberal Gladstonian retrenchment as the reason for abandoning Liberal Gladstonian free trade. Likewise, during the second reading of the Unemployment Insurance Bill he sounded like an Edwardian New Liberal accommodating himself to the Conservatives' call for retrenchment. He ticked off Snowden for 'not drawing the line which separates the self-supporting element in the community from those who are compelled to incur the bounty of their fellow subjects' in the Unemployment Insurance scheme. He also took the opportunity to remind the Commons of his own role in framing the original legislation as well as establishing labour exchanges in the pre-war Liberal Government.[13]

Relieved of any formal position on the Conservative Party front bench, Churchill's decision to reassociate himself with the great social welfare reforms of the past twenty-five years did not necessarily confirm suspicions that he was moving with Lloyd George, Mosley and the Conservative progressives on the road to 'Tory socialism'.[14] Indeed, it was with the profoundly un-left-wing Neville Chamberlain that he had widened the scope of welfare provisions in the 1920s. This did not make Churchill a committed socialist, still less a closet Mosleyite. He briefly toyed with the concept of an economic sub-Parliament. This had nothing to do with the corporatist institutions of a quasi-fascist state.[15] In contrast, he was interested in it as a purely advisory body of specialists wholly subservient to the will of Westminster. This had some foreshadowing of the planning councils of British politics in the 1950s and '60s, but as an intellectual exercise, Churchill soon dropped the idea. Far from supporting interventionist measures, he wanted to reduce the burden of the state. He had led the assault on the economics of Lloyd George's proto-Keynesian proposals at the last election. Mosley's programme of May 1930 he chastised as 'a less efficient variant' of the Liberal leader's scheme of proposals which were 'examined in every aspect . . . [and found that they did] not hold water'.[16] That Mosley's economic ideas had become progressively more interventionist since his Commons resignation speech[17] only made alliance with Churchill less likely. Churchill's Indian diehardism has been seen as the great estrangement between him and the younger generation of left-wing Tories since they found him wholly outdated on the issue.[18] Yet, in 1931 it was also as much his rejection of interventionist economics in favour of the Chamberlainite line which kept him divorced from the Tory left. For these reasons, Churchill was not interested in forming a new centre group. Discounting the possibility, the *Daily Telegraph*'s diary column recalled that it would be like Lord

Randolph Churchill's attempt at it, 'all centre and no circumference'.[19] Churchill was not prepared to adopt the policies of economic planning to gain support from Lloyd George, Mosley or the 'progressives' of the Conservative Party. He was prepared instead to speak up for imperialism to gain support from his historic enemies on free trade and Ireland – the diehards of the Tory right.

II

Although King George V had requested that a non-partisan approach to unemployment policy was delivered in his government's King's Speech, it was only over Indian constitutional reform that moderate opinion between the leadership of the three main parties clearly converged. This made the attempts by the Tory diehards to break up the consensus on India harmful to the construction of Conservative/Liberal cooperation in 1931. For Churchill, this was ironic given that in 1929 he had hoped that India was going to prove a useful link between the diehards and Lloyd George. Restrained by the leadership of a minority government, the possibility was certainly in MacDonald's mind from late 1930 onwards that, if the financial situation deteriorated further, then there might be the need for a National Government of some ill-defined sort. He was not sure whether he wanted to lead it and he confided in his diary that he was tempted 'to go out altogether, give a pledge that I shall not hamper the govt., but be free to express views of my own which party responsibility renders impossible'.[20] That such a possibility was in the mind of a Prime Minister boxed in by the political arithmetic of the time is understandable. Indeed it would have been surprising if, under the circumstances, he did not ever give any consideration to politics beyond his administration's apparently imminent demise. However, it later became an accusation – made by socialists on the basis of a number of offhand comments – that MacDonald had been consciously conspiring to ditch his own Labour Government in favour of a national coalition with the Conservatives. In fact, there is little evidence to suggest that this was his concerted will. What he was hoping for as an embattled Prime Minister was that the official Opposition would restrain their assault to hitting him above the belt during a time of great financial peril for the country. Baldwin categorically rejected calls to enter a coalition of national unity, whether from outspoken business leaders or letters to the press from the retired public figures of yesteryear.[21] He had already damaged his own credibility in his party by supporting the Labour Government's constitutional talks on India and any attempt to join those across the floor in a deeper embrace could only risk a more fatal response. Baldwin, Chamberlain (who told his sister that he hated the very idea of it) and Lord Stonehaven (who had succeeded him as Party Chairman in April) were agreed that the Conservative Party 'would not stand for it for a moment'.[22] This made the turn of events even more unexpected.

MPs retired for the summer holidays in July 1931 conscious that the government might not see out the year. Everything hinged, or so it seemed, on events within the Liberal Party, upon whose fractious forbearance rested the continuation of a Labour Government without a Commons majority. Although Lloyd George's leanings were now clearly towards the interventionist left, he was never interested in selling his goods at a personal loss. His price was the replacement of the first-past-the-post electoral system by proportional representation. MacDonald was prepared to consider the 'alternative vote', a procedure more likely to redistribute Liberal votes between the two major parties. Churchill, by no means an opponent of the principle of electoral reform, regarded the 'alternative vote' as a device guaranteed to institutionalize 'blind chance' in deciding victory by giving prominence to the second preferences of 'the most worthless votes given to the most worthless candidates'.[23] This did not matter to Chamberlain who – with Sir Samuel Hoare's support – had come down in favour of scrapping the first-past-the-post system and was worried that the House of Lords' obstruction of the government's alternative vote proposals could give Labour an excuse for appealing to the electorate on a 'peers versus people' mandate.[24] Meanwhile, Lloyd George's intimations to the Tories suggested that he would bring down the government if the Conservatives withdrew their candidates in constituencies where Liberals looked likely to beat Labour, and if they also agreed to introduce urban proportional representation. Whilst helping out the Liberals was an unappealing prospect, the maintenance of a Labour Government that looked like being able to get the alternative vote on to the statute books anyway motivated Chamberlain sufficiently to keep in communication with Lloyd George without telling Baldwin – 'lest it should go to Ramsay!' He did, however, tell his brother Austen, Samuel Hoare and Lord Hailsham, presuming that (unlike the leader of the Conservative Party) they would not be in the habit of warning the leader of the Labour Party about plots to undermine his government.[25] Yet if Chamberlain could not trust his own leader (and Baldwin therefore had reason to mistrust Chamberlain), there was even less ground for trusting the motives of the notoriously slippery Liberal leader. The latter appeared no less receptive to informal approaches from MacDonald in July that may even have involved him being brought into the Cabinet. In any case, the House of Lords could be relied upon to delay or disfigure a Commons majority for the alternative vote. According to Chamberlain's intermediary, Kingsley Wood, during July Lloyd George began wondering aloud whether 'a crisis might arise in the autumn so serious that no one party could deal with it.'[26] The idea of an institutionalized coalition government run by Lloyd George and MacDonald was singularly unsavoury to the instincts of both Chamberlain and Baldwin. Even so, they still resisted the deterrent to this eventuality: that if there really was going to be some form of National Government, then the Conservatives might be better being a part of it. No matter how unpalatable the circumstances it was better to have a partial lever within government than none at all.

This was the climate, then, in which circumstance brought together strange bedfellows. Mutual antipathy did not prevent channels being kept open between Chamberlain and Lloyd George, whilst the cordial relations between Baldwin and MacDonald had not yet produced any concrete understanding. Churchill too was keeping his options open. As we have noted, his India diehardism and support for orthodox economics distanced him from the Tory left wing, who were the natural constituency of support for the dynamic duo of Lloyd George and Mosley. This said, Churchill still chose to keep abreast of all developments as the financial and political crisis unfolded. By July, Mosley was of the view that the deteriorating situation would lead to a National Government – led by Lloyd George with Churchill as second in command. In other words, Mosley was misjudging the situation sufficiently to believe the crisis would discredit the leadership of both the main parties. Since he was himself now disconnected from these two leaderships, his foresight into government suggested wishful thinking. Yet Mosley was not the only figure at this time conjuring up fantasy Cabinets for the coming crisis. Equally improbable combinations had the interest, and intermittently the support, of many of the key figures in the media at the time. These included Beaverbrook, Rothermere and the *Observer*'s editor, J.L. Garvin, the last of whom wanted to see Mosley and Lloyd George in the same coalition as MacDonald, Baldwin and Churchill.[27] According to Harold Nicolson (who was in the course of leaving Beaverbrook's employment in order to assist with the creation of Mosley's New Party), Lloyd George had described his intended strategy after dinner at the house of the Liberal MP, Sir Archibald Sinclair. Amongst the other dinner guests present were Churchill and Mosley. Lloyd George suggested that if a Labour–Conservative National Government was to be formed, then they should 'form a National Opposition' which would soon come to power itself given the supposed incompetence of MacDonald and Baldwin. What was clear from the discussion was, however, that Lloyd George, whilst master of ceremonies, had no real plan as to how this

coalition of talents was to operate. Nicolson noted that Churchill, who
had brought along his young supporter, Brendan Bracken, was 'very
brilliant and amusing but not constructive'. Nonetheless, Nicolson
thought that they all departed 'on the assumption that although nothing
has been said, the great Coalition has been formed. [Mosley] is very
pleased.'[28] In fact, nothing had been said because nothing tangible was
seriously in the offing. Churchill always retained a considerable deference
towards the pronouncements of Lloyd George but he was increasingly
prone to avoid putting them into action. This became clear when the crisis
arrived.[29]

In the meantime, it was perfectly understandable that Baldwin and
Chamberlain should have resisted a National Government being formed
prematurely with, or without, their participation. The evidence from by-
election results between April and June 1931 suggested a strong recovery
of support was under way for the Conservatives. Upon this basis they
could expect a clear majority if the results were translated at a general
election.[30] Furthermore, they were increasingly successful in preventing
government legislation like the Education, Agricultural and Trade Union
Bills. Scenting electoral victory to be close at hand, for Conservatives a
National Government was therefore an unwanted and still seemingly
unlikely prospect in the early summer of 1931. Instead Chamberlain's
strategy was now primarily concerned not with Lloyd George but with
those other Liberals who had sufficiently fallen out with their irascible
leader that they wanted to help the Tories bring down the MacDonald
Government. Having resigned as Home Secretary in 1915 over the
introduction of conscription, Sir John Simon had subsequently followed
Asquith into the wilderness rather than support Lloyd George's coalition
government in 1918. His relations with the Welshman had never been
easy since. Unwilling to help prop up the government any longer, he had
now chosen to make public his split with Lloyd George on the pages of
The Times. By March 1931 Simon was to be found dining in the Garrick
Club with Leo Amery, to whom he implied that those Liberals he could
bring with him would be prepared to swallow protective tariffs if their
constituencies could be guaranteed against a rival Conservative candidate.
Simon also let the idea germinate that he had an interest in the Foreign
Office if such a deal could be brokered.[31] This seemed acceptable to
Chamberlain. Simon also had the advantage of being sceptical about the
worth of the government's platitudes over Indian constitutional reform, a
stance which would make him more acceptable as a Tory alliance partner
if those further on the right wing were worried about the lack of
ideological depth to his commitment to tariffs. In fact, like Churchill,
Simon now saw that there was a case for tariffs based upon the need to

find extra revenue at a time of acute budget deficit. This encouraged Lloyd George to quip at a meeting of Liberal candidates that protection was 'one of the subjects to which Sir John has lent one of his countenances'.[32]

If the support of Simon and his group of Liberals could be guaranteed when Parliament reconvened after the summer, the Conservatives appeared poised to bring the Labour Government down in the Commons. All the indications pointed to a famous Tory victory in the resulting general election. Yet, over the summer, a financial crisis was to alter everything.

III

The Great Crash had not hit the City of London with the ferocity that it had struck Wall Street in 1929. When in May 1931 the Credit Anstalt bank collapsed in Austria, the Bank of England still felt itself to be in a position to lend money to the failed bank's guarantor in Vienna. Similarly, when the financial virus spread to Germany the following month, the Bank of England helped pump funds into the German financial sector in a belated attempt to prevent the destruction of all the Reichsbank's reserves. The accompanying international freezing of Germany's foreign debts for six months failed to stem the drain in confidence in its banking sector and that of eastern Europe. During July the extent of London's exposure to the collapses became clearer. It was now the City's turn to succumb. In extending funds to these ailing countries it had incurred short-term debts of £250 million above current assets. The collapse in these markets had the result of depleting the reserves which London could have fallen back on (if only temporarily) when her own currency came under fire. Funding unemployment benefits had drained the Exchequer. Without a restoration of confidence, a run on the pound threatened the maintenance of the gold standard. This was the immediate source of the political crisis that was now to follow. However, insofar as the confidence in London's ability to ride out the storm was further dented by the soaring burden to the Exchequer of unemployment, it can be said that the crisis was also the wider product of failure across the whole spectrum of the British economy.

The report of the May Committee, received the day after MPs had separated for their summer holidays, suggested that the Treasury was facing a £120 million budget deficit. It proposed spending cuts of £96.5 million to be achieved by cutting public sector pay, a 20 per cent cut in unemployment benefits, and raising taxation to net a further £24 million. These proposals were naturally unpalatable to different sections of the House. Conservatives balked at the prospect of yet higher taxation

(Britain as the highest taxed country in the world was a regular contention in speeches from the opposition benches at this time). Meanwhile, the suggestion of swingeing welfare cuts was inevitably going to attract the acute hostility of backbench Labour MPs, few of whom had entered Parliament inspired by the opportunity to kick the working man when he was already down. In fact, the unemployment cuts proposed would still have left the benefits at a real value of two shillings a week more than had been the rate in 1928 and over four shillings a week more than had been dispensed by the last Labour Government in 1924. Snowden himself commented that, taking into account the cost of living, those on unemployment benefit in August 1931 were 36 per cent better of than in 1924.[33] For many in the Labour Party this was small print compared to the principle of the matter. Nonetheless, without a revolution in economic management, the deficit would have to be reduced somehow. The published warning of the May Committee not only frightened the government, it alerted international lenders to the prospect that Britain was an enormous liability. This sentiment was encouraged by some of the more sensational headlines in the national press, *The Times* excelling itself in particular. Yet now that attention was firmly focused on what was to be done to restore confidence, the government had to be seen to take the report's warnings seriously. The alternative was to face an even worse panic in the financial markets, one which could withdraw the government's essential lines of credit. Twenty-five million pounds was raised from the Bank of France and the US Federal Reserve at the beginning of August to plug London's fast-depleting gold reserves. This soon proved inadequate and, with the run on the pound continuing, it was estimated that the sum would be exhausted within a month. The alternative option of devaluing the pound by taking Britain off the gold standard was quickly dismissed by Snowden. Officials at the Bank of England estimated that as much as £80 million might be needed. Such confidence could seemingly only be bought by a firm government commitment to getting its own house in order by cutting expenditure and balancing the budget. The human manifestation of the crisis was the collapse of the Governor of the Bank of England, Montagu Norman, who was incapacitated by a breakdown throughout the vital weeks. He announced belatedly to the press that 'I have not being feeling as well as I should like and I feel that I should like a little rest'.[34] Like a metaphor for the Bank's reserves, he duly left the country.

Given the certain hostility of much of the Labour backbench to major cuts, it was essential, if the government was to survive, that it convinced the Conservative and Liberal leaderships to support the measures with which their rhetoric of retrenchment was, in any case, consistent. In being a minority government, the political arithmetic of the situation would have necessitated liaison with the leaders of the Liberal and Conservative parties anyway, and the suggestion by the Bank of England that this should take place as soon as possible only consolidated the need to face up to this reality. Returning urgently from their respective French and Scottish holidays, Baldwin and Neville Chamberlain heeded the call and raced back to Whitehall to confer with Snowden and MacDonald on 13 August. Chamberlain made clear his position that while all of the May Committee's recommendations should be met, he could not guarantee support for the proposals for increasing taxation. Baldwin too was reluctant to help shoulder MacDonald's burdens, whilst Chamberlain, writing to his sister, felt sure that 'to secure such a measure of relief and to do it through a Socialist Government seems to me so important in the national interest that we must give it our support'.[35] Clearly he was not thinking at this stage that the Conservatives should join a government headed by MacDonald.

Supporting the Labour Government's attempt to enforce economies presented Chamberlain and Baldwin with a dilemma. Just at the moment when they had the government on the ropes and looked sure to win an overwhelming majority, they were now being asked to prolong its life. Indeed, they were potentially giving it the chance of redemption. On the other hand, they could only logically attack Snowden's efforts to cut the budget deficit on the grounds that it was insufficiently aggressive. Such a stance opened up a risk that fighting the ensuing election campaign on a platform of even more severe cuts might be unpopular. Although they naturally regarded spending cuts to be welcome in any environment and especially in view of the unfolding crisis, Conservatives genuinely believed that the long-term problems in the economy could not be solved without a tariff control on imports. The obvious course therefore was to let the government make the economies, and then, by fighting the ensuing election on a platform of protective tariffs, promise a medicine which neither Labour nor the mainstream Liberals looked likely to support. Suspicious of being trapped into making commitments to MacDonald that would restrict this necessary room to manoeuvre later, Baldwin decided to resume his holiday in Aix-les-Bains. Chamberlain was left to monitor the situation. In this way the party leader would not become too entangled in the government's strategy whilst the position remained confused. This, of course, was not the first time that Baldwin had employed this tactic. Faced with what was to him an even more unpalatable possibility, he had used Churchill in the same way to explore the possibilities of parliamentary alliance with Lloyd George in the hung Parliament only two years previously. Baldwin was a past master at letting his colleagues mine the most dangerous seams for him. If the props collapsed, the rubble would fall down on them leaving him unscathed.

The Cabinet convened at 11 a.m. on 19 August to discuss public spending cuts and did not break until 10.30 in the evening. Set the target of finding £78.5 million, they could agree on only £56.25 million. The following day, Snowden and MacDonald met to discuss the dire situation, with Chamberlain and Sir Samuel Hoare representing the Conservatives and Sir Herbert Samuel and Sir Donald Maclean representing the Liberals (Lloyd George was incapacitated, following a serious operation). Chamberlain's initial warmth towards Snowden's proposed cuts quickly froze over when it was revealed that the projected budget deficit had suddenly increased by £50 million to a total of £170 million. Nonetheless, the May Committee's proposed programme of cuts (which was more than the Cabinet had yet brought itself to endorse) was welcomed as a firm basis for action. The meeting then adjourned. This gave Hoare and Chamberlain time to consult with the Bank of England, those senior Tory colleagues contactable at short notice[36] and with the Liberal delegation. All agreed with the demand for stringent retrenchment.

The following day the Conservative and Liberal delegations reconvened with the Prime Minister, who was still unable to balance their calls for the original proposal of £78.5 million worth of cuts with the smaller figure of £56.25 million. Any increase on the smaller figure risked the resignation of at least some Cabinet colleagues. Labour was further constrained by the knowledge that the sort of cuts that appeared necessary had the opposition of the General Council of the Trades Union Congress. Walter Citrine and Ernest Bevin made sure the Prime Minister and the Chancellor were in no doubt as to the TUC view on the matter. In conference with the Conservative and Liberal negotiators, MacDonald, seemingly at his wits' end, riposted a complaint from Hoare by parrying whether he was 'prepared to join the Board of Directors'. This was a throwaway line not intended to be analysed by subsequent propagandists and historians, but it became the subject of such conjecture nonetheless. To Hoare, Chamberlain, Samuel and Maclean, however, if they wanted the economies to take place, then it seemed a far better strategy to threaten the government with annihilation if it did not implement them than to join in the burden of office and share out the blame amongst themselves for administering the strong medicine.

On 22 August, Chamberlain looked more favourably at a revised offer from MacDonald which, in supposedly increasing the cuts to £68.5 million, was regarded by the Bank of England to be sufficient to secure fresh foreign credit. If this was indeed to be enough to staunch the outflow of reserves, then the government appeared to have lived to fight another day. Chamberlain seemingly felt as much: that a deal was all but done on this basis and that, as he reported to his wife, 'the crisis is over'.[37] Such thoughts quickly proved to be premature. Even if the proposals, which included the political totem of a 10 per cent cut in unemployment benefit, were going to command the support of the majority of the Cabinet, MacDonald thought they would bring about the resignation from it of at least Arthur Henderson and William Graham. This, he told King George V, would unavoidably lead to the collapse of the government.

By Sunday, 23 August, Baldwin had returned to London and the King was now determined to confer with him and with Herbert Samuel who, in Lloyd George's medical incapacity, was now the acting leader of the Liberal Party. Over lunch, the editor of *The Times*, Geoffrey Dawson, strongly advised a sceptical Baldwin that it was his duty to prop up MacDonald. By the time the Conservative leader reached Buckingham Palace, the King had already consulted with Samuel and the two had agreed that the creation of a National Government headed by MacDonald was the preferred course of action. When this was put to him by the King, Baldwin felt unable to decline, but doubted its plausibility. The King made clear that he would ask him to form a government if MacDonald was unable to do so. MacDonald's position seemed impossible and Baldwin therefore naturally expected to become Prime Minister within the next day or so. It was Chamberlain who reminded him that, at least before a general election could be called, he would have to ask Samuel and the Liberals, plus MacDonald and Snowden, to join or support the government if it was to secure a parliamentary majority whilst the emergency legislation was passing through its stages.[38] Although it was possible that a straight deal with Simon could have just scraped a majority, this option seems suddenly to have been forgotten about. In any case, it would have produced a majority too narrow to depend upon. It was, therefore, the immediate situation which demanded some form of short-term National Government – not merely the personal dictate of George V. What the King preferred was that MacDonald, rather than Baldwin, should head the new government.

It would have been scarcely human for MacDonald to react with anything other than despair at the position in which he found himself. Despite his placing of a revolver to the head of his Cabinet in warning that any resignations would bring the whole Labour Government down, the full package of economies was more than ten of the twenty-one ministers could accept. The reductions in unemployment benefit was the major sticking point. In the end, it was the issue which caused the Labour Government to self-destruct.

MacDonald now proposed resignation, but the King urged him to think again, reassuring him that the Liberal and Conservative leadership would support him. MacDonald was still inclined to resign and told the opposition leaders as much. Yet, at this moment, with the Prime Ministerial succession poised to pass to Baldwin, Chamberlain suddenly told MacDonald that as Labour leader he should join rather than merely support the new government. This also had Samuel's agreement although, intriguingly, Chamberlain noted that Baldwin 'maintained silence and we did not pursue the matter further'.[39] This was despite the fact that he had reluctantly accepted the logic of the proposal earlier in the day. It is not difficult to imagine that Baldwin was by now finding Chamberlain's practical observations increasingly annoying.

The next day, the King informed the party leaders that he expected MacDonald to stay in office and the Liberals and Conservatives to support him. Whatever his personal inclinations may have been, it was difficult for the Prime Minister to shirk such a request. MacDonald's acceptance of this royal vote of confidence, supplemented by Samuel's intimation that he was ready to pull the Liberals in behind the Premier, curtailed Baldwin's room for manoeuvre and he now felt obliged to serve under MacDonald as well. The King further pressurized them all by suggesting that they had to work out the details immediately so that the press could be informed. MacDonald then had the unenviable task of telling the Cabinet that although they were now out of office, he would be proceeding to form a new government with their political enemies.

Neville Chamberlain's biographer, Keith Feiling, stated majestically that in the creation 'of this great political change' Chamberlain 'was the constructive engineer'.[40] Although he has at times been painted as the *eminence grise* of the whole operation, this has now been shown not to be the case.[41] It is true that he was involved in the day-to-day negotiation and referral during the August crisis whilst Baldwin was away on holiday but Chamberlain did not direct events down a course of his own making. His essential role was to monitor the situation, not to take executive decisions without consulting the leader. He did not foresee the creation of a National Government with Tory participation until the last moment. Indeed, far from fostering a cross-party coalition, he worked on the assumption that it was the Conservatives' role to bolster a *Labour* Government, led by MacDonald, to push through economy before an election could be fought on the usual party grounds. Chamberlain's advice to MacDonald to stay on as Prime Minister and to Baldwin that he should serve under MacDonald did not influence these eventualities. Neither Chamberlain nor Baldwin created the crisis; they did not consciously subvert the procession of events, nor initiate the political realignment that was its result. Rather, their contribution was supplementary to the far more important directives of King George, whose own views in turn hinged less upon personal calculation than upon a reasonable analysis of the practicalities of the situation.

King George V's role was that of a catalyst, a position well within the confinements of constitutional precedence. He had every right to consult as to who could most ably perform the task of Prime Minister. He had every right to encourage his existing Prime Minister to stay in office. He had every right to warn his preferred choice that in his view the alternatives were less agreeable. He could not force MacDonald to continue any more than he could force the Liberal and Conservative leaders to fall in behind him. By firmly pressing his views he made it awkward for the leaders to refuse his request – but it was still ultimately their decision. Their compliance may have been due either to personal weakness or respect for their monarch. More likely, their compliance was based upon a realization that what the King proposed truly was the best solution. Baldwin could have refused point blank without appearing personally discourteous to the King by arguing that *regrettably* such an arrangement could not command the support of the parliamentary Conservative Party and was therefore dead in the water. If Baldwin's bluff had then been called by the formation of a formal Lib–Lab coalition, then he had the perfectly constitutional option of organizing the undermining of His Majesty's Government, on the floor of the House of Commons. This was, after all, the normal courtesy of British politics even if the national crisis asked for a more generous response.

Baldwin chose not to pursue the more narrowly drawn partisan approach. In part this may have been because, with an expected outright crash in the City feared to be only hours away, he did not responsibly have the time at his disposal to waste in conniving ways of bringing down a Prime Minister who had honourably agreed to stay at his post to try to steer the ship of state through the storm.[42] Furthermore, Baldwin may have feared the adverse publicity of appearing to repudiate the King's bipartisan request in favour of personal advantage. Such a fear would therefore suggest that the King's actions were in tune with, rather than contrary to, the general desire of the nation. This further contradicts the charge that the monarch was acting purely on some personal whim of his own devising. Baldwin also had to consider the implications for his party if a MacDonald–Samuel government was formed which then succeeded in restoring financial confidence. Such an eventuality might undermine a subsequent Conservative electoral message based on its well-worn theme that only the Tories could command the confidence of international finance and the economy at large. Certainly to an extent that has seldom been employed by a British monarch since, King George V used his powers of persuasion to their utmost. It was, for comparison, no secret that his son, George VI, was to prefer the prospect of Halifax as Prime Minister in 1940 but ultimately tolerated an alternative outcome without interfering to the extent that his father did in 1931. It is questionable whether, without George V's warning, advice and encouragement MacDonald would have continued as Prime Minister in 1931 not least because he himself seemed to lack the will to continue.[43] In truth, the influence of the crown was only as strong as the personal repute its wearer had built up. In character and in deed, George V had established considerable esteem and Baldwin agreed to accept his advice. In contrast, five years later, George's successor, Edward VIII, commanded much less personal respect and it was Baldwin who was to reverse the constitutional balance between King and his first minister by effectively asking Edward to toe the line or abdicate.

IV

Whilst the leaderships of the Conservative and Liberal parties promised to swing the full voting power of their MPs and peers in Parliament behind the new government, the inclusion of MacDonald as Prime Minister failed to deflect the bulk of the Labour Party from the course of opposition despite the growing sense of emergency. Besides his main supporters from the former Cabinet (Snowden, J.H. Thomas and Lord Sankey) and a further four lesser ministers, MacDonald was supported by only eight Labour backbenchers, one of whom was his son, Malcolm. The events of 24 August had removed the obstructive ministers and redrawn the lines of parliamentary division in favour of giving an administration the majority it had lacked for the previous two years.

The official statement announced to the press that: 'The specific object for which the new Government is being formed is to deal with the national emergency that now exists. It will not be a Coalition Government in the usual sense of the term, but a Government of Cooperation for this one purpose. When that purpose is achieved the political parties will resume their respective positions.'[44] This desire that the National Government would only last a matter of weeks in order to bring in the necessary emergency economic measures manifested itself in Baldwin's insistence that only a small ten-man Cabinet should be appointed. Of the ten members selected for the emergency Government's Cabinet on 24 August, four were Labour (MacDonald as Premier, Snowden continuing as Chancellor of the Exchequer, Thomas as Dominions' Secretary and Sankey as Lord Chancellor) and two were Liberals (Samuel became Home

Secretary and the former Indian Viceroy, Lord Reading, became Foreign Secretary). Only four places, therefore, were consigned to Conservatives: a Cabinet minority obviated by the fact that a Conservative withdrawal risked bringing down the whole edifice. Baldwin chose for himself the post of Lord President of the Council, an office which allowed him freedom to cast an executive eye over the whole range of Cabinet business. By retaining the Conservative leadership he had an effective right of veto on all policy. In other words, he could enjoy power without responsibility. Neville Chamberlain returned to the Ministry of Health, the post he had held during the 1924–9 government. In the view of *The Times* this was 'a most important matter' since it was 'the one spending Department included in the Cabinet, which will certainly be concerned with a vast number of inevitable economies, and where his proved administrative ability will be specially necessary'.[45] Sir Philip Cunliffe-Lister likewise returned to the Board of Trade, the same post he had held in the previous Tory Government. The up and coming Sir Samuel Hoare became Secretary of State for India.

The concept that a small executive was best able to deal with a crisis had been used by Lloyd George in the First World War. In streamlining decision making it had been much credited for its contribution to the war's successful outcome. It had since become an ongoing panacea for administration championed not only by the great war leader but by his impersonators and acolytes, Oswald Mosley and the young Tory progressives. It was ironic that in 1931 it was a device which was to be employed by the political establishment they despised. The restricted size of the emergency Cabinet was useful in making more acceptable the exclusion of all figures of the Tory right wing, including the party's leader in the upper chamber, Lord Hailsham, and the Tory 'old gang' ex-coalitionists. Sir Austen Chamberlain was the only former coalitionist offered a portfolio in the government (that of First Lord of the Admiralty) but even this was denied Cabinet rank. Hailsham's exclusion dampened the prospects of Churchill's most likely right-wing contender for the leadership succession and, offered only office outside the Cabinet, he chose not to take it. Lunching with Leo Amery and the idiosyncratic Lord Brentford (the former Home Secretary, William Joynson-Hicks), Hailsham did not demur from the judgement that his Cabinet exclusion was based upon the fact that Baldwin was 'jealous and afraid of [him] as a person who has been acclaimed as an alternative leader'.[46] When later in the year, in November, a new Cabinet was formed following the general election, Hailsham was appointed to run a contracting and wholly marginal War Office.

Amery was one of the senior Conservatives most apprehensive about the creation of the National Government. He feared it might prove to be a device which would sideline his chief priority – protectionism and the creation of the imperial trading bloc. He later suggested that the major attraction for Baldwin of a National Government was that it could be formed without Lloyd George and Churchill.[47] Baldwin's *bête noir*, the Liberal leader, was still convalescing and therefore could not have been accorded office in the circumstances. Churchill was out of the way, holidaying in France. In fact, such considerations were not the focus of Baldwin's attention in August 1931. If one of his primary reasons for joining the National Government had been the permanent exclusion of the ex-coalitionist element, he would not have been so reluctant to enter it in the first place and would not have, on so doing, insisted that it should dissolve itself as soon as its immediate task was accomplished in order to give place to old party politics. It was only later that he was to see how effective the new alignment was in making the victory of the Carlton Club *putsch* of 1922 more permanent. Nevertheless, others shared Amery's instinct at the time. Sir Samuel Hoare wrote to his 'greatest friend in political life',[48] Neville Chamberlain, that 'as we have said several times in the last few days, we had some great good luck in the absence of Winston and Ll.G'.[49] Did Hoare mean that had the two of them been available they would have tried to wreck the process, or did he mean that places would otherwise have had to be found for them in the government? Considering that both Lloyd George and Churchill gave their initial support to the government's formation, it could hardly be the former proposition. Hoare's later publicized view – that essentially because of their political position, 'no one even suggested that [Lloyd George and Churchill] should be associated in any way with what was happening'[50] – contradicts the sigh of relief over their absence that he shared with Chamberlain at the time.

In fact, whilst a fit Lloyd George could not have been excluded from the government, save by his own command, a post for Churchill was much less probable. The new Government may have been in part constituted to save the very device that Churchill had been responsible for restoring – the gold standard – but his eclipse on economic questions by Chamberlain and his concentration upon the Indian Question came at a time when economy was much more important than events in the subcontinent. With Hoare appointed to the India Office and the Chairman of the Indian Round Table Conference, Lord Sankey, sitting on the Woolsack, the personnel were in place for the further constitutional reform scheduled for a second Round Table Conference. However, if the National Government was to be temporary, then there was no need to address the

Indian issue in any committed way. Therefore consideration as to how best to play Churchill would scarcely have been a primary consideration in the minds of the Cabinet-makers. Indeed, the fact that the National Government was not formed with the intention of lasting long enough to address the Indian agitation conclusively also undermines the established view on the subject that it was Churchill's India diehardism which kept him out of the Cabinet in August 1931. In view of this, his position on India and his much commented upon resignation from the Business Committee on the issue back in January had little to do with his exclusion from the Cabinet. Equally, his earlier resistance to protectionism had marginal relevancy to his failure to share office with his Conservative colleagues in August 1931. Men like Philip Cunliffe-Lister who 'would never again work with Winston as Chancellor [because in the last Tory Government] he defeated all tariff proposals'[51] found themselves, under the special circumstances of the crisis, working with Philip Snowden, whose free trading sentiments ran deeper than those of the backsliding Churchill.

Churchill's exclusion from the August Cabinet was not, therefore, primarily because of his views on India or his free trading past. He was excluded for the same reason as Hailsham. Churchill's colleagues thought that his natural temperament would be antagonistic to the Labour members in a small Cabinet determined to maintain a 'national' and united front. This was an irony that was to make the events of 1940 all the more refreshing. India was the most pressing of Churchill's supposedly objectionable right-wing views, but his renowned and age-old combativeness towards the Labour Movement stood to disqualify him from office even if he had waxed lyrical about Indian constitutional reform. Further, it has been suggested that if Churchill had still been in the Business Committee in August 1931, he could not have been so effectively marginalized in the process of forming the National Government.[52] Certainly, Churchill would have been consulted, and would have had no shortage of comment. However, there is no reason to believe that with only four seats available in the August Cabinet for Conservatives, he would have emerged from the process with a portfolio, when, thanks to MacDonald's veto, other qualified right-wing men like Hailsham did not. Amery who, like Churchill, had his reservations about the new Government, but unlike Churchill *was* on the Business Committee at the time of the new Government's formation, felt unable to prevent the Government from being created.[53] Although he had been more loyal to the party over empire free trade despite his divergent views, than had Churchill on India, he was nonetheless excluded from Cabinet office, even after the October

reshuffle confirmed Tory predominance in the Government. Even allowing for the popular falsehood that alleged that he had ordered troops to
gun down peaceful Welsh striking miners in Tonypandy in 1910,[54]
Churchill had rejoined the Conservative Party specifically as an anti-
socialist who had reckoned the Liberal Party was no longer up to that
task. His rhetoric then and his bullish behaviour during the 1926 General
Strike, quite apart from his splendid oratorical destructions of the hapless
MacDonald in early 1931 (which were much more memorable than any
imagery Baldwin and Chamberlain had ever coined), were at the root of
his exclusion from a National Government of level headed inter-party
unity led by the leader of the Labour Party.

At best it has been suggested that Churchill might have filled a minor
Cabinet position had an all-Tory Cabinet been formed in mid-1931
instead of the National Government.[55] Supporting the status quo, whether
it was to be a National Government or an exclusively Tory one, would
have effectively marginalized Churchill's chance of the Premiership in
either scenario. Chamberlain was now the obvious choice in either of
these options. In seeing Churchill's differences with the party and
Government leaders over India and rearmament as the reason for his
exclusion from office, historians have confused cause with effect. Mis-
attributing the inevitability of his long walk in the political wilderness in
the 1930s has clouded their estimation of the political judgement behind
his great campaigns on India and rearmament that were to result. This is
unfortunate for, as we shall see, we cannot comprehend the underlying
reasons for the relative failure of these campaigns during the thirties
without understanding the consensual strategy underpinning the political
realignment of August 1931, to which his style of partisanship was victim.

Given the rough ride they had inflicted upon Baldwin during his period
out of office, the failure of the Tory right wing to attack the deal he had
struck with MacDonald could only have been exceptionally gratifying to
the party leader. When in July Churchill had first departed for his holiday
in Biarritz, he had left behind a Conservative Party intending to form a
government in its own right, not serving an administration fronted by the
Labour Prime Minister. Such was the speed at which events overtook
natural sentiment that by the time of Churchill's return to London there
was no official Conservative opposition to the formation of such a
government. Churchill now made it clear that he endorsed Baldwin's
actions. This was a volte-face. He had previously returned briefly to
England on 17 August for a couple of days before the decision had been
made to create a National Government and had spoken to Sir Robert
Horne about the situation. Horne had relayed to Neville Chamberlain,

who passed it on to Baldwin, that Churchill was, in common with 'a definite body of Conservative opinion ... aggressively of [the] view' that the Tories should 'take no responsibility whatsoever for Government plans ... This perhaps you would expect and discount.'[56] If this was Churchill's view, then he, like the 'definite body of Conservative opinion', adapted to the new situation very quickly, although no more quickly than did the previously sceptical Stanley Baldwin himself. In arranging a deal to write articles for the *Daily Mail* with Esmond Harmsworth the day before the National Government was formed, Churchill wrote to Brendan Bracken from France that he 'must reserve liberty to terminate the contract should I be called upon to take Office, and decide to do so'.[57]

Still in Biarritz when the National Government was formed, Churchill was anxious to find out how the balance of forces were assembling and was wisely still keeping all his options open. Reasoning that the 'Tory toughs' (largely the diehards) and 'the young men' (largely the left-wing Conservatives) would be naturally inclined to oppose the Baldwin–Mac-Donald axis, Churchill wondered whether perhaps Mosley could be a coordinating bridge bringing together these otherwise disparate groups in opposition. At the end of August, Churchill's impetuous son Randolph was dispatched to talk to Mosley and report back on developments.[58] Mosley, of course, was the very last person capable of squaring such a circle. He showed no inclination towards being dragged along as a mere team member when he had the ultimate leadership of his own destiny-driven party to keep him occupied. This was the manifestation of the attitude that was soon to propel him from being the wayward constitutional politician still accessible in polite dining society in 1931 down the divergent road of Fascism as *führer* manqué. His position was the same when he was approached by Neville Chamberlain, who was also interested in whether he could be brought on side. There was natural interest in keeping Mosley involved in mainstream politics and Chamberlain had always feared what mischief Mosley might get up to if left to drift along with other malcontents like Lloyd George.[59] Mosley told Harold Nicolson that he had had a covert meeting with Chamberlain in the hope of doing 'a secret deal'.[60] Nothing came of it. Events during this period have been well summarized by Mosley's son, who has written with particular reference to the discussions involving his father that much of the dinner-table talk came to nothing because 'everyone on the fringes of power seemed to be trying to charm everyone else, and to be waiting to see what would happen.'[61] None of the politicians in mid-1931 had any real plan to deal with an unpredictable situation that changed by the hour.

V

The sense of imminent disaster as the run on the pound continued was the major motivation for the speed at which the party leaders came together in a National Cabinet. As a consequence, there was scarcely time to consult party colleagues and members. This state of affairs was compounded by the fact that Parliament was not in session when the crisis unfolded. This gave the leaders a further degree of leeway which they could not have expected had events taken place under the full scrutiny of the Houses of Parliament. Ratification for the deal struck was only sought once the decision had been taken. This was unanimously granted by the Conservative Business Committee and at a party meeting on 28 August. Baldwin stifled any opposition by making clear that he had not sold the pass: the National Government would last only as long as needed to balance the budget and cut down the borrowing on unemployment benefit, after which a general election would be called and the Conservatives would fight alone and united in 'a straight fight on tariffs and against the Socialist Party'.[62] Despite the unanimity of approval for this line, those on the party's right wing retained worries as to its consequences. Hailsham put down a marker that an election on the old party lines should not long be delayed.[63] Beaverbrook was even more insistent for a quick election to be fought on tariffs and was annoyed that Chamberlain took a longer-term view.[64] Lord Lloyd was furthest wide of the mark in expressing delight that the whole business would finish off Baldwin altogether.[65] However, whatever their private doubts, even diehard MPs like Colonel John Gretton and Brigadier General Sir Henry Page Croft spoke up at the party meeting to endorse Baldwin's action.[66]

Parliament reconvened on 8 September to discuss the financial crisis and take stock of the momentous changes of the previous fortnight. MacDonald spoke first, followed by Arthur Henderson, the new leader of the Opposition. Churchill spoke next, the first Tory to do so. Initially Churchill's description of Baldwin's 'high motives' appeared decidedly lukewarm conceding, in a minor adjustment to the words of Lady Macbeth, that since 'the deed is done . . . we have got to make the best of it'. With Labour opposing the new coalition, he warned the Conservative Party that as the majority partner they would, as time went by, have to shoulder the 'new discontents and new disappointments' of a vast, unorganised electorate' if they long delayed calling a general election. Whilst he wanted Baldwin's assurance that no substantial step in Indian policy should be taken by the interim government, the main issue was that the country would now accept protection if it was put to them. Without it, Conservatives would be reduced to merely 'enforcing unpopular economies, and levying new and burdensome taxes'. Turning to the

Liberals, and paying particular tribute to his friend Sir Archibald Sinclair (the new Scottish Secretary), he 'rejoiced' that at last 'the Floor was broader than the Gangway, and long may it remain so . . . Now we are all together. Now we see our common opponents arrayed against us.' Since the British electorate 'are a great people . . . at their best on great occasions' they would respond warmly to a national appeal in a general election if it were called soon.[67]

Churchill's pronouncements corresponded with the *Evening Standard* diarist's observation that being now 'weak' and 'slightly the worse for drink' Churchill was 'like a schoolboy trying to get into the team'.[68] In fact, his call for an early election on protectionist lines was 'by no means pleasing to the Front Bench'[69] and Baldwin speaking shortly after him did not address directly the content of his speech.[70] Instead Baldwin restated the intent of Conservative Party strategy to disband the National Government, once the currency and budget had been stabilized without a sweeping tariff policy. The ensuing election would then be fought by the Conservative Party on a strong protectionist programme. Here, then, was Churchill arguing for the virtual opposite: that the Liberals should drop their archaic attachments to free trade (as he had done) so that the National Government could implement protection as soon as possible and fight a quick election on this national, rather than party, basis.

In the midst of a period of enormous international dislocation, the National Government was setting itself a Herculean task in seeking to restore confidence within the stated timetable of a matter of weeks. In fact, it was its failure to achieve its objectives in the allotted time that contributed to its longevity. In the first place it failed to steady the run on the pound. Snowden's emergency budget increased both direct and indirect taxation in the hope of raising a combined £75.5 million, to be supplemented with reductions in public sector salaries and the 10 per cent cut in unemployment payments. Even so, the total economies totalled only £14 million more than the Labour Cabinet had agreed upon, a fact which made the decision of Henderson and his group of Labour ministers to resign all the more politically doubtful.

By 28 August, the Government had secured £80 million of new credit from Wall Street and Paris. However, the Bank of England's prediction that this would be enough to plug the run on sterling proved wildly inaccurate. Indeed, the persistent socialist charge that the City and Threadneedle Street in particular had panicked the late government into making rash and inequitable decisions can hardly be sustained. One of the key features of the crisis was that the Bank persistently *under*estimated the credits needed to plug the flight from sterling. Yet the economies needed to secure even those credits that were obtained proved too much for some of the victims. To many, the Royal Navy was as much a symbol of British supremacy as the pound sterling and when sailors at Invergordon effectively mutinied rather than accept the proposed economies in their wages, international finance again took fright. Gold to the tune of £18 million was withdrawn from the country on 18 August alone, part of the £200 million lost since late July. Completely exhausted by the attempt to sustain the parity of the pound, the Bank recommended suspending the gold standard the following day and on 21 September Parliament did what it was told in a matter of hours, dissent emanating largely from 112 Labour MPs who defied the line adopted by the opposition leadership.

The immediate effect of coming off the gold standard was that sterling fell from its fixed rate of $4.86 by a whole dollar and then by the end of November began heading towards $3.20. By Christmas it had rallied to $3.40. As with future devaluations, the expected calamity not only failed to occur but, rather, the economic situation (at least in the short term) appeared to improve. At one level, it should have surprised no one: British exports were depressed by an overvalued currency. Devaluation encouraged the exchange rate to move towards a level more reflective of economic conditions. This advantage, it must be added, was to some extent undermined when it encouraged foreign competitors to raise tariffs further against Britain. Yet with the received wisdom so strongly haunted by the fear that devaluation would lead to soaring inflation and the reduction of the incomes of all – as had happened in Germany when the mark had collapsed – it is more understandable that those in positions of authority took the stance that they did. On 11 September, Snowden had broadcast to the nation claiming that if sterling was to go off the gold standard, wages, pensions and all incomes would have followed the same downward course of those in Germany, Austria and France:

> You would still have got your same paper pounds for your wages, incomes, and other receipts, and they would have been worth perhaps half or less than half of their present value in purchasing power.
>
> It is idle to suppose that world trade could go on as usual if this country's currency collapsed. We should have great difficulty in finding customers for the exports we have to sell, and that we must sell, to pay for our food and the raw materials for our factories. Our whole industry would be thrown into chaos and unemployment would rise by leaps and bounds.[71]

It was an incisive argument, particularly embarrassing when ten days later Snowden found himself taking Britain off gold. For his own reasons, when the Labour Government devalued the pound in 1967, Harold Wilson decided to place a rather different emphasis to that explained by

Snowden as the consequnce of such action – 'devaluation does not mean that the value of the pound in the hands of the British consumer, the British housewife at her shopping, is cut correspondingly. It does not mean that the pound in the pocket is worth 14 per cent less'.[72] The National Government and its supporters, of course, rushed to make light of the decision which only days before they had regarded as tantamount to supping with the Devil. Having backed the maintenance of the gold standard well into its injury time, *The Times* even had the audacity to claim that 'it has long been evident to observant people that the trend of events, both at home and abroad – and particularly abroad – pointed to the possibility of a temporary suspension of gold payments.'[73] All that can be said here is that none of those observant people had been writing for *The Times*.

That there was no panic may in part have been testimony to confidence in the National Government. It is unlikely that had devaluation been initiated by the former Labour administration the international markets would have taken such a sanguine view.[74] Yet if confidence was there, then it was not reflected in the run on the pound, even if this was based on the fear that Labour might return to power in the future. Churchill's legacy, one which had been supported by all his colleagues at the time, was the failed experiment of returning to the gold standard. The economic conditions which accompanied its collapse in 1931 were to greatly help the career of Neville Chamberlain. Ironically, it was an assistance Chamberlain tried to prevent.

VI

Had the National Government achieved all its objectives quickly, then it might well have decided upon its own voluntary euthanasia. Instead, just as its failure over the gold standard encouraged it to believe the situation was still too precarious for a return to normal party alignments, so the undermining of the political certainties upon which it had rested gave it a further *raison d'être* for survival.

The evidence suggests that when MacDonald agreed to form the new government he did not see that it would necessarily involve him being forced out of the Labour Party. After all, when in 1922 Conservatives had divided over whether to stay in the coalition with Lloyd George or split off and form their own government, the Lloyd George collaborators had not been forced out of the Conservative Party. Lloyd George had never been expelled from the Liberal Party when he led the coalition government, to which Asquith, the Liberal leader, had been opposed. Indeed, despite his apostasy, Lloyd George had succeeded Asquith as party leader, even though he had led his own coalitionist National Liberal Party against it in the general elections of 1918 and 1922. Whatever the precedence of British politics, MacDonald had underestimated the degree of venom his membership of the National Government had created with the overwhelming majority of the Labour Party. His decision not to attend their party meeting on 28 August won him no plaudits from that quarter. Instead, Ernest Bevin of the TUC General Council launched an unprecedented personal attack and carried with him both the Labour Party's national executive and its parliamentary party in outright opposition to the new government's proposals. This dashed any hope that the opposition Labour Party would support at least the most important measures towards balancing the budget. A month later MacDonald and his colleagues were condemned in their absence and formally expelled from the Labour Party. This was a crushing blow from a party which had once proclaimed MacDonald as its chosen one. It was the party he had led out of obscurity. His expulsion had not quite the consequences of a Stalinist show trial but the hatred and mutual condemnation between former colleagues that it encouraged was an unedifying spectacle which left poison in the Labour Movement's bloodstream for decades thereafter. Snowden, Sankey and Thomas too were expelled from the party and with so few Labour backbenchers supporting them they, like MacDonald, had no political future once the national combination broke up. This created its own expediency but it was not the only consideration at work. Whilst Snowden remained an implacable champion of free trade, the desperation with which both MacDonald and Thomas viewed the state of Britain's trade balance now led them to concede that protective tariffs could reduce imports and provide the necessary source of revenue to balance the budget. With this conversion in place there was no bar to the Conservatives fighting a subsequent general election in favour of protectionism whilst keeping MacDonald and his small band of like-minded supporters on their 'national' masthead. If such an appeal could not command the acquiescence of Samuel's Liberals, then this was no real loss, especially since a large section of Liberal MPs gathered around Sir John Simon were now firmly intimating that they would be prepared to accept tariffs. With these developments taking place, far-sighted Conservatives could see a way in which they could get their own agenda adopted and win a huge election endorsement for it by fighting with 'National' allies committed to their policy.

Simon had announced his support for tariffs on 15 September, and jumping on the bandwagon of a situation which encouraged old acquaintances to be forgot, his group of MPs declared independence from the rest of the Liberal Party on 5 October, styling themselves 'Liberal

Nationals' thereafter. This was an important move by Simon. During the August crisis he had still been sheltering under the rather less than waterproof umbrella of a Liberal Party led by Lloyd George and Samuel, and he had therefore no real claim to Cabinet office as of right. Now that he was autonomous he could offer Baldwin and Chamberlain what Samuel could not – Liberals in favour of Conservative economic policy. Henceforth, the National Government would be able to boast the support of 'Liberals' whilst, if necessary, dispensing with the troublesome free traders like Samuel whose blocking power over protectionism would now be broken by the calling of their bluff. They could choose either to swallow their principles and stay with a government that they no longer directed or they could resign. If they resigned they could view from the political sidelines the nauseating sight of traitors like Simon being offered power and preferment in their place.

Despite the weakness of their bargaining position following the acceptance of revenue tariffs by MacDonald and Simon, Samuel and the Liberals still tried to prolong the life of the government on terms suitable to themselves. This they attempted by playing on MacDonald's worries about calling an election at a time when the state of the currency suggested the country was far from out of danger. Chamberlain had no sympathy for this obstruction, noting that 'the Prime Minister is worn out and seems unable to make his mind to decisions'. If Samuel continued to block advances towards protectionism, then MacDonald should 'decide by a majority to adopt it, to accept Samuel's resignation, and go to the country on a programme of the full tariff and a free hand'.[75] Conservatives were now moving definitely towards a quick election. On 16 September, *The Times*, edited by Baldwin's friend, Geoffrey Dawson, began in earnest to canvass the idea that rather than go their own separate ways, the 'National' parties should fight together on a common front at a general election but that, conveniently, 'The appeal, no doubt, would in effect be for the support of the Conservative platform, for the present Government's true claim to be National involves no illusion about the attitude of the greater part of official Labour ... but the result would be assured.'[76] Dawson had already done his homework, putting the case to Baldwin, then transmitting general approval to MacDonald whom he claimed to find 'quite prepared for a National Government appeal and to serve under Baldwin subsequently' in an administration committed to introducing tariffs.[77] Dawson's views were shared by Chamberlain who thought that 'Our idiotic party thinks it has the game in its hand and wants to fight on party lines ... I believe the only way to secure the sort of majority which would give the world confidence is to go as a National Government, perhaps even as a National Party, carrying MacDonald and his colleagues with us together with as many Liberals as we could get.'[78] Thus spoke the great heir to Joseph Chamberlain's Liberal Unionism.

Fortified by the apparent failure of existing economic policy, and encouraged by the effect of going off the gold standard, Conservative MPs stepped up their demands for protective tariffs.[79] At first, Churchill observed that in fact a downward-floating pound, making exports cheaper and imports more expensive, actually undermined the case for protectionism, an argument which was also briefly championed by John Maynard Keynes.[80] Now was not the time for logic of this kind, and Churchill quickly fell into line with the majority of his party.

Backbench Conservatives, gathering in their own forum, the '1922 Committee', and the protectionist Empire Industries Association declared on 21 September their support for an immediate election with the commitment to protectionist tariffs at its forefront. A resolution from the '1922' supported maintaining MacDonald as Premier in such circumstances so long as he supported the tariff. Baldwin now told Snowden that he was unable to resist such pressure and gave Tory MPs in the Empire Industries Association the impression that by the time of the election, Samuel's Liberals would already have been forced to resign. According to Amery, Baldwin even implied that after the election he would be called upon to be Prime Minister as leader of the largest party.[81] Such an option suited neither Baldwin's alleged commitment to fair play nor the likely preferences of the King. He repeated it in a slightly more hesitant form to the front-bench strategists in the Business Committee the following day. Interestingly, this was not what the assembled wanted to hear. Supported by Hailsham, it was Chamberlain who 'very bluntly pointed out that if Ramsay wished to stay on after the election he would and that there was nothing likely to occur for eighteen months or more to create any difference unless he wished before that to become Ambassador at Washington'.[82] Yet again it was Chamberlain who had spoken up in defence of MacDonald retaining the Premiership over Baldwin.

The Conservative front-bench decision was to fight an early election in the 'National' colours, retaining – as proof of the fact – MacDonald as Prime Minister. There was a condition, however, and it was that the 'National' manifesto gave top billing to the programme of protectionism for which a 'free hand' would be asked. This was the stance that Chamberlain had established as Conservative Party policy in 1930. Amery scoffed that Baldwin had announced his support in the Business Committee for this as the 'result of an hour's thinking at 3 a.m'.[83] Actually the position gave rigid protectionists like Amery about as much as they could realistically have campaigned for had the Conservatives been fighting alone on the issue. If the Samuelite Liberals were not prepared to fight on these protectionist lines then, as far as much of the Tory Party was concerned, it was time to say goodbye and good riddance.[84] There is no evidence to suggest that Baldwin had pre-planned these developments, any more than his assertion that the National Government would defend the gold standard was a deliberate deceit given that the government subsequently abandoned gold. Whilst allowing for his scepticism about the whole process, Amery probably best analysed the decision by stating that 'a few weeks ago the idea of being under MacDonald was resented by most of our party. Now they have got converted to the national notion they are terrified of standing alone and being accused of having broken up the "national unity".'[85]

Whilst it was tempting for Tories to cut themselves adrift from those who were ideologically opposed to their economic strategy, the broader the election appeal the better was the expectation of defeating Labour. For protectionists like Chamberlain, the dictates of practical politics pointed to the wisdom of a call for a 'free hand' to take whatever measures were necessary to control imports rather than a manifesto commitment which spelt out in detail preordained tariff measures. This ensured that, since there was no commitment to any policy in detail, those like MacDonald could go into the election without being embarrassingly tied to the letter of Conservative ideology. However, Samuel was still being fortified with the strident views of the invalid Lloyd George who vehemently opposed the calling of an election, and proceeded to oppose any workable wording. This further induced despair in MacDonald, whom the King again had to encourage not to resign. If Chamberlain's explanation to Amery can be taken at face value, then the 'free hand' was a policy consciously intended to keep MacDonald in and shut Samuel out.[86] However, undermined by the Liberal group led by Simon, Samuel and the free traders backed down in the Cabinet and swallowed the contrived ambiguity of the so called 'doctor's mandate'. This maintained that each of the National parties would go into the election with their own manifesto but that MacDonald should also sign a moderately worded National appeal to which they would give support. In agreeing to share the National platform with MacDonald and Baldwin, Samuel annoyed both those Conservatives who wanted shot of him[87] and, at the same time, irrevocably parted company with Lloyd George, whose opposition to an election on such terms was unequivocal.

Once again, Baldwin was blessed by surprisingly little opposition from within the Conservative Party over actions which in any other context would have been regarded bizarre or inexplicable. On 6 October, the eve of the dissolution of Parliament, he addressed a further meeting of the parliamentary party. Amery noted that although a little hesitant, Baldwin:

promised to make no negative pledges and it was clear that we all should have
the freest possible hand. A propos of a question about L.G., S.B. said 'you had
better ask Churchill' who then got up, deplored L.G.'s attitude and utilized the
occasion to get back into favour with the Party by a very happily phrased vote
of confidence in S.B. . . . So we all broke up very happy and still happier to
hear that the Liberal meeting had been full of confusion and recrimination and
that Hore Belisha had actually moved a vote of censure on Samuel in the
chair.[88]

Parliament was dissolved on 7 October almost a month after it had
convened following the August crisis. Voting was scheduled for 27
October.

VII

Whatever had been his private worries and concerns about the new
Government's composition and chances of success, Churchill was never
slow to perceive that compared to a socialist challenge from the left wing
of the Labour Party, every effort should be extended to ensure a National
victory and that he should be seen to be doing everything in that cause.

With so little to agree about amongst themselves, the three National
groups targeted the actions of the Labour Opposition. In this, Labour
played into the government's hands. Portrayed as having walked away
from the crisis, Labour now called for state control of the financial sector.
A barrage of fiercely anti-capitalist rhetoric made it easy for Snowden,
their erstwhile Chancellor, to describe Labour's manifesto as 'bolshevism
run mad'. The National Liberal, Walter Runciman, suggested that those
with post office savings would have their money sequestrated by such a
Labour Government. Quite understandably, Labour denied these inflated
charges. Nonetheless, smears of this kind were a useful weapon for the
divided Liberals to distance themselves from their fellow free trading
brethren in the Labour Opposition. Echoing the anti-protectionist
warnings of the new leader of the Labour Party, Arthur Henderson, it was
Lloyd George, leader of the non-national Liberals, who inconveniently
addressed this point: 'Government supporters of all shades, including
those who are preaching protection, state with emphasis that free trade is
not the issue. Let there be no mistake. Free trade is at issue. If the
Conservatives secure a majority . . . there can be no doubt that after a
farcical pretence of investigation a general tariff will be insisted upon by
the will of the protectionist majority. The "open mind" is an open trap.'[89]
In view of this he offered advice to electors to vote for a pro-free trade
Labour candidate over a pro-protection Conservative. This was his

political death knell, finally divorcing him from the mainstream of the Liberal Party which he had done so much to use for so long as his own personal political convenience. He was, of course, correct in his analysis for the future of free trade, with or without Liberal participation in a National Government. At the same time as Lloyd George was giving his advice on tactical voting, Neville Chamberlain was telling his Birmingham audience: 'I must frankly say that I believe a tariff levied on imported foreign goods will be found to be indispensable . . . I hope to take my part in forwarding a policy which was the main subject of my father's last great political campaign.'[90]

Given the comments of Chamberlain and those like him, it appeared appropriate that the National appeal was summed up by the pre-printed Conservative Party posters whose slogans remained the same but whose attribution was hastily patched over with the motto 'Vote National'. As events transpired it is easy to see the whole event as a masquerade, or in George Lansbury's later phrase, a 'national humbug', in which the Conservatives paraded the name of their allies only to ignore them once victory was secured. It has been estimated that around one hundred Conservative candidates owed their subsequent election to the withdrawal of a Liberal candidate which allowed them a straight fight against Labour. In return, only in about ten constituencies did a Conservative with a serious chance of victory stand down in favour of a Liberal. However, the price of the National ticket involving this great reduction in the Liberals' number of candidates masked the truth that the bankrupt state of the party's coffers (Lloyd George had refused access to any of his political funds) would have prevented the Liberals from covering the country with more than a patchy campaign anyway. Had the election been fought under normal party conditions, the Liberals would probably have fared far worse than they did under the 'National' banner. For local Conservative Associations who were cajoled into complying with the arrangements for cooperating with the other national alliance groups, the key issue with regard to withdrawing their Tory candidate was whether the Liberal surrogate was amenable to protectionism. Thirty-five Conservative candidates stood down in favour of Simon's Liberal National Party (only four Conservative candidates could not be so persuaded) and MacDonald's group went similarly unhindered. But in contrast, only nineteen Tory candidates withdrew in favour of Samuel's National Liberal Party (the remnants of the official Liberal Party) with its clear adherence to the principles of free trade. As a result, eighty-five clashes took place between Conservative and Samuelite candidates. Targets included five of the eleven Liberal ministers in the government, of which Samuel in his Darwen constituency was the most desired scalp. This extraordinary state of affairs was not surprising in view of the thinly veiled hostility they received from Samuel's men in turn. Ninety Conservatives were opposed by their other National partners, and in the main this meant from Samuel's Liberals.[91]

The dislike between Conservatives and Samuel was mutual, although Churchill played little part in it. This made Samuel's endorsement of a National Liberal candidate to fight Churchill in his Epping constituency all the more foolish. After all, Churchill's election addresses were conventional for a Tory in the 'National' appeal[92] and he specifically supported the 'doctor's mandate' so that the Liberals would not have 'to commit themselves to any scheme' against their will.[93] Indeed, Samuel was being particularly ungracious given the fact that Churchill, like Baldwin, had, albeit mildly, manifested disapproval of a Conservative standing against Samuel in Darwen.[94] It was, after all, hard to see what future the Samuelite Liberals would have had in the election if they had been forced to fight it on their own. Samuel's audacity in attempting to dictate to his alliance partners the terms of engagement strengthened the Tory desire to humiliate him as soon after the election as propriety allowed.

VIII

The election result was a triumph beyond the hopes of even the most determined 'National' supporters. The Conservatives gained over 200 seats. Not a single Conservative seat was lost. In all, 471 seats were won by them and this was supplemented by 35 Liberal Nationals who under Simon's direction could be regarded as firm allies. Added to this were Samuel's National Liberals with 33 seats and MacDonald's National Labour with 13. Opposing the 'National' ticket, Lloyd George's Liberal group returned 5 members, two of whom were not his close relations. Polling less than half the number of votes cast for the National groups, Labour was humiliated with a mere fifty-two returned MPs (of which 6 were Independent Labour). This was a staggering drop of 235 seats on the result of 1929. With every single constituency in Birmingham, Sheffield and Manchester going to the Conservatives, George Lansbury was the only one of Labour's former ministers to be re-elected and, by this extraordinary default, succeeded Henderson as party leader. It was the biggest landslide in British electoral history.

The result offered two possibilities. On the one hand, it vindicated Baldwin's moderation and the party's electoral attractiveness when in harness with its National allies, thereby reinforcing Baldwin against his right-wing critics. Alternatively, as Tom Jones feared, the enormous size of the Conservative vote gave near-dictatorial powers to a party from within whom 'the Tory wolves will howl for high tariffs and will give S.B. hell.'[95] For these wolves, the opportunity was created to adopt the protectionist policies which a moderate leadership led by Baldwin and Churchill had denied them when they had last won power in 1924. Yet, with Churchill's cautious role now replaced in the Cabinet by that of the free traders Samuel and Snowden, the right wing would again have to fight hard to move the government towards their goal if this fresh chance was not to be let slip. The ideological purist, Leo Amery, returned with a 15,000 majority in his Birmingham Sparkbrook constituency, reflected:

> I went to bed very sad at the thought of how easily we could have attained a substantial majority for a clear and definite policy, and how great may be the difficulties which will now confront us with a coalition of old gangs and old gangsters with no policy and probably incapable of finding one. For myself it was anything but a pleasant election. I disliked the whole humbug about National Government and every day saw our people putting their foot into it more and more and getting tied up in a position in which they would be hopeless whatever the size of the majority. It seemed to me 1924 all over again, perhaps in an even worse form.[96]

Or, if the new government did not listen to its Tory backbenchers, would it be 1922?

Four

THE EMINENCE GRISE

I

In 1937 Churchill recalled the politics of the turn of the century as a time when 'the venerable, august' Lord Salisbury had been Prime Minister 'since God knew when' and Arthur Balfour had displayed his 'airily fearless' intellect in the Commons. 'But', Churchill concluded, it was Joseph Chamberlain 'who made the weather'.[1] In the government of 1931–5, Neville Chamberlain did not create the political climate, but he showed considerable adeptness in being able to adapt to its ever shifting thermals. This made all the more appropriate his unintentionally characteristic strolls with a rolled umbrella under his arm. Despite playing a prominent role in the negotiations which led up to the establishment of the National Government, he neither foresaw the manner of the crisis's outcome nor tried to direct the discussion against the trend of events. Having at first tried to avoid binding involvement in such a coalition, he soon saw how it could entrench the electoral appeal of the Conservative Party for the 1930s. Indeed, after the sweeping election victory under the National colours, Chamberlain noted: 'I hope that we may presently develop into a National Party, and get rid of the odious title of Conservative, which has kept so many from joining us in the past.'[2] Similarly after 1932, his stewardship of the economy as Chancellor of the Exchequer was affected by matters which were beyond his calculation or ran contrary to his original preference. He had supported the gold standard, but instead made the most of inheriting a currency which was no longer 'as good as gold'. Another example was the settlement of a tariff arrangement with the British Dominions. Understandably, he portrayed the deal reached as the fulfillment of his father's great imperial crusade but, in truth, the settlement achieved was more a demonstration of the dream's practical limitations. In each of these situations, Chamberlain tried to make the best of them. If the results were not miraculous – unemployment was tamed but never conquered – they were certainly more successful than those of many other industrialized competitors at that time. Joseph Chamberlain had asked the questions which transformed public debate. He saw few of them answered to his satisfaction in his own lifetime. Neville Chamberlain was less concerned with asking new questions than with trying to find answers to old ones. His social and economic doctrine was coherent and demonstrative of his phenomenal attention to detail and practicality, but it never had the vigour or intellectual originality of that pursued by his father. Judged by the criterion made famous by Rab Butler, however, Neville Chamberlain was a master politician. Unlike his inspirational father, he narrowed his professional canvas to the art of the possible.

II

In contrast to the government created in the emergency of August, the new administration formed after October's reassuring election victory at last gave a Cabinet majority to the Conservatives. Nonetheless, with eleven Tories facing nine from the other coalition parties (five Liberal and four National Labour), this was a level of representation hardly reflective of the Conservatives' overwhelming domination in Parliament. As respective leaders of the two different Liberal factions, Simon became Foreign Secretary and Samuel Home Secretary. Churchill was now clearly superfluous to requirements, unnecessary as far as making up a Tory majority was concerned and only likely to divert the Cabinet on to fresh issues of creative discord when there was already a fundamental chasm over tariff policy to be bridged. In contrast, Neville Chamberlain, promoted in the new Cabinet to the post of Chancellor of the Exchequer, was at the heart of the new government. This confirmed his position as the most senior Conservative in the administration after Baldwin and the one with the most demanding portfolio. Given his different approach to the Liberals on matters of trade, the future of the coalition would depend upon his command of economic affairs.

MacDonald remained at the helm as Prime Minister. He viewed his options without enthusiasm. Duty – as he saw it – propelled him on, although the election campaign had left him in no doubt about the company he was keeping. In his diary he recorded his sense of bitterness and betrayal: 'The Conser[vative] Head Office pretended to do what it never did & indeed played a shoddy game. It saw its advantage & took it, & unfortunately the size of the victory has weakened me. Once again I record that no honest man should trust in too gentlemanly a way the Conservative wirepullers.'[3] Baldwin continued next door in Number 11 Downing Street as Lord President in Council. From the backbenches, Amery thought that Chamberlain's capture of the Treasury would ensure

that Baldwin would become 'more and more identified with MacDonald
and when the break comes between the House of Commons and the
Government S.B. will be thrown out with him'.[4] If Chamberlain proposed
tariffs which his non-Tory Cabinet colleagues rejected, then he would feel
obliged to resign. Lord Randolph Churchill had done this over his
thwarted spending plans in 1886 and had never resurfaced from the
quicksand of political wilderness into which he plummeted. He had
chosen the wrong issue upon which to resign and paid the penalty
accordingly. Chamberlain's position after the 1931 election was much
stronger. If Tory backbenchers did not rally to save him, then the whole
policy upon which they pinned such hopes would go down with him.
Imperialists like Amery were more obsessed by the detail of tariff policy
than most, but it was clear what the fate of the government would be if it
attempted to prevent its new Chancellor from delivering an economic
policy compatible with at least the minimum demands of Conservative
MPs. There would be another Carlton Club revolt, with the intention of
replacing the government with a new Tory administration free to deliver
sufficiently protectionist measures. It seemed inevitable that in such
circumstances Chamberlain would be called upon to lead it.

The election result had delivered such a terrific blow to the leverage of
the Labour Party as the official Opposition that Chamberlain's chief
concern was not criticism from across the floor but from those Liberal
free traders grouped behind the new Home Secretary in the Cabinet.
Lloyd George's decision to oppose the new government meant that
Samuel was formally elected Liberal leader on 4 November. Tellingly,
Simon and his Liberal National group had divorced themselves from the
process, further underlining their independence. Comparing himself to
Samuel and Simon, Lloyd George contented himself from the sidelines
that 'he might be only half a man, but he was a bloody sight better than
two Jews.'[5] It said much about his relationship with former colleagues
that he could not only speak of them in these terms but that in Simon's
case he could not even identify the right race. Ironically, Simon's
antecedents were Welsh.

In terms of political leverage, Lloyd George was now as impotent as
Churchill, although by wisely staying within the governing party,
Churchill could hope for more influence on policy in the years ahead. In
his first speech before the new Parliament Churchill made clear that as far
as the government was concerned 'my relations with foreign Powers
continue to be friendly . . . My attitude will be one of discriminating
benevolence.' He was not slow to identify the potential weaknesses in
Baldwin's position. Speaking with the disarming whimsy reserved for
brutally trenchant observation, Churchill protested his surprise at finding

Baldwin 'now the champion coalitionist . . . I am sure he will be reminded of those dangers whenever he should chance to walk across the portals of the Carlton Club'. MacDonald, 'the Saviour of the Gold Standard – no, I beg pardon, of the pound sterling' who had attacked Churchill's economic policies during the election campaign, could equally expect no mercy from his oratorical tormentor. In economic affairs Churchill regarded the new administration's priorities to be the immediate introduction of protectionism and measures to reinvigorate the depressed agricultural sector. On top of this, he wanted to see the convening of an international conference to settle the war debt problem and the release of the gold reserves of the United States and France, whose stockpiling he attributed to the breakdown of the gold standard.[6] Whilst he made no attempt to associate himself with strict adherence to the party line, he wished the government 'Godspeed' in its endeavours. Impressed by Churchill's call to move swiftly in the adoption of a tariff policy, Amery thought it 'an admirable speech' after which 'nearly the whole House emptied itself to adjourn to the EIA meeting'.[7] Churchill, it appeared, was content to support the main thrust of government economic policy. Henceforth, his alienation from the government would not be over domestic issues.

With the front bench now rather crowded, Churchill's adaptation to the situation demonstrated the strategic wisdom for which he has been so infrequently praised. His acceptance of the principles of tariff economics made sense if he wanted to stick with the Conservative Party whatever the fate of its possibly temporary National associations. Indeed, if the party should lose its moorings and float off to the right, then his views on India and rebuilding national defence stood to endear him to a large section of the likely separatists. After all, his previous role in high politics as the conduit between the Conservative leadership and Lloyd George was now superfluous given the former Liberal leader's decline and fall. Churchill had no marketable relationship with the new crop of influential Liberals: Simon, Samuel and Runciman. Lloyd George's refusal to follow Churchill on the path of national rectitude, 'an absence we all deplore' as the latter told the post-election Parliament,[8] was a source of disappointment. Churchill had felt free to confess to the voters that 'I did my best to bring him along. I am sorry indeed that the great wartime Prime Minister should not be with his country in the perils of peace as he was in the perils of war.'[9] An underlying theme of Churchill's strategy from 1929 to 1931, a desire to keep Lloyd George involved in the balance of power, had therefore come to nothing. In the event, Churchill could not resist a jibe as his former colleague hobbled into electoral insignificance with a party for the most part composed of his own family: 'the most united party in the country – small, but united by bonds far above the ordinary connections and associations of political life'.[10]

III

Meanwhile, Neville Chamberlain's most pressing concern was not the opposition of Lloyd George and the Labour rump across the floor, and clearly not of Churchill whose support on the outline of likely economic policy now appeared to be forthcoming. Instead the challenge that the new Chancellor had to face concerned how to balance the pursuit of protectionism with the political implications that this might have for the future participation of the other 'National' groups in the government. The ensuing battle between Samuel at the Home Office and Chamberlain was to be the first major test to determine the viability of dissent from within, rather than outside, the National Government. It would also demonstrate the extent to which Chamberlain would put the 'National' ideal above the sort of reversion to party politics likely to promote him into 10 Downing Street.

It has been noted that Samuel and his Liberal group had gone into the October election on a platform that made clear their preference for free trade whilst leaving the final judgement to a 'doctor's mandate'. Given the mood of the Conservative Party this was always likely to produce a majority for protectionism. It was, therefore, clear that the Samuelites would be powerless to stop much of the substance of free trade being jettisoned but it was up to their political skill to contrive a position through which they could stay in the government without appearing to concede the central principles of their belief. The omens for success were not good; Churchill's experience on the front bench of the opposition Conservative Party in 1930 suggested that it would be difficult to stay there without at least conceding a food tax. Samuel therefore had to discover whether Tories were prepared to make concessions to him which they had denied Churchill.

The National Government had been elected to restore order to the country's economy. This clearly made Chamberlain at the Treasury the pivotal figure. MacDonald had not wanted him there but, given that the Tories had accepted only eleven out of a total of twenty Cabinet positions, he was scarcely able to deny them the Chancellorship as well as the Home Office and the Foreign Office. The appointment to the Board of Trade of the Liberal, Sir Walter Runciman – in Snowden's misguided words a free trade supporter of 'unshakeable tenacity' – was therefore intended to act as a counterweight to the protectionist Chamberlain at the Treasury. However, with a global shift towards free trade seemingly impossible, Runciman, like the Prime Minister, had lost faith in the ability of Britain to mount a unilateral campaign of free trade. Instead, in a world circumnavigated with tariff barriers, Runciman sought to use tariffs as a form of negotiation for bilateral agreements with other countries. To outraged free traders like Snowden and Samuel, this was a capitulation. Yet Runciman's intent was very different from that of Beaverbrook, Amery and the imperialist right wing in the Conservative Party who wanted to establish a well-defined empire trading bloc and welcomed tariffs against the rest of the world as a permanent step towards establishing an imperial single market. The major battleground of this policy division was now to be the fight between the right wing with their demand for food taxes to bind together the empire, versus the last legatees of Peel, Cobden, Bright and Gladstone.

With the anticipated adoption of a comprehensive protectionist policy appearing to draw near, fears grew over the attempts by foreign exporters to swamp the British market whilst free trade remained. To counter this, Runciman piloted through the Abnormal Importations Bill with its six-month-long import duties of up to 100 per cent on manufactures thought to fit into this conveniently vague category. Rushed through with little discussion (and certainly none of the language of impartial inquiry which the 'doctor's mandate' had expressed) the legislation was reminiscent of the panic tactics that had marked out many of the early decisions of the National Government. It also denoted the essential irrelevance of Liberalism to the direction in which the government was moving.

From Samuel's perspective, however, there was little to be gained from resigning over emergency measures to prevent an expected import swamp if by hanging on in office there was still the possibility of moderating future trade policy as a whole. Theoretically, Samuel's strongest weapon of obstruction was through his membership of the Balance of Trade Committee, which would set out the groundwork for trade policy. Here he could hope to work with fellow free trader Philip Snowden in taming the protectionist zealots. The problem with this strategy was that both the composition and the mechanics of the committee worked against the free traders. Protectionists were in the majority and Chamberlain chaired the group. Furthermore, with the Board of Trade virtually controlling the evidence over which the committee deliberated, the result was destined to be a foregone conclusion, given Runciman's desertion to the protectionists. Samuel and the National Liberals could cry wolf and threaten to resign from the government, but such a cry could only be of value if Conservative colleagues genuinely wanted to keep them on the inside. Unfortunately for Samuel, many did not.

The Board of Trade's advocacy of a general tariff left Samuel to fight a rearguard action in the Cabinet. With all the zealotry of the new convert, it was Simon and Runciman who did much of the arguing against their fellow Liberal. For the Conservatives, Baldwin overcame all the academic technicalities by offering 'a few observations as Leader of the largest political party in the House of Commons' which demanded protectionism – enough, it would be thought, to kill any argument.[11] In these circumstances, the free traders were completely outmanoeuvred. Whilst Chamberlain had expected Snowden to resign he was surprised to find that the Liberal Cabinet members, Samuel, Sir Archibald Sinclair and Sir Donald Maclean, were all contemplating departure as well. However, such a walkout would not necessarily lead to the dissolution of the National Government so long as the Simonite Liberal Nationals and the National Labour group stayed put; and MacDonald's affirmation that he now supported the tariff proposals was a favourable pointer. With this state of affairs, there was a good party case for the senior Tories to rid themselves of the fractious Samuelite clan. Equally, a converse argument also operated to the effect that if these Liberals could be overruled on the essential questions and still lend their names to the government then, like MacDonald, they might still have their uses as far as the electorate were concerned. Building on an idea Chamberlain had thought plausible for retaining Snowden, it was the War Minister, Lord Hailsham, who encouraged the dissenting Liberals to stay. He suggested that on this one issue the principle of Cabinet responsibility should be suspended and the free traders could stay in the Cabinet whilst voting against its adoption of protectionism. Representative of Conservative protectionists who would have been happy to lose Samuel and his allies, Leo Amery noted in his diary that 'the whole world would rock with laughter at the fatuity of the proposal.'[12] It was a sign both of the Liberals' desperation and of the desire of some of those in the Cabinet to keep them on board for the time being that this bizarre tactic, running wholly to the contrary of British constitutional precedent, was adopted. For the time being at least, fatuity kept the government together, if not exactly united.

In the first place, the measures which the Liberals complained about were less comprehensive than could reasonably have been feared. The problem was that they also appeared to keep open the door for yet more devastating circumventions of free trade in the future. The protectionist tariffs proposed placed a 10 per cent duty on most previously untaxed imports save produce from the British Empire and its mandated territories (which were to be considered later by way of the Imperial Economic Conference). Direct government preferment would be kept at arm's length by an independent board which would make fresh recommendations to the Treasury. The key staples – cotton, wool, wheat and meat – would still be imported without restriction along with a variety of other imports on the 'free list' including iron and tin ores, scrap steel, zinc, lead and rubber. In other words, these initial measures fell short of what Conservatives had been proposing to do whilst in opposition in 1930. They avoided the major food taxes without which the prospect of an imperial economic community was seemingly unobtainable. However, symbolism attracted a reverence of its own: the protectionist principle had at last been enacted, and by the son of Joseph Chamberlain who had commenced the crusade against free trade in 1903. Few could deny Chamberlain junior his encounter with destiny. Even Sir Donald Maclean, one of his Liberal opponents in the Cabinet, scribbled him a quick memento – 'I think your great father would, and mayhap may be, proud of your work today. This from an unrepentant Free Trader.'[13]

When Chamberlain rose in a packed House of Commons on 4 February 1932 to present his measures he carefully took his notes out of an old and rather battered red dispatch box he had placed on the desk in front of him. It was the box his father had last used as Colonial Secretary when he resigned from the Cabinet in 1903. The homage to family piety was completed by the presence of Joseph Chamberlain's widow (Neville's stepmother) gazing down on him from the gallery and his half-brother Austen, sitting, as always, on the third bench below the gangway.[14] So unemotional in most circumstances and towards most people, on the issue of his family and its legacy, Chamberlain was, understandably, proud and sentimental:

> There can have been few occasions in all our long political history when to the son of a man who counted for something in his day and generation has been vouchsafed the privilege of settling the seal on the work which the father began but had perforce to leave unfinished. Nearly twenty-nine years have passed since Joseph Chamberlain entered upon his great campaign in favour of Imperial preference and tariff reform. More than seventeen years have gone by since he died, without having seen the fulfilment of his aims and yet convinced that, if not exactly in his way, yet in some modified form his vision would eventually take shape. His work was not in vain. Time and the misfortunes of the country have brought conviction to many who did not feel that they could agree with him then. I believe he would have found consolation for the bitterness of his disappointment if he could have foreseen that these proposals, which are the direct and legitimate descendants of his own conception, would be laid before the House of Commons, which he loved, in the presence of one, and by the lips of the other, of the two immediate successors to his name and blood.[15]

When Neville sat down at the end of his speech, Austen got up from his seat, walked over to the Treasury Bench and in full view of the chamber shook Neville by the hand. Cheering broke out. The two brothers had not always had an entirely easy relationship, separated by six years and Neville's ongoing touchiness at being condescended to by the elder brother who had always been the one marked out as the prodigal son. This made the hand-shaking episode all the more poignant a display of the junior Chamberlain's coming of age.

That the legislation was only a small step along the path laid out by Joseph Chamberlain did not hinder Conservative endorsement of it, particularly since it was regarded as the beginning rather than the completion of the new policy. The Import Duties Bill passed the Commons by 454 to 78, the opposition comprising of the Labour Party and 32 Liberals. However, if Conservatives viewed the measure as only the start of a new programme, then this was exactly what worried the Liberals and called into question their future strategy. Samuel tried to interpret the 'agreement to differ' policy as one which also covered all subsequent tariff decisions springing from the basis of the legislation. His heated Commons' exchanges with Runciman in May on the proposals for further increases led even Churchill to moralize about the 'indecent, even scandalous, spectacle of Ministers wrangling upon the Treasury Bench'.[16] However, such dissent was inevitable given that, to the delight of the protectionist majority, the committee established by the legislation proceeded to recommend raising tariffs well beyond the 10 per cent range.

For his part, Churchill privately conceded to his former PPS, Bob Boothby, that MacDonald and Baldwin 'ceased to command my allegiance'.[17] In April he demonstrated his wit as the guest speaker at a Royal Academy dinner (he was, of course, a painter himself). His technique was to compare the leading politicians as if they were exhibiting their work before the hanging committee. Thus MacDonald's decision to desert Labour for the National Government came in for analysis: 'I have watched for many years his style and methods. For a long time I thought he used too much vermillion in his pictures. Those lurid sunsets of Empire, and capitalist civilisations, began to pall on me. I am very glad he has altered his style so fundamentally . . . [and that he] uses blue now like Sargent, not only for atmosphere, but even as foundation.' He went on to make good-natured fun of Baldwin's countryside scenes whilst noting they were a 'little lacking in colour, and in precise definition of objects in the foreground. . . . Still I must admit there is something very reposeful in his twilight studies in half-tone.' Greatly amused upon hearing these comments, Baldwin was moved to write Churchill something approaching a fan letter. Of his own future, Churchill made clear to the Royal Academy audience that he was 'not exhibiting this year' because of 'differences with the Committee'. Nonetheless, he had 'still a few things on the easel which I hope some day to present to the public'.[18]

The speech was broadcast on the radio. This was a rare opportunity afforded Churchill and it would not have been made available to him had he wanted to adopt a more contentious line of argument. When he sought air-time for the latter, the BBC fell back on increasingly absurd excuses in order to deny him a microphone. When he offered to be broadcast discussing political matters 'from an entirely independent standpoint', the Corporation refused on the grounds that allowing him (a backbencher at that) to air his views on monetary policy might upset the delicate negotiations taking place at the Lausanne Conference.[19] On this basis, it was a wonder the BBC could ever bring itself to bear the grave responsibility of broadcasting any topical insight at all. Churchill's attitude to the realignment of British politics was probably best summarized when he claimed that he had 'always been able to keep [his] enthusiasms for the present National Government within the bounds of decorum' but that internationally it had raised the prestige of Britain, and her ability to cope with the world economic crisis.[20] Meanwhile, Beaverbrook did not want him to lead the next step in the cause of empire free trade because he was 'utterly unreliable', even if he had been apparently 'sincere' in every conflicting political stance he had ever adopted.[21] Much of the content of Churchill's speeches on the 1932 Budget and the Import Duties Bill was not so much devoted to the measures, which he broadly supported and to which he had little that was original to contribute, but to repaying old scores against Snowden and Samuel.[22] As Cuthbert Headlam, a leading light amongst the 'Northern group' of Conservative MPs, put it, whilst Chamberlain might be 'a dreary man', 'Winston made the House laugh – that is all he is capable of doing – but it is not the way to stage a comeback.'[23]

In fact, both Churchill and Chamberlain nearly had their political careers cut off at this juncture. In May 1932 Chamberlain suffered a severe attack of gout. In no way reflective of his abstemious lifestyle, this was a hereditary complaint which dogged him repeatedly throughout the decade and forced him to contemplate the possibility that he might have to quit politics altogether, his destiny only part fulfilled. Churchill too had experienced a narrow squeak in December 1931. On a lecture tour in New York, he looked the wrong way whilst crossing the road and was run over by a car. A less robust figure might not have recovered. Churchill instead turned the experience into a newspaper article which was profitably syndicated all over the world, netting its author the then considerable sum of £600.[24]

IV

Protectionism had been instituted as a revenue tax largely against manufacturing imports, but the more contentious issue of food taxes awaited the Imperial Economic Conference. The conference was convened in Ottawa and lasted from 21 July to 20 August 1932 with the British delegation chaired by Baldwin. The imperialists' argument maintained that in a world in which contracting markets were choosing to isolate themselves further, moves towards empire free trade offered opportunities for commercial expansion. However, as before, these hopes were dogged by the Domimons' insistence that the protection of their industries was necessary at a time when they were still developing into maturity. The British delegation found it difficult to realize their own objective of increasing manufacturing penetration of the protected empire markets without making a suitable quid pro quo to encourage empire agricultural penetration of Britain. They had also to safeguard the British farmer from unlimited cheaper empire produce. Furthermore, the case for creating a self-sufficient economic bloc was undermined by the fact that the export trade of empire countries was also dependent on non-imperial trade. In Britain's case, two-thirds of her exports went to countries outside her empire.[25] These were facts which could not be altered without interventionist policies clearly inimical to maximizing markets and profit.

Canada induced the British delegation to accept tariffs on foreign grain together with free entry for Dominion flour. Australia pushed for Britain to institute restrictions on imports of foreign meat. Coupled with restrictions on wheat, this was a step too far both for non-Tory members of the delegation (Runciman and J.H. Thomas) and the Prime Minister back in London, who wrote warning that such a resolution could break up the National Government itself. In Ottawa, Chamberlain himself now threatened to resign unless meat tariffs were introduced, since there seemed little prospect of the conference coming to an agreement without them. As if this was not serious enough, MacDonald upped the stakes by telling Thomas on the telephone that if meat duties were accepted, a quarter of the Cabinet would resign. With this dangerous impasse far from resolved in London, the final accepted compromise in Ottawa involved Britain agreeing on a five-year restriction of foreign meat.

The negotiations exhausted Chamberlain. Near the very end when, exasperated, he walked out of a meeting, the project had appeared to be in jeopardy. He was particularly annoyed with Leo Amery who had decided to go on a busman's holiday to Ottawa whilst the conference convened and was spending much of his time buttonholing the delegates. Chamberlain suspected that his zealous colleague was responsible for encouraging the Dominions to make unrealizable demands. No doubt

Amery thought that if strong demands led to the break-up of the National Government, then two birds might be killed with one stone. Meanwhile, he had heard the rumour that the strain had become so great on Chamberlain that he had 'more or less collapsed' and that Hailsham was taking on much of his work.[26] Certainly, the conference and the prospect of failure, coming on top of his recurrent ill-health, had driven Chamberlain close to the edge. 'I was in despair', he wrote in his diary late in the evening of 15 August, 'after the others had gone to bed, I stopped at S.B.'s request and told him that, if the conference broke down because of our refusal to put up a duty on meat, I should have to fade out.' But for a near-run thing, Chamberlain's supposedly inevitable rise to the top almost ended in 1932, close but crucially short of the summit – just like his father and brother before him.

When the Ottawa agreements were finally signed, it was clear the extent to which Britain had ceded authority to its own Dominions. Whilst Britain agreed measures designed to help Dominion agricultural penetration of her own market, no real attempt was made by the Dominions to make it easier in return for British exports to enter their markets. Their concession was a marginal one: that they would make it even more difficult for non-British exports to enter. The limits of Joseph Chamberlain's imperial dream had apparently been reached.

At the end of a twenty-year battle, the imperialist visionaries could only be disappointed at the deal reached, no matter how they tried to put an optimistic face on the outcome. Paradoxically as a result, the protectionism introduced by the National Government was closer to the position accepted by renegade Liberals like Simon and Runciman or ex-Liberals like Churchill than that of the disciples of Joe Chamberlain. The quasi-Liberal interpretation had proved victorious not so much as a result of superior playing of Westminster and Whitehall politics. Rather, it coincided with the fact that the Dominion governments realized the horizons of imperial preference stopped with their own self-interest, a point so-called imperialists in London had never been prepared to face. The empire remained a family, but one in which its members were growing up and moving on.

Despite its limited advances, Ottawa nevertheless came as the final straw for the real free traders in the Cabinet. Snowden wrote to MacDonald on 15 September 1932 grumbling that the Conservatives had 'sacrificed nothing, but have used the enormous Tory majority we gave them at the Election to carry out a Tory policy and to identify us with it. We have sacrificed our Party and ruined the political careers of a score of young Labour MPs.'[27] Snowden's bitterness was not surprising. Being held hostage by Tories was hardly a dignified end to the career of a great

Labour pioneer. Yet it would have been optimistic beyond reason to have expected anything other from a government and a Parliament in which his views were so clearly in a minority. Given the likelihood that the Tories could have won a smashing election victory on their own in 1931, the electorate would therefore have voted for protectionism even if Snowden and his fellow 'National Labour' politicians had stayed clear of the coalition. Snowden was right as far as his wing of the Labour Party was concerned – nothing had been gained by sharing power with the Tories. Samuel had to consider whether Snowden's logic applied equally to the participation of the Liberal Party. Fearing the prospect of being left marooned amongst the Tories, MacDonald was insistent that Samuel should be encouraged to stay. The Prime Minister claimed he would be reduced to being 'a limpet in office' as Samuel's resignation would undermine his position as the 'head of a combination'.[28] Realistically, however, MacDonald's position was not personally threatened so long as Baldwin wanted to maintain cooperation. If there remained a prospect of MacDonald's political death, then it was more likely to be the result of suicide than as the victim of domestic violence. Indeed, without the Liberals, MacDonald's position became more, rather than less, essential to Tories wanting to maintain the front of a National Government. This was shallow comfort, and he inevitably found himself lamenting that 'this is nae my ain hoose.'[29]

After much soul searching, the free traders finally accepted that the Ottawa agreements could not be accommodated within their own beliefs. Whilst less keen to resign from the government than Samuel, Lord Lothian concluded that many of his fellow Liberals felt that they were being forced back 'between submerging Liberalism in another 1885 Liberal Unionist combination' or 'trying to infuse the Liberal spirit of reason and tolerance into the left parties'.[30] The former proposition held no appeal to Samuel. Once he had ensured that the rest of the party would follow him, he resigned from the government, along with the other Liberal ministers within his group, on 28 September.

Samuel retired to the backbenches with thirty-two supporters and complete control of the Liberal Party organization (Simon and Lloyd George having both separately established their own party bank accounts). For a year, Samuel's Liberals stayed on the government backbench, increasingly uncomfortable with the situation. Faced with mounting criticism from the wider party, Samuel finally crossed the floor with his loyal colleagues to the opposition benches in November 1933, an action summed up in an example of the doggerel of the day (collected with relish by Lloyd George) that

Slippery Sam has crossed the floor,
He won't help the Government any more;
He's sitting now on the opposite benches,
But nobody worries and no one blenches,
Or cares – to be brutal – a tinker's dam,
What has become of Slippery Sam.[31]

The resignations of Snowden and Samuelite Liberals significantly altered the balance of the National Government. This weakened the brake on the Conservatives accordingly. What was not disturbed was the maintenance of that government in power. Chamberlain certainly saw the loss of the free trade Liberals as a way of binding together all those groups that remained, assisting the process of 'the fused party under a National name which I regard as certain to come'.[32] Chamberlain was drawing his own historical conclusions from the comparison with the Liberal Unionists that Lord Lothian had raised. Whilst Baldwin appeared to be genuinely enjoying the compromises involved in coalition management, Chamberlain evidently viewed it merely as a shop window with which to entice more custom for his own brand of Chamberlainite Conservatism. Amery had noted the characteristics of this difference when the 'agreement to differ' clause had been proposed: 'The real mainspring of the trouble is that S.B. is afraid of forcing the pace, partly because he is afraid of the responsibility of being Prime Minister, partly because he is afraid that he may not be Prime Minister and Neville displace him.'[33] With MacDonald's continuing acquiescence, National Labour at least retained in the Premiership the ultimate symbol of their participation in the government (although MacDonald was naturally concerned that his role was precisely that – symbolic). National Labour also retained the Lord Chancellorship and the Dominions Office which, given the diminutive size of the party, was about as much representation as it was reasonable to expect. Content to work with the new fiscal arrangements that had proved too much for Samuel, Simon retained the Foreign Office. In most domestic matters he was now clearly indistinguishable from the Conservatives in any case. Indeed in many ways Simon and his Liberal National group were the real winners through Samuel's departure. They had been excluded from the Cabinet formed in August 1931 in favour of the Samuelite Liberals. Now, whatever their tenuous association with the traditions of liberalism, they were the sole Liberal representatives in power and were assured of office for this reason so long as they did not determine to upset the major objectives of the government.[34] In this way, Cabinet reshuffles came and went during the course of the decade without unseating Simon, who hopped from one great office of state to another – Foreign Secretary, Home Secretary, Chancellor of the Exchequer and

Lord Chancellor. He was a clever man, a KC and a fellow of All Souls, but his success was more a reflection of his political indispensability than (despite his best efforts) his ability to win friends. Churchill once referred to his 'marble smile', and his habit of slapping colleagues on the back and addressing them by the wrong Christian name was legendary. Later in life, he found himself on the same station platform as the socialist intellectual, G.D.H. Cole. Trying to escape the former Lord Chancellor's conversation, Cole cried that he only travelled third class and scurried off into the appropriate compartment of the train. To Cole's horror, Simon announced that he did likewise and followed him. When the ticket inspector arrived, both men produced first-class tickets.[35]

Although Simon's analytical mind was one of the finest in the legal and political world, his logic for staying in the government was refuted by Samuel in his decision to quit. In resigning, Samuel's Liberals had concluded that if they could not influence the policy of the government from within, they would be better so doing from without, and inevitably in full opposition. From there they played no further significant part in determining the country's political destiny. With the government prepared to push through Indian constitutional reform, Churchill and the Indian diehards would have to decide whether they could escape the fate of Samuel and the Liberals.

V

The dream of those Tories who had viewed protectionism and imperial preference as one of the major reasons for their political calling had at last been realized. The limits of the pleasure derived were all too obvious. The economic recovery came – eventually – but its source was at best indirectly related to the tariff negotiations. The trade deals negotiated at Ottawa did not significantly bind more tightly the political union of the British Empire. In the years ahead, the British Dominions were by no means always yodelling in unison. Ever the pragmatist, the Chancellor of the Exchequer rearranged his repertoire accordingly. Following Ottawa, Chamberlain appeared to lose interest in much of the imperial dimension of his father's economic teaching. Instead, he concentrated upon extending the preferences won between the Dominions and colonies of the British Empire by using the tariff as a negotiating counter in the seventeen trade agreements concluded between 1932 and 1935 with countries as diverse as the Scandanavian states, Argentina and Stalinist Russia.

If protectionism did not live up to the hopes of its zealots, it also did not live down to the warnings of the classical liberals. In 1930, protective duties had affected less than 3 per cent of imports (by value) to Britain, with revenue duties payable on a further 15 per cent. After the deals struck at Ottawa, three-quarters of imports paid duties and even some of those that did not were liable to other restrictions and obstructions. Whilst around a half of the imports ended up paying in the 10 to 20 per cent duty band, some, like imports of steel, paid far more.[36] Although it was true that protectionism now coincided with a movement in the British economy away from foreign trade and towards concentration on domestic demand, this was a trend already discernible before the tariffs had been imposed. The much feared equation between protectionism and higher prices did not affect the standard of living dramatically. Since one of the legacies of the world slump was low commodity prices, the retail price index was in 1937 still only modestly above its 1931 level; indeed, in the immediate aftermath of the Import Duties Act, it had actually fallen.[37] Meanwhile, quotas and tariffs did not appear to generate on their own the degree of prosperity in British agriculture that their advocates had for so long promised. Other measures, including the creation of marketing boards, had to be established as well. Whilst output (but not employment) did increase as the decade proceeded, this was at considerable expense to the Exchequer. Fortified with additional measures of financial ameliora-tion and market-rigging, farmers became the recipients of large-scale subsidies, a different kind of cash crop which was – with increasing difficulty – to support Britain's rural sector for the rest of the century.

Certainly a perceptible tilt in trade towards the empire was evident in the years which followed Ottawa. This may have been helped by a period of relative exchange stability within the sterling bloc – although the correlation between such stability and trade has often proved clearer in principle than has transpired to be the case in practice. Between 1932 and 1938, Britain's exports to imperial markets rose from around a third to two-fifths of her total export share. The proportion of imperial imports into Britain rose even more dramatically over the period.[38] This was a process already under way regardless of the measures adopted at Ottawa. It is a matter for debate whether the acceleration in the trend was the natural continuation of a redirection of economic activity or the product of protectionist policy distorting the market in a direction less profitable than free trade would have encouraged.[39] Less contentious is the suggestion that protection eased the pressure on the balance of payments and the pound. Together with depressed world commodity prices the effect of this was to reduce the necessity for deflation. The resulting relaxation of monetary policy led to the low interest rates that were to be the most constant feature of Neville Chamberlain's tenure at the Treasury between 1931 and 1937.[40]

In the panic of September 1931, base rates had been raised to 6 per cent. By June 1932, they had been successfully reduced to a mere 2 per cent. But for a brief period in the special circumstances of 1939, they were to remain at this rate until 1951. Now the absence of inflationary pressure ensured an inflow of funds back into the country. As a result, London had no difficulty paying back the emergency loans from France and the USA raised during the crisis of the previous year. The most important gain of the cheap money policy was that it made possible the conversion of the war debt at a lower rate of interest. The result was dramatic. Supporting the National Debt had accounted for 40 pence in every pound paid in taxation to the Exchequer in 1929. By the middle of the 1930s, this had fallen to less than 25 pence in the pound.[41] Financial stabilization and the migration of gold back to London had also been assisted by the intervention of the British Government in India, where the rupee was kept pegged to sterling. Agrarian recession and the high premium India had to pay for gold encouraged an outflow of the commodity, greatly to Britain's benefit, and India's sterling debt remittances were now being paid on time.[42] Writing to his sister, Chamberlain rejoiced that 'The astonishing gold mine we have discovered in India's hoards has put us in clover. . . . We can accumulate credits for the repayment of our £80m loan and we can safely lower the bank rate. So there is great rejoicing in the City and sterling remains steady.'[43] Whether these developments were so felicitous for India was a different matter. Like his father before him, Chamberlain's primary concept of empire focused upon the relationship between Britain and the white Dominions, and he expressed no particular interest in the culture and everyday politics of the Indian subcontinent.

With a low bank rate now sustained, the Bank of England's interest rate policy remained a strategic rather than a short-term tactical lever of economic management. Chamberlain sought to entrench sterling's stability in April 1932 with the launch of the Exchange Equalization Account which, with a (later expanded) base of £175 million, was used to buy up large amounts of foreign currency at a time when those currencies were relatively weak in relation to sterling. The fund was then used to iron out temporary fluctuations. The necessities of the situation thus ensured that Chamberlain became the unlikely architect of the managed currency.

Hoping that conditions of world confidence would ultimately return, Chamberlain viewed measures like Exchange Equalization as a temporary stopgap. He wanted to find a modus vivendi with France and, in particular, the United States, in order to recreate currency stabilization by international agreement. Temperamentally attracted to international junkets of every kind, MacDonald exercised his Prime Ministerial prerogative to chair the World Economic Conference which convened in June 1933 at the ill-chosen venue of the Geological Museum, Kensington. Following reported platitudes of hopefulness from the new President of the United States, Franklin D. Roosevelt, the occasion presented an opportunity to break out of the isolationist attitudes which had been reinforced by the contraction of world trade. Yet given the new American President's decision to take his country off the gold standard in April and pursue a national policy of regeneration, such an outcome proved forlorn. On the issue of the gold standard, the British Government could hardly lecture him from a position of strength. Hope that the USA would use its gold reserves to assist a revival in world trade were thus dashed. Instead the $10 billion gold inflow into the United States between 1934 and 1939 was hoarded without any alteration to the dollar's value.[44] Nevertheless, the reflationary policies pursued during those years by Roosevelt in the United States made it safer for Britain to modestly enlarge the cash supply in its wake. Harsh deflation was avoided. Provisions for the Sinking Fund aside, 1933 was the only year between 1921 and 1939 in which there was an actual budget deficit.[45] The reaction of the Canadian and South African Premiers to the American position at the World Economic Conference was to push for a more integrated imperial monetary framework to ensure greater stability for the currencies in the sterling area. The closer formation of such a financial bloc was therefore to emerge without the foreplanning of the supposedly so imperially minded Neville Chamberlain. It was also to include many countries that were far outside membership of the empire.

The legacy of war debts clouded the European and transatlantic financial picture and Chamberlain viewed the Americans and the French as the chief culprits. In December 1931, within days of having become Chancellor, he was grappling with this problem. He thought that the French in particular were keeping 'the whole of Europe in a state of nervous anxiety and are thereby precipitating the advent of Hitler' in their insistence on reparations which Germany could not pay. However, France's position in turn was coloured by the policy of the United States, which, before Roosevelt succeeded President Hoover, was also proving uncooperative. Chamberlain noted that

> Any reparations settlement or adjustment must be accompanied by a corresponding settlement, or adjustment, of war debts. Hoover knows it, but daren't say so. Unless he says so, France daren't move, and so we are all locked in a suicidal embrace which will probably drown the lot of us! Reflect on this: (1) we remitted nearly £400 millions of France's debt to us. (2) if the USA had agreed to fund our debt on the same terms as she gave to France, we should have so overpaid that to put it right we should pay *nothing* for another nine years! Did ever a country exploit her misfortunes more successfully than France?[46]

At Lausanne, in June and July 1932, Chamberlain worked hard to persuade the French of the need for a total settlement of both reparations and war debt. The conference succeeded in bringing Germany's reparation payments to an end. Central to Chamberlain's financial credo was the notion of confidence. Despite the drying-up of payments from the other former combatants, the idea that Britain should default on her debt repayments to the United States – other than as part of an international settlement – was therefore naturally anathema. In late 1932, Chamberlain resisted the temptation to default. In this he was 'strongly' supported by Baldwin and, as Chamberlain recognized, 'on those very rare occasions when he expresses an opinion of his own, he is generally right.' Having originally negotiated the terms of Britain's debt repayment back in 1923, Baldwin told the Cabinet on 28 November 1932 that debt 'repudiation might bring the world within sight of the end of capitalism. Our word was unique in the world.'[47] Unfortunately, the outstanding nominal debt of $4.7 million was now larger than the original advances of $4.3 million, of which half had already been paid. Britain paid only part of her scheduled repayment for 1933 and could only reasonably resume paying the full amount by demanding that London's war debtors paid up in turn. This had long been the problem. In view of the economic chaos on the continent and the political instability it was creating, Britain had allowed her debtors to default. To demand repayment now, if it were to achieve any response at all, might only provoke further unhelpful European upheavals. Indeed, Britain had some grounds for feeling aggrieved by the manner in which she was singled out by the Americans. Whilst the rest of Europe owed a quarter more in debt to the United States than did Britain, Britain had already repaid three times more than they had, and on less favourable repayment terms than the Americans had made available to countries like France. The decision of the US Congress to declare Britain's 1933 part-payment a 'default' made matters easier for Chamberlain. With reparations cancelled and a concomitant lack of further debt repayments in sight from the rest of Europe, in 1934 Britain joined the bandwagon and ceased her payments to the United States. The decision helped the Treasury's more general battle against debt. The total debt service burden fell from over 8 per cent of national income in 1932 to under 5 per cent in 1935.[48] Given that he was breaking a deal that had originally been struck by Baldwin, Chamberlain was fortunate to concede so little political capital to the Opposition. One of the advatanges for the government of Labour's drift to the left was that in adopting the rhetoric of opposing international capitalism per se, Labour lost any chance of being an effective critic of Chamberlain on the details of financial policy.

The other side of the nation's finances was the fiscal measures upon which the National Government had put such store when coming to power. Seventy per cent of the £81.5 million increase in taxation in Snowden's 1931 Budget had been paid for by rises in income tax. Chamberlain's years at the Treasury coincided with a switch of emphasis from direct to indirect taxation: in part, a manifestation of a country moving from free trade to protectionism (tariffs netted £40 million per annum). A ratio of 4:1 in 1918 between direct to indirect taxation became 3:1 in 1932 and neared parity the following year, an evolution naturally lamented by the Labour Opposition.[49]

Chamberlain resisted the more active reflationists, making clear that he was not prepared to cut income tax at the risk of unsettling the national finances. As far as he was concerned, the experience of other nations which had followed the path of unbalanced budgets gave no hope that such a policy led anywhere other than to economic uncertainty and, thereby, to the higher interest rates from which Britain had largely escaped.[50] Onlookers were unimpressed by his performance at the dispatch box when he delivered his Budget statement for 1933. One of Labour's chief finance spokesmen even (perhaps rather self-consciously) decided it was an occasion to catch up on some sleep in the chamber.[51] No doubt, given the paucity of colleagues on the opposition benches, he had considerable room to stretch out. Other politicians were less soporific. Frustrated by the failure to find a more imperially minded solution, Amery thought that Chamberlain's 1933 Budget 'was a cheerless performance and very distinctly depressed the House. Nor did the customary vindications of financial soundness, though acquiesced in by the House, evoke any applause at all ... Nor did he even go out of his way to indulge in any little excursus which might have suggested that he had a policy on the general problem.'[52] In fact, Chamberlain's excursus was restricted to influencing the policies of the spending departments. He did not regard the Treasury as the proper place for inventiveness, if by that term was meant travelling the road of unsound finance. Brought up by his father in the traditions of protectionism and municipal utility socialism, he was no zealot for the free market: his attempt to ensure that sterling was a managed currency, his introduction of tariffs and in particular agricultural protectionism, his support for transforming the iron and steel industries into a cartel and his use of Treasury funds to ensure that London Transport was a publicly funded monopoly were testament to that fact.[53] Nonetheless, he believed the surest way a Chancellor could help create the conditions for business confidence was to keep the budget balanced. In this respect, the scion of Tory imperialism had much in common with the nostrum of Gladstonian liberalism. For the likes of Amery, this was insufficient. In his diary he recorded that he

Listened to Winston delivering a slashing onslaught on Neville and MacDonald. Neville I fear has put his foot into it badly by talking about abnormal unemployment lasting for ten years. It is a pity to be too honest in the expression of your opinions; especially if they really are wrong as well as unpopular. This defeatism of the Government is really getting beyond bearing. They have no plan beyond balancing the Budget.[54]

Whatever alternative schemes may have promised, Chamberlain's dour economic policy met at least with modest success. In the eyes of his supporters, vindication came in his Budget of 1934. A small surplus allowed him the room for manoeuvre denied up until that time. As a result, the contentious 1931 cut in unemployment benefit (the immediate cause of the formation of the National Government) was revoked, along with half of the cuts that had been imposed on public service salaries. The income tax increases which had been introduced in the crisis of 1931 were also reversed, the standard rate falling from 5 shillings (25 pence) to 4 shillings 6d. (22.5 pence) in the pound. The worst of the recession was over. Chamberlain put it in typically Victorian terms to the Commons: the country had finished *Bleak House* and could now look forward to *Great Expectations*.[55]

By the time of his Budget in 1935 virtually all the emergency economy measures of 1931 had been reversed. Critics compared unfavourably the Chancellor's efforts to reduce unemployment with the 'New Deal' schemes being developed in the United States and elsewhere. In response Chamberlain mused that 'in view of our incorrigible habit of self-depreciation, it does not seem unpardonable to point out that nowhere else can you find a parallel to the results which have been achieved here.'[56] He was right, even if the comparison gave little cause for domestic smugness. The relative success of Nazi Germany and the Stalinist Soviet Union in reducing unemployment was tainted by the manner of the regimes executing the task. Even democratic industrialized nations which indulged in unbalanced budgets had by no means outperformed Britain. As the decade progressed, so the shadow created by the dole queues shortened more quickly per head of population in timid, prudent Britain than in countries like Sweden and the United States which attempted to finance growth through budget deficits.

Instead of opting for deficit financing, Chamberlain clung to his policy and the bank rate remained at 2 per cent. The role of cheap money in pulling Britain out of recession has been disputed. Capital investment, for instance, only picked up in 1934 by which time it could be linked with the general improvement in the trade cycle everywhere. However, building societies had by now emerged as a major presence in British life, financing three-quarters of the houses built in the 1930s. Low interest rates made mortgages more accessible, providing a further stimulus to the building of new homes and the upturn in the construction industry.

Even though they only covered the insured workforce, the unemployment statistics painted a depressing enough picture when the rate peaked at a quarter of the workforce in the summer of 1932. This represented an all-time high for Britain, a level to which subsequent recessions in the century scarcely came close in comparison. Real improvements did not emerge until late in 1934. For the next four years, employment figures continued to brighten. The case for a major public works scheme was weakened by this favourable trend, especially by the fact that such a project's main beneficiary – the construction industry – was already flourishing as a result of the house-building boom. Instead of the outsize concrete monuments of a British Mussolini were three million new homes built by private enterprise during the 1930s. The state's main role was to add to this process by continuing to supplement subsidies to local authority slum clearance programmes and new housing schemes. In all, the building boom created nearly a third of the new jobs generated during the 1930s. Between 1932 and 1935, it was responsible for 40 per cent of the rise in investment.[57]

The problem was that much of the housing boom concentrated on middle-class demand. As a result, pockets of unemployment in Wales, Scotland and northern England where the traditional staple industries had irretrievably lost their markets were left behind as defiant and indelible blots on the human landscape. Over 60 per cent of the insured workforce were unemployed in Merthyr in South Wales in 1934, compared to 37 per cent in Motherwell, just over 6 per cent in Neville Chamberlain's Birmingham and under 4 per cent in St Albans.[58] The government's response was the development of 'special areas' legislation. Perhaps inevitably, this achieved only marginal succour, the funds allocated to the projects proving insufficient to the scale of the task.

VI

The parliamentary situation in November 1934 was summed up by the Conservative MP, Cuthbert Headlam:

> Neville's speech on the distressed areas pleased no one ... – but I doubt whether there is any real falling off in the Government's supporters in the HofC, whatever the feeling may be in the country – and even if some Conservatives in the HofC are disgruntled with the Government, they are not the kind to follow Winston – they are our progressives who are shrieking for what they call a policy of reconstruction.[59]

In March 1935, fourteen MPs, amongst which Harold Macmillan was one of the most active, launched *Planning for Employment* as the centrepiece of their campaign to reconstruct and rationalize industry. The result was a cross-party think tank, the 'Next Five Years Group', fronted by the chairman of the MacDonaldite National Labour Party, Lord Allen of Hurtwood. Sixteen MPs, most of whom sat on the government benches, put their name to its published proposals to bring under public or semi-public control major utilities on the home front. This was combined with support for collective security through the League of Nations in Geneva as the cornerstone of British foreign policy.[60] Macmillan was an ambitious but earnest product of Eton and Balliol. He had served bravely in the trenches but was troubled in his private life by his wife's infidelity with a fellow left-wing Tory MP, Bob Boothby. These events appear to have further driven Macmillan on to succeed in the public sphere. He had completely distanced himself from Mosley who – having evolved the New Party into a pseudo-paramilitary British Union of Fascists – was now considered beyond the pale as far as the liberal establishment was concerned. After his movement's violent meeting at Olympia in 1934 Mosley lost what remaining shred of empathy he might have attracted from any serious figure on the Tory right, including the indulgence of even Lord Rothermere. Macmillan, by contrast, channelled his sympathy for the poor (his Stockton constituency was a particular black spot for jobs) through constitutional parliamentary means. As a member for a nearby constituency, Headlam saw much of Macmillan during this period and had a cautious regard for some of his views on industrial reconstruction, but regarded him, not without justification, as a self-obsessed 'colossal bore'.[61] Furthermore, Headlam thought of Macmillan that

> I fancy that the one thing he really is hankering after is political success and I feel that he would accept any job that was offered to him. His idea, therefore, may well be that, if he makes a nuisance of himself and can form a small and effective group to assist him in the job, he may persuade *hoi en Telloi* (sic.) to offer him a billet to silence his opposition. He is such an odd unforthcoming man – so tremendously absorbed in himself and his own affairs . . .[62]

Once again, the question of how best to gain influence with the Government arose. With no shortage of lobby fodder ready to do the Cabinet's parliamentary business in return for the prospect of preferment or just a quiet life, it was virtually inevitable that some groups would try a more confrontational route to make their presence felt. As we shall see in the chapters that follow, this was the line adopted by Churchill and his diehards over Indian reform, and later, in opposition to the appeasement of Hitler, in the belief that they could command an indispensable parliamentary group whose inclusion in an administration would become a reality once the government got into trouble or had its majority slashed at the next general election. This was the strategy which animated Lloyd George. Having proved little obstacle to the first three years of the National Government, he now reasserted himself in time for the expected disillusion. He calculated that by gathering a group around him who shared his economic views, he would become the power-broker in a new Parliament in which MacDonald, Baldwin and Chamberlain were shorn of their great majority.[63]

Lloyd George's campaign promoted state funding of a massive investment programme in town and country, organized by a new statutory council to combat unemployment and encourage emigration back to the countryside. By asserting that his campaign was non-partisan, he was able to attract the commendation of Conservatives like Sir Arthur Steel-Maitland, Lord Eustace Percy and Lord Londonderry. Churchill immediately issued a statement to the press, avoiding both detailed analysis and criticism of the Chancellor, Neville Chamberlain, but comparing favourably Lloyd George's 'refreshing' speech which deserved 'the closest attention' with 'the recent utterances of the deplorable politician who now maunders at the head of the Government'.[64]

In 1933 Churchill had seemed enthusiastic about Roosevelt and his 'New Deal' economics, but by 1935 he was speaking out against the level of interference and regulation it was spawning in the US economy. That he chose to commend Lloyd George's campaign was surprising in that it was little more than a reworking of the 1929 *We Can Conquer Unemployment* programme of which Churchill (then at the Treasury) had been prime castigator. After the first rush of enthusiasm had subsided, however, Churchill's doubts about Lloyd George's 1935 campaign resurfaced. He chose not to offer further support in the ensuing months at a time when even the government was going through the motions of studying its possibilities.[65] Although Lloyd George had previously cooperated – not without self-interest – with Austen Chamberlain and Churchill over their condemnation of the government's grip on which politicians could be allowed to broadcast on the BBC,[66] this was not the basis for a new alliance of the past masters. Churchill had been trying to enlist Lloyd George's support over air rearmament[67] but the latter opted for League of Nations' sponsored disarmament instead, dashing any such hopes of the two pulling in tandem. Any serious talk of a Churchill–Lloyd George ticket, while both still remained true to their principles, was by now essentially doomed to failure.

Lloyd George's initiative came at a time when the government was desperately looking for something to pep up its tired public face. Amazingly, given all that had gone on before, discussion took place as to whether he should now be welcomed into the Cabinet. He had given Austen Chamberlain the impression that he wanted a Cabinet reshuffle which, while bringing him (Austen Chamberlain) in to replace Simon, would include MacDonald's relinquishment of the Premiership. If Churchill's future was discussed, then no record of the fact remains.[68] More to the point, Neville Chamberlain claimed that he would not sit at the same Cabinet table as Lloyd George. After some vacillation, Baldwin reassured his Chancellor that 'he could not serve with L.G. since that would inevitably split the party.' Lloyd George himself concluded that Baldwin could not offer him an olive branch without 'shifting Neville, Runciman and possibly Simon [therefore] he advisably shrinks from quarrelling with them and the Diehards simultaneously'. Whatever the electoral capital to be made out of it, with so much opposition to Lloyd George on personal grounds alone from indispensable members of the Cabinet,[69] Baldwin would have had great difficulty bringing his old enemy into the government.[70]

From his side of the fence, Lloyd George was receiving contradictory advice. The Liberal, Lord Lothian, encouraged him to keep his movement 'entirely non-party'[71] whilst Rothermere told him to do the reverse. Rothermere's logic was that there was no point in Lloyd George appealing to the left because the Liberals did not want him back and Labour did not think they needed an ally. Since much of Europe had swung decisively to the far right, Lloyd George should convert the British right wing to the economics of the 'New Deal' and by coming 'out very strong on India and air armaments' he would in two years 'be the leader of the Conservative Party and once more Prime Minister'.[72] As with similar suggestions in the past, Rothermere did not appear to be conscious of the difference between fantasy and reality. There was plenty in Lloyd George's 'New Deal' which would have been iniquitous to much of the Conservative Party, particularly those in the general mindset of Neville Chamberlain. Equally, Rothermere seemed oblivious (as Churchill had briefly been in 1929) to the fact that Lloyd George's lack of imperialist views made a diehard link-up on India out of the question. The same was true for his championing of air disarmament on the back of a campaign which boasted the support of nonconformist churches and various assorted pacifists. For these reasons, Lloyd George's admirers in the Tory Party were the left wingers and most certainly not the diehards.

As one of the chief megaphones of the Tories' left wing, Harold Macmillan argued that Lloyd George was wasting an opportunity in associating himself with the socialists. He should instead join forces with the 'Next Five Years Group' (of which he was spokesman) to work for change from within the National Government's parliamentary ranks.[73] In the meantime, Macmillan was amongst those Conservatives who had private talks with Lloyd George and even appeared publicly on his 'Council of Action for Peace and Reconstruction' platform. However, the approaching general election necessitated a degree of circumspection and propriety – neither commodity of which was normally associated with the dynamic former Prime Minister.[74] It was perhaps felt that open support for Lloyd George's campaign was hampered by the unavoidable danger of commending him personally. His chance would only come if the next general election returned Parliament to the minority arithmetic of 1929–31.

VII

The increasingly isolated resident of 10 Downing Street, MacDonald was now as much a prisoner of his failing mental faculties as of the political situation. Even his society confidante, Lady Londonderry, had rather unkindly started calling him 'Ramshackle Mac'. Baldwin was content as Lord President to sit and bide his time, resisting sudden spasms of activity which might throw caution needlessly to the wind. Simon was kept active at the Foreign Office. Having to tailor Britain's international commitments to the skimpy economic cloth provided did not add to his general popularity although he would no doubt have been in even deeper trouble if he had got Britain involved against Japan in the distant conflict in Manchuria. After Samuel's departure, the Home Secretary was Sir John Gilmour. A Scottish Conservative, Gilmour provided the sober reassurance necessary for the post, even if his assaults on the betting industry annoyed more than one Tory MP. Neither remarkable for being one of 'the great reforming Home Secretaries' nor for being an eccentric reactionary in the mould of the saxophone-hating William Joynson-Hicks, he had, as Headlam put it, 'all the qualifications that are needed – a good sort, pleasant manners, long tenure of a seat in the House, enough to live upon – has been a whip'.[75]

This was the team in which Neville Chamberlain stood out as the great all-rounder. Combining the Treasury with the chairmanship of the Conservative Research Department, during 1934 he was to further strengthen his omnipotent presence in policy formation by taking the lead in a new unit, the Cabinet Conservative Committee. He may not have been a painter of the political canvas with the visionary strokes of the broad brush, but he did have an unmatched grasp of pointillist detail and of the practicalities of a set composition. As a result, his influence was to be detected in most areas of administration and planning. Already in October 1932 he could write to his sister about how much it amused him 'to find a new policy for each of my colleagues in turn'.[76] The government's agricultural initiatives, its housing policy (which carried forward fresh legislation to decongest some of the worse slum areas) and the Unemployment Assistance Board, were all examples of legislation with which he was primarily and intimately involved. That the Chancellor interfered in the affairs of domestic spending departments was unsurprising, especially given his previous innovations in local government in Birmingham and at the Ministry of Health. That he found time to involve himself in the actual legislation of so many other departments, amongst all his own cares at the Treasury, was perhaps more remarkable. Yet he did not always get his way. Reform of the House of Lords had long been a matter of unfinished business for the Tory right wing. They hoped to see a transformed upper chamber regain some of the powers and authority lost in 1911 when the Asquith Government had neutered its veto following its belligerent rejection of Lloyd George's Budget of 1909. Chamberlain favoured a scheme which would have effectively invented the life peer. One hundred of them would be created and the hereditary peerage reduced to the same number. Gently becalmed in the tranquillity of the marina, Baldwin felt this to be a voyage into the unnecessary.

Both the strengths and limitations of the Chancellor's hard work were demonstrated with his collaboration with the Minister for Labour, Henry Betterton, in establishing the Unemployment Assistance Board. Out of the varied jumble of benefits organized by local authorities, the Unemployment Act of 1934 sought to bring jurisdiction for the transitional payments (benefits usually made to those jobless who had exhausted their insured payments) under a new statutory commission. This body was to be charged with preventing regional variation by setting national rates and ironing out irregularities. Contrary to the impression the legislation had created at the time of its passage, when it came into operation in January 1935 its practical effect in many cases was the reduction of benefit. This was a situation which should have been provided for before the levels were made public. In November 1934 the Cabinet Committee dealing with the legislation had received advance warning of the low levels to be imposed and although Chamberlain had forced them to be readjusted upwards, the tinkering was wholly insufficient. Politically, this was a gift to the Labour Party for whom dole benefit cuts had been the cause célèbre of their opposition to the National Government's creation in the first place. More damaging was the wider public outcry and the Conservative backbench rebellion in the Commons. It was possible that the revolt could act as an example of one of the paradoxes of Westminster politics. So long as a Cabinet is sufficiently united, it can usually face down even the most determined of long-term rebellions from the backbenches. Clashes of this kind are inevitably turned into matters of confidence, in which the government can mobilize all but the most single-minded or least ambitious of its supporters. In contrast, a sudden and unforeseen event can unexpectedly bring together a tidal wave of indignation, incorporating with it otherwise government-loyal individuals and opportunistic ministers looking for their lucky break. The spontaneity of the outpouring can be enough to unbalance even the most confident of administrations. In rare cases, it can even reverse the whole drift of policy. Here was an outcry which unless addressed quickly could do serious damage to the administration's credibility.

Baldwin had, it would appear, been unaware of the effect of the legislation and panicked. He even stuttered in exasperation to Lord Salisbury that it was 'the worst mess I have ever been associated with'.[77] After his negotiation of the war debts payment, his calling of the 1923 general election and his failure to inspire the confidence of his colleagues in 1930–1, this was saying something. Tellingly, it was Chamberlain who was rushed in to chair a Cabinet Committee charged with performing the quickest possible U-turn. With his usual clarity of purpose, he proved up to the task. The new Minister for Labour, Oliver Stanley, was prepared to countenance an almost total reversal of policy. Chamberlain, however, steered a steady course and within a fortnight of the rebellion, fresh legislation had been pushed through Parliament. The benefit cuts were restored and full refunds were issued, but the essential feature of the legislation – the removal of local authority control – was retained. Chamberlain had saved the day, although his failure to spot the cause of the upset had been at the root of the crisis in the first place. His apparent disregard for the public reaction to his initiatives caused much resentment from MPs having to defend marginal constituencies and highlighted a potential shortcoming should he take over the reins from the more emollient Baldwin.[78]

Major headaches like the Unemployment Assistance Board ensured that by 1935, the role of a Cabinet action man was beginning to pall for Chamberlain. The politician who had once rejoiced in his capacity to direct other ministers' departments now lamented the increasing burden of 'carrying this Government on my back'. Simon's tenure at the Foreign Office was generating enthusiasm from no quantifiable quarter, and it briefly looked as if Chamberlain might replace him. Ultimately the change did not come and Chamberlain had in any case feared that it would have looked as if 'I had worked for the change because I saw Budgetary difficulties ahead.'[79]

There is a sense in which Chamberlain's period at the Exchequer has been seen as the inevitable precursor to the Premiership and certainly after 1935 this appeared increasingly to be the case. There were times during the 1931–5 Parliament, however, when this inevitability seemed much more doubtful. Baldwin had made the deceptively long leap from 11 to 10 Downing Street in 1923, as had several before him, but the transmutation was by no means automatic. Since Chamberlain's time, it has become yet more rare (of the seventeen Chancellors between 1945 and 1990 only three – Macmillan, Callaghan and Major – subsequently became Prime Minister). The Treasury was an opportunity, but it was also a graveyard, an all too apt analogy in the case of Chamberlain whose demeanour and couture was mocked by his opponents as the latest fashion in the municipal undertaker look. He was conscious of the challenges that went with the post, writing to his sister when first faced with the prospect of the job in 1923 that it would involve putting 'a spoke in other people's wheels'.[80] These other people were invariably Cabinet colleagues upon whose support he would hope to count. Holding down the position during the mass unemployment of the 1930s was an unenviable task, particularly in his first three years when the economic upturn seemed inadequate to the scale of the grim inheritance. That his approach would attract the hostility of the young Keynesians and self-appointed commissars of planning like Harold Macmillan was inevitable. Chamberlain's personal skills were not enough to endear him even to those more ideologically agnostic northern Conservative MPs like Cuthbert Headlam. Holding a normally marginal seat in County Durham, Headlam was aware of the case for prolonging the 'National' appeal whilst being personally disappointed that his own talents were not being recognized beyond junior ministerial office. These were sentiments no doubt shared by a good many other MPs. To the acerbic Headlam, Chamberlain's Budget performances at the dispatch box were 'dull and boring' and 'not a very inspiring effort'.[81] These were marked contrasts to the sort of comments that used to be passed by even normally hostile MPs towards Churchill's Commons orations as Chancellor in the 1920s.

Chamberlain preferred the company of his family to that of his colleagues and lacked the indiscriminate outpouring of warmth necessary to make new friends. Confiding to his diary reflections of a lunch spent sitting next to Chamberlain, Headlam recorded that the Chancellor was 'quite affable but with whom, as usual, I found it difficult to get on with – any forwarder, I mean. He and Baldwin always seem to me impossible people to know any better. There is an element of inhumanity about them – a kind of "negativeness" which I find it impossible to surmount – and I don't fancy that I am peculiar in this lack of acrobatic skill.'[82] A study of

Chamberlain's correspondence papers during this period reveals that his primary preoccupations were not chiefly directed towards mastering the small print of the economic recovery. Low interest rates and a competitive currency came about almost accidentally because of the destruction of a system Chamberlain had wanted to sustain. Indeed, he privately confessed in October 1934 to being 'puzzled to account for our continuous improvement, even in exports'. His attention to detail was more often channelled towards the legislative options of other departments than towards the measures producing the economic recovery that his Treasury officials monitored. What did considerably exercise his mind whilst at the Treasury were the great international economic issues: represented by the Ottawa agreements, reparation and the war-debt issues discussed at Lausanne, American and French gold hoarding and the 1933 World Economic Conference. As we have seen, he was not always able in these exchanges of diplomatic judgement to effect an outcome favourable to perceived British interest. This did not shake his tenacious self-belief nonetheless. Tied in with the disarmament negotiations stop-starting in Geneva, these attempts at international settlement were the occasions in which Chamberlain began to see for himself a role beyond the confinement of the home front. It was during his years at the Treasury that he started to act and think himself into the role of an international player. This would later forever link his name to the search for the political stability of Europe through the appeasement of the fascist dictators.[83]

Five

INDIA: 'THE MAKING OF A
FIRST-CLASS CRISIS'

I

In 1931, the architect Sir Edwin Lutyens completed the grandest commission of his career. He had begun work on the Indian Viceroy's house in New Delhi back in 1912. When at last it was finished it was a structure of monumental splendour, its great walls of Dholpur sandstone starkly decorated in a style that combined classical order with Moghul ornament. At its heart, a giant dome capped the 'Durbar hall'. On top of the dome a very large Union Jack fluttered from a very tall pole. This was the centrepiece of a new axial layout for the city of New Delhi, based on a triangle of sixty degrees, and deriving inspiration from Washington DC. From the Viceroy's house, a great avenue stretched out, passing on its way the other government edifices in the complex, designed by Herbert Barker. These were not the buildings of a people ready to move out.

The grandeur of the architecture reflected the self-confidence of its occupants. In the early 1920s there were only a little over 150,000 Europeans in an India of 320 million inhabitants.[1] Furthermore, the Indian population was growing at a rate of 34 million a decade. It took a certain assuredness of purpose for the British to retain administrative overlordship for such a mass of humanity – more than 200 main languages, several major religions (although two-thirds Hindu) and four main ethnic groups – with a civil service of whose staff only 500 were British. Force, of course, underwrote the British Raj, but even here it was more by implication than by physical presence. A third of the total manpower of the British Army was stationed in India but this only represented 60,000 men. Supplemented by a further 174,000 Indians in the force, India's status quo in the early 1930s was kept by two million fewer men under arms than in Europe, a continent with a similar size of population.[2]

Outside those provinces governed directly by British administration (what was referred to as 'British India'), the subcontinent was still a patchwork of over 600 princely states which had emerged out of the collapse of the Moghul Empire. Ruled by the local nawabs and maharajahs, these states varied greatly in size and status and covered around one quarter of the subcontinent's population and almost half her land mass. The princes had signed treaties with the East India Company whereby they retained internal sovereignty but surrendered their jurisdiction in military and external affairs. As the 1858 Government of India Act made clear, they were bound to pursue 'sound policy' aimed at 'loyalty to the [British] Crown'. Further encroachments on their rights materialized as the nineteenth century wore on. British administrators found themselves intervening to sort out the indebtedness, corruption and general incompetence of some princes' exchequers. The result was to push the princes (not always unwillingly) into becoming feudatory chiefs – pampered, but essentially subordinate to the British Paramount Power.[3] For the ordinary Indian, these developments did not alter what for the most part remained the hazy visibility of the British presence.

Yet behind the apparent ease upon which Britain's hold over the subcontinent rested, changing conditions necessitated a constitutional framework capable of adaptation. One and a half million Indians had volunteered to fight for the British Empire during the Great War. This was one of the biggest volunteer armies the world had ever seen. Whatever misconceptions may have existed, it was a testament to the acceptance of British order. But it proved to be a war with revolutionary consequences. The (British-run) Government of India had made an enormous financial contribution to the empire's war effort. The measures taken to plug this budget deficit and reinforce sound finance had a paradoxical effect: in order to help Britain out financially, India became more independent fiscally. The money found to assist the war effort came partly from doubling India's general tariff to 7.5 per cent and this hit Lancashire's already ailing cotton textiles trade. After the war, the right of the Viceroy and his administration to set India's own tariffs was guaranteed. No time was lost in exercising this power more fully, and British exports became the target – by 1931 the general tariff had reached 25 per cent.[4]

London had to balance the need to keep control of India's financial sovereignty (in order to avert the possibility of her repudiating her debts) with the intention of making concessions to Indian aspirations elsewhere. The Great War had been fought, after all, amongst much pious talk about the self-determination of nations. Under pressure from the Viceroy, in 1917 Lloyd George's Government had sanctioned (after much judicious editing) the Secretary of State for India, Edwin Montagu, to announce that it was British policy to encourage 'the increasing association of Indians in every branch of the administration, and the gradual development of self-governing institutions with a view to the progressive realisation of responsible government in India as an integral part of the Empire.' The discussions in Cabinet made clear that this did not involve in the foreseeable future the sort of home rule which had, in principle, been promised for Ireland or existed in Britain's white Dominions. Nonetheless, a process of expectation had been put in motion. The 1919 Government of India Act embodied this spirit by giving Indians a greater say over the provisions of local government and also created a democratically elected lower chamber at the level of central government, the Central Legislative Assembly.[5] The Viceroy would retain the power of veto (as a weapon of last resort) and the most important aspects of central government, including law and order, defence and revenue remained firmly in his hands. Nonetheless, a rolling process had been started: a statutory commission was to be established within ten years to report on the effect of the reforms and to make fresh recommendations for a system of government whose stated intention for the states of India was to be 'increasingly representative of and responsible to the people of all of them'.[6]

These were limited reforms, but no less contentious for that fact. Unrest in India followed the implementation of the 1919 Act, the worst outburst of which resulted in the notorious Amritsar massacre. Although not all of the disturbances were directly related to the legislation, Tory diehards at Westminster were quick to draw the parallel. Justifiably outraged that the Act had been rushed through both Houses of Parliament without a division, they were determined to make sure further reforms received a proper scrutiny a decade later.

By the mid-1920s, the Indian civil disobedience campaign appeared to be under control. With Muslims and Hindus fundamentally divided and as much in opposition to domination from each other as from Britain, the prospect of a concerted campaign for national self-determination appeared far off. Yet it was not long before Britain's relief at this prospect appeared dangerously complacent. In 1927 the Statutory Commission reporting on the operation of the 1919 reforms, under the chairmanship of Sir John Simon, was boycotted by Indians furious at their exclusion from its membership. In 1928, Hindu supporters of *swaraj* (home rule) convened and passed the 'Nehru report' which called for full government by Indians, with control over internal affairs and adult suffrage. This was far beyond what the Simon Commission was investigating or the new liberal-leaning Viceroy, Lord Irwin (the future Foreign Secretary, Lord Halifax), could countenance. It was also unacceptable to the Muslims, who feared the tyranny of the Hindu majority in the political entity that Motilal Nehru and his colleagues were proposing. Irwin's declaration the following year, affirming dominion status as the goal, was an attempt to encourage the pro-*swaraj* National Congress Party leaders to participate in a workable framework rather than to pursue the unobtainable.

During 1930 the civil disobedience campaign in India escalated again. This convinced Lord Irwin and the Labour Government in London of the need to call the Round Table Conference in which British and Indian delegates would jointly shape a new constitution. The unrest equally convinced Churchill and the Tory diehards that, as after 1919, the promise of fresh reforms would only encourage the more extreme demands of the Congress Party with a resultant collapse of law and order in the subcontinent. In marching to the sea to collect salt (a taxed and government-restricted commodity) Mahatma Gandhi was seen to be allowed to break the law. The boycott of British goods escalated. Finally in May, Gandhi was arrested and gaoled, but the disobedience movement had by now taken on a fresh momentum. The Government of India found itself imprisoning more than 20,000 civilians. British rule was being challenged.

II

Baldwin's bipartisan approach to Indian constitutional reform has been noted in Chapter 2 and his support for the convocation in November 1930 of the Round Table Conference was its manifestation. His first choice to represent the Tories in the talks was Sir Austen Chamberlain but he refused on the grounds that his earlier negotiations with the IRA over the creation of the Irish Free State in 1921 had made him a marked man by the right wing. The Conservative delegation was therefore led by the ambitious MP for Chelsea, Sir Samuel Hoare, who had by then already emerged as the Tory leadership's spokesman on Indian affairs. By the time the conference broken up, many of the Indian delegates seemed to be broadly supportive of creating a federal structure. Significantly, this now had Hoare's backing.

Hoare's reasons for supporting federation had little in common with the liberal sentiments of the Labour Government or the aspirations of the Indian representatives. Since Congress support was strongest in British India, increasing responsible government in that part of the country seemed the quickest route to debasing British authority over the whole subcontinent. In contrast, India's princely states were by nature more reactionary. Their inclusion in a greater political structure convened through a federal assembly could, therefore, dilute the influence of the elected central legislature, which was otherwise likely to be an easy platform of protest for the National Congress Party. As Hoare told his

Conservative front-bench colleagues on 12 December 1930, the replacement of the British India Legislature by an all-India federal assembly
would strengthen control over the subcontinent by rescuing 'British India
from the morass into which the doctrinaire liberalism of Montagu had
plunged it'. It would also leave in British hands all the essential machinery
of control including the viceregal powers over the army, law and order,
currency exchange controls and trade agreements.

Hoare was hard-working, able and rather too evidently had high
personal aspirations. His stiff public manner and hard, determined face
was balanced by a less than scrupulous approach to office and personal
gain. He did not make a favourable impression amongst press lobby
correspondents to whom he offered to leak information in return for
being personally lauded in newsprint.[7] In August 1931 he became
Secretary of State for India in the emergency National Government and
stayed in the post after the general election in October. He was
responsible for calling a second Round Table Conference and on this
occasion, in contrast to the events of its predecessor, Gandhi and
Congress delegates participated in the discussions. This helped to
underline the fundamental differences between Congress demands and
those of other Indian groups. Congress wanted to assume absolute power.
This was disturbing to the other Indian representatives, especially the
Muslims and the Indian princes who were not attracted to the prospect of
subservience to a polity likely to be dominated by Congress activists. It
was this very inability amongst the Indian politicians to agree on what
they wanted that presented Hoare with his opportunity to drive through
legislation of his own making, even when the Government of India had
grave doubts about its prospects for success. Hoare wanted to proceed
with greater Indian provincial autonomy along the lines proposed by
Simon's Statutory Commission whilst binding the princely states to an all-
India federation. There was no need for immediacy on this latter point as
long as the princes continued to give the impression that they were
working towards the federalist goal. For so long as this state of affairs
was maintained, Congress demands for increased responsibility in central
government could be held back. Hoare was determined to prevent any
retreat from this scheme and advised Irwin's successor as Viceroy, Lord
Willingdon, that there was no chance of the British Conservative Party
endorsing legislation which increased responsibility at the centre in British
India unless it was part of an all-India federation.[8] Not all of Hoare's
Cabinet colleagues were quite so enthusiastic: Simon and Hailsham were
sceptical. Neville Chamberlain had little more sympathy for Gandhi than
had Churchill. At the time of the Mahatma's negotiations with Irwin,
Churchill had memorably described his horror at this 'Middle Temple

lawyer, now posing as a fakir of a type well known in the East, striding half-naked up the steps of the Viceregal Palace, while he is still organising and conducting a defiant campaign of civil disobedience, to parlay on equal terms with the representative of the King-Emperor'.[9] Chamberlain's description of him was not much better. He told his sister that Gandhi was 'a revolting looking creature, without any redeeming feature in his face that I could see. Not that it was wicked or ugly looking – there was just no charm whatsoever.' The Chancellor further satisfactorily concluded on the basis of the Round Table talks:

> It looks to me as if presently we should have one or more provinces asking for autonomy without waiting for the centre, and in that case we shall try and give it to them . . . let them make their experiments in self-government so that they and we may see what they make of it. If they are successful, well and good. That will give us confidence in going further. If on the other hand (as I think more likely) they fall down directly [and] a really nasty situation arises, then there will still be strong central Government to step in and clear up the mess.[10]

Although he appeared not to acknowledge the fact, Chamberlain's instincts on India were not diametrically different from those of Churchill. The latter was also prepared to countenance greater provincial autonomy whilst keeping resolute the British grip at the centre. The difference was that – unlike Chamberlain who was preoccupied with matters at the Treasury and in domestic legislation – Churchill thought that Britain's grip on India's central government would be undermined by the rest of Hoare's legislative proposals. Furthermore, he was prepared to make a fuss about it.

Meanwhile in India, the Viceroy, Lord Willingdon, confronted the return to civil disobedience with tough action of his own. Gandhi and the other Congress leaders were imprisoned for their support of law-breaking and 48,000 Indians were to find themselves behind bars by May 1932.[11] Hoare then proceeded to work on his own plans – they differed little from the line adopted by the Conservative front bench before the formation of the National Government. Congress was the most dangerous political force to oppose the British Raj and so reform should seek to minimize the importance of the institutions in which Congress performed most strongly. Britain's interests were to hold on to military and strategic control of the subcontinent, to safeguard commercial interests in India and to ensure that powers were not devolved that would allow her to renege on her sterling remittances. On all these strategic points, control would remain in British hands.[12] Indeed, with these 'reserved powers' for the Viceroy's Council, and agriculture, health and education policies largely devolved to provincial government, the dangers of furthering

Indianization of central government were dismissed by the fact that there was not much left for central government to do. Other competencies kept out of the hands of Indian politicians would include those guaranteed to the minorities, those which were the responsibility of (largely British) bureaucrats in the Indian Civil Service and viceregal appointments dealing with the remaining 'reserved' areas.

All-India federation would take place once the princely states comprising half of their combined total population had agreed to enter it. The federal legislature would have two chambers. Direct elections from the 30 million voters in the provinces would determine the lower chamber. Representatives for the upper chamber in British India would for the most part be decided through indirect elections. The princes would have around forty per cent of the seats in the upper chamber and around thirty per cent in the lower chamber. The Muslims would have around a third in each of the chambers. Thus only a third of the seats in federal central government would be for elected Indian representatives from British India. This meant that, as Hoare told the Cabinet, 'short of a landslide to the left in both British India and the States it would seem almost impossible for Congress to get a majority in the legislature.' With the Viceroy given new powers to produce his own legislation, the Westminster principle of scrutiny and responsibility seemed to be ignored by the fact that the federal government could not be removed by a vote of either the lower or upper chambers of the federal assembly. The principle was not too difficult to discern: divide and rule.

The Cabinet approved Hoare's scheme, publishing it on 17 March 1933 as a White Paper, *Proposals for Indian Constitutional Reform*. Only Hailsham expressed concern about what might happen if the princes ultimately refused to join the federation and noted that the transferral of control over police forces to the provinces levered law and order enforcement out of British hands. On this basis, he now confessed that 'from the first he had misgivings' about the government's India policy. It was rather late in the day to be coming out with these sort of doubts and Hailsham did not press the matter. The man who had suggested the 'agreement to differ' principle to keep the Samuelites in the Cabinet despite their differences with it over tariff reform policy was content in his own case to impose an agreement to keep quiet in public on the potential perils of Indian reform. It was Baldwin's sentiment that perhaps best captured the hope of the moment: that the proposals stood a chance of keeping India for the empire, whereas without them the subcontinent would be lost.[13]

The framework established showed Hoare's political and strategic skills at their best. With the supportive patronage of Lord Beaverbrook, his position was now played up in the *Sunday Express*:

> The outstanding Minister in public esteem, the man who has gained more than any other is Sir Samuel Hoare ...
>
> Sir Samuel is a prospective Prime Minister. He is talked about as a likely man for the leadership of the Conservative Party in the course of time.
>
> I am convinced that he will go up not down, provided only that he maintains the control by Great Britain of the Army in India and of the finances of the Indian Government.[14]

But if the successful passage of Indian reform really could make Hoare the next, or future, Prime Minister, would the doom-mongering Churchill succeed if Hoare's work ended in disorder and failure? By the time the India White Paper was launched, it had already become clear that Churchill would fight it every step of the way.

III

The dilemma facing Tory diehards over Indian reform was similar to that experienced by Samuel and his Liberals on the issue of protectionism. One option was to work with the Cabinet proposals, seeking to scale down and moderate them but essentially accepting that their basic principles could not be overturned. Alternatively, the diehards could regard such collaboration as futile and fight a guerrilla war in the hope that the Cabinet would concede that pursuing the reforms was not worth the price of dividing their backbenchers. The Samuelites' strategic weakness was the fact that the overwhelming majority of the Conservative Party did not support their cause. In contrast, the Tory diehards knew they could command considerable sympathy from across the ranks of their party. The government could survive one of its Liberal coalition partners going into opposition, but it could not survive the implosion of the Conservative Party. Appeased or confronted, Tory diehards were a significant and fundamental force within the Conservative body politic and, if antagonized, they were not afraid to prove the point.

The diehards' ability to mount a sustained attack on their own government was dependent upon the resources they could field. Here the government had a clear inbuilt advantage against its rebels. Diehard support had seemingly remained steady in the parliamentary Conservative Party before and after the 1931 general election at around fifty MPs. However, as a proportion of the whole party this had slipped from a ratio of 50:261 to 50:473. If the other National allies were to be included, then the ratio was even more lopsided at 50:554. Furthermore, there were no

MPs sitting on the opposition benches with diehard sentiments, the main charge against the government that came from Labour members being that the proposed reforms did not go far enough in addressing Indian aspirations. The government could use this fact to call the diehards' bluff by arguing that weakening the government meant enhancing the prospects of Labour returning to power – and pursuing an even stronger policy of Indian appeasment. The chances of the diehards' defeating government legislation on India outright therefore appeared remote and the case for trying to moderate the legislation through conciliation correspondingly stronger. On the other hand, even if the diehard opposition could be overcome in the division lobby, their potential for creating nuisance knew no bounds. If they were intent on conducting their parliamentary tactics with the resolute house-to-house defence of street-fighting partisans, then they could delay legislation, derail the government's timetable and distract it from its main tasks. Faced with this prospect, the government might think again about bothering with constitutional reform in the Raj, and this realization was what the diehards had to count upon their campaign bringing about.

Hoare was aware of the pitfalls that lay in his way. His strategy was to bring the diehards into the discussion process but to ensure that they could not determine its findings. The marginalization of Samuel and Snowden on the Trade Committee charged with investigating the case for tariffs had already been a recent pointer to the success of this strategy. A Joint Select Committee of both Houses of Parliament was therefore proposed, charged with the task of analysing the White Paper on Indian constitutional reform. Only after it had reported its recommendations would legislation be set before Parliament. Spokesmen for the diehard point of view would be invited to participate in the committee but it would have an inbuilt majority in favour of reform.

Hoare felt that the adoption of a Joint Select Committee on Indian reform undermined 'Winston's most damaging line of attack, namely that Parliament was going to be edged out of the final settlement'[15] as had been the case with the 1919 Government of India Act. On top of this, Hoare thought that it presented the government with 'a great gain when we have got the whole question safely into the hands of the Joint Select Committee' since it was a way of circumventing 'the extreme right [from] mobilising an extensive attack' in Parliament.[16] The government hoped that debate could be silenced by the assertion that public discussion would be premature until the Joint Select Committee had issued its report. If the report then proceeded to recommend the proposals of the White Paper (always likely given that its composition was going to be controlled by its supporters) then its enactment would proceed, having muzzled many a divisive diehard speech in the meantime.

A Joint Select Committee also gave Hoare some breathing space. This was a commodity that he needed since it would be a matter of time and diplomatic attrition to win even lukewarm acquiescence of the Indian princes to the cause of all-India federation. If, after this gruelling process, the princes' support for federation could be confirmed, it might make the resulting Bill's passage at Westminster much easier because of its reassurance to hesitant Tories that the Indian nationalists' power in a new constitution would be greatly diluted by the presence of the princely states. As Hoare told the Viceroy, Lord Willingdon, 'the attitude of most Conservatives is one of suspended animation. They are waiting to see whether the White Paper really does make the safeguards as effective as possible, and also whether the Federation looks really like taking shape.'[17]

There were dangers for the government in a protracted procedure, however. The very scale of the White Paper could defeat its implementation. Hoare feared that the end of the session might arrive before the completion of the Joint Select Committee report. The committee would then lapse and a new session would have to reconstitute a fresh committee from scratch, if, indeed, it was prepared to do so at all. 'In any case', he gloomily concluded, 'the effect would be to delay everything for at least another year and I do not then believe that we should get any Bill through this Parliament at all.'[18] Even if the committee did produce a coherent report, Hoare was well aware of the difficulty of 'getting a Bill of about two hundred clauses through Parliament with half the Conservatives in the House of Commons doubtful or hostile, and the House of Lords suspicious of almost every detail'. Whilst hoping that Churchill was 'overbidding his market', Hoare could well see how Churchill could believe that by the autumn 'he will have captured most of the Conservative organisation'.[19]

At first the diehards appeared to play by the rules set out by the government. Churchill wrote to Lord Lloyd that whilst it was 'quite probable' that in the end the diehards would lose the fight, the protracted parliamentary process ensured that there was no danger of them 'being rushed'.[20] He regarded as advantageous the presence of peers on the Joint Select Committee and expressed the hope, which he believed was shared by Hailsham, that Lord Salisbury would chair the committee. When in February 1933 the government did confidentially approach Salisbury to chair the committee, he refused.[21] Nevertheless, both Churchill and the executive of the pressure group, the Indian Empire Society, still persisted in looking for ways in which the diehards could cooperate within the government's procedures in order to limit the radicalism of the legislation.

The diehard policy was laid out in a Commons motion of 22 February 1933 by one of their more able spokesmen, the MP for Bournemouth, Brigadier General Sir Henry Page Croft. It called for binding the Joint Select Committee's competence to the strict discussion of the Simon Report's recommendations for the extension of self-government in the Indian provinces. In other words, Hoare's plans for the federation of central government were to be outside the Committee's remit and, therefore, of subsequent legislation.[22] If the government had accepted the Page Croft motion, then the diehard campaign would be curtailed to constructive criticism rather than open warfare. But to make this concession would be to undermine the whole strategy of Hoare's policy of appeasing Indian aspirations whilst creating a structure which kept India bound under the British Paramount Power.

Reporting on the progress of Page Croft's motion in Parliament, *The Times* noted that although Churchill 'did not himself take part (except by occasional interjections)' in the debate, some of the diehard speeches in favour of Page Croft's motion might have been regarded 'consciously or unconsciously the product of his galvanic inspiration'. The motion 'was quite frankly intended, as everyone realised, to be a preliminary trial of strength between the Government and the extreme right wing'. The newspaper further moralized that the revival of interest in India amongst MPs would be beneficial so long as they were progressive in their views on the issue and did not 'set their faces firmly against the appalling levity which would treat it as an opportunity for personal or party scores'.[23] This was the line that Geoffrey Dawson was to take throughout *The Times*'s coverage of the Indian issue.

If the Commons debate was a trial of strength, then the diehards came out of it well. Although they mustered only 42 MPs in the lobby, 245 Tories had defied a three-line whip by abstaining or absenting themselves. Indeed, it was despite, or rather because of, the fact that Page Croft's motion had come top of the private members' ballot on a matter which vitally affected the parliamentary programme that the government was panicked into putting the Whips out on all Tory and National MPs. This was an unusual response to a private members' motion. If the diehards could entice the sceptics and abstainers into outright opposition to the policy, then any resulting Bill, and perhaps the future composition of the government itself, would be open to question – although this prospect risked scaring the waverers into backing the India policy. Nonetheless, the government, having done some quick calculations of their own as to backbench support, knew that the party was too finely poised for comfort. Drawn up by Rab Butler, the 'black list' was bigger than the 'white list'.[24]

Hoare observed that 'the Winston crowd', as he revealingly termed the diehards, had 'been very active with meetings, lunches, and propaganda of every kind'.[25] The dying Lord Sydenham, who had been largely responsible for the Indian Empire Society's own statement of policy,[26] had written to Churchill encouraging him that he 'alone [could] now stop this surrender of India'. In replying that he would take up the cudgel, Churchill inferred that the prospects for success were not good given the likely antics of the Whips' Office.[27] Control of the party caucus was, therefore, the best way to challenge the whips' grip on the parliamentary party. Sir Louis Stuart, the *Indian Empire Review*'s editor, noted that two years ago Churchill had been 'standing almost alone [even if] he was not quite alone' on India. By comparison the 'march of events' was now much more favourable and signs were now emerging of disquiet towards the government position from the constituency associations.[28]

In seeking to win over the activists of the Tory caucus, the diehards targeted the constituency and area representatives on the Conservative Central Council. The Council's next meeting was to be at the end of February, the final hurdle that the government had to jump before presenting the India White Paper to Parliament. During the summer of 1932, Churchill had already begun to plan the mobilization of the party caucus as the springboard for an autumn campaign on India with assistance from Lord Rothermere.[29] Addressing the Anti-Communist and Anti-Socialist Union, Churchill maintained that the grip of the Whips' Office over the parliamentary party could be sidestepped on the grounds that 'one deep-throated growl from the National Union of Conservative Associations would be enough to stop the rot.'[30] In fact, the party was not bound to listen to its caucus, but if it received a firm public slap in the face from such meetings, then it would both be embarrassing and would cause considerable unease amongst MPs. Since the diehards were unable to offer preferment for office, a vigorous campaign in the constituencies was their way of pressurizing backbench MPs to join their side, presenting sitting Conservative MPs with the worry of a rebellion from their own constituency associations.

When the Conservative Central Council met on 28 February, *The Times* reported that 'there was a general belief that it would adopt' Churchill's resolution criticizing the creation of a democratic all-India government. Both Churchill and Hoare were greeted with 'loud cheers' (although *The Times* then went some way towards contradicting its own evidence, five pages further on in the same edition, by also admitting that Hoare began his speech to 'a very critical audience'). Hoare's Achilles heel was exposed by Churchill's use of the argument that the Indian proposals were being forced upon the reluctant princes against their will and that, as

The Times summarized, 'in his opinion, the present policy of the National Government was nothing but a Socialist policy'.[31] Even Hoare had to admit afterwards that Churchill had 'made one of his very effective speeches'.[32] The claim that the policy was a socialist one, to be repeated throughout the diehards' campaign, was bound to appeal to the more partisan party workers, particularly those in southern England where the dependence on 'national' votes had been less essential to the re-election of Conservatives. As a result, the government's victory of 189 to 165 was embarrassingly narrow. Hoare confessed in a state of near panic to the Viceroy that the Council, attended by the 'leading Conservatives in the constituencies who take a part in electioneering and the local organisa-tions', was full of Churchill's 'partisans'. Unless the White Paper was issued soon and in detail he feared that 'there is the making of a first class crisis here and a breakaway of three-quarters of the Conservative Party'.[33] It was, therefore, possible in February 1933 that Churchill was backing a winning horse after all. The caucus politics of the party's Central Council which Lord Randolph Churchill had tried to stir in the 1880s appeared at last to have come of age and come, potentially, to the salvation of his son.

Following on from their parliamentary performance, the vote of the Central Council was, in the *Indian Empire Review*'s words, 'a remarkable portent'[34] for the diehards. It enabled Churchill to write to the Chief Whip, Captain David Margesson, asserting that since the diehards represented 'three-quarters of the Conservative Party in the constituen-cies' (of which they could 'prove half'), they should have eight places on the Joint Select Committee to the twelve from those who supported the Round Table policies. Churchill was flexing his muscles prior to playing a full part in the committee.[35] Preparing for this, the diehards formed a new organization, the India Defence Committee (IDC)[36] charged with coordi-nating collective action. Sir Alfred Knox became its Chairman and a new young right-wing recruit from the 1931 landslide, Patrick Donner, its Secretary. Also invited were all those Tories who had voted against the government in the previous India divisions.[37] Initially, fifty Conservative MPs became members. Churchill also began to plan the creation of a group of '8 A1 peers' to marshal diehard cohesion in the House of Lords.[38]

The government's India White Paper was released on 17 March and Hoare opened its debate in the Commons ten days later. Given his need to win over sceptical Tory opinion, much of Hoare's speech concentrated on defending the White Paper not for its advances but for its constitutional safeguards and he tackled some of the diehards' oldest topics and newest recruits head on. In contrast to the 1921 Irish Treaty which had failed, 'even [with] the signature of my right hon. friend the Member for Epping' (i.e. Churchill), because it had not provided the safeguards necessary to keep the Irish loyal to the imperial crown, the Indian White Paper ensured that the British Government would still appoint the Viceroy, the provincial Governors and other high officials. The security services, the executive affairs of the federal and provincial governments and 'the ultimate power', the army, would still be under British control. 'Those', emphasized Hoare, were 'no paper safeguards'.[39]

For the diehards, it was Viscount Wolmer, Lord Salisbury's nephew and a member of the Commons, who most directly countered Hoare's arguments. Parliamentary democracy tempered by safeguards had never worked anywhere because the two principles were fundamentally incompatible. Indians were being encouraged to believe they were being given 'responsible self-government . . . leading them on to Dominion status'. As soon as they attempted to exercise the rights normally associated with this status it would be 'filched away from them' by the British Governor whose 'responsibilities and rights [would] inevitably bring him into conflict with his Parliament'. If Hoare's safeguards had existed in the Irish Treaty, then they would merely have involved increasing the use of the British Army, a response to – but not a solution for – the Irish question.[40] Throughout the long campaign over India, neither side could escape the haunting memory of Ireland and her painful progression towards home rule. For the government, it allowed the opportunity for another gratuitous mention of Churchill's own involvement in handing over the empire to gunmen.[41] For the diehards it seemed to support their argument that the concession of significant powers to the natives only undermined the validity of retaining other restraints on their sovereignty.[42] The ensuing bitterness of the debate was, as the historian John Charmley has pointed out, because 'it was a civil war between two conceptions of what Conservatism was about; . . . those who argued that accommodation with change was necessary to preserve what could be preserved, and those who knew that tactical concessions always led to strategic ones'.[43]

For all Wolmer's efforts, it was Churchill's oration which was most anticipated, as pro-government speeches made clear. On the floor of the Commons at least, he was the undisputed front man for the diehards. In Samuel's backhanded compliment, despite the poor judgement which Churchill had shown over the past fifteen years in military, financial and political matters which had been '[un]helpful to the nation', at least he 'prevents our debates from being dull'.[44] This was perhaps his problem: as the *Indian Empire Review* suggested 'when he rose there was a stir. He was expected to be funny.'[45] The diehard MP Colonel John Gretton was possibly correct in his compliment to Churchill that his and Baldwin's speeches were the only ones that the House 'cared to hear'.[46] According to

Hoare (whose analysis of Churchill's views on India always included the calculation that his real target was the Cabinet men themselves)[47] the second day's debate on India had encouraged Churchill to go 'about the House saying that he had not only smashed the scheme but that he had smashed the Government as well'.[48] *The Times* was certainly of the view that the diehards were getting the better of the debate until Churchill stood up to speak.[49] His 'much advertised' speech on the third day was, Hoare pleasantly reflected, 'one of the greatest failures of his life'[50] due to his wholly unproven assertion, and his failure to withdraw it when challenged, that promotion in the Indian Civil Service was being linked with support for 'modern' pro-government views.[51] *The Times* agreed with Hoare, gleefully reporting that the House subsequently 'appeared to combine pity for Mr Churchill with apathy towards his argument'.[52] Austen Chamberlain, writing to his sister, could 'recall no parallel' to Churchill's oratorical flop and thought that 'he ha[d] become hysterical' and that 'it is impossible to discuss [India] with him even privately'.[53] Churchill's hysteria over India probably suggested that he was, or at least had become, absolutely genuine in his opposition on the issue. Yet whilst diehards defended his motives, one Tory backbencher peddled the line that Churchill's opposition to government policy on unemployment, foreign affairs, India and doubtless other issues in the future were all symptomatic of his ambition and lack of sincerity.[54] These were familiar charges.

One of the worst aspects of the debate for the diehards was that it offered them little gain. Without any public objection to the principle of a Joint Select Committee,[55] the diehards had decided not to place an amendment to the government motion. This left only the Labour Party to provide the opposition in the division lobby. The government had, therefore, won the first round in the Commons. The Joint Select Committee would consider the proposals of the White Paper rather than merely the Simon Report and Churchill had been made to look foolish into the bargain. Hoare hoped not only that Churchill's humiliation in the debate would give the government an advantage in winning back wavering backbench support but that 'the papers that are backing him so strongly will begin to wonder whether he is the divine leader that they had assumed'. Writing to his allies, however, Churchill was determined that the campaign would be fought to the bitter end, with or without the prospect of ultimate victory.[56] The debate was, however, clearly a setback and Churchill was thus in a correspondingly less commanding position when the following day Hoare wrote to him to encourage his acceptance of the offer to sit on the Joint Select Committee.[57]

The government proposed to give sceptics of the White Paper nine seats on the committee. This would be clearly outweighed by the twenty-five supporters of the Paper. Churchill appears initially to have been undecided what to do.[58] H.A. Gwynne, the veteran editor of the sympathetic *Morning Post*, lobbied Churchill to accept the offer if Lord Salisbury could not be dissuaded from accepting a seat since there was no point in refusing to join the committee unless all diehards likewise undermined its authenticity by boycotting it. If any diehards sat on the committee, then their claim that it was 'packed' with government supporters would be weakened and their cohesion as a united opposition undermined.[59]

At the last moment, Churchill, in telling Hoare that he wanted 'neither part nor lot in the deed you seek to do', firmly decided not to sit on the committee.[60] This came as an annoyance to some of those diehards who accepted membership[61] and as a surprise to Hoare who had expected his cooperation. Indeed Hoare only prevented all the diehards from boycotting the committee by manoeuvring Salisbury into staying, and by agreeing that two fresh diehards take the places of Churchill, and of Page Croft and Lord Lloyd, who had also followed his decision to withdraw.[62] Hoare suspected that Churchill's decision not to stand had been encouraged by the demon bogey of the National Government, Lloyd George.[63] More likely, Churchill had made a simple calculation that since on the terms offered there was nothing that could be gained by cooperation, there was more sense in mounting a public campaign against the proposals.

Churchill's decision not to sit on the committee has been largely regarded as a political blunder.[64] It made him the target of considerable criticism and allowed him to be portrayed as unduly factional in his approach. On the other hand, it is surely surprising that Churchill contemplated sitting on the committee at all. Membership of the Joint Select Committee was intended to prevent partisan expression on the Indian issue whilst the committee was deliberating. Yet Churchill's verbal command of this form of protest was his strongest card. Salisbury's decision to accept the responsibilities of a seat on the committee ensured that he never put his name to, or publicly recommended, the diehards' campaign before the committee's report was published. Page Croft made it clear that he had been advised that he could not honourably speak up for the diehards and sit on the committee simultaneously.[65] In contrast, Hoare could safely sit on the committee without any diminution of his authority as Secretary of State for India. For Churchill to have done so would have virtually bound and gagged him on the Indian issue whilst the committee was sitting. In the meantime, the diehards would have been deprived of their only really first-rate platform performer.

On 10 April the membership of the Joint Select Committee was presented to Parliament. Only five of its thirty-two-strong composition supported the diehard position whilst six were government ministers, a proportion which even senior party figures like Austen Chamberlain thought totally unwise.[66] When a Commons motion was laid down requesting the removal of the ministers from the committee, it attracted the support not only of the hard-core diehards but of 118 votes in the division to 209 for the government. This was another huge vote by backbenchers against their own government and it made clear that Tories of all hues were not calmly going to take being hoodwinked by a biased committee. Churchill naturally made the most of this success, suggesting that had the Whip not been applied, a majority of Conservatives might actually have voted against their own government. Instead, the Cabinet had composed the Joint Select Committee 'not looking for advice but for advertisement'.[67]

Hoare suspected that Churchill, watching events in Germany where Hitler had recently become Chancellor, thought that England was 'going Fascist' and saw himself as a potential British Mussolini (ironically, it was later to be Hoare who was to be found compromising with Fascist powers). Churchill's motive, as interpreted by Hoare, was that since he had 'convinced himself that he will smash the Government sooner or later [therefore] if he joins the Committee he will be muzzled at any rate for a time'.[68] The decision not to cooperate in the Joint Select Committee was therefore the point of no return, opening up fresh opportunities for Churchill and his fellow diehards to associate themselves vigorously with the campaign in the constituencies. In choosing confrontation over cooperation, they were virtually declaring a Tory civil war.

Six

'THE WINSTONIANS'

I

By 1933 the National Government had survived the natural maladies of infancy. Reneging on its promise to be a short-term combination concerned only with saving the currency and balancing the budget, it had won a resounding general election victory. The economies had been made. The currency had been saved – albeit by action opposite to that which the Cabinet had originally proposed to defend it. The government had overturned nearly ninety years of free trade orthodoxy by introducing protectionism. Samuel's Liberals had split off into opposition, unloved and unlamented. These events, combined with the failure to reach international agreement at the world disarmament talks in Geneva, encouraged the Opposition's allegations that the National Government had become, in effect, a Conservative administration to which the likes of Ramsay MacDonald and Sir John Simon clung because it was their only means of continuing to hold Cabinet office. Conservatives like Neville Chamberlain were content to maintain this 'National' coalition precisely because it required them to make so few concessions whilst affording the benefit of a broader and more popular face to the electorate. Economic and international circumstances – rather than the political make-up – was all that prevented the government's realization of Tory aspirations in full.

Next door to the Prime Minister in Downing Street, Baldwin in his office as Lord President of the Council remained aloof from much of this interpretation of Conservative Realpolitik. He knew what it meant to be at the beck and call of a blood-baying Tory Party and was now at far greater ease in the more diffuse structure of a national coalition. When in October 1932 delegates at the Party Conference in Blackpool voted in favour of maintaining the National Government but were against changing the Conservative Party's name, Baldwin encouraged them 'to carry our share in the letter and spirit of the National Government; our aims must be national and not party; our ideals must be national and not party'.[1] He was aware that some of the non-Tory ministers, and MacDonald in particular, were resentful at being held hostage, even if voluntarily, and he was keen to make sure that they continued to play their part. To Baldwin, support for Indian constitutional reform was a token of faith in his coalition partners and a recognition that their more liberal input had a place at the centre of government policy. This was scarcely a major concession on Baldwin's part since he shared their views on such questions anyway. In any case, the Indian reform proposals were being piloted by Hoare, a Conservative, and were merely the extension of proposals he had formulated for his party's adoption during the 1929–31 period in opposition. At that time, the rumpus caused over Irwin's declaration and subsequent parley with Gandhi worried Baldwin that he would experience considerable difficulty getting the Tory Party as a whole to accept Hoare's policy in normal political circumstances. In contrast, ongoing membership of a National Government gave Baldwin his opportunity to get Indian reform accepted by his party as a token of their commitment to the electorally beneficent coalition to which they were bound. He sought, therefore, to use the post-1931 situation not so much to further Tory Party advantage in the crude sense but rather to use the rhetoric of coalition to pressurize his *own* party to adopt his *own* particular brand of centre-liberal conservatism. This was an important cause for Baldwin, so much so that he chose to put the whole future of the national project on the line in defence of his position on India.

In asserting in a public speech at Worcester on 29 April 1933 that the fate of the legislative proposals for India and the future of the National Government were inseparable, Baldwin was playing a dangerous game. From the editor's office at *The Times*, Geoffrey Dawson wrote to Baldwin to assure him that he was 'at [his] service' to fight against the 'Winstonians' who were 'all "traitors" to their party'.[2] Dawson reinforced this high-risk strategy a little over a month later in a *Times* leader article entitled 'The Conservative Choice'. There, Baldwin's Vicar on Fleet Street interpreted the party scriptures to the Tory laity. Either the India White Paper was approved or Baldwin and the Indian Viceroy, Lord Willingdon, might resign. This would end the National Government at home and any chance for a consensual settlement in the subcontinent.[3] Enemies of Indian federation were to be regarded as outright opponents of the government itself.

Preoccupied with matters at the Treasury, Neville Chamberlain had no more time for the antics of Churchill and the diehards than he had for the Indians themselves, inhabitants of a faraway country of whom he knew nothing. Usually eager to muscle into the affairs of other government departments, he had little to offer when it came to the remit of the India Office. This attitude may have been shaped by the fact that he had always got on well with Hoare and trusted his judgement. Chamberlain and

Hoare shared a sober-minded and unsentimental approach to policy which naturally led them to repudiate as heady distractions the instinctive romantic and idealistic posturing of diehards and Congress activists alike. Yet if the reform package should be brought down by a successful parliamentary revolt and Baldwin, MacDonald and Hoare found themselves forced to step aside as a result, Chamberlain remained the obvious Tory to assume the leadership. He was sufficiently divorced from the proposals not to be held culpable for them and was in the ideal position of being the hostage of no one wing of the party. This was an advantageous position in which to be and much less risky than turning against his own colleagues in order to rub shoulders with those whose attitude he did not instinctively share. Baldwin's fate was tied to that of the government's India policy. Conservative MPs might well pay homage to the anointed successor of an assassinated leader but that successor was rarely the usurper who had wielded the knife in the first place.

Churchill was equally aware of the realities of power. He wanted to be back in office and believed India offered him an opportunity in this respect, but even he was not vain enough to think he would gain the Premiership in only one jump from the backbenches. Instead, he envisaged his return to Cabinet rank to come when the government, having been damaged by the Indian confrontation, sought to broaden its base by including the other survivors from the Lloyd George coalition and representatives of the Tory right with whom he currently shared the backbenches.

In an important letter, inexplicably ignored by historians, Sir Austen Chamberlain reported to his sister a weekend that he had spent with Churchill at Chartwell, the latter's country home in Kent:

> He anticipates that he and his Indian Die-Hards will continue to hold about 1/3rd of the Party, that the India Bill will be carried but that the fight will leave such bitter memories that the Govt. will have to be reconstructed. Only Ramsay, S.B., Sam Hoare, Irwin and perhaps the Lord Chancellor are so committed that they would have to go. Simon could stay and it would still be a National Government, but who is to lead it? Obviously I am the man! And so he led me up into a high place and showed me the kingdoms of the world. I was not greatly tempted.[4]

Ever since his first speech to the Commons after the emergency formation of the National Government, Churchill had hoped that a 'real' broad-based administration would be formed bringing back with it all his old friends with whom he had served in the Cabinet during the dark days of the war and the years of reconstruction thereafter. At the top of his list were Lloyd George, Sir Austen Chamberlain and Sir Robert Horne

(Churchill's greatest brother in arms, Lord Birkenhead, having burned out and died in 1930). The charge, so frequently employed by his opponents, that he was merely using the issue of India to destroy the National Government thus held some water, although his target was more who should run its executive, not that it should be dissolved and replaced entirely. What was not true was that his opposition to Indian reform was based purely on this personal agenda alone and that it was, thereby, devoid of principle. As Paul Addison has observed, 'historians who believe that Churchill's Indian campaign was purely a tactical struggle against Baldwin need to explain why throughout the Second World War Churchill conducted a tooth-and-nail struggle in private against all attempts to introduce representative central government in India.'[5] Churchill cared passionately about the future of the British Raj in India and had come to the conclusion that none of the existing members of the Cabinet had the will to defend it. His own political comeback and the preservation of the centrepiece of empire thus became inextricably linked in his own mind, regardless of what this meant for the future tranquillity of the National Government.

II

The tone of Baldwin's denunciation of Churchill and the diehards at Worcester made clear that the government was not going to pull any punches once hostilities had been declared. He specifically accused the diehards of attempting to 'destroy national unity' by 'going about the country'.[6] This was a reference to the fact that the diehards were building up support in the constituency associations and the first challenges to sitting members were being made.[7] Hoare had already warned the Viceroy that the Conservative Party could expect 'embarrassing resolutions out of a good many constituencies'.[8] He expressed the fear to Sir John Anderson that if the government was seen to fail more generally as it approached its mid-term, then 'Winston and his army would gain a great deal of support and might even force a political crisis'.[9] By the summer of 1933, fifty-eight constituency branches had passed motions critical of the White Paper policy.[10] By early May, Churchill was boasting that the India Defence Committee had already attracted the support of nearly seventy MPs.[11]

Churchill had made no direct public denunciation of Baldwin over the previous two years (allegedly because of his 'personal regard' for his leader).[12] This restraint came abruptly to a close when in his Worcester speech Baldwin warned that Churchill's attempts to 'split the Conservative Party' could help bring about 'some form of Bolshevism or fascism' in Britain.[13] This was a grave charge to make against the man to whose judgement Baldwin had once entrusted the Treasury. Churchill immediately fired off a lengthy press statement which highlighted the extent of the breach between the party leadership and the India Defence Committee. The battalions of the past were marshalled to spearhead his attack: Gladstone's campaign for home rule had riven the Liberal Party, not Hartington and Joseph Chamberlain's defence of the Anglo-Irish Union; the Conservative Party had been broken by Peel's free trade conversion and not Bentinck and Disraeli's defence of the status quo. On this basis, it was not those who were defending traditional Tory imperialist values who were to blame. Rather the fault lay with Baldwin's attempt to force 'upon his party a policy on which it has never been consulted and which runs directly counter to its deepest instincts and traditions . . . Those who drive the wedge into the oak are accountable, and not the oak which splits in accordance with its natural grain.'[14]

To sustain the fight, Churchill had to be able to rely on as many buttresses of support as possible. His relations with the press underlined the difficulty he faced in keeping a solid constituency of encouragement throughout the period. The *Morning Post* was resolutely pro-diehard but its readership was famously going down with each fresh announcement in its obituaries column. Cultivating his stooge Hoare as the future party leader, Beaverbrook's *Daily Express* gave the diehards at best lukewarm support.[15] It was the Rothermere press which promoted the diehard viewpoint through the mass media.[16] Churchill wrote eleven articles for the *Daily Mail* in 1934 and thirteen in 1935, although he found no time to write any in the five months between October 1934 and late March 1935. His son Randolph wrote for another Rothermere publication, the *Sunday Dispatch*. Against this were ranged the media forces of the Establishment. Although its owner, Lord Camrose, avoided any personal hostility towards Churchill, the *Daily Telegraph* backed the government with 'a particular presentation of views calculated to mitigate differences among Conservatives'. The former Party Chairman, J.C.C. Davidson, was particularly delighted that Camrose wanted the *Telegraph* to help the government with the 'education' of the party on India and suggested that Hoare should 'visit him . . . and give him in broad outline the general policy of the Government, and also consult him as to how best to deal with Winston's opposition'.[17] Even more strident in its support for Baldwin, *The Times* lost no opportunity to denigrate both Churchill and the diehards.[18] Equally partisan, the BBC used its monopoly control of broadcasting to deny Churchill access to the airwaves until after the Joint Select Committee Report had been adopted as party policy.[19] In the end, the diehards lost the fight to influence the media. Twenty-two of the twenty-six leading national and provincial morning newspapers supported the resulting legislation.[20]

The diehards failed to win the media battle generally. Nonetheless, it gave them the great opportunity to take their campaign beyond the narrow confines of Westminster where the government's majority was the most sure-footed. Churchill saw the *Morning Post* and the *Daily Mail* as advertising boards for subscriptions to the new campaign. In this even Beaverbrook, Churchill recorded, had 'been helpful too'.[21] The resulting creation, sprouting out from the parliamentary India Defence Committee, was a larger movement called the India Defence League (IDL). Whilst technically non-party, Churchill thought that party 'constituencies might be associated with the League by resolution. We ought eventually to get the best part of a hundred Conservative seats definitely pledged.'[22] Rothermere wanted to go further, suggesting that if the Tory candidate in a forthcoming by-election in Hitchin did not support the IDL line, then he would be happy to fund an India diehard candidate to run against him.[23] This was the sort of divisive strategy that appealed to the great press lord. He had clearly drawn different conclusions from his anti-Baldwin by-election stunts in 1930 and 1931 to those of everyone else. For MPs like Churchill whose career was anchored to the Conservative Party, it was important to discourage maverick action of this kind. Nevertheless, in June 1933 Conservative Central Office refused to fund the selected Conservative candidate at Hitchin precisely because of his alleged pro-diehard sentiments. Central Office even intervened at Altrincham to foist upon the constituency a pro-Indian reform candidate, Sir Edward Grigg, against the will of most of the local association.[24]

Far from being a crank operation of negligible significance, the India Defence League (IDL) was launched in June 1933 with the committed support of ten Privy Councillors, twenty-eight peers, fifty-seven MPs, two former Governors and three former Lieutenant-Governors of Indian provinces and other representatives from the armed forces and the judiciary.[25] At the end of a distinguished legal career, Viscount Sumner became its Honorary President.[26] Churchill opted to become Vice-President, a position he shared with Rudyard Kipling (Baldwin's cousin and the original author of Baldwin's quip about the press lords having 'power without responsibility') and the doughty Sir Henry Page Croft.[27] Other Vice-Presidents included the Duke of Devonshire's heir, the Marquess of Hartington, and the old hero of Irish Unionism, Lord (formally Sir Edward) Carson side by side with the Duke of Norfolk's son, Viscount FitzAlan, Catholic aristocrat and last Viceroy of Ireland.[28] Indeed, one of the most striking aspects of the diehard leadership was the political genealogy of its patrician membership. Scions of three of Britain's greatest aristocratic political families (Churchills, Cavendishes and Cecils) were involved in the cause.[29] Had it successfully courted the nouveau riche's greatest political family, the Chamberlains, it would almost certainly have succeeded.

Funding for the diehard movement was provided by the famously wealthy 'Bendor' Duke of Westminster, the eccentric right-wing heiress, Lady Houston, and by a number of the Indian princes who were concerned about being subjected to Hoare's federation. Other donations came from Rothermere, the IDL's parliamentary members, and included £4500 from the rusty coffers of the diehards' fighting fund which had been established to undermine the previous national coalition in 1922.[30] Campaign headquarters were set up at 48 Broadway in Westminster. Patrick Donner became Parliamentary Secretary, whilst a Chief Organizer and his assistant were appointed to conduct the nationwide campaign. Colonel John Gretton, Chairman of the Bass brewing empire, became the IDL Treasurer. A redoubtable and seemingly eternal diehard who had first been elected to Parliament in 1895, Gretton symbolized the Colonel Blimp image tagged in the popular imagination to the diehard cause. He was affectionately described by a previous Chief Whip as 'one of the best-hearted fellows one ever met, kind, generous, self-effacing; ugly as possible, blinking at one through gold-rimmed spectacles; inarticulate, for it is almost impossible to hear a word he says'.[31]

Despite the occasional Gretton figure, the perception of the diehards as a group of walrus-moustached stalwarts was greatly (and deliberately) overdrawn by their opponents both at the time and in the subsequent writing of history. Many had held high rank in the armed forces, although this was hardly unusual in the post-First World War Conservative Party.[32] Insofar as they differed from the Tory MPs who supported Indian reform, the diehard MPs also tended to be older, with longer parliamentary experience and predominantly safe seats.[33] However, their social backgrounds were not wildly different from those of other Tory MPs. Most were comfortably middle class.[34] The most geographically cohesive group were the eleven diehard MPs who sat for Lancashire or Cheshire constituencies, a reflection of that area's concerns over ceding to Indians greater control over the cotton textile trade. There were as many diehard MPs who did not represent southern English constituencies as did[35] – a point seldom stressed when we consider the traditional image of them, amusingly described by John Charmley in terms of the 'seaside resorts of England resound[ing] with the growls of red-faced colonels' backed by 'the conservative denizens of the genteel watering-places'.[36] The diehards may not have been liberal progressives but they were geographically and personally somewhat more evenly representative of middle-class Britain than their opponents liked to admit. In seeking to become their spokesman, Churchill was identifying himself with an essential ingredient of the Tory tradition.

III

The first prong of the diehards' attack was to use their support in the Conservative constituency associations to gain control of the organs of the party caucus to which the associations sent representatives. In this respect the National Union's Annual Conference (i.e. 'the Party Conference') and the National Union's governing body, the Central Council, were the chief targets. They were platforms upon which to launch a direct power challenge to the party leadership.[37] The second prong of the attack was to use activity in the constituencies to influence the voting intentions of their MPs. The establishment of local India Defence League branches was one way of expressing the widespread concern of right-wing politically aware constituents, but this in itself was of minimal worth unless they also influenced the control and personnel of the local Conservative Associations. These would have more leverage in persuading wavering MPs not to pursue a pro-Indian White Paper line against the will of their own constituency workers and voters. In all, sixty local branches of the India Defence League were established.[38] The constituencies which they covered were represented by one hundred and twenty-seven MPs. Yet, judged by results in Parliament, the influence of the League where it mattered was muted. For the most part, India Defence League constituency branches failed to convert sitting Conservative MPs to the diehard cause.[39]

Baldwin loftily condemned the diehards' campaign in the constituencies as if it were a subversive intrusion upon popular democracy. His government was, in fact, covertly doing exactly the same as the India Defence League. Hoare, in particular, was concerned about the 'Winston propaganda in the country', telling the Viceroy that he wanted to launch a rival organization with the assistance of the former President of the European Association in India, Edward Villiers. So keen was Hoare to enlist Villiers' help that he telegraphed to Willingdon about the desirability of 'getting him a Knighthood.'[40] R.A. ('Rab') Butler, the young and purposeful Under-Secretary at the India Office, became 'very busy' in establishing the group with the former Party Chairman and current Chancellor of the Duchy of Lancaster, J.C.C. Davidson.[41] As members of the Joint Select Committee on the Indian proposals, pledged to avoid partisan and prejudicial activity whilst it was adjudicating, Hoare, Butler and Davidson were consciously breaking their pledges and had to cover their own tracks of involvement accordingly. Nevertheless, on 17 May 1933 their organization, the Union of Britain and India (UBI), was launched, professing to be non-party but setting itself, in its own words, 'the object of furthering the Government's programme of Constitutional advance as outlined in the White Paper, while insisting on the maintenance of adequate safeguards'.[42]

The Union of Britain and India was necessary since as its Chairman, Sir John Thompson, put it, 'it is impossible for the [Conservative] Central Office to arrange for meetings in constituencies where the local Association is hostile. It is just in those constituencies that meetings are most wanted.'[43] Since the government had claimed that campaigning on the Indian issue should be suspended until the Joint Select Committee Report had been published, the UBI was a way in which they could secretly campaign whilst pretending to be officially doing no such thing. Given what were to be the government's successful attempts to muzzle the party caucus on this issue, it was more cunning than commendable. Of course, the India Defence League were already campaigning hard, but at least they had always argued against the placing of a gag on the debate in the first place. Furthermore, unlike Hoare, Derby and Davidson, the diehards who had accepted places on the Joint Select Committee fully complied with the so-called gentleman's agreement to avoid public comment whilst the committee was going through its deliberations.[44]

Devoid of famous personalities at its helm,[45] the Union of Britain and India was a pale shadow of the India Defence League in terms of support and organization. Its leaders tried to make a virtue out of this necessity; Thompson boasted that 'the Union itself is not constituted as an association in the strict sense of the word with members and periodic meetings . . . [but] of ex-Governors and ex-Members of Council who have had experience of the Montagu–Chelmsford Reform [i.e. the 1919 Government of India Act], we have twenty-seven as compared with two on the India Defence League list.'[46] The UBI listed 192 members and supporters.[47] In the spring of 1934, the IDL responded both to this and to Baldwin's charge that they had few members who had served after the introduction of the Montagu–Chelmsford reforms, by publishing a list of 300 of their own members with Indian experience, 200 of whom had been there since the reforms' establishment in 1919.

Rab Butler, whose flat was often used for the UBI's meetings, admitted from the safe distance of his memoirs that 'initially it was very difficult to find anyone willing to join it.'[48] Even before its great recruitment drive of December 1934, the India Defence League boasted 'eight or ten thousand subscribing members'[49] and had three times as many branches as were subsequently established by the UBI. Thompson himself admitted that he could not find enough 'well-wishers' to get branches started because the chairmanship 'class of provincial society' permeated 'so strong a diehard atmosphere'.[50] Instead, he felt it more profitable to hold meetings in constituencies without setting up an organization on the ground itself.[51] Eventually the need to imitate the IDL became too great and twenty UBI branches were launched in all, half of them during 1935, which was after the effective cessation of hostilities in the party caucus anyway but when it was still important to keep constituency pressure on wavering MPs.[52] No branches were ever established in the diehards' designated battlefield of Lancashire where they found it impossible to generate any support.[53] The UBI Bulletin was virtually a leaflet in comparison with the monthly fifty-odd-page Indian Empire Revue.[54]

What particularly rankled with the diehards was the belief that Conservative Party funds were being used against them at a time when the leadership was pretending to be open-minded.[55] Viscount Goschen, the UBI President, made clear in The Times, after continuing speculation,[56] that his organization had 'never at any time received any financial assistance from any party organization or from the Government'.[57] Such protestations were almost certainly economical with the truth. The UBI was little more than a front for Conservative Central Office.[58] The Health Minister, Sir Howard Kingsley Wood, was one of those involved, and although he preferred not to invest his own money he told Butler to extract as much as possible from 'the same source as helped us before', making clear that 'the anonymity of the source of supply' had to be maintained.[59] Once the campaign was wound up, Edward Villiers got his promised knighthood. None of this was very surprising or unique. Nonetheless, it showed up in a poor light the moralizingly lofty tone adopted by a government officially committed to the prevention of campaigning on the Indian issue whilst the Joint Select Committee was in deliberation. It added to the sense of recrimination with the diehards. This poisoned the manner in which the debate proceeded, to the detriment of all concerned.

IV

The lesson of Lord Randolph Churchill's political undoing suggested that diehard concentration upon winning over the party caucus did not of itself hold the government to ransom. Even if successfully persuaded, the caucus had no claim on the right to determine policy. The last major diehard campaign, in 1921 against the proposals for settling the Irish question, was little more encouraging. Beaten in the Commons division lobby against the massed ranks of the then Lloyd George coalition government by 439 votes to 43,[60] but aware of greater sympathy for their cause out in the constituencies, the diehards had taken their case to the Party Conference in Liverpool. Had Colonel John Gretton's motion been successful, with its implicit assault on Austen Chamberlain's leadership, serious embarrassment would have been caused. Chamberlain himself had realized that 'if we are beaten there it won't be the end, but it will be unpleasant' but he did not seem exactly overconfident of the fact, concluding in the same breath that he was 'fighting for my political life'.[61] His hopes had rested with the speech delivered by Archibald Salvidge, the leading wire-puller in Conservative Liverpool politics. Such was the tension on the conference floor that minor scuffles broke out between some overwrought delegates. Salvidge, however, hit precisely the right note, highlighting the leader's personal integrity and pointing out that if the Conservative Party was to be broken up on the issue, then power would be handed over to the opposition parties who would be even less likely to safeguard Ulster and loyalist interests in Ireland. The tactic bore fruit and when Gretton insisted upon taking the motion to a vote, confident in the belief that in their hearts he had the support of much of the caucus, he was humiliated by securing the support of fewer than 70 of the 1800 delegates present.[62] Thereafter, Austen Chamberlain arrived at the conference and was able to deliver his keynote appeal for unity.

If by 1933 historical precedence was not on their side, then the India diehards could content themselves that there were no hard and fast rules in history and certainly not in power-broking within the Conservative Party. Furthermore, it could now be perceived that the diehards had advantages which they had lacked in 1921. Then, they had not enjoyed the support of any senior party figure of the eminence and the skill of Winston Churchill. Indeed, over Ireland, one of their greatest advocates, Lord Birkenhead, had defected to the side of the government of which he was member. Furthermore, talks with Sinn Fein had begun in October 1921 and were concluded with the Irish Treaty in December. This had given the diehards far less time to mobilize an effective opposition than the timescale resulting from the elephantine inquiries into Indian reform now provided. The meeting of the Central Council of the National Union of Conservative Associations on 28 June 1933 was the first test of the effectiveness of their campaign amongst party activists since the launch of the IDL. Churchill and Sir Henry Page Croft from the Commons, and Lloyd and Carson from the Lords were pitched against Baldwin in the speaking order.

Baldwin had opened the debate with a familiar chestnut by warning about the dangers of paralysing British politics over India in the manner in which it had once been paralysed over Ireland. His main argument, though, was based not on the merits of the White Paper but rather on the relationship to the government of the Joint Select Committee. Baldwin claimed that because the latter was reviewing the policy with 'semi-judicial consideration' (words which, as we shall see, came to haunt him) it was not appropriate for the caucus to intervene in the issue since this might prejudice the committee's verdict. In return for the Central Council's acquiescence on this point, he promised that once the committee's report was published he would 'take counsel together' with the caucus before framing the resulting legislation.[63]

Although Lord Carson claimed otherwise,[64] if the delegates were to rebuff their leader, particularly in the light of his statements implying the indivisibility of Indian reform and the continuance of the National Government, then the whole direction and composition of the administration would have been open to question. Despite Baldwin's speech, however, Rab Butler, present at the Council, later thought that it was Neville Chamberlain's 'presence [that] decided the result of the meeting'. After all, if a Conservative of his credentials could stomach the proposals for the greater good, then what had the delegates to worry about? In comparison, Hoare's interpretation that Churchill performed badly was borne out by the repeated heckling meted out to him for his refusal to sit on the Joint Select Committee.[65] Churchill even interrupted his flow to murmur indignantly that there was being 'run propaganda to victimize' him.[66] Unimpressed, the delegates agreed to be bound by the party leadership's suggested gagging act by a vote of 838 to 356. Baldwin had gambled heavily by banking on the Tory partisans being naturally more interested in maintaining a National Government at home than in reversing constitutional proposals in far-off India. This point was to act crucially in favour of the advocates of Indian reform. The Conservative MP, Cuthbert Headlam, felt about the Central Council meeting that 'It was obvious from the first that S.B. would score again: however tired people may be of him, they are not going to depose him in order to put Winston in – and, however sick they may be of the present Govt., they are not going to run the risk of destroying the "National Govt."'[67] Many of those who voted to gag themselves may have been suspicious of the India White Paper but genuinely believed that it was best not to prejudice matters before the great and good of the party had had a chance to examine it properly. The beauty of the Joint Select Committee's deliberation in acting to gag the Tory caucus was that it gave all the momentum to the Cabinet view. From his sounding board in the editorial page of the *Indian Empire Review*, Sir Louis Stuart prophesied, writing after the Central Council had voted not to be heard until the report was published, that when the time did eventually come for them to 'take counsel':

> Mr Baldwin will make another opening address containing a brief statement of the proposals, will continue that the proposals are accepted by him, by the Cabinet, and by all the other eminent men who support him, and will state that non-acceptance of the proposals will imply a lack of confidence in himself and will emphasize that at all costs there must be no difference of opinion on the Indian question, because the Indian question is not a party question.[68]

This is exactly what Baldwin proceeded to do.

Having failed to gain control of the Central Council in June, the diehards' next target was the India debate at the Party Conference, ominously held on the Chamberlain home ground in Birmingham, on 6 October. Almost 10,000 IDL leaflets were distributed and posters were displayed not merely on hoardings but also on passing motor cars circling the venue.[69] It was almost as if a rival political party was trying to gatecrash their opposition's conference. Although in proposing the diehards' motion, Viscount Wolmer insisted that its acceptance was consistent with 'this conference record[ing] its confidence in the National Government', it was once again Neville Chamberlain who came to the rescue of the platform party by claiming that the diehards' motion represented a 'direct challenge to the Government'. The conference duly decided by 737 to 344 (with 121 abstentions) to follow the now familiar line that it was not competent to comment on party policy until after that policy had already been settled.[70]

However, the government were not to have it all their own way. Hoare attempted to get his colleagues to put every pressure on constituents attending the Conservative Womens' Conference in May 1934 to vote for the pro-government resolution rather than that of the diehards.[71] Instead, the 2500 delegates passed overwhelmingly the Duchess of Atholl's amendment criticizing the White Paper policy. The forerunner of the Young Conservatives, the Junior Imperial League, voted likewise at its annual general meeting. Earlier, on 9 February, Churchill had spoken at the Essex and Middlesex Provincial Area National Union, where his resolution expressing 'anxiety' over the White Paper's police and central government proposals was endorsed, despite the interventions of loyalist MPs, by 92 votes to 47. Given that areas like Essex and Middlesex were represented by thirty-two Tory MPs, such votes boosted diehard hopes that they were beginning to shift opinion on the ground.[72] Yet, while it was one thing for the diehards to win votes in meetings of this kind which the government could scarcely be expected to take seriously, it was quite another matter to win over the nationwide central institutions that were

part of the consultative structure of the party itself. When Viscount
FitzAlan attempted to overturn the gag on the Central Council on 28
March 1934, nine Cabinet ministers, the Chief Whip and a regiment of
party managers were wheeled into position to face the Tory delegates.
Once again the impression was left that a call for a debate was a direct
revolt against the party leadership and thus, the stability of the
government itself. The voting went against FitzAlan by 419 to 314.

Having gone through the strain of the Privileges case and the
commencement of the Lancashire campaign (described in the next
chapter), Churchill decided to go on a three-week Mediterranean cruise
rather than attend the National Union's 1934 Conference in Bristol.
Other diehards were less lethargic about the occasion and 600 copies of
the September edition of the *Indian Empire Review* were distributed.[73]
The diehards' Chief Organizer, Hugh Orr-Ewing, even arranged that all
IDL members took up residence in the Grand Hotel since 'The Royal
Hotel ha[d] been taken over by the Central Office'.[74] This really was a
party within a party. However, Wolmer in particular was keen that the
diehard attack was conducted in a way that did not intimidate the middle-
ground party activists into believing that their party was being bullied by
an aggressive exterior force.[75]

On 4 October, Page Croft spoke at the 1934 Party Conference for the
diehard resolution, begging the delegates that since the Central Council
had been 'persuaded to muzzle itself', then 'you are the democratic parent
of the Council ... It is positively your last chance to influence the
situation.' He claimed that the India policy was:

> a reversion to the ideals of Cobden, whose one aim was to quit the Empire.
> Why should 460 Conservative [MPs] be asked to surrender their principles at
> the behest of 30 Liberals and 10 Socialists? [in order to] risk the fate of one
> fifth of the human race [and] the final ruin of Lancashire and the destruction of
> our greatest market ... There is only one force which can now save India for
> the Empire – the Conservative Party – and the heart of the Party is this
> conference.[76]

There was nothing new in his claim that the policy was the unnecessary
by-product of the Tories' involvement in the National Government, since
this was one of the main thrusts of the diehard attack. The link between
Lancashire's future and India's level of fiscal autonomy was also a well-
rehearsed routine. However, the whole drift of Page Croft's argument,
particularly the reference to the long-dead Cobden, exuded the protectionist rhetoric of the Empire Industries Association and its age-old fight
against liberal free trade. On this imperialist line of attack – the vision of
Joseph Chamberlain and Lord Beaverbrook – Page Croft was a more

convincing champion than Churchill. Unable to lay claim to the appropriate pedigree, Churchill lacked the bond that men like Page Croft had with the Conservative caucus's deep-seated desire to find, in a world dominated by economic protectionism, an added justification for imperialism. This calls into question the suggestion that Churchill's failure to attend the conference was a fatal error, robbing the diehards of their star turn just at the moment when the caucus came closest to deserting their official party leadership.[77] When the vote went to a show of hands (on a loyalist amendment to Page Croft's motion calling for the conference to gag itself so as 'to have faith in their leader'), the conference Chairman's assertion that the government had won led to such 'angry protests' that 'amid intense excitement' a ballot had to be organized.[78] When the result was read out, the pro-government side was found to have won by a mere 543 votes to 520. Page Croft comforted himself with the narrow margin of his defeat, writing to Churchill that he thought 'the White Paper had not a score of friends in the Hall.'[79]

The publication of the Joint Select Committee's Report in November 1934 removed the gag on the caucus that had worked so effectively for the party leadership. The diehards realized that the resulting meeting of the Central Council on 4 December was the most important caucus division in the campaign and so Lord Salisbury's pamphlet and the IDL manifesto were sent to all the Chairmen of Conservative Associations, spurring the government to set about producing a counter-leaflet.[80] For its part, the caucus was also aware of the magnitude of the event, with 67 per cent of the Council's total nationwide membership present for what was acknowledged to be a debate of high quality from all sides.[81] Yet everything that the diehards feared about the issue being declared a fait accompli came true. Present at the Queen's Hall for the meeting, Cuthbert Headlam noted: 'a great crowd there: the Government had whipped up all their supporters and so presumably had Winston & Co. Baldwin made an admirable speech which clinched matters – Page Croft made an ass of himself but both Winston and Eddie [Marquess of] Hartington who also spoke for the Winstonians did well – Eustace Percy ranted quite successfully and Austen Chamberlain was good.'[82] Salisbury's motion condemning federation was defeated by 1102 to 390. This was a clear vote of confidence in Baldwin. Beaverbrook, who a month earlier had thought that the government was being driven close to having to abandon its Indian policy, now thought otherwise.[83] Given the threat the caucus had posed to his government over Ireland in 1921, it was not surprising that it was Sir Austen Chamberlain who re-emerged to play a prominent part to help quell the revolt. As with the situation in 1921 with the Irish Treaty, defeat for the government would not have necessitated the abandonment of the Joint Select Committee's Report as the basis for legislation (in effect, the underpinning of the whole India policy). It is nonetheless hard to see how Baldwin could have got out of such a hole without sparking a civil war in the party far bloodier than anything which had so far materialized since the formation of the National Government. The fear that he might be prepared to face this prospect was possibly responsible for encouraging many delegates to follow Disraeli's dictum to damn their principles and stick to their party. After Salisbury, the diehard speakers, in marked contrast to those for the government, lacked members of the Joint Select Committee and this may have told against them. Hoare's ability to convince the supposedly non-partisan Sir Austen Chamberlain and his group of the report's merits was certainly advantageous in winning over the doubters. However, given the way in which the caucus was denied a chance to debate the policy until it had been effectively enshrined as a major pillar of party doctrine (and upon which the future of the National Government supposedly depended), the result should never really have been in doubt. The delegates were not taking counsel with their leadership, as Baldwin had once promised that they would. The leadership were presenting them with their policy and making its acceptance a matter of confidence. This, after all, was the ultimate test of leadership over who governed the party – one which was, in the final analysis, a parliamentary one. Few delegates were prepared to risk an action which would so publicly hole their own government below the waterline. This was an unchanging sentiment. It had proved to be the case over Lord Randolph Churchill in 1886 and Austen Chamberlain's Irish policy in 1921. It would prove so again later when John Major survived the instinctive scepticism of delegates over his defence of the Maastricht Treaty and the possibility of scrapping sterling in favour of the Euro-currency.

Seven

THE MONSTROUS MONUMENT
OF SHAMS

I

For over twenty years, the imperialism of a resolutely led empire – sure of
its purpose and bonded together by economic preferences – had been a
litmus test readily able to demonstrate the deepness of the 'true blue' hue
of Conservative Party members. Churchill's hostility to what he believed
was Britain's signal of retreat from India had brought him into the orbit
of this Tory tradition. Yet outside his own suzerainty in Epping, his
mahogany-framed portrait had not yet joined those of Benjamin Disraeli
and Joe Chamberlain on the walls of constituency associations up and
down the country. Neither, for all his majestic poetry about far pavilions,
had he become the darling of the Party Conference, a forum where
admiration for the older troopers of the Tory right lingered. These
realities ensured that the diehard campaign for the control of the caucus
was not won by the son of its great champion, Lord Randolph Churchill.

On the floor of the House of Commons, the situation was very
different. No other diehard parliamentarian could lay claim to Churchill's
reputation. It was on this platform that he made his great gamble for the
diehard cause by attacking what he saw as a grievous breach of privilege
by the architects of Indian reform against the rights and rules of
Parliament. If he succeeded with this audacious line of attack, then the
government's strategy would be in total disarray.

At the beginning of April 1934 the *Daily Mail* handed Churchill
documents suggesting that pressure had been put upon the Manchester
Chamber of Commerce to alter its evidence to the Joint Select Committee
on Indian reform by Lord Derby, a member of that committee.[1]
Furthermore, he had done this with the acquiescence of another member,
no less than the Secretary of State for India himself, Sir Samuel Hoare.
Originally, the Manchester Chamber of Commerce had asserted that
Lancashire's cotton industry would be jeopardized by giving increasing
powers to nationalist Indian ministers. Despite being long on the decline,
in 1930 the cotton textile trade still accounted for a third of British
exports to India and was regarded as essential to the prosperity of

Lancashire. One hundred copies of the Manchester Chamber's evidence expressing concern at the proposed Indian reforms had been sent to the India Office in advance of it being shown to the Joint Select Committee in June 1933. However, the copies had not been distributed. In the meantime Lord Derby had dined with the then President of the Chamber, first in London and, so it appeared, thereafter in Manchester. When the document was presented before the Joint Select Committee the contents were far removed from the original copy sent in to the committee – the objections to Indian reform having been largely expunged. Like a juror secretly advising the accused, Derby's actions appeared to contravene the House of Commons 'sessional order number four' which forbade tampering with evidence being brought before a committee.

When he was handed this potential bombshell, it was significant that it was to his old former coalitionist friends, Sir Robert Horne and Lloyd George, that Churchill turned for advice.[2] Frances Stevenson, Lloyd George's secretary and mistress, certainly got it into her head that Churchill was 'working extremely hard to undermine the Gov[ernment] and appears to be gaining ground'.[3] That would have been the message that 'The Goat' would want to hear at any rate. Duly impressed by the evidence, Lloyd George found Churchill 'excited and excitable' about the case.[4]

Churchill considered that the best course was to raise the point with the Speaker in the Commons as a breach of privilege.[5] On 12 April he wrote to the most senior diehard on the Joint Select Committee, Lord Salisbury, hoping to enlist his support. Salisbury's response was that the deception was 'disgusting' and that it had been obvious 'when the Manchester witnesses appeared before [the Committee] that they had been got at'. Despite this, he could not allow himself to be 'involved' in a course of action which hinged upon the use of 'confidential' documents.[6] This was typical of Salisbury's interpretation of seemly conduct and also of his failure to attain any of his own objectives in politics. Yet, given his reputation for honourable behaviour, his refusal to associate himself with the action was a setback for Churchill. Unlike Rothermere, Beaverbrook disassociated himself from the attack, writing to his ally Hoare to assure him that he had refused to give support to the campaign.[7]

It is now clear that, at Hoare's instigation,[8] Derby had indeed interfered in the Chamber of Commerce's submission, persuading them to withdraw their evidence and to substitute it with 'a very harmless document'.[9] Despite this, Derby wrote to Churchill assuring him that he was mistaken and that the changes were the result not of pressure from him but from further information sent from the Chamber's Indian Mission.[10] This was untrue.[11] Proving it as such was a different matter. Furthermore, at a meeting at the India Office between Hoare and Lord Hailsham on 26 April, it was decided to temporarily lose particularly incriminating correspondence between Derby and the Deputy Under-Secretary at the India Office, Sir Louis Kershaw.[12] Whilst the circumstantial evidence suggested that Churchill had identified an infringement, without access to these documents, it was going to be difficult for him to prove his allegations under scrutiny. Having conspired to withhold the key evidence to the parliamentary inquiry, Hailsham was appointed Lord Chancellor the following year.

By the time Churchill raised the case as a breach of privilege in the Commons, he had decided to implicate Hoare fully in his charges.[13] This decision transformed the scope of his strategy to one of all-out war against the government itself. If his case was sustained, he would not only disable the government's attempt to pacify the strategic battleground of Lancashire, he would publicly disgrace the architect of the government's India policy. The resulting resignation of Hoare would endanger the 'Joint Select Committee and all its works', probably killing the India policy. Hoare admitted to the Viceroy, Lord Willingdon, there were 'not thirty' Conservative MPs 'genuinely keen to go on with the Bill, that the great mass is very lukewarm and that a very strong minority is actively hostile'. Even more extraordinarily given the public display of solidarity, Hoare thought that 'most of' his 'colleagues in their heart of hearts would say that it was impossible to get through a Bill at all'.[14] Modern interpretations asserting that Churchill's actions over the breach of privileges were misguided and counter-productive[15] appear unaware of how close they were to success in this respect. The Daily Telegraph speculated that should a general election follow (although there was constitutionally no necessity for one), Churchill would certainly be recalled to the Cabinet on his own terms.[16] In 1915, Churchill had sought by his Gallipoli offensive to break through the stalemate on the western front with a daring surprise move to knock out the weakest part of the enemy from the rear. His tactics in 1934 worked on the same principle. The analogy was not auspicious.

II

The Conservative leadership were 'staggered' by Churchill's act of treachery against his own party colleagues. Hoare was particularly taken aback that Churchill could plan such an action, sit next to him at lunch as if nothing was about to happen and then the following night have dinner 'with Lloyd George and Horne for the purpose of arranging an attack, [whilst] the following day he was trying to bring the leader of the Labour party . . . into it on his side. Can you imagine a more treacherous way of treating not only two former colleagues in various Governments, but two prominent people in his own party.'[17] Another government loyalist on the Joint Select Committee, J.C.C. Davidson, thought that the episode demonstrated that Churchill 'never discriminates between his friends and his enemies, but treats them alike. A man may have quite recently been working intimately with him, and yet he will attack him with the same venom and bitterness as a Communist . . . perhaps that is why Winston has no friends.'[18] The Indian Viceroy also chipped in with the statutory condemnation, expressing his belief to Hoare that Churchill 'with this great obsession about India has become orientalised' as only a 'bitter, disgruntled Oriental' could launch such an 'unscrupulous attack'.[19]

Hoare was already worried that the timetable for the India policy was being dragged dangerously close to the end of the parliamentary session and he thought that Churchill's strategy would succeed insofar as it would hold up the work of the Joint Select Committee still further. To investigate Churchill's allegations, a Committee of Privileges had to be convened, using up the valuable time not just of Hoare but also of the India Office, the Prime Minister and the leader of the Conservative Party. As it transpired, the resulting two-month delay of the Joint Select Committee's work prevented it from meeting until after the intervening summer recess, ensuring that five months were lost in total. To make matters even more embarrassing, Derby's brother was about to become acting Viceroy.

These were issues of magnitude and it is not surprising that the government played foul in order to defeat Churchill's charges. Hoare and Hailsham's deliberate removal of the vital incriminating evidence from the files submitted to the Committee of Privileges was part and parcel of a more general gagging of debate elsewhere – be it against those in the party who wanted to question the policy whilst the Joint Select Committee was deliberating or on the airwaves of the BBC. When he was called before the Committee of Privileges inquiry, Churchill was annoyed to be refused the right to cross-examine and question witnesses.[20] Although it was supposed to act with complete impartiality and went through the motions of being so, the committee's composition of MacDonald, Baldwin, Sir Thomas Inskip (the Attorney-General), four government backbenchers and three opposition MPs (all of whom supported Indian reform in one form or another) was not exactly stacked in Churchill's favour: there were no diehards represented whatsoever.[21] Extraordinarily, MacDonald, the Prime Minister, may even have given Churchill the impression that if he dropped the case, he might be given a government appointment to improve relations with the Dominions.[22]

Terence O'Connor, who was providing Churchill with legal advice,[23] thought that if the Committee of Privileges Report found against him, then he should save face by accepting the decision and expressing relief that his Conservative colleagues had been proved innocent from such grave charges. Hoare also felt that if he had adopted this emollient line, he could 'have regained much of his lost position'.[24] Given the composition of the committee, it might have been advisable to work on the assumption of such a defeat. The report's findings, drawn up by Sir Thomas Inskip and released to the public on 9 June, argued that the Joint Select Committee was not 'in the ordinary sense'[25] a judicial body and therefore the normal orders against tampering with witnesses were not strictly applicable. At any rate, it concluded, witnesses had not been tampered with but merely advised, a distinction perfectly acceptable to the Privileges Committee. Frightened about how the Commons might receive the report, MacDonald took the precaution of putting the Whips on the House. The committee refused to publish the evidence used in the case and demanded the return of all copies of the evidence held by Churchill so that they could be destroyed.[26] Even if the committee really believed that the sort of activities in which Hoare and Derby had indulged were legitimate, a year later they surreptitiously made sure that no one else would be able to act in that way in the future, when they changed the Parliamentary Standing Orders accordingly.[27]

Churchill ignored his legal advice in the Commons on 13 June. The Privileges Committee had concluded that the Joint Select Committee was not a judicial body. Baldwin, however, had argued to the Conservative Central Council in June 1933 that they should not debate Indian reform whilst the Joint Select Committee was still undertaking its 'semi-judicial' duties.[28] This was a fair debating point, but it was wasted on the occasion. Rising to speak after Churchill, Amery launched a savage offensive on the man he had been growing closer to over the need for rearmament. He implied that Churchill's motive was to cripple the government. Churchill fell into Amery's trap by asking him to translate his jibe '*fiat justitia ruat caelum*'. Amery replied, 'If I can trip up Sam, the Government's bust.'[29] The Chamber laughed. Churchill was reduced to being a source of ridicule. Another MP described him as a 'menace' to peace, unfit 'to be selected for any responsible post in any Administration in the future'.[30] Convinced of the honest intent of Derby and Hoare's behaviour, the Commons were in no humour to listen to Churchill's muckraking and accepted the report without even a division.

Friend and foe alike agreed that Churchill's position in the House had been greatly weakened. Unaware of the truth, even the Lancashire diehard MP, Sir Joseph Nall, thought that the committee's refusal to publish the evidence was probably a good thing since publication would cause 'a re-action against Winston and our group in quarters which up to now have looked to us to support their cause'.[31] The *Indian Empire Review* accepted unequivocally the committee's findings that no impropriety had taken place but defended Churchill against 'the insinuations as to his motives [which] reflect no credit on those who made [them]'.[32] Although Page Croft and a number of the other leading diehards spoke or wrote in support of Churchill,[33] many friends of the fair weather variety were reluctant to associate themselves with him in public. Dumping the blame on him on the morrow of failure was particularly ungracious given the fact that he had only raised the case after taking their counsel on the issue in the first place.[34] Returning from India, the assistant editor of the *Morning Post*, Edward Russell, wrote to the IDL Parliamentary Secretary, Patrick Donner, to complain that since Churchill was the only diehard politician taken seriously by Indians, his 'desertion' in the Privileges debate by the other diehards 'was the gravest tactical blunder'. Donner made sure that this revealing letter, which spoke of 'the internal jealousies on our side, particularly in regard to Mr Winston Churchill' being 'plainly apparent for some time', circulated to Churchill and a couple of other members of the IDL Executive.[35] The embarrassment which some of the diehards felt about their cause being championed by Churchill was now at its peak. When Churchill went up to address a diehard rally at the Manchester Free Trade Hall before an audience of 3000, not a single Manchester MP agreed to sit on the platform with him.

III

In November 1934, the Report of the Joint Select Committee was at last published. Its four Labour members dissented from its findings because they felt it had not gone sufficiently far in realizing Indian aspirations. On the other extreme, Lord Salisbury was joined by the other four diehards on the committee in drafting a minority report which largely restated the entrenched diehard position. Aside from these marginalized voices of discontent, the Joint Select Committee Report proposed only three significant changes to the original White Paper. The first two concerned implementing a firmer anti-terrorist provision and clarifying the anti-economic boycott strategy. The third change proposed that indirect election by the provincial chambers should replace direct election (on a narrow franchise) to the Central Assembly. This was done to keep Sir Austen Chamberlain's support but appears not to have worried the India Office in any case.[36]

Despite his personal regard for Churchill, Austen Chamberlain made clear to his former coalition colleague that he would still put his weight behind the government.[37] There was no surprise in this as Chamberlain, for all his lingering doubts about the India policy, did not share the diehard analysis and had no intention of doing anything which might encourage (in a reference to the left-winger, Sir Stafford) 'the greater danger of a Socialist dictatorship on the Cripps pattern'.[38] Writing to his sister, Sir Austen was of the all too typically self-important view that 'the Gov[ernment] ought to be grateful to me, for if I had gone against them, there isn't a doubt but that they would have been beaten and indeed, unless I had exerted myself, I don't think they could have obtained a working majority.'[39] Given Austen Chamberlain's failure to change radically India Office policy, this quotation may support Churchill's view of him as always playing the game and always losing it. The government got more out of his support than he gained in return and he couldn't help noticing subsequently that he was being 'used whenever India gets difficult'.[40] Churchill might have followed Austen Chamberlain's lead and accepted the inevitability of the Indian policy, thereby placing himself in an advantageous position to return to the Cabinet at the head of a united pro-rearmament group after 1935. This hypothesis fails to address Chamberlain's own failure to reap tangible benefits by such tactics.

Further, it is not clear that being a diehard was necessarily to be despised by other Conservative parliamentarians. According to Salisbury, who was not given to outbursts of partisan overstatement, it was doubtful whether, Hoare included, 'there was a single member of the [Joint Select] Committee who liked the White Paper' but that many had thought it 'better than the alternative'.[41] Hoare confessed to the Governor of Bombay, his former parliamentary private secretary, Lord Brabourne, that he did not see how the Bill could reach the statute books unless the proposed safeguards could be viewed as sufficient, since he had already 'taken the Conservative Party up to the utmost limit of their endurance'.[42]

Despite this, Churchill was under few delusions about the problems of conducting an effective opposition to all the main party leaderships in the Commons, when the diehards would be allocated only one speech to every three for the White Paper supporters and unable to wind up on the crucial motions.[43] He had made an unimpressive opening speech in the new session which, Hoare had heard, had annoyed other diehards for its 'bad tactics'.[44] Furthermore, Churchill was showing signs of confusing the India issue with personal allegiance to himself, writing to the IDL's Chief Organizer to complain that only twenty of the seventy IDL MPs had backed his opposition to the Betting and Lotteries Bill.[45] Whatever the argument for Churchill's opposition to the Bill, with its crackdown provisions against petty gambling – another instance of his removal from the party line – it had little to do with Indian diehardism. His expectation of loyalty on this unrelated topic suggested that he saw IDL members as his own praetorian guard. This was not necessarily how the other diehards would have chosen to identify their role.

As for the bookmakers, Churchill was confident enough to place bets with other MPs that the India Bill would not receive the Royal Assent in the existing session with federalism included in it.[46] Viewing events from the Governor's residence in Bombay, Lord Brabourne thought that neither the Indian Civil Service nor the Indian Police supported the White Paper but did not see how, once its proposals had developed impetus, they could be scuppered.[47] However, whilst opposition from the Congress movement could be taken for granted, it now became clear that the Indian liberals also rejected the reform proposals, even stating that they would rather work under the existing constitution. As Churchill reported gleefully to his wife, 'the Government have not a single section of Indian opinion behind their plan.'[48] Paradoxically, this did not resolve the tactical problem for the diehards. If events in India now militated against the likelihood of the most controversial aspects of the White Paper becoming immediately enforceable, so sceptical MPs at Westminster might judge that there was no imperial harm served by playing safe and bowing to the government three-line whip. Some counselled Churchill to accept this reality, drop his outright opposition and work to improve the proposed legislation by a series of considered amendments. This act of statesmanship, Lord Melchett assured him, would rejuvenate his flagging popularity in the country and place him 'in a predominant position in the Conservative Party'.[49] Yet, such an action would have been to retrace all the steps back to Churchill's reason for refusing to sit on the Joint Select Committee in the first place. Subsequent events had not necessarily pointed to that decision being misconceived, given Lord Salisbury's failure to secure any tangible gains from cooperating within a system in which minority status was always guaranteed. In any case, Churchill had established his bridgehead. It was too late to go in search of evacuation craft.

On 12 December 1934, the Commons debate on the Joint Select Committee Report was concluded with speeches from Churchill and a conciliatory Baldwin.[50] Churchill's 'fine'[51] speech was in Austen Chamberlain's opinion 'the best that he has made for some time'.[52] Seventy-five Tories rebelled, joined for different reasons by fifty-three Labour MPs. This figure was larger than had been anticipated.[53] With the help of the former Viceroys, Reading and Halifax (as Irwin had now become), the

House of Lords then rejected Salisbury's amendment by 239 to 62, despite an able performance from Lord Lloyd. This was a poor result for the diehards, considering that there were over one hundred members of the IDL amongst the peerage.[54] With unconscious temerity, Churchill attributed their Lordships' timidity to their emasculation by the 1911 Parliament Act (which he had helped instigate). Nonetheless, he still believed it possible that he could defeat the federal proposals.[55]

Although now busy writing an absurdly hyperbolic script for an unexecuted patriotic film to celebrate the life of King George V for Alexander Korda, Churchill studied the division list closely on the Commons debate.[56] Six members of the IDL had actually voted with the government. Nonetheless, Hoare was not complacent. Given the centrality of keeping Lancashire on side with its swathe of MPs, Hoare feared that without further tariff concessions on cotton textiles, there could be a defection of all or most of the Lancashire MPs. Yet, as he appreciated, the government still retained an advantage in that even some of its sceptical backbenchers did not want to see all the remaining time in the session squandered on the India Bill when the ensuing general election would be essentially fought on other issues.[57] On the other hand, Hoare wrote to Willingdon that on top of the doubts created by the Indian princes' scepticism over the benefits of federation, 'many Conservatives who are doubtful about the Bill are wondering whether in face of the German situation [Hitler was rearming Germany in breach of the Treaty of Versailles] it is wise to go on with a programme that divides the party.'[58] With Amery, Churchill was also warning about the threat from the emerging Nazi Reich and the government was conscious of the danger of the India diehards and the rearmers coalescing. Their reaction to this threat was to be one of Churchill's most important and most overlooked achievements during the period.

IV

One of the effects of diehard strategy was that the attempt to push the Joint Select Committee's deliberations out of parliamentary time lengthened the Indian campaign and drained the IDL's funds accordingly at a time when the pro-government forces could be bolstered from the coffers of Conservative Central Office.[59] In pressing Rothermere to dig deeper into his pocket, Churchill maintained that as well as increasing the number of IDL branches, it was 'possible that after the National Union has pronounced in January [1935] we shall decide to carry the war into the constituencies and fight every bye-election which affords that opportunity' but that 'it would be fatal however to intervene in bye-elections before the National Union has pronounced [since] anything like that would upset the delegates.'[60] Churchill was possibly losing sight of political reality to the extent that he was preparing to encourage the electorate to vote against the party to which he officially belonged. More likely, he was merely trying to excite Rothermere and his personal fortune with the tantalizing (but illusory) hope of such activity.

Whatever Churchill actually thought, Lord Lloyd seriously advocated that the IDL should 'fight whatever by-election offered any reasonable chances of success' since failure to do so would ensure 'accepting certain defeat on the India cause [and] also gravely jeopardis[e] any real revival of Conservative strength inside our party'. He had to admit, however, that this view was not shared by the rest of the IDL Executive, except possibly by Sir Alfred Knox who was on the far right of the party.[61] Neville Chamberlain had feared that if the government were to call a snap general election, as Simon was recommending, before 1935 (and thus without an India Act yet on the statute books), then the IDL would indeed probably run their own candidates against those of the National Government. This was one of Chamberlain's reasons for arguing that a general election should be postponed until after the legislation had become law.[62] What could happen when rival Conservative candidates fought against each other was demonstrated in the new year by Randolph Churchill.

The decision of the 23-year-old Randolph Churchill to fight the Wavertree by-election in Liverpool against the official Conservative candidate came as a bombshell to friend and foe alike. He made his decision without his father's knowledge and approval. Churchill was furious that his own son had taken this action but decided to stand by him publicly, fearing the damage that could be done if Randolph was left alone to destroy himself and the cause with it.[63] Naturally rude and impulsive, young Randolph seemed to embody his father's rashness without his *gravitas*. It was fortunate for Churchill that he was only one of a long line of public figures whose offspring decide to embarrass them in public. At least Randolph was stirring up trouble on the same side as his father. This was more than could be said for the son of the leader of the Conservative Party. Oliver Baldwin was a left-wing socialist who in the 1929–31 Parliament had been the Labour MP for Dudley, the constituency adjacent to that for which his father sat – a public repudiation of his father which caused particular unhappiness to his mother.[64]

At last presented with the sort of showdown which he had long been anticipating, Rothermere decided, without waiting for encouragement from Churchill, to throw full newspaper support behind Randolph who was, in any case, one of his employees on the *Sunday Dispatch*. The *Daily Mail* gave him not only newspaper coverage but also littered the constituency with placards on his behalf. The Duke of Westminster promised £500 towards Randolph's fighting fund, Churchill gave £200, and a further donation of £100 was made by the right-wing eccentric Lady Houston, famous for her funding in 1931 of the winning British aircraft in the Schneider Trophy and the 1933 flight over Everest.[65] Meanwhile, the Indian Assembly at Delhi unconsciously assisted Randolph's campaign by rejecting the proposed trade deal, further casting doubt on the future of Lancashire's perilous textiles economy when placed increasingly at the mercy of Indian politicians.

The decision on 22 January 1935 of the IDL Executive and its parliamentary committee to campaign actively on Randolph's behalf, came as a surprise to Churchill who had anticipated a more cautious approach.[66] In pledging themselves to oppose the official candidate of their own party, these Conservative MPs were doing what they had up until that date resisted. Having previously been unsure whether to travel up to Liverpool to join the campaign,[67] Churchill felt that the IDL's decision now made it easier for him to do so. Naturally the leading diehards were annoyed that Randolph had decided to stand without consulting them and felt that the action stood to lose the group members and possibly, although Churchill disagreed, the party Whip.[68] However, the psychological effects of the IDL backing down from a fight might well have been worse. Instead, Randolph's meetings were blessed by the presence of supportive Tory MPs, and a proper agent and campaign organization were established. Given that the Liverpudlian electorate was marked by sectarian divisions as well as ideological ones, Lord FitzAlan was dispatched to encourage the Catholic voters to back Randolph, and Lord Carson did likewise for the Protestant electorate.

Fortified by the size of their own constituency majorities, some of the diehards were sufficiently obsessed by the Indian issue to risk the Whips' removal. Churchill fired a pre-emptive salvo at the party machine, warning that diehard MPs would not back down under intimidation. Further, he asserted that if the Whip was removed, then IDL members merely needed to win a vote of confidence from their own constituency Conservative Associations in order to act as 'a rebuke' to the government from 'a number of the strongest and safest Conservative seats throughout the country'. He even asserted that the full use of 'the party machine' to stop his 23-year-old son from representing the Conservative interest in 'Parliament where for so many generations his forbears had borne their part' was 'pitiful'.[69] This counter-offensive was strengthened when the respected party figure, Sir Robert Horne, made a public declaration that if the government attempted to intimidate diehard MPs, then he himself would refuse the Whip.[70] Like Austen Chamberlain, Horne was one of those senior figures whose natural scepticism towards the India policy had been seemingly squared, and whom the government had no desire to drive into the rebel camp.

On 30 January 1935, Churchill was finally permitted to deliver his BBC broadcast on India, four years after he had first requested to do so. It proved to be the only broadcast speech on the subject he was allowed to make during the whole controversy. As he could not resist reminding his listeners, of the thirteen speakers the BBC had chosen to broadcast, he was one of only two to represent the diehard point of view. For rhetorical power, his performance was a masterpiece of nationalistic oratory, denigrating the Bill as 'a monstrous monument of shams built by pigmies'. The more discerning listener might have noted the triumph of vivid conjecture over more reasoned prediction.[71] Hoare hoped that the broadcast 'was too extreme for the BBC hearers who are on the whole rather a quiet lot'.[72]

On 2 February, Churchill, aware of the sort of havoc his son was capable of creating, telegraphed Randolph to forewarn him that if he attempted to turn the by-election into an issue of smashing the National Government, then he would not come and speak on his behalf. Churchill's pronouncements, not least his radio broadcast, certainly implied that the National Government was undermining true Conservatism, but to his son he now fumed that the 'mass party rightly favour real National Government' which would be achieved with the destruction of the Liberal vote at the next election and that he himself was intending to stand as the 'Conservative and National' candidate.[73]

The same day as Churchill was hurriedly imparting this advice, the Nazeing branch of his stronghold in the West Essex Conservative Association passed a motion condemning his 'consistent opposition to the National Government'. Further, it suggested that if his son was going to stand as an Independent Conservative in Wavertree, then there was a 'highly dangerous precedent for the adoption of an Independent Conservative candidate in the Epping Division, who would undoubtedly now be welcomed by many loyal supporters of Mr Baldwin and the present Government'.[74] Churchill replied that he had been authorized by the West Essex Conservative Association 'to oppose the Indian policy of the late Socialist Government, which has now become the policy of the present National Government'. Churchill stated that he was a supporter of the concept of the National Government but objected to one headed by the 'international socialist' Ramsay MacDonald. Arguing that 'the Conservative Party . . . must recover its pre-eminence and cohesion' before the next general election, Churchill looked to his imaginary National Government which would be a 'reunion of all those forces which carried us through the Great War and broke the General Strike'.[75] Not for the first time, Churchill reflected upon the mythical golden age during which he had held office before the political realignment of 1931, and to which he was yearning to return.

Churchill continued his theme on the disabling of Conservatism within the National Government when he spoke at the eve of poll at Wavertree. Arguing that the future of the empire was more important than loyalties 'to a leader like Mr Baldwin or MacDonald', he claimed that with a 'Socialist' as Prime Minister and – rather less surprisingly – 'a Socialist at the head of his Majesty's Opposition', to say nothing of the socialist Lord Chancellor and Disarmament Conference representative, it was intolerable that it was 'the Socialists who had foisted this Indian Federal policy upon the Conservative party . . . which lies tame and dumb'.[76] These propositions were at the heart of the diehard discontent which maintained that Indian reform was really the most obvious expression of the more general capture of the Tory Party by its non-Conservative National allies in the government. In fact, it was not the existence of the National coalition which determined the policy so much as the determination of the leadership of the Conservative Party, and of Baldwin in particular, to pursue a centre-liberal agenda. Insofar as the Tory leadership associated it with their National allies, it was to cloak their own intentions. Amongst the diehards, Wolmer was closer to understanding this state of affairs and he maintained that even if they lost the battle over the Indian reforms, their campaign must nonetheless 'lay the foundations of a new Conservative Party which is true to Conservative principles'.[77]

Wavertree went to the polls on 6 February. With over 10,000 votes, Randolph was just over 3000 votes short of the official Conservative and 5000 behind the Labour candidate who won as a result of the split Tory vote.[78] The 'little brute Randolph', as the 55-year-old Hoare described the boy thirty-two years his junior, 'got more votes than we expected' whilst, unsurprisingly, Churchill (senior) and the Duke of Westminster thought the prodigal child's performance 'magnificent' and 'glorious'.[79] Churchill's belief, however, that the result meant 'no harm done' was less realistic than Hoare's musing that Randolph's intervention in losing the official Conservative the seat 'will undoubtedly do both Winston and him a good deal of harm in the party'.[80] The Secretary of State for India would have to savour this moment of retribution. Events in the subcontinent itself were about to deal him a terrible blow.

V

On 11 February 1935 Churchill wound up for the diehards on the second reading of the Government of India Bill. Despite five years of debate and rancour, the legislation was scarcely altered from the proposals Hoare had drawn up for Indian federation back in 1930.* For his own part, Hoare felt he had gone 'as far as I could without the gravest risk of endangering the Bill with the moderate Conservatives'.[81] When the division took place, 84 Conservatives made up the 133 votes against the 404 cast for the government. Thus, more Conservative MPs rebelled on a three-line whip against the second reading of this legislation than over any other in the twentieth century.

Fortified by the mustering in the Commons, Churchill's attention now focused upon the preparations for the India Bill's ascension to the committee stage. Here, the campaign would continue and Churchill informed Rothermere that the IDL had

> formed an 'Amendment Committee' which will be able to furnish a continuous brief to all our MPs for their use during the protracted debates of next year. Lord Rankeillour formerly a Deputy Speaker and versed in every detail of Parliamentary procedure will be the Chairman, and Professor Lindemann, Sir Michael O'Dwyer and probably Mr J.H. Morgan, the well-known constitutional lawyer, will be the members. Thus the entire opposition to the Bill will be considered as a whole and the danger of mutually contradictory amendments avoided. It would not be possible to form a more competent group.[82]

Churchill pulled no punches and at one point in the thirty-six days allotted to the committee stage, even sought to insinuate that the only Indian princes prepared to enter federation had been bribed. Throughout, he attempted to force Hoare into statements which would put him at odds alternately with the interests of Indian politicians in British India and the princes in their states. This made the Secretary of State for India all the more nervous about the response of the princes to the project and how that response would be interpreted by those seeking to maximize division.[83] Yet, regardless of how well the debates proceeded, Churchill conceded privately to his wife Clementine that with a regular diehard turnout of around fifty, there was no cracking the government's unsinkable majority and, therefore, he contrived to force as few divisions as possible.[84]

It was just at this moment that extraneous events suddenly intervened to throw a lifeline to the diehard cause. Meeting for a conference in

---

* See pp. 145–8 above.

Bombay, the Indian princes declared outright their rejection of federation. Churchill wrote in jubilation to his wife that the princes' statement, on top of the rejection of the government's plans from virtually every other section of the Indian political classes including the Congress Party, 'wrecks the federal scheme against which I have been fighting so long. It may also lead to the withdrawal of the whole Government policy.'[85] Hoare claimed to the Viceroy, Lord Willingdon, that the princes' decision came as 'a surprise'. Such a statement suggests that he had up to that point ignored or disregarded all the obvious indications that had been increasingly apparent to others. Certainly the Cabinet were genuinely taken aback by the princes' declaration, to the extent that many 'were asking whether it was worth going on with the Bill at all'. Quoting Austen Chamberlain as being 'horrified at the state of affairs' Hoare decided to blame the Viceroy, at least having the brutal honesty to write to him personally and assuring him of the fact that men like Austen Chamberlain thought that the Cabinet 'were getting little or no help from your end and that whilst the die-hards were kept fully informed as to what was happening and were daily using great influence with their friends amongst the Princes, we appear to be inert and helpless'. Hoare assured Willingdon that if his ministers were happy about federation being dropped, then they could forget about the rest of the Bill proceeding since he would have nothing more to do with it. Furthermore the Bill's withdrawal 'might very well mean the fall of the Government, but it would certainly mean the end of Indian legislation for this Parliament and probably for many years to come'. King George V was reportedly so angry that he was even threatening to snub the three ringleading princes at his forthcoming Jubilee.[86] Of course Hoare's reproaches were deliberately intended to frighten Willingdon into action. At the same time, Hoare knew that the situation was extremely serious. If the Viceroy couldn't be bullied into achieving success, then his own job as Secretary of State for India – and perhaps those of others in the Cabinet – was on the line.

For the moment the government's majority in the Commons could still be whipped into shape, although on 26 February the diehard vote on a motion proposed by Churchill reached an all-time high in attracting eighty-nine Conservative rebels. This was the largest backbench rebellion against the National Government in the division lobbies of the decade (or against any other Conservative Government in the century). Far more diehards had been brought out to defy a three-line whip over India than the anti-appeasers would ever manage to attract later on in the 1930s. Hoare was in no doubt that they were now on the 'edge' of a 'first-class Parliamentary crisis'. It was the Cabinet which had forced the Indian constitutional initiative upon Parliament and it was the Cabinet's will which was now under the greatest strain. Furthermore, the Cabinet were determined to keep the support of Sir Austen Chamberlain and the swathe of moderate supporters outside the government who thought like him. Technically, this gave Sir Austen considerable bargaining power. However, in practice he could not retract from the position of loyal support for the proposed legislation which he had spent the previous weeks broadcasting so authoritatively to Commons and Party Conference alike. As Hoare pointed out – not only to Willingdon but to his old colleague the Governor of Bombay, Lord Brabourne – Sir Austen had agreed with him that all-India federation was the only workable framework for the Bill and that if they 'could not proceed with Federation', then they would 'almost inevitably have to drop the Bill altogether'. Indeed, there was a considerable danger that if the Bill was passed without the princes entering a federation, then a future Labour Government could easily build on the legislation to produce something much more offensive to Tory sensibilities. Hoare was aware of the stories circulating that with Rothermere's money Churchill and the Conservative MP J.S. Courtauld were in daily correspondence with some of the princes, gaining information about their intentions before the government did, leaving 'the House astonished' that Churchill 'seemed to know everything that was happening' whilst Hoare 'seemed to know nothing'.[87] Furthermore, Hoare believed that it was the princes' Counsel, Denis Pritt (the left-wing lawyer), and J.H. Morgan, 'the constitutional jackal of the *Morning Post* and the die-hards', who, because of their dislike for the government, had provided the princes with the biased interpretation that encouraged them to reject federation.[88] It had seemingly not occurred to Hoare that the princes, rather than being the undiscriminating victims of devious lawyers, might have employed them precisely because of the line they proposed to take. The true picture was a complicated one. The statements issued by the Chamber of Princes were not eternally binding nor could they claim to represent all the affected princelings in the subcontinent. Nonetheless, what had emerged was damaging enough. In the Commons, Hoare could do little but stall for time, claiming that the negotiating process with the princes was ongoing and that a negative result in the short term was still compatible with introducing federation when the time was right. Churchill, however, leaped at the opportunity to print and circulate the princes' speeches – demonstrating the essential incompatibility of their demands with that of a workable federation – to all members of both Houses, the press and to the membership of the IDL.[89]

Just when events in India seemed to be moving favourably towards the diehards, the home front was suddenly upset once again by young Randolph. 'Entirely against my wishes', fumed Churchill, his own 'uncontrollable' son had chosen to back publicly an Independent Conservative candidate with Lady Houston's money against the Conservatives in the Norwood by-election scheduled for 14 March. Without support from his father or the IDL, and in backing a candidate who had briefly flirted with Mosley, Randolph's actions were certainly ill considered. He had clearly learned nothing from the political fallout from his Wavertree adventure. Only one MP, 'and he a crack-pot' in Churchill's words, appeared on the platform with him. Even Rothermere's press failed to rally to Randolph's call and Beaverbrook personally tried, without success, to dissuade him from his course.[90] The only good news (or so it then appeared) was that whilst out campaigning with her brother, Diana Churchill got her first glimpse of the official Conservative candidate, Duncan Sandys, whom she went on to marry later that year. When Norwood went to the polls, Sandys retained the seat for the Conservatives. Randolph's candidate lost his deposit, winning only 2698 votes, his failure to split the Tory vote and the non-involvement of the IDL leaving Churchill to muse optimistically that his own reputation had not been seriously damaged by the incident.[91]

In fact, Churchill was being undermined by the ongoing manifestations of internecine conflict. The bushfires in the constituency associations which the IDL had ignited two years previously now embarrassingly looked like being fanned back in the wrong direction. The situation in Churchill's own constituency appeared to be fast deteriorating: by early March, the Nazeing, Waltham Abbey, Buckhurst Hill and Epping branches had all passed censorious motions against his actions. 'Against this', he wrote to his holidaying wife, 'Chigwell and Harlow have passed strong resolutions of support and encouragement, and the great voting masses of Woodford and Wanstead seem quite solid. There is some trouble however in South Chingford. Loughton chilly. Woodford magnificent.' Churchill was taking no chances. At last aware that his son's antics had proved a major irritant to his constituents, he saw advantage in being able to postpone his constituency's annual meeting – on account of its Chairman's illness – until the end of March, by which time he hoped that 'the excitement of Wavertree' would have subsided. This prospect was not helped by Randolph's interference in Norwood, which Churchill asserted he would 'have nothing to do with . . . except to bear a good deal of the blame'.[92] However, his position was bolstered when an attempt by party activists to deselect another diehard, Victor Raikes, in the nearby constituency of Ilkeston, was defeated by an overwhelming 594 to six at a meeting of his association. Churchill reported to his wife that it was being said that 150 MPs of all hues were prepared to support MPs' rights of conscience against 'the intrigues of the Central Office'.[93] When the West

Essex Unionist Association meeting was finally held, although the debate lasted two and a half hours, of the 200 party members in the meeting, only 24 voted against Churchill. This silenced further opposition from within his constituency for the time being.

Meanwhile, Churchill's opinion of the government and its leaders had reached an all-time low. They were, he assured Clementine, 'like a great iceberg which has drifted into warm seas and whose base is being swiftly melted away, so that it must topple over. . . . You cannot run the British Cabinet system without an effective Prime Minister. The wretched Ramsay is almost a mental case – "he'd be far better off in a Home". Baldwin is crafty, patient and almost amazingly lazy.' In bemoaning the absence of someone with a 'commanding mind ranging over the whole field of public affairs' in his party, Churchill was looking for a leader who closely resembled himself, or failing that, Lloyd George. He thought Lloyd George wanted 'to come in and join' the Cabinet in a 'kind of War Cabinet' – one which Churchill would also be invited to join. This was not going to be immediately realizable. In any case, Churchill protested to his wife that he was 'disinclined to associate [himself] with any administration this side of the General Election'.[94] Hoare was still of the opinion that Churchill was 'determined to smash the National Government and believes that India is a good battering ram as he has a large section of the Conservative party behind him'.[95] According to Thomas Jones, Baldwin was adamant that Churchill should be excluded from entering the government and that 'the Party would resent taking him in', certainly before the general election.[96] Baldwin had already lifted him once out of the political wilderness (in 1924) and was in no rush to do so again.

Churchill told Clementine that both Lord Hugh Cecil* and his elder brother, Lord Salisbury, despite 'seemingly at the point of death, continue to exert themselves with unshakeable conviction . . . Of course the Government will get their beastly Bill through, but as the Princes will not come in, all the parts I have objected to will remain a dead letter.'[97] In May, Churchill asked Victor Raikes to give him a list of up to thirty MPs who 'had borne the brunt of voting and speaking' so that he could invite them to a dinner at Claridges that he was organizing for 'our team'.[98] The dinner was held on 31 May and attended by forty-one MPs, twelve peers and five others with Churchill proposing the toast to Salisbury as the Bill would shortly be passing up to the Lords.[99]

The Bill's report stage was completed on 30 May with Hoare almost

---

* The leading free trader within the Edwardian Conservative Party who had been Churchill's best man at his wedding to Clementine in 1908.

lamenting to Willingdon that the debates it produced always became duller once Churchill 'drifted away towards cocktail time'.[100] The Bill had 473 clauses and 16 schedules. During its passage it had spawned 1951 speeches (many of them by Hoare who had also answered 15,000 questions) filling 4000 pages of *Hansard* with 15.5 million words.[101] On 5 June 1935 Churchill finally conceded defeat on the third reading, lamenting that 'all the machinery, prestige, and loyalty of the Conservative party [had been] used contrary to its instincts and traditions'. Concluding his oration, he warned Hoare that 'in the crashing cheers which will no doubt hail his majority tonight, we pray there may not mingle the knell of the British Empire in the East'.[102] When he sat down, the chamber emptied, leaving Amery to address a much sparser audience. This reality was cruelly emphasized when his opening words, 'Here endeth the last verse of the last chapter of the Book of Jeremiah,' were met with the catcall, 'Followed, oddly enough by Exodus.' Eighty-four Conservatives and (for contrary reasons) 38 Labour members divided against the 386 government votes, ensuring the legislation's passage by a majority of 264. Two days after his last speech on the India Bill, Churchill was back in the Commons urging increased spending on the RAF. The following day, Ramsay MacDonald resigned as Prime Minister and Baldwin moved next door into Number 10.

The India Bill passed its second reading in the House of Lords on 20 June by 236 to 55, without a division on the third reading taking place. The Royal Assent was granted on 2 August. Yet a new dawn for the Raj did not rise with it. The central provision of the Government of India Act, the longest piece of legislation in British history, was effectively stillborn. Without the princes being prepared to enter the proposed federation, the active part of the legislation was largely confined to greater provincial autonomy, the principle of which even the diehards had not opposed. Initially, this did not worry Hoare, a politician whose ability to say one thing, do another and, if found out, manage to imply the compatibility of one to the other, led to his being more concerned with the concept of federation as a block to alternative advances than to its immediate realization. In this he was more cunning than his Cabinet colleagues, but inevitably his bluff would be called sooner or later. As a result, his unexecuted scheme melted away into irrelevance when the Second World War transformed the relationship between Britain and India and made a reality out of Indian aspirations for independence.

It is difficult to imagine that a fully operational federation would have prevented or subverted the reaction to events that the Second World War created in the subcontinent. The princes would not enter the federation to counterbalance the threat of the Congress Party. In any case, recession in

the countryside weakened the princes' power base and the government
increasingly began looking to the Muslim League as the counterweight to
Congress. The limited advances of 1935 strengthened Congress's position. War in 1939 made Congress even more of a threat and the 'Quit
India' campaign of 1942–3 when Japan was at the gates was dealt with
sternly. Economic factors were no less important than political ones.
India's role as a captive market for British manufactures had been on a
prolonged downward curve. In dislocating trade and encouraging import
substitution, the war speeded up the process. Furthermore, the war turned
India from one of Britain's major debtors into one of her major creditors.
This removed the previous concern of London financial interests that
control of the subcontinent was necessary in order to prevent her
defaulting on her debts. These considerations combined with the strain of
holding on to an increasingly fractious population set the timetable for
conceding Indian independence. Whatever the government's boasts at the
time, the 1935 Indian reforms did not work and did not save India for the
empire. Only in the cosmetic and sometimes artificial world of Westminster had the government really won the battle and even here Baldwin had
reason to thank with relief Captain David Margesson, the Chief Whip, to
whom he confided that he felt 'so close'.[103]

VI

History has not been kind to the diehards. Many of them were not
particularly thoughtful, inspiring or agreeable figures – although much the
same could be said of fellow Tory MPs who backed the Indian reforms.
Unwilling to accommodate the desires of politicized Indians for a greater
measure of control over their own lives, it is hard to see how the diehards'
proposal for limiting constitutional change to the further devolution of
power towards Indians in provincial government could have provided a
long-term framework in which the British Raj could have survived *and*
retained popular consent. Yet historians of inter-war politics have
dismissed the diehard campaign too casually. The diehards' primary
criticism of the National Government's proposals for the subcontinent
were proved to be well founded. They had always maintained that all-
India federation, the centrepiece of Hoare's strategy, was unworkable.
Events proved that on this, they were right. Nor were the diehards merely
one more example of the perennial 'awkward squad' with which every
administration has to contend. Even Hoare acknowledged that they had
more sympathizers than the division lists suggested, telling Willingdon
that the 'big majorities I have behind me in the debates are no guarantee
of the position. If it looked as if I was withholding information from the

House or misleading them upon essential matters, the Conservatives would go against me almost en masse.'[104] Outside the biographies of Churchill (and not even all of these), few published histories of the 1930s have devoted much space to the Indian diehard campaign. The issues raised were those that primarily concerned a small and politicized class in Westminster, the Home Counties and Lancashire. But if (like most political issues) they were not felt universally, their importance to those in positions of authority was crucial. Beyond its attempt to shape imperial policy, the diehard challenge threatened to destroy the careers of several Cabinet ministers and nearly undermined the whole balance of the National Government. Re-examining the private papers of the senior figures in the administration leaves the reader in no doubt that the diehards had them running scared. This was particularly the case when events in the subcontinent bolstered diehard arguments in Parliament; in March 1935, with the prospect of federation wholly discredited by the actions of leading Indian princes, the Cabinet wobbled and seemed on the verge of shelving the whole scheme. It is hard, in this light, to go along with the established consensus that the diehards were an irrelevant gang of losers with whom the government could always wipe the floor. When it came to being mobilized to vote against a three-line whip, there were more India diehards in the 1930s Conservative Party than there were anti-appeasers on foreign policy. It might be argued that the ultimate failure of appeasement proved the small band of anti-appeasers (many of them natural misfits) right and thus justified their being magnified in the lens of history far beyond the minority status they endured at the time. To this, it must be added that the government's India policy also failed to work. In little more than a decade Britain would lose India entirely. Diehards may not have had better solutions, but they said that the framework that Hoare attempted to construct could not hold up. On this, they were right. If history is written by the victors then, on Indian reform, it has been written by the pyrrhic victors.

The impressive performance of the diehard challenge against the full machinery and preferment of a seemingly impregnable National Government must, inevitably, lead us to reappraise the general consensus that Churchill's association with the diehards was a strategic blunder that sealed his fate in the political limbo. Churchill was the front man that the diehards needed and had so visibly lacked in their previous tussle with a coalition government over Ireland in 1921. This is not to say that he was fully trusted by them. His support was regarded as a mixed blessing, as the failure over the Hoare–Derby breach of Privileges case had demonstrated.[105] By the end of the campaign Lord Salisbury tended to share the fear of his nephew, Viscount Wolmer, that Churchill had become 'an awful incubus' to the diehards.[106] Nevertheless, political history is full of individuals who were doubtfully compatible with one another but who saw personal or ideological advantage in working for a common cause. Other prominent diehards, like the IDL. Parliamentary Secretary, Patrick Donner and Lord Lloyd, realized the debt they owed to Churchill's leadership.[107] A political opponent, the Liberal leader Sir Herbert Samuel, was probably closest to the mark when he claimed that if Churchill 'were not there to give leadership and energy and to form a centre for this movement, I believe that very little would have been heard of it from the beginning'.[108] Churchill's links with wealthy donors and, in particular, with the Duke of Westminster, were to prove a vital conduit of revenue for the campaign. The regularity in which Chartwell, Churchill's Kent country home, was used as the meeting forum for the diehards also confirms the centrality of his position within the group's structure.

In 1933 Churchill had prophesied to Austen Chamberlain that the India campaign would end the Cabinet careers of MacDonald, Baldwin, Hoare and Irwin. If this was his hope, then he had fallen well short of achieving this complement of scalps by the time of the final passage of the India Bill. Had Churchill improved his own political position nonetheless? Historians have been happy to fall into line behind Robert Rhodes James' analysis, one of the most influential commentaries on his efforts:

> The obvious losses from Churchill's lengthy campaign on the India issue can be swiftly assessed. By breaking with Baldwin in January 1931 he had forfeited a very substantial expectation of becoming a leading member of the National Government appointed in August. By his violent attacks on the Government for the following four years on this issue he had cut himself off from any consideration for inclusion while the struggle continued, and certainly did not assist his claim for office when it was ended. . . . What is more curious – if Churchill's egocentricity and obsession [with India] is forgotten – is the fact that Churchill was genuinely surprised by the rejection of his overtures after the passage of the Act. . . . It is impossible to extract anything of advantage in this lamentable struggle. Certainly the price exacted has been a bitter and an enduring one. Duff Cooper did not exaggerate when he described Churchill's resolve to fight the granting of Dominion Status to India as 'the most unfortunate event that occurred between the two wars.' For, by 1935, Hitler had come, and the uneasy fabric of European peace was crumbling ominously.[109]

Contrary to the analysis expressed above, as we saw in Chapter 3, Churchill's opposition to Baldwin over India was not the reason for his exclusion from the National Government. In this chapter we have seen how close Churchill came to forcing the government to climb down from a policy that proved ultimately to be a failure. In the following chapter we shall examine how the India campaign actually resurrected Churchill's case for inclusion in the Cabinet and go on to see how the India campaign aided his crusade to rearm Britain against Hitler.

Baldwin had gambled on linking the future of the National Government with the successful passage of the Indian reform legislation. For many, any price was worth paying if the administration was kept in power. In June 1934 more than a hundred Tory MPs had written to the press advocating that the cooperation between the component political parties within the National Government should become a permanent objective. In effect, this was to urge the case for 'fusion' into the sort of centre party which Austen Chamberlain had envisaged in 1922 or 'national party' for which Neville Chamberlain had hoped in 1931. It was as if Lord Randolph Churchill's call for a 'centre party' as far back as 1887 was being answered at last. The overwhelming majority of these signatories were those who had won their seat for the first time in the landslide conditions of 1931 and who could reasonably expect to be defeated in the next election if they could not again maximize the non-socialist vote.[110] Mainly representing safe seats, diehards were not amongst them. Indeed, the prospect of strengthening the bonds holding together the National Government ran wholly counter to the sectional interests of the Tory right. Before the political earthquake of 1931, they had expected representation in the next Conservative Government. Indeed, it was Baldwin who had at that time claimed that the wide spectrum of views from left to right amongst Conservatives meant that they alone could best 'hope to form a national party'.[111] This strategy had been jettisoned by the creation of the cross-party National Government. With MacDonald, Simon and Baldwin at its head, the Cabinet was composed of the former Labour and Liberal parties' right-wing refugees in alliance with the left and centre of the Conservative Party. This meant excluding from the government the Tory right wing despite the fact that with over eighty MPs, they had more parliamentary support than the National Labour and Liberal allies combined.

The diehard campaign over India failed to force the inclusion of Churchill in the government as its representative to counterbalance the more liberal elements. However, it scared the party leadership off moves to fuse the National forces together into a centre party. This was because Conservative Central Office dared not take action that would precipitate an irrevocable split with as many as eighty of its own MPs, most of whom represented large and wealthy constituency associations. This fear, combined with reluctance amongst the Liberal National and National Labour groups themselves, strengthened the hand of the Conservative

Party Chairman, Lord Stonehaven, to argue against submerging the Tory Party into a new centre 'National' party.[112] Thus, the diehards, and Churchill in particular, played their part in preserving the independent existence of the Conservative Party at a time when many of its leaders, including Neville Chamberlain, would have been prepared to see it submerged into a new broader organization.

This last point was ironic. Baldwin had actually contemplated resigning the Tory leadership once the India Bill had become law, believing that the diehards would not return to the party fold if he became Prime Minister. He foresaw that the only way to keep the diehards united to the party was if Neville Chamberlain took over for five years before giving way 'to a younger man'.[113] The problem with passing the baton to Chamberlain – as the Daily Telegraph's owner Lord Camrose warned Baldwin – was that the Liberal coalition partners might refuse to serve under him, ending the National coalition.[114] Thus, the diehard campaign failed to get rid of Baldwin despite the fact that he was prepared to step down in order that diehards might be reunited with the party, whilst Chamberlain, who had hoped to fuse all the National parties together, was not handed the Premiership because of the fear that he might drive the National parties apart. Far more extraordinary than bringing back Churchill, in 1935, Baldwin even considered offering a place to his eternal bête noir, Lloyd George, in the belief that doing so would demonstrate that the government had not run out of constructive ways of dealing with unemployment.

It is in this light that Churchill's strategy can be best understood. Like Lloyd George who believed his bargaining position would be stronger once the government's majority had been cut, Churchill warned the government that after the next general election had lost the Tories their northern marginal seats and returned the party to its southern English power base, the diehards would proportionately have a stronger voice. Churchill wrote to Willingdon's successor as Viceroy, Lord Linlithgow, 'As long as the Princes are not nagged and bullied to come into Federation, you need not expect anything but silence or help from us [i.e. the diehards]. We shall count more in the new Parliament than in this fat thing.'[115] Churchill saw the Indian issue, the cement which had bonded him to the diehard group, as likely to be less adhesive in the near future. Other issues would now dominate the group. Lloyd George hoped his crusade for economic reconstruction would remould British politics. But, with the economy recovering, it was events in continental Europe that promised to be more likely to shape the course of the next five years. On this front, Churchill, whose recreations suitably included building brick walls, was ready to campaign for the rebuilding of Britain's defence forces.[116] He had most of the diehards' support on this fresh crusade and appeared to be broadening his appeal to other sections of the Conservative Party as well. Far from being destroyed over India, he was still an indomitable obstacle in the way of the direction in which Baldwin and his government hoped to travel. Furthermore, on the defence of the realm, Churchill was making his stand on an issue even closer to the hearts of committed Tories than the future of India. With this fresh momentum building up behind Churchill's attack, it was Neville Chamberlain who now decided to act.

Eight

THE DEFENCE
OF THE REALM

I

It was not until the end of the 1920s that many of the most famous literary accounts of the Great War were published. Amongst those to reach the bookshelves between 1928 and 1930 were Sherriff's *Journey's End*, Blunden's *Undertones of War*, Remarque's *All Quiet on the Western Front*, Graves' *Goodbye to All That* and Sassoon's *Memoirs of an Infantry Officer*. The critique of the war came not only from those who had experienced it at the sharp end; those who gave the orders also felt that they had to account for themselves. As a counterweight to Churchill's magisterial *The World Crisis* published in five volumes between 1923 and 1931, Lloyd George and Lord (Sir Edward) Grey had come to view the war respectively as the product of overzealous militarism and excessive secret diplomacy. Best-sellers, Lloyd George's *War Memoirs*, published between 1933 and 1936, proved to be a publishing phenomenon.

On top of the sentiments expressed by these old combatants, socialists charged that the armaments trade itself – with a commercial interest in human misery – was partly to blame for what had happened. By putting an end to this form of capitalism, socialism would bring about an end to war. It was a contention which accompanied the familiar left-wing critique of military conflict as the inevitable by-product of imperialism and capitalist power politics. With these arguments in mind, undergraduates at the Oxford Union in 1933 famously declared that there were no circumstances in which they 'would fight for King and Country'. Appointing themselves to speak for the 'lost generation', this particular testament of youth provoked a degree of public controversy not usually sparked by proceedings on the floor of a student debating society. When Randolph Churchill went back up to Oxford in an attempt to get the motion expunged from the Union's records he was lucky to escape with his trousers still on. Pursued off the Union premises by a throng of angry young pacifists, he avoided indignity only by seeking sanctuary in a public lavatory, which as one of his pursuers later admitted was 'an odd place to keep your trousers on.' The pursuer in question was John Hackett, later General Sir John Hackett, MC, DSO and Bar.[1]

Whatever weight was given to the posturings of the young, a general reaction against the more strident manifestations of jingoism and power politics was discernible across the country and was mirrored in the language of the leading politicians. With the exception of the most pure socialists and the diehard right, there was widespread support for the League of Nations in Geneva, the international body established after the war. The forerunner to the United Nations, but in the early 1930s lacking the membership of both the United States and the Soviet Union, the League promised to find an alternative to the traditional methods of settling breakdowns in international diplomacy by providing a forum for arbitration, cooperation and collective security. Having opposed Britain's entry into war in 1914, the Prime Minister, Ramsay MacDonald, was well placed to demonstrate the government's commitment to fostering a more pacific world order.

The Labour Movement was firmly committed to internationalism. Although this was necessarily a vague concept, it drew upon a sense of the brotherhood of man and the detestation of the way in which national borders got in the way of class loyalties. Socialist internationalism was certainly distinct from liberal internationalism. The latter included the global free flow of capital, an evil which socialists believed had conspired to suffocate the life out of the 1931 Labour Government. In January 1933, Adolf Hitler became German Chancellor and began transforming his country from an economic tragedy into a humanitarian one. A Marxist sense of historical determinism led some on the left to see Hitler's coming to power as a temporary aberration which would only speed the counter-offensive of European socialism. In May 1933, Hitler suppressed Germany's free trade unions. In July a one-party state was created. In October the Labour Party met for its annual conference and voted in favour of complete British disarmament. In the event, or possibility, of war, the party committed itself to disable the economy and bring down the government with a general strike. The Labour Party leader, George Lansbury, a Christian pacifist, made his position absolutely clear, announcing that 'I would close every recruiting station, disband the Army and dismiss the Air Force. I would abolish the whole dreadful equipment of war and say to the world "Do your worst".'[2] Lansbury's concept of world socialism was further divorced from liberal internationalism in his initial mistrust of the League of Nations, which he saw as a tool of the old militarist powers (in large part meaning the liberal democracies, Britain and France). Only when Stalin entered the League in 1934 did the Labour left transform their position and begin campaigning for adherence to the counsels of Geneva as the cornerstone of British foreign policy – concomitantly making the Tory right regard the League with mounting suspicion.

The triumph of the pacifists in the Labour Party was to be a temporary phenomenon but it cast an evening shadow. It reinforced the National Government's determination to stick together in the face of the Labour alternative, and retarded the attempts of anti-appeasement socialists to be taken seriously by many pro-rearmament Conservatives. Labour scored a memorable victory over what had become a safe Conservative seat at a by-election in East Fulham in October 1933 and made gains in March 1934 in the London County Council elections. These advances may have been inspired not so much by guns as by butter (or at any rate hostility to the means test and the pressing need for affordable housing). However, Baldwin was amongst those Tories who interpreted them as electoral rebukes over the government's failure to achieve disarmament. What was true was that the results hammered home a clear message that large sections of the electorate were voting Labour regardless of the party's pacific defence and foreign policy and, in many cases, even welcomed the latter. This was not an environment in which Baldwin wanted to be seen as a trigger-happy Tory, oblivious to the higher moral challenge.

It is impossible to understand the psychological trauma of the period without comprehending the enormous cost to Britain of the Great War. The driving force behind the War Graves Commission, Sir Fabian Ware, calculated that if the British Empire's 921,000 dead were to march four abreast down Whitehall it would take three and a half days for the end of the queue to pass the Cenotaph. France had fared worse and in the years after the Armistice, a yet greater amount of iron seemed to have entered the soul of her political class as a result. The war had not, after all, been a one-off fall from grace but had followed Germany's previous and successful invasion of France in 1870. Four years of warfare on her soil had turned much of north-east France into a wasteland. This had been made worse in 1918 by the retreating German Army operating a scorched earth policy, stealing, into the bargain, 460,000 tons of French industrial material in order to re-establish it in Germany. The British and French decision to finance reconstruction on the back of reparations that Germany could not pay proved subject to immense criticism. Now generally regarded as a colossal mistake, it was at the time the most obvious way in which the western allies could afford the huge war debts they themselves had rung up in the course of the carnage. Although most of the reparations bill was never paid, by the time of its effective cancellation in 1932, it had become a source of serious discontent.

Whatever the residue of hostility amongst many Britons towards

Germany during the 1920s, the French more particularly felt need of protection from their eastern neighbour. Written into the Versailles Treaty were the clauses preventing Germany from possessing a military air force and limiting the tonnage of her armed fleet. She was permitted an army of only 100,000 men. This removal of Germany's offensive capability was intended to stimulate the corresponding disarmament of the victors. In 1925 Austen Chamberlain (who received the Nobel Peace Prize as a recognition of his work) brokered the Treaty of Locarno in which Belgium, France and Germany agreed to respect their existing borders with each other, with Italy and Britain acting as guarantors. For a while there was much optimistic talk of the 'spirit of Locarno'. Unfortunately, international guarantees are made solid by the signatories' ability to meet their obligations, not merely by the spirit in which they are signed. Britain had no effective field force in which to make such a continental commitment. Thus, she could only defend France without an effective army for as long as Germany was prevented from having an effective army with which to invade. The problem was that Germany wanted to break out of the limitations placed upon her armed forces. Despite promptings from London, France did not feel confident about reducing her armaments to levels corresponding to those of Germany. Complaining about being denied equality of rights, between September and December 1932, the German Weimar Government absented itself from the world disarmament talks in Geneva.

Ramsay MacDonald was particularly irritated by France's refusal to disarm. However, Britain's diplomatic bluff was successfully called when France agreed to disarm if Britain made a more substantial military commitment to France's defences. The pacifist left in Britain would not stomach a military pact. The empire-minded right (and most forcefully of all, the Empire Dominions themselves) would brook no continental commitment. The Treasury would not tolerate additional expense. When France pressed on, suggesting equality for Germany if she proved herself a good neighbour for the next four years, the new German leader, Hitler, chose his moment to take umbrage. On 14 October 1933, Germany walked out of the World Disarmament Conference and the following week exited from the League of Nations. Effectively pointless without German cooperation, the Disarmament Conference continued its deliberations until April 1934, carried on by the momentum of its own bureaucracy, frightened to stop travelling in hope for fear of the inevitable arrival in disappointment.

II

The Tory right wing had no obvious backbench spokesman on foreign affairs. Few of them had much confidence in the League of Nations, an organization to whose existence a number even took offence. Many rekindled a dislike for the French. Other right wingers equally keen to maintain Britain's isolation argued that this was best guaranteed by a strong France prepared to keep order on the continent and, if need be, keep Germany in check. This was the position held by Churchill who, in contrast to many of his colleagues, anticipated the problem of a resurgent Germany even before Hitler's ambitions had become more fully evident.

Churchill made his first major speech in the Commons on the subject on 23 November 1932. In a light-hearted vein, he mused that MacDonald had led British negotiations at the disarmament talks and that opposition to the Prime Minister was 'one of my most consistent themes'. Paying a rather token courtesy to the League of Nations as 'a priceless instrument of international comity', Churchill did not waste platitudes on the work of the Disarmament Conference. It would not work and rested only on the utopian unreality of 'the poor good people of the League of Nations Union' which was the British pressure group of enlightened folk committed to advancing Geneva's cause. Churchill took the view that Britain with its 'Imperial responsibilities ought to be very careful not to meddle improvidently ... in this tremendous European structure', whereby France watched over the interests of small countries like Belgium, Poland, Rumania, Czechoslovakia and Yugoslavia in the same way that the British Navy had protected small nations through its mastery of the seas. To undermine French security at the Disarmament Conference was to unsettle the territorial integrity of all these countries in the face of a re-emerging German militancy which, in direct conflict with the British Empire, would seek 'the restoration of lost territories and lost colonies'.[3]

Perhaps the most noticeable feature about these observations was the argument that, by not undermining the French, Britain could best be kept out of a continental conflagration. Churchill repeated this theme in subsequent speeches. Far from joining in the spirit animating those pressing for progress at the disarmament talks at Geneva, he exclaimed in the Commons 'Thank God for the French Army'. Britain, he went on to tell his constituents, should be sufficiently armed to be 'strong enough if war should come in Europe to maintain our effective neutrality, unless we should decide of our own free will to the contrary'. In contrast, MacDonald's aim of 'interfering on the continent and trying to weaken France and strengthen Germany, was a Socialist foreign policy'.[4] This belief that the problems of Europe were the province of French policy was far removed from the generally anti-French tone of considered opinion at the time. Ironically, in this confused situation, to be pro-French on Churchill's terms was to be open to a charge from a Liberal MP, Geoffrey Mander, that 'he and his friends are really a lot of miserable Little Englanders'.[5] Churchill's desire to see a degree of British rearmament also ran against the grain of those pro-Geneva Conservatives who were still hoping for multilateral disarmament, like Anthony Eden, who decried Churchill's unconstructive quips and arguments for armed isolation.[6]

The brutal Japanese invasion of the Chinese province of Manchuria in 1931 presented the first serious challenge to confront the member states of the League of Nations. The response did not bode well for their collective effectiveness on the international stage. When the League condemned the method of the Japanese action, the Japanese merely left the League and carried on as before. Short of an all-out war, there was not much, in any case, that the international community (in military terms the fleets of Britain and France) could do about it, unless the United States wished to cut off all its dealings with Tokyo as well. Of its own volition, the USA was not a member of the League and had no intention of getting embroiled in some half-hearted measure, let alone a wholehearted one. Indeed, Manchuria was hardly a model state, China's nominal rule leaving much to be desired. Both Churchill and the grand old man of Conservative foreign policy, Sir Austen Chamberlain, were amongst those Tories who were at first broadly sympathetic to Japan's attempt to stabilize her interests in that volatile part of the world. Leo Amery even hoped that by concentrating on pickings from the Chinese territories like Manchuria, Japan would be diverted and satiated, and consequently pose no expansionary threat to the sphere of influence in the area of Britain and her Dominions. Unfortunately, if Manchuria was not a model state, then neither was Japan's occupation. Whatever the interpretation of her motives and her intervention in China, there was considerable agreement in London that Tokyo's ambitions posed a real threat in the Pacific and Australasia. If Japan was suddenly to launch a strike, the British bases in Singapore and Hong Kong were ill equipped to offer solid resistance. Indeed, already in 1932 the Committee of Imperial Defence was being informed by the Chiefs of Staff that all of Britain's possessions in the Far East were vulnerable, 'as well as the coastline of India and the Dominions and our vast trade and shipping, [lie] open to attack'.[7] Prior to Hitler's consolidation of power in Germany, it was understandable that Britain's first strategic requirement should be the defence of her empire, rather than the balance of power in central and eastern Europe.

The commitment to prioritize imperial defence had two main consequences. In the first place it ensured that defence resources were directed towards that goal and not the French objective of a European continental commitment to contain Germany. Secondly, the attitude of the Dominions suggested that they did not intend to back Britain up if she should declare war on the European continent. This remained broadly the Dominions' general attitude at least up until late in 1938. Forcing a breach in this unity would have badly disrupted the British Empire as an entity in international affairs. Instead, the Cabinet agreed to gradually reinforce the defences of Britain's base at Singapore, the linchpin port for the Royal Navy to guard Australasia. The effect of these changes was more symbolic than practical and during 1933 the £5 million increase in defence spending only brought the figures back in line with the already low figures of 1931.

III

The strain caused by the financial crisis of 1931 dictated not only the complexion of the political combination that would hold power for the rest of the decade in Britain but also underpinned the rationale of its foreign policy. In March 1932 the Treasury responded to the Chiefs of Staff review by stating that policy should look towards creating a 'period of recuperation, diminishing taxes, increased trade and employment'. Military commitments threatened the reverse and therefore 'today's financial and economic risks are far the most serious and urgent that the country has to face.'[8]

In Neville Chamberlain, the Treasury had found a champion. The Chancellor of the Exchequer was determined to bring the nation's finances into order, without which any militaristic adventure would be precarious. Churchill at the Exchequer between 1924 and 1929 had cut defence budgets mercilessly – the Admiralty in particular bearing the brunt of his assault – but this had been in a world in which Germany was virtually disarmed and Japan a recent ally. In such an environment, the 'ten-year rule', in which the British Government worked on the assumption that it would be embroiled in no major conflict for a decade, was understandable, if optimistic. This confidence was not to last, and even before the re-emergence of the German threat, by 1932 British strategists had, as we have seen, found cause for concern in the Far East. The dispatch of British troops to Shanghai to foil aggressive Japanese encroachments convinced the Cabinet in March 1932 to abandon the ten-year rule. Neville Chamberlain's immediate response was to present Treasury figures for defence estimates lower than at any time since the Great War.

Even if the Foreign Office had wished to exert military influence in Europe, the Chiefs of Staff reported in October 1933 that the British

Army was in no position to fight a continental war against Germany. Considering there were only two divisions that could be immediately dispatched to such a conflict, this was hardly a pessimistic conclusion. Importantly, however, and despite his natural prudence, it was Neville Chamberlain who was amongst the first to argue that the military risks to Britain had at last overtaken the financial ones.[9] A Defence Requirements Committee (DRC) was established as a subcommittee of the Committee of Imperial Defence (CID). There being no single Defence Minister, the CID was advised by the three service Chiefs of Staff and coordinated by the Cabinet itself. On the new DRC sat the Chiefs of Staff with Sir Robert Vansittart, permanent Under-Secretary at the Foreign Office, and Chamberlain's adviser, Sir Warren Fisher, the experienced Permanent Secretary at the Treasury and head of the civil service. Sir Maurice Hankey was appointed to chair the new DRC to coincide with his other roles as Secretary both to the CID and the Cabinet.

This was the arrangement within which Chamberlain's control over defence priorities grew immeasurably. After February 1934 the Cabinet accepted Fisher's recommendation that they should only receive proposals for defence expenditure once they had already been fully reviewed by the Chancellor of the Exchequer. Together with Lord Hailsham at the War Office, Sir Bolton Eyres-Monsell, the First Lord of the Admiralty, was appalled that the latest idea for coordinating defence requirements was to place them in the care of the Treasury – of *all* departments.[10] This was a great gain for Chamberlain who, as described in Chapter 4, had already extended his authority into most of the domestic departments as well.

The Defence Requirements Committee refocused British defence policy towards viewing Germany as the most likely international troublemaker. Meanwhile in order to prevent Britain succumbing to strategic overreach, the balance in the Pacific should be maintained by trying to re-establish an understanding with Japan. Discussing proposals in May 1934, the Cabinet considered the case for committing an expeditionary force to the defence of the Low Countries in the event of their invasion by Germany. The Low Countries had a historic strategic significance given their proximity to the Channel and Britain's maritime defence. Now their defence was argued to be vital since they provided forward bases for the RAF to strike Germany's economic vertebrae of the Ruhr.[11] Despite the Cabinet's general approval for avoiding a European commitment, Baldwin, mindful of the range of German bomber aircraft, told the Commons in July 1934 that 'when you think of the defence of England you no longer think of the chalk cliffs of Dover; you think of the Rhine. That is where our frontier lies.'[12] The statement, issued as part of Baldwin's commendation of proposals to increase spending on the Royal

Air Force, was a thinly veiled reassurance aimed towards the French to the effect that German violation of her border (or perhaps even German remilitarization of the Rhineland) was for Britain an act justifying war. This followed the announcement that the Foreign Secretary, Sir John Simon, had made to the Commons earlier in the month that 'the integrity of Belgium is no less vital to the interests and safety of this country today than it has been in times past'.[13] Considering that Britain had declared war on Belgium's behalf in 1914 this was a weighty judgement. However, other Cabinet ministers, notably Chamberlain and Lord Halifax (the former Viceroy, Lord Irwin), dissuaded Simon from giving the Belgians what they wanted: an automatic guarantee. These ministers feared that consequent military discussions would be seen as a reversion to the sort of military alliances that had ended up in the Great War.

The government's stated preference was for international agreements that were inclusive of traditional enemies rather than the reconstruction of pacts that were designed to recreate the old enmities. In consequence, France's attempt to build an 'Eastern Locarno', binding France and the Soviet Union to guarantee each other as well as Poland, Czechoslovakia and the Baltic states against German invasion, was modified with Britain's agreement, to include equal guarantees to come to the aid of Germany against invasion from any of the signatories. If implemented, the scheme would effectively settle as final the borders of eastern Europe. For more than one potential signatory this was its drawback. Neither Poland nor Germany was happy to do anything that involved making guarantees with Stalin. Indeed the whole notion of settling the boundaries of eastern Europe on their existing lines ran counter to Hitler's objectives.

Events then moved in quick succession. The publication in London of a modest acceleration of the spending programme in the government's Defence White Paper of 4 March 1935 allegedly rendered Hitler speechless – which, if true, would have been no small achievement in itself. He soon recovered and retaliated by announcing that, in breach of the Versailles Treaty, a German air force was being built. In fact, the Luftwaffe had been covertly under construction for some time – as Britain and France well knew. This was followed on 16 March with the news that conscription was being introduced and a German army of half a million men created. Two days later, it was Chamberlain who again took the lead when the Cabinet discussed what to do in the light of these developments. He pressed Simon to tell Hitler frankly that if Germany did not accept the French offer of mutual guarantees with the Reich's main eastern neighbours, the consequence would be a Europe of armed camps and pacts. 'Hitler's Germany is the bully of Europe,' Chamberlain wrote; 'it will be necessary for Simon to talk plainly in Berlin.'[14]

After meeting the *Führer*, Simon was depressed to find that far from a multilateral guarantee, Hitler wanted the reverse: rearmament, no collective security, Germany's eastern borders to bring Germans living in the countries of eastern Europe back within the Reich and the return of former colonies that as a result of Versailles had passed to British administration. This was not good news. However, Hitler re-emphasized his desire not to compete with Britain for naval supremacy or meddle in the affairs of her empire. He also highlighted Britain's other great fear, aerial bombing, as an area where agreement might be possible. The French proceeded to draw their own conclusions from Hitler's refusal to accept as final the borders of his eastern neighbours. Consequently, France signed a mutual alliance with the Soviet Union, an unholy marriage which shocked the Tory right wing at Westminster. Rather more casual about the sanctity of the national borders of eastern European countries that had only been around for fifteen years, the British Government's policy concentrated upon reaching agreement with Berlin on the prevention of a naval race and the horrors of strategic bombing. Without first ascertaining the views of the French on the proposals, Simon's last act as Foreign Secretary was to sign on 6 June 1935 the Anglo-German Naval Agreement under which Germany bound herself to build a fleet no larger than 35 per cent of the tonnage of the Royal Navy. By now the Versailles Treaty placed on Germany all the constraining features of a teabag. The British, however, had no desire to start another naval race comparable to that which had preceded the Great War. By limiting the German presence on the seas it was felt that the Royal Navy could thereby cope with the growing menace of Japan towards the British and Dominion interests in Australasia. Over air-force limitation, Hitler was now to prove less accommodating.

IV

Outside law and order operations on the fringe of her empire, Britain had every reason to want air-force limitation. The Royal Air Force was only the fifth or sixth largest in the world. In 1923, the RAF's planners had suggested that fifty-two squadrons were needed to defend Britain from attack. It was a sign of the times that the requirement had not been fully implemented and that it was based on the assumption that the attack would come not from Germany (which as a result of Versailles had no air force) but from Britain's increasingly nominal ally, France. The realization that Hitler was covertly building up the *Luftwaffe* with the capacity to strike both the easily exposed and densely populated London as well as Britain's industrial heartlands now increased public alarm and called for a vigorous reappraisal. Baldwin had already added official voice to these fears in 1932 when he told the House of Commons with complete fatalism that there 'was no power on earth' that could protect the British people from being obliterated from the skies since 'the bomber will always get through'.[15] From June 1934, estimates of the bombing damage that the *Luftwaffe* could inflict upon British cities reached apocalyptic proportions. Mindful of the perceived hostility of the electorate to arms spending other than to specific measures to counter what Baldwin called 'the semi-panic conditions which existed now about the air' (a semi-panic that his comments had helped fuel), the Cabinet ignored the objections of Lord Hailsham at the War Office about the state of the army in order to back RAF funding instead.[16] Such was the public fixation about a future in which war would be conducted in the air on the helpless multitudes below that when Baldwin came to discuss the new defence programme in the Commons, the measures for the air force were the only ones that he mentioned.

Chamberlain was the most important proponent of concentrating defence spending on the air force rather than the army. During 1934 he backed up this strategy by arguing that the public would only understand funding those areas of the armed forces most obviously committed to the nation's defence. Protection from aerial attack and maintaining maritime supply and communication channels were the most obvious necessities in this respect. Funding the full £76 million five-year package proposed by the Defence Requirements Committee was far beyond the means of the Exchequer. After all it also had to meet the desire before the next election came to cut taxes and restore the public sector cuts made by the austerity Budget of 1931. This was a point of concern not only to the Chancellor of the Exchequer, but also to Baldwin and MacDonald during the summer of 1934.[17] Baldwin suggested solving this problem by creating a defence loan, but borrowing of this kind was immediately slapped down in a memorandum from Chamberlain as 'the broad road that leads to destruction'. The Chancellor reminded his Cabinet colleagues that 'it was necessary to cut our coat according to the cloth'.[18] Chamberlain was well placed in the Cabinet to take the lead in subverting the resource requests of rearmament into a framework that did not further unbalance the books. In this, he got his way, reducing the DRC's £76 million figure for defence spending down to £50 million. Instead of the recommendation that spending on the army over the next five years should reach £40 million, only £19 million was to be provided. An army funded on this derisory scale could not participate meaningfully on the continent and foreign policy would have to reflect this fact accordingly. In effect, the

Chancellor was advertising the strategic outlook that would make appeasement inevitable later in the decade.

The army's loss was to be the RAF's gain, with Chamberlain seeking to confront Britain's vulnerability from attack from the air. Fighter technology was still at a primitive stage, with the first prototypes for the Hawker Hurricane only getting airborne by the end of 1935. In view of this, priority was particularly given to the RAF's bomber capacity in an expression of faith in the preventative medicine of mutually assured destruction. With this in mind, Chamberlain argued for increasing the number of RAF squadrons to eighty. On 10 July 1934, the Cabinet subcommittee had been informed that at present only five RAF squadrons had reserves, a disturbing observation which prompted the Secretary of State for the Colonies, Sir Philip Cunliffe-Lister, to suggest that 'there was no necessity to inform the House of Commons what the actual state of the war reserves was.' The subcommittee's report made bleak reading. Without the addition of a further £10 million, the RAF would be able to sustain a war footing for no more than a fortnight.[19] A week later, the Cabinet agreed to 'Scheme A', which at the cost of £20 million proposed to double the number of the British-based squadrons to eighty-four by March 1939, roughly equal to what it was anticipated the *Luftwaffe* would have. With Scheme A approved, it was not long before the German air strength estimate was reassessed – upwards.

The public's fear of the bomber aircraft and the strategic implications involved in prioritizing the German threat ahead of that of the Japanese, were powerful motors driving the National Government's defence allocation policy. An extra incentive came from the wing of the Conservative Party not represented in the Cabinet, and from the irrepressible Winston Churchill in particular.

Churchill had been Air Minister in the Lloyd George coalition government from 1919 to 1921 and had retained an interest in air technology. He had strongly deprecated Baldwin's claim that the 'bomber would always get through', loftily reminding the leader of his party on the floor of the Commons that 'the responsibility of Ministers to guarantee the safety of the country from day to day, and from hour to hour, is direct and inalienable.'[20] Churchill proceeded to write an article for the *Daily Mail* arguing for the redevelopment of the RAF in the event of the Geneva disarmament talks' failure.[21]

The immediate response of his detractors to Churchill's latest campaign was to wonder whether it was another stunt designed with self-promotion in mind. In supporting Churchill's speech against disarmament at the Conservative Party Conference in October 1933, Amery noted in his diary 'that there were those in the audience who knew how hard

[Churchill] had fought to weaken the Navy both as Home Secretary and more recently as Chancellor of the Exchequer. I was near Car Bridgeman and could not help reminding her that Willie [her husband – the former First Lord of the Admiralty] and I had had to threaten resignation together to stop Winston's onslaught.'[22] It was not long before the emergence of the scale of Britain's defence deficiencies encouraged Amery to build bridges with Churchill, being 'only too willing to work with him if he would throw himself on the defence and imperial side of things and give India a rest'.[23] In fact, their differences on India did not noticeably weaken their attack on the government's defence preparations; if anything they strengthened the assault by conducting it in the form of a synchronized pincer movement from different sides. None of the five Conservative MPs who in November 1934 signed Churchill's Commons amendment calling for increased air rearmament was an India diehard; indeed two of them were actively involved in the pro-Indian reform camp.[24] Here was an example of how the cross-currents created over the diehards' campaign did not prevent understandings with other Conservatives on different issues. Indeed, the very nature of the cross-currents was to contribute to the government's nervousness. Whilst the Conservative Party caucus was with considerable effort being prevented from declaring for the India diehards, a motion from the diehards' leaders – Lord Lloyd and Churchill – calling for British rearmament was passed unanimously at the 1933 Party Conference. Amidst what the event's annual report described as 'scenes of great enthusiasm', Churchill told the delegates that they needed to 'give a strong indication to the government that a change must now be made'. Noting that none of the armed service ministers was in attendance and knowing their feelings about the restraints upon their departments, he mischievously told the delegates that the ministers would 'welcome a feeling that the party as a whole wished to see the defences put into better order in the dangerous times of to-day'.[25]

Sensing that the government was still moving too slowly, the 1934 Party Conference passed the same motion that it had advocated the previous year. This was a thinly disguised rebuke from the party caucus and one that had to be either crushed or accepted. This time Chamberlain decided to call a spade a spade, conceding that although it was true that imperial defence 'had reached a dangerously low level', this was not the fault of the current administration but instead was 'due to the deliberate policy of successive Governments for the last eight and a half years. That includes the last Conservative Government when the Chancellor of the Exchequer was Mr Churchill.' With Churchill away, holidaying in the eastern Mediterranean, Chamberlain then wryly invited the resolution's mover to add to his motion Churchill's words about placing national security above other benefits so that the mover 'could pay a compliment to his absent colleague, Mr Churchill'.[26]

It was noted towards the end of Chapter 7 that a number of politicians and historians have argued that the Indian campaign injured Churchill's ability to mount an effective campaign for rearmament.[27] This was not how some of those in authority saw it at the time. The Military Assistant-Secretary to the Committee of Imperial Defence, Colonel Pownall, recorded in his diary for 30 July 1934 'it is extraordinary the effect of (so called) public opinion, the press and the Lord Lloyd–Churchill group on the minds of Ministers. It is slow working perhaps, but if continued it has inevitable effects.'[28] Indeed, Pownall was concerned that although the movement was helping the RAF, this was too much at the expense of the other armed forces. That afternoon, Baldwin made his Commons announcement that in view of the importance of the aeroplane, Britain's defences were on the Rhine, not the chalk cliffs of Dover. Indeed, the belief that Churchill's diehardism undermined his call for rearmament presumes that diehards and rearmers were not only different but irrevocably contradictory constituencies. Yet certainly before the Abyssinian crisis of 1935–6 brought into immediate question the manner in which Britain should involve herself in major international disputes with the dictators, there was no pressing division on foreign policy between different Tory advocates of rearmament nor did any prominent diehard oppose the campaign to rearm. During 1935 Baldwin became aware that the Executive Committee of the India Defence League wanted formally to widen the scope of their organization 'to include not only India but also all Imperial questions including Defence and the general maintenance of Conservative Principles'.[29] This was very worrying for the government, implying permanent opposition within the Tory Party from the right wing even if they could be defeated on their original Indian battleground. As the most prominent spokesman on both India and rearmament, Churchill seemed to be at the forefront of a yet more menacing organization, creating for the National Government the conditions of the pressure cooker. If it was too late to make concessions on India, then it was sensible for the government to let out some of the steam on rearmament.

The government's leeway to make concessions on rearmament to the Tory right wing was facilitated by Churchill himself. Whilst doggedly keeping up the pressure on India where compromise had become politically impossible, his tactics on defence were consciously less confrontational. Armed by information supplied from public servants (in breach of the Official Secrets Act),[30] Churchill sought to demonstrate that the government's figures on the supposedly embryonic *Luftwaffe* were serious underestimates. Aware that Germany was illegally building an air force, the government found it actually quite useful to have Churchill telling the world these uncomfortable truths. Before his amendment to the Address of 28 November 1934, Churchill wrote to Baldwin outlining the general line he intended to take.[31] He repeated this conciliatory course of action sending a full Memorandum to Baldwin on 28 April 1935 with 'the main outline of the case which I propose to unfold to the House when the promised debate on Air Estimates takes place in the early part of May'.

Yet Churchill was not just a public megaphone trying to take the credit for what the government was slowly getting round to doing anyway. His repeated requests for the government to come off the fence proved, as the Cabinet minutes make clear, that he was an annoyance to those ministers who wanted to scale down the pace of rearmament. Preparing for Churchill's amendment on air defence in the Commons in November 1934, Simon drew attention to:

> the speech made by Mr Winston Churchill in the House of Commons on 30th July last, and in particular to the series of questions which Mr Churchill had then asked in regard to German rearmament and more especially to her air rearmament. He (the Secretary of State) in winding up the Debate had evaded these questions, but Mr Churchill had made it clear that he proposed to revive the subject next week and on this occasion he would, no doubt, press for specific replies to his questions. Were the Government prepared to state in the Debate as a fact that the Treaty of Versailles is not being complied with? If so, they must also be prepared to state what further steps they contemplated.[32]

Simon was concerned that Churchill might damage Anglo-German relations and he hoped to apologize to the German Ambassador for being unable to prevent the debate from taking place. The Cabinet agreed with Hoare that Baldwin should counter Churchill's figures directly whilst holding on to the momentum of steady rearmament. The attempt by the Air Staff to bounce the Cabinet into bringing forward the completion of 'Scheme A' from 1939 to 1936 was blocked, however, by Chamberlain, who maintained that 'there was nothing in our information in regard to German preparedness to justify the proposed acceleration'. He reminded his colleagues that rather than wasting money, the financial balance 'was a serious one and he felt bound to warn the Cabinet against incurring any fresh commitments'.[33]

Churchill was now calling for the strengthening of scientific research into defence measures against bombers. He alleged in a Commons amendment to the Address that on current projections the *Luftwaffe* would be double the size of the RAF during 1937 and that it should become government policy over the next decade to maintain an air force larger than that of Germany. Lloyd George's secretary and intimate, Frances Stevenson, viewing the debate from the Gallery, wrote in her diary that when Churchill sat down he received 'almost an ovation' since there was 'no doubt that [his] line greatly pleased the Tory Party'.[34] Whilst disagreeing with Churchill's figures and maintaining that the *Luftwaffe* was currently less than half the size of the RAF, Baldwin salvaged the situation for the government by agreeing to an extra 300 first-line aircraft to maintain the RAF's superiority. He announced to the Commons that 'in air strength and in air power this country shall no longer be in a position inferior to any country within striking distance of these shores.'[35] Sir Samuel Hoare recorded for the benefit of the Indian Viceroy that this concession halted Churchill's attempt 'to bring on to the centre of the stage and to gather round him the very many people who are worried about German rearmament and what they believe to be the weakness of the Air Force'. Hoare nonetheless concluded that it was a relief that Churchill had not been answered upon the technicalities by the armed forces ministers since Churchill 'would have scored heavily'.[36]

Churchill's rearmament campaign got no support from the opposition parties. The leader of the Liberal Party, Sir Herbert Samuel, had already complained that Churchill's 'blind and causeless panic' in favour of building up the RAF resembled more 'the language of a Malay running amok than a responsible British statesman'.[37] Strident appeals for rearmament appalled liberal thinkers across the country as well as in Parliament. In contrast, Churchill's campaign to ensure that, whatever arms limitation might be achieved, the RAF must have at least parity, was a political triumph within the Conservative Party. This was the forum that mattered most to him. What he was proposing was not contrary to government policy, but rather a call to speed up its implementation. Thus, unlike over India, Churchill could champion a popular campaign whilst protesting support for the government.

Baldwin's assurance to the Commons of 28 November 1934 that Britain was still well ahead in the air race and the impression he gave that this would continue to be the case for some considerable time, had kept the momentum with the government. To this was added an extra £10 million on defence spending in the White Paper of 4 March 1935. Only six days after the Air Under-Secretary had accused Churchill of exaggerating German air strength figures in the Commons, Hitler, with impeccable timing, informed the Foreign Secretary, Sir John Simon, that the *Luftwaffe* had actually surpassed the size of the RAF already. Hitler was lying but this was not at first clear to informed opinion back in London. Almost immediately, the news of the *Führer*'s announcement played into Churchill's hands, making him appear better briefed on the comparative air strengths than the humiliated government. These events only further underlined his call to rearm quickly. Writing triumphantly to his wife, Churchill confided that 'a good many of those who have opposed me on India now promised support on this'.[38] Events looked brighter still when the *Daily Telegraph* published wildly inaccurate statistics that appeared to show that the *Luftwaffe's* front-line strength was now double that of the RAF.[39] Looking for support and seeking to gain influence for his views, Churchill wired several politicians encouraging them to read the *Daily Telegraph's* article. These nine politicians were not just the Liberals – Lloyd George, Sir Archibald Sinclair and General Seely – but also those he was gaining support from: his Tory ex-coalitionist colleagues Sir Austen Chamberlain and Sir Robert Horne, together with Lord Winterton and Frederick Guest and the India diehards Sir Henry Page Croft and Lord Wolmer. Churchill could therefore be forgiven for mentioning in the course of the Commons debate on 2 May that Baldwin's statement of November 1934 claiming that Germany's air-force size was half that of the British, and the Air Under-Secretary's assertion of March 1935 that the RAF would still retain superiority by the end of 1936, 'made in the most sweeping manner and on the highest authority, are now admitted to be entirely wrong'.[40]

By the summer of 1935, with the India debacle rounded off, the rearmament issue placed in Churchill's hands a number of valuable cards. With a little help from Hitler, he had made the government look dangerously under-prepared. Keeping Churchill excluded from the discipline of government therefore presented difficulties for Baldwin. Having at last succeeded MacDonald as Prime Minister in June 1935, he did not want to have to face from Churchill a further assault, launched with less public abuse but no less subversion than over India. Furthermore, an opportunity to make peace with Churchill seemed to be made easier by the latter's developing enthusiasm for the League of Nations which was perfectly suited to the government's new window dressing for foreign policy.

With a general election due in 1936, changes were made in the Cabinet reshuffle that Baldwin announced in June 1935. The main alteration was the removal of Simon from the Foreign Office, where he had been regarded as a failure by all wings of the party, although not always for the same reasons. With his no-nonsense approach to international negotiations, Chamberlain had at one point been regarded as the front runner for Simon's replacement as Foreign Secretary, but Baldwin decided to keep his housekeeper where he was. Instead, the Foreign Office was given to the long-suffering architect of the Government of India Act, Sir Samuel Hoare. With Conservatives now occupying 10 Downing Street, the

Treasury and the Foreign Office, efforts had to be made to maintain the appearance of a 'National' Cabinet. Simon, therefore, was given the Home Office together with the Leadership of the House. MacDonald took on Baldwin's previous position as Lord President despite a level of physical and mental incapacity that made the appointment border on cruelty – and not just to MacDonald. A smattering of other Liberal National and National Labour politicians held other Cabinet positions.[41] It was significant that independently minded senior Conservatives on the backbench who had loyally supported the government on India, like Leo Amery and Sir Austen Chamberlain, were not rewarded with office. At the same time, with the India legislation only just out of the way, a recall for Churchill would have been premature. However, he felt he could expect that, once the approaching general election was out of the way, it would be acknowledged that he had earned himself a Cabinet place both as a sop to the diehard wing of the party as well as a recognition of his popular campaign in the party for rearmament. This would be even more likely if, as was being touted, the National Government was returned at the polls but with a much smaller majority: a cue for which Lloyd George was also waiting in the wings. In the meantime the omens were good. Only the month after the conclusion of the India Bill, Baldwin asked Churchill to join the new Air Defence Research Committee. Having secured the new Prime Minister's agreement that acceptance would not prevent him from speaking out in public on the issue (in other words, that it was not a gag like the India Joint Select Committee), Churchill gladly accepted what was the first formal invitation to participate in an organ of government since he had left office in the election defeat of 1929.

Anticipating a happy conclusion to his years in the wilderness, Churchill did everything to repay the favour Baldwin at last appeared to be showing him. Far from joining five diehard MPs who wrote to Baldwin resigning the party Whip,[42] he and Page Croft now spoke openly of wishing to see the National Government continuing into a new Parliament, with Churchill favouring going to the country in the autumn.[43] No better manifestation of his desire to be seen to be at one with the leadership can be found than at the pre-election Conservative Party Conference at Bournemouth in October. His amendment was unanimously passed, stating that it was 'the duty of His Majesty's Government forthwith to repair the serious deficiencies in the defence forces' and that the conference supported 'any financial measures which may be necessary for the national safety, no matter how great the sacrifices may be'. Thereupon, he delighted the delegates by praising Baldwin as 'a statesman who has gathered to himself a greater volume of confidence and goodwill than any public man I recollect in my long career'. Baldwin responded that he rejoiced that the differences he had experienced with the diehards, and with Churchill in particular, were now 'at an end'.[44]

If anything, it was not the prospect that Churchill might be unpopular that ruled out his return but rather, almost regardless of the India schism, it was his strengths that made Baldwin uneasy about bringing him back. As we shall see, Baldwin specifically opposed the public promotion of comprehensive rearmament in 1935 which both Churchill and Chamberlain wanted to see underpinning the Conservative election campaign. Churchill's bad judgement and individualistic temperament were the most frequently quoted reasons for Baldwin and Chamberlain's desire to exclude him from the Cabinet 'team'. However, both these men had reason to fear that Churchill's call for rearmament, in being broadly popular both to the parliamentary party and to the caucus, might lead to his re-emergence as a contender for power. It is with this qualification that we should temper the observation of one Churchill biographer, John Charmley, in his analysis that rearmament 'provided the means for a rapprochement between him and the Party leaders'.[45] In any case, the party leadership did not yet know whether it was the discipline of a coming general election alone that was producing a new spirit of loyalty in Churchill. What he would do once the threat of a Labour administration receded remained to be seen. In the meantime, however, his claim to rehabilitation had to be considered, if postponed.

V

With unemployment falling steadily (in August it fell below two million for the first time since 1930) and by-election swings to Labour much reduced, Baldwin left 10 Downing Street for his annual summer holiday in Aix-les-Bains having still not decided when to call an election. Chamberlain, who resolutely supported the continuation of the National coalition, was frustrated by this, noting that the Prime Minister was 'in the condition that usually overtakes him at this time of year, when he is quite unable to set his mind to anything or even to listen to what you say'.[46] Baldwin certainly had much to weigh up in his mind. The approach of a general election begged questions about the purpose and continuation of the National Government as an entity. Although non-Tories still continued to play a part, it was now clearly dominated by Conservatives in the Cabinet as it always had been in Parliament. With the Indian legislation on the statute book, there was no obvious manifestation of liberal/centre-left input into policy. Furthermore, if the government had been formed to tackle the crisis of an endangered currency and an unbalanced budget, and had won the 1931 election on the grounds that it had not completed its rescue mission, then this excuse could surely not still be employed in 1935. Chamberlain's budget in April had brought income tax back down and completed the task of redressing the cuts made in 1931. The currency was now relatively stable. The budget was as balanced as the Treasury was content for it to be. On the criteria that it had set itself in August 1931, there was no case for prolonging the National Government's existence. However, when it suited the Tory high command, wholly different conclusions to these questions could be made just as easily. After all, what positive purpose was served by shaking off MacDonald's National Labour and Simon's Liberal National addition to the Tory majority, especially since in any case they clearly no longer determined the course of government policy contrary to the aims of the Conservative leadership? But if the National Government could no longer be credibly seen as the only possible bulwark to stand between Britain and financial catastrophe, could it not instead be portrayed as the only combination that could stand up to the totalitarian menace in Europe? Indeed, contrasted to the disarray within the Labour Party and the spread of extremism abroad, could not the National Government be seen as the very epitome of Britons keeping their heads when all about them in Europe were losing theirs? If so, who better to portray this state of affairs than the honest, pipe-smoking Stanley Baldwin?

The decision to make foreign affairs the centrepiece of the National Government's rejuvenation presented Baldwin with an opportunity. Whatever he did on this score would have to be seen to command the adherence of the (supposedly) liberal middle ground. The National Government had made it easier for Baldwin's moderate brand of Conservatism to hold the ascendancy over the Tory Party and in capturing the floating liberal vote in the country it had greatly boosted the parliamentary majority. With Herbert Samuel's Liberal Party having crossed the floor to join Lloyd George on the opposition benches in 1933, Baldwin had every reason to fear that much of the liberal vote would not stay with the National Government as it had in 1931. The 1933 World Economic Conference had scuppered any realistic expectation of an international return to free trade, curtailing the Liberal Party's traditional *raison d'être* in economic policy accordingly. Whilst a return to multilateral freeing up of world trade remained a central tenet of the Liberal programme, the Covenant of the League of Nations had replaced the shibboleth of free trade as the focus for liberal internationalism. Consequently, it was important that the government give the impression that it too was a signed-up supporter of Geneva. In June 1935 the Lord Privy Seal, Anthony Eden, was moved to the freshly created Foreign Office position of Minister for the League of Nations. Eden was young, dashing, a war hero and a recognized advocate of the League in international affairs. Whatever the influence on minds, he was just what the Tories needed in order to seduce liberal hearts.

If the government needed confirmation of the importance of being seen to be supportive of the League of Nations, then it came on 27 June 1935 when the results of a non-official national referendum conducted in the previous November were published. The referendum, known as the 'peace ballot', was organized by the League of Nations Union, an interest group dedicated to furthering the work of Geneva and led by what in a later generation were to be known as 'the chattering classes'. Whatever the nature of these activists, the result of the ballot revealed that support for the principles of the League of Nations was widespread across the whole country. Over 11.5 million voters responded – a figure only marginally smaller than the total number of votes cast for Conservative candidates at the previous general election. Enormous majorities were recorded in favour of Britain remaining a member of the League, for the international reduction of armaments and even for the abolition of their production and sale for private profit. Of those expressing a clear preference, 85 per cent wanted to abolish military aircraft by international agreement and 94 per cent wanted to punish aggressor nations with collective economic and non-military sanctions. If this failed, 74 per cent were prepared to go to war against the aggressor for the common good (although on these last two questions there was a large number of abstentions, on the last question over 2.3 million).[47]

Much might be said about the limitations of the ballot, in terms of scope, method and distribution. Answers to abstract notions were always likely to favour 'love thy neighbour' platitudes over Old Testament judgement. A very different response might have been solicited to a real situation, as the nation's attitude to later events was to show. Nonetheless, not even the most sceptical observer could deny that the ballot was answered by a huge proportion of the electorate and that their mood, forcefully expressed by it, was essentially pacific. What none knew was whether the British electorate's view on combating aggression was universal or whether it altered depending upon who the victim was and whether the aggressor posed a direct threat to Britain.

Whatever the question marks over theory and practice, Baldwin had to consider the expression of public opinion represented by the peace ballot. He furthermore had to deal with the complication created by the possibly hostile reception his party's right wing might give if he was seen to be too clearly a pilgrim of Geneva. As far as praying for the peace of the world through the League of Nations was concerned, Churchill was at this time an agnostic wanting to be converted. Amery remained a militant atheist.

Always preferring the political religion of good deeds rather than justification through faith alone, Chamberlain had offered the Cabinet a 'limited liability' proposal for an international peace-keeping force. When it was rejected, he realized the likely limits of national governments agreeing collective security at Geneva. Neither Churchill, Amery nor Chamberlain had any time for the view expressed by Clement Attlee, Lansbury's new and apparently interim replacement as leader of the Labour Party, that adherence to the League should come before all else and that he, personally, had abandoned 'all idea of nationalist loyalty'.[48] The brotherhood of man as a plenary session in a Swiss auditorium was not a glimpse of eternity congenial to the traditional Tory frame of mind.

The right-wing critique of the League of Nations was primarily ideological. It was additionally reinforced by an understanding of the reality that undermined the organization's objectives. The ability of the League to coerce an aggressor rested on the belief that collective security – the combined resources of all members to gang up on an aggressor – would prevent, or reverse, wrongdoing. Great emphasis was placed on the ability of economic sanctions to achieve this end. Unfortunately, this underestimated the extent to which economic self-sufficiency as practised by totalitarian states could keep an aggressor nation going for years on end. Indeed, such sanctions could not even be watertight since Japan, Germany and the United States were major industrial nations that were not even members of the League in 1935. Of existing members, only Britain, France, Italy and Stalinist Russia could go to war against a major foe with any real sense of making a vital contribution. Indeed, Stalin's help was an assistance that many Tories wanted to do without. If the aggressor to be punished was Germany, then to join offensive collective security measures against her, the Red Army would have to march through eastern European countries like Poland which had no intention of letting them enter for fear they would never leave. With a navy stretched by global commitments and only a small army, Britain's contribution to a conflict would take time to assemble. France, with mounting domestic problems of her own, was understandably reluctant to take the burdens of the world on her shoulders. Italy, the other significant power, which under Mussolini's leadership threatened Germany's encroachments on Austria, was a possible confederate. Unhappily, Il Duce's temperament was more in the nature of opera buffa than steely resolve (and the supporters of Geneva would eventually help to drive him out of the League as well).

These considerations stiffened the Tory right's resistance to involvement in a system of 'collective security' that threatened to make the under-resourced Britain an overstretched global policeman. Security could only be guaranteed by rearmament (the opposite of the goal to which supporters of the League were still committed). If it was going to be necessary to box Hitler in, then power pacts and military understandings with specific allies were the way forward – alliances that might involve turning a blind eye to some of the actions of other partners in the enterprise. Such Realpolitik was anathema to all those who held the work of Geneva dear, who saw it as the antidote to the secret diplomacy and armed ententes that preceded the catastrophe of the Great War. In actuality, the League of Nations assumed responsibility without power – the prerogative of the eunuch throughout the ages.[49]

Here was a fresh problem for Baldwin. As an ally, Italy was a bulwark against Hitler's apparent designs to annex Austria into his Reich: when in 1934, Germany had appeared poised for such an intervention, Mussolini had moved his troops up to the Austrian border. If he was converted into an enemy, Mussolini was an enormous headache to British strategic operations in the Mediterranean, through which passed the maritime route to India and many of Britain's imperial possessions. To have to face possible conflict in different geographical theatres with Germany, Italy and Japan simultaneously was not a viable option. Therefore, in order to firm up Italy's opposition to Hitler's interest in Austria, Britain and France had talks with Mussolini at Stresa in April 1935. Unfortunately, Mussolini was preparing to invade Abyssinia (modern Ethiopia). Ruled by Ras Tafari, who as 'Emperor' assumed the name Haile Selassie, Abyssinia was a slave-trading autocracy and an unlikely source of liberal enthusiasm. However, she was also a member of the League, under whose Covenant she was entitled to the protection of fellow members from attack. Either the British Government kept in with Mussolini and betrayed both Abyssinia and the principles of Geneva, or it would have to stand up for international law, face the possibility of war and lose a potential ally in constraining Hitler's Germany. It was an unenviable choice, made worse by the knowledge of an approaching general election.

Shortly before the announcement of the League of Nations Union's 'peace ballot', the Cabinet had agreed to a plan sketched out by the new Foreign Secretary, Sir Samuel Hoare. Mussolini would be effectively bought off by the partitioning of Abyssinia. Italy would gain the major portion of the country, all of which, if the invasion went unchecked, she would sooner or later capture in any case. However, following the peace ballot's result, the Cabinet began to talk of honouring League commitments in order to confront Italy since this was the 'present trend of development of public opinion in this country'.[50] In late August Hoare conferred with a number of the great and the good, including prominent supporters of the League like Lord Robert Cecil (President of the League of Nations Union and the liberal-Tory brother of the diehard Lord Salisbury), Sir Austen Chamberlain and the Liberals, Sir Herbert Samuel and Lloyd George. The common advice that Hoare received was that Britain should be guided by her obligations under the Covenant of the League or else, as appeared to be borne out by the response in the media, 'a great wave of public opinion would sweep the Government out of power.'[51]

Whatever secret diplomacy proceeded to try to heal the breach with Mussolini, it was clear that the government would now have to speak up in favour of the League in public. Having gained Cabinet approval for this last course, Hoare went off to address the League in Geneva on 11 September. In between the appropriate platitudes, he made it clear that Britain's foreign policy would be guided by its commitment to the Covenant of the League. Hoare returned to London in time to inspect the bouquets. On 23 October, Baldwin ended mounting speculation and announced that a general election would be held on 14 November.

VI

Labour was not slow in suspecting that the suddenly so effusive commitment to the League and the announcement of a general election were cynical moves by the government to exploit the international situation for electoral gain – as it had supposedly done over the financial situation in 1931 – to avoid the real issue of unemployment. To this was soon added the claim that the government was secretly seeking a mandate upon which it could then start a new arms race.[52]

The substance for this last allegation was based not only upon the increasing air defence spending estimates that had gone through Parliament despite Labour opposition but on the actions and words of both Churchill and Chamberlain. Despite the verdict of the 'peace ballot', Chamberlain had argued in August 1935 that the government 'should take the bold course of actually appealing to the country on a defence programme'. Baldwin, however, had moderated this by placing the emphasis on the 'long and anxious foreign affairs arguments rather than rearmament per se'.[53] Chamberlain recorded his prescient fears in his diary:

> Germany is said to have borrowed over £1,000 millions a year to get herself rearmed and she has perfected a wonderful industrial organisation capable of rapid expansion for the production of the materials of war. With Mussolini hopelessly tied up in Abyssinia and Great Britain disarmed, the temptation in a few years to demand territory etc. might be too great for Goering, Goebbels, and the like to resist. Therefore we must hurry our own rearmament and in the

course of the next 4 or 5 years we shall probably have to spend an extra £120 millions in doing so.

We are not yet sufficiently advanced to reveal our ideas to the public, but of course we cannot deny the general charge of rearmament, and no doubt if we tried to keep our ideas secret until the election we should either fail or if we succeeded lay ourselves open to the damaging accusation that we had deliberately deceived the people.[54]

Days before the election was announced, Chamberlain stuck to this theme publicly at his party's Scottish annual conference in Glasgow. There he assured delegates that rearmament was precisely what Britain needed to mend her defences and what the depressed areas (in which Clydeside was prominent) needed by way of job creation. This theme echoed that of Churchill, whose campaign on the issue Chamberlain was keen to prevent becoming the monopoly of backbench rebels.

For his part, Churchill was excited at the prospect of getting a crack at the socialists and was revitalized by the election campaign. With whatever trepidation, Conservative Central Office felt unable to reject his offer of assistance on the campaign stump, from where he further expounded his views on rearmament. Yet, regardless of Churchill's relish for action, it was Chamberlain who had laid out much of the party's election strategy. It was he who chaired the committee that composed the manifesto and he who had personally the greatest hand in its drafting. Inevitably, his work was modified and, in its published form, some of the manifesto's language showed the decidedly un-Chamberlainite trait of trimming to public tastes. It committed the National Government to uphold its duties to the League of Nations, with 'no wavering' of line taken over Italy's transgression in Abyssinia and stated that the collective security of the League 'alone can save us from a return to the old system which resulted in the Great War'. Whilst claiming to seek multilateral disarmament whenever an opportunity arose, the manifesto made clear in more Chamberlainite fashion that support for League collective security was only possible with the means to implement it and that 'the fact is that the actual condition of our defence forces is not satisfactory. We have made it clear that we must in the course of the next few years do what is necessary to repair the gaps in our defences, which have accumulated over the past decade. The defence programme will be strictly confined to what is required to make the country and the Empire safe and to fulfil our obligations towards the League.'[55] Despite the obvious hedging and qualification in which the commitment to rearmament was made, Labour chose to highlight any sign that the Conservatives were canoodling with their capitalist bedfellows in the arms trade. Commenting on what a returned National Government would mean, one of Labour's election posters featured a baby in a gas mask. Although Labour had moderated its policies since the resignation as leader of George Lansbury and its manifesto now accepted the need for armed forces consistent with home defence and League obligations, it was abundantly clear that the party was going to take a lean view of the defences deemed to be necessary. In 1940 Labour supporters were to be at the forefront of hounding out the dying Chamberlain as one of the 'guilty men' who failed to prepare Britain for war. It is noteworthy that during the 1935 election campaign it was Chamberlain more than any other Cabinet minister whom they chose to portray as a warmonger. Arthur Greenwood proclaimed that the Tories were responsible for 'the merest scaremongering, disgraceful in a statesman in Mr Chamberlain's responsible position, to suggest that more millions of money needed to be spent on armaments'. The rising star of the Labour Party, Herbert Morrison, on the hustings reportedly condemned Chamberlain for being 'ready and anxious to spend millions of pounds on machines of destruction. He had no money, however, for the unemployed, the depressed areas and social services. He would spend on the means of death, but not on the means of life.' Morrison even uncharitably compared Chamberlain's face to that of a death's head moth. Although reticent at attempting humour in public, Chamberlain responded the following day that he would not attempt to compete in looks with 'such a magnificent specimen of humanity' as Morrison.[56] Morrison was no Adonis. Labour's trump card was Chamberlain's seeming willingness to find funds for rearmament that he claimed did not exist to assist the poor. Labour intended to abolish the means test and cure unemployment with an undefined 'vigorous policy of national planning'. As Chancellor therefore, it was Chamberlain who again found himself at the forefront of the Labour attack on rearmament. With the official version of the events of 1931 now well rehearsed that Labour had presided over a financial crisis which they had proceeded to run away from, the idea that the economy was not safe in socialist hands needed no fine tuning. It was upon this platform that Chamberlain was able to contrast the crisis of August 1931 with the conditions of October 1935. With confidence restored, cheap money, he maintained, had brought about recovery. A million homes had been built since the last election. On top of this, he announced a £100 million road construction programme, one of a number of measures designed to boost employment and head off any impact the reconstruction campaign for public works advocated by Lloyd George's 'Council of Action' and others might have generated. Unemployment was falling and, importantly for the voter, there was the expectation that this trend would continue. Indeed, never one to underestimate the mischief Lloyd George could make, Chamberlain spent much of his own election broadcast countering the claims of the septuagenarian Welsh Wizard, as if, like Rasputin, he wouldn't be killed off until he had been poisoned, shot at point-blank range, tied in a sack, thrown in a river, drowned and then fished back out again in order to have a clobbering administered just to be on the safe side.

In fact, neither Lloyd George's 'Council of Action' nor the main Liberal Party under Samuel were to pose a serious threat to the National campaign. This was despite the extraordinary performance on their behalf of Philip (by then Viscount) Snowden. Genuinely embittered by what he saw as a betrayal, Snowden delivered an election broadcast of scarcely concealed venom, condemning his former compatriots in the National Government and repeating the allegation that what they were really seeking was a new term of office in order to trigger an arms race. Needless to say, his contribution was immediately condemned by Simon, Chamberlain and Churchill (who knew a turncoat when he saw one). Indeed, none of the opposition leaders on offer could match the popular impression that Baldwin generated for the National team. Clement Attlee had been rushed into the Labour Party's leadership upon Lansbury's resignation of 3 October over the Labour Movement's resolution in favour of collective security. Inexperienced and scarcely known to the wider public, Attlee failed to make much impact in the campaign. Tories adopted Churchill's jibe that he was the locum tenens leader who could not even lead his own party. A sign of the Labour Party's desperation was demonstrated in their choice of platform slogan – 'A VOTE FOR THE TORIES IS A VOTE FOR WAR' – which rather exceeded the normal boundaries of negative campaigning.

Although they had little to teach the National politicians in the art of scaremongering, Labour's attempt to paint their opponents' programme in the lurid colours of death and destruction may conceivably have been counter-productive in that it focused upon the international tension at the expense of the domestic hardships endured by those in the depressed areas. This was likely to work in the experienced National Government's favour. Baldwin, however, had acutely sensitive political antennae. He was determined both to prevent Labour's warmongering attacks from finding their target and to ensure that the liberal floating vote, presumed to be broadly pacific, was not put off voting for government candidates. As a result, he took the gamble of effectively contradicting the pro-rearmament message proclaimed by Churchill and Chamberlain, by stating that 'There has not been, there is not, and there will be no question of big armaments or materially increased forces. What we do want, and what we must have, is to replace our pre-war construction in ships in the Navy with modern ships. It does not mean increasing the Navy.'[57]

Baldwin's most-quoted remark of the campaign came at Wolverhampton on 28 October where, in an address to the Peace Society, he pointedly declared, 'I give you my word there will be no great armaments.' Speaking in Newcastle on 12 November, only two days before election day, he linked the commemoration of Remembrance Sunday with the need to preserve peace and prosperity, twin goals with which he associated the continuing work of the National Government.[58] The message was clear: Baldwin was in control and he would not tolerate a full-scale rearmament programme.

By the end of the campaign, Baldwin had once again proved himself to be the Conservative Party's most effective and, in particular, most reassuring communicator. The idea that he was the man the voter could trust had firmly taken hold, a double-edged weapon when within a very short time his honesty was to be called into question. For the moment, though, he reigned supreme and unchallenged. Behind the political shop window, his Chancellor, Neville Chamberlain, had worked the longest hours and produced the most impressive turnover as well as being the only member of staff to develop practical strategies for future trading. No one seriously doubted that he was the one most likely to take over the firm in the event of the 68-year-old Baldwin's retirement. Yet, this presumed that nothing unforeseen would disrupt best-laid plans in the meantime. Chamberlain, after all, was not infallible, nor was he immortal. He was only two years younger than the Prime Minister and there was clearly the possibility that he might end up being too old himself for the succession, bypassed by someone younger, if Baldwin carried on in office for long. Hoare was fifty-five and Eden only thirty-eight years old. In the meantime, Baldwin's ability to sideline publicly Chamberlain's pro-rearmament efforts from the debate demonstrated that when he could be moved to action, the Conservative leader was not to be easily discounted.

The nation went to bed on 13 November expecting the return of the National Government the following day. Tipsters in the newspapers made their bets on the size of the majority. Excluded from power in the Parliament that had at last come to a close, Churchill could reflect on his prospects for rehabilitation. They seemed good. When he had lost office in 1929 he had commanded the support of not a single coherent group in the Conservative Party. As a result of his campaign on India and his clarion call for rearmament, he was now seen as the finest advocate of causes dear to the right wing of the party which, because of the scale of the 1931 majority, Baldwin had felt no need to indulge. That majority was sure to be cut and Baldwin would be expected to broaden his reduced base by calling into his confidence the spokesman for this other major section of Tory opinion. At almost sixty-one, Churchill was still in the prime of life, his health sufficiently robust to absorb the relentless supply of tobacco and alcohol thrown at it. On the eve of the electorate's verdict, he prepared himself for the likely spoils of the morrow, the opportunity to regain one of the great seals of office.

BOOK TWO

Nine

THE TANGLED WEB OF
COLLECTIVE SECURITY

I

'Well, you're finished now' were the words with which Beaverbrook
greeted Churchill when he arrived at the newspaper tycoon's election
night party: 'Baldwin has so good a majority that he will be able to do
without you.' Convinced that the Prime Minister was about to ask him
back into the Cabinet, Churchill was aghast at his host's bluntness,
putting it down to 'a Canadian outlook on British politics'.[1] Yet
Beaverbrook's judgement proved the more accurate. The general election
was a triumph for the National Government and for Baldwin in
particular. The Conservatives retained 388 seats, supported by 33 Liberal
Nationals and 8 National Labour MPs.[2] For the Opposition, Samuel's
Liberals had slipped to 21 MPs. Labour, although trebling its number of
seats to 154, still hardly formed any effective parliamentary barrier to the
government. For its part, the Cabinet suffered only two high-level
casualties – a father and son: Ramsay MacDonald was defeated in the
Seaham constituency which until the election campaign he had made the
mistake of only visiting twice since that of 1931. His son, Malcolm,
drafted into the Cabinet as Colonial Secretary in June, also lost his
Nottinghamshire seat. Regarding their immediate return to the government to be a necessity, safe seats had quickly to be found for them in the
new year. In Ramsay's case, this meant the Scottish Universities seat, a
berth he had previously condemned as an electoral anomaly. In
Malcolm's case, finding a constituency would lead to a run-in with the
parliamentary ambitions of Randolph Churchill.

At the dissolution, the National Government had enjoyed a 400-seat
overall majority. After the election this figure was still an overwhelming
240. This sank Churchill's whole strategy which had been to make
himself the indispensable voice for the views of the Conservative Party's
diehard wing – to be called upon when, with a reduced majority, Baldwin
needed to broaden his number of allies. With each fresh declaration in the
government's favour confirming the leadership's independence from the
dictates of sectional opinion, so Churchill's hope was dimmed and finally

extinguished. The only personal comfort was his own popularity in his Essex constituency of Epping. In an improvement on the national trend, his 20,000 majority remained virtually unchanged against his chief opponent, a Liberal.

Baldwin's refusal to shift the emphasis of his government to the right was confirmed by his decision to keep a Cabinet scarcely altered from that with which he had gone into the election: with fifty to sixty MPs, the Tory diehards were rewarded with no supporters in the government whilst seven Cabinet seats were occupied by National Labour and Liberal National politicians, who were represented by a mere forty-one MPs. One Birmingham Tory MP, Oliver Locker Lampson, wrote to Churchill suggesting a hare-brained scheme to 'oppose the return of Ramsay and Simon etc., into the Cabinet and that our opposition to these personalities at this juncture might offer Baldwin an excuse not to take them, and therefore increase your chances'.[3] Aside from the political unreality of destroying a 'National' component days after the electorate had over-whelmingly returned a National Government, Locker Lampson was naive to think that Baldwin might want to discard the convenient cover for his own beliefs in moderate 'new Conservatism'. Meanwhile, Churchill's long-term *bête noir*, the anti-gambling pro-temperance Christian Scientist Tory MP for Plymouth Sutton, Nancy Astor, wrote to Baldwin, to beg: 'Don't put Winston in the Government – It will mean war at home and abroad. I know the depths of Winston's disloyalty – and you can't think how he is distrusted by all the electors of the country.'[4]

Indeed, for all his public display of reconciliation with Baldwin, Churchill still kept an eye on the opportunities for factionalist advantage, asking the former India Defence League's Secretary, Patrick Donner, to draw up a list of those diehards not returned at the election. Donner assured him that he would 'certainly keep in touch with our "whips": I anticipate little difficulty in keeping the Group together. It has become a habit with them.'[5] Almost a quarter of the diehards no longer sat in the Commons after the election, twelve having retired from the House and eight having been defeated. However, none of the ringleaders had gone down, and some of the new MPs who had replaced those who had retired might be expected to have right-wing views equally congenial to their constituency association.

The editorial section of *The Times*, a page that attempted to articulate intellectually what Baldwin thought instinctively, analysed the election result bluntly, stating that 'Mr Baldwin will be under no obligation to make reluctant concessions to the extremists of either wing' of his party.[6] This, according to the newspaper, was a relief because the Tory right wing's 'sub-acid hostility to the Government' and their 'clamour for indefinitely large armaments' had been an electoral liability. For good measure, the paper's editor, Geoffrey Dawson, rubbed in Baldwin's victory over the diehards by asserting that his majority circumvented 'the mischief which might have been wrought by special groups in a more evenly divided House of Commons'. In consequence, Parliament could 'proceed with its work without fear of interruption from purely political intrigues'.[7]

Churchill was furious with *The Times* for suggesting that Baldwin ought to ignore the fifty or sixty 'Right-wing Conservatives' who were allegedly interested only in 'purely political intrigue'. In an unsent letter to the newspaper, Churchill asked, 'What reason is there for a quarrel at the present time?' The Indian issue was dead; the government were finally grasping the necessity to increase defence spending; if differences did emerge, the right wing might 'have worthier motives than place-hunting and intrigue'.[8] Interestingly, despite the continuation of long-term unemployment in parts of the country, Churchill did not ever raise domestic issues as a possible source of division. This suggests a definite refutation of any alliance with progressive elements on the left wing of the Conservative Party. Right wingers like Oliver Locker Lampson recognized that defence issues were now central to the circle of MPs around Churchill. J.L. Garvin, the editor of the *Observer* (a post he had held since 1908 – an enviable degree of job security in the journalistic profession), had already written to Churchill along similar lines to encourage him that his 'greatest hour' was his 'for the taking'. Whilst only a quarter of the parliamentary Tory Party had supported him on India, three-quarters would support him on defence, an issue on which the only other serious contender for the party leadership, Neville Chamberlain, was supposedly out of his depth. Garvin had advised Chamberlain to work with Churchill, telling the latter that 'Neville is sound in heart and character but has never had the chance to master these matters of *haute politik* which have engaged you and me all our lives'.[9]

With the successes of his rearmament motions at the 1933 and 1935 Party Conferences and the reward of a growing Commons audience on the issue, there were plausible reasons for Churchill to believe that his career was back on the ascent. This was not the only consideration for Baldwin in his desire to exclude him from the government. The new Foreign Secretary, Hoare, had been informed that Churchill's acceptance of an armed forces portfolio would have serious repercussions for relations with Germany, possibly even throwing into doubt the future of the Anglo-German Naval Treaty (after initial indecision Churchill had voiced concern about the agreement because it breached the Versailles Treaty).[10] There is, however, little documentary evidence to suggest that the foreign policy implications of a Churchill appointment weighed as heavily on Baldwin's mind as the domestic, or rather the personal, considerations. Churchill's growing popularity in the party over rearmament seemed to cause Baldwin more fear than pleasure. Seemingly oblivious to the fact that the Prime Minister appeared not to be susceptible to this form of rough wooing, Churchill continued to push himself forward as the anxious suitor. Consequently, when his ambition to return to the Cabinet as First Lord of the Admiralty (the office he had held in Asquith's Government on the outbreak of war in 1914) was thwarted, he found rejection by Baldwin hard to accept. Far from believing the verdict final, he nurtured the desire that if he was not going to be offered office immediately, then he might be brought into the Cabinet in the new year.[11]

In fact, Churchill's desire to walk hand in hand with Baldwin risked detaching himself from the imperialist right on a major issue of foreign policy – adherence to the Covenant of the League of Nations. The implications of the Abyssinian crisis now put to the test the cohesion of the Tory right in the face of a major misjudgement from the Prime Minister.

II

On election night Chamberlain could take fresh reassurance from the verdict of the electorate in his Birmingham Edgbaston constituency. He had retained over 80 per cent of the vote, his majority against the Labour candidate slipping harmlessly from almost 28,000 to over 21,000. Once again, the Conservatives won all of the great industrial city's twelve seats. Resolved to keep him as his Chancellor in the new Parliament, Baldwin had written to Chamberlain during the election campaign suggesting that 'you and I are complimentary: each puts into the pool his own contribution and we make a jolly effective unit!' To one of his sisters, Chamberlain concluded 'that if I supply the policy and drive, S.B. does also supply something that is perhaps even more valuable in retaining the floating vote'.[12] In fact, Chamberlain's role in the election campaign and his semi-detached association with the pro-League of Nations position of his party's campaign were soon to play dramatically in his favour. However, in the hours after the election triumph it was inevitably Baldwin who had cause to take the greatest satisfaction. Noting how he had avoided the pitfalls of 'Winston's enthusiasm for ships and guns', the former Deputy Secretary to the Cabinet, Tom Jones, recorded that the Prime Minister had 'thrown that halo of faith and hope, free from meretricious ornament, which inspires confidence. The effect is to gather to the Tories a large voting strength of Liberals and unattached folk who like his sober and sincere accents, and who are afraid of the menace to small owners and investors associated with Socialism.'[13]

Baldwin's decision to fight a general election on a policy of backing League of Nations sanctions against Italy in the wake of Mussolini's invasion of Abyssinia had ensured that he had fought the election on an issue that seemingly commanded overwhelming public support. At the same time it diverted attention from the National Government's failure on the domestic front to crush unemployment in the depressed regions.[14] Since both the government and the opposition parties all commended the League of Nations, Labour and the Liberals had been justified in questioning why Baldwin had chosen such an issue on which to go to the people.[15] Cynically inspired or not, almost immediately his strategy would backfire, with extremely damaging consequences for the Prime Minister.

Italy's invasion of Abyssinia in October 1935 had presented the government with a major dilemma. If they antagonized Mussolini over his act of aggression, then they ran the risk of alienating a potential bulwark against Hitler, an important chip in the political poker game which had seemingly been gained at the Anglo-French-Italian talks at Stresa in April 1935. Furthermore, condemnation of Italy might provoke resentment not only in Rome but in Paris, since the French Government were also keen to strengthen the front created at Stresa; in June, the French and Italian Chiefs of Staff had participated in conversations with the purpose of coordinating action in the event of an attack on either by Hitler.

The Abyssinian invasion had not taken London by surprise. Yet despite having been forewarned eleven months previously of Italy's likely intentions (the first border incident in December 1934 paving the way for the actual invasion in the following October) the government had taken no decisive course of action. No forceful objections had been communicated to Mussolini at Stresa and he could have been forgiven for regarding the cordiality of the conference there as evidence that Britain was not going to stand in his way over the fate of a slave-trading despotism.[16] Simon's message in May 1935, informing him that there was widespread public feeling in favour of settling disputes peacefully through the League, was not taken seriously – after all, public condemnation had not stopped Japan's occupation of Manchuria.[17] Indeed, in June Simon's successor as Foreign Secretary, Hoare, told the Cabinet that the French 'in the event of a Clash were showing every sign that . . . they would be on the side of Italy . . . Either we should have to make a futile protest, which would irritate M. Mussolini and perhaps drive him out of the League and into the arms of Germany, or we should make no protest and give the appearance of pusillanimity.'[18] During the summer recess on 21 August,

Baldwin had called together MacDonald, Chamberlain, Simon, Hoare and his deputy at the Foreign Office, Anthony Eden, to discuss what should be done about Abyssinia. In typically dismissive form, Chamberlain confided afterwards to his sister that he did not know why Baldwin bothered breaking up his summer snooze in Aix-les-Bains, when he clearly had nothing worthwhile to contribute to the discussion.[19] Chamberlain thought sanctions would be imposed against Italy but that, without Germany or the USA joining the effort, they would fail and would be seen to do so. Hoare bluntly spelled this strategy out to the British Ambassador in Paris, making clear that he did not think economic sanctions, with or without the French, had much chance of success but that 'whatever may develop, it is essential that we should play out the League hand in September' and 'on no account assume the impracticality of sanctions until the League has made this investigation. It must be the League and not the British Government that declares that sanctions are impracticable and the British Government must on no account lay itself open to the charge that we have not done our utmost to make them practicable.'[20] Chamberlain approved of Hoare's duplicitous strategy. The two discussed 'at considerable length' what line to take in public, Chamberlain noting to his sister that Hoare 'first asked my opinion and then, when I have given it, he produced bits of his draft which showed that he had been on the same idea. He then modified the emphasis or elaborated the argument in accordance with my suggestions.'[21]

The result was the formula Hoare articulated at Geneva on 11 September when he assured the world that Britain would back the League in 'steady and collective resistance to all acts of unprovoked aggression'.[22] During the endurance test of the Indian reform campaign, Hoare had shown a machiavellian approach to policy. He had endeavoured to concoct a stance that was all things to all men: reform-minded in order to appease British liberal opinion and diminish the scepticism of the Indian political class; couched in the language of controls and safeguards in order to keep Tory MPs in the fold. His attitude to Indian federation – that it could be postponed in practice so long as it was enacted in principle since even a void was a barrier to the onwards march of the Congress Party – demonstrated an intellectual dexterity that was well beyond the comprehension of most of his fellow Cabinet members. Hoare displayed the same cynicism with regard to the League of Nations and, as with India, he was to prove to be too clever by half. When he spoke at Geneva, what Hoare actually said was that Britain supported collective security so long as all the other League members did likewise. This was the softly spoken let-out clause. As A.J.P. Taylor has put it, Hoare 'seemed to be betting on a certainty either way. If collective security worked, the prestige of the National government would be enhanced and the League could then be used effectively against Germany; if it failed, others could be blamed and the way would be open for rearmament.'[23]

With economic sanctions duly applied against Italy, Hoare received Cabinet approval to hold secret talks with Pierre Laval, his opposite number in Paris. There was an obvious need to try to find agreement. France had already given Mussolini the impression that he had carte blanche in Abyssinia. In August the French Ambassador to London had instructed Vansittart, the British Permanent Under-Secretary at the Foreign Office, that France would not back Britain if she instituted sanctions against Italy unless Britain agreed to impose sanctions against Germany if it invaded Austria – a course London was keen to avoid. Following considerable equivocation, it was not until 18 October that France reluctantly assured Britain that she would come to her aid if, as a result of sanctions, the Royal Navy was attacked in the Mediterranean by Italy.[24] However, by agreeing to go along with a minimal interpretation of sanctions, the Quai d'Orsay (the French Foreign Office) then went further than Hoare had foreseen. This upset his calculation that Britain would be able to escape her collective security commitments by being able to blame France for not keeping her side of the bargain. Whilst the National Government went to the polls on its pro-League sanctions policy, Hoare and Anthony Eden, the Minister for League of Nations affairs, spent much of the campaign in touch with Laval trying to see what deal could be done with Mussolini.

Short of declaring war, Italy could only be stopped through all her oil imports being cut off (without supplies of her own, this would have shut down her military effort). However, this form of economic sanctions ran the risk of goading Mussolini into declaring war on the key perpetrators, Britain and France (Mussolini had responded to the oil sanctions possibility by moving troops on to the French border and threatening to bomb the French Riviera; the British fleet and garrison in Egypt were similarly at risk). An oil embargo might not, in any case, prove watertight due to the hesitancy of Italy's neighbours to apply it and of non-League countries to be bound by it. The British Government had committed itself to collective security and sanctions against Italy but had certainly not sought or received endorsement during the election campaign for all-out war. This Hoare had explicitly made clear in the Commons on 22 October. Whether or not it was naive to believe that international diplomacy and collective security in particular could be successfully conducted without the ultimate sanction of the threat of war was another matter. Briefly encouraged by the possibility that the USA would cooperate with an embargo, Chamberlain came round to arguing that oil sanctions should be imposed. On 29 November he convened a meeting in his room with Hoare, Simon, Eden and Sir Walter Runciman, the President of the Board of Trade. Chamberlain noted in his diary later that day that Runciman 'showed great reluctance to agree to our joining in oil sanctions but would not face the alternatives. [Hoare], rather against Eden's inclinations, was inclined to hold up the embargo long enough to allow further conversations in Paris to test out the possibility of a general settlement. I was prepared to agree to this.'[25] Baldwin made clear to the Cabinet on 2 December that a war with Italy had to be avoided and that if Mussolini was thrown overboard 'no one would be willing to tackle Hitler.'[26] Consequently, it would be hazardous to proceed with oil sanctions; the need to reach an accommodation with Mussolini was thus all the more pressing. The basis upon which Hoare had been negotiating with Laval to settle the problem was endorsed and the Foreign Secretary and his Permanent Under-Secretary, Vansittart, travelled to Paris for further meetings at the Quai d'Orsay on 7 and 8 December.

With Mussolini's troops now two months into their invasion of Abyssinia, the best the British and French could do without direct intervention was to persuade the Italian dictator to limit the scale of his conquest. Hoare and Laval agreed to concede to Italy the lowlands of Abyssinia that bordered Italian Somaliland and to which (had it not spuriously been recognized in international law) the Emperor of Abyssinia had only a tenuous and ill-defined claim anyway. In return, Mussolini would be prevented from occupying the highlands of Abyssinia but would instead enjoy a zone of economic interest, guaranteed by a League of Nations mandate that would provide an effective cover for Italian control. Furthermore, to increase the remaining part of Abyssinia's viability by giving it a sea outlet, Britain would agree to cede to it Zeila in adjoining British Somaliland. Laval's information was that Mussolini would probably agree to this plan and so Hoare, fearing that the alternative was a wild Italian declaration of war against Britain, returned to London believing a deal to be all but signed and sealed. On 10 December the Cabinet agreed, and Eden instructed the British Ambassador to urge Emperor Haile Selassie to accept.

That same day details of the agreement were prematurely leaked in the French press. Uproar followed. The deal appeared to reward Italy for her aggressive action whilst going behind the back of Geneva at the same time. It was a pretty bad day for Baldwin when even the leader page in *The Times* attacked his government – its deputy editor, Robin Barrington-Ward, penning some evocative lines about the remaining rump of Abyssinia surviving only through 'a corridor for camels'. As Brendan Bracken reported to Churchill, who was holidaying in Majorca whilst the news broke, 'the Foreign Minister of a country that has just re-elected a Government in order to sustain the principle of collective security, went to Paris and dealt a mortal blow to the principle he was supposed to sustain.'[27] Tory MPs were inundated by letters of complaint from constituents who felt that their trust had been betrayed. Many more were added by League of Nations Union activists burning the midnight oil to churn them out. Seventy MPs on the government side of the House signed a motion attacking the proposal.

Taking a brief respite in Switzerland and with a certain portentous symbolism, Hoare chose this moment to go skating out on the ice. He fell over and broke his nose. On the instructions of a doctor, he was ordered not to return to London for fear of infection.

Whilst the Foreign Secretary recuperated from his fall, Baldwin was left to hold the fort at Westminster. Amid howls from the opposition benches that he had betrayed the League and the very election pledges upon which he had won a general election only a month previously, the Prime Minister stalled for time, telling the Commons that 'I have seldom spoken with greater regret, for my lips are not yet unsealed. Were these troubles over I would make a case and I guarantee not a man would go into the lobby against us.'[28] In fact, the only thing sealing Baldwin's lips was his inability to conjure up a convincing explanation. On 17 December the Cabinet backtracked and Eden was instructed to tell Geneva that the Hoare–Laval plan was off.

Forlornly leading the rearguard opposition in Cabinet, Chamberlain was aghast at this about-turn. When Hoare at last returned to London, he paid him a visit and told him to stick to his guns. Baldwin visited as well, and pledged his support. This was not something upon which Hoare should have placed much confidence. Baldwin was acutely conscious of public and political opinion. These sensitive barometers were tilting away from the Foreign Secretary. The Conservative backbench Foreign Affairs Committee was baying for his blood and so, ominously, was the Chief Whip. Undaunted, at the Cabinet meeting on 18 December, Chamberlain tried to defend him. The minutes of the meeting record him claiming that 'the Foreign Secretary probably felt himself to be on his trial, though, of course, the Cabinet were with him.'[29] This was an optimistic appraisal of his colleagues' selfless nature.

Chamberlain had been up late the previous night going over a draft of what the Foreign Secretary proposed to say in the Commons. In Cabinet, however, indignation was expressed that the implications of Hoare's case – fear that Britain would have to fight Italy alone and that this was too risky – would be treated with derision in the Commons. Four ministers expressed grave concerns about making this excuse.[30] The most decisive die to be cast came with the intervention of the Lord Privy Seal, Lord Halifax. In his prosecution of the Government of India Act, Hoare had done much to realize the reformist goals Halifax had pursued when (as Lord Irwin) he had been Viceroy to India. Now Halifax repaid him by hoping that he would be sacrificed, since 'the whole moral position of the Government before the world was at stake'. Considering that Halifax had sat happily enough in Cabinet meetings that had approved the basis upon which Hoare had negotiated, this was a disagreeably sanctimonious washing of hands from the High Church man. That he would later write to Chamberlain claiming that he did not see what all the fuss had been about over the Hoare–Laval proposals was even more extraordinary. Nonetheless, at the vital Cabinet meeting, Halifax's contribution was critical. He raised the stakes by telling those assembled that if Hoare was not dismissed, then the situation was so serious that it might bring down Baldwin himself and 'if the Prime Minister were to lose his personal position, one of our national anchors would have dragged.'[31]

Chamberlain attempted to retrieve the situation and scribbled a note to Halifax suggesting that Hoare should announce that he was offering his resignation but that it would then only be accepted if the government lost the ensuing debate in the Commons. Unsurprisingly, this idea got nowhere. Characteristically, Baldwin had not yet made up his mind. It seems that he thought Hoare might be able to renounce his own scheme whilst refusing to resign – a proposal that rather went against the spirit of ministerial responsibility. The Prime Minister confessed that 'though he was not rattled, it was a worse situation in the House of Commons than he had ever known' and that 'he did not wish to express a view at the Cabinet as he had not yet settled his opinion.' In preparing to meet the Commons, he declared that he 'would stand or fall by what he said on the morrow. He had found the present conversation very useful. It was essential that everyone should speak his mind. For the moment he would say nothing.'[32]

Following the meeting, Chamberlain again visited Hoare. It would appear that this visit was made at Baldwin's request, with Chamberlain shamelessly instructed to inform Hoare that he would be found a new job quickly so long as he went to Parliament and made a speech explaining that the deal had been all his own doing and had never had the blessing of the Cabinet. Baldwin then called round and told Hoare to resign immediately. Betrayed, the Foreign Secretary began to draft his resignation speech.

Despite his claim to his colleagues that he was not 'rattled', Baldwin was certainly aware of the magnitude of the division in the Commons and suspected that his majority might fall to 'about 100'. It was not surprising that the Baldwin who a month before was the all-conquering hero was now fighting for his political life. After all, this was the Prime Minister who had gone into the election campaign intoning that, however difficult collective security might be, the only course was to 'hitch your wagon to a star', as the alternative to 'a race in armaments' which would light 'a fire that mankind will not be able to put out before it has destroyed them'.[33]

From his holiday spot in Majorca, Churchill received Brendan Bracken's reports on the unfolding situation. Hoare's actions were opposed by 'all the Liberals, and most of the Conservatives', most world opinion, the *Daily Telegraph*'s owner Lord Camrose and even the normally loyal Geoffrey Dawson of *The Times* (although Hoare was supported by the anti-Genevans, Rothermere and Beaverbrook). As for the Foreign Secretary himself, he was entirely isolated in Parliament, being deprived of the support of the anti-Geneva Tory right wing who would 'never forgive him for India [whilst] the pussyfoot Tories who backed him up in India [were] now his most bitter critics'.[34] Randolph Churchill confirmed this impression, adding that 'even anti-Sanctionists like Alan Lennox-Boyd are . . . horrified that the Government should have involved themselves in such a humiliation' whilst Bracken, like Beaverbrook, was 'torn between his desire to see sanctions terminated and Baldwin exterminated'.[35]

The tactic of the Whips' Office was to panic Tory backbenchers into believing that a defeat in the division lobby would force not merely Cabinet resignations, but also a general election.[36] There was no constitutional precedent for such a nonsensical suggestion – especially since the government had won a resounding general election victory only a month previously. Nonetheless, this type of suicide pact was later employed by John Major's Government over the European Communities Finance Bill in 1994, with equal success (if success be measured by the fact that the government majority was maintained at the cost of the Cabinet appearing to be 'in office but not in power'). According to his brother Neville, Sir Austen Chamberlain had gone to the Conservative backbench Foreign Affairs Committee of which he was Chairman on 17 December intending to speak in the Hoare–Laval agreement's defence. Finding that the policy was regarded with great hostility, he instead fuelled it further with what Amery described as 'a speech of high moral indignation'.[37] This volte-face may also have been encouraged by Baldwin, who implied to Sir Austen that he would be rewarded for his support with Hoare's place at the Foreign Office. Consequently, in the Commons debate, the senior statesman weighed in to defend Baldwin from Attlee's accusation that he had behaved dishonourably, a 'challenge which every Member of the National party will resent and resist'.[38] Labour's motion (with its implication of no confidence in the government) was defeated without difficulty in the division. Almost all of the Tory MPs also backed Lord Winterton's loyalist amendment, which cleverly managed to combine rejection of the Hoare–Laval talks with a more general commitment to the government. In fact, Winterton's amendment, so helpful in getting the government off the hook, had actually been drafted with the assistance of Baldwin, Simon and Neville Chamberlain.[39] Only a handful of MPs who had supported the Hoare–Laval scheme like Amery, Gretton and Page Croft could not bring themselves to vote on the Winterton amendment, but virtually all the other familiar India diehard names trooped through the Lobby with the government. Even so, the threat of a large number of Conservative MPs voting against the government had given the Cabinet a tremendous jolt. It owed the comfort of its victory to the decision at the vital moment of those like Austen Chamberlain to suspend their better judgement in order to put party unity first. Never one to underestimate his own importance in these matters, the senior Chamberlain later told his sister that his intervention had done much to save Baldwin 'when an adverse vote would have been a direct vote of censure & necessitated his resignation'. But if he now expected to receive his reward he was to be cruelly disappointed. Having got him to play his own game, Baldwin promptly denied his accomplice the Foreign Office, half-heartedly offering an ill-defined and untempting Cabinet position instead. Worse, the Prime Minister managed to give Sir Austen the impression for good measure that he thought he was 'gaga'.[40] No stranger to political disappointment, and no admirer of the Prime Minister's interpersonal skills, Austen Chamberlain made a note for posterity of their meeting. He felt that Baldwin's 'repeated reference to Ramsay MacDonald's condition and to the danger of men becoming senile without being aware of it were offensive in their iterations. I could perceive no prospect of public usefulness in the acceptance of such an offer so conveyed and I came to the conclusion that what he wanted was not my advice or experience but the use of my name to help patch up the damaged prestige of his government.'[41]

Hoare had wanted Austen Chamberlain to succeed him at the Foreign Office. Instead his replacement was Anthony Eden. It was an appointment intended to signal that the government was seeking forgiveness for its trespasses. Churchill had also wanted Austen Chamberlain's return and was not inspired by Baldwin's choice of the 'lightweight' Eden.[42] Indeed, although the Foreign Office would have been out of bounds, this might have been a moment for Baldwin to have asked Churchill to rejoin the Cabinet as someone of stature untainted by the Hoare–Laval scandal.

This was especially true given the signs that Churchill was now believed to be accommodating the views of the majority of the Conservative Party on League collective security whilst continuing to champion the still-vocal right wing on the question of more armaments. Eden wrote to him (not entirely in jest) about the possibility of his return to the Government.[43] From his journalistic perch, Randolph Churchill's information for his father was that 'the disgruntled elements in the Cabinet' – by which he chiefly meant the War Minister, Duff Cooper, and Eden as well – wanted his 'inclusion as an offset to Baldwin'.[44] Hitler had supposedly expressed with great alarm to Beaverbrook his fear that Churchill's return to office was a 'forgone conclusion' although Beaverbrook had reassured him that 'there was no possible chance of it'.[45] Rather than return at this moment to participate in the high politics of Westminster, Churchill stayed out in Marrakesh with Rothermere and Lloyd George, ruminating that Baldwin was 'a fool' given the 'terrible situation on his hands, not to gather [Lloyd George's] resources & experience to the public service'.[46]

Writing with the tremendous benefit of hindsight, Churchill later wrote in his memoir of the approach of the Second World War, *The Gathering Storm*, that had he decided to return from the Mediterranean in the midst of the crisis, he 'might have brought an element of decision to the anti-Government gatherings which would have ended the Baldwin regime. Perhaps a Government under Sir Austen Chamberlain might have been established at this moment.'[47] This was wishful thinking. Churchill's absence allowed him to avoid taking sides. Had he done so he would have discredited himself either with the right or the left of the party depending on the line he chose to adopt. His speeches and correspondence suggest that he seemed genuinely unable to decide whether Geneva or Stresa represented the best hope of containing Germany, the country that he was sure represented the chief threat.[48] In this respect, his approach was little different from the faltering indefinite lurches that represented the government's foreign policy at the time. In contrast, by holding his fire he seemed sure to benefit from the one inevitable result of the government's diplomatic fiasco: a call to increase spending on the defence forces. Viewed from distant Morocco, Baldwin seemed either to be poised to retire or likely to opt for 'a strong reconstruction', which would surely involve, with a little help from destiny, calling the advocate of rearmament to the Admiralty.[49] In the meantime, Churchill urged his son in the strongest terms not to publish any personal attacks on government ministers, especially Baldwin and Eden, since this would be 'very injurious' to his own position.[50] The government was bruised, but would survive. Churchill's hopes had to accommodate themselves to this fact.

III

Having gone 'to see Sam [Hoare] to say goodbye', Chamberlain noted in his diary that 'when I said something about returning presently to the Cabinet, he said "It's all right between you and me, but I am not so sure about some of my colleagues."'[51] The two of them had thought along similar lines in their strategy for dealing with Italy and the League of Nations. If Baldwin had chosen Chamberlain rather than Hoare as Foreign Secretary back in June 1935 (as he had contemplated doing), it might have been Chamberlain's career that would have been dealt the blow of enforced resignation in December, destroying his hopes for the Premiership. Instead, by remaining at the Treasury, Chamberlain had been lucky: he had agreed with Hoare's plan but escaped the responsibility for it.

The majority of the Conservative Party in the Commons had been horrified by the Hoare–Laval scheme. Their sudden and spontaneous convulsion against it threw the whole foreign policy of the National Government into disorder. Yet there were also important factions within the parliamentary party which did not share the adoration of the League of Nations. Shortly before the general election, Amery had led a delegation to see Baldwin in order to express apprehension about the implications of sanctions against Italy. The core of this delegation was twenty Conservative MPs, brought together as the 'Imperial Policy Group' with a number of peers, including Lord Milne who had previously been Chief of the Imperial General Staff (CIGS). For some on the imperialist right, opposition to collective security was merely the continued expression of the isolationist viewpoint. The more sophisticated thinkers, like Amery, believed collective security was a direct contradiction of the Tory policy pursued by Austen Chamberlain at the Foreign Office between 1924 and 1929. This argument insisted that the 1925 Locarno Pact had symbolized the abandonment of the ill-starred League, reheralding the age of regional pacts. After all, if the League's Articles of its own Covenant were still to be in force, then 'Locarno was clearly superfluous and meaningless.'[52] Sharing the belief that an Anglo-French-led pact was the only hope against Hitler, Churchill had taken this argument a stage further. With the departure from Geneva of Japan and Germany, Britain and France had the opportunity to lead the League of Nations. On this logic, by adopting the language and institutions of the League and collective security, Anglo-French objectives in restraining Germany could avoid the chastisement of liberals concerned about the re-emergence of 1914-style balance of power politics. At first, Churchill was undecided whether the Soviet Union could or should be included in this alliance, as Imperial Russia had been against the Kaiser's Reich. This was the spectre that most put off the Tory right wing from sharing Churchill's desire to exploit the language of 'collective security' for the re-creation of the anti-German entente.

An indication as to the balance of forces within the Conservative Party for and against the use of collective security through the League of Nations was provided by the response to the Hoare–Laval debacle. In the upper chamber, Lord Lloyd put the strategic benefits of alliance with Italy above the rhetoric of the League.[53] In the Commons, other prominent diehards, including Sir Henry Page Croft, were amongst those who signed Early Day Motions (EDMs) supporting the Hoare–Laval scheme and, by implication, opposing the League. A much smaller proportion of the surviving diehards signed pro-League EDMs. Whether on the left or the right of the party, most Tory MPs did not declare in this fashion one way or the other.[54] A few independent thinkers, like the diehard Duchess of Atholl, supported the League but also agreed with the Hoare–Laval plan as the best option on offer.[55]

Signatures on EDMs did not tell the whole story. What can be deduced is that those India diehards who expressed a preference and wanted to sideline Geneva were more in evidence that those who clung to the League. Yet at the time of the Hoare–Laval crisis this view was dwarfed by those Tories who were aware of the great public hostility to such a stance. Eden's appointment to the Foreign Office in place of Hoare was seen as an attempt by Baldwin to buff up the government's image as a supporter of the League. His appointment was followed by a brief period in which it looked as if limited economic sanctions against Italy might be successful after all. It soon became apparent, however, that the Italians would complete their invasion of Abyssinia before the next rainy season forced them to take cover. Determined to show that he was willing to risk pain in pursuit of his ideals, Eden decided to grasp the nettle and argue for the implementation of oil embargo measures. Baldwin agreed and the government began to draw up plans for the League's action.

The French chose this moment to deal a body blow to Eden's plans for oil sanctions. The Quai d'Orsay felt that it had already been pushed more than enough by Whitehall. Now Paris suggested that support for Eden's initiative was conditional upon a British guarantee to support French insistence on the maintenance of the German Rhineland as a demilitarized zone. The deadlock was broken not by Eden nor his new French opposite number, Pierre Flandin, but by Hitler. The German Army marched into the Rhineland on 7 March 1936, unopposed.

Although the Locarno Pact had committed Britain to guarantee France's borders, the agreement only obliged Britain to resist with force the remilitarization of the Rhineland if it was seen as a precursor to the German invasion of France. It was not yet clear that this was Hitler's intention. However, Britain was officially bound to implement whatever course of action the Council of the League of Nations might recommend in view of Germany's breach of the treaties of both Locarno and Versailles. There was never any serious likelihood that the British Government would fight to remove German troops from what was part of their own country. Only two days before the remilitarization had taken place, both Baldwin and Chamberlain had argued forcefully in the Cabinet that neither France nor Britain was in any position to fight back in the event of the Rhineland coming under German military authority. When that eventuality came to pass, the German Ambassador to Britain, Leopold von Hoesch, seized the moment. In virtually the same breath in which he informed Eden of the remilitarization, he spoke of Germany's desire to rejoin the League and share its obligations, to reach an air-force agreement with Britain and to sign non-aggression treaties with Germany's eastern neighbours. With these inducements dangled before him, Eden's immediate instinct was to see what he could do to disassociate Britain from the likely French reaction to their citizens being brought within the range of a pair of standard-issue *Wehrmacht* binoculars.

The Cabinet was no more interested in mobilizing the armed forces against the Rhineland's remilitarization than were thought to be the British public. The Labour Opposition could hardly make capital out of a government that acted pacifically in this way. Chamberlain made a positive suggestion: that a multinational (but essentially British) force should be stationed on the Franco-Rhineland border as a guarantor to the territorial integrity of both countries. On 19 March this was agreed in principle with the Locarno signatories, France, Belgium and Italy. Being necessarily dependent on the acceptance of the other Locarno signatory, Germany, it was – unsurprisingly – a non-starter. In the Commons, Eden played down the significance of staff talks with the French, underlining that Britain had no intention of getting involved in a 'quarrel that is not ours'. This line received approval from virtually every section of political opinion. For the moment, there was still a general hope that the conditions for creating a new atmosphere of trust (Germany's re-entry into the League, as well as an air pact with Britain and a demonstration of good neighbourliness with the countries of eastern Europe whose integrity France promised to guarantee) could advance – despite Germany's suspicious reticence in discussing specific measures.

IV

In April 1935, Britain, France and Italy had appeared to be in agreement that they should act together to thwart the possibility of German aggression, particularly if Hitler should interfere further in Austria. By the end of the year, Britain's actions in response to the invasion of Abyssinia had tested the patience of France and earned the enmity of Italy. Britain's failure to stand by France over the Rhineland further soured cross-Channel relations whilst convincing the Quai d'Orsay that France could not act alone without Britain by her side. The election of a French centre-left variant on the theme of National Government, the 'Popular Front', with the assistance of the Communists in May 1936, concomitantly encouraged right-wing policy makers in London to despair of France's usefulness. The ensuing wave of strikes and capitulation to workers' demands in France only confirmed these fears.

To add to this woeful strategic picture, collective security failed against Italy – although with oil sanctions never introduced because of the poor relations between Britain and France and the likely existence of sanction-busting countries, the measures were no more collective than they were secure. Despite the hardship that non-oil sanctions had created in Italy, the Abyssinian invasion re-established sufficient momentum to mop up what was left of the African state before the rains came and Haile Selassie fled the country. In these circumstances, maintaining sanctions against Italy served no purpose, or at least not the specific purpose for which they had been intended.

The League's failure to restrain Italy encouraged the anti-Genevan faction to believe that their stance had been vindicated and that the future lay in a return to the détente of Stresa. With rather more sadness, others were forced to agree that the debacle had proved the futility of the League in practice, whilst still concerned about what this meant in principle. Even before the *coup de grâce* had been delivered, the right-wing MP Sir Henry 'Chips' Channon hoped that he was discerning a mood within the Conservative Party, as in the country, that standing by the League had been an expensive folly and that the Hoare–Laval pact should have been implemented after all. Indeed, on the strength of his resignation speech, he even rather optimistically thought that some Tory MPs expected that Hoare 'would be Prime Minister before the end of this Parliament'.[56]

Taking the view that Italian sanctions were a distraction from the main challenge – which came from Hitler – both Austen Chamberlain and Churchill saw no gain in prolonging the agony and by May 1936 they had both spoken out for their termination.[57] By the end of that month, Neville Chamberlain too was arguing in Cabinet for the sanctions to be lifted. In contrast to Eden, he saw rapprochement with Italy as a prime objective of

British foreign policy. Baldwin again tried to postpone taking a firm decision. Exasperated by the indecisiveness of the Prime Minister and several of his Cabinet colleagues, Chamberlain decided to force the issue. The opportunity to do so was inadvertently presented by a demand by the League of Nations Union and the opposition parties to increase sanctions against Italy. At a publicized meeting of a Conservative dining club on 10 June, Chamberlain stated emphatically that such a policy was 'the very midsummer of madness'. This was a clear bid to bounce the Cabinet into action. Despite apologizing to Eden for speaking out of turn, in his diary he conceded that he had done 'it deliberately ... I did not consult Anthony Eden, because he would have been bound to beg me not to say what I proposed.'[58]

Chamberlain's gamble concentrated the minds of his colleagues. Seven days after he had made his views public, the Cabinet agreed to begin the process of lifting sanctions. This announcement, which would have been derided had it come more immediately after the Hoare–Laval imbroglio, was accepted by the vast majority of the parliamentary party as inevitable. Chamberlain had got his timing right where Hoare had previously got it wrong. Only two Conservative MPs, the left wingers Vyvyan Adams and Harold Macmillan, voted against. Macmillan's resignation of the party Whip was hardly a cause for alarm in Conservative circles bearing in mind the general tenor of his support over the last six years. All would have been surprised to learn that twenty years later he would end up becoming party leader. In the meantime he went off to write a book advocating replacing the stock exchange by a committee ('a National Investment Board') and various other schemes 'to bring the economic system under conscious direction and control'.[59] For these rather radical measures, he chose the title *The Middle Way*.

Macmillan would later make capital out of his opposition to the dictators, but for the moment it was Chamberlain who had shown that he had the more striking qualities of leadership. Some saw his intervention in the sanctions debate as a deliberate attempt to wrest the command away from Baldwin. In fact, his attitude was more subtle. By speaking out for sanctions termination without going as far as taking a line of outright hostility to the League of Nations, it was he who combined decisiveness with moderation.[60] For the vast majority of Conservative MPs who found their position on the League of Nations at neither of the opposing extremes of Macmillan and Amery, it was Chamberlain who was the most commanding advocate of the middle way.

Ten

ROCKING THE BOAT

I

The Hoare–Laval fiasco had left the government battered and bruised. Baldwin's reputation for plain dealing had been damaged and enormous reliance was being placed upon the young Anthony Eden to regain the trust of liberal opinion which Hoare's diplomacy had so deeply offended. Although Chamberlain continued to steer a steady course from the Treasury, it was the high politics of foreign affairs that caused most comment in the leader pages of the press in early 1936. These were auspicious circumstances for Churchill to make a comeback with his campaign to boost rearmament as part of a commitment to international collective security. Unfortunately, it was also the time for Randolph Churchill to again embarrass his father by opposing the return to Parliament of Ramsay MacDonald's son, Malcolm.

Briefly Colonial Secretary in 1935, Malcolm MacDonald had lost his seat flying the National Labour colours in the general election. The Conservative domination of the Cabinet made his return to Parliament a priority in the cause of conveying the impression that Baldwin was still presiding over a truly National coalition. Unfortunately, Conservative Central Office's attempt to clear a path for him in the Scottish highland seat of Ross and Cromarty ran into the opposition of the local Unionist* Association. Rather than back MacDonald as the official National Government candidate, they decided to field their own Tory candidate and chose Randolph Churchill.

Whilst naturally sympathetic towards his son's views and ambitions, Churchill wrote wearily to his wife, Clementine:

how unfortunate and inconvenient such a fight is to me. 'Churchill v MacDonald'. If they get in, it would seem very difficult for Baldwin to invite me to take the Admiralty or the [Defence] co-ordinating job, and sit cheek by jowl with these wretched people . . . How will Baldwin take it? Will he regard

* As the Conservatives were still more popularly known in Scotland.

it as a definite declaration of war by me? I have of course expressed no opinion whatever, and Randolph will make it clear he is acting entirely on his own.[1]

Whilst Randolph was not technically standing against the National Government – he reminded *The Times* that he was 'the official Unionist candidate in support of the National Government'[2] – he was nonetheless publicly challenging its favoured candidate in the sort of contest guaranteed to generate maximum newspaper attention. *The Times* tried to insinuate, incorrectly, that his candidature was at his father's prompting, which encouraged another of the senior Churchill's now regular letters to the newspaper's proprietor accusing misrepresentation.[3] Rothermere and Beaverbrook both gave Randolph newspaper support (although the constituency was hardly their target market). Rothermere even approached Baldwin's socialist son, Oliver, to 'write up Randolph' and, as Winston reported to Clementine, 'write down Malcolm, which of course is what all other Socialists revel in. So we shall have Ramsay's son, Baldwin's son and my son – all mauling each other in this remote constituency ... When the contest gets a little further developed, I propose to utter the following "piece". "I wish Mr Baldwin would tell me the secret by which he keeps his son Oliver in such good order."' Musing (correctly as it transpired) that Hoare would probably go to the Admiralty after a decorous interval, Churchill sighed that his son's campaign would finish off his own chances of returning to the Cabinet.[4] The junior MacDonald's victory over the junior Churchill – beating him into third place – seemed, once again, to demonstrate not only Randolph's rash judgement but perhaps more worryingly that the historic family name was not necessarily an overriding electoral asset.[5] Yet if this was the message, then it made little lasting impact in Westminster where talk of creating a government minister responsible for coordinating defence was intensifying. This, it was rumoured, would be Churchill's great chance to return to the Cabinet.

II

During early 1936 the argument over the levels of expenditure needed to sustain Britain's security was complemented by discussion about how it could be better organized. In February, the Commons debated a proposal to create a new position, a Minister for the Coordination of Defence. Freed from any remaining pangs of loyalty to an administration whose Prime Minister he believed had snubbed him so badly, Austen Chamberlain criticised the government for its indolence and advocated making a single member of the Cabinet responsible for chairing the Committee of Imperial Defence and coordinating it with the Chiefs of Staff Committee.[6]

To his sister, Sir Austen wrote that if there was any truth in the rumour that Baldwin proposed 'to hand over Defence to Ramsay MacDonald there will be a howl of indignation & a vote of no confidence'. Sir Austen took the view that 'there is only one man who by his studies & his special abilities & aptitudes is marked out for it, & that man is Winston Churchill.' Nonetheless he doubted whether either Neville or Baldwin wanted him back in the government.[7]

Churchill had also at last come to recognize that Baldwin did not, by choice, want him back.[8] This was not because the Prime Minister thought Churchill a political has-been. Writing to Neville Chamberlain, Hoare explained that he had been offered a choice of returning to the Cabinet with either the new Defence portfolio or as First Lord of the Admiralty, since 'on no account' would Baldwin 'contemplate the possibility of Winston in the Cabinet for several obvious reasons, but chiefly for the risk that would be involved by having him in the Cabinet when the question of [the Prime Minister's] successor became imminent'.[9] Unknown to Churchill at this moment, Baldwin was contemplating making Neville Chamberlain the Defence Coordinating Minister, filling his vacancy at the Exchequer with his half-brother Austen. To make clear that he was still heir apparent, Baldwin seemingly proposed that Neville would continue to live in 11 Downing Street as the Prime Minister's right-hand man. Presented with these proposals, Neville replied that he would 'consider it' despite the fact that he 'did not want to leave the Exchequer'. He thought that Hoare or Austen were 'the only possible appointments' but hoped that Austen would not be given the job 'especially as after his speech it wd be said that he had been given the post to shut his mouth'. Meanwhile Austen counselled Neville not to take the Defence job since Churchill was the 'one man in his opinion really suitable'.[10] This was an interesting exhibition of the Chamberlain family's attitude to each other and the call of public service.

Around the Cabinet table, enthusiasm for Churchill was noticeable by its absence. The Health Minister, Kingsley Wood, thought 'it would never do to have Winston' and supported Austen for the job. Walter Runciman thought Churchill's genius at the post would soon wither away and believed Hoare 'would be best and that we ought not to be too "squeamish" about taking him in so soon'. Meanwhile, the Chief Whip, Captain David Margesson, also deprecated Churchill and 'suggested Inskip or (preferably) W[alter] Elliot'. On this basis Neville Chamberlain told Baldwin that he did not want the job and 'after reviewing the whole field came back to my original view that Sam [Hoare] was the best man'. Baldwin thought that it 'looked as if' it would have to be so, and reluctantly took Chamberlain's advice that the matter 'was too urgent' to postpone the appointment until after Easter.[11]

Meanwhile, the *Daily Telegraph* was writing up Churchill's chances for the Defence Coordination post as being 'prominently mentioned' with 'great interest'.[12] Churchill's problem was that his supporters were not in the government, nor were they strong enough to force the Prime Minister's hand from outside it. Nonetheless, whilst protesting that it would not 'break his heart whatever happens', Churchill began to think that the ineligibility of all the other likely contenders in one way or another pointed to his being offered the post, despite Baldwin's reluctance.[13] When the Conservative MP and former India diehard, Sir Roger Keyes, told Baldwin that Churchill's appointment was in both the party and the national interest, Baldwin implied that he would be a disruptive force in the Cabinet – or, as he put it, a disturbance to 'the smooth working of the machine'.[14] In the event, the ineligibility of the other candidates led Baldwin to make the unlikely appointment to the Defence Coordination Ministry of the Attorney-General, Sir Thomas Inskip, a decision likened to Caligula appointing his horse as consul.[15]

Much might be said in favour of Inskip's subsequent conduct at his new post. In particular, he was prominently involved in the decision to switch the emphasis from concentrating on the production of bombers in favour of making more fighters – which proved an important factor in the outcome of the Battle of Britain. In March 1936, however, his appointment was, as Amery pronounced, 'astonishing'.[16] Inskip had shown no particular interest in defence matters and offering him the job seemed to suggest two things, both of which were related: that Baldwin did not take rearmament seriously; and that he would not have Churchill back in the Cabinet under any circumstances whatsoever. Only days before, Amery had rather grandly recorded in his diary that 'smoking-room talk' had reached such a level of 'dissatisfaction' that he was being told not to be surprised if eventually he was 'forced to take the lead and call the Conservative Party out of the coalition'. Now he recorded that the choice of Inskip would 'prove to have greatly shaken [Baldwin's] authority in the House of Commons'.[17] The German remilitarization of the Rhineland had begun shortly before the creation of the new post was announced and, on top of his party political worries, Baldwin may have feared that a Churchill appointment at this time would be interpreted as a virtual declaration of war in Berlin. Austen Chamberlain thought that Baldwin had denied Churchill office 'for fear lest Hitler take his appointment ill and because the Prime Minister has a little mind and is both jealous and unforgiving'.[18]

The episode convinced Churchill that he could not ease himself back into the Cabinet solely through ingratiating himself with key groups inside the Conservative Party or with its leadership. Instead he would appeal above party labels to the broader constituency of all those, from left to right, concerned by the militarist intent of Nazi Germany. He was also determined not to be sidelined by the shimmering mirage of a junior appointment in the government. When he called for the creation of a Ministry of Supply to deal with munitions, he 'went out of his way to explain that he did not want the job for himself' and suggested Kingsley Wood for the post.[19] Meanwhile, Churchill's reputation with the government was certainly dented by his friendship with his scientific adviser, Professor Frederick Lindemann, whose dogmatic promotion of eccentric schemes on the Air Defence Research Committee of the Committee of Imperial Defence brought its respected Chairman, Henry Tizard, to the brink of resignation. Tizard wrote to the Air Secretary, Lord Swinton (formerly Sir Philip Cunliffe-Lister), complaining of Churchill's 'gross discourtesy' in 'circulating an attack on the Committee without taking the trouble to learn my views beforehand'.[20] Swinton himself complained bitterly to the Cabinet about Churchill's attitude on the committee insinuating that, like Lindemann, he was extremely disruptive, intransigent and wrong.[21] In the eventide of his tenure as Prime Minister, Baldwin was disinclined to welcome aboard those who behaved in this way.

III

Their cause articulated in the pages of the *Observer* by its editor, J.L. Garvin, the Conservative right feared that by alienating Italy over Abyssinia, Britain had a potential enemy to contend with in the Mediterranean – from where Britain's supply route to much of her empire could be cut off. This view was supported by a 'deluge of eloquence' from Churchill, who deduced the need to strengthen the British naval presence in the Mediterranean rather than leave British communications 'at the mercy of so unreliable a thing as Italian friendship'.[22] He was particularly concerned about the proposed withdrawal of British troops from Cairo. His response was to get together a deputation of MPs to speak to Baldwin on the subject.[23] The deputation included his fellow old comrades in the fight against the Indian reforms, John Gretton and Sir Roger Keyes, but was largely composed of those who had been on the government side in the Indian dispute.[24] In fact, the thread binding these colleagues together was less their ideological cohesion than the fact that they were senior backbench figures. The majority of them were members of the 'Other Club' which Churchill had co-founded back in 1911 with F.E. Smith (later Lord Birkenhead) and in whose hospitable dinner-table discussions he remained a leading light.[25] Austen Chamberlain was particularly keen to fuse those concerned with the situation in the Mediterranean with those who were informally gathering into 'the Defence Group'. In this way he sought to cement with Churchill the leadership of the pre-war politicians to petition Baldwin on rearmament. Churchill wrote to Eden at the Foreign Office to complain about the way in which the government would force through their policy of reducing Britain's military presence in Egypt and the Mediterranean without 'Parliament having an inkling'.[26] However, with more pressing concerns, there was no question of Egypt becoming an obsession in the way that had India. Instead, the tactic of organized deputations became the form in which Churchill and those who thought similarly would make their views known to the leadership without actually going so far as to vote against the government in the Commons. On 28 July, Austen Chamberlain and Churchill led a further delegation to meet the Prime Minister in synchronization with one led from the Lords by Salisbury. This time the demand was for a secret session in which Parliament could be properly informed about the extent of the defence deficiencies (something the government had no intention of conceding). With Labour refusing to get involved,[27] this 'Defence Group' consisted 'only of people who were all associated in one way or another in the pre-war days, and nearly all of whom have served in the Cabinet or held office'.[28] Diehards were well represented.[29] A further deputation on 23 November from the same group proved equally unable to prod the government into greater action. As a tactic, it was virtually worthless.

Reluctant to vote against Baldwin, Churchill nonetheless had no compunction about speaking out against the Prime Minister's professional torpor. This provoked the former Air Minister, Lord Londonderry (Churchill's Germanophile second cousin), to warn him about the dangers 'of hitting the poor little man too hard because it will evoke a wave of sympathy which he will be able to stimulate by platitudinous broadcasts'.[30] This view was shared by another parliamentarian and cousin, Frederick Guest, who advised Churchill to stick to 'smashing the hypocritical humbug of the Pacifist Socialist Party' and thus shore up the government rather than trying to 'break down SB' since 'the party will simply and immediately crown [Neville Chamberlain]. You can lead the Conservative party but you cannot break the Party machine.'[31]

It was generally accepted that Baldwin, now in his thirteenth year as party leader, would probably not wish to remain at the helm for much longer. Neville Chamberlain was the clear successor and with the economy continuing to prosper it looked as if only the unpredictable eruptions of foreign affairs could hamper a smooth handover. This was indeed the one potential tripwire for, as Austen Chamberlain reportedly observed to his brother, 1936 was the first time since Lord Salisbury's Government that the House of Commons had been primarily divided on foreign policy.[32] In this sense, defence did indeed provide a platform for Churchill to emerge as the Tory spokesman on the great issue of the day. However, without a Carlton Club-style *putsch*, there was no clear route by which he could succeed Baldwin when he was not even in the Cabinet. He had tried playing the party loyalty card and had not been rewarded for it with the Defence Coordination portfolio and it seemed as if Baldwin would not have him at any price. Indeed, even had he been so minded, it was not clear whom the Premier could sack in order to give Churchill an appropriate job. Eden was at the Foreign Office with pro-Genevan credentials and was, at any rate, only six months into the job. Baldwin had just given the Admiralty to Hoare, Swinton was genuinely working hard to rebuild the RAF from the Air Ministry, Duff Cooper was a 'hawk' at the War Office and Inskip was hardly going to be replaced only three months after his appointment. Churchill had ruled himself out for a Ministry of Supply and there was no question of him taking a post that did not involve the defence issue. For all these reasons, it was hard to see how Churchill could supplant Chamberlain as Baldwin's successor merely by repeatedly demonstrating loyalty. His only chance lay in the possibility that the course of events would completely discredit the government's approach, calling for a complete reconstruction. In the meantime, he would have to make the most of support from the infantry. Lord Bayford, a former junior minister in the Lloyd George coalition and current Chairman of the Association of Conservative Clubs, told his association that Churchill's inclusion in the Cabinet would 'give great satisfaction in many Conservative circles'.[33] The MP, Oliver Locker Lampson, wrote to Churchill encouraging him that his stance on defence issues marked 'a peak point in your national importance'.[34] What was more, far from being alone in the parliamentary party, Churchill was now in regular contact with disaffected senior backbenchers.

Writing in his memoirs in 1948, Sir Henry Page Croft recalled that for two years after the end of the Indian rebellion Churchill led a 'little band' who regularly met up over dinner and at weekends to discuss their response to Britain's defence deficiencies. Whilst Page Croft implied that this grew out of their activities fighting the India Bill, in terms of those who regularly met up the group was not exclusively diehard.[35] Once they had been 'working together [for] about a year'[36] their meetings suddenly became public knowledge. Under the banner headline 'ANTI-BALDWIN "SHADOW CABINET" MEETS' the left-liberal *News Chronicle* reported that 'Mr Baldwin's most notable critics', Churchill, Sir Austen Chamberlain, Sir Robert Horne, Sir Edward Grigg and Sir Henry Page Croft, had met at Lord Winterton's Sussex country house, Shillinglee Park, presumably to discuss the forthcoming Cabinet appointments to the Colonial Office and the Admiralty. Denied an interview with Winterton, the roving reporter was left to speculate and glean the musings of some locals in a nearby pub.[37] Sir Austen assured his brother Neville, who relayed the information to Baldwin, that the group was motivated by a genuine concern about the state of national defence rather than any wider hostility to the government. This encouraged another of Baldwin's observations about Churchill's lack of judgement.[38] Nonetheless, the incident rattled the front bench. One Cabinet minister (sadly unnamed) was sufficiently incensed at this senior backbench factionalism to shout 'Traitors' at the alleged conspirators when they walked into the Commons chamber. Baldwin made matters considerably worse by referring to the meeting as occurring at 'the time of the year when midges come out of dirty ditches'.[39] The previous month, Austen Chamberlain had spent the weekend at Churchill's Kent residence, Chartwell, where he had discussed the German threat with Churchill, Page Croft, Horne, Grigg, Bob Boothby and Professor Lindemann. Writing to his sister about the weekend, Sir Austen wrote, 'Is it a Cave? Well some would like to make it so, but I am not a Cave man.'[40] Yet in the aftermath of the Rhineland invasion and Baldwin's appointment of Inskip instead of Churchill, the increasingly incensed elder Chamberlain was forced to admit that 'I am being driven into opposition or nearly so'.[41]

Correspondence with senior statesmen did not, in itself, give Churchill a commanding platform from which to return to office. Lloyd George felt that 'Winston has no following in the country. He has no "region" on which he is based for support like the Chamberlains in the Midlands, the Stanleys in Lancashire, the Aclands in the West. He's a stunter. He can put things neatly: "SB has chosen between the devil and the Neville", and last year "between the devil and the deep LG."'[42] Halfway through 1936, Churchill found himself lacking more than a territorial base. The Prime Minister was the ultimate arbiter of patronage and as the wealthy émigré American socialite and Conservative MP for Southend, Sir Henry 'Chips' Channon, perceived the situation in his diary: Baldwin 'hated' Churchill, just as the latter was 'consumed with contempt, jealousy, indeed hatred for Baldwin, whom he always denigrates'.[43] For all his alleged popularity amongst certain sections of the party and the readership of the *Daily Telegraph*, Churchill seemed to be no nearer to office than at any time since 1930.

IV

By the middle of 1936 Churchill's views straddled all wings of the party. The right wing agreed with his call for greater rearmament, his rejection of giving back Germany's old colonies, his call to end sanctions against Italy and his plea for British non-involvement in the Spanish Civil War, which began in July that year. Yet these were all to greater or lesser degrees party policy anyway and only a few Tory mavericks disagreed with them in principle. Whilst the Conservative right wing was not interested in joining France in her attempt to build an eastern European security pact against Germany, the Locarno Treaty commitments to defend France against German invasion were generally accepted, and Churchill's Francophilia was shared by Austen Chamberlain and, if a little more ambiguously, by Amery.[44] Churchill's support for the League of Nations was also still party policy although, with the Italian sanctions in the course of being abandoned, it was clear that the commitment was now extremely shallow, despite Eden's occupancy of the Foreign Office. Noting that Churchill wanted to bury Britain's differences with Italy, Amery thought that 'it is amazing to see how far he has come round since he declared himself an out and out sanctioneer last October.'[45]

Following the remilitarization of the Rhineland, Churchill tried to explain his views to the Conservative backbench Foreign Affairs Committee. The League of Nations, he told them, might be a relatively new mechanism in international affairs but it could be used for the same traditional ends that had always guided British foreign policy: the prevention of the continental hegemony of any one power. It was, he elucidated to Lord Londonderry, a continuation of the four-hundred-year tradition in which 'to oppose the strongest power in Europe' Britain had involved herself on the continent 'by weaving together a combination of other countries strong enough to face the bully'.[46] Many Tories questioned his interpretation of the League's function. When Amery suggested that it might force Britain to abandon its security mechanism on 'some technical or minor issue' of 'universal collective security', Churchill backtracked that 'he was not thinking of the Covenant but of more specific arrangements under the aegis of the League'. This would have come as news to Churchill's forthcoming band of non-Tory collaborators who joined him under the banner 'Arms and the Covenant'. Even his admirers pointed out to him that the case for rearmament and peacetime encirclement of Germany was hardly in the spirit of the League of Nations.[47]

For the most part, Churchill failed to allay the Tory right's fear that the League was essentially antagonistic to British national interest. As well as its international character, it was partly the League's legacy of supporting disarmament and attracting liberal-minded intellectuals that made it so unappealing to the right. Perhaps the main barrier, however, was that it was a mechanism through which the Soviet Union could interfere in international affairs. Churchill's interest in bringing Stalin into the collective security system against Germany was anathema to those Tories who felt that, whatever Hitler's many flaws, he had the one redeeming feature of being a vigorous anti-Bolshevik. Amery regarded the Foreign Affairs Committee to be 'practically solid' against Churchill's 'continental arrangements that committed us to Russia', leading Churchill – whilst 'against declaring that we washed our hands of Russia and Eastern Europe' – to make the qualification that neither could Britain commit herself to military intervention on Russia's behalf. Austen Chamberlain remained initially silent on the issue of appealing to Moscow, seemingly unsure where he stood.[48] Far from wanting Churchill's anti-German 'league of coercion', Amery expressed his view to the Germanophobic Permanent Under-Secretary at the Foreign Office, Sir Robert Vansittart, that 'Germany could only come into a satisfactory and stable European system if Russia is left out of the picture'.[49] As far as Amery was concerned, 'instead of leaving the three sources of danger, Germany, Russia and Japan to neutralise each other, we were committing the world and ourselves to participation in their struggles (and as far as our interests were concerned on the wrong side)'.[50] This was not merely a right-wing response but one shared by both Neville Chamberlain and Stanley Baldwin. Meeting the delegation on defence matters led by Churchill and Austen Chamberlain in July 1936, the Prime Minister hoped that 'if there is any fighting in Europe to be done, I should like to see the Bolshies and the Nazis doing it'. Britain should not be drawn into such a conflict even if France went to aid her Russian ally 'owing to that appalling pact they made'.[51] To Amery, the logic of this was to rebuild the Stresa front with Italy as a means of encircling Germany without Russian help.[52]

Following the Great War, Britain had been given an international mandate to govern former German colonies like Tanganyika. Tory imperialists were adamant that Hitler's request for their return should be denied. Page Croft seconded Duncan Sandys' motion at the Party Conference in October 1936 demanding a government assurance to this effect, Baldwin having been characteristically vague on the issue.[53] Patrick Donner's little coterie of Tory MPs[54] may have been formed in the backlash to Hitler's Rhineland remilitarization, but it was stopping Hitler in Africa that inspired some of their most concerted action.[55] Whilst old diehards made up the core of these concerned MPs, two Early Day Motions on the subject from Duncan Sandys together attracted the signatures of a quarter of the parliamentary party.[56] Since all those MPs who held ministerial and government payroll positions could not sign, this was a clear indication of massive support within the Conservative Party for a firm line. The general position for a discernible section of the Tory right was summarized by its parliamentary 'Imperial Policy Group': no colonial concessions to Germany (nor in Egypt to Italy), removal of the League of Nations' coercive clauses, British rearmament, defence of France and Belgium from attack, but no military commitment to the states of eastern Europe where, instead, concessions to Germany should be made.[57] Further evidence of the scrambled viewpoint within the parliamentary Conservative Party was demonstrated by those who signed up to an Early Day Motion of 29 June 1936 which called on the government 'to eschew any military or other commitment which would have the appearance of an alliance between Great Britain and France and Soviet Russia and adheres firmly to the desire for closer relations between Great Britain, Germany, and France'. Signed by Amery, this was a right-wing motion that failed to attract many traditional diehards. In truth, united in the need to rearm to face a possible threat, the old diehard element were every bit as divided over the options for British foreign policy as were their former adversaries on India and disarmament.[58]

Whatever the hesitations of others, by the summer of 1936, Churchill was convinced that all other considerations were subservient to the goal of restraining a resurgent Germany and that, if need be, this meant calling upon 'the aid of Russia and all the minor countries in the East and South of Europe'. Action through the League of Nations was 'the means by which all these overwhelming forces can be assembled' and 'by which the greatest unity can be obtained in this country'.[59] In conversation with the Cabinet Secretary, Sir Maurice Hankey, Churchill was highly critical of anti-League Tory MPs. Under 'no illusions' about the League's weakness, he saw 'that the British people will not take re-armament seriously except as part of the League policy'. Churchill wanted the government to undertake with France a detailed study as to whether the Soviet Union was 'a fit ally worth having or not'.[60]

If the British electorate would not support rearmament unless it had the support of the League, then it was equally crucial that Churchill should try to make sure that the traditional supporters of the League should become supporters of rearmament.[61] In April he had written to Lord Robert Cecil, the tireless President of the pro-Genevan pressure group, the League of Nations Union (LNU), on the growing totalitarian menace in Europe. In his letter, Churchill suggested that once the LNU had addressed the 'ways and means' of adopting its principles, they would 'need a secular arm' and that he 'might help in this'. This was not an unconditional surrender to the LNU by the bellicose senior statesman. As he made clear, the LNU would also have to come round to his thinking since 'It seems a mad business ... to try and tame and cow the spirit of our people with peace films, anti-recruiting propaganda and resistance to defence measures. Unless the free and law respecting nations are prepared to organise, arm and combine they are going to be smashed up. This is going to happen quite soon. But I believe we still have a year to combine and marshal superior forces in defence of the League and its Covenant.'[62] In promoting the seemingly blank cheque of collective security, Churchill risked outpacing Austen Chamberlain who, although a supporter of the principle of the League, saw regional pacts as the more immediate form in which to practise German containment. During 1936, Churchill was to identify himself much more closely with the LNU than Sir Austen, their former honorary Vice-President, was prepared to do. Churchill's contemplation of rapprochement with the Soviet Union (he avoided committing himself to a full-scale alliance) signalled a major departure from the method in which he had tried and failed to regain office since 1931, as the tribune of the right-wing faction. Only when the Tory right were especially offended by the spectre of international Communism by Soviet intervention in the Spanish Civil War did he retract his campaign for making a diplomatic approach to Moscow.[63]

As well as pushing the LNU in the direction of rearmament, Churchill had to ensure that it focused on the German danger rather than on its ongoing obsession with Italy. He was also increasingly in communication with the Anti-Nazi Society, a pressure group charged with drawing attention to the menacing nature of Germany, in particular its anti-Semitism. It was from this association that the 'Defence of Freedom and Peace' movement under its slogan 'Arms and the Covenant' sprang.[64] This latter group, often referred to as the 'Focus', avoided publicity, meeting largely in private until its calling of a public meeting at the Albert Hall in December 'under the auspices' of the LNU. In May, Churchill spoke at a private lunch for the 'Focus' circle which included several concerned members of the Liberal Party, including his friends Sir Archibald Sinclair (Samuel's successor as Liberal leader) and Lady Violet Bonham-Carter. Churchill made clear, despite initial hesitancy, that Britain would have to pursue a policy of full-scale rearmament if it was to stand up to Germany and he suggested a manifesto be drawn up setting forth the group's aims 'and on this basis enlist members and supporters from every section of public'.[65] The burden of the group's funding was met by three of its members: Eugen Spier, Sir Robert Waley-Cohen (the Chairman of British Shell) and the chemical industrialist, Sir Robert Mond.[66] As Jews, these three men had good reason to loathe the Nazi Reich.

The eclectic nature of the anti-Hitler confederacy with whom Churchill now mixed was demonstrated in July when he tried to fit as many as he could round the lunch table in his London flat. Liberals and captains of industry rubbed shoulders with the Tory MPs Oliver Locker Lampson and Duncan Sandys (Churchill's new son-in-law) and the General Secretary of the TUC, Walter Citrine (with whom Churchill had crossed swords during the General Strike ten years previously). Keeping such a politically diverse group united was a difficult task, but over lunch a few ground rules were established: Russia would be looked to as a potential bulwark against German eastern expansion; a research committee would be set up to keep all the 'Focus' members fully briefed and the group should start organizing nationally in October.[67] In the meantime it was agreed to adopt the title of 'Defence of Freedom and Peace Union' and it was also agreed, as Churchill argued, that it should not form a 'new and rival society to existing organisations, but only a welding together of those organisations'. Cheered by the fact that the TUC Conference had voted for rearmament, Churchill deduced from this that 'Labour is more alive than many of the Conservatives.' He hoped that the group would therefore be in a position to get 'large numbers' of prominent Labour men to join, helped by the fact that Walter Citrine should chair their great launch meeting.[68] This sounded like a man who had lost all interest in becoming leader of the Conservative Party through the traditional process. Nevertheless, he was keen to entice the ultra-respectable Austen Chamberlain to come to the group's meetings even if only in an observatory role.[69] However, nervous after his former experiences on the LNU Executive, when he had found it full of 'some of the worst cranks I have known', Austen Chamberlain preferred not to be associated in the group's public launch.[70] When Citrine objected to Lord Lloyd being present because of the difficulties it would create with trades unionists, Churchill appears to have agreed not to press for his India diehard colleague's inclusion.[71] Few better examples of Churchill's abandonment of the right wing at this particular moment could be presented than this concession and he even planned to 'get in touch' with the Labour leader, Clement Attlee, once the 'Freedom and Peace Union' was properly launched.[72] As he put it to his son, 'all the Left Wing intelligencia [sic] are coming to look to me for protection of their ideas, and I will give it whole heartedly in return for their aid in the rearmament of Britain'.[73] Ultimately, though, he knew where power lay: in December he warned Lord Robert Cecil, who was busy collecting signatures amongst his left of centre friends that 'unless you have hope of strong Conservative support, it will only concentrate the Tory antagonism upon the League of Nations Union'.[74]

Since the passage of the India legislation and the winding up of the

India Defence League, there had been no effective popular movement with which Churchill could associate the promotion of his views. In contrast to the Indian campaign, he had avoided dividing against the government in Parliament in favour of the less openly confrontational course of leading private deputations to the Cabinet on defence issues. Now there was the prospect that the 'Defence of Freedom and Peace' group promised to act like a new India Defence League, providing him with a rather more broadly based platform. Indeed, one of its prominent members, Sir Norman Angell, thought that 'if and when Churchill goes into the cabinet, [the Freedom and Peace Union] will ... simply dissolve'.[75] However, whilst Churchill was their ablest platform speaker and his support was a boon to the group, some of its members were extremely distrustful of his motives.[76] The central intention of the group was to enlighten public and 'informed' opinion by providing information in support of their anti-German objectives. This, of course, corresponded with championing Churchill's but the latter was not its *raison d'être*.

Beside his membership of the 'Freedom and Peace' group, Churchill accepted the presidency of the British Section of the New Commonwealth Society.[77] Although committed to 'the promotion of International Law and Order through the creation of a Tribunal in Equity and an International Police Force', it was the sort of organisation which senior individuals from all parties and distinctions felt obliged to join – including Neville Chamberlain, whose advice Churchill sought out before accepting the presidency. Having made clear that he would not consider himself bound by all of its views,[78] Churchill associated himself with the New Commonwealth Society because it was influential. When he addressed it at the Dorchester Hotel on 25 November, there were around 450 people in attendance, including politicians and diplomatic representatives from over forty countries and, as the *New Statesman* put it, 'numerous Tories, some of them the most extreme Diehards'.[79] Inevitably, it was all too much for the eccentric benefactor of right-wing causes, Lady Houston, who despaired at Churchill's 'coquettes with these disarmament fanatics'.[80]

Churchill's relations with the New Commonwealth, the LNU and the 'Freedom and Peace' group all suggested that he was looking outside the Conservative Party for support. Nonetheless, he remained mindful of the need not to divorce himself completely from the Tory right. A case in point was his reaction to the Spanish Civil War – a conflict in which liberal and socialist sympathies lay with the left-wing Republican forces but, as Churchill recognized, 'the great bulk of the Conservative Party [were] very much inclined to cheer the so-called Spanish rebels'. Favouring non-intervention, Churchill wrote to the French Ambassador to warn him that if his country intervened to help the Spanish Government, then there was a danger of a British realignment against Communism that would leave Britain and France 'estranged'.[81]

With some qualification, Churchill supported the British Government's call for non-intervention as the safest option for preventing the escalation of the conflict into a European war. Since it also worked to the advantage of Franco who received arms and assistance unhindered from Italy and Germany, it contented figures on the Tory right who were openly supportive of Franco.[82] Churchill had no desire to destroy his credibility amongst Tories by appearing overly sympathetic to the Communists as the MP and sometime diehard, the Duchess of Atholl, proceeded to do. He had no intention whatsoever of accepting the Duchess's invitation to him to listen to her case and attend the 'Annual Congress of Peace and Friendship with the USSR'.[83] Such a move would have been entirely counter-productive in trying to convince the Conservative Party to stand up to Hitler, and he made a point of condemning Moscow's interference in Spain, to the annoyance of his new occasional dining partner, the Russian Ambassador.[84] If such zealous organizations as the Anti-Socialist and Anti-Communist Union were not disturbed by Churchill's new friends on the left, then he was probably pretty safe from charges of fellow-travelling.[85] Indeed, it was individuals from the Tory right wing who expressed admiration for his speech on defence in the Commons on 12 November in which he criticized the government for not responding sufficiently quickly to the need to rearm.[86] Baldwin made what Amery thought 'a most lamentable confession and one which filled the House with dismay' by stating that he had not commenced rearmament earlier because it would have been unpopular with the electorate.[87] Stripped of the qualifications in which it was originally couched, this statement was to do enormous damage to Baldwin's reputation after the Second World War broke out.

On 3 December the LNU and the 'Movement for the Defence of Freedom and Peace' held their great rally in the Albert Hall. The occasion had received much advance billing as the effective launch of a crusade in favour of collective security – 'Arms and the Covenant'. Churchill's speech was to be the star attraction. The previous month the *Oxford Times* had commented that when Churchill came to speak at the Oxford Union he drew 'the largest crowd of undergraduates since Mr Lloyd George came to the same hall in 1912'.[88] Amongst the twenty MPs from all parties seated on the platform at the Albert Hall was the Liberal leader, Sir Archibald Sinclair.[89] With typical pedantry, Sir Austen Chamberlain had declined to take part in the meeting or join the organization's committee, despite agreeing with its programme and being prepared to have a statement of his support read out at the meeting.[90] In the chair for the occasion, Walter Citrine made clear that the speakers were making a personal contribution and that this was not the launch of a 'Popular Front or Centre Party'.[91] This was probably a reference to rumours articulated in the *New Statesman*, that whilst for the moment 'no new party or organisation is to be formed . . . the logic of present politics is surely the formation of a Centre front with Winston Churchill as the effective leader, if not as the potential Prime Minister' of a coalition of moderate left and right forces.[92] The *Spectator* had likewise predicted that the meeting would further elevate Churchill's reputation, commenting that 'if he bids for the role of democratic leader there may be considerable stirring in the square half mile south of Trafalgar Square.'[93] Such possibilities were not in the minds of the organizers.[94] Yet the success of the Albert Hall meeting was only a demonstration of the forces that could be marshalled once a momentum was established. The difficulty was in sustaining this momentum when in competition with other distracting issues. With this in mind, Citrine had managed to prevent Churchill at the Albert Hall from tying his message in favour of collective security to a statement about the King.[95] It was the revelation of Edward VIII's desire to marry Mrs Simpson, then in the process of divorcing her second husband, that now diverted Churchill's energy and threatened to destroy his political leadership of the coalition of supporters of collective security.

V

An American divorcee, Wallis Simpson was regarded in court circles as a spectacularly unsuitable choice of consort to the new King. The son of an American mother, Churchill was unlikely to have been as insufferable about the transatlantic connection as some chose to be. More important was the reaction to the visible wreckage of her private life; divorced persons were still barred from the royal enclosure. Furthermore, Mrs Simpson's personality, an acquired taste even for those with a hardened palate, compounded her difficulties, denying her support amongst those in positions of influence who might otherwise have wished to make an exception for her. To most, she was a disaster poised to bring down a gifted and handsome monarch. Only to those who regarded the young King as lazy, self-willed, disturbingly right wing and on an inevitable collision course with his government did she seem to be a godsend.

The Prime Minister had already spoken to Lord Salisbury about the coming difficulty over the King's marital intentions. Together with Lord Selbourne, Salisbury had suggested that Baldwin receive a deputation of 'the elder statesmen . . . Austen, Winston, Crewe, Derby etc', as well as the Labour leader, Clement Attlee, to 'strengthen [Baldwin's] hands'.[96] Having developed a rapport with the King when the young man had been Prince of Wales, Churchill told Salisbury that he could not join the delegation since by doing so he would 'lose all influence over the King' in the likely event that he should seek his counsel. The implication was therefore that Churchill would seek to exert his independent influence on the King to end his relationship with Mrs Simpson.[97] It was also a means of keeping his own options open should the political Establishment be brought down over the issue.

Churchill had been briefed on Edward's attachment towards Mrs Simpson by the King's legal adviser, Walter Monckton, in July and had indeed expressed a desire that the King should end the damaging liaison. However, according to his own recollections, he did not see the King on the subject until 4 December, the day after the LNU/'Focus' group rally at the Albert Hall. Edward had sought his Prime Minister's approval before seeing Churchill, whom he had selected, as Churchill prophesied, as a trusted adviser independent of government patronage. Such was the rift and extraordinary role reversal between the King and his first minister that Baldwin soon wished he had not given permission for the meeting between Edward and Churchill.[98] On meeting the King, Churchill was given the impression that if Edward insisted on marrying Mrs Simpson, then Baldwin was equally determined to force an immediate abdication. To Churchill, the King pleaded that what he desired was a fortnight to weigh up the options. Churchill was shocked at the effect the stress was having on the monarch's health and believed that his desire for time could not be denied. He wrote urgently to Baldwin urging him not to rush the King into a hasty decision.[99] However, what worried the Prime Minister was what Edward might do with the extra time. He might decide to finish his relationship with Mrs Simpson – considerable pressure was already being put on her via Lord Beaverbrook to end the affair herself.[100] Alternatively, the King might launch a direct appeal to the country, in the process gathering around him a 'King's Party' and manoeuvring Baldwin into a position where, unwilling to do his monarch's bidding, he was forced to tender his resignation.

The question of delaying a decision was pivotal. Churchill toyed with various proposals to keep Edward on the throne, including one that would have involved making Mrs Simpson Duchess of Cornwall rather than Queen whilst barring from the succession any children she had by Edward.[101] Baldwin, however, refused to countenance such a scheme and made the fact clear to Edward, ensuring that the issue was a stark one between denial of Mrs Simpson or immediate abdication. According to the Secretary of State for India, Lord Zetland, who wrote to the Viceroy on the subject, if the King ignored his Prime Minister's advice, 'It was pointed out at the Cabinet that this might involve the resignation of the Government and that in this case it would give rise to a Constitutional issue of the first magnitude, viz the King v. the Government. It seemed that the King had been encouraged to believe that Winston Churchill would in these circumstances be prepared to form an alternative Government'.[102] The Tory MP, Victor Cazalet, noted down almost verbatim what Amery was also recording in his own diary, that 'stories are rife about a plot to make [Churchill] Prime Minister, have an election, supported by Rothermere and Beaverbrook – a kind of "French Revolt". What folly.' No admirer of Churchill, Sir John Reith, the Director-General of the BBC, feared that one of the possibilities was indeed that 'we might have the King as a sort of dictator, or with Churchill as PM, which is presumably what that worthy is working for.'[103] With these rumours circulating in official circles, Salisbury wrote to Churchill expressing his 'great anxiety' lest Churchill's position was changing from counselling the King to finish with Mrs Simpson to that of championing the King whatever the decision to which he came.[104] Salisbury had some reason to be apprehensive on this account for Churchill advised Edward to consult with his supporters, Lord Beaverbrook and the Ulster Premier, Lord Craigavon, and told him that by gaining time he was 'gaining good positions and assembling large forces behind him'.[105] It is a matter of personal interpretation as to whether these forces could be a reference to forming an alternative government if need be, or merely, that there was a body of influential people prepared to ensure that the government did not bully the King into making a hasty decision one way or the other.

Disastrously, in what Amery regarded as 'a most mischievous manifesto'[106] in the Sunday newspapers on 6 December (the story of the King's private life had broken in the national press three days earlier), Churchill allowed his detractors to suggest personal motives by writing that 'If the King refuses to take the advice of his Ministers they are of course free to resign. They have no right whatever to put pressure upon him to accept their advice by soliciting beforehand assurances from the Leader of the Opposition that he will not form an alternative administration in the event of their resignation, and thus confronting the King with an ultimatum.'[107] This seemed to raise the prospect of a scenario whereby if the King challenged his ministers (and the Opposition had committed themselves to support the government on the matter), Churchill would be the obvious person to whom he would entrust the formation of an interim government. Even if Churchill had not intended, or foreseen, this interpretation of his comments,[108] it could easily be used by his opponents to suggest that he was primarily looking out for himself in the crisis.

Now that the affair was at last public knowledge, the desired period of reflection for the King was cut short. Churchill's public contribution to the debate was not only that the King must be given time but that the Cabinet had not, alone, the authority to force his abdication. Parliament would also need to be consulted. All this raised the spectre of what Baldwin least wanted – a divisive public debate about where the monarch's duty lay.[109] Churchill argued that the reverse was true because 'if an abdication were to be hastily extorted, the outrage so committed would cast its shadow forward across many chapters of the history of the British Empire.'[110]

The assertion that Churchill genuinely wanted to force the government's resignation so that he could form a fresh administration of 'King's friends' is fatally contradicted by the advice he gave to the King. The advice was that 'The only possibility of Your Majesty remaining on the Throne is if you could subscribe to some such Declaration as the following:- "The King will not enter into any contract of marriage contrary to the advice of His Ministers."'[111] This formula would have ensured that the King could not have insisted both upon marrying Mrs Simpson and remaining King. It would have prevented any circumstances in which the government would have felt obliged to collectively tender its resignation. The charge that Churchill desired such a course so that he could lead the King's Party therefore collapses. Unfortunately for Churchill, others were unaware of the advice he had given, which may also explain the failure of those dependent upon secondary sources to get to the truth of Churchill's real motives. Only those who were with him during the restless weekend working out the formulae (Lord Winterton, Archibald Sinclair and Bob Boothby) could vouch for his actual strategy.[112] It was through these sources that such disparate voices as Sir Henry 'Chips' Channon and the New Statesman were able to pronounce Churchill's innocence to what remained a sceptical audience. The New Statesman pronounced that 'when all is known [Churchill] will be found to have played no intriguer's part . . . His advice to the King, my informer says . . . will be found to have been impeccable from every constitutional point of view'.[113]

Part of the problem seems to have been that Churchill genuinely believed that, given time, Edward would either agree to drop Mrs Simpson or, as he later said to Baldwin, 'if for any reason the Simpson divorce does not go through it will be felt by many millions of people throughout the Empire that the abdication could have been avoided . . . Surely the Prime Minister will lie under the charge of having left his Sovereign in ignorance of the legal facts, and thus confronting him with an unreal dilemma?'[114] There was, after all, some grounds for believing that Mrs Simpson's divorce might not go through unchallenged. The decree nisi had been granted in Ipswich on 27 October but it would only become absolute six months later. The law stipulated that if the grounds for divorce (Mr Simpson's adultery – conveniently enough in the public location of a hotel) were faked by deliberate collusion between the couple petitioning for divorce because the plaintiff (Mrs Simpson) was already involved with another man, then the divorce would not be legal.[115] On these grounds the divorce should not have gone through. It is interesting that there is no surviving evidence of Baldwin trying to use his influence with sections of the press (or the security service) to try to expose the dubious legal basis for the divorce – which, if leaked, would have destroyed any chance of Mrs Simpson marrying the King.[116]

Monday, 7 December was the first parliamentary opportunity to raise the matter following its public disclosure. When Baldwin announced that he had no further statement to make on the royal situation, Churchill, as Amery recorded in his diary, 'tried to get an assurance that "no irrevocable step would be taken before the House had received a full statement" and tried to develop the question into a little speech. He was completely staggered by the unanimous hostility of the House, as well as being called to order by the Speaker.'[117] Lord Winterton, who sat in the Commons, later reflected that Churchill had received 'one of the angriest manifestations I have ever heard directed against a man in the House of Commons'.[118] The National Labour MP, Harold Nicolson, watching how Churchill had 'collapsed utterly in the House', was not alone in feeling that Churchill had 'undone in five minutes the patient reconstruction of two years'.[119] Bob Boothby agreed, telling Churchill in exasperation that his intervention had 'reduced the number of potential supporters' of their position on the crisis 'to the minimum possible' which he thought was 'now about seven in all'. Victor Cazalet described Churchill's flop as 'almost pitiable, if he did not deserve it for what he has done'.[120]

Still struggling to digest the enormity of the damage he had caused to himself, Churchill was warned by a member of the 'Focus' group that if he persisted in his stance, then 'those of us who have worked with you in the Freedom and Peace movement [would have to] dissociate ourselves from your standpoint.'[121] This reinforced the fears of 'Focus' activists who had been wary of giving him too prominent a role in the first place.[122] In the aftermath of his Commons humbling, Churchill found himself surrounded in the Commons smoking room by some of his 'most loyal supporters' roundly accusing him of 'playing for his own hand'. As Boothby informed him, these supporters could no longer follow him blindly 'because they cannot be sure where the hell they are going to be landed next'.[123]

Churchill backtracked in the Commons on 10 December following the King's announcement of abdication. Amery thought that, despite rising 'in face of a hostile House', Churchill's strategic retreat was 'an admirably phrased little speech'. Even Geoffrey Dawson wrote to him claiming to be impressed by the speech's 'thoroughly sound, constitutional point of view'.[124] The episode had, however, done nothing to dispel the continuing doubt over Churchill's judgement and motives and it is little wonder that he was seen a few days later still looking 'distraught'.[125] The false accusation that he had wanted to use the issue to seize power personally was perhaps the most damaging aspect of his intervention. That the King was also supported by the notoriously anti-Baldwin press lords, Rothermere and Beaverbrook, seemed to add credence to the claim.[126] It took time for others to follow Amery's revised view that such allegations had been 'unjust' since as Churchill was 'personally very fond of the King' it was primarily his horror at 'the King's difficulties [which] may also have helped upset his judgement'.[127] This was a fair analysis of the trouble into which Churchill's emotional and sentimental nature could land him. Yet he had bounced back from seeming political death before. By 12 December he was back in the Commons making what Winterton regarded 'one of the best speeches of his life' on defence policy.[128] Whatever its long-term implications, the short-term effects of the crisis reversed the fortunes of Churchill and Baldwin.[129] As Amery recorded for posterity, the Prime Minister 'a few weeks ago [had driven] us all to despair by his fatuous confession that he had done nothing about defence because public opinion was pacifist, and it seemed clear that the sooner he was got rid of the better. And yet for this particular [abdication] crisis he was ideally fitted.'[130] Boothby's not disinterested advice reflected his desire to coax Churchill further towards the left and the advocates of collective security since 'the Die-hards are not fundamentally loyal to you, ... the Press Lords (and especially one of them) are your most dangerous enemies, and ... Brendan [Bracken] is the best friend and the worst counsellor in the world'.[131]

VI

The first half of 1937 found Churchill in subdued mood. His antics during the abdication crisis had overshadowed the launch of the 'Defence of Freedom and Peace' movement. Quoting the Spectator's view that 'the reputation which he was beginning to shake off of [sic] as a wayward genius unserviceable in counsel has settled firmly on his shoulders again', one historian has concluded that the crisis 'brought to an abrupt end the moves to put Churchill at the head of a popular front ... [although even without this] it would almost certainly have been killed by other serious differences among those who hoped to bring it about'.[132] The most public manifestation of this was the contrasting responses of those on the left and those on the right towards the Spanish Civil War. However, this was not the only factor at work. With no sudden alarms emanating from Berlin in early 1937 public attention briefly moved away from defence and foreign policy; this was the case regardless of the fracturing of Churchill's supporters. Acknowledging the temporary calm in international affairs, Churchill feared that the gestures of the government had so reassured MPs 'that it is a matter of public comment that it is difficult to keep a House when the gravest matters are being discussed'.[133] In view of this apparent absence of a discernible continental threat, it was not surprising that the 1937 King's Speech devoted only a quarter of its space to external affairs where previously they had occupied almost half. In a clear rejection of comprehensive collective security, for the first time since 1931, the Speech also made no pledge towards the League of Nations.[134] Churchill's desire to involve the Soviet Union in attempts to restrain Germany were made to look even more worthless when in June 1937 Stalin appeared to disable Russia's military machine by purging it of its High Command. Meanwhile, Russian intervention in the Spanish Civil War had confirmed the right wing's worst fears that whatever its now dubious capability, Moscow was still inspired by the spirit of international Communism and was a completely untrustworthy ally.

By March 1937, Churchill was writing to the increasingly estranged Lord Rothermere that 'Parliament is dead as mutton and the Tory party feel that everything is being done for the best and the country is perfectly safe.'[135] The previous month, Churchill's friend and scientific adviser, Professor Frederick Lindemann, standing as an Independent Conservative, had become a victim of this sense of security by coming third with only a quarter of the votes in the Oxford University by-election.[136] Baldwin, back in public favour because of his handling of the abdication crisis, was now making no secret of his preparations to retire once the coronation had taken place of the new king, George VI. Chamberlain's own succession to 10 Downing Street had become a certainty. It seemed equally certain that he would not be inviting Churchill to join him round the Cabinet table. Working with him was, complained Chamberlain, 'like arguing with a Brass band'.[137] Furthermore, as far as the government was concerned, Churchill's counsel was, it seems, scarcely worth having. He was 'irritable' as to whether his memorandum on the Luftwaffe had been circulated to the Committee of Imperial Defence and anxious to know if he would be continuing to receive the Air Staff's criticisms which had previously been made available to him as a member of the Air Defence

Research Committee (ADRC). In fact, the Air Secretary, Lord Swinton, had come to the conclusion that compared to his own Ministry's estimates of *Luftwaffe* strength, Churchill's figures were valueless overestimates and that there was little to be gained in sharing secret information with Churchill if he was not going to accept it. Yet despite his continual criticism of it, Churchill was not removed from the ADRC[138] – the act of snubbing him being, presumably, more trouble than it was worth.

Churchill was making little headway with the front bench. His attempts to unite the Conservative backbench behind him also seemed to have stalled. Back in November 1936, Amery had been afraid that Churchill 'had captured a good many Conservatives' for the cause of League collective security against Germany.[139] By March 1937, however, the veteran *Observer* editor, J.L. Garvin, was expressing the views of a 'growing' section of the Conservative Party that Germany should be allowed to expand her hegemony over eastern Europe, creating the *Mitteleuropa* she had been suspected of seeking to create before the Great War.[140] Writing to Churchill, Sir Norman Angell fearfully put this view down to the Tories' desire to build a bulwark against Soviet Communism and felt that unless more Conservatives joined the LNU, thus preventing it from being 'captured by the Left, more and more will that collective resistance to German domination which you have urged become unpalatable to Conservatives, and the greater will be the tendency to accept the surrender solution'.[141] Churchill shared with Chamberlain the strong characteristic of tenacity. Despite his tendencies towards depression – the notorious 'black dog' – Churchill was incapable of finally conceding that his own career was effectively over. Whilst completely out of the running for the leadership, he never gave up hope, despite all the evidence to the contrary, that he would be brought back into the Cabinet to help with the rearmament effort. In writing to the exiled ex-King Edward (now styled the Duke of Windsor) he stated that he was delaying paying him a visit until later in May since he did not wish to be out of the country when the Cabinet reshuffle came. Whilst he was 'not very keen upon office' he would, nevertheless, 'like to help in defence'.[142]

Amongst those who feared the consequences of what Churchill might do if he returned to the Cabinet was the Southend MP and perceptive diarist, 'Chips' Channon. Nonetheless, he thought that Churchill had a better rapport with Chamberlain than with Baldwin and that after his 'brilliant speech on Spain, Churchill's "stock" has soared, and today people are buying "Churchills", and saying once more that he ought to be in the government, and that it is too bad to keep so brilliant a man out of office'.[143] Churchill described himself to Channon as 'really the leader of the Opposition as the Labour people are so ineffectual, weak and uneducated'.[144]

Meanwhile in March, the Chief Whip, Captain David Margesson, had written to Chamberlain suggesting popular appointments for the proposed Cabinet reshuffle. He had not suggested Churchill 'for obvious reasons' but felt that

> if, however, you should ultimately decide to include him, I suggest for your consideration that he might go to the Board of Trade. He has the experience and drive, his friends in the Party are right wing, but he himself is a low tariff man. As there is so much to do in that Department, he would be kept thoroughly busy and out of mischief. His appointment to the Board of Trade would keep him well away from the Defence Departments, where he would be a great nuisance.[145]

It is worth noting from this that Margesson, whose eye was unflinchingly trained on the parliamentary Conservative Party, still regarded Churchill's allies to be predominately right wing, despite his flirtations with the centre-left enthusiasts for collective security. Indeed, H.A. Gwynne, the editor of the true blue *Morning Post* (which was shortly to be merged with the *Daily Telegraph*), also thought that a Churchill appointment to the Cabinet with command of one of the fighting services would actually 'offend' the supporters of Geneva with their 'leaning towards pacification'.[146] This suggests that many Tories realized that Churchill's commitment to the League of Nations was primarily to make his case for rearmament more palatable and that his new friendships on the left were designed to further this end.[147] Furthermore, it is interesting to note that Margesson's advice suggests that Churchill's comments on rearmament were clearly not regarded as helpful to a government supposedly wanting to move public opinion down that path. Indeed, the Chief Whip concluded his analysis of Churchill's worth by stating that a post at the Board of Trade 'would minimise the alarm which his return to the Cabinet might otherwise occasion in some quarters'.[148] Perhaps this is a reference to the views of the ever-diminishing band of non-Tories in the National Government or even to the Official Opposition (although it is unclear why that should have been off-putting to the Conservative Chief Whip). Alternatively, Margesson may possibly have had in mind the delicate sensibilities of Adolf Hitler, whose confidence Chamberlain would hope to win through the policy of appeasement.

When the new Secretary of State for War, Leslie Hore-Belisha, reported to Chamberlain Churchill's desire to serve in the Cabinet that he would shortly be forming on becoming Prime Minister, Chamberlain's reaction mimicked that of Baldwin: 'if I take him into the Cabinet . . . he will dominate it. He won't give others a chance of even talking.' This sense of avoiding what Chamberlain described as 'anyone who will rock the boat'[149] was at the core of Churchill's exclusion from high office in the 1930s. The National Government included everyone except the right wing and the left wing – those who would 'rock the boat'. It was a coalition of different shades but of no contrasts. It was the reason why, whatever choice of tactics he employed, Churchill was always going to be excluded from major office in the peacetime endeavours of the National Government.

Eleven

MR CHAMBERLAIN'S
WALK WITH DESTINY

I

On 8 December 1935, the day before the Hoare–Laval negotiations developed into a political crisis, Chamberlain had pondered the prospects for his own political future:

> I suppose the answer is that I know no one that I would trust to hold the balance between rigid orthodoxy and a fatal disregard of sound principles and the rights of posterity. And, perhaps, when I come to think of it, I don't really care much what they say of me now, so long as I am satisfied myself that I am doing what is right. For it isn't as if I had ambition which might be ruined by present unpopularity. I believe S.B. will stay on for the duration, and by next election I shall be 70 and shan't care much, I dare say, for the strenuous life of leader, even if someone else hasn't overtaken me before then.[1]

Confidence in his own ability combined with strenuous denial of personal ambition for the glittering prizes of political life were common features of Chamberlain's jottings both in his diary and in the regular letters to his sisters, Ida and Hilda. It was understandable that he did not want to tempt fate on the issue of the Premiership. It had eluded both the ambition of his father and the expectation of his brother, in spite of their obvious talents. Neville remained cautious even when it became almost certain that he would succeed in becoming Prime Minister after all. As the appointed hour drew near, he could be forgiven for writing to his elder sister that whilst he was not superstitious, 'when I think of Father and Austen, and reflect that less than 3 months of time, and no individual, stands between me and that office, I wonder whether Fate has some dark secret in store, to carry out her ironies to the end.'[2]

Chamberlain had never had more than a working relationship with the man he was poised to replace. He was conscious of Baldwin's political skills and his adeptness at interpreting the national mood. When it came to the Prime Minister's role as an administrator and shaper of policy, he had markedly less regard for him, although this disrespect was tinged with none of the contempt which Sir Austen held for the man. In February

1936 Baldwin had hoped to remain at 10 Downing Street until 1938 but the burden of office, even for one of its more relaxed executors, was taking its toll on his mental and physical well-being. At the Party Conference in October 1936, Chamberlain had been forced to deputize for Baldwin who was under doctors' orders to rest. It was with some satisfaction that the Chancellor concluded from the reaction of the delegates that there appeared to be 'a general acceptance of my position as heir-apparent'.[3]

Set against the trough benchmark of 1931–2, the economy continued to provide grounds for cautious optimism. Nonetheless, it was a mark of the recovery's inability to touch the depressed regions in South Wales and in the North that even by 1937 national unemployment still stood at over 14 per cent of the insured workforce (higher than at the worst of the recessions of the early 1980s and early '90s). That this situation continued whilst the economy was by almost every other indicator doing well reinforced the despairing realization that, regardless of the increasing level of block grants to the worst-hit areas, Chamberlain's medicine provided no cure for those whose sickness looked increasingly terminal. The ailing regions were now the political ghettos of the Labour Party, in turn giving that party the aspect of a guardian of the dispossessed rather than that of champion of the prosperity for the many. This was not, in itself, a recipe for nationwide electoral recovery.

The extra money specifically earmarked for alleviating the depressed areas was small change compared to the sums needed to maintain the rearmament programme. This was a comparison not lost on Labour, although it was to some extent offset by the government's deliberate policy of favouring the award of defence contracts to the work yards of the depressed areas even when they were the least cost efficient. In the midst of the foreign exchange crisis of the early '30s, Chamberlain had prioritized the sanctity of good financial house-keeping above directly mitigating the immediate poverty of the dispossessed. Yet during the second half of the decade it was he who orchestrated the Treasury orthodoxy's subversion in order to strengthen military defence. The expanding needs of the Defence Budget from 1935 to 1936 increased by £50 million to reach £186 million in the financial year 1936–7. Nonetheless, the primary economic policy of cheap money had meant that the amount borrowed to pay for the Defence Budget was almost covered by the savings in debt charges engineered since Chamberlain had taken over as Chancellor. For the year ahead, he had calculated that the Exchequer would be around £15 million in the red. In his Budget of April 1937, he grasped the nettle and raised income tax to the equivalent of 27.5p (5s 6d) in the pound. It was his announcement that this was to be supplemented by his own idea for a 'National Defence Contribution' (NDC) that led to uproar.

During his tenure at the Treasury, Chamberlain's interest in interfering in the proposals of his Cabinet colleagues was infrequently reciprocated in turn. In part, this may have reflected the general level of confidence that his colleagues had in his operational competence and the dearth of it that he had in theirs. This state of affairs, supplemented by the constraints of pre-budget purdah, ensured that his great new proposal for a National Defence Contribution had been insufficiently analysed and discussed before it was launched. This was particularly unfortunate given the complicated and contentious nature of the scheme. Instead of a simple tax on profits, it involved a sliding scale business tax on the rate of profit expansion. Once the full implications of what was involved had sunk in, the reaction was extremely hostile. Such an explosion was not likely to faze the Chancellor. On the contrary, he had been working on more strategic assumptions. Worried that the economy was on the verge of 'a feverish and artificial boom followed by a disastrous slump', he confided his fears to his sister, Hilda, that this could only result in 'the defeat of the Government and the advent of an ignorant, unprepared, and heavily pledged Opposition, to handle a crisis as severe as that of 1931'. He felt sure that the NDC would help to calm down this danger but conceded that the scheme was 'the bravest thing I have ever done since I have been in public life, for I have risked the Premiership'.[4] Brave decisions in politics are often shorthand for decisions that lose general elections and terminate their exponent's career.

For many years, the left had drawn attention to the profiteering of 'big business' from rearmament and war. Chamberlain hoped that as a tax on quickening profits, the NDC would help to undermine Labour's contentions. The left, however, were not, nor were ever likely to be, the Chancellor's constituency. The Conservative Party and the business interest were and they resented the new levy. In fact, the fiscal burden of the NDC called the bluff of some of the Tories who had posed as proponents of rearmament. What it showed was that they were unrealistically all for tanks and aeroplanes so long as business was not having to pay for it. In fact, since German business was being subjected to a 40 per cent levy on profits, Chamberlain's scheme was modest by comparison. Certainly, if MPs were not prepared to sanction his proposal, then appeasement was the logical foreign policy to follow despite the risk of ultimate subservience to Germany. If, however, Britain was to pursue diplomacy from a position of strength, then either income tax or borrowing would have to be raised. Tories faced a future of hard choices and few favours. Not all of them immediately grasped this reality.

As a result, Chamberlain found himself assailed from all sides, from industrialist contributors to the party's coffers and local constituency associations, to the economist and journalist, John Maynard Keynes. The City too was appalled and called once again upon its unofficial spokesman within the party, the veteran Sir Robert Horne, to convey its displeasure. Most extraordinarily of all, Joseph Ball, a noted Central Office Svengali at the Conservative Research Department, appeared to be aiding and abetting the revolt. Given that Ball was one of Chamberlain's most loyal lieutenants, this was an indication of the fear that if it was allowed to proceed, the NDC would sever the party from its business support. By the end of May, more than thirty Tory MPs had signed hostile Early Day Motions. One hundred and fifty MPs crowded into the Conservative Finance Committee which demanded that the scheme be scrapped. Humiliatingly, the Chancellor was forced to climb down. In June, it was replaced by a new proposal which introduced a much more simple 5 per cent flat-rate tax on business profits. The Chancellor announcing this extraordinary climbdown was Sir John Simon. The real architect of the catastrophe had just become Prime Minister.[5]

II

The momentum behind Chamberlain's succession to the Premiership had developed such force that not even the fiasco of the National Defence Contribution could check it. Had the crisis come amidst a different political atmosphere and implicated a less respected politician within the government's ranks, the Chancellor might have been leaving the Treasury for the backbenches rather than for 10 Downing Street. Instead, it did not damage him precisely because those who wanted the scheme scrapped did not want to damage him.

When Joseph Chamberlain died in 1914 he had no inkling that it would be his younger, rather than his eldest, son who would end up Prime Minister. Unfortunately, in dying on 16 March 1937, Sir Austen Chamberlain missed by only two months seeing his brother succeed where he had himself been pipped at the post. Neville had always been emotionally much closer to his sisters than to his aloof and somewhat fastidious brother. Nonetheless, to the Archbishop of Canterbury, he confided that 'from the earliest days I have looked up to Austen with perhaps much more deference, as well as affection, than is usually the case where the difference of years was so small.'[6] Without a mother and with a father engrossed in his own political career, this was perhaps not so surprising. With the news filtering through Westminster of Austen's death, Chamberlain recorded in his diary the scene in Parliament: 'I had stood behind the Speaker's chair to listen to the tributes, as I did not feel equal to sitting on the bench. . ... As I came out of the Chamber, 3 Labour members . . . put out their hands, and said something, of their respect and admiration for Austen. The House of Commons is a wonderful place.'[7] Churchill was amongst those who wrote offering their condolences. Chamberlain, in essence a private man, replied to Churchill assuring him of the 'great admiration and affection' that Austen had always had for him.

Having seen off the previous monarch, Baldwin saw it as his duty to see in the new one. George VI's coronation on 12 May commended itself to the Prime Minister as a suitably successful occasion upon which to bow out and he timed his resignation for a fortnight afterwards. On 28 May 1937, Chamberlain at last became Prime Minister.

Why had Neville Chamberlain succeeded where his father and brother had not? As ever, time and chance had played their parts. Joseph Chamberlain had been hampered by the need to establish himself in Conservative circles having walked out on his former career in the rival political party. Such acts inevitably create a chasm of mistrust. Through sheer mental agility combined with an imaginative approach to devising mould-breaking policies he sought to narrow this fissure within his adopted party. To achieve this, he attempted to divert the party's existing and self-defining lines of understanding away from their customary thoroughfare and to channel them instead down a highway of his own construction. In different circumstances this might have succeeded, but on the issue of tariff reform it created in its wake new divisions within the Conservative Party. Even if, after 1906, he had managed to unify the party behind a policy then considered to be electorally damaging, the incapacitating stroke that he suffered removed any such possibility of his own elevation to the role of party leader, let alone Prime Minister. Austen's career had benefited from deeper roots within the party (although he too had at first been a Liberal Unionist) and from less of the ideological discord that had accompanied his father's trail-blazing career. Yet Austen lacked the feel for the grass-roots mood that had animated his father. As a result, he was a victim of the political game of musical chairs. When in 1922 the band stopped playing and the more nippy Tories dashed to reclaim their chairs he was caught in the spotlight, still tangoing with Lloyd George across the dance floor.

Joseph and Austen had severely damaged themselves in battering to create the great breach through which Neville Chamberlain unassumingly walked. Unlike his father, he had not been faced with the difficulties of having to establish his credentials in the Conservative Party in the first place. Subsequently (and unlike Austen in 1921–2) he had not been forced to lead it by the scruff of the neck down paths it had been hesitant to journey. By the time Neville arrived on the scene in earnest, the party had a much clearer idea of where it wanted to travel and he was not interested in hatching plans to divert its chosen course. On this, he had the good fortune of being able to swim with the current rather than be diverted by 'dynamic' contra-flow politicians like David Lloyd George. Without these clashes of ideology and personality, he was left to prove himself as an able administrator. His one truly fundamental strategic gamble, the decision to join the National Government, was not primarily his and, in any case, worked out successfully. If it had not (as it easily might not) it would have brought down Baldwin, not himself. Indeed, at virtually all the vital moments, circumstance had conspired to keep Neville out of the direct line of fire whenever the government came under attack. The personal qualities that his very name implied, the sober rectitude of a diligent man of affairs, were great advantages for an aspiring Prime Minister. He worked hard and deserved respect. He was a public servant with a spotless private life. His own thoughts on his character were telling too, having previously written that he thought that his brother Austen

> has not the eagerness of temperament and the inexhaustible vitality of Father, which kept him ever revolving some constructive idea ... I believe I lie somewhere between the two ... there are very few and brief moments when I feel I can't bear to talk or think of the politics that have become my main purpose in life. Indeed, my fear is always lest this prime interest should obliterate my other interests in art or music, or books, or flowers, or natural history.[8]

At the end of Baldwin's last Cabinet meeting as Prime Minister, Chamberlain paid tribute to him. The event was something of an anticlimax. MacDonald, also the subject of Chamberlain's praise, had already left the room and Baldwin's words of thanks struck Chamberlain as being not 'quite happily worded or adequate to the occasion'.[9] Chamberlain was worried about the party's response to the NDC and his last weeks as Chancellor had also been marred by what he described as Baldwin's 'shirking responsibility'. Rather than undertake the unappealing task of getting the Dominions ministers to agree that Mrs Simpson in becoming Duchess of Windsor should not be made a Royal Highness, the Prime Minister got Chamberlain to do it. The latter grumbled that Baldwin 'takes all the credit for saving the monarchy but shirks what he thinks is a disagreeable job'.[10]

Chamberlain was sent for to go to the Palace on the morning of 28 May. Waiting for his audience, a point of protocol suddenly occurred to him. Did he literally have to kiss hands with his monarch or was the term only figurative? The King's private secretary did not know and Chamberlain was ushered in, unsure what to do. He spent the first few minutes of the interview glancing at the King's hand for a sign of any sudden gesture or twitch. None was forthcoming and eventually the King asked him to sit down.[11]

On becoming Prime Minister, the position which he modestly told his sister Hilda was the 'post which ought to have come to the two senior members of the family', Chamberlain reflected on the fact that 'it has come to me without my raising a finger to obtain it, because there is no-one else and perhaps because I have not made enemies by looking after myself rather than the common cause.'[12]

Churchill, a man regularly accused by his enemies of putting self before party, accepted Chamberlain's success with good grace. Writing later in the year in Colliers magazine, he acknowledged that 'there never was any doubt that Neville Chamberlain would succeed Baldwin. No rival candidate was even discussed by serious people.' Whilst it was true that Chamberlain 'had few friends and shuns society' Churchill felt that 'he is a man of the highest character' who 'carries the flag of righteous endeavour'.[13] On 31 May, Churchill, who in the light of Austen Chamberlain's death had become the most senior Conservative Privy Councillor in the Commons, seconded Lord Derby's motion nominating Chamberlain to the party leadership. After praising Baldwin as a 'massive figure' Churchill announced to cheers that 'no one was so active in pressing forward the policy of rearmament' as Neville Chamberlain. The occasion demanded that he sing the new leader's praises, but his choice of identifying Chamberlain with his own campaign suggested that he wished to be welcomed back into the party mainstream. This said, he could not help giving the double-edged commendation of Chamberlain as a parliamentarian who would 'not resent honest differences of opinion' in party debate.[14]

III

Chamberlain's biographer, Keith Feiling, wrote that in office he was 'Masterful, confident, and ruled by an instinct for order, he would give a lead, and perhaps impart an edge, on every question. His approach was arduously careful but his mind, once made up, hard to change; he would make relevance a fundamental and have the future mapped out and under control, thus asking his departmental ministers to envisage two-year programmes.'[15] The contrast with Baldwin could not have been more pronounced. Baldwin could afford the luxury of detachment because in Chamberlain he had the benefit of a Chancellor of the Exchequer who was also prepared to take on the burden of most aspects of government business. When it was his proprietorial turn to ascend the 10 Downing Street staircase, Chamberlain on the other hand was not to be so assisted. His choice of successor at the Exchequer was Sir John Simon, still the leader of the Liberal National Party. Blessed with a first-class legal mind, Simon certainly had the mental capacity to back up the new Prime Minister. Indeed, the last pre-Keynesian Chancellor, he maintained Chamberlain's own economic mindset which in itself was an interesting reflection on where thirty years of argument had left the respective positions of the spiritual son of the Edwardian Liberal H.H. Asquith, and the second son of the Edwardian imperialist, Joseph Chamberlain. Yet Simon, who was without personal support within the massed ranks of the Conservative Party, could not provide Chamberlain with the wider political strategy with which Chamberlain had been able to drive the Baldwin administration. When after February 1938 the Foreign Secretary-ship was to pass to Halifax – a member of the House of Lords – Chamberlain also found himself expected to be the main articulator (and target) of foreign policy in the Commons. This was a lot for one man to do, even for one as sure of his own talents as Chamberlain.

Here was the second problem. Baldwin's contribution to his party was primarily one of mood and this allowed for latitude in framing (and more importantly readjusting) policy to the course of events. Chamberlain's disciplined and unmalleable approach, in which the future was 'mapped out and under control', could work well in planning a legislative future for a peaceful nation being gently nurtured by the warm underblanket of commercial recovery. It was Chamberlain's misfortune that the prospect of war was to chill and then freeze the conditions needed to maintain this climate. Instead, the mind that planned everything ahead was unsuited to adaptation in the face of changed circumstances or of a reality different to that which he first perceived. There was truth in the charge that his mind ran on rails. Following unofficial discussions with Hitler and Goering, Lord Halifax (who was over in Germany for a hunting festival) had reported back to his Cabinet colleagues that an understanding on the future of central and eastern Europe was quite possible. With this interpretation backed up by the fanatically pro-appeasement British Ambassador in Berlin, Nevile Henderson, Chamberlain concluded of the Germans at the end of November 1937 that 'of course they want to dominate Eastern Europe; they want as close a union with Austria as they could get without incorporating her in the Reich, and they want much the same things for the Sudetendeutsche as we did for the Uitlanders in the Transvaal.'[16] On this basis, Chamberlain all but excluded the use of force to prevent these changes so long as Germany likewise did not use force in making them in the first place. His policy was drawn up in this expectation. Articulated, it proved difficult to alter in the face of what Hitler really intended: the full annexation of both Austria and the Sudetenland into the German Reich by any means necessary.

Chamberlain's awareness of the centrality of prioritizing relations with Germany was constantly distracted by the outrage not only of the opposition parties but also of the wider public, first on the issue of sanctions and Abyssinia and then with regard to the stacked funeral pyres of the Spanish Civil War. On this last matter, the League of Nations had no power enshrined in its Covenant to deal with an internal struggle as opposed to one between nation states. For the most part, the government's stated position of non-intervention satisfied all but the most freethinking of its supporters.[17] However, the issue was by now greatly complicated by the involvement of Germany and Italy in supplying and assisting Franco's insurrectionists and by the reciprocal help the Soviet Union gave to the Republicans. The struggle fundamentally stirred the left-liberal conscience and the German bombing raid on Guernica became the most symbolic expression of the fear that civilians would be the primary targets of a future 'total war'. It was not long before the left became suspicious about the stance of the Foreign Office. Britain's standing aside, the left alleged, was essentially of more help to the Nationalists than to the Republicans. Faced with a barrage of criticism, even Eden found himself referring to the 'war of the Spanish obsession'.

The Spanish conflict had implications far beyond the Iberian peninsula, the publication output of the Left Book Club and the rhetoric on the floor of the House of Commons. Chamberlain hoped to rebuild the understanding seemingly reached between Britain and Italy that had been severed as a result of the Abyssinian conflict. Italy's involvement in the Spanish Civil War made public rapprochement with Rome politically sensitive. Furthermore, in view of Eden's distrust of Mussolini, Chamberlain had to tread with even greater care if he did not wish to lose his notoriously temperamental Foreign Secretary.

A man of tact and detachment far greater than that possessed by Chamberlain would have been needed to deal with the volatile Anthony Eden. Indeed in many ways the Premier and his Foreign Secretary were polar opposites. Eden's outward smooth charm and inner insecurity was matched by Chamberlain's outward aloofness and inner self-confidence. On the need to avoid an unnecessary war with Germany the two were agreed, although Eden was more sceptical of Hitler's ability to be controlled by sweet reason than was the relentlessly over-optimistic Chamberlain. On the relationship that Britain should try to reconstruct with Italy they were fundamentally divided. To Eden, Mussolini was devious and untrustworthy and at best a valueless ally. Indeed, on 9 January 1938, Eden went as far as to tell his Prime Minister, 'there seems to be a certain difference between Italian and German positions in that an agreement with the latter might have a chance of a reasonable life, especially if Hitler's own position were engaged whereas Mussolini is, I fear, the complete gangster and his pledged word means nothing.'[18] In contrast Chamberlain thought that the detachment of Il Duce from the *Führer* and the neutralization of an Italian threat to Britain's vulnerable strategic interests in the Mediterranean were prizes well worth pursuing. Without control of the Mediterranean, the British Navy would have to go all the way around Africa in order to reinforce its Asian and Pacific empire and interests, which were guarded from Singapore. The torpedoing by covert Italian submarines of vessels presumed to be reinforcing the Spanish Republicans was evidence enough of the damage to British lines of communication that a hostile Italy could present. When British-registered vessels were also briefly the target of Italian torpedoes, the case for a detached approach from London was further undermined and it was in part the fear of drawing France into the Spanish conflict against Franco that encouraged Mussolini to call off his submarines. Chamberlain wanted to seize this opportunity of improving Anglo-Italian relations. This, however, was hampered by Mussolini's insistence on British recognition of his Abyssinian conquest. Even Chamberlain was reticent to do this without having the international approval of the League of Nations – a sanction that appeared to be far from forthcoming and would be politically sensitive at home where it would offend liberal-minded sensitivity.

Chamberlain knew the course which he wanted to steer British foreign policy and the need to keep Eden on board during the journey. Although he had not been happy about Lord Halifax's hunting visit to Germany, Eden nonetheless fell in behind Chamberlain's line with regard to trying to maximize the areas for agreement with the Reich. Chamberlain reciprocated by having Sir Robert Vansittart, the Foreign Office Permanent Under-Secretary, with whom Eden endured poor relations, removed out of harm's way to the ill-defined post of 'Chief Diplomatic Adviser' from where he could be politely ignored. Vansittart was one of the FO's most anti-German hawks. Indeed, despite their differences of temperament and emphasis, Chamberlain and Eden seemed to work together sufficiently well at least until 1938. Eden several times wrote to the Prime Minister making clear that he welcomed his intervention in foreign policy.[19] This was not to last.

Tensions were reignited in China where renewed Japanese aggression again threatened Britain's enormous commercial interests in Shanghai.

With relations towards Italy and Germany still so delicate, Chamberlain was resolutely opposed to threatening Japan at this time. He was all too conscious of the Chiefs of Staff warning that Britain could not take on more than one Fascist militaristic state at a time. Eden was keen to solicit the support of the United States which would be essential if Britain found that it had no option but to confront the Japanese offensive. Chamberlain was much more sceptical of the likelihood of Washington's desire to prop up the British Empire against Tokyo at a time when opinion on Congress Hill was isolationist and periodically Anglophobic in temperament, if not in deed. Following the realization that Chamberlain had deliberately neutered one of his telegrams to the US State Department on the case for economic sanctions against Tokyo, Eden tried to correspond with Washington beyond the Prime Minister's prying eyes. Trust between the two men was clearly deteriorating fast.

Japanese attacks on British and American vessels brought the two leading countries of the English-speaking world more closely together than had any of their more recent acts of attempted diplomacy in the months prior to the Japanese operations along the Yangtse River. For a brief moment the prospect was held out that Roosevelt was interested in serious Anglo-American naval talks in the Pacific. Chamberlain's hope that for once the British might be able to count on the support of more than words from the US Government soon faded, leaving him exasperated at the failure of 'the Japs' to miss their stage cue to 'beat up an American or two!'[20]

On 12 January 1938, Roosevelt contacted Chamberlain. Surveying the areas of real and potential conflict in Europe, the President was perturbed at the state of the Old World, not least if it should have to be rescued once again by the New World, which had problems enough of its own to be getting on with. Believing economic problems to be at the root of the political points of friction, Roosevelt wanted to make himself available for a world conference to try to alleviate the tensions. At the centre of these talks would be the greater availability of natural resources, Germany's and Italy's absence of which was encouraging their search for enlargement and their theft. In return, arms limitation and codes of international conduct would be signed by all those countries participating. Fearing isolationist opinion at home, the President let Chamberlain know of his scheme in conditions of the greatest secrecy. Only if London agreed would he then take up the matter with Paris, Rome and Berlin.

It would appear that Roosevelt did not want to supplant Chamberlain's appeasement policy but rather to reinforce it. Washington made no attempt to enlist Eden behind the scheme and consciously chose to communicate with Chamberlain rather than his Foreign Secretary. Indeed, given the 'America First' views of Congress and the existence of the Neutrality Acts, the room for Roosevelt's involvement was narrowly circumscribed in any case. However, whatever its helpful intent, Roosevelt's suggestion was inadvertently at odds with Chamberlain's modus operandi: – an intense dislike of others interfering in areas in which he only trusted himself as the arch problem solver. For all his diligence and integrity, this was one of the Prime Minister's weaknesses. When Roosevelt's telegram arrived, Eden was conveniently on holiday in France. Chamberlain got back to London first and altered the telegram that Vansittart's replacement at the FO, Sir Alexander Cadogan, proposed to send to Roosevelt. Instead of suggesting that the plan be deferred but promising British support if the President decided to go ahead, the telegram merely said that the plan should be deferred. This was as good as an outright rejection. By the time Eden got back to London, Chamberlain had sewn up the whole situation.

In contrast to Chamberlain's dismissiveness of American involvement in European affairs, Eden felt that Anglo-American rapprochement was a goal well worth the sacrifice. Furthermore, appearing agreeable to Roosevelt could also encourage Anglo-American naval conversations without which the Japanese menace to British interests in the Pacific developed frightening proportions. It is far from clear that this was at all what Washington had in mind and Eden's position became more attractive in hindsight than it was in any sense realistic at the time.[21] Nonetheless, he decided that he must stand up to Chamberlain on the issue and a series of bruising encounters took place between the two men. Eden's resolve was fortified by the advice of Oliver Harvey, his supportive private secretary, who encouraged him to 'take a very strong line' since in view of his importance to it, the government 'couldn't let you go on this'.[22] Threats and counter-threats, veiled and not so veiled, passed between Eden's lieutenants and those loyal to the Prime Minister. If Eden did not get his way, then his parliamentary private secretary (PPS) threatened to leak the contents of Roosevelt's offer to the press. Chamberlain's closest adviser, Sir Horace Wilson, made clear that in such an event he would crank into operation 'the full power of the Government machine in an attack on [Eden's] past record with regard to the dictators'.[23] On this particular field of battle at least, Harvey's calculation proved right. Chamberlain backed down and telegraphed Roosevelt to say that he would support the proposals when they were launched. However, Roosevelt now made clear that his offer was on hold until a more auspicious moment and that in the meantime he was backing Chamberlain's own attempts to solve Europe's problems.

The crisis between Eden and Chamberlain over the Roosevelt offer calmed down as quickly as it had arisen and there seemed every hope, at least for the moment, that the two would return to a normal working relationship. Eden, however, soon found fresh cause for anxiety in the antics of Lady Ivy Chamberlain (Sir Austen's widow) who had set herself up in Rome as an informal go-between with Mussolini. Eden had justifiable grounds for concern. Even if she was no more than a conduit of information, the Prime Minister's sister-in-law was insufficiently schooled in the exacting discipline of high diplomacy to undertake such a task with someone as duplicitous and unpredictable as the Italian dictator. This placed the Prime Minister in an invidious position since he had to reassure Eden that his sister-in-law would not be allowed to become a player in the game although he had regarded her role as extremely useful in developing a personal touch with Il Duce. Accepting the pleas of the Italian Foreign Minister, Count Ciano, Chamberlain was particularly aware of the case for urgency in rebuilding the Anglo-Italian understanding. The manner in which Hitler was interfering in Austrian affairs indicated that the threat of a Nazi coup or a German invasion had re-emerged as a real possibility. Eden, on the other hand, feared that Rome's concern on this point was a bluff and that Britain should be careful not to entangle herself with Mussolini's uncertain motives. Keen to discern the nature of the beast before sticking his head in its mouth, Eden wanted to make the removal of Italian troops from the Spanish conflict a precondition for talks. Aware of the deteriorating Austrian situation and believing himself to be battling against the clock, Chamberlain now sought to overrule his Foreign Secretary and press on regardless.

Count Grandi, the Italian Ambassador, arrived at 10 Downing Street on 18 February. Reporting back on his negotiations, he claimed to have found Chamberlain and Eden to be 'two enemies confronting each other, like two cocks in true fighting posture'. This was not surprising. Eden had wanted to have private talks of his own with Grandi in the first place, but Chamberlain had used his own ex-MI5 agent, Joseph Ball at the Conservative Research Department, to make sure the Italians knew that they stood a better chance talking to the Prime Minister than going through the supposedly unsound Foreign Office.[24] Chamberlain had flinched when confronted with the prospect of losing Eden over the response to the Roosevelt initiative but this time, as he told Sir Horace Wilson, he was 'determined to stand firm even if it means losing my Foreign Secretary'.[25] Failing to resolve their differences between themselves, both Chamberlain and Eden argued out their respective positions to a hastily convened meeting of the Cabinet. The Prime Minister insisted on the whole Cabinet having their say. It was evident that he commanded their overwhelming support. Eden then made clear that for him this was a resigning issue and after a break to digest this fact, Chamberlain convened a further meeting of the Cabinet. A compromise package put together by Halifax in which Italian troop withdrawals from Spain would be part of the final treaty proved of no avail. The Foreign Secretary was determined to go.

Without any real semblance of support from his Cabinet colleagues, Eden resigned in a manner that almost bordered on relief. In various portfolios, he had been dealing with matters of foreign policy for six years. He had pinned his career to the success of the League of Nations, during which time the League had effectively collapsed as a forum for deterring aggression. He did not now want to carry the can for a policy orchestrated by the Prime Minister that he believed was even more ignominiously doomed to failure. He saw that a German invasion of Austria could not be far off and that he would be impotent to stop it but would nonetheless lose further credibility were he still responsible for foreign policy when the *Anschluss* took place. In these circumstances it would have been an understandable conclusion for Eden to come to that he was – for the moment – better off avoiding the responsibility for it all.[26]

Eden's resignation has been seen as a turning point in British foreign policy. A large section of public and political opinion had viewed him as a less partisan figure than Chamberlain. The grey-haired leader of the Conservative Party could be easily caricatured as the manifestation of almost pre-1914 Tory ideological insularity. In contrast, the fresh-faced Eden was seen to represent a more modern and progressive bi-partisan approach that was in keeping with what was supposedly still a National Government. Central to this interpretation was his obvious and genuine support for the League of Nations. A comparison has naturally been made with the fall of Field Marshal von Blomberg, the German War Minister who was forced to resign when it was discovered that he had married a woman whose virtues were best appreciated from a standpoint of moral relativism. Hitler's assumption of Blomberg's powers as Commander-in-Chief of the Armed Forces, the forcing out of several other 'conservative' generals, and the replacement of Neurath as Foreign Minister by Ribbentrop, appeared to represent a turning point in removing the last vestiges of control on the *Führer*'s all-or-nothing ambitions. Likewise, Eden's fall and his replacement by Lord Halifax has been viewed as the removal of the last brake on Chamberlain's all-out drive for appeasement as the centrepiece of British foreign policy. Halifax seemed to share Chamberlain's views. Furthermore, as he was a member of the House of Lords, his appointment to the Foreign Office left Chamberlain in charge of serious discussion of foreign policy in the Commons. In this task he was to be aided by R.A. Butler, whom he appointed as the new parliamentary under-secretary of state (Lord Cranborne having resigned with Eden). Butler had shown considerable ability as Hoare's lieutenant during the passage of the India Bill. Chamberlain knew that he had found someone naturally suited to the same task in dealing with the nuts and bolts of Commons discussion on what would now be the administration's central purpose, the appeasement of Europe.

It is tempting to imagine that Chamberlain had deliberately gone out of his way to engineer Eden's resignation so that he could, in effect, become master of his own foreign policy. In the final hours, Chamberlain may have worked for this end. However, there is no evidence that he had planned it until the Austrian emergency accelerated the urgency with which he sought alliance with Italy. Until that time, and perhaps indeed until the very last hours, Chamberlain had tried to overcome his differences with his Foreign Secretary.

Amery, who took a dim view of Eden's adherence to the League of Nations, was able to contain his sense of loss at the Foreign Secretary's fall. Discussing the resignation with the Home Secretary, he noted that Hoare 'told me the whole Cabinet were unanimous in agreeing with the PM. He was inclined to think that Eden's attitude had been influenced by personal vanity; generally speaking Sam thinks him vain, unstable and not really a heavyweight. This may be with a touch of personal bias.'[27] Labour hoped to embarrass the government over Eden's resignation with a vote of censure – the threat of which bound the Conservatives closer together. On this, Chamberlain chose to fight. He had cleared a common line with his Cabinet first and the Whips' Office did its best to ensure that backbenchers similarly did not stray from it. Furthermore, the Prime Minister chose this as the occasion to make absolutely clear that, until it could be reformed, the League of Nations was a redundant form of international pacification.

Amery believed that only around twenty to thirty Tory MPs 'really felt that a great mistake had been committed' in letting Eden go but that it had sent Churchill into 'one of his excited moods'. When it came to the Member for Epping's speech, Amery observed that Churchill 'spoke with pretty hostile intent but great restraint of diction, evidently sensing the feeling of the House and realising that there was no hope of any cave worth mentioning. Over this affair as over Edward VIII, he instinctively rushed off in the wrong direction – from the Party point of view at any rate.'[28] Amery felt that the result of a meeting of two hundred members at the Foreign Affairs Committee on 24 February was clear in its swing towards Chamberlain's position.[29] Not prepared to damn an administration of which he had so recently been a prominent part, Eden's resignation speech was a damp squib and received little support even from Conservative MPs who had until that moment been keen to identify themselves with him.[30]

In his war memoirs published in 1948, Churchill made great play of his foreboding on learning that Chamberlain had let Eden resign. At the time his was one of the more prominent signatures on a list of Conservative MPs expressing their confidence in Chamberlain.[31] Whether or not by design, Chamberlain had got his way. A supposedly rival magnet for power in the Cabinet, stubborn with his own ideas, had fallen on his own sword with little obvious loss to Chamberlain's credibility and general level of comfort. The ripple that this had created in the parliamentary party had been easily containable and Eden indicated a reluctance to generate needless trouble on the backbenches. He was certainly not in cahoots with Churchill, and the potential rebels on foreign policy were divided in personnel and incohesive in message. The appointment of Lord Halifax appeared to produce a situation in which Prime Minister and Foreign Office would work towards similar ends and through the same means. Indeed, the loss of votes amongst otherwise centre-left liberals that Eden's departure might have caused the National Government could even be recouped by Halifax's image as a man of Christian purpose who as Viceroy of India had demonstrated the convictions of a liberal reformer. Indeed, if he had really won the respect of the troublesome Mr Gandhi, then there was every hope that he might prove the figure who could also pass Hitler a teacup of soothing English Breakfast.

In April, Chamberlain got what he wanted, an understanding with Italy. Recognition of Italy's Abyssinian conquest was to be granted in return for the ending of Rome's anti-British propaganda in the Middle East and for the reduction in Italian troop numbers in Spain and Libya. Important from Britain's strategic perspective, it reduced the potential for fresh upset in the Mediterranean. The event, however, was accorded secondary publicity compared to the upheaval that had in the meantime taken place in Vienna.

IV

Enraged that Schuschnigg, the Austrian Chancellor, had announced that his nation's electorate would decide by a national referendum whether or not to join Germany, Hitler demanded that he resign in favour of the Nazi, Dr Artur Seyss-Inquart. Responding to Seyss-Inquart's call for German intervention (which had actually been drafted by *Reichsmarshall* Goering), the *Wehrmacht* invaded Austria on 12 March.

There was no question of Britain threatening Germany over its

Anschluss with Austria even although it was a breach (now one of many) of the Treaty of Versailles. Any international response was compromised by the scenes of cheering Austrians saluting the occupying German forces and by the fact that at the time France did not even have a government in office with which to coordinate a response. Despite the fact that the British talks with Italy had already commenced, Mussolini refused to discuss the Austrian *Anschluss*. Eden's supporters saw this as vindication for his view that II Duce was not to be trusted. Chamberlain, however, concluded that but for his late Foreign Secretary, an understanding with Mussolini could have been entrenched much earlier and that consequently the *Anschluss* might have been prevented.[32]

It has been alleged that it was not until the Munich crisis that Churchill seriously challenged British foreign policy.[33] In this debate much depends upon what is meant by the word 'challenge'. Nonetheless, his response to the *Anschluss* was very different to that displayed by Chamberlain. Whilst the Prime Minister wished not to be deflected from the policy of appeasement that he saw as the only means of avoiding a general European conflict, in the Commons debate of 14 March Churchill called for a warning to be dispatched to Hitler making clear that if he invaded any further country, then Britain would intervene to stop him. This was a commitment that the Prime Minister was keen to avoid.

Chamberlain had still not ruled out the possibility that Hitler was a man with whom he could do business. He was disappointed that Hitler had chosen violent means to realize his goal of incorporating Austria into the German Reich, but he hoped to get back on terms with him as soon as possible. Indeed, Chamberlain informed his sister that he would tell the *Führer* that 'it is no use crying over spilt milk and what we have to do now is to consider how we can restore the confidence you have shattered.'[34] The Prime Minister still saw the return of colonies as a powerful gesture which it was hoped would calm down Germany's expansionist ambitions in eastern and south-eastern Europe. Halifax seemingly placed even more emphasis on this point, having articulated the belief that colonial concessions were the only vital question between Britain and Germany. This was despite the reality that British-administered colonies were amongst Hitler's secondary rather than primary demands and were, in any case, being stoutly defended by a vocal right-wing group within the Conservative Party. In fact, obscure colonies were hardly a substitute for European *Lebensraum*. They had little economic potential for whoever owned them. In any case, they would be useless to Germany in the event of war given the fact that they could be easily blockaded by the British fleet.[35]

Chamberlain's apparent belief that Hitler's ambitions were of a scale that could be satiated by being given the likes of Togoland demonstrated his inability at this stage to grasp the full measure of the man with whom he was dealing. Only weeks before Hitler's invasion of Austria, Chamberlain had asked for a paper on the practicalities of bomber disarmament, convinced that Hitler might yet be persuaded to dispense with the tool of the *Luftwaffe* that Britons feared most. During his tenure as the Reich's Foreign Minister, Neurath had played along with this fancy, hinting at the *Führer's* desire to abolish bomber aircraft whilst being reticent, as always, to be pinned down on details. Nonetheless, this remote glimmer of opportunity continued to fuel Chamberlain's preference for hope over experience. In April he wrote to the British Ambassador in Berlin, Nevile Henderson, suggesting that if the Germans could be persuaded to talk seriously about disarmament, then 'we might conceivably get to something not unlike the general settlement we have always worked for.'[36] This meant appeasement in the purest sense of the term. With the support of the Chiefs of Staff, Chamberlain had overruled Eden's enthusiasm for the request from Paris for Anglo-French military conversations. The British Field Force, so the reasoning went, was so small that no worthwhile conversations could be had. More important still, nothing was to be done to make Germany suspicious of British good intentions. This argument, if logically sustained, should have called into question why Britain was daring to rearm at all. Even Eden had opposed a French proposal that Paris and London should warn Berlin against enlarging Germany's boundaries. For his part, Hitler told Nevile Henderson that it was none of Britain's business how Germany defended German-speaking people in central and eastern Europe, that the issue of colonies could be put on hold and that there could be no disarmament until the Soviet Union had disarmed. This might have been seen to be the final rebuff. To Chamberlain it was only a temporary setback. In the meantime Hitler's unhelpful stance commended the case for Britain to reach a deeper agreement with Italy as soon as possible. In the aftermath of the *Anschluss*, Chamberlain told his sister:

> For the moment we must abandon conversations with Germany, we must show our determination not to be bullied by announcing some increase or acceleration in rearmament, and we must quietly and steadily pursue our conversations with Italy. If we can avoid another violent coup in Czechoslovakia, which ought to be feasible, it may be possible for Europe to settle down again, and some day for us to start peace talks again with the Germans.[37]

Chamberlain feared that rival power pacts would be more likely to provoke rather than prevent war. He believed the rather limp gatherings of the League of Nations were particularly ill suited to the task of providing an effective brake on the Nazi appetite. He had no time for Churchill's window dressing of the alliance system through the League. Ganging up on a police state like Germany with the support of Stalin's Soviet Union was, as Chamberlain fully realized, the pot calling the kettle black. There was, in any case, the suspicion that Stalin's purges had destroyed the military capacity of the Red Army. Given the destruction of the Russian officer class, this was a reasonable assumption to make. The fact that events after 1941 did not bear this out did not make it necessarily untrue three years previously. Similarly, Chamberlain distrusted involvement in France's bellicose pronouncements in the face of the resurgent Germany. The destruction in France of political stability, indeed of confidence itself, gave the British Prime Minister little comfort in believing that Paris could deliver its promises when called upon. If these two views of the effectiveness of France and the Soviet Union were going to be borne out in reality, then his policy of appeasement appeared to be the rational course of action.

The possibility that Czechoslovakia was Hitler's next target had tremendous implications for British policy. Prague's treaty with Paris, if honoured, would trigger a war between France and Germany. In such an event, the Soviet Union had also agreed to intervene on the side of France. Europe would be plunged into war by an alliance system similar to that which had led to the Great War, only with the initial catalyst being Czechoslovakia rather than Serbia. Chamberlain had to think carefully how Britain could best anticipate this tripwire. In 1914, the cause of Belgium had tilted the scales in favour of Britain's involvement in the Franco-Austro/German-Russian conflict. It was therefore now up to British diplomacy to ensure that actions with regard to the Czech state did not create for Britain a latter-day Belgian *casus belli*. In 1938, as in 1914, Britain was loosely allied to France but this did not necessitate a declaration of war on behalf of a central European third party with whom Britain had no such formal understanding.

Chamberlain had to consider the practical effectiveness of the diplomatic minefield that had been laid to prevent the German Army moving beyond its own national borders. The first question concerned the efficacy of this Soviet-Franco-Czech alliance system. Would France honour her obligation to Czechoslovakia and, indeed, given her apparent lack of self-confidence, had she the determination to see through such a gamble? If Stalin honoured Russia's alliance with France, then what use could the Red Army be in the fight against Germany if the countries of eastern Europe would not (for good reason) let the Russians on their soil? Britain was committed to defending France from invasion from Germany, but what if that invasion only came once France had first declared war over the issue of the Czech state for which Britain had no obligation?

Whatever its attractions on paper, Chamberlain thought that the prospect of a Grand Alliance was unworkable in practice. As he put it in a letter to one of his sisters in March: 'you only have to look at the map to see that nothing that we or France could do could possibly save Czechoslovakia from being overrun by the Germans if they wanted to do it.'[38] All his subsequent manoeuvres and humiliating contortions before Hitler in the succeeding months have to be seen in the light of this perception of the impossibility of preventing the country from being crushed by means of force. The second point was that Chamberlain was not prepared to take on Germany before Britain's rearmament programme was complete, nor was he prepared to go all out to complete the programme imprudently. The case was best articulated by the Chancellor of the Exchequer, Simon, who pointed out that 'at the present moment . . . we were in the position of a runner in a race who wants to reserve his sprint for the right time, but does not know where the finishing tape is. The danger is that we might knock our finances to pieces prematurely.'[39] This was an important point and one of which the Prime Minister was only too well aware. It did, however, mean that the pace could be slowed as well as quickened. An extraordinary signal was sent to Berlin when London chose to respond to news of the *Anschluss* by announcing a cut in the British Army's budget. If diplomacy hoped to keep Hitler guessing as to whether Britain would or would not intervene in the event of his invading Czechoslovakia, then the *Führer* needed only to look at the concomitant stripping of the British Army to make his assumption that London was not going to cut up rough.

In the Cabinet committee dealing with foreign policy the Home Secretary, Sir Samuel Hoare, advocated making a pro-French declaration. In this he was joined by the President of the Board of Trade, Oliver Stanley, although the latter's view that Czechoslovakia was not worth fighting for demonstrated that he had not thought the matter through very closely. The Minister for Defence Coordination, Inskip, voiced the view of the military men that the Czechs would be quickly beaten before the Anglo-French response could do much about it. To this was added the voice of Ramsay's son, Malcolm MacDonald, at the Dominions Office, who pointed out that Britain would go into war with a divided empire since Canada and South Africa appeared not to want to shed their manhood's blood for the sake of the Czech boundary. The committee's view, backed up by that of the Chiefs of Staff (who presented the worst case scenario as if it was the most likely one), was then presented to the

Cabinet on 22 March. With this, Chamberlain had a mandate to step up the pace of appeasement.

Despite the earlier procrastinations, Anglo-French discussions – political and military – finally commenced in April. The view of the French Prime Minister, Edouard Daladier, was that the defence of Czechoslovakia was a necessity since if it fell, Hitler could be expected to move further east, aggrandizing Romania's grain and oil resources. Thus stocked up, Hitler could then turn west. At all costs, Germany had to be prevented from gaining the natural materials that it needed to fight a long war. If it could be denied these (for it had precious few of its own), then in a prolonged conflict Germany could not expect to defeat the combined resources of the Russian, French and British empires. Chamberlain disputed the logic that underlay Daladier's thesis. Did Hitler even want all of Czechoslovakia, never mind the rest of eastern Europe? Was not the fear of encirclement as much likely to make Germany want to strike out as to make it cower? Might not the effort to create a better atmosphere with Hitler improve the situation as Chamberlain's efforts with Il Duce had between Britain and Italy? In all of this, Chamberlain was not seeking to postpone an inevitable war to a moment most advantageous to Britain and least advantageous to Germany. Although he recognized the possibility of war if matters were handled badly, he believed that with the right diplomacy there need be no war at all.

Chamberlain's formal position was to adopt the guessing game advocated by Halifax in which Britain would keep open the possibility of armed intervention whilst making no explicit commitment that would have to be welched upon. In May 1938, when it looked momentarily as if Hitler was poised to invade and the Czech Army mobilized, Halifax warned Ribbentrop that Germany should 'not count upon this country being able to stand aside' since 'if once war should start in Central Europe it was quite impossible to say where it might not end, and who might not become involved.' This was to restate almost exactly the words that Chamberlain had used to the Commons in March.[40]

V

Hitler's stated interest in Czechoslovakia concerned the welfare of the German-speaking areas of the Sudetenland that ringed the country's northern, western and southern frontiers with Germany (and Austria which was now part of Germany). The Sudetendeutsch had never been part of the unified Germany but had enjoyed a favourable status in the former Austro-Hungarian Empire. Following that empire's collapse and the Sudetenland's absorption into the new state of Czechoslovakia which was created after the First World War, these German speakers felt themselves to be second-class citizens. Certainly they had some cause for lamenting their reduced circumstances. Against this it has to be pointed out that as citizens of Czechoslovakia they enjoyed the liberties of the only remaining democracy in eastern Europe and as such they were treated better than many other minorities in 1930s Europe.

Self-determination had been a great cry of the liberal diplomat for a century, but strategic necessities prevented the Sudeten question being framed in these singularly uncomplicated terms. If the Sudetenland, much of which was mountainous, was absorbed into the German Reich, then the remaining rump Czech state would become virtually indefensible against invasion. The rights of the Sudetendeutsch to self-determination and the rights of the Czechs to national security were thus entwined and seemingly indivisible. Against this, Britain's Ambassador in Prague, Basil Newton, was advising London that even the existing Czechoslovakia with the Sudetenland intact could not beat back a German invasion especially now that the *Anschluss* had created a semicircle of German territory around the Czech state. Furthermore, if a lengthy European war fought by proxy on Czechoslovakia's behalf led eventually to Germany's defeat, Czechoslovakia's pre-existing boundaries 'had already proved unacceptable and . . ., even if restored, would probably again prove unworkable'.[41] In short, the country was so strategically and racially ill composed that it was not worth fighting for. Harsh strictures of this kind do not read well with the hindsight of the country's subsequent torture. Nonetheless, it is with the benefit of the same hindsight that it has to be conceded that there was some truth in Newton's analysis. When Czechoslovakia was restored after 1945 its unity was created by driving out the German speakers of the Sudetenland as if by way of acknowledgement that Czech and Sudetendeutsch could never live together amicably in the same country. This was not the end of the readjustments. Czechoslovakia had scarcely begun to breathe the air of post-Communist independence following its 'velvet revolution' of 1989 before it became devorced from Slovakia. In this light, we might come to admire – for all their mistakes – the political abilities of Prague's politicians in the 1930s to keep their country free and together against such odds. At the time, admiration was in short supply.

Chamberlain's task in 1938 was to see that Czechoslovakia's difficult circumstances did not produce the friction that would generate the spark of war. Believing that Hitler's ambitions could be restricted to the country's German-speaking areas and that he was not necessarily hell-bent on world domination, Chamberlain backed the application of pressure on the Prague Government to make concessions to its Sudetendeutsch minority. No avenue should be opened that would give Hitler an excuse for hasty action in defence of the German-speaking minority's rights. If the Prague Government refused to make concessions to Konrad Henlein's pro-Nazi Sudetendeutsch party, then they were assured that they would receive no British help in the event of a German invasion. What Chamberlain seemingly did not realize was that Henlein was under strict orders from Hitler precisely not to reach agreement with Prague. The assumption that Hitler's interest in Czechoslovakia could be limited to the welfare of its German speakers, the assumption upon which Chamberlain based his diplomacy, was erroneous. In July Chamberlain announced that he was proposing Lord Runciman as an impartial mediator between the Sudetendeutsch and the Czechs. Runciman was certainly impartial in the sense that he came to the problem with none of the preconceived ideas that someone with any knowledge might have had. In fact, his task was not really to be impartial at all but to tell the Prague Government to make concessions. In the beginning of September, Prague accepted his advice and made most of the concessions for which Henlein's Sudetendeutsch party had called. This looked dangerously like a solution so Henlein, obeying His Master's Voice, broke off negotiations. Runciman's mission could never succeed. Too much was invested by the Reich Chancellery in the hope of its failure. By the time this was fully appreciated in Downing Street, it was too late.

Whilst Runciman was attempting to work miracles in Czechoslovakia, the Cabinet moved to take action of its own. On 30 August it agreed not to issue Hitler with a formal warning of Britain's intent to fight on Czechoslovakia's behalf in the event of it being invaded by Germany. Halifax pointed out that such a declaration would have neither the united support of the Dominions nor of the British electorate and Chamberlain maintained that it might increase rather than diminish Hitler's frustrated anger. Yet this decision only addressed part of the predicament. It has been noted that Britain's supposed ally, France, was pledged to go to war on Czechoslovakia's behalf against a German invasion. The question, which Chamberlain deliberately kept off the Cabinet agenda at this stage, was how France's position affected that of Britain. On this question, Halifax was of the view that Britain would have to stand by France. This was all the more reason to play up France's growing reluctance to fight in the first place.[42]

Whilst no one in the Cabinet had been prepared to challenge Chamberlain's conclusion that they were united in refusing to guarantee Czechoslovakia, a minority of Cabinet ministers maintained a sceptical view about the direction in which their Prime Minister was guiding foreign policy. Together, Oliver Stanley (President of the Board of Trade), Walter Elliot (Minister for Health), Earl Winterton (Chancellor of the

Duchy of Lancaster) and Earl de la Warr (Lord Privy Seal) all had doubts. Whilst this had the makings of a cabal, it was hardly a force to be reckoned with against the rest of the Cabinet. Chamberlain had made sure that the big guns were on his side and the support of the Foreign Secretary (Halifax), Home Secretary (Hoare), Chancellor of the Exchequer (Simon) and Lord Chancellor (Maugham) easily overpowered the objections of the only major Cabinet figure to object forcefully to Chamberlain's line – the First Lord of the Admiralty, Alfred Duff Cooper. An exponent of a field force sufficient to make a reality of a continental commitment, Cooper was not much impressed with the troops he might otherwise have hoped to command within the Cabinet. He had regard for Oliver Stanley but realized that the ministerial sceptics were 'three of the lightest weights in the Cabinet'. To his wife, Lady Diana, Cooper sighed that Elliot, Winterton and de la Warr were 'more liabilities than assets'.[43]

Chamberlain's mind was made up and evidence to the contrary was thus an inconvenience. From his ill-defined vantage point as 'Chief Diplomatic Adviser', Vansittart maintained contact both with British opponents of Chamberlain's policy and with anti-Hitler dissident forces in Germany. One of those who kept in touch with Vansittart was Lord Lloyd, the old India diehard who was now Chairman of the British Council. Lloyd was receiving information from his contacts that elements within the German Army's General Staff were deeply uneasy about Hitler's ambitions. At considerable personal risk (he was later executed by the Nazis in 1945) one of their emissaries, Ewald von Kleist-Schenzin, came to London on 18 August to brief Vansittart, and subsequently Lloyd and Churchill. The message from dissidents like von Kleist was clear. Hitler was planning to invade Czechoslovakia in mid- or late September. If Britain publicly made clear that it would go to war with him in these circumstances even at the risk of provoking a pan-European conflict, the *Führer* would have to back down or face being overthrown by disgruntled German officers who would bring into being a more agreeable regime. Vansittart briefed Chamberlain on von Kleist's mission and Lloyd and Churchill both wrote reports to the Foreign Office. Although it gave Chamberlain a feeling of 'uneasiness', in which 'I don't feel sure that we ought not to do something', the Prime Minister was not minded to gamble on threatening war on the basis of the unsubstantiated talk of anti-Hitler 'jacobites' whose open strength was so far noticeable by its absence and might prove to be no more than a mirage when put to the test.[44]

With both Cabinet and Parliament dispersed on their holidays, the Foreign Office continued to receive intelligence reports that pointed to a German invasion of Czechoslovakia on 19 or 20 September. The

Permanent Under-Secretary at the Foreign Office, Cadogan, now wondered whether a formal if private warning should not be dispatched to Hitler after all. Denied the rest of an all too brief Scottish holiday following his audience with the King at Balmoral, Chamberlain was sent for and returned to Downing Street on 7 September. In contrast to the situation a little over a week previously, he at last agreed to issue Hitler with a private warning that restated Britain's support for a negotiated settlement along lines set out by the Runciman mission. In the event of Germany ignoring this procedure and becoming embroiled in war with France, Britain would not 'stand aside'.

The ultimatum was prepared for Henderson to deliver to Hitler via the Reich Foreign Minister, Ribbentrop. Henderson, however, seemed close to a breakdown. The conditions in which he was having to endure the Nuremberg rally would have been enough to unhinge those of stronger stomach than he, but his reaction to the occasion suggested that he had lost what little fire in the belly he had ever possessed. Far from stiffening his resolve, the sight of the Nazi machine in full cry only confirmed his belief that Britain could never take on the Master Race and should do everything and anything to avoid doing so. Now of all times, Henderson argued desperately, was not the time to upset Hitler with bellicose warnings of the kind London proposed. Rather, he advised, the British press should be instructed 'to write up Hitler as the apostle of Peace'.[45] Halifax still wanted the ultimatum delivered but through the sheer weight of his insistence, Henderson got his way and the warning to Hitler was not given.

Henderson's support was an important fillip to Chamberlain's position. That appeasement was also counselled by Britain's Ambassadors in Europe's other relevant embassies, strengthened the Prime Minister's hand yet further. It would have taken considerable nerve for London to have ignored the advice of those of its diplomats closest to events.[46] Henderson's reluctance to issue Hitler with a warning at this time even attracted the support of those like Halifax's private secretary, Oliver Harvey, who wanted a stiffer line generally. Harvey perceived 'the danger of Hitler going off the deep end if confronted with the risk of a diplomatic defeat which his regime – none too strong – might not survive'.[47] Von Kleist had been wasting his breath.

Meanwhile, the position in the Czech Sudetenland had deteriorated. Whipped up from Berlin and by Hitler's Nuremberg speech of 12 September, riots had forced the introduction of martial law in the German-speaking areas within the Czech boundary. Hitler had now manoeuvred his opponents into a position from which he could construct his pretext to invade. Furthermore, Chamberlain feared that his suspicions were being borne out with the apparent wavering of the French in their commitment to the Czechs. A sign of backsliding, Paris said it wanted to hold a conference with the British and German governments.

Events were in danger of overtaking the timetable upon which Chamberlain had made his calculations. He had been planning his personal visit to Hitler, 'Plan Z', since the end of August, and the last thing he wanted was for the French, racked by their transparent sense of insecurity, to get in on the act. Without consulting either his Cabinet (Simon, Halifax and Hoare were the only Cabinet members who were told, along with Cadogan at the FO and the Premier's adviser, Sir Horace Wilson) or the French Government (a fact that went down poorly with Daladier who had had the decency to include Britain in his diplomatic plans), Chamberlain communicated to Hitler the following message: 'I propose to come over at once to see you with a view to try to find a peaceful solution. I propose to come across by air and am ready to start tomorrow.'

It is difficult at the end of the twentieth century to imagine the impression that Chamberlain's shuttle diplomacy must have made. No British Prime Minister had ever intervened in this manner before. Indeed, Chamberlain had never been in an aeroplane before, let alone one making a trip to the heart of Europe. Chamberlain was to be the first British Prime Minister to set foot in Germany for sixty years. When the Cabinet assembled on 14 September, it was to be told that the request had already been sent and that Hitler had accepted. A fait accompli is not the basis for argument. In contrast, the basis of Chamberlain's negotiating position was the source of considerable discussion. He suggested that he would start by commending a scheme whereby the Sudeten areas would hold plebiscites on their future membership of the Czechoslovak state. Since their likely option to join the German Reich would undermine Czechoslovakia's strategic defence capacity, Britain might have to guarantee what was left of the rump state. Winterton and Hailsham (now Lord President) were uneasy about holding plebiscites, whilst De La Warr and Oliver Stanley felt that rushing into them at Germany's bidding was tantamount to surrender. Duff Cooper now became more certain that war could not be avoided. Simon, who was also worried about overhasty plebiscites, suggested that Chamberlain should use his mission to confer with Hitler. The visit would not be an ultimatum, but part of an exercise in toning down the manner in which Hitler would realize his ambition.

On 15 September Chamberlain was received by Hitler in his mountain retreat near Berchtesgaden. Chamberlain's weak spot had always been his belief in his own ability to surmount difficulties. Hitler played upon this conceit to maximum effect. The result of the German dictator's exercise was to leave the ageing Premier twittering to his sister about how Hitler's advisers had assured Horace Wilson that the *Führer* had 'been very favourably impressed' by Chamberlain, declaiming that he had 'had a conversation with a *man*, he said, and one with whom I can do business and he liked the rapidity with which I had grasped the essentials. In short I had established a certain confidence, which was my aim, and in spite of the hardness and ruthlessness I thought I saw in his face I got the impression that here was a man who could be relied upon when he had given his word.'[48] More importantly, Hitler told Chamberlain that he was intent on unleashing the *Wehrmacht* across the Czech border in order to absorb the Sudetenland into Germany and was 'prepared to risk a world war' if need be. Taken aback that Hitler seemed to have let him travel all this way in order to state his intentions rather than to negotiate a compromise, Chamberlain looked for a way of feeding the tiger: 'I said I could give no assurance without consultation. My personal opinion was that on principle I didn't care two hoots whether the Sudetens were in the Reich, or out of it, according to their own wishes, but I saw immense practical difficulties.' Chamberlain thus made clear that he was not objecting to the act of Germany seizing a part of a country to which it had no legal claim, but rather that he would only object if the confiscation of Czech property was carried out in an aggressive fashion. As one military historian has said (with reference to the Austrian *Anschluss*), 'as usual British leaders were more concerned with Germany's bad form than with the actual event.'[49] Having stated his position, Chamberlain prepared to return to London for consultation whilst Hitler conditionally agreed to do nothing precipitate in the meantime.

Back in London, Chamberlain immediately squared his position with the big three in his Cabinet, Halifax, Hoare and Simon, before seeing the full Cabinet the following morning. Chamberlain said that he thought Hitler's appetite could be limited to the Sudetenland and that so long as he was bought off here, this would mark an end to his ambitions. The sceptics, unsure of themselves, played for time rather than attempting to force the issue to a head. Duff Cooper took the most hostile line, but he too was not prepared to resign at this moment and instead grudgingly backed the holding of plebiscites in the disputed areas. Reconvening after lunch, the Cabinet supported the notion of Britain guaranteeing the new Czech borders once the Sudetendeutsch had been absorbed into the Reich. This particularly made sense (by being harmless) if the Sudetenland was the summit of Hitler's territorial ambitions.

Daladier and his defeatist Foreign Minister, Georges Bonnet, arrived in London the following day, 18 September. Talks which commenced before lunch stretched into the dead of night. The French delegation were unhappy about the tool of plebiscites and so it was agreed instead that the territory ceded by international agreement to the Reich would be those areas where German speakers comprised the majority. The redrawn boundaries of the Czechoslovakian state would likewise be guaranteed by an international rather than merely a Franco-Russian agreement. On Monday, 19 September, Chamberlain had a resounding success in keeping his Cabinet, sceptics included, united upon the approach he had now agreed with the French. When on the 20th, the Czechs at first said the proposals were unacceptable, both London and Paris made clear that Prague could either think again or prepare for the German invasion unassisted. After further arm-twisting and semi-menacing visits to the Czech President in the middle of the night, the Czechs at last gave in to this pressure. Chamberlain prepared to fly back to Godesberg on the Rhine to cement the deal with the *Führer*. First he again convened the Cabinet so that he might have their backing and sanction for the line he proposed to take. The result was a mandate for him to negotiate a redrawing of the Czech boundary in Germany's favour. Hitler would be asked to sign a non-aggression pact with what was left of the free rump Czech state. The Cabinet agreed that Chamberlain was not to countenance any attempt by Hitler to champion the opportunistic claims on Czech territory by Poland or Hungary. Even Hoare backed Duff Cooper's demand that Germany would have to abide by the adjudication of an international boundary commission before moving the *Wehrmacht* into the Sudetenland. A German refusal would lead to war. This formula agreed with his colleagues, Chamberlain set off to parley with Hitler.

Chamberlain arrived at Bad Godesberg on 22 September. He had secured a deal that he believed would give Hitler what he wanted. Out of the jaws of war, peace had been extracted. Contrary to the Prime Minister's expectations, Hitler was furious at the antics of this meddlesome old man. He had no wish to be cheated out of his lightning conquest by some international commission and made clear that he was not interested in what Chamberlain had achieved on his behalf. Instead he was going to order the German Army to invade in six days' time, advancing as far as it saw fit, and not so much as a cow was to be removed by the Czechs from the German-speaking areas in the meantime. Chamberlain's logic had presumed that since Hitler was determined upon the ends of annexation, the task was to provide him with means that would ensure a peaceful and limited transfer. Now it seemed that violent means were as much a part of Hitler's intentions as the ends of annexation. Chamberlain was shaken by Hitler's Bismarckian desire for blood and iron, yet he did not concede defeat. Instead he exceeded his remit from London by implying that an international guarantee of Czechoslovakia's redrawn boundaries did not mean that they could not be driven back further in Germany's favour at some later stage. Even this did not impress the *Führer*.

Hitler dismissed the concept of a guarantee unless the Polish and Hungarian claims against Czechoslovakia were also granted and insisted that German occupation of the Sudeten areas must precede any international supervision of the changeover. This intransigence left Chamberlain in a difficult position and he tried to moderate Hitler by implying that his own political future was in doubt if an acceptable solution could not be achieved. When he told the *Führer* that he had been booed on his way to the Heston aerodrome, Hitler riposted that this was merely left-wing critics with whom Chamberlain need not bother. Chamberlain insisted that this was not so and that it was the hostility of sections within the Conservative Party that he feared.[50]

In fact, events at Godesberg were creating trouble for Chamberlain at home, and especially where it mattered most – in his own Cabinet. This was augmented by the logistical problem of being in Godesberg and separated from the rest of his colleagues in London. In fact, he was given cause for concern by the immediate reaction of some Cabinet ministers as soon as he was out of their sight. The Foreign Secretary, Lord Halifax, had been left in London to keep a check on possible dissent. Chamberlain briefed him from Godesberg at 10.30 p.m. and, more fully, the next morning. Halifax, however, was more disturbed by what he heard than was Chamberlain in recounting it. He even contradicted Chamberlain's withholding of approval to the Czechs to begin mobilizing to defend their country. Horrified, Chamberlain tried to block the message and Halifax acquiesced.[51] However, Halifax telegraphed Chamberlain telling him what he certainly did not want to hear: public opinion was turning against selling out on the Czechs and he was to tell Hitler that if he rejected a peaceful solution he would be committing an 'unpardonable crime against humanity'.[52] Furthermore, Halifax instructed Rab Butler (who was in Geneva) to find out whether the Soviets really would fight for Czechoslovakia if push came to shove.[53] Faced by an intransigent dictator and disobedient colleagues at home, Chamberlain intimated that he would have to return to London to confer with the Cabinet. Extraordinarily, given the way he had been treated, he left proclaiming (according to the German record of the meeting) that 'a relationship of confidence had grown up between himself and the Fuhrer as a result of the conversations of the last few days' and that if they could overcome the current difficulty over Czechoslovakia, then 'he would be glad to discuss other problems still outstanding with the Fuhrer in the same spirit.' In the meantime Hitler's grudging gesture, to 'the only man to whom I have ever made a concession', was to postpone the German invasion until 1 October.[54]

Following a meeting of the Foreign Policy Committee, the Cabinet convened in full in the late afternoon of 24 September. Hitler's brinkmanship had gone too far. The Czechs would not, and should not, be persuaded to accept an ultimatum that was tantamount to the result of a military defeat. The Secretary of State for War, Leslie Hore-Belisha, called for the British Army to be mobilized and was backed by Duff Cooper, Walter Elliot, Earl Winterton and Oliver Stanley. Chamberlain opted to have the discussion put on ice in order to be resumed the following day. Giving the Cabinet his considered opinion that Hitler was sincere in claiming that his ambitions were limited to the Sudetenland, not the domination of Europe, the Prime Minister reportedly argued that:

> In his view, Herr Hitler had certain standards. (He now spoke with greater confidence on this point than after his first visit.) Herr Hitler had a narrow mind and was violently prejudiced on certain subjects; but he would not deliberately deceive a man whom he respected and with whom he had been in negotiation, and he was sure that Herr Hitler now felt some respect for him. . . . The Prime Minister said that he thought it would be a great tragedy if we lost this opportunity of reaching an understanding with Germany on all points of difference between the two countries. A peaceful settlement of Europe depends upon an Anglo-German understanding. He thought that he had now established an influence over Herr Hitler, and that the latter trusted him and was willing to work with him.[55]

Public opinion was hard to gauge. Nonetheless there were some signs that a loud and vociferous body had emerged that was opposed to what it saw as the betrayal of Czechoslovakia. Lord Hailsham, possibly influenced by the experience of his son Quintin who was at that time fighting the Oxford by-election against an anti-Chamberlain alliance led by the Master of Balliol, even expressed the view to Duff Cooper that the Prime Minister's line would never survive a mauling on the floor of the House of Commons.[56] From the Conservative backbenches, Amery thought like-wise.[57]

By the time the Cabinet reconvened on 25 September, Halifax had endured a restless night troubled by his conscience. Since his appointment to the Foreign Office he had articulated a policy that had marched in harmony with that of the Prime Minister. Events at Godesberg forced him now to reassess the situation. He made clear that he did not think that Britain should press Czechoslovakia to accept the Godesberg terms. He felt that Hitler 'was dictating terms, just as though he had won a war but

without having had to fight'. Nor was this all. In words that Churchill
would later echo, the Foreign Secretary confessed to his colleagues that
'the ultimate end which he wished to see accomplished, [was] the
destruction of Nazi-ism. So long as Nazi-ism lasted, peace would be
uncertain.' This entirely contradicted Chamberlain's belief that assisting
Hitler to dispose of the Czech state was the prelude to a greater and more
general settlement with the Third Reich. Not surprisingly, Halifax's line
entirely took Chamberlain by surprise. He scribbled a note to Halifax
stating that 'your complete change of view since I saw you last night is a
horrible blow to me' and implying that he might have to consider
resigning the Premiership rather than declare war. Halifax scribbled back
that whilst he felt a 'brute', he had been unable to sleep for the torment of
the decision he felt that he had to express. Chamberlain's typically
unsympathetic response was to remind his Foreign Secretary that 'night
conclusions are seldom taken in the right perspective'. Halifax's actions
were motivated by honourable intentions but personal calculations gave
him the opportunity to act. Chamberlain could not survive a second
Foreign Secretary resigning in seven months.[58]

Halifax's declaration tilted the balance in the Cabinet. The sceptics
were reinforced and apart from those like the Lord Chancellor, Maugham, who were determined to avoid war at almost any cost, Chamberlain's usual supporters now appeared to be contemplating joining a
French declaration of war in the event of a German attack across the
Czech border. In this sense, in saving Chamberlain from getting his own
way, Halifax's intervention may have prevented the extremely damaging
resignation of perhaps three or more members of the Cabinet.[59] The
Godesberg terms would not be acceptable after all. Realizing (as he had
not previously) that Hitler was not to be bought off by fair-minded
appeasement, Halifax adjusted accordingly and his resolve stiffened.
However, he had been implying for some time that Britain would have to
stand by France in the event of a Czech invasion. By refusing to cajole
France or the Czechs into what he regarded as dishonourable surrenders,
he now seemed prepared to make standing by them a reality where
previously he had sought to minimize the chances of having to do so. It
was Hitler who had moved the goalposts. The difference between Halifax
and Chamberlain was that the former was not prepared to play on this
new ground whereas the latter was. The Prime Minister had inaugurated
the peace process to solve the Czech problem and had pinned his political
colours to its successful conclusion. In sinking so much personal capital
into keeping Britain out of war, he was more prepared to be forced by the
process's momentum into concessions he found disagreeable than to stand
up for the previous position he had advocated. The result of this was that

he gripped on to the peace process with the dogged tenacity of one who no longer controlled its destination but who feared the inevitable bruising that jumping off would entail.

Chamberlain's great remaining hope was the self-doubt of the French and of their Foreign Minister, Georges Bonnet, in particular. Nothing could better undermine the growing readiness of the British Cabinet to fight alongside France than the hesitancy of France to fight in the first place. In fact, the French position was not easy to gauge, not least because they seemed unsure of it themselves. Cross-examined by Chamberlain and Simon (himself a leading KC) on 25 September, Daladier prevaricated when asked blunt questions about the exact nature of his country's response to a German invasion across the Czech boundary.[60] Nonetheless, France was still committed to standing by the Czechs, even if Chamberlain had grounds for doubting how well thought out that position was in practice. Following a meeting the next morning with the Chief of the French General Staff, General Gamelin, Chamberlain made clear that Britain would stand by France in the event of her going to war with Germany. Any other position would have certainly brought about Duff Cooper's resignation and possibly that of several other members of the Cabinet as well.

The position was now desperate. Chamberlain was nonetheless determined to keep lines of communication open with Hitler. As a result, the Prime Minister's trusted adviser, Sir Horace Wilson, was dispatched to appraise the German dictator of the position. Wilson informed Hitler that the Godesberg ultimatum was unacceptable to the French and that the previous formula outlined after Bertschesgaden should be the basis of a Czech–British–German understanding. Wilson had been instructed to tell Hitler verbally that if he did not accept this, then there was the danger of Britain joining the resulting war. Upon meeting the *Führer*, Wilson was subjected to such a tantrum that he did not feel able to deliver the verbal warning until the following morning. This was certainly convenient. Chamberlain had not wanted to issue a warning at all, believing that 'anything in the form of a threat would destroy any chance of acceptance of the appeal.' He further acted to circumvent Cabinet opposition and that of Halifax and the Foreign Office in particular. Wilson telephoned Henderson (presumably at Chamberlain's bidding) to tell the Germans to disregard any statements that did not come directly from the Prime Minister.[61]

Chamberlain had been prepared to swallow the Godesberg ultimatum if it meant avoiding war, but, without the full support of his Foreign Secretary or the French Government and with the opposition of the Czechs, this was not a position that could be sustained. With no clear response from Hitler to Wilson's mission, Chamberlain's last throw was to open communications with Mussolini in the hope that Il Duce could persuade his fellow dictator to seek an arbitrated settlement. The Prime Minister had invested much in cultivating Italy's friendship and now was the time to see whether or not the effort had been in vain.

The Royal Navy mobilized on 27 September. This was a clear sign of warlike intent, the impact of which Chamberlain tried to mitigate by publicly announcing that it was only a 'precautionary' measure that did not necessarily imply 'that we have determined on war'.[62] No orders to mobilize the army or RAF were given. Hitler had vowed to begin his invasion by 1 October and time for a peaceful settlement was therefore running out. Gas masks were issued. Anti-aircraft guns were set up along the Embankment. It seemed that Britain was only hours away from war.

'It seems to me incredible,' announced Chamberlain in a desperate appeal for common sense to prevail, 'that the peoples of Europe, who do not want war with one another, should be plunged in a bloody struggle over a question on which agreement has already been largely obtained.' The wording of Chamberlain's broadcast to the nation was carefully chosen. Britain would fight to prevent world domination from a militaristic state. However, he seemed to hint that even at this late stage the crisis of the moment might yet be avoided for war being a 'fearful thing', 'we must be very clear, before we embark on it that it is really the great issues that are at stake.' This comment was significant, since it followed what became his most famous comment on the crisis: 'How horrible, fantastic, incredible, it is that we should be digging trenches and trying on gas-masks here because of a quarrel in a far-away country between people of whom we know nothing . . . I would not hesitate to pay even a third visit to Germany, if I thought it would do any good.'[63] It was hardly surprising that, even at this late hour, Chamberlain was searching for a way out. France was hoping that an appeal from Mussolini to prevent war might save the day; the half-hearted mobilization of the French Army did not augur well for the anti-German alliance. The likely action of the Soviet Union was still not clear. Attempts were being made in which the Romanian Government would let the Red Army pass through her territory in order to come to the Czechs' aid, but even if this came about, would Prague already have fallen by the time the Russians arrived and was the westward march of the Soviet forces a welcome development anyway? Meanwhile, the attitude of the British Dominions demonstrated less than full-hearted commitment to the possibility of war. In the Cabinet, Duff Cooper tried to downgrade the importance of this state of affairs. 'Perhaps the really extraordinary thing,' he postured, 'was that the Dominions should ever take part in a

European war' at all. He maintained that, in any case, Britain's position now 'in regard to the co-operation of the Dominions was more favourable than it had been in 1914'.[64] He was determined to guard against a last-minute attempt by the Prime Minister to latch on to an excuse for backing down. Similarly, Halifax took a lead in opposing further concessions which 'amounted to complete capitulation to Germany . . . We could not press the Czech Government to do what we believed to be wrong.'[65] Nonetheless he came to the Prime Minister's aid with a reworked compromise. He suggested that Hitler should be allowed to march into the border areas of the Sudetenland by 1 October with the remaining areas under dispute to be settled by agreement by the end of that month.[66]

Whilst the Cabinet was still sitting, Hitler's response was handed to Chamberlain. It demanded that the Sudetenland be united with the Reich but in a process comparable to that sketched by Halifax. German troops would march into the areas that the Czechs had been prepared to concede after the Bertschesgaden summit and plebiscites would be held in the remaining areas. Germany would join in guaranteeing the new Czech borders once this had been achieved. This was not the language of one bent on world domination. In this light, stopping German speakers from joining the Germany Reich did not appear to be such a clear-cut case for a British declaration of war. Chamberlain now contacted Hitler, offering to come to Berlin to negotiate a more sensible handover that would avoid war. He also made a further attempt at enlisting Mussolini's support in finding a peaceful solution.

Chamberlain did not know for sure whether his offer would be accepted when he arrived in the Commons chamber. MPs knew that war was potentially hours away, yet for all the talk of rebellion, Chamberlain received for the most part a rousing reception when he arrived to take his place. An hour into his speech, Cadogan arrived with a message that was forwarded along the front bench. Simon passed the note to Chamberlain whilst he was approaching the end of his solemn and inconclusive recitation of the state of play. The Prime Minister looked at the note and looked back at Simon for reassuring confirmation that he should announce its contents. Hitler had made his reply. He would be convening a conference in Munich the following day with Mussolini and was inviting Daladier and Chamberlain to it. This was a moment to treasure. Chamberlain made clear that he would accept and begged that the chamber should let him proceed with haste to fly to Germany. Shouts of joy broke the tension – MPs cheered deliriously. After Attlee gave the nod, Labour MPs joined in.

Hitler had agreed to postpone mobilizing his army for a day in order for the conference to take place. This left no time for prevarication and there remained a distinct possibility that Chamberlain would be bounced into accepting terms that were as bad or worse than Godesberg. Whatever happened, the Czechs would play no part in the conference concocted to determine their fate. Chamberlain's suggestion that they be included was rejected out of hand. The conference got under way shortly after noon on 29 September. It was 2 a.m. the following morning before it was concluded. By then a deal had been done. Ready to sign, Hitler dipped his pen into the inkpot. Nothing came out. The pot was empty.[67] This symbolic shortcoming was hurriedly rectified. The German occupation of the Sudetenland was on and a war with Germany was off.

The agreement that Chamberlain signed appeared to be a significant improvement on the ultimatum issued at the Godesberg summit. Instead of a lightning German invasion on 1 October, the movement of the *Wehrmacht* into the first part of the Sudetenland would be spread over ten days. An international commission would supervise the full absorption of the German-speaking areas into the Reich, and also oversee both the manner in which it was carried out and the holding of plebiscites in the affected areas. In view of the Sudetendeutsch claims to self-determination, it would not have been easy for Chamberlain to reject these proposals, given that Britain had in response to the Bertschesgaden summit already made clear that a transfer of territory in Germany's favour should take place. War had become a likelihood because of Hitler's stated intent of violently seizing territory. Now that he seemed prepared to back down and accept an orderly and internationally supervised transfer, the case for agreement seemed overwhelming. This was the position at the time of signing. By the time Hitler had broken almost every aspect of the understanding, it was too late, and too inconvenient to do anything about it.

Whilst the exact text of the agreement was being transcribed, and despite the lateness of the hour, Chamberlain secured a commitment to have a further conversation with Hitler (without involving the French) in the morning. Without prevarication, Hitler agreed to sign a one-page document that Chamberlain and Horace Wilson had knocked up earlier that morning. It was a further sign that Chamberlain believed Hitler to be a man of his word and that agreements reached with him would be binding and would secure the long-term peace of the continent. The full text read:

> We, the German Fuehrer and Chancellor, and the British Prime Minister, have had a further meeting to-day, and are agreed in recognising that the question of Anglo-German relations is of the first importance for the two countries and for Europe.
>
> We regard the agreement signed last night and the Anglo-German Naval

Agreement as symbolic of the desire of our two peoples never to go to war again. We are resolved that the method of consultation shall be the method adopted to deal with any other questions that may concern our two countries, and we are determined to continue our efforts to remove possible sources of difference and thus to contribute to assure the peace of Europe.'[68]

VI

'Peace with Honour' announced Benjamin Disraeli on his return from the Congress of Berlin in 1878. These were the words that Chamberlain was now to echo himself. Both Prime Ministers had used different sorts of diplomacy in their negotiations to avert war. Disraeli (by then Earl of Beaconsfield) had famously sent orders for his train at the station to be prepared for his imminent walk out. Characteristically predisposed against the diplomacy of the theatrical bluff, Chamberlain had shown a greater sense of willing to agree to peace at virtually any price. Paradoxically, his bargaining strength came not from his own approach but from that of his more sceptical Cabinet colleagues. Whilst he might be prepared to accept whatever terms Hitler stipulated, his Cabinet were not. This became evident when Halifax made clear that peace on the basis of the Godesberg ultimatum would be unacceptable.

The reception that Disraeli had been accorded in 1878 was overshadowed by the serenade that greeted Chamberlain on his return from Munich. Arriving at Heston aerodrome, he read out the text of the new Anglo-German accord, holding up the piece of paper that bore his and Hitler's signatures. Relating the events of the day to his sister, Chamberlain wrote that 'Even the descriptions of the papers give no idea of the scenes in the streets as I drove from Heston to the Palace. They were lined from one end to the other with people of every class, shouting themselves hoarse, leaping on the running board, banging on the windows, and thrusting their hands into the car to be shaken.'[69] Chamberlain posed with the royal family on the balcony at Buckingham Palace to acknowledge the cheers. The exuberance of the moment overcame any doubts about the wisdom of the royal family associating themselves with a policy that was soon seen to be extremely contentious. At the time, it seemed the most natural thing in the world. It was as if a great national victory had been scored. Despite rain the crowds were enormous. The next time London's streets were to be so packed was when the crowds who cheered Chamberlain for not fighting Hitler, cheered Churchill for having successfully done just that. Eventually Chamberlain made his way to Downing Street. Here, he recorded: 'I spoke to the multitudes below from the same window, I believe, as that from which Dizzy announced peace with honour 60 years ago.' From that window, he declaimed in his alto voice his shortest and most famous speech of all: 'My good friends, this is the second time in our history that there has come from Germany to Downing Street peace with honour. I believe it is peace for our time.' This phrase, from the English *Book of Common Prayer*, had in 1925 been used by Baldwin to describe his hopes for settling industrial unrest. What may have also been in Chamberlain's mind was that it had been used in 1928 as the title for a book of the collected speeches of his brother Austen.[70] The speeches had concentrated on European security at the time of the Treaty of Locarno. In repeating the phrase, Neville believed that he had completed his late brother's unfinished business: the pacification of Europe.

VI

These events would have strained the mental constitution of a young man, let alone one who was almost seventy. As Chamberlain acknowledged to his sister, by the time he got to the Prime Ministerial country retreat, Chequers, 'I came nearer there to a nervous breakdown that I have ever been in my life.'[71] He received over 20,000 letters of congratulation in the first few days after news of the Munich agreement was announced. The Dominion governments, relieved that their loyalty to Britain was not now going to be put to the test, were delighted that he had prevented a war in which they would have been expected to contribute.

Munich did not alter the reality of Germany's confiscation of the Sudetenland. Without the agreement, the *Wehrmacht* would have marched in immediately, rendering unto the *Führer* that which the *Führer* deemed his. Munich was considered a victory for Chamberlain because it reversed the Godesberg ultimatum's terms, and more closely resembled those that Britain and France had forced the Czechs to concede after the Bertschesgaden summit. This was why, although the Sudetenland was ceded to Germany, no war ensued. The Munich Agreement set up a framework, internationally monitored for an agreed and supervised occupation. An international commission would set in motion plebiscites in the affected areas which – if they so voted – could opt back into Czechoslovakia.

As we have seen, Chamberlain believed that, despite being 'half mad', Hitler was a man of honour who would keep to his bargain. Nothing could have been further from the truth. Indeed, perhaps sensing that he was confronted by politicians who were happy to be duped if it meant avoiding war, Hitler lost no time in double-crossing Chamberlain and Daladier. The terms that made Munich politically acceptable were never implemented. The international commission was convened but only to be steamrollered into impotent irrelevance by the Nazis who proved that possession was nine-tenths of the law. The promised plebiscites were never held. The guarantee to the rump Czech state, denuded of its defence lines, was never given. In fact, once implemented, the Munich Pact secured for the Czechs no long-term benefit that they were not given by the Godesberg ultimatum after all. This was the ultimatum over which Britain and France had been seemingly prepared to go to war.

That Munich was a broken promise that was to destroy Czechoslovakia is not in question. Chamberlain was not primarily concerned with saving the last democracy in eastern Europe. His comments of support, condolence and understanding for the Czechs' predicament were few and far between. His mission was to find terms that would not so affront the decency of his colleagues that they would decide that they could take no more of Hitler's bullying. The Munich agreement is the pivot upon which Chamberlain's subsequent reputation has swung. To those who saw it as a betrayal, a stain upon Britain's history and a missed opportunity to hit Hitler hard before he was ready, the Prime Minister's negotiation eternally damned him as the foremost of the 'guilty men'. To his supporters at the time, it was a valiant attempt to preserve peace that failed only because of Hitler's subsequent and unimaginably dastardly behaviour. In this interpretation, Chamberlain was the apotheosis of an English martyr. He was a decent man who had done his duty in a stiff collar and matching upper lip, rolled umbrella in hand, an innocent sacrificed to one who was the embodiment of Man's Fall. To his defenders amongst historians today, Chamberlain was not the dupe of the devil incarnate but a shrewd politician who knew that war would very likely be a disaster not just for the Czechs and the British but for western civilization itself. This interpretation of his motives subdivides into two camps: those who believe Chamberlain hoped that war could be postponed indefinitely and those who believe he was seeking to postpone it only until Britain was in a position to right its military deficiencies and take on Hitler from a position of strength. Evidence in support of the latter includes the views of military figures at the time like General Ironside, who concluded in his diary that 'Chamberlain is of course right. We have not the means of defending ourselves and he knows it . . . We cannot expose ourselves now to a German attack. We simply commit suicide if we do.'[72] No analysis of Chamberlain as a politician can dodge attempting to weigh up all these contradictory positions in evaluating his motives and legacy.

At least since March 1938, the argument against Britain fighting Germany over Czechoslovakia had been made plain to the government.

The Chiefs of Staff Report presented in March, 'Military Implications of German Aggression Against Czechoslovakia', claimed that 'no pressure which this country and its possible allies could exercise would suffice to prevent the defeat of Czechoslovakia.' At the Cabinet Foreign Policy Committee's meeting of 18 March, Inskip, the Minister for Defence Coordination, echoed this viewpoint, stressing that he believed that Germany could overrun all of Czechoslovakia in a week and there was nothing Britain could do about it other than launch a naval blockade of Germany, which would take two to three years to work. By September, the Chiefs of Staff had tempered their previously pessimistic prognosis but only to an extent that encouraged Halifax to tell the Cabinet that he wanted to avoid war not because he thought Britain would lose but because the suffering needed for victory would be too great.[73]

Since British strategists assumed they could not, the first consideration was whether the Czechs could mount a sustained resistance to invasion. At the time of the Munich Agreement the Germans could field forty-eight front line divisions. However, less than a quarter of these were motorized or mechanized and only three were Panzer divisions. These Panzers, it should also be pointed out, were of inferior capability to those that were to smash through France in 1940. In September 1938, the vast majority of German divisions were not appreciably better armed or trained that those of the French Army. Artillery was for the most part horse-drawn and, particularly at the heavier end of the scale, presented considerable problems for the Germans. At the time of the Munich crisis they appear only to have had enough ammunition to last for six weeks of hard fighting. Furthermore, the reserve divisions were not yet fully developed and with only eight of these ready, they would have to fall back on a second line made up of old Great War veterans in the twenty-one divisions of the *Landwehr*.[74]

British attempts to rubbish the value of the Czech Army came ill from a country that had only two divisions up and ready to commit to the fray. The Czechs could field thirty divisions against the thirty-seven German divisions directly facing them. However, even allowing for the perceived advantage of defensive positions, the overall quality of the Czech divisions was inferior to those of the attacker. Where fully developed, the Czech fortification lines were impressive but they were patchy and could probably not have kept out the *Wehrmacht* for a prolonged period. Nevertheless, the nature of the terrain, the proposed dispersed use of the Panzers and poor weather conditions that would have hampered *Luftwaffe* operations, all stood to blunt key weapons of the blitzkrieg that were to be of such considerable assistance to future German victories.

That the Germans would have been successful in overrunning Czechoslovakia in late September 1938 cannot be seriously doubted. There was, however, every likelihood that (in terms of time, loss of life and matériel) it would have been a more costly operation than the subsequent conquest of Poland. Significantly, it was figures on the German General Staff who were amongst those most concerned that the Czechs would be no pushover.[75]

In contrast to the situation later, Germany's western frontier in September 1938 was dangerously exposed to attack. The massing of the German Army around the Czechoslovak border, together with the need to keep a watch on the Polish border, left only five divisions guarding Germany's western front and three spare. Effective reserves could take weeks to mobilize and German industry was by no means ready to switch immediately to an all-out war capacity. In other words, if Britain and France had declared war in September, the French could have launched fifty-six divisions against only eight German ones. The German defence against a French invasion from the west would have been further weakened by the fact that both its land-mechanized units and its air force were for the most part engaged on the Czech border. During 1938, production along Hitler's defensive Siegfried Line was massively stepped up but at the time of Munich it was still far too shallow and insubstantial to withstand assault for more than three weeks. Thus whilst Hitler fantasized about his west wall's invincibility, his officers realized that the soldiers needed to defend it were instead miles away, tied up facing the Czechs. By the time reserves could have been mobilized to meet the incursion, the French should have been through the Rhineland and in a position to strike at the industrial heartland of the Reich, the Ruhr.[76]

Unfortunately, this level of penetration was the best that the French had in mind. The simple arithmetic of a walkover victory was complicated by other considerations. For one thing, the French Army was being led not by Napoleon but by General Gamelin. Gamelin had no intention of seizing the initiative to knock out the Reich. Instead, he proposed halting the invasion of Germany as soon as Hitler was in a position to dispatch troops from the Czech campaign to meet it. Thereupon, rather than press home their early advantage, the French would destroy all the industrial and military installations that they had conquered and fall back into French territory behind the Maginot Line. By this time (estimated to be early 1939) it was anticipated that the British would be in a position to send across the English Channel an army worthy in quantity of the name. In all of this role-playing, there is an inevitable temptation to blame the French political and military elite for their timidity and lack of self-confidence. Such a temptation might well be fuelled by the knowledge of the swift collapse of France in 1940. These are accusations that an impartial observer might be able to lay – but at the time, in September 1938, the British contribution was just as hesitant. Indeed, the British Chief of the Air Staff wanted to start a series of staff talks with the French in order to dissuade them from offensive action.[77] It was in the light of this percussion of pessimism from Chiefs of Staff that Chamberlain and his ministers were encouraged in their sense of inadequacy against a Reich that was in reality hugely overexposed.

Britain's strategic conception was underlined by the strength of her navy and the weakness of her army. The way to defeat Germany, it was argued, was not to pursue a head-on clash with her impressive-looking army but to use economic strangulation. This was an understandable line to take, but it logically demanded that Britain prevent Germany moving east rather than stand aside and let it happen. By going east, Germany gained the very resources that made economic suffocation a redundant policy. At the time of Munich, the Germans could not count on the armed support of any eastern European country. This had an importance beyond the direction of (un)diplomatic language. Romania, for example, proposed in the event of increased hostilities to cut off supplies of oil to Germany.[78] Here the difference between the questionable strength of eastern Europe as a military bloc and her real strategic significance as a resources bloc must be emphasized.

British policy makers worried that a war over Czechoslovakia would summon the unwanted attention of Stalin's Russia into the heart of European affairs. Two contradictory positions were held. On the one hand, the Red Army was useless. On the other, its movement through eastern Europe was something to be feared. In contrast to the situation later, the Red Army in offensive mode was possibly of limited value in 1938 (it did not, after all, impress when taking on the Finns). If anything, this was an ideal situation. Russia could be on the Anglo-French side but could make no territorial advantage. Meanwhile, the Russian Baltic fleet could do genuinely useful work, harassing Germany's supply of ore from Sweden. Indeed, the Reich's naval inferiority added to its sense of strategic weakness. All its major battleships were still in construction, there were no aircraft carriers and only twelve submarines capable of Atlantic diving. Germany could not, therefore, expect to receive imports through the North Sea and even doubted whether the Swedish ore trade could be maintained, especially if the Russian Baltic fleet really was mobilized in hostility. Furthermore, a Russia that was on the Allied side would deny Hitler the resources he wanted to buy from her. In 1938, Russia's great importance to the Anglo-French cause lay not so much in the debatable quality of the Red Army but in a repository of natural resources that would be of great use to the side she chose to supply it to in a prolonged war. Germany's absence of raw materials was made more serious by the lack of foreign exchange throughout the decade with which to pay for them. During 1938, this position worsened further and the German economy showed every sign of mounting crisis, manifesting itself in the shortage of supply to meet demand. There was, for instance, petrol left for only four months in Germany if the country was to go on to a war footing and neither Romania nor Russia looked poised to help her out. During September, most of the countries of Europe began withdrawing contracts to supply Germany with the resources it needed. The tragedy of Allied, and in particular British, diplomacy in 1938–9 was that it failed to stop the Molotov–Ribbentrop non-aggression pact being signed in August 1939. Apart from anything else, this guaranteed Russia as the supply agent to Germany of many of the essential resources that the Reich required to prosecute a world war.[79] This would not have been the case had war broken out in September 1938.

Britain's understanding of the balance of forces – military, political and those of resources – could certainly have been better. The fact is, however, that it was not. Chamberlain was not blessed with hindsight nor, failing that, with superior wisdom to those who advised him. He could only draw up his plans on the basis of the (flawed) information in his possession. This led him to believe that the balance of forces was more favourable to Germany in September than it would be later, an assessment that was, if anything, the reverse of the truth. Added to the advice of the British Ambassador in Paris that all decent Frenchmen opposed war was the advice of his Ambassador in Prague that the Czechs were going to be crushed unless they stopped being obstinate, and the advice of the Ambassador in Berlin that on no account was the *Führer* to be made upset, creating a formidable body of opinion that no responsible Prime Minister should lightly cast aside. On the day of Chamberlain's meeting with Hitler at Bad Godesberg, Hankey's successor at the Committee of Imperial Defence, General Ismay, concluded that whilst postponing war for another year would allow Germany to increase its economic and military potential, the *Wehrmacht* would no longer be able to win a quick war because the Maginot Line would prevent it marching on Paris. The build-up in the RAF and anti-air defence systems would prevent the *Luftwaffe* from delivering a knockout blow against Britain from the skies. On 27 September, the Chiefs of Staff drew comparable conclusions, stating that since Britain was 'in bad condition to wage even a defensive war at the present time' the 'balance of advantage is definitely in favour of postponement'.[80] Postponing war was, of course, not the ultimate goal of Chamberlain's policy since he still believed the greater goal was in his grasp – peace in our time. Nevertheless, at worst, he believed that a possible war fought later would be more likely to be successful than a certain war fought now.

British defence policy had concentrated upon maintaining a sizeable naval advantage which the Anglo-German Treaty of 1935 had recognized and preventing the creation of an army that could fight on the continent since this was regarded as the job of Frenchmen. Yet, ironically, the unprepared state of the RAF – the service that had received the most attention and the greatest advocacy both from Chamberlain and from rebels like Churchill – was seen to embody one of the reasons why Britain could not risk a war in 1938. In trying to get his Cabinet colleagues to agree to Hitler's Godesberg terms, Chamberlain had played on this fear. According to the official minutes, he had reminded them that in the morning, 'he had flown up the river over London. He had asked himself what degree of protection we could afford to the thousands of homes which he had seen stretched out below him, and he had felt that we were in no position to justify waging a war to-day in order to prevent a war hereafter.'[81] Only 200 pilots were considered to be fully trained and ready for Bomber Command. It was estimated that they could drop at best a fifth of the bombs on Germany that the *Luftwaffe* could unleash on Britain. Only five of Fighter Command's twenty-nine squadrons had up-to-date aeroplanes. This was the Hawker Hurricane (the Spitfire had not yet come off the production line). The British estimated that they commanded a first-line strength of 1606 planes (with 412 in reserve) and the French 1454 (plus 730 reserve). French figures were also the triumph of quantity over quality. In contrast, the *Luftwaffe* were believed to be ready with 3200 supplemented by a reserve of 2400 planes. Certainly, had the *Luftwaffe* attacked Britain at the time of Munich, then it would have met little resistance. It would not have been tracked by a comprehensive radar system, the anti-air defences would have proved little more than pinpricks and it would have been counter-attacked by few Hurricanes and no Spitfires.[82] London was therefore at the mercy of the bomber which – as Baldwin had warned – would *always* get through. To have declared war on Germany in these circumstances would have been nothing short of suicidal. In contrast, by delaying war at Munich Chamberlain ensured that when the battle over the skies of Britain did finally take place it was, in his successor's words, Britain's finest hour. When that battle arrived, the strength of Fighter Command was almost ten times that of September 1938.[83] This, however, was not the whole story.

Had the *Luftwaffe* attacked in October 1938 using the calculations upon which the Cabinet had to base their decisions, then the consequences would have been disastrous. Yet, as with virtually everything else, the Cabinet were in possession of the wrong statistics. The *Luftwaffe* did not have a combined first-line and reserve strength of 5600 but rather a total of 3307. Without bases in the Low Countries (and in October 1938 if the *Wehrmact* could scarcely defend the Siegfried Line, it could certainly not overwhelm Dunkirk), the German bombers available in quantity at the time had not the range nor the bomb load to do to London, let alone to the industrial belt in the Midlands, the damage that they were to achieve in 1940–1. In September 1938 the *Luftwaffe* had only 1128 bombers and lacked the proper navigation instruments for truly effective bombing in Britain. It took the time that Chamberlain 'bought' at Munich for the Germans to achieve aircraft figures approaching the scale Britain had estimated for 1938.[84] In any case, as the French were well aware, the *Luftwaffe* had no intention of bombing Britain in September 1938 because they were fully committed to striking out Czechoslovakia.[85] Indeed the *Luftwaffe* had scarcely begun to think out the possibilities of strategic bombing on the scale Britain feared.[86] Chamberlain had based his calculations on a type of war which, it seems, was not an option. By preventing a war in 1938, only to concede one later, he created the conditions in which Germany could indeed deliver the punch upon which his dire predictions had been based.

In the light of these considerations, the justification for Munich seems threadbare. It did not guarantee the Czechs the security that it promised. Chamberlain signed away a Czech army of over thirty divisions at a time when he was the leader of a country that could commit only two divisions. The Germans gained not only a strategic position in which they could overwhelm the rest of Czechoslovakia but the military matériel of the Czechs when doing so. This included the Skoda armaments factory, which was one of the biggest of its kind in the world. The effect of transferring the works from Allied to German hands was considerable. Between August 1938 and Hitler's invasion of Poland, the Skoda works' output nearly equalled that of all Britain's armaments factories combined. Munich extinguished democracy's last arsenal in the east. It bought time for the RAF to win the Battle of Britain and to limit the destruction unleashed by the Blitz but had the conflict come in 1938 it would probably not have been necessary to fight an aerial war over Britain in the first place. Munich also bought Germany time to gain the resources it needed to fight a world war, construct the Panzer divisions and aeroplanes to fight the blitzkrieg, and neutralize Russia as an enemy and turn her into a supplier.

Although Britain ended up being in a better condition to defend herself, it is difficult to argue that the Allies were in a stronger position to fight a continental war against Hitler in September 1939 than they had been at the time of Munich when, on the western front, French divisions outnumbered German ones by over five to one. Yet, in all this, it must be remembered that (but for the noise emanating from mavericks like Vansittart and Churchill) the advice and information that Chamberlain received from almost every quarter at the time pointed to the imperative not to fight Hitler on the issue of which country German-speaking citizens wanted to live in. With advice that accentuated every negative and minimized every positive, what else was the Prime Minister expected to do?

Twelve

THE REBELLION

I

Back in London, Chamberlain had to overcome three separate sources of opposition to his signature upon the Munich Agreement. One source was to be expected – the Labour and Liberal opposition parties. He had little to fear from them during the remaining life of a Parliament in which he could expect to command a majority invariably in excess of 200. In undermining the size of that advantage, the second source was more serious: a rebellion led by Churchill and the malcontents on the Conservative backbench. Such an assault could no doubt be seen off, as Baldwin had seen off a larger 'awkward squad' over the Government of India Bill. Nevertheless, if the rebellion was to reach that scale of conflict, then the position would be very serious. Chamberlain wanted to capitalize on the Munich understanding with the dictators. He wanted a free hand to be able to react quickly to the fast-moving pace of events in continental diplomacy. He did not want to be constantly distracted with fending off biting insects at home whenever a cool head and an even temper were needed abroad. Churchill's talent for publicity and Eden's broad-ranging popular appeal could easily rouse passions in the constituencies and amongst caucus delegates at the Party Conference. In contrast to the Indian revolt, such a campaign would also attract the support of those outside the party and in other parties. This was particularly disturbing at a time when calls were growing for the base of the National Government to be broadened. The third source of discontent that Chamberlain had to stare down could potentially prove the most serious of all: dissent from within the government and at the Cabinet table itself. He had secured the support for Munich of the increasingly sceptical Halifax. This was crucial. Having lost Eden in February, Chamberlain might not survive the resignation of two Foreign Secretaries in less than eight months. However, he needed more than a loyal Foreign Secretary. Even if he retained the support of the three major figures in the government (Halifax, Simon and Hoare), for how long could he survive if a significant minority of his Cabinet colleagues walked out? There was nothing much he could do about the howls of indignation from the Labour front bench, but all Chamberlain's political skill would be called upon to limit the effect of dissent from the Conservative front and back bench. The First Lord of the Admiralty, Duff Cooper, was clearly likely to stir up the most trouble in the Cabinet. Recent events demonstrated that the Prime Minister would be no less called to account by an even more tenacious opponent on the backbench – Churchill.

II

At a personal level, Churchill had not been best placed to take on the Prime Minister in the months leading up to the Munich denouement. He was sixty-three years old. Losses on Wall Street and Beaverbrook's cancellation of his journalistic contract had left him in serious financial trouble. Reluctantly he was forced to put up for sale Chartwell, the Kent home on which he had lavished so much of his free time, redesigning and improving. Only the assistance of one of Brendan Bracken's wealthy associates, Sir Henry Strakosch, saved it from the hammer, and Churchill from debts that would have called into question his ability to stay in politics. The *Daily Telegraph* also did its best to come to his rescue, and he eagerly accepted its contract to write regular articles. At a time when a backbench MP's salary could not begin to support Churchill in the manner to which he had become accustomed, the generosity of friends and the advances of publishers were what kept him afloat. Necessary as these lifelines were, they were not without their cost. Supporters' generosity could easily be misconstrued in the whispers of political opponents. Publishers' deadlines limited the time available to take aim at the principal political target.

   Churchill had avoided voicing outright opposition to the government's foreign diplomacy over the summer of 1938. He was prepared to support the efforts of Lord Runciman to try to broker a deal in which peace would be salvaged honourably and the Czechs encouraged to lower the temperature by granting the Sudetendeutsch greater autonomy. Although entertaining dissidents at every opportunity, he chose to keep the government briefed on the discussions that took place. On 19 August, von Kleist had visited him at Chartwell. Afterwards, Churchill sent a memo to the Foreign Office, apprising them of von Kleist's case for standing up to Hitler. Receiving official endorsement to do so from Halifax, he also wrote von Kleist a letter of encouragement to show to his German monarchist allies. Churchill repeated to Halifax von Kleist's estimation that all the German 'Generals were convinced that they [Germany] could not possibly fight for more than three months and that defeat was certain'.[1] He also sent copies of his discussion with von Kleist to Chamberlain and to Daladier. The time had now come, he urged, for the British and French to address a joint warning note to Hitler. The Soviet Union should be asked to sign as well. This, Churchill maintained, would encourage President Roosevelt to intervene to put pressure on Hitler. When the Cabinet met on 30 August, it was clear that neither Chamberlain nor Halifax was greatly tempted by this proposal. Nor were they impressed by Churchill's information gleaned from a visit to Chartwell from the Russian Ambassador, Ivan Maisky, that the Soviet Union was keen to discuss what joint measures could be taken. Days later, the former German Chancellor, Dr Brüning, made the trek to Chartwell. Chartwell had become a sort of Jacobite court of St Germain. To Churchill's detractors, it had supplanted Oxford as the home of lost causes.

By September, Churchill's scepticism over the government's foreign policy had grown stronger, but with Parliament on its summer recess there was little he could do to challenge it formally even had he wished to do so. For his part, Chamberlain was keen to make the most of the absence of parliamentary scrutiny. To his Chief Whip, David Margesson, he wrote, 'you won't need to hear from me how anxious the situation has been and still is. But I hope we may avoid any premature summoning of the H of C.'[2] Nonetheless, it would be helpful to try to square the potentially troublesome Churchill, or at least give him the impression that the Prime Minister was taking into account his views.

The day before Hitler's eagerly awaited Nuremberg speech, 11 September, Churchill was granted a meeting with Halifax and Chamberlain at 10 Downing Street. The meeting bore no fruit. His case for making it clear that a German infringement of the Czech border would lead to a declaration of war from London got nowhere. Churchill had formed his views on the basis of his conversations with dissident figures and with the possibly duplicitous Russian Ambassador. Using their own channels and the advice of their resident diplomats, the government were much less sure than was Churchill that the French and Russians were ready to take on the Third Reich.[3] Three days after seeing Churchill, Chamberlain announced to his Cabinet that he was off to pay Herr Hitler a home visit.

On 19 September, following the Anglo-French talks in London, Halifax agreed to a further meeting with Churchill, this time at the Foreign Office. There he was told that the French were looking for a way out of having to fight. The following day, Churchill travelled to Paris with the Conservative MP Brigadier General E.L. Spears (who had run the British Military Mission to Paris from 1917 to 1920). On arrival they conferred with two of Daladier's more hawkish Cabinet ministers, Paul Reynaud and Georges

Mandel. Churchill's advice was for them to stand firm and not to be manoeuvred into resignation. Bonnet, the Foreign Minister, was particularly annoyed at what he saw as a British politician meddling in French affairs and complained to the British Government accordingly. He had already had to endure repeated telephone calls from Churchill whilst Chamberlain was in the air flying back from Bertschesgaden.[4] Returning to Britain on 21 September, Churchill issued an unequivocal statement to the press in which he prophesied the result of an Anglo-French capitulation to the threat of German force. He also underlined the strategic implications of deserting the Czechs to their fate: 'The neutralisation of Czechoslovakia alone means the liberation of twenty-five German divisions, which will threaten the western front. The path to the Black Sea will be laid open to triumphant Nazi-ism.' He was insistent that the unity of the Sudetens with the Reich was not the sole goal of Hitler's bayonet-tipped diplomacy: 'The menace, therefore, is not to Czechoslovakia, but to the cause of freedom and democracy in every country. The idea that safety can be purchased by throwing a small State to the wolves is a fatal delusion. The German war power will grow faster than the French and British can complete their preparations for defence'.[5] Whatever Churchill's standing amongst his parliamentary colleagues, his views still made good copy. This was not just the case in London. The Parisian newspapers published his statement as well.[6] It was now clear that he envisaged little prospect of a peaceful settlement to the Czech border and that, therefore, he was at odds with the likely product of Chamberlain's efforts to appease Hitler.

Yet this state of affairs did not lead him to believe he was *necessarily* on a collision course with Chamberlain. Churchill believed that the Prime Minister might not be prepared to pay the price that Hitler demanded and he was encouraged by the line the Cabinet was taking on the point. Whilst Chamberlain was on his way to Godesberg, Churchill went to Downing Street for a further briefing. There he was given an accurate summary of the negotiating position with which the Cabinet had licensed Chamberlain to proceed. Impressed by the firm stand that the government now appeared to be taking, in the evening Churchill summoned a like-minded group to his London flat in Morpeth Mansions near Westminster Cathedral. Present were four members of the House of Lords: Lloyd, Horne (formally Sir Robert Horne), Lytton and Cecil; and four MPs: Brendan Bracken, Viscount Wolmer, Harold Nicolson and Sir Archibald Sinclair. Bracken was Churchill's closest personal supporter, so much so that there was an ongoing (and entirely false) rumour circulating round Westminster that he was Churchill's unacknowledged son. Wolmer combined different dimensions of his own Cecil relations in being simultaneously a right-wing diehard and a supporter of international collective security. Writer, diarist and husband of Vita Sackville-West, Harold Nicolson had been a National Labour MP on the government benches since 1935. As a diplomat at the conclusion of the First World War, he had sat on the committee of the Paris Peace Conference that had drawn up the borders of Czechoslovakia from the old Austro-Hungarian Empire. A Scottish baronet, Sir Archibald Sinclair was the leader of the Liberal Party, having succeeded Samuel three years previously. He had served with Churchill as his second in command in the trenches in 1916 and had remained on good terms with him ever since. Churchill told this group the outline of his briefing from Downing Street. He felt that if Chamberlain succeeded in imposing such terms on Hitler, then he would be deserving of support. If he capitulated in the face of fresh demands, however, his climbdown should be fought tooth and nail.[7]

Chamberlain might prove impervious to all manner of threats from his backbench but leading malcontents hoped the devout Anglo-Catholic Halifax could yet be persuaded to convert to their sect. Between 24 and 25 September, the troubled Foreign Secretary was besieged with advice from the likes of Amery, Eden and Spears, urging him to oppose Chamberlain's intended acceptance of the Godesberg ultimatum.[8] As was noted in the previous chapter, Halifax's awakening conscience did indeed cause Chamberlain trouble in Cabinet. Churchill issued a further press statement on 25 September demanding the immediate recall of Parliament. This was exactly what Chamberlain wanted to avoid for as long as he could reasonably get away with. Postponing Parliament's recall for a further forty-eight hours would give him time to establish his position first, negotiate without precondition and then deliver to a reconvened Parliament a fait accompli.

On the afternoon of 26 September, Churchill was again received in the Cabinet Room at 10 Downing Street by the Prime Minister and the Foreign Secretary. He was present during the discussion that led to the issuing of the communiqué later that evening that warned Germany that Britain would not stand aside once an invasion of the Czech state had triggered a Franco-German war. Churchill believed that he was at one with the government's tactics, even although he wanted to go further by including the Soviet Union in the initiative.[9] In the evening, he gathered together a group of anti-appeasement politicians in his flat. Most of the regulars were in attendance, with those on the left of the Conservative Party like Bob Boothby and Harold Macmillan rubbing shoulders with right-wingers of the vintage of Lord Lloyd and Leo Amery. Eden was noticeable by his absence. To the assembled crammed into his pied-à-terre, Churchill reiterated his belief that the government would not accept the Godesberg terms and that the communiqué was not a retreat but rather a face-saving measure for Hitler to accept the original Anglo-French package. He believed that they should support Chamberlain in this objective. At the same time they should bolt the door behind the Prime Minister by advocating alliance with Russia, the imposition of national service and the creation of a cross-party coalition government.

When Parliament at last reconvened on 28 September, up until the point in Chamberlain's speech when he was interrupted by the news of Hitler's agreement to one last conference, Churchill had been sitting there receiving 'so many telegrams that they were clipped together by an elastic band'.[10] Accounts vary as to whether or not he applauded Chamberlain in the standing ovation that attended the Prime Minister as he prepared to leave the debate to fly to Munich. Nonetheless, he did shake Chamberlain by the hand as he was leaving, told him he was lucky, and wished him 'God Speed'. He subsequently cabled the press, making clear he supported the Prime Minister's initiative 'from the bottom of my heart': 'The indomitable exertions which he has made to preserve peace make it certain that should he be forced to declare that it is our duty to take up arms in defence of right and justice, his signal will be obeyed by a united nation and accepted by a united Empire'.[11] In a private room at the Savoy Hotel the following day, Churchill met with his colleagues in the 'Focus' group, the majority of whom were centre or on the centre-left of politics. Spurred on by the right-wing Lord Lloyd, they were keen to ensure that Chamberlain did not rat on the tough line once he got to Munich. Churchill wanted to send Chamberlain a telegram making clear that if he attempted to do Hitler's work for him in bullying the Czechs into surrender, then he would be opposed in the Commons. He wanted Eden to co-sign it. But where was Eden? Also he wanted the signatures of Attlee and Sinclair, the leaders of the two opposition parties, together with Lords Cecil and Lloyd. By the evening, Churchill was distraught to find few of the necessary key figures were prepared to sign his telegram. Concerned that it would be seen as an anti-Chamberlain vendetta, Eden refused to sign. Attlee equivocated, claiming that he would need endorsement first from the Labour Party, something impossible in the remaining time available.[12]

The first news of the Munich Pact came in whilst Churchill and some of his dining compatriots of the 'Other Club' were still in the Savoy. The only Cabinet minister present at the table, Duff Cooper, grabbed the newspaper from the journalist Colin Coote. He read out the report. A silence followed. He got up from his seat and without a word walked out of the building. Churchill returned to Chartwell to ponder the situation and add bricks to his wall. The following night he was telephoned by

Cooper's wife, Lady Diana, to tell him of her husband's resignation from the Cabinet. Lady Diana later recalled that Churchill's 'voice was broken with emotion. I could hear him cry.'[13]

III

At the Cabinet table, Duff Cooper had been the most vocal opponent of Chamberlain's desire to do a deal with Hitler. Cooper it was who had rescued the leadership of Stanley Baldwin in 1931 by stepping in to fight the press lords at the Westminster St George's by-election. It was asking a lot of his political skills to break the career of Baldwin's successor as leader and Prime Minister. To defeat Chamberlain or his policy (and the one would have involved the other), Cooper would have to marshal a large proportion of the Cabinet in opposition to the Premier's diplomatic policy. The number necessary to do this depended on their relative importance. The Chancellor, Simon, and the Home Secretary, Hoare, were staunchly behind the Prime Minister. Halifax was part of the reception committee that greeted so fulsomely Chamberlain's return from Munich across the tarmac at Heston aerodrome. The Foreign Secretary had made his stand over the unacceptability of the Godesberg terms. In getting Chamberlain (against his own wishes) to repudiate them, he had saved his Prime Minister from having to defend an unashamedly more odious and craven surrender than Munich could be repackaged to present. In doing so, he did Chamberlain an enormous favour. If none of the principal figures in the government was going to attack the Munich Agreement, then was there any point in the more minor Cabinet men creating trouble? Memories, inevitably, went back to the backbench and junior ministers' coup that underpinned the bringing down of the Lloyd George Government in 1922. MacDonald's Labour Government had collapsed in August 1931 despite the Prime Minister retaining the support of the key minister involved (the Chancellor) and a bare majority of his fellow ministers – but a numerical majority was not enough, and the government fell. If the same were to happen now, Chamberlain might not be the choice to form a new administration on a broader basis in the manner in which MacDonald had been the choice back in 1931. Chamberlain did not have the benefit in a crisis that MacDonald had enjoyed: it seemed doubtful that the opposition parties would come to rescue the career of one who so obviously despised them and everything they stood for – judgements, it must be said, that were returned with compound interest.

With delirious crowds lining Chamberlain's route from Heston aerodrome to Buckingham Palace, the atmosphere was not auspicious for

organizing a Cabinet ambush of the Prime Minister. The press overwhelmingly backed the man of the hour. The dissidents were neither
sufficiently senior nor sufficiently numerous to force out the Prime
Minister. The ultimate manifestation of a Cabinet minister's rebellion was
his own resignation. Even this would not now save Czechoslovakia. How
would resigning over something that had already happened help the cause
of anti-appeasement when by staying in the Cabinet there remained the
possibility of living to fight another day? What was the point of
threatening a war in defence of a country when it had already been signed
away without war? For the independently minded Cabinet minister, the
price of using the ultimate weapon of resignation was the self-defeating
removal of himself from the forum where he believed himself to have
most influence.

Duff Cooper's decision to resign might be seen as the worst of all
worlds. He left after the deed to which he had objected had been done and
in leaving removed himself from being a Cabinet brake on further such
action in the future. Not only did this mean the personal tragedy of
resignation from an office which he admitted he 'loved', but he failed to
trigger a mass walkout and therefore did little damage to the Prime
Minister and his policy which might have made the sacrifice worthwhile.
Here was the problem. Cooper was a man with a famously short temper.
Hobbies that included drink, gambling and women would probably have
led to his being hounded out of office had he the misfortune to be a
Conservative Cabinet minister in the 1990s rather than the 1930s. But he
was no base schemer and whilst several sober monogamists saw no
reason to sacrifice their own careers on a matter of principle, Cooper did
just that. He resigned purely and simply because the government had
done something he believed dishonourable. He was exasperated with
Chamberlain's antics, but he had no desire to bring down the government. This attitude affected his advice to others not to quit. When Walter
Elliot suggested that he should resign as well, Cooper disagreed, telling
him that 'it would be better for me to go alone, as I had no wish to injure
the Government.'[14] The other possible Cabinet rebels, de la Warr and
Oliver Stanley, decided they were better off continuing to fight from
within than without. Chamberlain could have survived even if they had
all decided to go, but their actions in effect gave him the smoothest ride
possible.

The essential decency of his Cabinet sceptics, together with the strength
of his own hand, gave Chamberlain a political 'catch-22' over his
critics. The very failure of the government to rearm Britain commen-
surably with the prospect of it being able to counter Germany with
confidence played paradoxically into Chamberlain's hands at a time when

the alternative was a war. When Parliament had been recalled on 28 September it was with the sombre prospect of war within hours. Munich had changed all that. What were those who opposed the settlement now to offer to Parliament and the British people? Did they want to snatch conflict from the prospect of peace? Furthermore, if they maintained that conceding the Sudetenland by negotiation only whetted Hitler's appetite and gave him a strong strategic foothold to take over the rest of eastern Europe, then Chamberlain could point to the Anglo-German accord not to resort again to war as a sign of Hitler's good intent. True, it might not hold, but it seemed a better hope for peace than a declaration of war whilst Britain was still unprepared for a fight. Walter Elliot's logic for not resigning reflected this:

> Being in the Cabinet, I am responsible for the fact that I am weaker than Germany. It is no use resigning – that does no get me out of my responsibility. That fearful timetable is a great crime and scandal, for which those of us who accepted it will be justly condemned, and I believe some day justly punished. . . . That does not get away from my desperate question – if I could rub out that agreement, and get us back to Tuesday night, would I do it? In the present state of our forces – French and British – I cannot say that I would. Therefore, I accept the Munich terms. Therefore re them, I do not, and cannot resign.[15]

To get round this line of argument, the anti-Municheers had to claim that a refusal to do Hitler's diplomacy for him would have prevented both the invasion of the Sudetenland and the descent into a second European war. If Hitler had been stood up to, their argument claimed, he would have backed down.

Chamberlain could not prevent a determined figure like Cooper from resigning any more than he needed to worry about the determination of the other sceptics to stay. Only in the case of Harry Crookshank, the Minister for Mines, did the Prime Minister show his adeptness in limiting the damage. Crookshank felt that whatever Munich represented it was not 'peace with honour'. He was not taken in by the suggestion that Chamberlain had outwitted Hitler, believing instead that 'the man is crazy and hypnotised by a looney.'[16] Unimpressed by Chamberlain's Commons performance in contrast to that of Duff Cooper, Crookshank wrote his resignation letter to the Prime Minister on 4 October. However when Crookshank gained an audience, Chamberlain persuaded him to think over the decision first and do nothing precipitate until he had addressed the Commons again. This he agreed to do whilst making clear that he expected Chamberlain to recant on his 'peace with honour' rhetoric and to reverse policy by trying to reach a military understanding with the

Soviet Union.[17] After hearing Chamberlain at the dispatch box, Crookshank concluded that he 'must gulp hard' and tell the Prime Minister that
'he could burn my letter of resignation'. The junior minister decided to
keep his scepticism 'mental not vocal'.[18] With this level of opposition
within government, it would be up to Churchill on the backbenches to
lead the revolt against appeasement.

IV

'Reputations,' wrote one historian, 'were made and destroyed in the
debates on Czechoslovakia which affected political careers for the next
quarter-century.'[19] Indeed, with the exception of the debate in 1940 that
was to break Chamberlain's parliamentary mastery, the four days of
discussion on the Munich Pact proved perhaps the most famous
Commons debate of the century. When the Prime Minister arrived to take
his seat by the government dispatch box, those on the benches around
and behind him rose en masse to applaud his work. Only Churchill, his
son-in-law Duncan Sandys, Harold Nicolson and two other MPs (Robert
Bower and Ronald Cartland) declined to join in the standing ovation.[20]
Making his personal statement on his decision to resign from the Cabinet,
Duff Cooper spoke first. Chamberlain loyalists were anxious to hear their
man in his moment of triumph but the former First Lord of the Admiralty
had, by precedent, the first say. He accused the Prime Minister of dealing
with Hitler 'through the language of sweet reasonableness' when he
would have been 'more open to the language of the mailed fist'. There was
no point talking in 'guarded, diplomatic and reserved utterances' to a man
who only comprehended the 'the headlines of the tabloid press'. Even if a
firm line had ended in war, Czechoslovakia was no more an obscure
reason for fighting than had been Belgium in 1914 since what was at stake
was a greater principle:

> We were fighting then, as we should have been fighting last week, in order that
> one great Power should not be allowed, in disregard of treaty obligations, of
> the laws of nations and the decrees of morality, to dominate by brutal force
> the Continent of Europe. For that principle we fought against Napoleon
> Buonaparte, and against Louis XIV of France and Philip II of Spain. For that
> principle we must ever be prepared to fight, for on the day when we are not
> prepared to fight for it we must forfeit our Empire, our liberties and our
> independence.

Furthermore, Chamberlain's diplomacy had 'taken away the defences of
Czechoslovakia in the same breath as we have guaranteed them, as
though you were to deal a man a mortal blow and at the same time insure

his life'. Cooper concluded that he had sacrificed much in his decision to resign from the government. He had lost his job, sundered associations of which he was proud and relations that he had maintained for years, sundered even his role with a leader he admired. He had, perhaps, ruined his own political career, but he had 'retained something which is to me of greater value – I can still walk about the world with my head erect'.[21] Returning to his seat after speaking for three-quarters of an hour without a note, he received a piece of paper from Churchill informing him that he had given one of the finest parliamentary performances the veteran statesman had ever heard.[22]

The pages of *Hansard* do not convey the effect that Chamberlain's speaking style had upon those who believed in him. His speech had none of the rhetoric and flair with which Cooper had held the House, but his mastery of detail, composure of delivery and certainty of argument was exactly what his supporters in the Commons chamber expected of the occasion and duly received. Chamberlain claimed that the agreement of the four powers had 'averted a catastrophe which would have ended civilisation as we have known it'. The task ahead was to complete Britain's rearmament programme combined with lightening international tension so that ultimately agreed disarmament could take place. This, the 'removal of hostility between nations until they feel that they can safely discard their weapons', was what he wished 'to devote what energy and time may be left to me before I hand over my office to younger men'.[23] There was never any doubt that he would carry the majority of the chamber with him even without the three-line whip that had been imposed.

Churchill did not speak until the third day of the debate. He started by making clear that the magnitude of the occasion demanded that he speak against the policy of a Prime Minister for whom had always had 'personal regard'. However, he did not see what Munich had gained the Czechs that differed from the earlier position in which Britain was prepared to go to war on their behalf: 'instead of snatching his victuals from the table', the German dictator 'has been content to have them served to him course by course'. Rather than clipping Germany's wings, Chamberlain's diplomacy had produced the reverse effect. 'The Czechs,' postulated Churchill, 'left to themselves and told they were going to get no help from the Western Powers, would have been able to make better terms than they have got – they could hardly have worse, after all this tremendous perturbation.' Further, he prophesied that, denuded of its frontier defences, 'you will find that in a period of time which may be measured by years, but may be measured only by months, Czechoslovakia will be engulfed in the Nazi regime.' The betrayal of Czechoslovakia ensured that 'the road down the

Danube Valley to the Black Sea, the resources of corn and oil, the road which leads as far as Turkey, has been opened.' In short, Germany would become economically invincible, and ready to turn her guns westward. The fault lay with the government, not just in the events of the previous fortnight, but since the emergence of the Hitler regime itself: 'what we have done and of what we have left undone in the last five years – five years of futile good intention, five years of eager search for the line of least resistance, five years of uninterrupted retreat of British power, five years of neglect of our air defence. Those are the features which I stand here to declare and which marked an improvident stewardship for which Great Britain and France have dearly to pay.' The National Government's handling of events had been a catalogue of disaster:

> the responsibility must rest with those who have the undisputed control of our political affairs. They neither prevented Germany from rearming, nor did they rearm ourselves in time. They quarrelled with Italy without saving Ethiopia. They exploited and discredited the vast institution of the League of Nations and they neglected to make alliances and combinations which might have repaired the previous errors, and thus they left us in the hour of trial without adequate national defence or effective international security.

The breach between Churchill's and Chamberlain's thinking was funda-mental. Chamberlain had spoken of his hopes of pursuing a prosperous and peaceful coexistence with Germany. Churchill believed this to be impossible with a regime 'which spurns Christian ethics, which cheers its onward course by a barbarous paganism, which vaunts the spirit of aggression and conquest, which derives strength and perverted pleasure from persecution, and uses, as we have seen, with pitiless brutality the threat of murderous force. That Power cannot ever be the trusted friend of British democracy.' Yet he feared that Chamberlain's diplomacy risked Britain becoming a pawn to every whim of the German *Führer*. This was the theme of his peroration, that:

> the whole equilibrium of Europe has been deranged, and that the terrible words have for the time being been pronounced against the Western democracies: 'Thou art weighed in the balance and found wanting.'
>
> And do not suppose that this is the end. This is only the beginning of the reckoning. This is only the first sip, the first foretaste of a bitter cup which will be proffered to us year by year unless by a supreme recovery of moral health and martial vigour, we arise again and take our stand for freedom as in the olden time.[24]

The *Daily Telegraph* stood up for him. Other papers did not. *The Times* spoke of his 'dismal sincerity'. The *Express* referred to 'an alarmist oration by a man whose mind is soaked in the conquests of Marlborough'.

V

The first question that the Conservative rebels had to consider was whether they should consciously act together as a bloc or go each according to his own judgement. This was a fundamental issue. It called into question whether there was a coherent anti-appeasement position or merely a miscellany of semi-detached politicians who happened to oppose the Prime Minister's policy for a variety of reasons. Indeed, even if there was a coherent common ground, it remained open to debate whether Eden or Churchill was the best equipped to lead it. The temperament that made Churchill supposedly an unsuitable member of the Cabinet also kept him out of the collection of younger anti-appeasement MPs who preferred to constellate around the less domineering personality of Anthony Eden. In the Commons, Churchill could count on the support of his loyal lieutenant, Brendan Bracken, and in the Lords, of Lord Lloyd. His work with the Arms and the Covenant 'Focus' and New Commonwealth groups endeared him to liberals in and out of the Commons. Tentative steps were being taken with the Labour Party as well. Crucially to his later success, Churchill had also begun to praise the trades union movement – correctly identifying it as an essential ally to a full-throated war effort. Whilst Eden was a Conservative politician with cross-party appeal, Churchill was fast becoming a cross-party politician.

Resigning from the Foreign Office in February 1938, Eden had found himself surrounded by a group of like-minded admirers on the backbenches. More than twenty predominately younger members formed this loose association and were derisively known in the Whips' Office as the 'glamour boys'. Those who had worked with Eden at the Foreign Office, like Lord Cranborne and J.P.L. Thomas, were prominent within its discussions as were two admirers of Churchill, Harold Macmillan and Harold Nicolson. Further to the right, Bonar Law's son, Richard Law, also counted himself in this number together with the former Indian diehard, Viscount Wolmer.[25] Yet their meetings had more the feel of the discussion group than the tight political cabal. Eden was certainly not minded to transform these private gatherings into a coherent attack on the government. He had not given up the hope of the Premiership, especially in the event of a broader coalition being formed. He decided that conditional appeasement of those in authority was a better course than confrontation. This was not a line he had followed through when it came to foreign policy.

The Glamour Boys were predominantly supporters of collective security, which now pivoted upon bringing the Soviet Union into an Anglo-French alliance. This was equally Churchill's war cry. Yet, except for a few individuals, there was little in the way of cooperation between the respective acolytes of Churchill and Eden. At one level, the gap was generational. At another, it demonstrated the unease felt in the Eden camp about associating with a man who might easily charge off on some new departure of his own devising without consulting them and for whom the abdication crisis had been the final nail in an impressively airtight coffin. Yet, it would be a mistake to regard such attitudes as definitive and unyielding. An MP like Anthony Crossley was so determinedly in the Eden camp that he had been keen not to be associated with Churchill in mid-September. Nonetheless, he found himself attending several of Churchill's group meetings and was so horrified at talk he heard elsewhere that was critical of Churchill's honourable intentions that he wrote to him offering to publicly declare that no intrigue had taken place at these convocations.[26] Ultimately, MPs thought individually rather than collectively. Few were by nature so subservient to any one individual that they could not readapt themselves as circumstance demanded.

Leo Amery was certainly an MP whose mind made him a hostage to no fad or fashion. His opposition to the ideology of the League of Nations and his failure to see Mussolini as a demon prevented him from being in the Eden camp, although he occasionally attended their informal get-togethers. Continual disappointment at having been passed over for office by men who were his intellectual inferior had long cooled his enthusiasm for the Chamberlain regime. Despite these attitudes, he was not out for blood and was not attracted to the actions of some of the young hotheads. Following the Godesberg summit, he noted in his diary with disapproval that Harold Macmillan was 'very wild, clamouring for an immediate pogrom to get rid of Neville and make Winston Prime Minister before the House met [on the following day]. I poured cold water on that sort of talk.'[27] His scepticism over joining Russia in an alliance further isolated him from the Glamour Boys, and from Churchill as well. Sensing the mood of much of the Tory Party on the eve of what was to be the Munich settlement (but was at that moment anticipated to be the start of a war) Amery had managed to persuade the anti-appeasers not to parade their campaign to bring Russia into the alliance until war had actually commenced. Once war started, he prophesied that it would be all right to call for Russian assistance since Tory MPs would by then 'only too readily welcome help from the Devil himself'.[28]

Amery's suspicions about premature Russian involvement were repli-cated amongst many of those Tory MPs who had been India diehards in the last Parliament. This naturally led them to give Chamberlain's diplomacy the benefit of the doubt. Even still, it is wrong to think that the former diehards had a corporate view any more than had any other collection of Tory MPs at the time. India had bound them together in a way that subsequent debates could not. Earlier in the year, Churchill had failed to rally them in opposition to Chamberlain's appeasement of the Irish leader, Eamon de Valera. Despite being the son of Joseph Chamberlain, the Prime Minister had allowed Ireland's remaining 1921 Treaty obligations to be torn up in his desire to build bridges with southern Ireland. The negotiation had shown that nothing was sacred to Chamberlain in the search for appeasement – even a treaty signed by his brother Austen. Churchill had failed to rouse the diehards on the issue, despite his insistence that Britain's strategic position would be imperilled in wartime by the loss of her naval bases in Ireland. Even for imperially minded politicians, that country was by 1938 yesteryear's issue. Most were content to accept Chamberlain's assumption that winning Irish friendship was of greater long-term value than holding them to obligations they might try not to honour anyway. Most diehards were enthusiastic rearmers and, as has been noted previously, the India campaign had indirectly forced the government to take calls for rearmament more seriously. Nonetheless, on appeasement, the diehards split as many ways as did those who had once opposed their Indian alarm.[29] Only a minority of the diehards backed Churchill at the time of Munich. An even smaller minority backed him amongst those who had supported the Indian reforms.

Conservative opponents of the Munich settlement were spread across the political spectrum of the party. Nonetheless, they also had some elements in common. On the whole they tended to be somewhat younger than the average Tory member. They were also more likely to represent a constituency in the south-east of England, and more likely to belong or be related to a titled family than was the average Tory MP. Furthermore, anti-Munich Tories were also far more likely to be public school educated than those who supported Chamberlain. Indeed, anti-Municheers were disproportionately the products of Eton and Oxbridge (these facts rather contradict the tendency of egalitarian commentators to claim that appeasement and the 'Establishment' were irrevocably entwined).[30]

Munich provided particularly difficult ground for the anti-appeasers to fight on since they were battling against a natural reaction of relief. On 28 September, Parliament had assembled, resigned to a war that it would – with some exceptions – have supported. Now it had reassembled brightened by Munich's sudden deliverance from evil. A way had been seen out of the catastrophe. Sons would not be sent to the slaughter.

Houses would not be destroyed from the air. Lifetime savings would not be squandered by the state in the production of shells and mortars. It might not prove a permanent peace but it seemed a better risk than putting an ill-equipped and inadequately sized army into the field. The last time had been bad enough.

Undaunted, anti-appeasers pressed on in varying degrees of hostility. Richard Law summarized the essential point: 'I believe that we have now obtained, by peaceful means, what we fought four wars to prevent happening, namely the domination of Europe by a single Power.' Chamberlain had allowed Britain to associate itself in the work of 'the most cruel, the most inhuman tyranny that the world has ever known', 'the firm we have joined as a junior partner'.[31] This was not the normal badinage traded across the floor of the debating chamber. It was a frontal assault delivered at a time of international tension by a Conservative MP, the son of the party's late leader, against the policy of the incumbent leader. The aspirant leader-in-waiting, Eden, attacked the settlement along similar lines, although noticeably with less vehemence.

In fact, Conservative rebels had to consider the tenor of their remarks carefully. The leadership had a further trump card to play. Word quickly got around that Chamberlain was considering calling a snap general election. Few in the party doubted that he would sweep the country, capitalizing on his apparent triumph in preventing war. Worse, it was rumoured that those Tories who voted against Munich in the division lobby would be regarded as opponents by Conservative Central Office. Every attempt would be made to have them deselected in their constituencies. Failing that, 'official' Conservative candidates would be run against them on polling day. By speaking out now, the Tory rebels risked being denied their platform to speak out later. But if they did not fight now, when would they?

Faced with the prospect of annihilation, the Tory rebels had to consider their options. They could hardly climb down in public and vote for a policy against which they had made their opposition absolute. Instead they tried to take the sting out of the attack. On the night of 3 October, with the Commons debate under way, Churchill and Eden, together with their respective lieutenants, Brendan Bracken and J.P.L. Thomas, were joined by Macmillan. Together they held a meeting with the Labour politician, Hugh Dalton. If Labour's assault on the government came in the form of a vote of censure, then the Tory rebellion would be at sixes and sevens, caught between abhorrence of the deal struck with Hitler and the need not to provide a pretext for being ousted from their own party. Dalton noted their plea for Labour to act in a way that would not leave Tory dissidents open to accusations of betrayal. He nonetheless felt unable to offer a guarantee or make any assurances as to whether Labour would field candidates against the Tory rebels in the event of their being opposed in a snap election by Conservative 'loyalists'.[32]

Threatened with his resignation from the junior ranks of the government, Chamberlain had privately assured Harry Crookshank on 4 October that he was not planning to hold a snap election.[33] This fact was not communicated to the rebels. But if Chamberlain was still keeping the option of an election as a public threat, his bluff was called from the backbenches by Sir Sidney Herbert. Herbert had started off his political career in 1919 as Churchill's private secretary and had subsequently served during the 1920s as Baldwin's parliamentary private secretary. His ringing condemnation of any attempt to fight a snap election to hound out Tory dissidents was made all the more effective by the fact that he was not commonly regarded to be one of the 'awkward squad' himself. Furthermore, he was terminally ill and gave his speech (as it transpired, his last) in obvious pain. Afterwards Churchill wrote him a note: 'You stopped the General Election by your speech; and as you spoke I seemed to hear the voice of that old Conservative Party I once honoured and not of this over-whipped crowd of poor "whites".'[34]

Churchill had called together a number of the rebels for a meeting in Bracken's house in Lord North Street on 3 October. They knew that the government could scarcely withdraw the Whip from thirty members especially if Duff Cooper and Eden were amongst the number. In the same way, the India diehards had been given confidence at the time of the Wavertree by-election in 1935 by the knowledge of the sheer weight of their numbers when combined with that of other MPs supporting their right of conscience. Indeed, it was not until the government of John Major in the 1990s that the Whip was removed from any group within the parliamentary party for opposing on principle a major plank of policy. Even still, the anti-Munich rebels had to consider the arguments in favour of restraining the vehemence of dissent. A further meeting on 5 October failed to gain agreement on whether to abstain or vote against the government. Churchill favoured voting against, whilst Amery cautioned in favour of abstention.[35]

The Commons debate concluded on 6 October. Chamberlain's closing speech made Amery and Eden waver. Amery had always understood the strategic reality of the problem but had been horrified by Chamberlain's handling of the crisis. It was the knowledge that so many of his young supporters were determined to abstain that persuaded Eden not to divorce himself from them by voting with the government, even though he agreed with 90 per cent of what Chamberlain said.[36]

Three Eden supporters voted with the government. Bob Boothby absented himself from the key government division whilst contenting himself to vote against the Labour amendment. More surprisingly, normally pro-Chamberlain MPs like Victor Raikes and John Gretton were amongst four traditional right-wingers who did likewise. Twenty-two Tory MPs rebelled against their own government by abstaining in the votes that marked the end of the Commons debate.[37] Churchill was the most prominent of the thirteen who went so far as to remain seated in the chamber whilst the division was being counted.

Chamberlain was contemptuous of the machinations of Churchill and his group. Writing to his sister, the Prime Minister admitted that he had found the four-day debate 'a pretty trying ordeal': 'I tried occasionally to take an antidote to the poison gas by reading a few of the countless letters & telegrams which continued to pour in expressing in most moving accents the writer's heartfelt relief & gratitude. All the world seemed to be full of my praises except the House of Commons.'[38] Having won his division, Chamberlain proposed to disband Parliament again for the length of the original adjournment, until 1 November. This was opposed both by the opposition parties and by Conservative rebels. Harold Macmillan was the most outspoken, complaining that Chamberlain was treating Parliament 'more and more as a kind of Reichstag to meet only to hear the orations and register the decrees of the government of the day'. When Churchill claimed that the country wanted Parliament to remain in session whilst the international tension remained, a section of Conservative MPs laughed derisively.[39] Churchill's interjection also led to an acrimonious wrangle with Chamberlain who called his remarks 'unworthy'. Churchill wrote to his Prime Minister to object, but Chamberlain was clearly every bit as brittle: 'I considered your remarks highly offensive to me and to those with whom I have been working. I had not regarded these remarks, wounding as they were, as requiring a breach of personal relations, but you cannot expect me to allow you to do all the hitting and never hit back.'[40] The arsenal at the disposal of the Prime Minister to hit back was formidable. Appeasement was a foreign policy, not a creed for nearer to home. Churchill and the rebels would now feel the full force from the government's supporters in their own backyard. MPs returned from Westminster to face the wrath of their constituency associations.

VI

Running the gauntlet of the sanctioned thuggery of the Whips' Office at least gave Conservative rebels the soupçon of satisfaction that – like the early Christian martyrs – they were standing up for their beliefs against the agents of oppression. Somewhat more dispiriting was to be chastised by their own natural supporters, men and women who at the last election had given up their free time to canvass and campaign on their behalf. Many of the rebels returned to the constituencies to find themselves anything but heroes of conscience. A general election could be called at any time and suddenly their primary concern was not with attacking the Opposition but with fending off attempts by their own side to force them out.

Despite coming from a Tory family whose service to the state long predated popular democracy itself, Lord Cranborne (who was, despite his title, a member of the House of Commons) came in for presumptive lectures on Conservative duty from ordinary members of his south Dorset constituency. He survived nonetheless. Duff Cooper similarly kept his head above water in Westminster St George's although the motion expressing confidence in him effectively bound him to supporting the 'unity of the party' in future. He was being served a warning notice and it remained unclear whether he would be reselected to fight the seat at the next general election. All his efforts at party loyalty to save Baldwin's leadership against the intrigues of Lord Rothermere in 1931 were now cast aside and forgotten. Indeed, having thrown his weight around back then in an effort to remove the party leader, Rothermere now intervened again in Westminster St George's in an endeavour to achieve the reverse. The press lord went so far as to suggest his own nephew as a replacement candidate for Cooper. He also intrigued against Eden in the latter's Leamington Spa constituency.[41]

Some of the opponents of Munich were more lucky. Harold Macmillan had his constituency association effectively over a barrel. It was he, personally, who was bailing out its debts.[42] Elsewhere, grass-roots rumblings produced a much more threatening atmosphere. In Aldershot, Wolmer came under an attack of sufficient ferocity that the Prime Minister's sisters, Ida and Hilda, who were members there, decided they would not need to rally the women's association against him after all.[43] Only the threat of the constituency Chairman's resignation prevented moves to have Wolmer deselected. Bob Boothby was another who overcame opposition in his east Aberdeenshire constituency association with the help of a loyal chairman. Even so, the executive initially tried to block his holding meetings.[44]

The Duchess of Atholl was in deeper trouble. Her opposition to Munich had come after she had already been in trouble over her pro-Republican stance in the Spanish Civil War. Having been notified in May that she was deselected as the Conservative candidate to fight Kinross and west Perthshire at the next election, the Duchess had no particular reason to put up with being dictated to by her association for the remainder of the Parliament. Rather, she decided to resign and fight for the seat as an Independent. This gave her constituency association the opportunity to field their own, now the official, Conservative candidate against her. The Duchess secured the support of Labour and the Liberals who decided not to run their own candidates in an attempt to give her a straight fight. Alone amongst Conservative MPs, Churchill sent her a public letter of endorsement. Withdrawal of the Whip was threatened to any Tory who went up to speak on her behalf. Kinross went to the polls on 21 December. The Tory Party machine surpassed itself in bombarding the constituency with senior figures to endorse the official candidate, a local farmer. It was, in the words of one parliamentarian and noted historian of the period, 'one of the dirtiest by-election campaigns of modern times, from which only the Duchess emerged with any distinction'.[45] She lost by a little over 1300 votes. Chamberlain wrote to his Chief Whip, confessing that he was 'overjoyed' at the news.[46]

VII

One of the supporters of Munich with whom Churchill maintained cordial relations was Sir Henry Page Croft. By the end of October, Churchill was confiding to him his concerns. Whilst he wanted to continue the fight within the Conservative Party, he feared that the battle might be lost, that 'it might all go down the drain as it did in the India business, through the influence of the Central Office and the Government Whips.' If the party was prepared to accept 'a state of sub-subservience, if not indeed actual vassalage to Germany, and that you can do nothing to arrest this fatal tide, then I think the knowledge would simplify my course'.[47] Churchill was now extremely dissatisfied with the Conservative Party and nauseated by the witch-hunt being perpetrated against those who opposed appeasement. What was more, he knew that a campaign to remove him was fermenting in his own Epping constituency. Rothermere, whose regard for Churchill was higher than for most of the other anti-Municheers, wrote advising him 'to go slow' with his constituency workers. Chamberlain's popularity was such that any Tory who challenged him would 'suffer a complete eclipse'. The press baron warned further that 'the public is so terrified of being bombed that they will support anyone who keeps them out of war. . . . I don't trust the Epping electorate because Epping is on one of the routes by which enemy aeroplanes will approach London.'[48]

The Central Council of the West Essex Conservative Association met on 4 November in London to consider Churchill's stance. Churchill's chief antagonist was Colin Thornton-Kemsley (a 35-year-old chartered surveyor with political ambitions) who argued that a pact of friendship between Britain and the European powers had more chance of avoiding war than a concerted campaign to gang up on Germany. For the moment, Churchill managed to stay ahead of his pursuers with a resolution passed backing his stance. But he was far from out of the wood. Crucially for any embattled MP in such a predicament, he retained the all-important loyalty of his constituency Chairman, Sir James Hawkey. His other remaining card was that, given sufficient time, events would demonstrate him to have been right all along. In this respect, Hitler came up trumps.

On 6 and 8 November, Hitler made speeches specifically naming and castigating Churchill. This, as Churchill pronounced, was doing his own influence a power of good. The Tory rebels' case had rested not merely upon the specific fate of the Czechs but upon the larger question of the nature of Nazism. In contradiction of the government line that it was not for Britain to isolate countries on account of their own internal arrangement and ideology, the Tory rebels insisted that the Nazi ideology made war inevitable sooner or later. A glimpse into the nature of the beast was soon available. Hitler's speeches in the aftermath of Munich certainly provided little comfort for the view that negotiation rather than force would henceforth govern Reich foreign policy. Indeed, in his speech in Munich of 8 November, he spelled this out specifically, insisting the Germans would 'secure for ourselves our rights by another way if we cannot get them by the normal way'.[49] Scarcely twenty-four hours later, the Kristallnacht assaults on German Jewry shattered the last illusions that the Hitler regime could be treated on the same terms and through the same methods as a civilized entity. The fate of Mosley's blackshirt movement had demonstrated that Jew-hatred had a limited appeal in Britain. Even those Tories who had been prepared to avert their gaze from such aspects of the Reich up until this point were sickened by the pogroms that now took place. Even 'Chips' Channon, given to more anti-Semitic sentiments than most, was driven to despair, noting in his diary: 'No-one ever accused me of being anti-German, but really I can no longer cope with the present régime which seems to have lost all sense and reason. Are they mad? The Jewish persecutions carried to such a fiendish degree are short-sighted, cruel and unnecessary.'[50]

Events in Germany were particularly unwelcome to those in Conservative Central Office who were still scheming for an early general election. Market research was in its infancy and the evidence from the Tories' own in-house pollsters was contradictory. Nonetheless, it was clear that the hysteria in favour of Munich was quickly subsiding. During November, the Conservative Research Department's by-election analysis swung from interpreting that a fresh general election would leave the National

Government's majority virtually unchanged to prophesying a result too close to call.[51] The eight by-elections held between Munich and the end of the year gave no indication of a swing back towards the government and Chamberlain regarded the position, at home and abroad, to be too unstable to risk a snap election.[52] Only 15 per cent of those questioned by an opinion poll at the time thought that Hitler's campaign against German Jews should not affect Britain's attempts to build a peaceful understanding with him.[53] Even allowing for the limits of 1930s market research, this was as clear an expression of public opinion as any poll could present. In February 1939 the Conservative Research Department concluded that Chamberlain should not go to the country at this time, citing the popular revulsion against Hitler's Jewish persecutions as a key reason.[54]

Meanwhile, relations between Churchill and Chamberlain continued to deteriorate. The government's successful attempts to manipulate the press reached a new intensity, mitigated only by the enthusiasm of so many of those in the press to do the government's propaganda work for it without any prompting.[55] On 16 October, Churchill had commenced a broadcast to the United States with the words: 'I avail myself with relief of the opportunity of speaking to the people of the United States. I do not know how long such liberties will be allowed. The stations of uncensored expression are closing down; the lights are going out; but there is still time for those to whom freedom and Parliamentary government mean something, to consult together. Let me, then, speak in truth and earnestness while time remains.'[56] Chamberlain was infuriated by these remarks. Although he did not mention Churchill directly, he left the Commons in no doubt whom he was talking about when little more than a fortnight later he intoned censoriously: 'It is not one of the characteristics of totalitarian States, at any rate, that they are accustomed to foul their own nests. I do strongly deprecate all the statements made by persons in responsible or even irresponsible positions, who take opportunities of broadcasting to the world or in other countries in particular that their own country is in a state of decadence.'[57]

On 17 November, Churchill's interest in playing the party game snapped when, for the first time since the India debates of 1935, he voted in the opposition lobbies against the government. The occasion was Chamberlain's rejection of a Liberal motion favouring the creation of a Ministry of Supply. Churchill, who had long advocated such a department as a precursor to organizing a sustained war effort, had called in the chamber for the support of fifty backbench Tories to follow him through the opposition lobby. A rebellion on this scale, he maintained, would not threaten the life of the government but would force it to introduce the

Ministry. He was to be sorely disappointed. The government made the vote one of confidence in the government itself. With Eden and his acolytes keeping their powder dry, Churchill was only joined in the division lobby by Bracken and Macmillan. Duff Cooper even spoke in defence of the Prime Minister. For his part, Chamberlain mused to the House that Churchill had 'many brilliant qualities' but if anyone asked him whether Churchill possessed good judgement, 'I should have to ask the House of Commons not to press me too far.'[58] Churchill responded to Chamberlain's jibe in tones that made clear the breach: 'I will gladly submit my judgement about foreign affairs and national defence during the last five years, in comparison with his own.' Churchill then listed a series of supposedly gullible Chamberlain statements each followed by one German atrocity after another. Baldwin's failings were also brought up, but it was Chamberlain who 'knew all the facts. His judgement failed just like that of Mr Baldwin and we are suffering from the consequences of it to-day.'[59] This was tough talking.

The deselection threats in the constituencies encouraged the mood of caution trod by many of those Munich rebels who still saw Eden as their natural leader. Replying to the suggestion that Eden should come to a lunch of the 'Focus' group, Churchill doubted that the 'shy' former Foreign Secretary would want to show up.[60] Indeed, Eden had his own reasons for assuring Chamberlain privately that he supported his stand on Munich. Hoare felt that although there was no 'basis of a working agreement between Winston and ourselves', Chamberlain should get Eden back in the Cabinet 'if and when you can'.[61] Halifax advised similarly.[62] The Prime Minister remained unsympathetic. With 'trouble enough with my present Cabinet', he told his sister that he did not want to make it worse by including Eden and Labour politicians who 'would keep up a constant running fight' over his conduct of foreign policy, especially that part geared towards 'conciliation' with the dictators.[63] Eden's attempt to limit his campaign to one of constructive criticism curried no favour with Chamberlain no matter how mildly the criticism was phrased. Eden wanted to help an administration prepare for a likely war. Chamberlain was determined to lead Europe back in the direction of peace. In December Eden told Churchill that he would refuse offers to re-enter the Cabinet unless it was a part of a comprehensive reconstruction.[64] This entirely honourable attitude made his exclusion even more of a certainty. None of the Cabinet changes that Chamberlain proceeded to make gave any comfort to the anti-appeasers. His idea of broadening the government was restricted to a minor shuffling of the pack. The major innovation was to replace as Lord President in Council the ill Lord Hailsham with an even older man, the Liberal National architect of pressurizing the Czechs, Lord

Runciman.[65] The Premier had even wanted Samuel brought back into the Cabinet. Having resigned from it over Chamberlain's promotion of tariffs in 1932, the former Liberal leader was every bit as much a figure enjoying the long goodnight of British politics as his fellow 68-year-old, Lord Runciman. Chamberlain however, had been impressed with Samuel's outspoken approval for the Munich settlement from the benches of the House of Lords. Samuel's decision to decline the offer did the Prime Minister a favour. His appointment would have caused nothing but groans from all sides within the Conservative Party.

VIII

Churchill had been sufficiently concerned over the constituency meeting called to challenge him in November to sketch what he might do if defeated. In such an event, he considered standing in the resulting by-election as an Independent and he took the trouble to make sure that he would have the support of the Liberal Party and the League of Nations Union in the event.[66] Nonetheless, he did not wish to be manoeuvred voluntarily out of the Conservative Party if he could help it. So long as he remained the official candidate for Epping, the best that Central Office could do would be to run an alternative and unofficial candidate against him. As the Party Chairman, Sir Douglas Hacking, admitted, such candidates could not hope to beat the likes of Churchill, Duff Cooper or Harold Nicolson.[67]

With the new year, the campaign to oust Churchill gathered momentum. Epping was one of the largest constituencies in the country with over 100,000 electors grouped into twenty-six wards. The tactic of those Tories who wanted rid of their member was to try to take over the smaller ward branch committees. In this way they hoped to gain a majority on the constituency's central association even though the largest wards – making up the majority of the Conservative Association – remained loyal to Churchill. For his part, Churchill was particularly concerned that bogus new members were joining in order to vote out officers loyal to him in the smaller branch wards and to elect pro-Chamberlain officers in their place. Measures were instigated to have these suspicious proceedings reversed but in the meantime Churchill found himself having to form separate branch committees of his own supporters. He proposed to tell the Conservative Party Chairman that 'the consequence of your interference must be, namely, that two alternative Associations will gradually come into existence in all the districts where your tactics are successful.' If the insurgents managed to gain a majority of ward delegates in time for the association meeting on 17 April 1939, Churchill would be voted out. This would be despite the fact that he retained the support of wards which (according to his own calculation) represented four-fifths of the constituency. In the event of his defeat, he proposed to form 'a separate Association' and continue the fight from there.[68]

At the beginning of March 1939, a gathering of the Epping constituency's Nazeing branch became the focus for a series of members and office-bearers to denounce Churchill. Their ringleader, Colin Thornton-Kemsley, got himself elected as Chairman of the Chigwell branch. Having been selected as the prospective Conservative candidate for a constituency in the north-east of Scotland, he was quoted as saying that he thought 'that unless Mr Churchill is prepared to work with the Conservative Party, National Government, and our great Prime Minister, he ought no longer to shelter under the goodwill and name which attaches to a great Party.'[69] Other members echoed this line, one referring to Munich as 'one of the greatest acts in history' and describing Churchill as 'a menace in Parliament'.[70]

At Chigwell, Churchill defended his position and claimed that although he had been out of office for a decade, he was 'more contented with the work I have done in these last five years as an Independent Conservative than of any other part of my public life'. The description of his political affiliation was particularly telling. Four days later, on 14 March, he gave his definitive statement on dissent to constituents of the Waltham Abbey branch. Answering complaints 'in some of the outlying parts' of the constituency, Churchill maintained that his prophecies at the time of Munich were already coming to pass. His defence of an MP's responsibility for his own judgement encapsulated a classic attack on the power of the party machine:

> What is the use of sending Members to the House of Commons who say just the popular things of the moment, and merely endeavour to give satisfaction to the Government Whips by cheering loudly every Ministerial platitude, and by walking through the Lobbies oblivious of the criticisms they hear? People talk about our Parliamentary institutions and Parliamentary democracy; but if these are to survive it will not be because the Constituencies return tame, docile, subservient Members and try to stamp out every form of independent judgement.[71]

Churchill's determination to meet fire with fire checked the spread of the revolt against him. He had no difficulty overcoming the insurrection at the association meeting in April. Events moved decisively in his favour. His chief opponent, Thornton-Kemsley, was fortuitously removed from the constituency by winning the Kincardine by-election. His place as Chairman of the Chigwell branch was taken by one of Churchill's supporters.[72] But, in central Europe, events of greater magnitude had also come to substantiate Churchill's warnings. On 15 March 1939, Germany invaded the remnants of free Czechoslovakia. Without so much as a consultation with the British Prime Minister, Hitler had torn to shreds the Munich Agreement. Chamberlain's policy looked to be in tatters. At last, some began to suspect that Churchill, for so long a voice in the wilderness, had been right after all.

Thirteen

'IF THEY HAD ASKED NICELY . . .'

I

'When I was Prime Minister,' commented Baldwin to his former private secretary shortly after the Munich Agreement, 'I always had Neville, as Ramsay had me, to interpret my views to the Cabinet and carry them along. The trouble is, Neville has nobody.'[1] In fact, Chamberlain was to discover that his trouble was no longer the absence of an obvious deputy but rather the emergence of a qualified candidate for that role, and one with a different opinion on how policy should be directed. The developing counterweight in question was the Foreign Secretary. Around this parallel universe a constellation developed of those whom the Prime Minister regarded as 'the weaker brethren' on his front bench. The Cabinet rebellion on the Godesberg ultimatum had been the first manifestation of trouble from this quarter and Halifax's support for the Munich terms was by no means the end of the matter. This was soon evident in the contrasting attitudes expressed during Parliament's debate on the Munich Agreement. In the Commons, Chamberlain had spoken of his hopes that the signatures collected on his famous piece of paper would stand as guarantor to a peaceful European coexistence. In the House of Lords, however, Halifax's tone struck a more discordant note in which Munich had represented only the best of 'a hideous choice of evils'. Its lesson, the Foreign Secretary asserted, was that Britain must henceforth rearm quickly if she wanted to play the decisive role in international affairs.[2]

Halifax's insistence on speeding up the rearmament programme contradicted Chamberlain's wilder expectations that the instigation of a new understanding with the dictators could foreshadow an agreement on multilateral disarmament. According to Sir Alexander Cadogan, the Permanent Under-Secretary of State at the Foreign Office, the Prime Minister believed the sincerity of Hitler's desire, expressed at Munich, for the abolition of aerial bombing, and perhaps even the destruction of all bomber aircraft.[3] Chamberlain's problem was that few of his Cabinet colleagues shared this fantastic misinterpretation of the Fascist frame of mind. When on 3 October the Cabinet convened for the first time after

Munich, Buck de la Warr and Oliver Stanley led the plea for an acceleration in the pace of rearmament. Chamberlain retorted by restating the existing orthodoxy: concentration upon plugging defence 'deficiencies' without embarking 'on a great increase in our armaments programme' as a 'thank-offering for the present détente'.[4] By the end the month, Inskip (Minisister for Defence Coordination) and Kingsley Wood (Secretary of State for Air) had joined the campaign within the Cabinet for a broadening of the rearmament programme. Chamberlain, however, repeated that this was not what he had signed the Munich agreement with Hitler for:

> There had been a good deal of talk in the country and in the press about the need for rearmament by this country. In Germany and Italy it was suspected that this rearmament was directed against them, and it was important that we should not encourage these suspicions.
>
> The Prime Minister said that he proposed to make it clear that our rearmament was directed to securing our own safety and not for purposes of aggression against other countries.
>
> A good deal of false emphasis had been placed on rearmament, as though one result of the Munich Agreement had been that it would be necessary for us to add to our rearmament programmes. Acceleration of existing programmes was one thing, but increases in the scope of our programme which would lead to a new arms race was a different proposition.[5]

Chamberlain resented colleagues 'losing their heads', as he put it, 'and thinking as though Munich had made war more instead of less imminent'.[6] That his immediate thoughts were on improving relations between the four Munich signatories rather than on encircling Germany was clear to all who knew his intentions. Writing to his sister in February 1939, he claimed to be looking forward to establishing good relations with General Franco, who had all but won the civil war in Spain. He also hoped to get France and Italy to start negotiating together as a precursor to disarmament. As regards Britain, Italy and Germany:

> I myself, am going about with a lighter heart than I have had for many a long day. All the information I get seems to point in the direction of peace & I repeat once more that I believe we have at last got on top of the dictators. Of course that doesn't mean that I want to bully them as they have tried to bully us; on the contrary I think they have had good cause to ask for consideration of their grievances, & if they had asked nicely after I appeared on the scene they might already have got some satisfaction.[7]

This was a surprisingly buoyant attitude coming as it did so soon after the Kristallnacht atrocities against the Jews and the continuing boasts and taunts of the *Führer* implicitly and explicitly against British interference in European affairs. The truth of the matter, at Munich and in the months thereafter, was that Chamberlain was prepared to ignore an almost limitless number of uncomfortable truths if it meant escaping the haunting spectre of another Great War. For all the years he had been forced to endure the shouts and jeers of 'warmonger' from Labour politicians, he was a better pacifist than most of them.

II

The rearmament programme was designed to defend Britain, not to attack the Third Reich. Chamberlain told the Cabinet the day before he left to visit Daladier that

> If the French took the line that they were relying on us for the defence of Paris, then it would be necessary to make it quite clear to them that our AirForce was being built up for our own defence. . . . our attitude would be governed largely by the fact that we did not wish to see France drawn into a war with Germany on account of some quarrel between Russia and Germany, with the result that we should be drawn into war in France's wake.[8]

Chamberlain and Halifax visited Paris on 23 November. At one level, this could be interpreted as an overdue but no less symbolic gesture of support for joint Anglo-French will in the anticipation of future trouble from Germany. However, the main message that Chamberlain took away from the journey was the enormous enthusiasm he generated as the apostle of peace from the French crowds gathered to greet him. This was no less than he had expected. Indeed, he had planned the visit not just to 'strengthen Daladier' but 'to give French people an opportunity of pouring out their pent-up feeling of gratitude and affection' towards himself.[9]

Anglo-French relations were conditioned by the scale of Britain's military commitment. In Britain, the key to assuaging public concern over the defence deficiencies, as both Churchill and Chamberlain appreciated, was to step up the production of aircraft to meet the menacing threat from the *Luftwaffe*. It was with the backing of Simon and Chamberlain that emphasis was given to RAF fighter rather than bomber production.[10] This decision, taken against the advice of the Air Staff, was of fundamental importance in the winning of the Battle of Britain and for it the country was to owe Simon and Chamberlain a (largely unpaid) debt of gratitude. However, in early 1939 it was the enlargement of the British Army that was crucial to strengthening the alliance with France since without the dispatch of a sizeable expeditionary force, any continental commitment was restricted to that of supplying those allies left to take the full brunt of the assault. Since Chamberlain had sought to avoid having to make a continental commitment, he had opposed increasing the British Expeditionary Force beyond being ready to dispatch two divisions to the European theatre on the outbreak of a war. The Cabinet's decision in February to increase the total to four divisions and a mobile division backed up by four territorial divisions, only highlighted the feebleness of the commitment. With the first troops capable of leaving for France three weeks after the outbreak of war, it was clear that the government was not exactly contemplating facing a blitzkrieg. In contrast to Chamberlain, Halifax had come round to seeing that the prospects for cementing an effective Anglo-French alliance were jeopardized by France's suspicions that she would be facing the full force of the German war machine virtually alone if Hitler decided to go west. Halifax's support strength-ened the hand of the noticeably ambitious Secretary of State for War, Leslie Hore-Belisha, in his campaign to build up the army. In January, Halifax took on Chamberlain and Simon in the Cabinet's Foreign Policy Committee by demanding full staff talks with the French on the basis of a comprehensive commitment to prepare for war not only against Hitler but (to Chamberlain's horror) against Mussolini as well. Halifax was overruled.[11]

Chamberlain now had to be careful. Halifax had moved from a position of appeasement to one of preparation for a probable war and the broadening of the government's base. Hore-Belisha was not satisfied with the Lilliputian size of the British Army. Inskip, the Minister for Defence Coordination, had come round to supporting the case for a Ministry of Supply, Churchill's long campaign for which Chamberlain had set his hand against. All these potential troublemakers could be overcome but only if Chamberlain could prove that the chances of another war were continuing to diminish because appeasement was working. Here was a serious problem. How could he build understanding with Germany when there were those in the Foreign Office who were determined to support what Halifax described as 'the immediate objective' which was 'the correction of the false impression that we were decadent, spineless and could with impunity be kicked about'?[12]

The obvious course for Chamberlain was to conduct foreign policy over the heads of the more bellicose elements in the Foreign Office. As Margaret Thatcher discovered to her cost in 1989, Prime Ministers who try to rule through advisers rather than through ministers play a risky game. Halifax was soon alerted to the suspicions that his authority was being circumvented by Chamberlain who was using Downing Street's chief press officer, George Steward, to communicate with Berlin via a contact at the German press agency. MI5 intercepts were passed on to Halifax by Cadogan apparently confirming that these contacts were being made. Did Chamberlain sanction them or were they the work of his overzealous staff? On 29 November, Halifax demanded an explanation. Chamberlain claimed to know nothing about it. This was the sort of issue over which senior Cabinet ministers resign unless the Prime Minister could put up a convincing enough show that he was in ignorance. Whether or not truthfully, this is what Chamberlain managed to achieve.[13] Nonetheless, a warning shot had been fired and in future he would have to tread even more carefully.

III

The new year heralded a series of scares causing fear in London that Hitler really did intend to strike out westwards instead of east. One rumour had it that he was even planning a surprise knockout air raid on London. Despite the lack of reliable evidence, these Chinese whispers, mumbled with a variety of motives, quickly gained an avid hearing in a fog of uncertainty. In January 1939, the Cabinet agreed to initiate staff conversations with their opposite numbers in the Belgian military, on top of those with the French. The prospect of German troops and naval bases on the other side of the Channel clearly presented a challenge to the British Empire's strategic defence. Responding to a rumour that Hitler was thinking about invading Switzerland, the Cabinet also agreed to support French action in the event of this leading to a European war.

At Locarno in 1925, Sir Austen Chamberlain had committed Britain to defending France's boundary with Germany. Nonetheless, Neville Chamberlain was restlessly working out the arithmetic of every possible permutation. In consequence, he told the Cabinet that he was reluctant to make binding commitments to France because whilst 'France had undertaken to come to our assistance if we were attacked . . . France might be attacked from more than one quarter, whereas we were only liable to be attacked by Germany and that the obligations of mutual assistance in the event of attack would not therefore be equal . . . he would deprecate any attempt to define the position more narrowly.'[14] Which quarters were in Chamberlain's mind? It seemed improbable that General Franco would choose to attack France the moment he had just finished bleeding his own country dry. Instead, Chamberlain's fears were concentrated upon the deteriorating relations between France and Italy. This was particularly unfortunate as far as Chamberlain was concerned, given his perennial interest in appeasing Mussolini. It was to Rome that Chamberlain and Halifax now commenced upon a fresh pilgrimage.

Although the trip went ahead in January 1939 largely without incident there was little evidence to support Chamberlain's belief that this 'truly wonderful visit'[15] represented a fresh hope that Mussolini could yet be used to lean on Hitler. 'Hoping to get Mussolini to express his true feelings about Hitler,' Chamberlain is recorded in the Cabinet minutes as telling his colleagues that Il Duce 'had never taken the opportunity offered to him, but had remained throughout absolutely loyal to Herr Hitler. The Prime Minister said that at the time he had been somewhat disappointed at this attitude, but on reflection he thought that it reflected credit in Signor Mussolini's character.'[16] As if this was not credulous enough, Chamberlain stated that the 'fit and well' looking Italian dictator had at no time during the visit 'shown the slightest sign of jealousy at the great reception given to the Foreign Secretary and the Prime Minister', a reception which was 'heartfelt, spontaneous and universal'.[17] Chamberlain was desperately trying to convince himself that all was well, for to concede otherwise was to admit defeat. He would have been surprised and hurt to know that after he had left, Mussolini had discussed him with the Italian Foreign Minister, Count Ciano. 'These men are not made of the same stuff as the Francis Drakes,' concluded Il Duce of Chamberlain and his entourage, 'and the other magnificent adventurers who created the empire. These, after all, are the tired sons of a long line of rich men, and they will lose their empire.'[18]

IV

Economic considerations fundamentally affected Chamberlain's thinking. Whilst rearmament was providing jobs in parts of the country that had never experienced the consumer boom of the South, the nationwide picture was darkening. In January 1939 unemployment nudged back up to 14 per cent of the workforce. With disappointing economic figures, so receipts to the Treasury eased off. This was not a good time to implement a massive hike in taxation to fund armaments. In consequence, on 21 February (the day in which the Cabinet had discussed increasing the continental commitment to a mere four regular and four territorial divisions) Chamberlain announced to the Commons the doubling of the Defence Loan to £800 million. In the Great War, Britain had borrowed heavily from the United States to pay for the war effort. In fact, she had borrowed so heavily that, as we have seen, in 1934 she had in effect defaulted on her outstanding debts. The result of this and American neutrality legislation was that Britain was prohibited from borrowing from the USA again in wartime. Predictions might be made that in the event of a genuine conflict the American attitude would be more helpful, but it could not be assumed as a principle upon which to base calculations.

Rearmament increased the demand for imports. As a former Chancellor of long standing, Chamberlain took very seriously Simon's warnings from the Treasury about the interrelated problems of poor trade figures, a diminution of revenue and a run on the pound. Each year after 1931 there had been a net inflow to the country of gold and foreign exchange reserves, but in 1938 this situation had been dramatically reversed. Fears that Britain might suffer another financial crisis on a par with 1931 were never far from the minds of the political generation whose claim on office had rested upon their call to balance the books.[19] With assessments that British involvement in a continental war would be likely to last for three years, it was essential that this financial 'fourth arm of defence' was not disabled even before the fighting began. When in May 1939 Simon demanded a Committee of Control to rein in excessive defence expenditure, Chamberlain gave his backing, ensuring into the bargain that none of the ministers charged with defence portfolios sat on it.[20]

If the British economy was straining under the burden of rearmament, then it seemed probable that the German economy might also be in difficulties. This appeared all the more likely since Germany's rate of rearmament as a proportion of national income under Hitler had been much higher than Britain's in each year until 1939. Chamberlain was well aware of the rumours about the state of the German economy and that it lacked sufficient hard currency to pay for its essential imports. It had always been a totem of left-wing academic analysis that the struggle for necessary resources was the cause of imperialist adventure in inequitable non-socialist societies. Indeed, this view indirectly had its adherents within government itself, hence the belief that in a long war, the Anglo-French blockade would eventually lead to the collapse of the natural resource-deficient Third Reich. Chamberlain well appreciated that the looming economic crisis in Germany could only be tackled either by the *Wehrmacht* invading neighbouring countries to appropriate their resources or by a decision to switch activity from the armament programme to the creation of exports to pay for imports. Hitler was therefore at the crossroads between choosing a future based on conquest or a future based on opening up to international trade.

It is in this light that Chamberlain's support for financial talks with Berlin must be seen. In order to sustain the enormous burden of militarization, the German economy had switched decisively away from international trade and the free flow of capital, preferring to exist behind a barrier of exchange controls. The problem with this from a military perspective was that Germany still needed foreign exchange with which to pay for the importation of essential resources for its armaments programme. There were limits to her neighbours' interest in entering a barter-based trade with her. This, in effect, meant the Balkans and countries of eastern Europe. Halifax was amongst those particularly concerned that Berlin's attempts to bind these countries into an economic vassalage in which goods were provided like a Danegeld to prevent actual annexation would give Hitler his *Lebensraum* without his actually having to spill blood for it. Policy makers in Whitehall felt that the way to prevent this servitude was to encourage the opening up of the German economy. Where trade would flow freely across borders, the *Wehrmacht*, it was hoped, would not. However, to encourage this trade liberalization, Britain would have to help Germany to generate hard currency.

Chamberlain sanctioned talks between Montagu Norman (still Chairman of the Bank of England) and Hjalar Schacht, President of the Reichsbank. These were held in November 1938 in London and in January 1939 in Berlin. Schacht's pitch was that if Britain was interested in liberalizing German trade and making the Reichsmark a convertible currency, then she should offer Germany a loan or reduce interest charged on foreign debts. To sceptics, the problem was obvious. Would British financial assistance lead to détente with an opening up of the German economy or would it end up in British cities being bombed by a *Luftwaffe* built by British finance? In March, a British Foreign Office report revealed that sterling surpluses granted to Germany under the existing Payments Agreement were being used to gather raw materials of a 'strategic' nature.[21] Optimists still believed that a fresh deal could turn events in the right direction. After all, if British rearmament was curtailed by fears of it triggering a run on the pound, then encouraging the Reichsmark to become a convertible currency would logically have the same effect on the German war machine. Although Schacht was sacked from his post in January, his Nazi replacement continued to make positive noises towards these British offerings of economic appeasement. Chamberlain was encouraged too by trade agreements reached with the Reich. At the end of January, Germany conceded an agreement on coal export quotas on terms not unfavourable to Britain. On 14 March at Düsseldorf the Federation of British Industry and its Germay counterpart agreed to commence bilateral agreements and partnerships by way of the joint cartel arrangements that existed in the subsidy-driven world that had rejected the classical path of free trade.[22] These negotiations, surely, were encouraging signs that Germany was looking to build a peaceful coexistence with her economic competitors. It was not to be.

V

On 14 March 1939 the Czech President, Hácha, had been called to Berlin for talks. Hitler kept him waiting whilst he watched a film, a romantic comedy called *Ein Hoffnungsloser Fall (A Hopeless Case)*. Eventually at 1.15 in the morning Hácha was shown in and informed that in a few hours' time Germany would invade his country. Hitler told him to order his troops to lay down their weapons or the *Luftwaffe* would obliterate Prague from the skies. At this Hácha suffered a heart attack. Hitler's doctor was rushed in and administered an injection which revived the old man sufficiently to sign his country's death warrant. The *Wehrmacht* marched into Prague later that day.

Choosing to ignore information by MI6 that an invasion of Czechoslovakia was imminent, Chamberlain was taken by surprise by the *Führer*'s act. Indeed, when news of the invasion reached Britain, the Prime Minister was away on a fishing trip with his master of dirty tricks (but keen angler) Sir Joseph Ball.[23] Earlier that month, Chamberlain had told the press that the international picture was looking so favourable that disarmament talks could be initiated by the end of the year. By 12 March he was so sure that he had the situation under control that he wrote to his sister marvelling at how he had brought the Tory rebels to heel with the 'prodigal sons' Churchill, Eden, Duff Cooper and Wolmer 'fairly besieging the parental door' in praise.[24] Chamberlain's immediate reaction to the news of the Czech invasion was to play down its significance. Given that neither he nor the rest of the Cabinet had any intention of honouring the guarantee that they had given to Prague after Munich, it was essential that this line was adopted.[25] Hitler had provided Chamberlain with a pretext for breaking his pledge by ordering the former Slovak Prime Minister, Tiso, to declare independence from the Czech state or face invasion from neighbouring Hungary. Although keen to gain greater autonomy from Prague, the Slovak Government did not want to secede from the rest of the country but – faced with invasion – did Hitler's bidding just as the Czech President was forced to do under similar pressure. These events allowed Chamberlain to wriggle out of his guarantee to defend Czechoslovakia on the grounds that the country no longer existed. Indeed, in the Commons, he did not use the word 'invasion' once, preferring to describe the conquest merely as Czechoslovakia becoming 'disintegrated'. The events were a 'shock to confidence' making all the more necessary the need to rebuild it. 'Do not let us,' Chamberlain concluded, 'be deflected from our course'; whatever setbacks there might be 'the object that we have in mind is of too great significance to the happiness of mankind for us lightly to give it up or set it on one side.'[26] Not a word of sympathy was expressed for the Czech people.

Chamberlain had badly misjudged the mood of his parliamentary colleagues. In part his reluctance to attribute blame was a consequence of the sketchy amount of information at first available to him.[27] Nonetheless, what he did reveal to the Commons was rather less than was already known by many of the more informed backbench members or, indeed, what had already appeared in the national press. At Munich, Britain had connived with the Reich to deprive Czechoslovakia of its defences on the understanding that Hitler had no intention to use force against what remained of the country. Hitler's word had been shown to be worthless and the British Prime Minister's reliance upon it, manifested in his waving of the piece of paper with Hitler's signature upon it at Heston aerodrome, was seen to demonstrate a colossal error of judgement. Each of Hitler's previous acts of aggression had been backed by the pretext of uniting Germans with the Fatherland. This argument no longer held, since the invasion of the Czech state brought into the Reich a solidly non-German population. These and other facts were well established when on 16 March, Chamberlain came off badly in exchanges on the floor of the Commons:

> Sir Archibald Sinclair: Have the British Government lodged any protest with the German Government against the invasion of this territory?
> The Prime Minister: No, Sir, we have not done so.
> Sir Archibald Sinclair: Is it proposed to lodge a protest with the German Government?
> The Prime Minister: I could not answer that question without notice.

When asked by the Labour MP, Philip Noel-Buxton, whether the British Government proposed to make clear to Berlin that 'any attempt to attack the lives or liberties of the leaders of the Czech people will intensify the indignation in this country at their aggression', Chamberlain replied simply, 'I think it wrong to assume that the German Government have any such intention.'[28] It is not difficult to imagine that exchanges of this kind provoked more than one Conservative MP to shift uncomfortably on his leather-upholstered seat.

That same day, backbenchers gave their verdict in a meeting of the Conservative backbench Foreign Affairs Committee. Calls were made for the immediate institution of military conscription and the establishment of an Anglo-French alliance with the Soviet Union. In the Commons, Eden, supported by Wolmer and Richard Law, had already led the Tory rebels' response to events by calling for a reformed National Government to include members from all corners of the House.[29] The call for a broadening of the government directly conflicted with Chamberlain's continued tenure as His Majesty's first minister. Harold Nicolson recorded in his diary: 'The feeling in the lobbies is that Chamberlain will either have to go or completely reverse his policy. Unless in his speech tonight [in Birmingham] he admits that he was wrong, they feel that resignation is the only alternative. . . . The Opposition refuse absolutely to serve under him. The idea is that Halifax should become Prime Minister and Eden Leader of the House.'[30] The mood of anger and fear was shared by many of those who had supported Chamberlain at the time of the Munich démarche. The occupation of Prague, as Page Croft later put it, was the 'turning point of our times'.[31] Chamberlain now had to act quickly, first to recover from the negative effect of his detached performance in the Commons, and second to demonstrate that Britain was moving into a position in which she could prevent Hitler pulling off further stunts of this kind in the future. Again it was Halifax who – rather than giving Chamberlain enough rope to hang himself – offered him useful advice by persuading him to add a concluding peroration to his proposed speech in Birmingham on 17 March. As a result, Chamberlain told his audience how depressed he was that Hitler had 'shattered' the worthwhile achievements of Munich. At last a note of 'sympathy' was struck for the Czech people. Most importantly of all, the Prime Minister posed the fundamental question: 'Is this the last attack upon a small state, or is it to be followed by another? Is this in fact a step in the direction of an attempt to dominate the world by force?' If world domination was the goal, then 'no greater mistake could be made than to suppose that, because it believes war to be a senseless and cruel thing, this nation has so lost its fibre that it will not take part to the utmost of its power in resisting such a challenge if it ever were made'.[32]

Whatever his initial reaction to the news, once he had time to digest what had happened and to discover his party's views on the violation, Chamberlain realized that appeasement would have to be put on hold for the time being. In the Cabinet the day after his Birmingham speech, he conceded that whilst the hope for an accommodation with Germany must continue, 'Herr Hitler's attitude made it impossible to continue to negotiate on the old basis with the Nazi regime.'[33] This was a total turnaround from his utterances at the Cabinet table at the time of Munich when he intoned that Hitler was a sincere man. Furthermore, no sooner had the details come in over the Czech occupation than the Romanian Ambassador called upon Halifax with the news that Berlin had issued his country with an ultimatum as well. By the time the Cabinet convened on 18 March, the Foreign Secretary had already issued a verbal warning over Romania to the German Ambassador and had alerted Britain's potential

allies on the matter. At the Cabinet meeting, Chamberlain accepted that
Britain would have to seek support from Balkan and eastern European
countries if further German aggression was to be resisted.[34] In fact, the
Romanian Ambassador had greatly exaggerated the menacing nature of
Berlin's diplomacy with Bucharest. But by the time this was appreciated,
the belief had taken a firm hold that Romanian independence from the
Reich was an essential British interest. On 22 March, the *Wehrmacht*
occupied Memel, the German-speaking stretch of Lithuania.

VI

Attention now focused upon Poland. Wedged between its former German
and Russian masters, Poland had gained its independence as a result of
the Great War. In order to prevent the new Polish state from being
landlocked, the German port of Danzig (modern-day Gdansk) had been
turned into a Free City with its own autonomous administration under a
League of Nations High Commissioner, surrounded by a strip of land
ceded to Poland, known as the 'Corridor', which thus cut between
German East Prussia and the rest of the German Reich. On 26 March it
emerged that German-Polish talks on Danzig and the Polish Corridor's
future status had broken down. Three days later, Chamberlain was
confronted by information from Ian Colvin, a *News Chronicle* corre-
spondent in Berlin, of German plans for the immediate invasion of
Poland. Chamberlain was sceptical of this information; rightly as it
transpired. Nonetheless, British attention now switched instantly to what
appeared to be the next cause célèbre for the extension of Hitler's eastern
empire.

The immediate problem in Whitehall was to discern which way Polish
diplomacy would face. Being squeezed between the *Wehrmacht* and the
Red Army was an unenviable fate but, presented with the choice, Warsaw
gave the impression of preferring to appease Hitler rather than Stalin. In
1920, Poland and the Soviet Union had been at war. In 1934, Warsaw
had signed a non-aggression pact with Berlin and had also colluded in
grabbing a share of the offcuts from the Czechoslovak carvery. Halifax
even feared that the result of Polish appeasement of Berlin would be to
cover Hitler's eastern front so that he would be free to attack westwards.
Neither Whitehall nor the Quai d'Orsay trusted Colonel Jozef Beck, the
Polish Foreign Minister, whose cards were being played ominously close
to his chest. Intelligence reports backing up Colvin's claim that Hitler was
poised to invade Poland particularly concentrated Halifax's mind.
Requesting and being granted an emergency meeting of the Cabinet, he
argued for issuing an immediate British guarantee to Poland in the hope

of making Hitler rethink a quick strike. Here was an example of sudden events bouncing a government into action contrary to its long-term strategy. In fact, as Chamberlain appreciated, a British guarantee could be useful in more ways than one. It would prevent Poland from reaching an agreement with Germany that would make her, in effect, Berlin's vassal. Halifax had advised the Foreign Policy Committee on 27 March that the fifty-division-strong Polish Army was a better deterrent against Germany than the Red Army. This judgement, which made little sense in hindsight, was not quite so eccentric at the time. After all, the Poles had beaten back the ragged Red Army from the gates of Warsaw in 1920. The situation now was admittedly very different but Stalin's recent purges gave little ground for believing that the Red Army had transformed itself into a well-led, well-organized fighting machine. If Poland really was a stronger fighting power than the Soviet Union, then the British Government could have the best of both worlds: like the Kaiser in 1914 Hitler would have to fight a war on both a western and an eastern front. At the same time, the British could keep the devious Bolsheviks out of the equation.

Ignoring these considerations, the opposition parties were particularly adamant that Stalin should be enlisted in the fight to preserve the independence of the states of eastern Europe. These were Labour and Liberal politicians whom the Tory dissidents wanted brought into the administration. On 28 March, Eden tabled a motion calling for a new National Government 'formed on the widest possible basis' in order to direct a transformation of the economy on to a potential war footing. Forty backbench MPs put their names to this motion, including Amery, Churchill and Duff Cooper. This was quickly stamped on by a counter-motion inspired from the Whips' Office deprecating any attempt to undermine confidence in the Chamberlain administration. Nonetheless, both sides of the Commons chamber were now restless and the issue of what to do about the Soviet Union could not be dodged for much longer. In the Cabinet, the case for approaching Moscow was being put, somewhat surprisingly, by Sir Samuel Hoare. Chamberlain profoundly mistrusted the Soviet Union and questioned the altruism of its interest in European affairs. Given the subsequent nature of Stalin's involvement in the independence of the states of eastern Europe, the British Prime Minister was by no means a scaremonger in this respect. Destroying the wealth and manhood of the British Empire in order to condemn eastern Europe to a Communist police state rather than to a Fascist police state was of marginal benefit – especially considering the tendency of some of the eastern European countries (the late Czech state notably excepted) to be run by semi-Fascist governments of their own making in any case.

Nonetheless, the immediate problem was what to do about the accelerating pace of Germany's aggrandizement of territory. The French were warning that allying with the Soviet Union stood to cement Rome's embrace of Berlin and added to this, Halifax pointed out the hostility that a pact with Moscow would create in Portugal and Spain. Most importantly of all, if Poland was Germany's next target, then what was the good of Britain allying with the one country the Poles hated more than the Germans? Thus, Chamberlain felt that issuing Beck with a guarantee was particularly useful given the latter's continued opposition to Russian involvement in an anti-German security pact.[35] On 31 March, Chamberlain announced to the Commons that Britain had guaranteed Polish independence. France did likewise.

The proposals to guarantee Poland had met with little opposition in the Cabinet. The wording, which was largely Chamberlain's own work, gave Britain a deliberate let-out clause with regard to German designs on Danzig and the Polish Corridor, as he explained to his sister: 'It was unprovocative in tone, but firm, clear but stressing the important point (perceived alone by the Times) that what we are concerned with is not the boundaries of States, but attacks on their independence. And it is we who will judge whether this independence is threatened or not.'[36]

In 1935, Sir Samuel Hoare had made solemn pledges on the international stage that had encouraged people to believe that Britain was firmly committed to implementing a foreign policy of collective security. Privately Hoare had intended a more complicated, even duplicitous, strategy in which circumstances would have shown the commitment to be unworkable, thereby allowing the government to backtrack and pursue a diplomacy of Realpolitik. The result, the Hoare–Laval crisis, backfired horribly. At that time, Chamberlain had looked on Hoare with support and understanding and was sorry to see him fall victim to his excessively sophisticated scheme's failure. Yet, as Chamberlain's observations to his sister makes clear, the Polish plan in March 1939 was not so very different from the arithmetic that had made up Hoare's Abyssinian calculation in 1935. The Polish guarantee was not intended to make war with Germany inevitable any more than Hoare's pro-collective security rhetoric was intended to foreshadow definite confrontation with Mussolini. On the contrary, the commitment was intended to give Britain leverage in forcing Poland to come to terms with Hitler's demands over the Danzig and Corridor questions. In this way, Hitler could be satisfied without Poland being subjected either to a full-scale invasion (forcing a Europe-wide war) or succumbing to a treaty that reduced her to vassal status without a general conflagration. Because Chamberlain maintained that Britain was guaranteeing Poland's independence, not her border, redrawing the boundary in Germany's favour would thus not trigger British action. Only if Hitler attempted to smash all Poland as an entity would Britain declare war on the Poles' behalf. Given the clear incentives that Britain was offering the German dictator not to go this far, it was reasonable to presume that even he would not be so hell-bent on self-destruction. This was a shrewd policy and an understandable one. It was also one fraught with Byzantine subtleties. Not being able to spell out the nuances that underpinned its cleverness risked its being misinterpreted by parliamentarians and public alike who would see it as a clear and welcome drawing of a line in the sand against German aggression of even a more limited kind against Poland. When that aggression came, Chamberlain might not be able to overcome this tide of expectation for the great showdown with the Nazi state.

VII

In the days after the invasion of Czechoslovakia, Chamberlain had appeared to lose his grip over Parliament. Whatever the truth in Harold Wilson's later pronouncement that a week is a long time in politics, the favourable reaction created by the Polish guarantee certainly suggested that it is so of a fortnight. Chamberlain's mastery of the political scene was instantly regenerated. When the Commons debated the new policy on 3 April, the guarantee drew support from almost every quarter of the House – including from Churchill and the Labour front bench. That the guarantee appeared at first sight to be an abandonment of the appeasement policy would soon store up trouble for Chamberlain. For the moment what seemed a reversal strengthened rather than weakened his position. This caused disgruntled wonder from Harold Macmillan, who concluded that the fact the Prime Minister had 'made such persistent and bone-headed mistakes' did not undermine his position since 'if Chamberlain says that black is white, the Tories applaud his brilliance. If a week later he says that black is after all black, they applaud his realism. Never has there been such servility.'[37]

Almost immediately after he had re-established his position, Chamberlain came through a fresh trial of fire when his attempt to keep Mussolini briefed about British actions and intentions was humiliatingly not repaid on Good Friday. Without warning, Italy marched into its client state, Albania, shelling Durazzo into the bargain. Repeating his initial reaction to the occupation of Prague, Chamberlain appeared more annoyed by the newsworthy manner of Mussolini's aggression than by the act itself and wished Il Duce could have found a way of making it look as if the aggressive act was part of an agreed arrangement (as Hitler had attempted to do). Chamberlain complained to his sister that he was being 'badgered for a meeting of [Parliament] by the two Oppositions & Winston who is the worst of the lot, telephoning almost every hour of the day. I suppose he has prepared a terrific oration which he wants to let off.' He certainly was not going to allow 'reckless people' to deflect him from his steady course whilst crowds were still gathering to applaud wherever he went.[38] The problem was that Mussolini's sudden action made a mockery of the spirit in which Chamberlain and Halifax had hailed their visit to Rome three months previously. Mussolini, it had belatedly become clear, was no more solid an anchor upon which to moor British foreign policy than his German counterpart. Worse was to follow. Reports, fuelled by the Greek leader General Metaxas, circulated implying that Italy was poised to invade Corfu. Greece would then be at war with Italy. Like the English Channel, the Mediterranean was seen as an essential communication link holding together the British Empire, the loss of which could not be countenanced. British interests in keeping open the Suez Canal were paramount. It was the artery through which traffic with India and Australasia passed. Italian pretensions in the region were thus a cause of the utmost concern as were any attempts to encroach upon Britain's interests in the Middle Eastern oilfields. Halifax supported issuing Turkey and Greece with a British guarantee of their independence on lines similar to that issued to Poland. This was the logical extension of his words and deeds in recent months, including his attempts to get Britain to make bulk-purchases from south-eastern European countries so as to prevent them slipping further into Berlin's economic sphere of influence and ending up as part of German *Lebensraum*.

Events in the Balkans ruined Chamberlain's Easter secondment to the Scottish fishing streams. Indeed, there seemed to be an uncanny synchronicity between fresh European outrages and the donning of the Prime Ministerial tweeds and waders. Hastening back to Downing Street, he met the Cabinet on Easter Monday to take stock of the deteriorating situation in the Balkan countries. It was agreed that the Balkans could not become part of the orbit of Italy or Germany. In the same manner as with Poland, Britain would now issue Greece with a guarantee. Doing so left open the issue of Romania. That country's strategic importance, and in particular the need for its oilfields not to fall into German hands, was equally well understood. The French protested that guaranteeing Poland (and now Greece) but not Romania almost encouraged Germany to strike at it – either by force, or by treaty implemented under the threat of force. The Cabinet therefore agreed to join France in guaranteeing Romania. Negotiations got under way to bring Turkey into an alliance as well.

Hitler's attitude to Britain's diplomatic initiatives could be guessed by his secret instruction to his officers to commence preparations for Operation White – the invasion of Poland – only three days after Chamberlain had announced the country's guarantee. After all, how was Britain, with a mere four divisions ready for engagement on the continent, to honour its commitments there? Only the introduction of conscription could suggest to the Reich Chancellery that London was any more determined to honour its new guarantees than it had been that of the late Czechoslovakia. On 18 April, Hore-Belisha had an acrimonious interview with Chamberlain in which the latter, clearly irritable, gave the impression that he wanted to scupper the Secretary of State for War's campaign amongst his colleagues to introduce conscription. Later that day the Army Council came down in favour of partial mobilization as the only alternative to conscription. Halifax also had taken up Hore-Belisha's concerns. This was a dangerous situation for Chamberlain. He therefore determined to steal the initiative away from Hore-Belisha (of whom he had formed a personal dislike) by circulating his own proposals for conscription. In the Cabinet, Chamberlain even went so far as to state that he had personally 'long been in favour in principle of a scheme of compulsory military training' but had fought shy because of previous statements he and Baldwin had made not to introduce it and for fear of what the trades unions might think.[39] The Prime Minister's sensitivity to the Labour Movement was not one of his more renowned characteristics. Similarly it was a curious argument to claim that he had not done something that he believed in because he had said publicly that he did not believe in it. Nonetheless the Prime Minister recognized that there was now an irrepressible momentum in favour of conscription and that it was important to take hold of it by presenting his own modified scheme. The Cabinet agreed on 24 April to Chamberlain's proposals. Three days later, the Commons approved the resulting Military Training Bill which introduced conscription for males between the ages of twenty and twenty-one for a strictly limited period. The measure was opposed by the Council of the Trades Union Congress and by Attlee and the Labour Party. It also provided Hitler with his excuse for renouncing the 1935 Anglo-German Naval Agreement the same day.

VIII

Chamberlain's hope that these new guarantees would augment the case for *not* allying with Stalin was increasingly difficult to sustain. France had completely reversed its hesitancy of the previous month and was proposing a fresh mutual alliance with Russia in which either would come

to the assistance of the other in the event of war with Germany over
Poland or Romania. In this scenario, Britain would find herself on the
same side as Russia in a war whether she had concluded an alliance with
her or not. Moscow's own plans had been issued to both Paris and
London on 18 April. The scheme involved a mutual assistance pact
supported by joint military cooperation to cover all the states bordering
Russia from the Baltic to the Balkans. This was not as simple as it
sounded. Both Romania and Poland had in place defensive pacts against
Soviet invasion and – ominously – Moscow demanded that the British
guarantee to Poland was directed *only* against Germany. The Soviet
proposals also included a clause preventing any of the three signatories
from concluding a separate peace with Germany once the war had begun.

Chamberlain was wary of the sort of binding and potentially compromising alliance that Stalin was now promoting. It would both solidify a
Europe of two armed camps (the very destination that the appeasement
policy had sought to avoid) and could drag Britain and France into a
German war of Stalin's making. The Soviet plan involved an attack on
one of the signatories as a declaration of war on all. Chamberlain did not
want to go to war with Germany just because Hitler had declared war
(possibly after provocation) on the behemoth to the east. Moscow's
suggested three power pact, therefore, would not do. Understandably,
Chamberlain far preferred Halifax's much more limited suggestion that
the Red Army should be committed to helping Poland and Romania if
those countries requested it in the face of a German invasion. The
problem here was that this held limited appeal for Stalin who was already
being presented with more mutually binding proposals from Paris.
Furthermore, parliamentary opposition to Chamberlain's clear havering
over relations with Moscow was continuing to mount. This contrasted
with the all-important balance of forces within the Cabinet where the
existing position was still sustainable. Only Oliver Stanley, Malcolm
MacDonald and Sir Samuel Hoare were arguing for an alliance with the
Soviets on Moscow's three power pact terms and none looked to be
preparing to resign on the matter. Thus Chamberlain retained a clear
majority in favour of avoiding a binding alliance with the Kremlin.
Interestingly, the coda was added that Britain and France would *already*
have to be at war on the invaded country's behalf before the proposed
Russian offer could be acted upon. On 15 May, Molotov (who had
replaced the more amenable Litvinov as Soviet Foreign Minister)
categorically rejected the British proposal.

Chamberlain might well have had cause for annoyance that many of
the figures who now abused him in public for not clipping Hitler's wings
through alliance with Stalin's regime were the same ones who had

chastised his efforts to keep Hitler in check by building friendly relations with the less (if only by comparison) objectionable Italian dictatorship. Whatever the (minimal) likelihood of Mussolini acting as a brake on the ambitions of his fellow Fascist, there were few red rags more likely to bond him closely to Hitler than an Anglo-French attempt to encircle Fascist central Europe with the forces of Comrade Stalin. Chamberlain's problem was that as the international temperature rose, so it was becoming self-evident that Mussolini was not prepared to play the role that he had allotted to him as a restraint on Hitler. Yet if ideological considerations did not stand in the way of Britain negotiating with Nazism, then why should they debar a pact with Stalinism? Russia's proposals for a three power pact were now in the public domain and the Commons debate on 19 May had provided the growing alliance of anti-appeasers with a shooting gallery in which to pot at Chamberlain for his failure, in Lloyd George's words, to look 'this powerful [Soviet] gift horse in the mouth'.[40] Churchill reminded the government that whatever their ideological differences and reasons for mutual mistrust, on the central issue of future German expansion, the Soviets and British shared a common purpose. Downing Street had to 'get some of these brutal truths into their head. Without an effective Eastern front, there can be no satisfactory defence of our interests in the West, and without Russia there can be no effective Eastern front.'[41] On the triple alliance, Eden and Churchill were in complete agreement. Amery, however, was much more sceptical of alliance with Stalin.

Chamberlain remained unconvinced by the parliamentary pressure from yesterday's men for an alliance with a country that they themselves had originally tried to strangle at birth. He regarded their contribution as tiresome and potentially dangerous, telling the Foreign Policy Committee on 19 May that 'many influential persons in Germany were trying to persuade Herr Hitler that the time to strike was when the Three Power was concluded, and that the conclusion of such a Pact would unite Germany as nothing else could do.'[42] The following day, Cadogan noted in his diary that Chamberlain 'says he will resign rather than sign alliances with Soviet[s]'.[43]

The Prime Minister's problem was that his position was rapidly being cut from under him. Halifax reluctantly made clear that Britain would have to accede to the Soviet proposal (including a guarantee to defend Russia against Germany) or talks would collapse. This placed Chamberlain in a terrible quandary. Public admission that Britain had guaranteed eastern Europe but failed to gain the support of the massed divisions of the Red Army and the enormous resources of the Soviet Empire would intensify the hostility to which the Prime Minister was once again being subjected in the Commons chamber. Insofar as it could be gauged, popular feeling across the country appeared to be widely in favour of a Soviet alliance.[44] Writing to his sister, Chamberlain feared that an 'Alliance would definitely be a lining up of opposing blocs & an association which would make any negotiation or discussion with the Totalitarians difficult if not impossible'. He admitted though, that he was increasingly outnumbered in the Cabinet on this view. By late May, the only Cabinet minister who supported him was Rab Butler, the Under-Secretary at the Foreign Office, who was 'not' as Chamberlain conceded, 'a very influential ally'.[45] Crucially, the growing preference of the rest of the Cabinet was that it was better to do a deal with the Soviets on their terms rather than risk having no pact at all. It was reinforced by a transformation in the analysis of the Chiefs of Staff. Based on their estimates, Lord Chatfield (Inskip's successor as Minister for Defence Coordination) had at first told the Foreign Policy Committee on 25 April that he expected that only 30 of the 130 Soviet divisions could be maintained in the field for long. He soon had to report that the Chiefs of Staff had rethought the situation. The number of active Red Army divisions soared; the possession of 9000 good tanks and a navy that could keep its German counterpart tied up in the Baltic was suddenly thrown into the balance on the Russians' side. Furthermore, even if the Russians could not supply Britain and her allies with much war material, it was invaluable that they did not supply Germany with them. As a result of the Anglo-French staff talks of 3 May, Chatfield informed the Cabinet:

> The French intention in the event of a war between Germany and Poland was to stand on the defensive on the Maginot Line . . . The British Chiefs of Staff were considerably disturbed at the prospect of complete inaction on the part of the French and the consequent failure to exploit the two-front war. . . . If the French were going to do nothing to draw off the weight of a German attack on Poland, the assistance of Russia would be of great value to the latter.

The combination of the Cabinet's willingness and the Kremlin's unwillingness to bend left Chamberlain outmanoeuvred. The French too were determined that the existing Russian offer was better than no offer at all. If Chamberlain had been considering resignation, then he soon thought better of it. If he was to go, it was better that he did not do so on an issue where he clearly had lost the support of most of the country, much of the Cabinet and many within the party. Like the eleventh-hour salvation of Munich, events might yet come to his aid and it was important that he stayed at the helm in readiness. In the meantime a tactical retreat was the only option. On 24 May the Cabinet agreed with France to enter into alliance with the Soviet Union. Halifax made clear that not to do so could tempt Stalin into negotiations with Hitler. Later that day the Commons heard from Chamberlain's lips the intention of his administration to agree to the three power pact.

All did not go according to plan. Having conceded the essence of the Soviet proposals, the British and French chargés d'affaires in Moscow were now insulted by Molotov who objected to their intention of mentioning the League of Nations in the proposed text of the treaty. Tellingly, he rejected the insistence that the three powers would join in to repel aggression towards a state 'in conformity with the wishes of that state'. Molotov wanted to extend the anti-German pact to the defence of Finland and the Baltic states – countries that pointedly did not want Russian help. The full list he presented on 2 June consisted of Belgium, France, Greece, Turkey, Romania, Poland, Latvia, Estonia and Finland. The British representative pointed out that his country could scarcely be expected to be a party to guaranteeing countries that requested not to be guaranteed. In turn, Molotov refused the Anglo-French request for including Switzerland and the Netherlands on the grounds that those two countries had no diplomatic relations with the USSR.

The countries over which it was proposed to fight were not the only issue standing in the way of agreement. In the case histories of Austria, the Sudetenland and the remnants of Czechoslovakia (and shortly in the Polish Corridor as well), German intervention had been preceded by internal discontent deliberately stirred up from Berlin as a pretext for interference. Molotov posed the British and French representatives an important question arising from this tactic. What if a Berlin-inspired coup in a country resulted in that country's government being replaced with a leadership which then *invited* the German Army to come in for its protection? Given that in the remaining free capital cities of eastern Europe there were already many far-right politicians and future 'quislings' within an elevator ride of the corridors of power, it was crucial that any three power alliance knew what its line would be in the event of their taking office.

The British position remained one of extreme caution and the issue of the internal pro-German *coup d'état* an unwelcome variable for which an unequivocal answer was best avoided. By the end of June, Chamberlain and the Cabinet's Foreign Policy Committee were still insisting upon the inclusion of the Netherlands and Switzerland whilst being prepared to concede to the Soviet demand that there be no negotiation of a separate peace by the signatories once war had commenced. When General Ironside, the Inspector-General of Overseas Forces, told Chamberlain on 10 July that an alliance with Russia was 'the only thing we could do', Chamberlain riposted that it was 'the only thing we cannot do'.[46] Two days later the Prime Minister told the Foreign Policy Committee that on balance he thought Moscow would make an agreement with Britain but was 'probably in no hurry to do so'. Molotov, however, proposed to cut through the deadlock by suggesting that military staff talks should get under way immediately instead of waiting for the final text of a political agreement to be settled first. Given the mood in the Cabinet and elsewhere, Chamberlain had to accede to this. It was a dangerous policy telling an ideologically opposed foreign country Britain's military plans, especially when there was not yet in place a formal understanding. However, as the Prime Minister advised the Cabinet on 19 July, he 'could not bring himself to believe that a real alliance between Russia and Germany was possible'.[47]

The manner in which both the British diplomatic and military missions negotiated with their Soviet counterparts was a source of criticism at the time and an ongoing charge of hostile historians thereafter. If Chamberlain was fit enough to fly off at short notice to Germany to take tea with Herr Hitler, then his accusers wanted to know why he was not prepared to invest similar energy in a deal with potential allies. Halifax made no move to rise to the occasion and Chamberlain rejected the suggestion of other leading politicians to undertake the task. Churchill's offer of his services to David Margesson, the Chief Whip, met with no response. Eden's offer was also turned down and Chamberlain was annoyed that Halifax had been 'not unsympathetic' to the idea. He was particularly concerned about the opportunities for conspiracy provided by the situation, having learned that Lloyd George had told Rab Butler 'that if we did not approve of Anthony, Winston should go! I have no doubt that the three of them talked it over together, and that they saw in it a means of entry into the Cabinet and perhaps later on the substitution of a more amenable PM!'[48] In fact rejection of these offers to travel to the Soviet Union was understandable. As Chamberlain implicitly acknowledged, sending either Churchill or Eden without elevating them to an appropriate government responsibility would have been absurd and he had no intention of giving them that responsibility. That Chamberlain looked at the equation in terms of a political calculation against potential rivals demonstrated that he was still very much a politician even at a time when the fate of empires hung in the balance. Instead of a parliamentarian, the Foreign Office civil servant in charge of the Central Department, William Strang, was dispatched to join the British Ambassador to negotiate in Moscow.

The Anglo-French Military Mission under Admiral Drax was sent to Moscow on 5 August. Taking an aeroplane would have involved flying over German airspace and touching down to refuel. Understandably, this was not a favoured option. Nonetheless, there was a distinct lack of imagination when it came to investigating viable alternative routes. In consequence, the mission took six days to arrive, seventeen after the original decision to parley had been taken. As with the charge that insufficiently senior figures were sent on the political mission, so critics claimed that the tardy journey time of the Drax mission further underlined to the Russians that London was not serious in its negotiations. Certainly the British mission did not proceed with the sense of urgency that the occasion demanded, but neither did Molotov whose foot-dragging and pernicketiness was every bit as suspicious. In part, the British slowness was designed not so much to hamper agreement as to prevent premature collapse. Drax had been given specific instructions to prevent the talks failing by drawing out the process as long as possible, preferably until after autumnal weather encouraged a German postponement of any Polish invasion. In the circumstances this was appropriate since no worthwhile military exchanges between the Anglo-French and the Soviets could take place until Drax was in a position to confirm that the Poles would permit the Red Army to cross their frontier in the event of a German invasion. The Poles had still given no such undertaking when Drax was asked the question directly on 14 August. Indeed Beck argued that nothing would make a German invasion more likely than a Polish undertaking of this nature towards Stalin. This being the case, there never was likely to be any prospect of a deal between Britain, France and the Soviet Union. All expectations to the contrary were the product of wishful thinking. It was not the individuals dispatched nor the time they took to get to Russia that was the reason for the talks stalling. The problem was that Moscow wanted a deal that it was outside London's powers to deliver. But it was not outside the powers of Berlin.

IX

During the spring and summer of 1939, Chamberlain continued to ponder how best to deal with the sceptics within his own party. The eternal question facing any party leader was: should potential critics be brought into the Cabinet where they could do most damage (but might be capable of being tamed) or should they be left out and remain able to continue to create embarrassing disturbances from the newsworthy (but impotent) backbench? At the same time, the Tory rebels had to confront an even more fundamental question in deciding whether there was still anything left to rebel against. After all, Chamberlain was bending in their direction: Poland, Romania, Greece and Turkey had been guaranteed, the rearmament programme had been extended, military conscription had been introduced and a Ministry of Supply belatedly established. Certainly Churchill and Eden felt that had these measures been undertaken when they had first called for them, then the situation might not be as serious as it had now become. Nonetheless, the next battle was not going to be won by refighting those that had already receded into the past. The debate had moved on. It was time to act responsibly.

With these considerations in mind, Eden's main campaign avoided a detailed criticism of the government's plans in favour of pursuing a sustained call to broaden the administration's base to the opposition parties. This was an annoying line as far as Chamberlain was concerned but he was well aware that Eden was not plotting a palace coup. The Prime Minister knew this because his own close friend, Sir Joseph Ball, had taken the liberty of wire-tapping the telephone conversations of the former Foreign Secretary's political allies.[49] The head of the Conservative Research Department, Ball also kept in touch with his friends in MI5. He had been plucked from that organization in 1924 to 'run a little intelligence service' for the Tories (including planting agents in Labour Party headquarters) by J.C.C. Davidson who later described him as having had 'as much experience as anyone I know in the seamy side of life and the handling of crooks'.[50] Loyal to Chamberlain and the cause of appeasement, Ball also secretly ran a stridently pro-German weekly magazine, *Truth*, which rubbished Churchill (to the Prime Minister's amusement) and peddled anti-Semitic conspiracy theories about the motives of those who stood in the way of appeasing the dictators.

As with Eden's friends, Chamberlain was (thanks to Ball's wire-taps) able to eavesdrop on a number of Churchill's private telephone conversations.[51] The Prime Minister concluded that the best hope of keeping him quiet was to dangle the prospect of a return to the Cabinet before him without actually offering him anything. Baldwin had pursued a similar tactic with some measure of success in the period between the passage of the India Bill and the appointment of Inskip as Minister for Defence Coordination. There was every reason to believe that Churchill might be receptive to the ploy one more time. Before the Commons debate on the Italian invasion of Albania on 13 April 1939 Chamberlain had summoned him to Downing Street. He provided him with confidential information in return for which he hoped Churchill would not rock the boat. Churchill appeared to assent to this, but Chamberlain felt his subsequent speech in the Commons did not go far enough in doing so. Following the debate, the Chief Whip, Captain Margesson, told Chamberlain that Churchill had indicated his desire to serve in the Cabinet. He supposedly assured Margesson that

he could work amicably under the PM who had many admirable qualities some of which he did not possess himself. On the other hand he too had great qualities and could do much to help the PM to bear his intolerable burden, likely as it was to get worse as time went on. He would like the Admiralty but would be quite satisfied to succeed Runciman as Lord President. He thought Eden should be taken in too but observed that he could give much more help than Eden.

Chamberlain had already heard that on being summoned to Downing Street, Churchill had been under the misapprehension that he was to be made Minister for Supply and was 'smarting under a sense of disappointment, only kept in check by his unwillingness to do anything which might prevent his yet receiving an offer to join the Govt'. Chamberlain conceded to his sister that there would be benefits in having Churchill back in the front bench where his debating powers could be used for – rather than at the expense of – the administration. The question was whether this benefit was outweighed by the damage he could do in the Cabinet itself, where he would wear Chamberlain out with 'rash suggestions'.[52] Chamberlain concluded that this consideration *did* outweigh the benefits. The appointment of Leslie Burgin, a Liberal National MP, as Minister for Supply should have been a further indication that Churchill's exclusion from the Cabinet was written in stone. Nonetheless, the tireless campaigner still appeared to believe that his time would come.

It was not surprising that Churchill felt that his destiny had not yet been fulfilled. Hitler's actions continued to transform the member for Epping's warnings into prophecies. According to the *Daily Telegraph*, which was now assiduously backing him, to hear Churchill's Commons performance on the night the Military Training Bill was rushed through 'members hurried in, filling the Chamber and side galleries'. After his speech, the newspaper maintained that he had rarely 'been more warmly cheered after a speech, and when he sat down, there was reluctance among members to follow so brilliant an effort'.[53] Even *The Times*, which had not wanted to see him back in office, conceded that it was 'one of the finest of his Parliamentary performances'.[54]

In May, the liberal/centre-left *New Chronicle* had published an opinion poll showing a clear majority favouring Churchill's recall to the Cabinet.[55] By early July, the *Daily Telegraph*, the *Observer*, the *Manchester Guardian*, the *Yorkshire Post*, the *News Chronicle*, the *Daily Mirror* and the *Evening News* had all come out in favour of Churchill's recall. Even the pro-Communist *Daily Worker* had done so – although this may not have been entirely helpful to his cause. Despite his admiration for aspects of Hitler's regime and his belief that the Reich's power necessitated a policy of appeasement towards it, Lord Rothermere now threw his *Daily Mail* behind Churchill as well. Meanwhile, in its leading article on 3 July, the *Daily Telegraph* described Churchill's qualities and experience noting that 'every public man has made mistakes in his time. If they were to be counted as a bar to confidence, who would remain, except nonentities to carry out the King's Government?' It was Churchill, first and foremost who, the newspaper claimed, was on the minds of those who demanded the government's reconstruction: 'It is impossible to ignore the welling up of the feeling not only inside the rank and file of the party, but also among some of its most distinguished members, that Mr Churchill's inclusion in the Government is an urgent need.'[56] Lord Camrose, the *Telegraph*'s owner, had a revealing conversation with Chamberlain later that day. Chamberlain admitted that in the event of war, he would ask Churchill to join the administration but that essentially his reasons for excluding him in the meantime were the same as they had always been. His judgement was 'notorious'. Churchill would seek to dominate Cabinet discussion in the same way that he had when Chancellor in Baldwin's 1924–9 Government. Cabinet colleagues had tended to cave in to his barrage of argument and memoranda rather than endure the consequences of standing up to him. Chamberlain joked that when after 1886 the then Prime Minister (Lord Salisbury) had been petitioned to recall Lord Randolph Churchill to the Cabinet, he had replied, 'If you have once got rid of a carbuncle do you make an effort to get it back?' In any case, Chamberlain confided in Camrose the important news that he had not 'yet given up hopes of peace'. Polish independence may have been guaranteed, but 'if Hitler were asking for Danzig in a normal way it might be possible to arrange things'. Even the Polish Foreign Minister, Beck, could be persuaded of this, if the necessary guarantees were made:

> Winston was Public Enemy No 1 in Berlin, and Eden was the same in Italy. Their inclusion in the Cabinet might strike both ways. So far as the latter was concerned, he [i.e. Chamberlain] still clung to the idea that Italy being the weaker and now the unwilling partner of the Axis, we ought not to eliminate all idea of being able to seduce her away from her present entanglement. Eden's appointment might have a detrimental effect on such a chance.[57]

The press campaign to bring Churchill back was, according to Hoare, counter-productive. Writing to his PPS, the son of Viscount and Nancy Astor (who in a volte-face now advocated Churchill's recall), Hoare reasoned:

> Anything that Winston attempts is always overdone, and in this case it was so overdone that it has stirred up a great reaction against him. I believe that if there was a ballot of Conservative Back Bench Members on the subject, four out of five would be against him. This is to some extent the result of the papers

of the Left and the important papers of the Right shouting with one voice for his inclusion.

All this has made Neville's position stronger rather than weaker.[58]

Indeed, perplexed by the press campaign in favour of Churchill, the Prime Minister believed that the storm would soon pass. He put it down – not entirely jokingly, it seems – to a 'conspiracy' between Ivan Maisky and young Randolph Churchill. As for the *Daily Telegraph*'s participation, he was nonplussed, but believed it might have something to do with its owner: 'since his illness Camrose is a changed man.' In any case, the campaign was 'over-played' and had 'annoyed both my friends and Anthony's who don't see why their hero should be given such a second place'.[59]

Whilst Churchill still hoped to be recalled to the Cabinet table that he had last sat round almost ten years previously, he remained much more prepared than Eden to continue attacking the government when and where he thought it was in error. Together with Amery and a number of the other anti-appeasers[60] he voted against the government in May over its attempts to set a five-year time limit on continued Jewish immigration into Palestine. In a forceful speech, Churchill condemned a policy that he maintained would prevent the realization of the Balfour Declaration. An even more acrimonious exchange was to take place on 2 August during the Commons debate on the adjournment. Chamberlain proposed that Parliament should adjourn for its summer recess from 4 August until 3 October. Churchill, however, chose to call a spade a spade, complaining that the government's treatment of MPs was tantamount to saying:

> 'Begone! Run off and play. Take your gas masks with you. Do not worry about public affairs.' Leave them to the gifted and experienced Ministers who, after all, so far as our defences are concerned, landed us where we landed in September of last year, and who after all – I make allowances for the many difficulties – have brought us in foreign policy at this moment to the point where we have guaranteed Poland and Rumania, after having lost Czechoslovakia and not having gained Russia.

He had a further warning for his party's leaders: 'I noticed a sort of spirit on these benches to try and run this matter through on ordinary party loyalty and calling everyone who differs unpatriotic. If that sort of atmosphere were created I am sure that it would be absolutely swept away by the country.'[61]

Chamberlain made clear that failure to give him a carte blanche over the length of the summer recess was no technical matter. Instead he insisted: 'very well; it is a vote of no confidence in the Government and no confidence in the Prime Minister in particular.'[62] Ronald Cartland (the brother of the romantic novelist, Barbara Cartland, and MP for King's Norton – a neighbouring constituency of Chamberlain's) was infuriated by this announcement, and spoke out against Parliament being silenced when 'we are in a situation that within a month we may be going to fight, and we may be going to die.' Another Birmingham Tory MP, Sir Patrick Hannon, laughed out loud at this assertion. Incensed, Cartland retorted: 'There are thousands of young men at the moment in training camps, and giving up their holidays, and the least that we can do here, if we are not going to meet together from time to time and keep Parliament in session, is to show that we have immense faith in this democratic institution.'[63] Cartland even singled out Chamberlain, accusing him of seeking to make 'jeering pettifogging party speeches which divide the nation' rather than getting the whole country behind him.[64] This was an extraordinary outburst against his own leader and a number of Tories, furious at Cartland's strong language, demanded that the Whip be removed from him. Chamberlain considered trying to engineer Cartland's deselection before the next general election.[65] In the event there was no need. Cartland was killed in the retreat from Dunkirk.

At the time, the wrangle over the adjournment of Parliament appeared to demonstrate that Churchill's national stature did not impress his colleagues on the Conservative benches. Eden preferred to keep his head below the parapet rather than challenge the government on the issue. Despite being an Eden supporter (although increasingly despairing of the fact he was 'missing every boat with exquisite elegance')[66] Harold Nicolson decided that he could not 'let the old lion enter the lobby alone' and he joined Churchill in abstaining on the adjournment.[67]

MPs departed for their summer holidays on 4 August. Eden chose to spend time with his Territorial Army unit on summer camp. Over the past few months his decision to keep his concerns over Chamberlain's approach inside decorous boundaries had kept him within the party pale. This came at the expense of being eclipsed by Churchill in the popular eye as the leading Tory opponent of appeasement. For his part, Churchill continued to resemble an irritated bull, stamping his hoof, head lowered, and poised to charge. Having recently visited him at Chartwell, General Ironside reflected in his diary that he kept thinking about Churchill down there, 'full of patriotism and ideas for saving the Empire. A man who knows that you must act to win. You cannot remain supine and allow yourself to be hit indefinitely. Winston must be chafing at the inaction. I keep thinking of him walking up and down the room'.[68] The campaign in the media for his recall continued. Three hundred and seventy-five university academics, including seventy professors, wrote a letter in The Times requesting that he be brought back into the government. At the same time, huge advertising bill hoardings in central London proclaimed a new message, 'What Price Churchill?' It later emerged that the campaign was paid for – seemingly off his own bat – by a leading advertising agent.[69]

Whilst Chamberlain retired to Scotland to go fishing, Churchill opted for more of a busman's holiday. On 15 August he arrived with Spears to inspect the Maginot Line in north-east France. He was impressed by what he saw, although he expressed a prescient concern to General Georges that a German tank advance through the Ardennes could circumvent having to attack the line. Thereafter he lunched with the Chief of the French General Staff, General Gamelin. Driven on to the border with the Rhineland, Churchill peered over at the German side. Behind him on the French side, a large banner faced Germany proclaiming *Liberté, Egalité, Fraternité*. Opposite, on the German side, another banner replied *Ein Volk, Ein Reich, Ein Führer*.

X

The sense of foreboding and determination that animated Churchill as he gazed across to the German border was exactly the mood from which Chamberlain hoped to escape as he relaxed along Loch More, patiently waiting to feel a bite on the end of his fishing line. He had recently confided in his sister his expectation that Hitler had decided not to fight a war in the near future. Whilst the *Führer* might attempt to intimidate the British and French into a false move by holding troop manoeuvres near the Polish border, 'all my information' indicated that Hitler realized 'that he can't grab anything else without a major war and has decided therefore to put Danzig into cold storage'.[70]

Chamberlain was not the only player in the saga receiving 'information'. Through John King, its spy at the Foreign Office in Whitehall, Moscow had intercepted Nevile Henderson's communications from Berlin advocating further appeasement. This advice could not have encouraged the Soviets in their negotiations with the British for an anti-German pact. Yet the realization that there was a spy at work (King was eventually arrested in October) only added weight to Chamberlain's excuse (with Halifax's knowledge) to bypass the Foreign Office and to negotiate with Berlin through alternative channels. On 24 July, Dr Helmut Wohltat, one of Goering's entourage working on Germany's Four Year Plan, met with Chamberlain's special adviser, Sir Horace Wilson. With Chamberlain's full acquiescence, Wilson wrote down on 10 Downing Street writing paper a sketch for an Anglo-German non-

aggression pact that would also cover trade relations and – extraordinarily – disarmament. The account of these discussions from the German
side may have been deliberately over-optimistic as a means of trying to
steer Goering further towards the German 'peace party'. Whether or not
this was the case, it was reported back that Wilson, Sir Joseph Ball and
Robert Hudson (the Secretary at the Department of Overseas Trade) were
proposing that Britain and Germany should make a joint declaration
repudiating 'forcible aggression' as 'an instrument of international policy'.
Given that Hitler had already effectively promised this on the piece of
paper he signed at Munich – and had then proceeded to invade the Czech
state – such a proposal was surely the triumph of hope over experience. If
it was the basis of a serious British offer, then it suggested that experience
had also encouraged an overwhelming confidence in the power of the
three-line whip at Westminster. On the basis of his discussions with
Wilson, the German Ambassador reported to Hitler that Britain did not
regard itself unconditionally committed to Poland, that 'a programme of
negotiations' could be expected from London if the invasion of Poland
went ahead and that 'Wilson affirmed that the conclusion of an Anglo-
German entente would practically render Britain's guarantee policy
nugatory.' Trying to put his spin on events to the media, Robert Hudson
spoke freely to the *Daily Express* of his role in trying to organize a large
'peace loan' to Germany. Chamberlain was understandably furious to
read such loose talk in the national press. Attempting to limit the scale of
the damage, he claimed that Hudson had acted on his own initiative and
that no loan had been formally offered. Both the newspaper reports and
the German interpretation of the discussions may have been exaggerated,
but the central intent was clear enough: Britain was feeling the strain of
rearmament, believed Germany was too, and was desperately trying to
reach an agreement that would cool the atmosphere for both countries.
From such a détente it was hoped to draw the much needed peace
dividend.[71] Chamberlain was offering Hitler an inducement to turn away
from war and the Polish guarantee would only be honoured if the
German *Führer* really was determined to pursue war regardless of the
attractions of peace.

Whilst Wohltat and Wilson were engaged in talks, Chamberlain
unofficially sanctioned a commodity broker and doyen of the Germanophile Anglo-German Fellowship, E.W.D. Tennant, to visit the Reich's
Foreign Minister, Joachim von Ribbentrop, in Germany on 22 July.
Before leaving, Wilson had briefed Tennant 'that in no circumstances, was
he to mention to anybody the fact that he had had this conversation with
me or that he had been in any way in touch with the Prime Minister'.
Tennant had been told to make clear to Ribbentrop that there would be

British 'resistance' to 'further outbursts by Germany in Europe'. For his part, Ribbentrop stated that Germany wanted Danzig. Tennant floated the idea of a £100 million loan from Britain.[72] This was not all; Chamberlain proceeded to send Lord Kemsley to meet Hitler at Bayreuth five days later. Hitler told Kemsley that he was interested not in a loan but in the scrapping of the last vestiges of the Versailles Treaty. Next Chamberlain sanctioned Rothermere to write to Ribbentrop. For his troubles, Rothermere received a long diatribe about how Britain had poisoned relations with Germany. This was a dialogue of the deaf.

Relying on men like Wilson, Tennent, Kemsley, Rothermere and Sir Joseph Ball to transmit the diplomacy of hints and nudges to the Third Reich was a bizarre way for Chamberlain to try to improve international relations. The threat of espionage was not the only reason that had led him to resort to these unofficial means of conducting foreign policy. The official channels, and in particular the Whitehall end of the Foreign Office, had become clogged with too many sceptics of continuing with this sort of injury-time appeasement policy. Unlike official communications, if these unofficial links were revealed to public scrutiny, Chamberlain could always deny complicity. This was an admission that the Prime Minister was forfeiting his grip on the weaponry normally at a government's disposal. The reliance on covert diplomacy underlined that Chamberlain had, in effect, lost the public debate. There no longer existed any Cabinet consensus in favour of appeasement, still less of an all-embracing 'Establishment' attitude.

XI

On 19 August, Chamberlain was summoned back to London to address the unfolding crisis over Danzig. German pressure was mounting ominously on the Poles to cede the city and the surrounding 'corridor'. Halifax had reiterated to the Cabinet, shortly before it had gone its separate ways for the summer, that the fate of Danzig itself would not trigger the Polish guarantee but that if 'a threat to Polish independence arose from Danzig, then this country would clearly become involved'.[73] The manner of the latest Reich diplomacy gave grounds for apprehension that despite the official protestations, Hitler's appetite might not be limited to strictly former German areas of the Polish state any more than it had proved to be in the former Czech state. Against this general sense of foreboding, small glimmers of hope briefly sparkled. Rumours continued to circulate that Goering could yet be a bulwark for a peaceful solution against Ribbentrop and those Nazis identified in the 'war party'. Indeed, MI6 reported that Goering had indicated a desire to fly on a secret mission to Britain to meet Chamberlain. Covert plans were made to receive him at a deserted aerodrome on 23 August. From there he was to be driven to meet the Prime Minister at his country residence, Chequers. Secrecy would be maintained by giving the house's normal staff a day's leave. Their places would be filled by intelligence operatives. In the end there was no need for the secret service to be sent on a crash course in silver service. The prospect of a Goering initiative had to be shelved, overtaken by a momentous event. Late on the night of 21–22 August the Soviet Tass news agency announced that Ribbentrop was on his way to Moscow to sign a non-aggression pact.

The pact itself was signed on 23 August with the published details awaiting MPs as they hurried back to a hastily recalled Parliament the next morning. When the first news of the initiative reached Whitehall, Chamberlain had already drafted a warning letter to Hitler making clear that Britain intended to stand by her Polish commitment and that there would be no repetition of the uncertainty that had foreshadowed Britain's declaration of war in 1914 (although the unofficial diplomacy of the last few months had helped to do just that). By the time it reached Hitler that evening, it included a passage confirming that the Molotov–Ribbentrop pact would not alter Britain's determination.

None of the clues pointing to a rapprochement between Moscow and Berlin had been sufficient to dislodge the belief in Whitehall that something as ideologically illogical as a Nazi-Soviet pact could be imminent. Trade talks between the two rival totalitarian powers had been convened in February but they had not borne fruit. Nonetheless, Stalin's speech to the Party Congress in March had been low on the sort of anti-Fascist rhetoric that had become the stock-in-trade of such occasions and the propaganda war between the two countries had calmed down by the summer. As the summer wore on, more and more reports suggesting a thawing in relations between Moscow and Berlin were ignored or misinterpreted in Whitehall and by the intelligence services.[74] Given the number of spurious scare stories and deliberate misinformation emanating from sources 'close' to the Reich Chancellery at this time, the folly of not taking these rumours more seriously was understandable – at least until mid-August. By 17 August Molotov was aware that Ribbentrop was planning to visit Moscow within days with a comprehensive package of proposals.[75] When he arrived, Ribbentrop was able to offer Molotov in a matter of hours what the Soviet Foreign Minister had been unable to gain from French and British diplomats in months. British officials had procrastinated over Russian terms that appeared to give the Red Army the right to march into east European and Baltic countries on possibly dubious pretences and against the will of their governments. Anglo-

French diplomacy had sought to find a way in which an alliance could be concluded whilst preventing the Red Army from becoming such an uninvited guest. In contrast, the German proposals sought to encourage Stalin to regain countries that had once been within the domains of Tsarist Russia. The published text of the agreement proclaimed that the Soviet Union and Germany would enter into a non-aggression pact with one another for a minimum of ten years. Not only would they not attack each other, no support 'in any kind' was to be given to a third party at war with either of the two signatories. Left unpublished was a secret protocol delineating who would gain the spoils of this cynical marriage of convenience. Poland would be redivided between the two of them. Save for Lithuania which would be within the German sphere, the Baltic states would be regarded as within the Soviet 'sphere of interest' in the event of their 'territorial and political transformation'. Not just the Treaty of Versailles, but the Treaty of Brest-Litovsk was being reversed as both countries sought to reclaim what they had lost to the cause of 'self-determination' in the Great War.

Chamberlain and Halifax remained clear-headed about the bombshell that had been dropped. Neither of them had been overconfident about the military worth of the Soviet Union. Concerned primarily with diplomatic solutions, Chamberlain was not an expert on France's military preparation or strategic plans. His thinking implied considerable confidence in the ability of the French Army to hold back even the might of a *Wehrmacht* freed from having to fight simultaneously the Russians in the east. Furthermore, whilst the Molotov–Ribbentrop pact ensured the denial of Soviet resources to the Anglo-French in the event of war, it meant that the Reich would be supplied. This undermined one of London's central strategies: the gradual resource strangulation of the German fighting machine by an effective blockade.[76] These were considerable handicaps but Chamberlain could point also to a positive side on the balance sheet: Germany's new-found Communist associate made a mockery of Hitler's attempts to portray his ambitions as a crusade against the Red menace. In consequence, the prospect was further diminished of Germany being joined by any of the other Fascist powers in the event of war. When in May Italy had signed the Pact of Steel with Germany she had been told that there were no plans for war until 1942. Now that it was clear what Hitler really intended, Mussolini felt justified in excluding Italy from her obligations to stand by Germany. Japan was similarly unimpressed by Ribbentrop's initiative. Thus although the Molotov–Ribbentrop pact had dashed one British strategic hope – of the Reich having to fight a major war on two fronts – it had also (for the moment) removed any remaining

likelihood of the ultimate British nightmare of having to fight simultaneously against Germany in Europe, Italy in the Mediterranean and Japan in
Asia and the Pacific.

Recalled to Parliament on 24 August, MPs obligingly rushed through
an Emergency Powers Bill that day. Maintaining, however, that there was
little else for the legislature to do as the weekend approached, Chamberlain then saw to it that Parliament was adjourned again until the
following week. In fact, MPs needed to have few fears that this was a
deliberate ploy to prevent them obstructing a further act of Prime
Ministerial diplomatic audacity. Chamberlain's note to Hitler making
clear to him that the Molotov–Ribbentrop pact did not alter Britain's
guarantee was underlined the following day with the formal signing of
Britain's treaty of alliance with Poland. This gave legal status to the
guarantee of March and, coming with the news that Italy would not take
up arms, gave Hitler, poised to start the invasion, momentary pause for
thought. Whatever impression he may have given in the past, Chamberlain was now prepared to go to war if Hitler insisted on ignoring his
warning.

Britain's preparation for war did not preclude the hope for peace.
Making the warning to Germany emphatic was part of this process and
Chamberlain continued to watch in hope for a sign from Berlin that Hitler
was prepared to back down rather than go over the brink. If Hitler could
not be made to see sense, then it was hoped that he might be prevailed
upon to do so (or if not, to be overthrown) by those around him. To this
effect, rumours about Goering's efforts to prevent an Anglo-German war
continued to reach Whitehall. On 27 August Halifax accompanied
Goering's Swedish go-between, Birger Dahlerus, in a meeting with
Chamberlain at 10 Downing Street. Dahlerus insisted that Goering was
still working for peace. This was followed by the arrival of the hapless Sir
Nevile Henderson from Berlin. The British Ambassador brought news
that Hitler wanted Britain to appreciate that his proposed adjustments to
the Polish border were justifiable and that he wanted a new understanding
with Britain which included the safeguarding of her empire. Even at this
late stage, Henderson's analysis was certainly unrealistic and, according
to taste, craven. In the evening, Cadogan noted that Henderson's
suggestions for his talk with Hitler 'included offer of Non-Aggression
Pact with Germany! I managed to kill this with P.M. and H[alifax]'.[77]
Instead, Henderson was dispatched back to Berlin in order to deliver
Chamberlain's latest communication. Britain would welcome an attempt
at German-Polish negotiation to settle the outstanding border dispute.
Once any resulting agreement had received an international guarantee,
Britain would look to build a 'more complete understanding' with

Germany. Nonetheless, the Polish guarantee remained. Taking this line with Berlin, London proceeded to recommend to Warsaw that they negotiate terms with the Reich to settle the Danzig/Polish Corridor aspect of the dispute as quickly as possible. However, unlike the Czechs in September the previous year, the Poles knew that the guarantee prevented them from being left in the lurch. Combined with an overestimation of what patriotic zeal could do in the face of Panzer divisions, this reinforced their desire to stand up to the German menace. Chamberlain would have preferred the Poles to promote a spirit of self-sacrifice, but he was no longer prepared to desert them if they did not. In consequence, there was little of the pressure applied to the Poles that London had applied to the late Czech Government. As the historian John Charmley has put it, 'Beck was the beneficiary of Beneš calvary.'[78]

Birger Dahlerus returned to Downing Street on the morning of 30 August to assure Chamberlain that the Germans would offer a plebiscite in the Polish Corridor. For a brief moment the mood in Whitehall appeared to brighten under the impression that Hitler was looking for a face-saving way out of the crisis. This mirage soon disappeared. Rather than pursue a reasoned negotiation with the Polish Government, Hitler demanded that a top-level Polish delegation should arrive in Berlin and accept Germany's terms over Danzig and the Polish Corridor. If they did not arrive and sign up within twenty-four hours, Poland would be annihilated. Chamberlain suggested that this timetable was unrealistic and that the Germans should give the Poles more time to consider the situation. He allowed Dahlerus to use one of the telephones in 10 Downing Street to talk directly to Goering for clarification. Chamberlain then cabled the British Ambassador in Warsaw telling him to instruct the Poles to hurry over to Berlin to look at the terms. By the following day, Hitler's sixteen-point ultimatum had still not been communicated to the Poles despite his insistence that they had to sign immediately or face invasion. Nonetheless, shortly after 1 p.m., the Polish Ambassador to Germany, Josef Lipski, turned up to meet Ribbentrop. Lipski tried to telephone Warsaw for further instructions. He could not get through. The Germans had cut the line.

XII

Germany invaded Poland in the early hours of 1 September. The first reports of German bombing came through to the Foreign Office in London about three hours later, at 7.30 a.m. Churchill was awoken at Chartwell by a telephone call from the Polish Ambassador to inform him of the news, in itself an acknowledgement of his importance at the moment of crisis. Motoring up to London, he received a further message. It was from Chamberlain, asking him to meet him at Downing Street. This was not the first crisis in which Churchill had been called in to be briefed by the Prime Minister only to be released back to the backbenches at the meeting's termination. But if Churchill feared he would be shown enough detail to compromise him but not enough to offer him responsibility, his worries were soon laid to rest. The Chamberlain that greeted him in Number 10 was a seventy-year-old man who had given up on the quest for peace. The War Office had given the order for full mobilization and according to Churchill's later recollection, Chamberlain now 'told me that he saw no hope of averting a war with Germany'. Like Lloyd George in the last war, Chamberlain proposed to preside over a small six-member War Cabinet. That he was in earnest in his belief that peace could not be salvaged was clear – he asked Churchill to join in. 'I agreed to his proposal without comment', Churchill recorded, 'and on this basis we had a long talk on men and measures'.[79]

Since the occupation of Prague, Chamberlain had offered what one historian has called 'both a stick and a carrot'.[80] The carrot had dangled the hope that Germany and Poland would negotiate in a reasonable manner the detail of the border dispute over Danzig and the Polish Corridor (something neither party actually wished to do). If Germany turned away from the diplomacy of menace, Britain was willing to offer her considerable financial aid in transforming herself from a restrictive armaments-driven economy to a peaceful and more open-trading nation. But if Hitler refused this assistance, Chamberlain held the stick of the Polish guarantee: any attempt by Hitler to widen his interest in Poland beyond a peaceful settlement of Danzig and the Corridor would be regarded as a definite indication that he was intent on the sort of European domination that would have to be stopped by force. By 1 September Chamberlain appreciated that the carrot had scarcely even been sniffed: offered a transition to peace, Hitler had given the impression that he actually *preferred* war. Danzig could not be separated (as Chamberlain had originally hoped when issuing the guarantee) from Hitler's wider plans for a Poland whose independence as a nation he was determined to smash. Indeed, whatever may have been his hopes earlier in the year, when it came to the crunch Chamberlain showed every determination to declare war. For years he had been haunted by the Chiefs of Staff's worst case scenario: Britain dragged into war simultaneously with the three Fascist powers, Germany, Italy and Japan. September 1939 appeared to be an opportunity in which Britain would be restricted to war with only Germany. There would also be no complications in Britain having to promote the interests of the Soviet Union now that the

Kremlin had made a Faustian bargain with Berlin. These considerations eased Chamberlain's dilemma as did the news that the governments of the Dominions would come to Britain's aid. At the Cabinet meeting on the morning of 1 September, Chamberlain told his colleagues gravely that the 'events against which we have fought so long and so earnestly have come upon us. But our consciences were clear, and there should be no possible question now where our duty lay.'[81]

Although psychologically the decision had been taken, there was no immediate British declaration of war. France appeared to be wanting to delay and was insistent that Britain did likewise. With an expectant Parliament due to assemble at 6.30 p.m., the delay created difficulties and would be the natural parent of rumour and counter-rumour. Yet waiting for the French also had its uses. Fearing the possibility of an immediate *Luftwaffe* strike on London (as if the German Air Force did not have enough to do in Poland) Whitehall regarded every hour gained without the declaration going through as time won in which to crank the emergency regulations into action.

The impetus that seemed to be driving Britain inexorably towards war received a sudden check the following day. Hitler was said to be considering the prospect of an Italian-inspired peace conference and, despite Daladier's hostility, Bonnet was attempting to steer the French Cabinet towards advocating the scheme. Halifax, who had made clear to Mussolini's Foreign Minister, Count Ciano, that a conference could only take place if German troops were first withdrawn from Poland, argued in Cabinet that it was worth postponing until noon on 3 September the British declaration of war so that a chance could be given for this deliverance to take place. Ciano repeatedly made clear that he saw little prospect of the *Wehrmacht* moving back out of Poland. Given that Chamberlain agreed with his Foreign Secretary in stipulating that no conference could take place unless the Germans did first retreat, the prospect seemed a slim one. Nonetheless, in the afternoon meeting of the Cabinet both Prime Minister and Foreign Secretary put the case for postponing an ultimatum for at least another twenty-four hours so that Hitler might be given time to respond to the peace conference initiative. In fact, both men knew there was little prospect of this but it was worth exploring whilst they waited for Daladier to overcome the peacemongers in his government. It was primarily in order that London should not pre-empt Paris that it was proposed that no time limit on a British declaration was to be mentioned to the Commons. This was the major focus of division within the Cabinet. No one looked like making a stand in the cause of not declaring war. The divergence was between those who were prepared to wait, and those who were determined that a further delay would smack of irresolution. Hoare emerged as the most senior leader of this latter group of 'hawks' in the Cabinet, backed by Oliver Stanley, Malcolm MacDonald, Leslie Burgin, Walter Elliot and the ministers responsible for the army and the RAF, Hore-Belisha and Kingsley Wood. This was a sufficient quorum to demand immediate action or break the government. Since Chamberlain accepted the principle of war, there seemed little point in his destroying his own administration on the issue of how many hours should elapse before the deed was done. A prolonged delay in issuing the ultimatum was rejected. The Cabinet agreed that war would be declared at midnight. Nonetheless, Halifax telephoned Ciano asking him, rather desperately, to make a final effort to persuade Hitler to call off the attack and attend a conference. Ciano repeated his assessment that the *Führer* was not likely to do so.

By the evening a statement was expected in the Commons announcing a declaration of war. MPs had spent the afternoon congregating in the Smoking Room bar, fortifying their fighting talk with Dutch courage.[82] Chamberlain addressed the packed Commons chamber at 7.44 p.m. He did not mention a timescale for an ultimatum. What was he scheming? Although he made clear that no negotiations could take place until the Germans had begun retreating, the House was stunned to learn that

> If the German Government should agree to withdraw their forces, then His Majesty's Government would be willing to regard the position as being the same as it was before the German forces crossed the Polish frontier. That is to say, the way would be open to discussion between the German and Polish Governments of the matters at issue between them, on the understanding that the settlement arrived at was one that safeguarded the vital interests of Poland and was secured by an international guarantee.[83]

MPs had been here before. Eleven months previously on the brink of war, Chamberlain had appeased aggression and saved Czechoslovakia with guarantees that proved worthless in the face of the *Führer*'s uncontrollable appetite. The analogy was not lost on those MPs who had cheered then but were ready for war now. The mood in the chamber turned from expectation to anger. 'Chips' Channon noted 'the resentment against Chamberlain: all those who want to die abused Caesar'.[84] Standing in for Clement Attlee, Labour's deputy leader, Arthur Greenwood, rose at the dispatch box facing the Prime Minister. As he did so, Amery, demented with fury, shouted out from the Conservative benches, 'Speak for England.' It was a definitive moment. Greenwood announced that he was 'gravely disturbed' and that the whole House was 'perturbed' by the Prime Minister's statement. At a time when MPs were desperate for information, Chamberlain had spoken for only four minutes and had not even mentioned the nature or timing of a declaration of war. At 7.59 p.m., he rose again and in a brief statement that came close to pleading, he tried desperately to dispel the disastrous impression his earlier performance had given. He had now all but lost the House, and promising to try to give it a definitive statement the following day, he was relieved by the timely moving of the adjournment. By 8.09 p.m. he was back out of the chamber and hurrying down the corridor.

Halifax later noted that he had never 'heard the Prime Minister so disturbed' as when he reported the 'very unpleasant scene' he had just endured in the Commons chamber. Chamberlain realized that his statement had 'infuriated the House'. Worse, 'he did not believe, unless we clear the situation, that the Government would be able to maintain itself when it met Parliament next day.'[85] This opinion was confirmed by Margesson, the loyal Chief Whip, who feared the government might fall. Meanwhile, sitting up through a thunderstorm in his Morpeth Mansions flat with Boothby, Bracken, Sandys, Duff Cooper and Eden, Churchill was finding the silence from Downing Street increasingly ominous. The previous day, Chamberlain had asked him into the government but nothing had been heard since. Was he being double-crossed? Boothby assured him that this was the case and that tomorrow he should turn up to the Commons and oust Chamberlain from office. This was hot-headed talk. For the second time that day, Churchill wrote to Chamberlain encouraging him to end the delay and to confirm that he was sincere in the offer of the Cabinet place.

Chamberlain was not double-crossing Churchill, but the delay and his failure to bring either Churchill or other MPs more fully into his confidence naturally fuelled suspicious minds. Halifax again telephoned Paris, telling them to get a move on with their declaration. Meanwhile, the Chancellor of the Exchequer, Sir John Simon, shaken by events in the Commons, had joined the war party and with other members of the Cabinet holed up in his room, he insisted upon another meeting with Chamberlain in which a definite time would be confirmed for declaring war. Simon was the only minister who had also sat in the Cabinet of August 1914 that had declared war on the Kaiser's Reich. Then he had at first resigned and was only persuaded to stay when the German intention of invading neutral Belgium altered the complexion of the *casus belli*. The second time around, he had screwed his courage more firmly to the sticking place. Whilst Simon was impressing the French Ambassador with the need for a hasty declaration, Chamberlain got through to Daladier on the telephone, making clear that if France continued to prevaricate, 'it would be impossible' for the government 'to hold the position' at Westminster.[86] Big Ben struck eleven o'clock. Chamberlain agreed to convene the Cabinet again, the last time in its current composition that he would do so, at 11.30 p.m. A timetable was agreed: the Germans would be served with an ultimatum to withdraw from Poland at 9 a.m. If they had not intimated that they would do so within two hours, then Britain would declare war. On 3 August 1914, the Foreign Secretary, Sir Edward Grey, had looked out across the London night and observed that 'the lamps are going out all over Europe; we shall not see them lit again in our lifetime.' As Cabinet members went their separate ways just after midnight on 3 September 1939, there were few lamps to guide their way home. It was a blackout in preparation for an expected air raid. Rain lashed against windows and the only light came from the flashes of lightning that illuminated the night sky.

XIII

Britain declared war at 11 a.m., and France at 5 p.m. Chamberlain broadcast to the nation and at midday spoke in a similar and dignified vein to a House of Commons subdued and restrained in marked contrast to the previous evening:

> This is a sad day for all of us, and none is it sadder than to me. Everything that I have worked for, everything that I have hoped for, everything that I have believed in during my public life, has crashed into ruins. There is only one thing left for me to do; that is, to devote what strength and powers I have to forwarding the victory of the cause for which we have sacrificed so much. I cannot tell what part I may be allowed to play myself; I trust I may live to see the day when Hitlerism has been destroyed and a liberated Europe has been re-established.[87]

Five hours after war had started, a streamlined and reshuffled pack of ministers sat down around the Cabinet, now the War Cabinet, table. Simon stayed as Chancellor. Hoare too was included in his new office of Lord Privy Seal, his place at the Home Office taken by the nominally non-party Sir John Anderson. Chatfield, Kingsley Wood and Hore-Belisha retained their portfolios at defence coordination, the Air Ministry and the War Office. The addition was the new First Lord of the Admiralty, returning to the post he had held at the last outbreak of war with Germany in 1914. For ten years he had been a political pariah. To those in office during that time, he had represented the spectre of the uninvited guest, trying to rearrange the placements at the dinner table. Now his moment had come. The signal went out from the Board of Admiralty to the Fleet: 'Winston is Back.'

Fourteen

ASSASSINS IN THE SENATE

I

'Mr Churchill was born for Government,' declared the *News of the World*, 'and on rising to address the House for the first time in his new Office he placed his elbows on the despatch box with such easy familiarity that one could not imagine that he had been a back bencher for a decade.'[1] On his first day, he had returned to the same Admiralty House in Whitehall from where he had directed naval policy against the Kaiser's fleet a quarter of a century earlier. His secretary recalled him rushing up to the First Lord's Room and going 'up to a cupboard in the panelling. I held my breath. He flung the door open in a dramatic gesture – there, behind the panelling was a large map showing the disposition of all German ships on the day he had left the Admiralty in 1915.'[2]

In fact, it had not been Chamberlain's original intention to return Churchill to his old berth. Following the example set by Lloyd George in 1916, the Prime Minister had at first envisaged creating a small War Cabinet most of whose members – including Churchill – would be relieved of significant departmental concerns. In this plan, the three ministers responsible for each of the armed services would have been excluded from the War Cabinet. This, needless to say, was not to the liking of the indignant ministers concerned and it was only under pressure from them that Chamberlain – keen to avoid a major wrangle with colleagues at such a critical moment – backed down. Meanwhile the leaderships of the Labour and Liberal Opposition rejected the offer he made to them to join the government. The consequence of these developments was that the War Cabinet became a cumbersome nine-man committee of departmental heads. Listening to Chamberlain's first speech to the Commons after the declaration of war, Amery considered it 'good, but not the speech of a war leader'. An experienced observer of political life from both front and back bench over nearly thirty years, Amery thought that Chamberlain's oversized War Cabinet 'might work for a while, but I think I see Winston emerging as PM out of it all by the end of the year'.[3]

Amery's instinct about Churchill's fate reflected a marked shift in the new First Lord of the Admiralty's prospects. In the last months of peace, Anthony Eden had commanded the personal adherence of a larger coterie on the Conservative benches than had Churchill. Eden was also thought to enjoy more widespread appeal as a rival leader amongst the populace.[4] But, unlike Churchill, he had a tendency to limit the nuisance he was prepared to make of himself. This was a fatal flaw. Its reward was the Dominions Office, a position outside the War Cabinet. Resisting the temptation to create a fuss, the former Foreign Secretary's decision to accept this comparatively junior role excluded him from the high table of the war's prosecution. It was a commendable gesture of self-sacrifice, typical of his sense of patriotic duty. For his own career prospects it represented the worst of both worlds: membership of the government prevented him from leading backbench discontent if events took a turn for the worse whilst exclusion from the War Cabinet prevented him from developing his claims as a rival leader within the corridors of power. Unlike Churchill, he had made himself irrelevant to the course of events. This suited Chamberlain and Halifax. The refusal of the official Opposition to join a government of national unity ensured that the Premiership and the leadership of the Conservative Party would remain indivisible. Of the two 'anti-appeasement' Tories who could emerge to threaten Chamberlain's position, Eden, although attracting more adherents on the Tory benches, was now marginalized as a challenger whilst whatever success Churchill made of his new job, he was hardly a mainstream Conservative Party man.

Having overcome the parliamentary wobble of 2 September, Chamberlain's own position appeared as secure in war as it had been in peace. He was weary at the prospect of having to face Labour and the Liberals' continued jeers and sneers from across the Commons chamber, but he could hardly be surprised by their preference to pursue the role of loyal opposition rather than accept what would have been, in practice, a secondary role in a coalition government led by a man they despised. In some respects, their decision not to serve made matters simpler for him. He could bring their leaders into his confidence as and when the needs of national interest appeared to demand it whilst at all other times enforcing his overlordship with a Commons majority that still exceeded 200. Whatever their qualms at the nature of its prosecution, the Opposition were all but united in supporting the armed crusade against Fascism. A cross-party 'truce' was quickly concluded to ensure that the composition of the Commons would not be altered whilst the war lasted, the Quinquennial Act (the law limiting the length of a Parliament to five years) being suspended. This removed the spectre of a mandatory general election by November 1940 if the war had not been concluded by that time.

Despite Chamberlain's instinctive self-confidence, he was deeply anxious about the war's possible length and its consequences. He continued his regular correspondence with his two sisters, Ida and Hilda, admitting to them that his life had deteriorated into 'one long nightmare'.[5] Even the avoidance of serious fighting by the British and French forces in the first six weeks of the conflict did not prevent him confiding 'how I hate and loathe this war. I was never meant to be a War Minister.'[6] After visiting the British Expeditionary Force in France and inspecting the defences of the Maginot Line in December, he reported back that 'it sickened me to see the barbed wire and pill-boxes and guns and anti-tank obstacles, remembering what they meant in the last war.'[7] Nevertheless, he was in agreement with his French counterparts on the essential point of military strategy: that time was on the side of the Allies. Both Chamberlain and Daladier believed that the lead in armaments built up by Germany during the years of appeasement would be whittled away in the months of conflict ahead. In contrast to the enormous resources that Britain and France could extract from their respective empires, the Nazi Reich would weaken under the stranglehold of an economic blockade. In sprinting too soon, Germany would be outpaced by the more gradual and sustainable build-up of her two western enemies. It was therefore crucial that the Germans did not seize the opportunity to convert this long-distance marathon into a 100-metres dash. An armed stand-off was to be encouraged rather than the launch of a premature assault on the German war machine that would give it the incentive to strike back before the Allies had time to make up for their previous deficiencies in rearmament. It was particularly important during this period of frozen hostility – soon christened the 'Bore War' or 'Phoney War' – that the *Luftwaffe* should be provided with no excuse to launch reprisal raids on the great industrial cities that were working overtime to provide the Allies with an arsenal to match that at Hitler's disposal.

Back in July 1939, when Chamberlain had hoped that the then peacetime British rearmament programme would prove to be sufficient to make Hitler 'realise that it never will be worth while' declaring war, he had explained his military thinking to his sister. 'That is what Winston & Co. never [seems] to realise. You don't need offensive forces sufficient to win a smashing victory. What you want are defensive forces sufficiently strong to make it impossible for the other side to win except at such a cost as to make it not worth while'.[8] The assumptions underpinning this analysis were that France could hold off an assault in the west; Germany would be brought down by an economic blockade or an internal coup against Hitler; and that Germany could not withstand a war of three years' duration. 'It won't be by defeat in the field,' he further assured, 'but by German realisation that they *can't* win and that it isn't worth their while to go on getting thinner and poorer.' Getting the German people to turn on Hitler was the goal, and Chamberlain had 'a "hunch" that the war will be over before the Spring'.[9] Encouraging an internal coup was the rationale behind the decision to send the RAF over Germany to drop a bomb load of nothing stronger than propaganda leaflets. With hindsight, all of Chamberlain's assumptions were fantastic errors of judgement, exercises in the most hallucinogenic wishful thinking. The belief that the war could be won without carnage was understandably attractive to a Prime Minister contorted in revulsion at the prospect of having to refight the horror of the Great War. But he was not alone in this comforting delusion. It was shared by many of his advisers and colleagues and even those like Churchill who preferred a more active prosecution of the war believed that time and the French Army were invincible assets on the Allied side.

Chamberlain's aversion to fighting the Germans head-on equally suited the French. With a landscape scarred by two previous German invasions within the living memory of the elderly, it was an understandable French attitude to seek an away fixture third time around. A variety of alternative fronts, including the Balkans, were canvassed instead. Even bombing Germany's oil supply in Baku was suggested – despite the fact that this would mean attacking the non-combatant Soviet Union. Whilst the *Wehrmacht* was engaged in invading Poland in September 1939, the French had mobilized eighty-five divisions to face Germany's thirty-four on the border. Yet the desire to postpone the date and move the location ensured that, minor excursions apart, nothing was done to take advantage of this predominant position. French political differences and insecurities were added to by the sense that perfidious Albion was not really sincere. Given that only four British divisions had arrived in France by the end of the first month of the conflict it was hardly surprising that the German propaganda loudspeakers picked up the incantation 'Where is the British Army?' to bray over the French border. This was the price paid for Chamberlain's long-held refusal over the previous five years to guarantee western Europe with anything more than another 'contemptible' little army (as the Kaiser had referred to the British Expeditionary Force in 1914) rather than a field force worthy of the name. Unfortunately although Britain had more ships and better aeroplanes than France, this preponderance in the Allied cause's division of labour was not particularly visible to worried French citizens who were wondering whether London really was going to fight down to the last Frenchman.

News that Britain's figure of one million unemployed had actually risen higher in the first few months of the war further contributed to the belief that the Chamberlain Government was failing to transform the country into a war economy capable of closing the gap with the German Reich.[10]

The overwhelming pre-war desire to preserve peace had resulted in a paucity of thought on the subject of how, in the event of an armed conflict, war with Germany might be prosecuted and what would be the objective of victory. Over at the Foreign Office, Cadogan at last exercised his mind on the question of Britain's war aims. Posing the questions proved much easier than finding the answers. War had been declared to save Poland but almost nothing had actually been done to this effect. With Poland's speedy liquidation, Britain's attempts to force the Germans to surrender their conquest were complicated by the fact that the eastern half of the country had meanwhile been seized by the Red Army in conjunction with the secret protocol attached to the Molotov–Ribbentrop pact. If Britain was fighting for the freedom of Poles, then ought she not now to be equally at war with the Soviet Union? The more the possibilities were pondered, the less palatable they became. Cadogan therefore settled on the safer and more limited objective that Hitler's removal should be the central war aim. Chamberlain felt likewise and was not interested in the peace offer Hitler made in his Reichstag speech of 6 October that would have left Germany in possession of all her conquests. 'The difficulty is that you can't believe anything Hitler says,' Chamberlain reminded his sister; 'the only chance of peace is the disappearance of Hitler and that is what we are working for.'[11] He elaborated on this theme a month later:

> To my mind it is essential to get rid of Hitler. He must either die, or go to St Helena, or become a real public works architect, preferably in a 'home'. His entourage must also go, with the possible exception of Goering, who might have some ornamental position in a transitional Government. Having once got rid of the Nazis, I don't think we should find any serious difficulty in Germany over Poland, Czechoslovakia, Jews, disarmament, etc.[12]

At times Chamberlain seemed to articulate the fight against Fascism in the language of a nursery governess. It is surprising to find him so simplisticly convinced that major wars could be ended as easily and unmessily as they were started. Furthermore, believing in the folly of the Versailles Treaty and the prospect that a fresh Carthaginian peace might be demanded of the Germans, he feared that 'our real trouble is much more likely to be with France.'[13] Obsessed with the 'fanatic' who had double-crossed him at Munich, he did not see Germany as a threat without him. This contrasted with the approach of French policy makers who, facing the prospect of a third invasion of their soil by Germany since 1870, believed that the aggressive polity within Germany ran deeper than the poison emanating from the one man and his inner clique currently at the country's head. According to this view, the problem would not be solved merely by fighting a war to shuffle which group of right-wing German nationalists continued to direct their country's affairs. The trouble was that neither London nor Paris wanted to see the Red Flag flying from the Reich Chancellery; many wanted to see it even less than the swastika. Considerable precision within the fog of war was needed to engineer a result in which a new regime in Berlin would be strong enough to maintain the pre-1938 status quo, but not sufficiently self-confident to seek to hold on to its subsequent thefts. A war to surgically remove Hitler and his inner circle was as problematic as one to crush all the militaristic elements within the German nation once and for all. The only thing more desirable than an easy and bloodless victory was one that was likely to produce a lasting peace.

Refusal to deal directly with the *Führer* encouraged the attempt to seek out those in the German High Command who might achieve Chamberlain's goal – Hitler's overthrow. Goering's Swedish go-between, Birger Dahlerus, continued to flit around Whitehall for a time but with the *Reichsmarshall*'s claim to be a potential leader of the peace party increasingly resembling a mirage, there were no more than half-hearted attempts made to engage seriously with Dahlerus. In fact, Chamberlain's colleagues appeared to be resigned to the fact that there was little they could do to instigate an internal coup in Berlin. When in October the possibility was raised with the War Cabinet of discussions between two British agents and representatives of German 'generals' who were said to be keen to negotiate, ministers were at first uneasy. Cadogan noted that even Halifax had spent too much time listening 'to Winston on the subject of "beating Germany". We must try every means of helping G[ermany] to beat herself. . . . PM frightened by the Cabinet.' According to a new recruit to his secretariat, John Colville, Chamberlain believed that these links might form the basis for serious negotiation whilst 'stipulating that Hitler himself shall play no part in the proposed new order. In return for a change of régime (or at least a modification), restoration of frontiers and disarmament, the PM would be prepared to agree to economic assistance for Germany, to no demand for reparations, and to Colonial discussions. He wishes, however, to insert some safeguards for the Jews and the Austrians.'[14] These hopes crashed when at Venlo on the Dutch-German border the two British agents instrumental in setting up the negotiations were arrested by the SS. The discussion with German dissident figures had, it now embarrassingly transpired, actually been with Nazi double-agents.[15] The deception ended any meaningful attempt sanctioned by Chamberlain to negotiate peace along these lines – such subsequent feelers as there were to German dissident figures never got round the simple truth that, ultimately, the would-be conspirators could not deliver.

Early indications suggested that most Britons supported the general manner in which Chamberlain was conducting the war.[16] Nonetheless, he was a seasoned enough politician to know how quickly public moods and appetites could change. Even greater than his apprehensions that French revanchists would prolong the war unnecessarily was his fear that British pacifists would try to stop it prematurely. He confessed that he had 'always been more afraid of a peace offer than of an air raid' since 'it was too early for any hope of a successful peace negotiation, the Germans not yet being sufficiently convinced that they could not win.' In the space of three days in the week leading up to Hitler's October peace offer, more than three-quarters of the 2450 letters Chamberlain received from the public favoured – in some shape or form – suing for peace.[17] If Britain should suffer serious reverses, then there remained the possibility that this mood would find expression in Parliament. A small number of Labour MPs centred around Richard Stokes and George Lansbury were promoting the pacifist cause in unlikely tandem with those fellow travellers of the right who, for a variety of motives, still hoped to find some accommodation with Germany. Apart from businessmen whose motivation in this respect ran little deeper than a simple calculation of profit and loss, those who took this desire for peace to the perimeter fence of high treason were for the most part an eccentric collection with minimal following. Even the amateur dictator, Sir Oswald Mosley, had urged his Fascist sympathizers to support the British war effort (although in 1940 this was not enough to prevent his incarceration). More worrying was the attitude of the former war leader and the politician whom Chamberlain had always hated most. Lloyd George had adopted an extremely defeatist attitude and was said to be keen to seek out a peace offer possibly brokered by Roosevelt if Britain's chances of winning through were thought to be less than 50/50.[18] Whatever role the Welsh Wizard was proposing for himself in the event of a further deterioration in the country's position, Chamberlain did not trust him and was determined to avoid a situation in which he would be forced to call upon his talents.

Within the government, the Under-Secretary of State at the Foreign Office, Rab Butler, gave the impression of being the minister keenest to keep an open mind on how far the war should be taken. In early 1940 he appeared prepared to explore the possibilities of a negotiated peace and was looking to an unholy trinity of the Pope, the American President and the Italian dictator to find a way out of the minefield. If his diary is to be believed, Butler maintained that Halifax held out a similar, if distant, hope.[19] Again, little was done to encourage the initiative. Luminaries of the National Peace Council, a collection of thinkers, thespians and theological faint-hearts, who wrote to Chamberlain begging him to find a realistic peaceful solution, misunderstood the Prime Minister's resolve. What drove the 71-year-old was the stubborn tenacity that had driven him as a young colonist to continue growing sisal long after the crop had repeatedly failed and as an ever hopeful statesman had led him to attempt the accommodation of Hitler's desires no matter how difficult the latter made the task. Now the task confronting him was to get rid of that 'accursed man' and Chamberlain was no less determined to see the task through to its successful conclusion whatever the likes of George Bernard Shaw and Sybil Thorndike might think.[20] This did not prevent some from seeking to make trouble. On 11 October the *Daily Mirror* gave Churchill the credit for insisting in Cabinet upon the rejection of Hitler's peace offer, despite the fact that Chamberlain had been equally opposed to it. Clearly intended to damage the Prime Minister, the story was an embarrassment to Churchill who wrote speedily to Chamberlain deploring the attempt 'to make mischief between us' and assuring him that he had not circulated the information to anyone 'outside the secret circle'. Chamberlain took a generous view, advising Churchill to pay no attention to it.[21] Churchill was speaking no more than the truth when on 12 November he broadcast to the nation that 'you know I have not always agreed with Mr Chamberlain; though we have always been personal friends. But he is a man of very tough fibre, and I can tell you that he is going to fight as obstinately for victory as he did for peace.' When Chamberlain showed him the telegram he had sent Roosevelt rejecting parley with Hitler, Churchill, momentarilly overcome, wept with admiration, before blurting out, 'I'm proud to follow you!'[22]

II

In the first months of the war, it was Churchill who asserted himself as the most newsworthy of Chamberlain's ministers. The navy was the only one of the three armed forces that had a technical and numerical superiority over its German counterpart. During the 'Phoney War' it was also the service that most regularly engaged the enemy. Although there were serious setbacks including the sinking of HMS *Royal Oak* in its base at Scapa Flow, there was also much to cheer about. Churchill made the most of successful action, especially the scuttling of the German pocket battleship *Graf Spee*, the rescue of captured British sailors from the hull of the *Altmark* and the defeat of Hitler's 'secret weapon' – the magnetic mine. The First Lord of the Admiralty possessed a natural flair for news management. This reached its most extreme limit when he claimed that the Royal Navy had sunk half of the U-boat fleet despite the wealth of evidence to the contrary. Nonetheless, Churchill was able to report accurately to the Commons that after the first six months of the war less than half the tonnage of war and merchant shipping had been lost than in the equivalent period in the Great War.

From the start, it was Churchill's speeches and broadcasts that did most to elevate his status. His statement to the Commons on 26 September detailing the fleet's work since the declaration of war was the first of his major bravura performances as First Lord. Harold Nicolson observed Chamberlain and Churchill sitting together on the government front bench, the one 'dressed in deep mourning', the other 'looking like the Chinese god of plenty suffering from acute indigestion'. After Chamberlain had sat down to barely a murmur of approval, Nicolson recorded the immediate effect induced by Churchill:

> One could feel the spirits of the House rising with every word. It was quite obvious afterwards that the Prime Minister's inadequacy and lack of inspiration had been demonstrated even to his warmest supporters. In those twenty minutes Churchill brought himself nearer the post of Prime Minister than he has ever been before. In the Lobbies afterwards even Chamberlainites were saying 'We have found our leader.' Old Parliamentary hands confessed that never in their experience had they seen a single speech so change the temper of the House.[23]

Thomas Jones now maintained that 'Winston is the only Cabinet Minister who can put things across in an arresting way to our people. The PM is costive and dull and talks of endurance and victory in the most defeatist tones.'[24] Indeed, the historian John Charmley has compared Churchill's position with that occupied by Kitchener in the Great War: 'he was taken by the nation as a symbol of the determination to win the war, and if he was damaged in the eyes of the public, then the war effort and the reputation of the Government would suffer accordingly.'[25] This attitude was shared by some of those who had worked for Churchill personally. In February 1940 Violet Pearman who had been his secretary throughout the period of his wilderness years wrote to him from her home where at the age of forty-four she was already fatally ill. She assured him of his 'heart of gold' and let him know that 'here in Edenbridge one humble person follows your joys and griefs with a very full heart. I am very proud to hear your name spoken frequently in this small market town by all sorts and conditions of men, and to hear the pride and confidence which your presence in so vital a post brings to all.'[26] So much for the aphorism that no great man is a hero to his butler. Indeed, it was ironic that the government minister who was most sniffy about Churchill's performances should bear that very name. Rab Butler described Churchill's broadcast of 12 November to John Colville, as 'beyond words vulgar'. Still, as Colville, who agreed that the speech was 'boastful', could not help observing, 'the City take a favourable view (War-Loan rose a point!).'[27] In his broadcast of 21 January Churchill compared the actions of the neutral countries in pandering to Germany to their feeding a crocodile in the hope that it would eat them last. This, Halifax maintained, undid much of the diplomatic work the Foreign Office had been undertaking to win over the neutrals' confidence. Churchill apologized to the Foreign Secretary whilst reminding him that 'asking me not to make a speech is like asking a centipede to get along and not put a foot on the ground.'[28]

In general, Whitehall regarded the invasion of the Churchillian rogue elephant with decidedly mixed feelings. Lord Stanhope, Churchill's predecessor at the Admiralty, was particularly sneering, gossiping to Amery that 'Winston's first act of state on reaching the Admiralty was to order a bottle of whisky' and doubting that he 'will stay the course of administrative work after years of soft living'. Amery, who knew Churchill rather better, thought that, whilst 'there is some force in that', Stanhope underrated Churchill's 'power of nervous output and willpower'.[29] Indeed, the problem was not whether Churchill could take the pace but the fact that those around him could not. Daily he dispatched a barrage of minutes in which he aired aloud ideas and questions as they came to him – often to the exasperation of those who had to answer them. Chamberlain got particularly irritated about receiving long letters from the First Lord whom he saw personally every day in any case, and after a frank talk, prevailed upon Churchill to curtail the annoying habit. During February 1940, Churchill began affixing labels demanding 'ACTION THIS DAY' on paperwork to which he wanted priority given. By April, with major operations being implemented in Scandinavia, Chamberlain told his sister that Churchill's work habits were 'most wearing' to all around him:

> He goes to bed after lunch for a couple of hours or so and holds conferences up to 1 in the morning at which he goes into every detail, so I am informed, that could quite well be settled by subordinates. Officers and officials in his own and other departments are sent for and kept up until they are dropping with fatigue and Service Ministers are worn out in arguing with him. I say to myself that this just the price we have to pay for the asset we have in his personality and popularity, but I do wish we could have the latter without the former.[30]

Churchill was not prepared to restrict his canvas to his own department, another technique destined to be unpopular with Cabinet colleagues. Having spent so long prophesying war, he was eager to take the lead in its prosecution, a trait aided by the rest of the government's desire to take as little offensive action as possible. The hope that the demands of his own department would keep him too busy to meddle as an amateur strategist for the whole war proved illusory. Churchill was determined to become a de facto Minister for Defence and involved himself in as many aspects of the policy structure as he could. By the time policy options reached the War Cabinet they had already passed through the Chiefs of Staff and the Military Coordination Committee. Established in October 1939, this last committee consisted of the three service ministers (Kingsley Wood, Hore-Belisha and Churchill), the Minister for Supply (Burgin) and the increasingly redundant Minister for Defence Coordination (Chatfield). Churchill was also a member of a further War Cabinet subcommittee under Hoare's chairmanship, the Land Forces Committee. From the outset Churchill argued in it for expanding the army to twenty divisions ready for combat on the continent within six months and forty within a year. Anything less, he maintained, would weaken the resolve of the French to stand their ground in the face of a German onslaught. With Hore-Belisha's backing, the committee proceeded to recommend to the War Cabinet eleven divisions ready to leave the country within six months, twenty divisions within a year and a total of fifty-five a year later (drawn from a slightly smaller population, the British Army had had a hundred divisions in 1918). Chamberlain, however, maintained that the needs of the air force should continue to have priority and that a decision on the equipping of the army should be deferred until a comprehensive study of all three services (and in particular the RAF) had been undertaken.[31] Churchill was adamant that the French could not be let down in this respect and when Chamberlain conceded the point in the Cabinet, Churchill sent him a note:

> My dear Neville,
>   I hope you will not think it inappropriate from one serving under you, if I say that in twenty years of cabinets I have never heard a more commanding summing-up upon a great question.[32]

Chamberlain, whose notorious susceptibility to flattery surely did not extend as far as this bit of trowel work, passed on the contents of the note to his sister Ida, concluding, 'I need hardly say perhaps that I had come down in favour of the solution he had advocated.'[33] As it transpired this was not quite the end of the matter and in February Churchill had to defend his position vociferously in the Military Coordinating Committee against attempts to scale down the rate of diverting resources to the army. 'It would be a most dishonourable thing,' Churchill assured his colleagues, 'if the size of our Army were reduced to a mere 36 divisions when the French, with a much smaller population and only half the manufacturing capacity, had 110 in the field.'[34] Although an expected German invasion of France in November failed to materialize, there remained continual cause for apprehension. Keen to preserve their neutrality, in September 1939 the Belgian Government had refused military discussions or joint operations with the British and French. Given that the Maginot Line stopped at the Belgian border, this was particularly inconvenient for Allied strategists who hoped to plug the gap between the Line and the English Channel with the British Expeditionary Force. A German push into the neutral Netherlands would bring London within range of the *Luftwaffe's* medium-range bombers and fighters.

These worries were compounded by the total breakdown of respect between Hore-Belisha and Lord Gort, the BEF's Commander-in-Chief. Informed by the Duke of Gloucester of the situation, King George VI was said to be horrified at the state of relations between his Commander in the field and the Secretary of State in London and, it seems, pressed Chamberlain to act against Hore-Belisha accordingly. This put the Prime Minister in an embarrassing position having previously given his colleague the impression of confidence to the extent that he wanted him to serve at the War Office throughout the length of the war. Nonetheless, Chamberlain decided to grasp the nettle and, without warning, on 4 January 1940 he summoned Hore-Belisha and offered him a transfer to the Board of Trade, or failing that, the Ministry of Information. Hore-Belisha refused the offer and was, consequently, sacked altogether. Churchill offered him his sympathy and his advice that he should have taken the Board of Trade, but no more. 'The world and particularly Whitehall love a victim,' noted a sympathetic 'Chips' Channon after listening to Hore-Belisha's resignation speech in the Commons: 'How he has fallen; a fortnight ago he was surrounded and flattered by MPs soliciting favours, today he is almost a political outcast.' There were few cheers when he sat down.[35]

If the Secretary of State for War was dispensable, then Chamberlain knew that the First Lord of the Admiralty, with his popular support in the country, was not. With their respective wives, Churchill and Chamberlain had dined together in the Admiralty on 13 October 1939. Despite years of association, four of which (1924–9) they had sat in the Cabinet together, it was the first time they had ever dined together socially. The Prime Minister impressed Churchill by reminiscing upon his career as a Bahaman sisal grower, the details of which the First Lord had not known.

Churchill later wrote that 'this was really the only intimate social conversation that I can remember with Neville Chamberlain amid all the business we did together over nearly twenty years.'[36] In fact, most of Chamberlain's political peers could have made a similar claim. There is little record of him socializing informally with Baldwin either. Chamberlain devoted his emotional energies to his family rather than his colleagues. He had got to the top by mastery of his job, not through back-room wheeling and dealing. 'He was quite conversational for once,' noted John Colville after a brief car ride with Chamberlain, 'but his favourite topic is the weather.'[37] Indeed Colville, who greatly admired the Prime Minister, later contrasted his manner with that of Churchill:

> Chamberlain was austere, and he seldom said to me anything not strictly related to business. At week-ends he retired to Chequers, where there was only one telephone (and that in the pantry). He disliked being disturbed, telephonically or otherwise, at weekends or after dinner at 10 Downing Street. He never took a Private Secretary with him to Chequers; nor did he ever invite the members of his staff to lunch or dine with Mrs Chamberlain and himself. That was in marked contrast to Winston Churchill, who treated his Private Secretaries as part of the family.[38]

By November 1939, Chamberlain was again labouring under another onslaught of gout. On at least one occasion the attack was so bad that he had to be physically carried from his rooms in Downing Street to the Cabinet Room.[39] A less stoic figure might have decided that this was cause enough to quit, but such was not in Chamberlain's make-up. In January 1940 thoughts of resignation were countered by the fact that (as he cumbersomely phrased it to his sister), 'I don't see that other to whom I could hand over with any confidence that he would do better than I.'[40] Whenever possible he kept to his routine. Every morning he would join his wife Annie for a perambulation around the lake at St James's Park, acknowledging the greetings of passers-by as they went.[41] Although a personal detective walked several paces behind, security in the midst of a war was felt less necessary than at the end of the twentieth century, after fifty years of peace.

Chamberlain made what appeared to be a recovery from the gout attack that hit him towards the end of the year and by April 1940 Colville was noting, 'his incredible capacity for hard work, and his apparent immunity from fatigue continue and seem even to increase as the problems become more difficult and the days heavier with work. His seventy-one years lie very easily upon his shoulders.'[42] Indeed it was the tenacity of temperament and capacity for hard work that most impressed both Churchill and Chamberlain about each other now that they found

themselves working together again. Asked by Chamberlain to accompany
him for the first time to the Supreme War Council in Paris, Churchill was,
according to Chamberlain, 'in the seventh heaven at being asked to come
and declared that he had never enjoyed two days more'. As Chamberlain
pointed out to his sister, for all Churchill's 'violence and impulsiveness' he
could be 'very responsive to a sympathetic handling. To me personally he
is absolutely loyal and I am continually hearing from others of the
admiration he expresses for the PM.'[43] On the return journey across the
Channel on board HMS *Boadicea*, one of the officers observed the scene:
'the neat figure of Neville Chamberlain approached, surrounded by his
retinue like a popular master at a preparatory school conducting the
Sunday walk. One or two of the boys preferred to trudge along by
themselves. Among these was Winston Churchill.' Chamberlain went up
to the ship's bridge but got cold and had to have soup brought to him.
Churchill meanwhile had ensconced himself in the warmth of the ward
room drinking port, sucking a cigar and leafing through the pages of
Blighty magazine, a glorified girlie mag popular with sailors. From deep
within the ward room could be heard his distinctive growl, 'Tell the Prime
Minister to come and have some gin.' The First Lord of the Admiralty
subsequently went missing. He was eventually discovered sitting on a
table in the stokers' mess deck, 'swapping yarns'.[44]

III

Two of the raw materials that Germany needed to sustain its war effort
were oil and iron ore. The non-aggression pact entitled her to continue
purchasing oil from the Soviet Union and, fearing the alternative of
invasion, Romania also supplied Germany on a limited basis. Cutting
these supplies appeared to the Anglo-French allies as an attractive quick
route to short-circuiting the German war machine without having to
confront it head-on across the western front. Although Chamberlain was
not prepared to risk a French plan for a landing in Salonika to open a
Balkan front, he found much more appealing the prospect of cutting off
Germany's iron ore supplies from Scandinavia. The French and British
navies were already preventing Germany from receiving ore from her
traditional Spanish supplier, and the other deposits in Lorraine were some
miles within the French border. As a result, neutral Sweden had become
Hitler's primary ore supplier. The source was in the Gällivare ore fields in
the far north of the country within the Arctic circle. Between May and
November it could be shipped to Germany through the Gulf of Bothnia
(the northern stretch of the Baltic between Sweden and Finland). During
the winter months, however, the freezing conditions in the Gulf meant

that the ore had to be exported through the North Sea from the Norwegian port of Narvik. To avoid ships being sunk by British action, the export route hugged the Norwegian coast so as to be within the neutral country's three-mile limit of territorial waters.

An operation to sever Germany from its Scandinavian supplier hinged upon action from the Royal Navy. As First Lord, Churchill had early on been working on various schemes to achieve this result. There were a number of logistical problems, not least of which was the likely attitude of the *Luftwaffe* to the presence of His Majesty's fleet blocking the route to the German ports. Churchill was slow to appreciate the devastating effect that air power could have on a flotilla and it was not until January 1940 that he was at last persuaded to give up the idea. Less risky than allowing the fleet to become sitting ducks was the alternative of mining Norwegian territorial waters. The problem with this was that in doing so Britain would be interfering with the sovereignty of a neutral nation. The argument in the plan's defence, that the sacrosanct nature of Norway's waters had already been violated by German vessels, would not necessarily be sufficient to calm non-aligned international opinion at a time when the attitude of the United States was potentially crucial.

The War Cabinet was still grappling with this problem when a further act of aggression provided an opportunity to act. On 30 November 1939, the Soviet Union attacked Finland. Yet, instead of being pulverized by its mighty neighbour, the Finns fought back and for the first few weeks of the war delivered a humiliating rebuff to a Red Army that appeared to exemplify the incompetence that its detractors had always said it would display in combat. Some of those on the right in Britain and (especially) France who had balked at guaranteeing Poland now became excited at the prospect of aiding the noble Finns. The far right in France believed that an opportunity had been created to switch the emphasis of the war into an assault on Bolshevism. In Britain, there had emerged a sentiment that saw – thanks to the Molotov–Ribbentrop pact – the ideologically rival Nazi and Communist regimes as the obverse and reverse of the same totalitarian coinage. Having proved unable to rescue Poland, Chamberlain feared that Britain and France would suffer an immense loss of international credibility as the defenders of small nations if they were seen to sit back and allow Finland to be devoured by the Soviet Union. On the other hand, directly assisting the Finns meant fighting the Soviets. This was inescapably the case even if the act was conveyed as an arm's length operation with a remit strictly localized and limited to seeing the Reds off Finnish property. On the evidence of the Russians' first few weeks of war, the operation could possibly be attained very quickly and without extending the conflict needlessly (after all, British military assistance to the 'Whites' in the Russian Civil War had not degenerated into a full-scale war between the two countries), but the hazards remained enormous, and potentially deadly. Against the risks, intervention offered a huge reward. Under the pretext of involving themselves in the Finnish struggle, the British and French would cross Scandinavia and occupy the Gällivare ore fields in the process. Chamberlain approved of this scheme in principle, believing that severing Germany from its ore supplies could be 'one of the turning points of the war', dealing the Reich 'a mortal blow'. Backed by the advice of the Chief of the Imperial General Staff who considered the Germans 'inexperienced in combined operations', Chamberlain maintained that even if the Germans retaliated by seizing bases on the coast of Norway, 'it was very doubtful whether they could ever over-run a large part of the country'.[45]

On 27 December, the War Cabinet agreed not to send British 'volunteers' or aircraft crew to the Finnish war, 'such action', as Chamberlain pointed out, 'being reminiscent of "non-intervention in Spain"'. But, the Prime Minister did back Churchill's alternative scheme of cutting off the ore trade from Narvik. As the First Lord pointed out, if this act provoked the Germans into invading southern Scandinavia, then Britain would be justified in moving in and occupying the Gällivare ore fields. The problem was the likely attitude of the Norwegian and Swedish governments, both neutral, to Britain's proposed action. Chamberlain believed that the two countries 'would protest, but not violently' and that British action could proceed shortly afterwards – but only once Britain was 'quite sure that there were no very alarming reaction to our communication'.[46]

The reluctance of the Scandinavian governments to fit in with Britain's strategy was a setback for those like Churchill who were keen to press ahead regardless. Nonetheless, he continued to have proposals sent to him for the mining of Norwegian waters around Narvik and the disabling of the port facilities at Oxelösund from where the iron ore made its summertime route. The Director-General of the Ministry of Economic Warfare advised the War Cabinet on 2 January 1940 that once the Swedish ore supply had been fully cut off, which could take a year, the effect would be 'decisive'. This was bad advice since German stockpiles were being badly underestimated, but it was the information on which the British Government had to make its decisions at the time. Chamberlain again raised the possibility that a British action to sever the supply might trigger a German invasion to get there first. When he asked what would happen if Sweden joined the German side, Churchill insisted that such an act would likewise give the British an excuse to move in and occupy the northern ore fields, an idea that the Chief of the Imperial General Staff (CIGS), General Ironside, regarded as militarily impractical.[47]

Increasingly, Chamberlain began to veer towards Churchill's position and in the War Cabinet of 12 January he agreed to have the plans to capture the ore fields – even if they involved Norwegian and Swedish opposition – examined by the Chiefs of Staff.[48] At the Supreme War Council in Paris on 5 February, Chamberlain agreed a strategy with Daladier that reversed previous hesitancy over entanglement in the Finnish conflict. Feeling the pressure of the French right, Daladier was insistent that the Finns should be aided. A 'volunteer' force of two to three divisions should be dispatched to help the Finns repel the Soviet invaders. In the course of this action the Swedes and Norwegians were to be leaned upon to provide a right of way for the Anglo-French initiative. Whilst exercising that right, the Anglo-French would occupy the Swedish Gällivare ore fields. The Norwegian ports of Stravanger, Bergen and Trondheim were also to be secured by 20 March. Delaying beyond this date, as Chamberlain subsequently told the War Cabinet, would be to risk their falling into German hands first. Backed by the Prime Minister, Churchill was keen to concentrate on seizing Narvik first, and only once this was achieved should Trondheim be occupied. Stravanger and Bergen would have to wait.[49] Vital weeks were lost without even the decision to lay mines being implemented. Consulted on the matter, Clement Attlee and the Labour leadership voiced objections to mining the territorial waters of neutral Norway. The Dominion governments were equally uneasy. Citing the likely attitude of the United States as a further consideration, Chamberlain argued for postponing the mine-laying until some act of German provocation provided a clearer pretext. Reluctantly, Churchill was forced to bow to his senior.[50] On 4 March, the Chiefs of Staff argued against the plan to assist Finland because of Sweden's refusal to allow Allied troops to pass through her territory.

This was not the end of the matter, and Chamberlain remained keen to send the Finns warplanes. The decision was a risky one, but so was doing nothing. If the Soviets succeeded in wiping Finland off the map, then there was the possibility that this would be sufficient to prompt the Germans to seize the Gällivare ore fields before the Red Army did. The other problem was that basing his evidence on the strength of their current performance, Chamberlain dangerously underestimated the military potential of the Soviet Union in the same fatal way as would Hitler in launching Operation Barbarossa the following year. Colville recorded Chamberlain on 15 February exhibiting an 'over-confident' attitude in thinking that 'once our Hurricane aircraft, and other, foreign aircraft, are in action on the Finnish side "there won't be a Russian left in Finland".'[51] On 11

March he agreed to send eight bombers to Finland immediately with a further forty-two to follow.[52] Daladier appeared to be on the brink of resignation and the British War Cabinet agreed to proceed with the dispatch of an expeditionary force to land at Narvik and proceed via Gällivare to the Finns' aid even although both the Norwegian and Swedish governments still refused to permit passage or get involved in anything that might make them a target for invasion by Germany. Of the force of 50,000 that Daladier had unrealistically promised the Finns by the end of the month, only 300 Anglo-French 'volunteers' had arrived by the time the war ended promptly on 13 March. Peace was achieved at the expense of the Soviets' shaving off a relatively minor amount of Finnish territory (in particular the Karelian isthmus) and imposing upon her restrictive ordinances, which nonetheless fell well short of the price of occupation suffered by the less fortunate Baltic states. Having digested the news, Chamberlain seemed relieved that this meant shelving an intervention plan that offered 'many possibilities of disaster'.[53] The episode quickly passed in British politics but not so in the affairs of France. Daladier's failure to dispatch 'volunteers' in time proved sufficiently contentious to bring about the fall of his divided government, his position as Premier passing to Paul Reynaud.

The conclusion of the Russo-Finnish War meant the jettisoning of the Gällivare ore field plan and the War Cabinet took the decision to disperse the forces prepared for the expedition.[54] However, it was not long before attempts to prevent the trade via Narvik were back on the agenda. Reynaud pressed not only for operations in Norwegian waters but also for the sending of British submarines into the Black Sea with action there and in the Caspian 'to paralyse the entire economy of the USSR before the Reich can succeed in mobilising it to her advantage'. Chamberlain was determined to resist this scale of action against the Soviet Union and consequently sought to refocus the enthusiasm for a forward policy to the Scandinavian war theatre. At the Supreme War Council on 28 March, Chamberlain successfully urged Reynaud to have the Rhine mined whilst the Royal Navy did likewise in Norwegian waters. Both these proposals had the backing of Churchill, who considered himself a personal and political friend of the new French Prime Minister. The Narvik operation was planned to commence on 5 April but was put back in large part because of dissent from the French (stirred up by Daladier) who were reluctant to agree to the Rhine being mined for fear of German retaliation.[55] The three-day delay proved particularly unfortunate. In the meantime, Chamberlain spoke publicly to the delegates of the Conservative Party caucus's Central Council. 'Hitler', he announced, had 'missed the bus'.

Mining the Norwegian waters commenced on 8 April. Butler had told Colville that the policy represented the triumph of the '"Winston" policy ... over the "Halifax" policy', the Foreign Secretary having only given his consent 'because of his loyalty to the PM', and that Chamberlain 'for his part is not over-optimistic, but feels that after the expectations aroused by the meeting of the Supreme War Council the other day some effective action must be taken. He does not believe (like some people) in "action for action's sake", but he recognises the importance of the psychological factor in the present war and the necessity of throwing occasional sops to public opinion.'[56] Hitler's rationale for taking action did not concern itself with sopping public opinion. The news that reached London on 9 April was astounding. Notwithstanding the recent signing of a non-aggression pact with Copenhagen, Germany was invading Denmark and was making landings in Norway. Germany had been planning the invasion since December and was seizing the opportunity before Britain's clumsily obvious operation could crank into action. Narvik, Trondheim, Bergen and Stravanger were seized by the Germans in a dazzlingly executed series of operations. Paratroopers were dropping from the skies everywhere. By nightfall, Oslo had fallen. Far from missing the bus, Hitler was driving it, right past the British waiting at the bus stop.

The daring German action did not confound Whitehall in the way that might be expected. Churchill remained optimistic, believing that the German action played into British hands by providing a carte blanche for a full-scale action. Halifax felt equally relieved.[57] Indeed, the early actions by the Royal Navy justified this optimism with seven German destroyers sunk in the Bay of Narvik. Relative to the size of the German fleet this was a loss of strategic importance. Encouraged by these early engagements, the War Cabinet decided to proceed with a landing at Narvik. Halifax favoured the French plan, believing that Trondheim, the ancient Norwegian capital, was of more strategic importance. Chamberlain also wavered towards this view. From Trondheim, Norway could be dissected and the northern German force cut off. Briefly dithering himself, Churchill eventually succeeded in impressing the need to prioritize Narvik's capture. However, taking Narvik was delayed by Major General Mackesy, the commanding officer for the assault, who wanted to hold off until the snow had melted and he could be reinforced by sufficient artillery to attempt a landing against a potentially larger force defending a naturally fortified position.

As late as 20 April, Chamberlain was confident of victory and believed the Germans would be ejected from Narvik within a fortnight.[58] In fact, the campaign was fast degenerating. Some of the reasons for this were the result of the shortcomings of Britain's rearmament programme over the previous years. It was even reckoned that a successful capture of Narvik and Trondheim would necessitate the use of almost all Britain's available anti-aircraft guns.[59] Other reasons had to do with insurmountable difficulties presented by the strategy for the campaign. Without a proper base within range, the British suffered from a lack of fighter aircraft support. An attack without air superiority could only be extremely costly and this was the price paid for vacillating long enough to let the Germans seize the Norwegian airfields first. Military officers charged with the assault blamed the politicians for providing them with insufficient resources to carry out the task. On the other hand ministers in Whitehall wanted to see officers displaying a measure of the risk and daring that the Germans had so brilliantly shown days earlier. The attempt to avoid a direct assault on Trondheim by making landings to the north at Namsos and to the south at Andalsnes ran into heavy air attack from the *Luftwaffe*. On 27 April the decision was taken to evacuate all operations except for Narvik. The British landing party was evacuated from Andalsnes on 1 May and from Namsos two days later. With the surrender of the Norwegian resistance to the Germans on 4 May it was debatable how long even a successful British assault at Narvik could be held without a relief operation tantamount to a full-scale invasion of the whole country. In any case, by the time the landing at Narvik took place on 12 May the ice in the Gulf of Bothnia was breaking up and ore exports could reach Germany via that route. The campaign had been misconceived and poorly executed. Briefed of British intentions by the work of his intelligence services, Hitler assured Mussolini that he had invaded Norway in order to deny the British Narvik and Trondheim: 'It is indeed obvious that the possession of Norway, or of Sweden, by the British would have had catastrophic consequences for Germany, while on the other hand a German success in those sectors cannot have a decisive bearing on the outcome of the war. The conflict will be decided solely in the West!'[60]

IV

The unfolding course of the Norwegian campaign put enormous strain on all the members of the War Cabinet. Churchill had not had an easy or productive time chairing the Military Coordinating Committee and was glad to hand it over to Chamberlain. Views and attitudes were changing with each twist and turn. Colville could record in his diary on 23 April that Chamberlain was 'depressed – more by Winston's rampages than by the inherent strategic difficulties'[61] whilst two days later noting Churchill's profession of 'absolute loyalty' to Chamberlain and that the two of them were getting on 'admirably'.[62] Colville's intelligence was that 'Winston himself was being loyal to the PM, but his satellites (e.g. Duff Cooper, Amery etc.) were doing all in their power to create mischief and ill-feeling.'[63] In truth, Chamberlain's support for Churchill was based on political calculations deeper than personal feeling alone. Colville maintained that the Prime Minister was wisely humouring Churchill because of the unassailably popular position the latter had built up in the country. Chamberlain simply could not risk the prospect of Churchill flouncing into the Commons chamber and claiming that after delay had been heaped upon delay over his plans, he had been denied responsibility to act effectively in the prosecution of the Norwegian campaign.[64] Tardy operations in the Scandanavian theatre of the war had already caused Daladier's replacement with Reynaud in France and Chamberlain had no wish to be usurped for similar reasons by Churchill. To Sir John Reith, formerly the BBC's Director-General, who had been appointed Minister for Information in the new year, Chamberlain gave the impression that he was rather less than overawed by Churchill's 'inflated' reputation – one which was ripe for some 'debunking' even if it 'would have to be done by someone else'.[65]

For his part, Churchill's main grumble was not with his Cabinet colleagues so much as with the Chiefs of Staff. Attempts to guide a coherent plan from a committee of three separate service chiefs, each determined to protect his own service's best interest, were inevitably difficult, whatever the rationale for the existing relationship. Churchill made clear to Chamberlain that he wanted real authority over the conduct of the war. From the perspective of his own personal security as Prime Minister and remembering the fate of Asquith at the hands of Lloyd George during the last war, there was something to be said for Chamberlain giving Churchill what he wanted. On the other hand, there was reason to worry about what strategic blunders an unfettered Churchill might commit in such a role. Chamberlain saw a way of squaring this circle by proposing to give Churchill a new outpost on the Chiefs of Staff subcommittee via Major General Ismay, who would lead a central committee. Retaining the chairmanship of the Military Coordinating Committee in Chamberlain's absence, Churchill would thereby 'give guidance and direction to the Chiefs of Staff Committee, who will prepare plans to carry out the objectives which are given to them by him'.[66] The War and Air Ministers, Oliver Stanley and Samuel Hoare (who had replaced Hore-Belisha and Kingsley Wood respectively), expressed deep unease about this arrangement and threatened to resign. Chamberlain called their bluffs by saying that in such a scenario he himself would return the seals of office and allow Churchill to become both Prime

Minister and Minister of Defence. Faced with this option, Stanley and
Hoare backed down. With his leverage over the Chiefs of Staff duly
strengthened, Churchill expressed himself gratefully to Chamberlain. In
fact, without the power to compel, the new arrangement still left him
short of becoming effectively defence supremo. This suited Chamberlain
perfectly.[67]

Keeping his team united was a key concern of the Prime Minister and in
the midst of the Norwegian campaign's hopes and disappointments, the
rival claims and contrasting advice, his handling of his colleagues was
assured. In contrast to the unity of the War Cabinet, division and
fractiousness were increasingly in evidence on the backbenches. Ceding
the additional powers for the war's strategic prosecution to Churchill was
one way of ensuring that the First Lord would not be tempted to appeal
for support from this quarter. Maintaining a united front was particularly
important at a time when a public split would have triggered a far more
serious crisis than that created by the sacking of Hore-Belisha in the
relatively quiet days of January 1940.

Despite his huge majority, Chamberlain was by May 1940 facing the
most serious expressions of parliamentary discontent since the outbreak
of war. News of the Norwegian situation was compounded by mounting
exasperation at Britain's evident rearmament deficiencies. Reports con-
cerning the weak state of the army's armoured back-up were causing
particular outrage (the British Army in France was supported by only
seventeen light tanks and a hundred infantry tanks – three-quarters of
which were armed with nothing heavier than a machine gun). It was clear
that the opposition parties would seek to capitalize on these shortcomings
in the two-day adjournment debate scheduled to commence on 7 May.
This was understandable and, regardless of the supposed 'truce', the
Opposition would have been doing less than its job, and no service to the
country, had it shirked its duty in this respect. Evidence was also
mounting that serious discontent on the Conservative backbenches was
spreading beyond the machinations of the usual suspects. This was
serious, although without a division expected from the adjournment
debate, the government front bench were bracing themselves for a
difficult cross-examination at the witness box rather than a verdict from
the jury. It was important in these circumstances that the ministers in the
dock all corroborated each other's stories.

One of the questions facing the government in preparing for the
adjournment debate related to whether discontent on the backbenches
could be reconciled and becalmed by emollient words and deeds. At least
three semi-organized groups could be discerned, with some of their
associates intermingled. Styling themselves as the All-Party Action Group,

one array of 'progressive' Tory MPs were convening with centre-left politicians under the chairmanship of Clement Davies, a future leader of the Liberal Party. Few of those monitored as associating in this circle had demonstrated much loyalty towards Chamberlain and their motives were presumed to be hostile. Another closely related group comprised those Tory MPs who had looked to Eden as their leader during 1938 and 1939. Again, there was antipathy towards Chamberlain from these members but some at least claimed a residual interest in party loyalty and might be tamed by judicious handling. In April a third body, the 'Watching Committee', was established by the diehard Lord Salisbury. This was not purely an anti-Chamberlain cabal, but rather a genuine attempt to monitor the government's activities and hold it accountable to backbench concerns. At its first convocation, Amery took the chair and Salisbury communicated its views to the Prime Minister and Foreign Secretary. The news was not good. By the end of April one of the Watching Committee's members, Harold Nicolson, recorded the 'glum' mood and 'the general impression is that we may lose the war.'[68] The question for members of the War Cabinet concerned which of them would be on the receiving end of this discontent.

The backbench malcontents were united in the belief that heads should roll, but divided over how many. This raised the inevitable problem facing revolutionaries – how far should the revolution be taken? On the one hand there were the latter-day Girondists, who wanted to reform the *ancien régime*. These were Tories satisfied with keeping Chamberlain and a Conservative-led National Government, but anxious to free it of its dead wood, in particular the Air Secretary, Hoare, and the Chancellor, Simon. More than any of the other senior politicians, these two men were being blamed for the failures not just of recent months but, with convenient selectivity, for those of the last few years. On the other hand there were Tory rebels who resembled Jacobins. They regarded it as cosmetic and dishonest to scapegoat the two least popular members of a government for policies and attitudes that were essentially shared by the Prime Minister. Pruning the rose would only revitalize it. What the Tory radicals wanted was not another Cabinet reshuffle – the fabled rearrangement of deckchairs upon the *Titanic* – but rather the creation of a genuine all-party coalition including the Labour and Liberal leadership in a government of national unity. Only then could the ship of state change course. Bringing Labour into the government would at last harness the full potential of the trades union movement to the war effort (strikes were still a commonplace in 1940). Furthermore, creating this latter-day Committee of Public Safety would complete the palace coup since because of Labour's likely reluctance to serve under him in a coalition of this kind, Chamberlain would be forced out of the Premiership.

Who would succeed Chamberlain and lead this new combination was a matter of debate. Some Tories still hoped there could be a new all-party government whilst keeping the old Prime Minister. According to the *Evening Standard*, briefed directly or indirectly by Salisbury, the Watching Committee was coming down in favour of a cross-bench coalition in which the existing unpopular ministers would be dropped (presumably Hoare and Simon). This again was reminiscent of the French Revolutionary Girondists who, with the intention of limited goals, allowed the creation of the Committee of Public Safety which, passing into the hands of Jacobins, was to become the instrument of their own persecution. Some Watching Committee members hoped that such a fate could be prevented even if Labour's joining the government was dependent upon Chamberlain's resignation. In such an event, they hoped that Halifax would hold the new coalition together as a replacement Prime Minister.[69] This last strategy was agreeable to the left-wing Labour politician, Stafford Cripps, who anonymously briefed the *Daily Mail* to call for a new War Cabinet with Halifax as Prime Minister and Churchill, Lloyd George, Eden and Labour's Herbert Morrison as non-departmental ministers.[70] All manner of other combinations presented themselves as the sense of crisis deepened. 'People are so distressed,' wrote Harold Nicolson, 'that they are talking of Lloyd George as a possible P.M. Eden is out of it. Churchill is undermined by the Conservative caucus. Halifax is believed (and with justice) to be a tired man.'[71] In fact Lloyd George was never likely to be chosen in a decision which ultimately rested with King George VI, particularly if the advice of an outgoing Chamberlain or any of his acolytes was to be sought and given prominence.

The government Whips were alive to the mounting danger from the backbench but unsure how best to counter-attack. For his part, Chamberlain tried to talk up the positive aspects of the Norwegian campaign. To sceptics like Nicolson, the attempt to suggest that 'the balance of advantage rested with us' was so obviously untrue as to be counter-productive.[72] Chamberlain's attempts to assert that the campaign was far from a disaster were also out of synch with the initial strategy of the government Whips who put it about that the campaign was all Churchill's fault.[73] However, maintaining that the paucity of weapons at the disposal of the armed forces was the fault of the man who had spent the last five years campaigning for rearmament was rather more difficult. No less importantly, with a major Commons debate pending, the government needed to keep Churchill's debating prowess harnessed to its own side. The pro-Eden MP, Jim Thomas, wrote to the like-minded Lord

Cranborne on 4 May, noting the tactics of the Whips' Office for the Norway debate, at first 'endeavouring to throw the responsibility' for the campaign's failure on Churchill 'but they eventually thought it wiser to make use of him'.[74] In the circumstances this was to prove more sensible.

V

The Commmons adjournment debate commenced ominously for Chamberlain on 7 May. As he entered the Chamber derisive jeers of 'Missed the bus!' rang out at him from the opposition benches.[75] His speech was less than entirely convincing. He tried to minimize the operation: the withdrawal was 'not comparable to the withdrawal from Gallipoli' (a sly reference to the First Lord of the Admiralty's great failure of the First World War); 'not much more than a division' was involved; 'the Germans had far heavier losses in warships, in planes, in transport and in men.' Finally he addressed the calls of those who wanted a War Cabinet composed of ministers without departmental responsibilities by pointing out that 'in taking decisions it is impossible to ignore those who have to carry them out' and he alerted members to the new arrangements regarding Churchill and the Chiefs of Staff Committee.[76] Once his bugbear, the First Lord was now both a shield and a sword for the Prime Minister.

Any thought that Chamberlain's performance would prove sufficient to restore order amongst his own ranks was almost immediately dispelled when the Great War naval hero and diehard Tory MP for Portsmouth North, Sir Roger Keyes, stood up to speak. Impressively decked out in his Admiral of the Fleet uniform with a full armoury of six layers of medal ribbons 'because I wish to speak for some officers and men of the fighting, sea-going Navy who are very unhappy', the sea dog unburdened his unease at a situation in which his own offer of assistance had been spurned. Maintaining that there should have been a full assault on Trondheim, he nonetheless distanced himself from one of the logical conclusions of his alternative strategy, that it was the First Lord who had got it wrong. Reflecting on the lessons of Gallipoli, Keyes said of Churchill:

> at that time, he had many enemies, who discredited his judgement and welcomed his downfall. Now, however, he has the confidence of the War Cabinet, as was made abundantly clear to me when I tried to interest them in my project; he has the confidence of the Navy, and indeed of the whole country, which is looking to him to help to win the war. . . . I beg him to steel his heart and take the steps that are necessary to ensure that more vigorous Naval action in Norway is no longer delayed.[77]

The words of a services' old hand were supplemented by those of a
political veteran. Like Churchill, Leo Amery had spent a decade in the
political wilderness, repeatedly passed over for office by those he regarded
(often with reason) as his intellectual inferiors. It was particularly irksome
to him that he had been denied the opportunity to complete the imperial
project of Joseph Chamberlain because of the preferment prejudices of
Old Joe's son, Neville. Inevitably, some of this bitterness crept into
Amery's speech as he reflected on the failings of a decade which had
produced 'peace-time statesmen who are not too well fitted for the
conduct of war. Facility in debate, ability to state a case, caution in
advancing an unpopular view, compromise and procrastination are the
natural qualities – I might almost say, virtues – of a political leader in time
of peace. They are fatal qualities in war. Vision, daring, swiftness and
consistency of decision are the very essence of victory.' This was, in effect,
a message to send for Churchill, and in doing so, Amery did not miss the
chance to pass his own 'locust years' testament on the decade of his
exclusion from office:

> In recent years the normal weakness of our political life has been accentuated
> by a coalition based upon no clear political principles. It was in fact begotten
> of a false alarm as to the disastrous results of going off the Gold Standard. It is
> a coalition which has been living ever since in a twilight atmosphere between
> Protection and Free Trade and between unprepared collective security and
> unprepared isolation. Surely for the Government of the last ten years to have
> bred a band of warrior statesmen would have been little short of a miracle.

He then quoted Cromwell's advice to John Hampden on the need to find
amongst Roundheads the temperament of Prince Rupert's cavaliers –
'men of a spirit that are likely to go as far as they will go'. Speaking 'with
reluctance, because I am speaking of those who are old friends and
associates of mine' Amery was the first of the senior Tory senators to
plunge the dagger into Chamberlain: 'This is what Cromwell said to the
Long Parliament when he thought it was no longer fit to conduct the
affairs of the nation: "You have sat too long for any good you have been
doing. Depart, I say, and let us have done with you. In the name of God,
go!" '[78] With that, Amery sat down. Following on from his 'Speak for
England' interjection on 2 September, he appeared to be getting the hang
of the punchy interjection, belying the oft-repeated suggestion that he
might have ended up Prime Minister if he had been half a head taller, and
his speeches half an hour shorter. Chamberlain had long since shut
himself off from the jibes and assaults of his more excitable detractors but
like Caesar wilting under the pain of Brutus's dagger, he appeared

particularly jolted by the words of a former colleague of long and honourable standing.

The extraordinary internecine blood sport unleashed on the floor of the Commons chamber encouraged the Labour leadership to rethink its strategy. When pressed by Clement Davies to make the debate a vote of censure, Attlee, aware of the size of the Conservative Party on a three-line whip, had originally argued that this strategy should be avoided as likely to be counter-productive. The spectacle of self-inflicted blows made him think again. When Herbert Morrison rose at the opposition dispatch box on 8 May it soon became clear that the Labour Party had scented blood. Morrison attacked 'the whole spirit, tempo and temperament of at least some Ministers' and of Chamberlain, Simon and Hoare in particular both before and during the war. 'If these men remain in office,' asserted Morrison, 'we run grave risk of losing this war.' In consequence, Labour would force a division, making a vote on the adjournment – for all intents and purposes – a vote of censure. As Morrison sat down, Chamberlain rose in his place and in a handful of ill-chosen words presented his tormentors with a stick with which to beat him: 'I do not seek to evade criticism, but I say this to my friends in the House – and I have friends in the House. No Government can prosecute a war efficiently unless it has public and Parliamentary support. I accept the challenge. I welcome it indeed. At least we shall see who is with us and who is against us, and I call upon my friends to support us in the Lobby tonight.'[79] The repeated reference to his 'friends' at a time when everyone was adopting a 'nation pulling together' tone was unfortunate. It was Chamberlain's lifelong hate figure, Lloyd George, who seized the moment to capitalize on the error. Having waited so long to get his own back, the political colossus of the Great War could not but have relished the moment of at last joining the dagger-plunging ceremony and his opening remark – 'I intervene with more reluctance than usual' – brought the inevitable horse-laugh from those around him. Criticizing the failure of Britain to make the most of her opportunities in Norway, he maintained that he did not think that Churchill 'was entirely responsible for all the things that happened there'. At this, Churchill jumped up to make clear that he took 'complete responsibility for everything that has been done by the Admiralty'. Lloyd George, however, advised him not to 'allow himself to be converted into an air-raid shelter to keep the splinters from hitting his colleagues'. A further attack on Chamberlain led the Prime Minister to demand 'the meaning of that observation'. This was another mistake and Lloyd George rubbed in the Prime Minister's comments about appealing to his 'friends'. According to Lloyd George, Chamberlain had

met this formidable foe of ours in peace and in war. He has always been worsted. He is not in a position to appeal on the grounds of friendship. He has appealed for sacrifice. The nation is prepared for every sacrifice so long as it has leadership, so long as the Government show clearly what they are aiming at and so long as the nation is confident that those who are leading it are doing their best. I say solemnly that the Prime Minister should give an example of sacrifice, because there is nothing which can contribute more to victory in this war than that he should sacrifice the seals of office.[80]

Revenge is a dish best enjoyed cold. It was, according to Colville, watching the debate from the gallery, 'the most forceful speech he has made for years: I could see that he held the House spellbound as he flung his arms about . . . The Opposition shouted themselves hoarse as L.G. became more vehement and less and less reasonable. Horace Wilson, who sat with me in the official gallery, said that the hatred written on their faces astonished him: it was the pent-up bitterness and personal animosity of years.'[81] Looking up into the Strangers' Gallery, 'Chips' Channon 'caught the eye of poor Mrs Chamberlain who has hardly left the House for two days: she is a loyal, good woman . . . She was in black – black hat – black coat – black gloves – with only a bunch of violets in her coat. She looked infinitely sad as she peered down into the mad arena where the lions were out for her husband's blood.'[82] The Prime Minister was taking blows from all corners; those who attempted to speak in his defence performed so poorly or were so discredited that they only succeeded in making matters worse for him. All now depended on the closing performance from his trump card. At 10.11 p.m., the First Lord of the Admiralty rose to wind up the debate for the government. Chamberlain's fate was in his hands.

Rather than accepting Lloyd George's invitation to distance himself from his colleagues, Churchill chose to accept the blame head-on. Most of his speech was devoted to defending the Norwegian campaign's execution, 'offering', as Amery noted in his diary, 'in his most persuasive manner a quite incomprehensible account'.[83] It was a courageous and barnstorming performance that took the fire back to the enemy camp. He was repeatedly heckled by Labour backbenchers, one of whom from the outspoken Scottish contingent – and in the early stages of inebriation – took unreasonable exception to Churchill's accusation of 'skulking'. These irrelevant distractions squandered the Opposition's attempts to put the First Lord on the ropes. When eventually he could be heard above these shifting frequencies of white noise, Churchill turned to the issue of using what was in effect a vote of censure in the form of an adjournment vote, one he condemned for being issued without proper notice, it having only been announced at 5 p.m. Turning on those who had been outraged that Chamberlain had called upon his 'friends', Churchill was not afraid to land punches: 'Exception has been taken because the Prime Minister said he appealed to his friends. He thought he had some friends, and I hope he has some friends. He certainly had a good many when things were going well!' He concluded by urging: 'Let pre-war feuds die.'[84]

Even a natural critic like 'Chips' Channon admitted in his diary that Churchill 'made a slashing, vigorous speech, a magnificent piece of oratory ... How much of the fire was real, how much ersatz, we shall never know, but he amused and dazzled everyone with his virtuosity.'[85] The question remained as to whether it had been enough to save Chamberlain.

VI

With the division called, MPs filed out of the chamber and into the lobby. Chamberlainites jeered 'quislings ... rats' at the Tory rebels as they passed through the 'noes' lobby, the latter responding with rather milder charges of 'yes-men'.[86] At least one MP was seen with tears streaming down his face as he betrayed his party leader. Tories who were spied passing through the opposition lobby included known mavericks and eccentrics – the eternal awkward squad of all political life. Familiar critics of appeasement trooped through from the diehard right of the party – Richard Law, Admiral Keyes, Lord Wolmer – and from the left – Bob Boothby, Harold Macmillan and those who had previously looked to Eden for salvation. They were joined by the former ministers, Amery, Winterton, Duff Cooper and Hore-Belisha. With five years' experience in the Whips' Office, Captain Charles Waterhouse summed up the rebels as 'the usual crowd of Anglo-American – gently disgruntled – sacked – aspirant – Glamour, with a few well-meaning sentimentalists and amateur strategists thrown in ... Hitler will thank Thor for our quislings.'[87] If this had represented the full picture, then the Whips might have been able to relax. Alarmingly though, the familiar malcontents were being joined by others, not only traditional loyalists but even some who had been prominent appeasers in the past. Amongst this group was Lord Hailsham's son, Quintin Hogg, who had won the 1938 Oxford by-election on a stridently pro-Munich platform. Salisbury had advised members of the Watching Committee not to vote against the government, but Nicolson found 'on reaching the House that so many unexpected people such as the Service Members and Lady Astor are determined to vote against the Government that we have no alternative'. He expected about thirty would do so.[88]

For their cause, the Whips too had been hard at work. The Chamberlain camp hoped to limit the damage, considering a majority of a hundred or more to be within the margin of safety.[89] Chamberlain's parliamentary private secretary, Lord Dunglass (the future Prime Minister, Alec Douglas-Home), had, as Amery put it, 'been tremendously busy trying to persuade the revolting Unionists to vote for the Government "just once more", promising them that Neville would see them next day and tell them about his plans for reconstruction, even hinting that he might sacrifice Sam [Hoare] and Simon to assuage them'.[90] This had only limited success. Iron had entered the soul, and the performance of Keyes, Amery and the others in striking down the Prime Minister in full public view had given courage to the timid.

Shortly after 11 p.m. the Tellers returned to face the Speaker with the result of the vote. A tense and packed chamber heard the news: 'Ayes to the right 281, Noes to the left 200.' There was a gasp. Then pandemonium broke out. The government's majority had been cut from over 200 to eighty-one. Forty-one of its MPs had voted with the Opposition.[91] Half of them had not previously shown marked disloyalty to the leadership. Another eighty-eight had not voted. Half of this last number were unable to be present in the House (through illness, infirmity, or overseas military service) or were absent on a pre-arranged mutual pairing with an opposition MP. Thus, almost 40 MPs deliberately abstained as a mark of protest.[92] Taken together with those who had voted with the Opposition, more than a fifth of the government's backbench were in open revolt. On a three-line whip, this was a disastrous result for Chamberlain. It was far worse than the division on Munich when twenty-two Tories had abstained and none had voted against him. With the announcement of the vote, the Labour MP, Joshia Wedgwood, stood up and started singing 'Rule Britannia', joined in the display by Harold Macmillan. Chamberlain was serenaded by a demented chant of 'Go, go, go, go!' The Chief Whip, Captain Margesson, signalled 'to his henchmen' to rise and cheer the 'pale and angry' Prime Minister as he 'stood up, erect, unyielding, sardonic, and walked out past the Speaker's chair and over the feet of his colleagues who then followed'.[93] 'No crowds tonight to cheer him', reflected Channon, 'as there were before and after Munich – only a solitary little man, who had done his best for England.'[94]

VII

What did the vote mean? Was it the end of the road for the Prime Minister? The first task was to separate the revolutionaries between Girondists and Jacobins, the former might yet be persuaded to support a

suitably contrite and reformed Chamberlain administration whilst Jacobins were irreconcilably and ideologically hostile. It was clear that some
of those who had abstained were doing so largely as a protest vote against
the continuation in office of the Cabinet's less popular performers, Simon
and Hoare. Chamberlain soon became the recipient of anxious assurances
from a number of Girondists pleading that their rebellious action on 8
May had in no sense been a personal stand against him.[95] He reflected on
the 'very painful affair' to his sister: 'The Amerys, Duff Coopers, and their
lot are consciously or unconsciously swayed by a sense of frustration
because they can only look on, and finally the personal dislike of Simon
and Hoare had reached a pitch which I find it difficult to understand but
which undoubtedly had a great deal to do with the rebellion.'[96] The
assumption that some of the rebels had been animated by personal
motives led the Prime Ministerial entourage to investigate the prospects of
buying them off. Horace Wilson apparently advised Chamberlain to offer
Amery the office of his choosing, even the Treasury or the Foreign Office.
This was to misjudge the man badly, with Amery noting in his diary that
the episode was 'truly typical of the Horace Wilson methods and of the
kind of opinion Neville's advisers have held as to the motives which
inspired criticism and opposition'.[97] After an early morning convocation
of the Watching Committee, Salisbury had passed on to Halifax its
general consensus that the vote had holed Chamberlain below the
waterline and that he should be replaced by a cross-party coalition under
either Halifax or Churchill. Without specifying whom the successor
should be, a similar conclusion was reached at a joint meeting of Clement
Davies' group and the young Tory 'glamour boys'.[98]

By mid-morning on 9 May, the Prime Minister was showing signs that
he was preparing to concede defeat. There would have to be a cross-party
coalition involving the Labour Party. Whilst he would lead this new
administration if he could, Chamberlain knew the chances of his being
allowed to do so were slim. If Labour refused to serve under him, then it
was important that they could be persuaded to serve under his preferred
choice of successor. He was sure in his mind which of his colleagues it
should be. He wanted Halifax.

The Foreign Secretary arrived to see Chamberlain at 10.15 a.m.,
already aware that he was the preferred candidate. Preferred, that is, by
all the individuals and parties involved in the making of a new Prime
Minister. He was Chamberlain's first choice, a point upon which he was
quickly reassured once the interview got under way. He could also expect
to command not only majority support from the parliamentary Conservative Party, but – importantly – could anticipate support from across its
spectrum with even many of the rebels content that he should succeed.[99]

Now that the Labour and Liberal Opposition were to be asked to join the government, he had also to be acceptable to their leadership. In effect, all depended upon which Conservative politician the Labour Executive were prepared to work with, although, as Lord Blake has put it, in this respect 'Labour had a veto, not a choice.'[100] By the time Halifax reached Chamberlain, Rab Butler had made him aware of his conversation the previous night with Hugh Dalton and Herbert Morrison to the effect that Labour would not serve under Chamberlain 'or in the company of Simon', but that 'Dalton said there was no other choice but you. Churchill must "stick to the war".'[101] Whilst prepared to serve under Churchill, Clement Attlee also gave the impression to Dalton that his preference was to serve under Halifax.[102] Able to command a parliamentary majority and tolerable to almost all groups in the participating parties, the Foreign Secretary fitted admirably the criteria the King would look for in choosing a Prime Minister for a new coalition government. That Halifax was a trusted personal friend of the royal family only made the King's task easier.[103]

The Premiership was Halifax's for the taking. The problem was that the noble Lord seemed reluctant to take it. Subsequently recalling his meeting with the Prime Minister in his diary, Halifax recorded Chamberlain telling him that:

> He thought that it was clearly Winston or myself, and appeared to suggest that if it were myself he might continue to serve in the Government. I put all the arguments I could think of against myself, laying considerable emphasis on the difficult position of a Prime Minister unable to make contact with the centre of gravity in the House of Commons. The PM did not think so much of this, arguing that, *ex hypothesi* in the new situation there would be comparatively little opposition in the House of Commons. The conversation and the evident drift of his mind left me with a bad stomach ache.[104]

The Premiership had not been occupied by a peer for thirty-eight years and it was understandable that as a member of the House of Lords Halifax would be apprehensive about how well he would be able to control the mood of the Commons. Dalton had intimated that Labour 'saw no objection in the Lords difficulty'.[105] The fight against Fascism had recharged Labour's resolutely patriotic fibres and this was an important concession from an instinctively egalitarian movement. Yet, however genuinely meant, there was always the prospect that in some future crisis this division between Prime Minister and the elected chamber would play to Labour's advantage. What appears not to have been discussed at length during the Chamberlain/Halifax interview of 9 May was a way round this problem. There was at this time no legal mechanism for Halifax to renounce his peerage. However, given both the sense of emergency and the apparent will of most MPs that he was the man best suited to tackle it, there was no bar to their changing the procedures of the House so that he could speak and answer questions in the Commons, even if he was denied the privilege of voting in it.[106] Such plans existed, but even if they had been more forcibly put to Halifax at the time it is doubtful whether they would have been enough to persuade him. To Chamberlain he was adamant: 'I told him again as I had told him the day before that if the Labour people said they would only serve under me I should tell them that I was not prepared to do it, and see whether a definite attitude would make them budge. If it failed we should all, no doubt, have to boil our broth again. He said he would like to have a talk to Winston and me together in the afternoon.'[107]

With a lifetime of public service and as a former Viceroy of India, it was certainly no lacking sense of duty that encouraged the Foreign Secretary to resist the highest prize in British politics. The interpretation of his most recent biographer and the recollections of Halifax's colleagues suggest other motives. In comparison to Churchill, Halifax was by his own admission relatively unschooled in military matters and as the war intensified he could expect the dynamic Churchill to be constantly seeking the upper hand on issues of strategic policy.[108] As Halifax made clear to Chamberlain in the afternoon of 9 May, he did not wish to suffer Asquith's fate during the Great War in 1916, pushed out by his colleague Lloyd George with his more active strategies for prosecuting the war. Churchill had 'qualities' preferable to his own 'at this particular juncture' and to leave him 'running Defence' in the Commons whilst Halifax was 'outside both these points of contact' would soon marginalize Halifax into becoming a 'more or less honorary Prime Minister, living in a kind of twilight just outside the things that really mattered'.[109] It would be far better that Churchill was given his opportunity to lead the country but with Halifax as a senior restraining influence within the War Cabinet. If Churchill proved successful, then well and good. If he did not – and there was now the prospect of a long war ahead – then Halifax would be able to step in as Prime Minister once the great human dynamo had burned out.

It was not in doubt that Halifax's refusal of the Premiership – at least at this juncture – meant that Churchill would succeed Chamberlain. The campaign for compromise candidates to enter the ring never got seriously under way. Indeed, Amery even discouraged Hore-Belisha from starting to lobby in his favour.[110] Yet it was possible that Halifax might yet be prevailed upon by Chamberlain to accept. Churchill had lunch with Eden, and was joined by Kingsley Wood, the Lord Privy Seal, who up to that point had been considered loyal to the old regime. According to Eden, who noted the episode in his diary, Kingsley Wood pledged support for Churchill and advised him to 'make plain his willingness' to become Prime Minister. In his memoirs, Eden maintained that he was 'surprised to find Kingsley Wood there giving a warning that Chamberlain would want Halifax to succeed him and would want Churchill to agree. Wood advised "Don't agree and don't say anything." '[111] Brendan Bracken later claimed that he had instilled similar advice in Churchill.[112]

In the afternoon, Chamberlain and Simon discussed what to do next. According to his own account, Simon offered to resign (and suggested Hoare should be encouraged to do likewise) if it would save the government. Without a final decision made, the Chancellor then took his leave with the Prime Minister's gratitude.[113] At 4.30 p.m., Halifax and Churchill both arrived in Downing Street where they met Chamberlain and Margesson, the Chief Whip. According to Halifax's diary, Chamberlain expressed his desire to resign and pledged that he would serve under either Halifax or Churchill. It was important to establish the position of the Labour leaders before they departed for a meeting in Bournemouth of their party's Executive. According to Halifax's account, 'Margesson said that unity was essential and he thought it impossible to attain under the PM. He did not at the moment pronounce between Winston and myself, and my stomach ache continued.'[114] In a recollection possibly embroidered with the telling, Churchill later told Colville that when he arrived at the Cabinet Room, Chamberlain had asked him whether he knew of any reason why a peer should not be Prime Minister. If Churchill had said that he saw no reason, it would have allowed Chamberlain to turn to Halifax and press upon him the case for assuming the Premiership. Churchill could hardly stab his colleague in the front and instead decided that it was an auspicious moment to study the view from the window on to Horse Guards Parade. In the meantime, Halifax filled the awkward silence with the suggestion that Chamberlain should advise the King to send for Churchill.[115] Whether or not this account is exactly what happened, it is clear that at some stage during the meeting Halifax again expressed his desire not to accept the Premiership, repeating his recitation about the historical analogy between Asquith and Lloyd George in the last war and the feeling of impotence he would have as a peer whilst Churchill ran defence and dominated the Commons. According to Halifax's subsequent diary notes, at this 'Winston, with suitable expressions of regard and humility, said he could not but feel the force of what I had said, and the PM reluctantly, and Winston evidently with much less reluctance, finished by accepting my view.'[116] Chamberlain then left Halifax and Churchill to share a pot of tea together whilst he attended to another engagement and awaited the arrival of a delegation from the Labour leadership.

Clement Attlee and Arthur Greenwood arrived in Downing Street at 6.15 p.m. In a subsequent letter to his sister, Chamberlain wrote that he had asked the Labour leaders 'the definite question whether the Labour Party would join a Government under me or if not under someone else. I did not name the someone else to them but I had understood that they favoured Halifax, and I had him in mind.'[117] Although they implied that it was unlikely that Labour would serve under Chamberlain, no firm decision was taken. The Labour delegation left intimating that they would go straight off to their party's conference in Bournemouth to consult the Labour National Executive and telephone back the result.

VIII

The news with which Chamberlain was awoken early on 10 May was far worse than anything that could emerge from Bournemouth. Hitler's armies had launched a lightning attack on Belgium and the Netherlands. The *Wehrmacht* appeared to be circumnavigating the Maginot Line and was heading through the two formally neutral Low Countries towards the English Channel before – presumably – striking into France. The great assault in the west had begun.

The War Cabinet met in emergency session at 8.30 a.m., 11.30 a.m. and 4.30 p.m. In the field, the army's plans were being cranked into operation with the British Expeditionary Force advancing into Belgium to meet the invasion. In Downing Street, Chamberlain now maintained that this was no time for a changing of the guard and that he was proposing to stay on as Prime Minister to see through the immediate crisis. At this Kingsley Wood bluntly told him that it was time to go. Having previously been a firm supporter of Chamberlain, the Privy Seal's defection may have been a well-intentioned act of kindness to protect the Prime Minister from an impossible position. It may also have been encouraged by hearing the rumour that Chamberlain was planning to throw him overboard as part of a Cabinet reshuffle.[118] Whatever the motivation, the advice was correct in the circumstances. Although Hoare rallied to Chamberlain's defence, no other member of the Cabinet did. Halifax made it clear that he agreed with Kingsley Wood. The news received at the third meeting of the War Cabinet – that Labour wanted to join the government but only if Chamberlain was removed as Prime Minister – finalized the matter. Chamberlain announced that he would resign.

Chamberlain's PPS, Lord Dunglass, made one last attempt via Butler to persuade Halifax to accept the Premiership but nothing had happened to change Halifax's mind and the Foreign Secretary went off to visit his dentist instead. Given to understand that Labour had in any case 'changed their minds and were veering towards Winston', Chamberlain 'agreed with him and Halifax that I would put Winston's name to the King'.[119]

With the news dominated by the outbreak of hostilities on the western front, there were no crowds at the railings of Buckingham Palace to see the motor car carrying Chamberlain speed into the forecourt. Receiving him inside, the King offered his sympathy, telling him 'how grossly unfair' he 'thought he had been treated'. He was sorry to hear that Halifax, his preferred choice, would not accept the Premiership but agreed, on Chamberlain's recommendation, to send for Churchill. Finally the King said goodbye and thanked his outgoing Prime Minister for all his help.[120]

For forty crowded years, Churchill's political career had been an extraordinary trek, attended by almost every conceivable reverse and recovery. In the final event, the crucial car journey that conveyed him from Whitehall to Buckingham Palace took just two minutes. He was received at 6 p.m. and accepted the commission to form a government. Returning to Whitehall, he worked into the night shaping his new War Cabinet. At nearly three o'clock in the morning he at last retired to bed, 'conscious', he later recalled, 'of a profound sense of relief' that he had at last 'authority to give directions over the whole scene. I felt as if I were walking with destiny, and that all my past life had been but a preparation for this hour and for this trial.'[121]

Epilogue

BURYING CAESAR

I

Churchill had become Prime Minister by default. He had only reached the top of the greasy pole because the pressure to remove some of the War Cabinet's more unpopular members had created a parliamentary crisis that coincided with a widespread mood nationally in favour of forming a new all-party coalition. Labour's refusal to serve under Chamberlain would have passed the Premiership to the apparently more acceptable choice of Halifax had he not declined the office – for the time being at least. Churchill knew that in these circumstances he could only cling to power for as long as Chamberlain, Halifax and the rest of 'the old gang' chose not to use their parliamentary majority to bring him down. Although he had lost the Premiership, Chamberlain was still leader of the Conservative Party, to which most members of the House of Commons belonged. He appeared to retain their loyalty in greater measure than did Churchill. Thus, the new Prime Minister could not afford the luxury of excluding from the Cabinet table potential troublemakers in the way that before the war Baldwin and Chamberlain had managed to exclude him. Keeping them on board was the price that had to be paid in return for their giving him the legitimacy he needed with which to govern – a parliamentary majority.

These were the circumstances which demanded that Churchill played the 'old gang' with the greatest tact. Returning from the Palace on 10 May, he immediately wrote to Chamberlain:

> my first act on coming back from the Palace is to write and tell you how grateful I am to you for promising to stand by me, and to aid the country at this extremely grievous and formidable moment. . . . With your help and counsel, and with the support of the great party of which you are the leader, I trust that I shall succeed. The example which you have set of self-forgetting dignity and public spirit will govern the action of many, and be an inspiration to all.
>
> In these eight months we have worked together I am proud to have won your friendship and your confidence in an increasing measure. To a very large

extent I am in your hands – and I feel no fear of that. For the rest I have faith in our cause, which I feel sure will not be suffered to fail among men.

I will write to you again to-night after I have seen the Labour leaders. I am so glad you will broadcast to our anxious people.[1]

Churchill intended to make Chamberlain Chancellor of the Exchequer or, failing that, Leader of the House. Violent Labour objections prevented either course from being pursued. Chamberlain confided to his sister that the latter post would 'involve me in much tedious sitting in the House, and very likely lead to ill-temper and bad manners. So I gave it up without a sigh.'[2] Instead, he became President of the Council, the position Baldwin had held from 1931 to 1935 during Ramsay MacDonald's National Government. The importance of this office was defined not by its competencies but by the political weight of its occupant. Just as it had conferred on Baldwin, the leader of the majority party in Parliament, the power at will to make or break the MacDonald National Government, so it bestowed the same authority upon Chamberlain in 1940.

The instinctive declarations of allegiance prompted by the leadership crisis had demonstrated the considerable support within parliamentary and official circles for Lord Halifax. Churchill realized the political necessity of keeping him on as Foreign Secretary, despite Eden's claims to the post. That the new Prime Minister also did not sack the Foreign Office's stridently pro-appeasement Under-Secretary of State, Rab Butler, or his PPS, 'Chips' Channon, was a further sign that he did not feel politically strong enough to wrest from the Chamberlainites this crucial department of government.

Churchill's central preoccupation on becoming Prime Minister was to assume command of the conduct of the war. The experience of the 'Phoney War' had demonstrated the inadequacy of piecemeal tinkering with the competencies of those responsible for strategic planning and decision making. Churchill placed the solution in his own hands by devising for himself the position of 'Minister for Defence'. A title of his own creation, the position came without defined powers but, as he later put it, this meant that he 'should assume the general direction of the war, subject to the support of the War Cabinet and of the House of Commons'.[3] It strengthened his direction of the Chiefs of Staff Committee, allowing him to downgrade the input over grand strategy made by the three service ministers. In so doing, Churchill was able to cut the composition of the War Cabinet to a more manageable membership of five.

The Labour leader, Clement Attlee, and his deputy, Arthur Greenwood, accepted the offer of the Lord Privy Seal and Minister without Portfolio respectively, thereby ensuring that two of the five members of the War

Cabinet were not Conservatives. Elsewhere in the government, Churchill took care to find positions for Chamberlain's former entourage in the ordinary Cabinet where they could be simultaneously kept busy and out of the direct management of war strategy. Simon was sent to the Woolsack. Kingsley Wood became Chancellor of the Exchequer, the seniority of the office encouraging the suspicion that he was being rewarded for his role in deserting Chamberlain at the peak of the political crisis. On bad terms with Churchill personally, Oliver Stanley huffily made clear that he would rather not serve the administration at all than be offered a post more lowly than what he felt was his due. He went off instead to serve with his regiment. This was an atypical reaction, since most of those who felt that their loyalty primarily was to Chamberlain maintained that they were prepared to serve in the new government precisely because they believed that Churchill's potentially dangerous instincts needed to be tamed by their own influence. Despite the criticisms that had mounted against him in recent months, Hoare was one of those who expected to continue in high office. Consequently, he was taken aback to find himself the only prominent former appeaser to be dropped from the government altogether. Disappointed, he asked Churchill for the not inconsiderable consolation prize of Viceroy of India. Although acutely aware of the political necessity of letting bygones be bygones, Churchill nonetheless drew the line at conceding this victory to the man he had so bitterly fought over the future governance of India between 1929 and 1935. Instead he made Hoare Ambassador to Spain from where he would be charged with keeping Franco out of the Nazi embrace.

With the completion of Churchill's reshuffle, Conservatives continued to make up the majority of appointments in the new coalition government. Given their parliamentary preponderance, this was the least that could be expected. Twenty of the thirty-four members chosen by Churchill had served in Chamberlain's administration (as, of course, had Churchill himself). In contrast, dissidents of the old regime received no special favour from its successor. None of the leading Tory anti-appeasers made it into Churchill's 'big five'. The new Secretary of State for War, Eden, had to make do with ordinary Cabinet rank as did the real martyr of Munich, Duff Cooper, who was appointed Minister for Information. Leo Amery had shared Churchill's wilderness years in the anti-appeasement dugout. He had also been one of the most forceful backbench opponents of Chamberlain in the Norway debate. Although he accepted Churchill's offer of the India Office, he was disappointed at not being elevated to the rank given to the chosen few entrusted with the strategic direction of the war.[4] Indeed, having supported Hoare's reforms, Amery had cause for surprise that Churchill had made him – of all positions –

India Secretary. Amongst the leaders of the remnants of the old diehard contingent on the subject, Lord Lloyd was delighted to become Colonial Secretary; outside the Cabinet, Page Croft was appointed to serve under Eden at the War Office whilst Wolmer went to the Ministry of Works. He was later to be put in charge of SOE – the Special Operations Executive – from where he oversaw Churchill's instructions to 'set Europe ablaze'.

Having spent so long, at loggerheads and at different ends of the greasy pole, Churchill and Chamberlain found circumstances conspiring in the moment of deadly national peril to make them dependent upon one another; Chamberlain could not form a government with cross-party support, and Churchill could not survive as head of that new combination without Chamberlain's support and the parliamentary majority that rested upon it. Churchill did his best to make sure the Tory leader was as comfortable as possible with these arrangements. Despite his own claim to the property, Churchill allowed Chamberlain to continue living in 10 Downing Street for a month after he ceased being Prime Minister and ensured that he was thereafter accommodated next door at Number 11. The 'one thing which struck' the civil servant Lawrence Burgis 'most forcibly' about the War Cabinet meetings at which he was present 'was the courtesy and deference with which Churchill treated Neville Chamberlain'.[5] As Churchill privately told W.P. Crozier of the *Manchester Guardian* on 26 July, 'I owe something to Chamberlain, you know. When he resigned he could have advised the King to send for Halifax and he didn't. . . . Chamberlain works very well with me and I can tell you he's no intriguer.'[6] Churchill was right not to suspect Chamberlain's motives. Although he disliked the fact that Churchill was 'surrounded by a different crowd from what I am accustomed to', Chamberlain admitted to his sister Ida, 'I must say that Winston has been most handsome in his appreciation of my willingness to help and my ability to do so. I know that he relies on Halifax and me.'[7] Churchill knew that he could not wrest control of the party leadership from Chamberlain and would be better off not trying. On 16 May he wrote to Chamberlain assuring him that 'I am, of course, a Conservative. But, as Prime Minister of a National Government formed on the widest basis, and comprising the three parties, I feel that it would be better for me not to undertake the Leadership of any political party. . . . The relations of perfect confidence which have grown up between us makes this division of duties and responsibilities very agreeable.'[8] Chamberlain wrote to his other sister, Hilda, explaining that his own retention of the party leadership 'was essential if Winston was to have whole hearted support'. In view of the attitude of some of Chamberlain's supporters who loathed the promotion of what they saw as 'the "Treachery Bench"' in the new government, Chamberlain feared that real hostility would 'certainly have broken out if there had been any change in the Leadership but I hope now that our party will loyally accept the change and follow my example'.[9]

Churchill would have been heartened by the tone of Chamberlain's private comments. The two men assured each other in writing of their mutual devotion with a regularity that indicated something of a sense of insecurity on the subject; Chamberlain's intention to use his power in order to shore up Churchill was therefore essential if there was to be any prospect of national unity at a time when the army was in retreat and the invasion of Britain looked imminent. It was an attitude that contrasted not only with the experience of Asquith and Lloyd George after 1916 but also with the division and mistrust permeating through the French Government as the Nazi blitzkrieg tore through Belgium and threatened Paris. There, Paul Reynaud had replaced Daladier as Prime Minister back in March. As with Churchill in London, Reynaud's allies looked to their new premier to prosecute the war more forcefully. However, with a Cabinet majority of only one and with Daladier as a non-cooperating Minister of War, his survival was in constant jeopardy. Chamberlain's greatest wartime service was to ignore the precedent set by his French counterparts. His support for Churchill was never unqualified, but it stayed the course.

II

Chamberlain's magnanimity in falling in behind Churchill was not shared by many of his more active supporters. Even whilst the new Prime Minister was still at Buckingham Palace kissing hands, the junior Downing Street private secretary, Jock Colville, and Chamberlain's PPS, Lord Dunglass (i.e. Alec Douglas-Home), had joined Rab Butler and 'Chips' Channon at the Foreign Office to drink to the health of Chamberlain, their 'King over the Water'. Channon recorded:

> Rab said he thought that the good clean tradition of English politics, that of Pitt as opposed to Fox, had been sold to the greatest adventurer of modern political history. He had tried earnestly and long to persuade Halifax to accept the Premiership, but he had failed. He believed this sudden coup of Winston and his rabble was a serious disaster and an unnecessary one: the 'pass had been sold' by Mr. C., Lord Halifax and Oliver Stanley. They had weakly surrendered to a half-breed American whose main support was that of inefficient but talkative people of a similar type.[10]

These sentiments were shared in even less measured terms by Dunglass.

The following month he told the wife of the Tory Whip Tommy Dugdale, that 'since W[inston] came in, the H of C had stunk in the nostrils of the decent people. The kind of people surrounding W are the scum and the peak came when Brendan [Bracken] was made a PC! For what services rendered heaven knows.'[11] This perfectly encapsulated the attitude of what Andrew Roberts has described as the self-appointed 'Respectable Tendency' of the Tory Establishment. The cousin of the Duke of Marlborough, Churchill had a better claim to being aristocratic than many of those who affected to look down on him (Dunglass would inherit an earldom, but Butler was primarily wealthy because he had married into the Courtauld family, the same path that Channon – a half-breed American – had taken into the Guinness family). To them, Churchill's adventurism was suspect, and his promotion of those like Bracken and Beaverbrook, in whom he detected the buccaneering spirit, doubly alarming. That Churchill had not, for the most part, put his own henchmen in the highest offices did not prevent his detractors from convincing themselves otherwise and forgetting about the fact that two-thirds of Chamberlain's ministers were still in the government. Rightly surprised not to be removed from his own Foreign Office duties, Butler was only one of a number of Conservatives who had to contend with the fact that they were now serving in an administration led by the man they had spent the best part of a decade briefing against and catcalling.[12] This was a sentiment shared not only by those who sat in Parliament. The junior Downing Street private secretary, Jock Colville (a Chamberlain loyalist who was soon to come round to admiring Churchill), summarized the view that Churchill's appointment 'sent a cold chill down the spines of the staff at 10 Downing Street . . . Our feelings were widely shared in the Cabinet Offices, the Treasury and throughout Whitehall . . . Seldom can a Prime Minister have taken office with the Establishment . . . so dubious of the choice and so prepared to find its doubts justified.'[13]

Evidence that Churchill's coronation had not been what many of those who had participated in the Norway debate had intended was embarrassingly in abundance when on 13 May Churchill arrived in the Commons chamber to speak for the first time as Prime Minister. As he moved across to take his seat on the Treasury bench opposite the dispatch box, he received the acclamation of some Labour members, but a decidedly muted acknowledgement from the massed ranks of the Conservative Party behind him. Churchill promised 'blood, toil, tears and sweat' in the endeavour for 'victory at all costs' against Hitler. It was clear that he would also have to move heaven and earth with his own parliamentary party, 'three-quarters' of which – according to the Chairman of its 1922

Committee of backbenchers – wanted Chamberlain back as Prime Minister.[14]

In normal circumstances, the attitude of Conservative MPs who continued to look to Chamberlain for a lead would have been an admirable expression of loyalty in a profession famous for lacking it. A handful of them wanted to make peace with Germany immediately, but this was as much a fringe view within the Conservative Party as was that of the similarly minded unilateral pacifists in Labour's ranks. A much larger number of Tories, who wanted to fight on but not – in Churchill's stark definition – 'at all costs', balked at what coalition with the Labour Party meant in practice. Aware that Labour's sense of non-partisan patriotic duty had not been much evident when Chamberlain had asked for their help in broadening the government back in September 1939, right-wing Tories were suspicious of Labour's motives in getting involved, now that they felt they could hit the Conservatives once they were down over Norway. Tories also recalled the years in which Labour had opposed Chamberlain's stepping up the rearmament programme beyond commitments to the League of Nations. In this, Conservatives allowed their long memories to divorce them from the more immediate instincts of the electorate which appeared to favour intensifying the war effort and believed that the more active cooperation in government of the Labour Movement was the best way to achieve it. This was not purely the product of an ideological drift towards collectivism, but a belief 'in getting the job done'. In this respect it was Churchill with his cross-party appeal and his slogan 'Let Us Go Forward Together' who captured the popular mood. By August, with the Battle of Britain swirling over the skies of southern England and the country under daily threat of invasion, Gallup recorded that Churchill's personal approval rating reached an unprecedented 88 per cent. Sir Frank Sanderson's experience was typical of that of fellow Chamberlainite MPs who found themselves blinking in the daylight of Churchill's mass popularity after spending so long in the gloom of their Westminster contempt for him. According to a report of his speech to the Ealing Primrose League on 1 June 1940, Sanderson told the assembled:

> 'There is not a more loyal man in this country than myself in regard to the late Prime Minister and still leader of our Party – Neville Chamberlain,' he said, to two apologetic little claps from a lady and gentleman in the back row as the rest of the audience sat in silence. After a moment he continued: 'But there comes a time when a specialist brain must needs fill a special position.' At this reference to Churchill, recorded the *Middlesex County Times*, Ealing Town Hall erupted into loud and prolonged applause.[15]

III

The events through which Churchill had to struggle to assert his will over fellow Conservatives could not have been more grave. He had become Prime Minister in the first hours of Hitler's blitzkrieg in the west. Overwhelmed by German paratroopers and with Rotterdam in flames, the Dutch were knocked out of the war on 14 May. Six days later, the German Panzer divisions advanced so rapidly that they reached Amiens. A lifelong Francophile, Churchill had shared the same general assumption upon which Chamberlain had banked his strategy: that the French would be able to hold a German invasion at bay. The simple arithmetic had certainly suggested that this would prove to be the case (135 Allied divisions in defensive positions faced 126 German divisions attacking through hostile territory). In the event, however, the Allies were totally overwhelmed by the ferocity of the assault unleashed upon them. They had nothing to match the Stuka dive-bombers which like shrieking Valkyries swooped out of the clouds to devastating effect in synchronized action with the advancing German armour. Whereas the French had dispersed their tanks across the entire front, the German Panzers were concentrated more effectively. Surprising the French by crossing the supposedly difficult terrain of the Ardennes, the German tanks made the crucial breakthrough at Sedan and proceeded to advance far behind the Allied positions, cutting their communication lines as a result. In almost every department of strategy and tactics, the Allies were outclassed. In Paris for emergency consultations on 16 May, Churchill was horrified to see clouds of smoke rising from the gardens of the Quai d'Orsay. Despite the fact that the Germans were still a long way from the French capital, 'venerable officials' were 'pushing wheel-barrows of archives' on to large bonfires. 'Already', concluded Churchill, the French were preparing to evacuate the city.[16] A French army which by supreme sacrifice had contained four years of wearying German attrition between 1914 and 1918 appeared now to be folding up in as many weeks.

The debilitating French sense of defeatism soon permeated through Whitehall. Hitler's push west meant that his bomber crews could take off from airfields even closer to Britain. Reports continued to suggest that from these forward positions aerial bombardment could incinerate the urban population and wipe out the factories upon which Britain's war effort depended. Britain's Dominions were sending what aid they could, but as far as the European theatre of operations were concerned, France's collapse would leave Britain outgunned and surrounded, alone and naked before a Nazi empire that stretched from the Atlantic to the redrawn Polish border with the Soviet Union. This was not all. If Italy entered the war on Germany's side – a declaration that looked imminent – then

Britain's strategic position in the Mediterranean would be imperilled, severing her ability to link up with her empire's resources. Britain appeared to be faced with only two options: to use for peace whilst she still had armed forces with which to bargain, or to fight on in the hope of some divine intervention. Churchill had no doubt which course he felt destiny compelled him to take, cradling the remote prospect that if Britain could hold out long enough, somehow Roosevelt might yet be prevailed upon to bring the full might of the United States down upon the Third Reich.

In the meantime, the position across the Channel continued to deteriorate alarmingly. The *Wehrmacht* entered Brussels on 18 May, the same day that Reynaud desperately reshuffled his Cabinet and tried to emulate Churchill's actions by assuming control of the Ministry of National Defence and War. Two days later, the Panzers had rumbled on to Abbeville, severing the communication lines between the mass of the French Army to the south and the British Expeditionary Force in Belgium. The British were now trapped in an enclave, miles from the coast. If the German armour could sweep up behind and take the remaining Channel ports, then there would be no prospect of the British troops being rescued. Consequently, on 21 May, the British attempted to fight their way out and link back up with the French to the south. Running up against the might of the Panzer divisions around Arras, the attempted breakout ground to a halt and the supporting French counter-attack failed to materialize. On 24 May the British pulled out of Boulogne. Churchill ordered the commanding officer to hold Calais at all costs. If it fell, little more than a single battalion would stand in the way of the Germans slamming shut the British Army's one remaining exit, Dunkirk.

Hoping to share his fellow Fascist's spoils, Mussolini was poised to join the war. Already wilting under the German assault, the French could not afford to face a further Italian invasion from the south-east. In consequence, Reynaud proposed buying them off. Halifax agreed that the possibility of an eleventh-hour appeasement of Mussolini should be investigated. In the process, the Italian dictator might prove able to mediate an all-round cessation of hostilities. Thus, a negotiated peace between France, Britain and Germany was the ultimate goal. Chamberlain recorded in his diary that the Foreign Secretary's proposal rested on the belief that 'there could be no harm in trying Musso & seeing what the result was. If the terms were impossible we could still reject them.'[17] Halifax made clear that 'impossible' terms from Berlin would be those that infringed Britain's essential sovereignty to defend herself and her interests. Although this was consistent with Hitler's oft repeated remarks that he wanted Germany to live in peace with a strong maritime Britain, the *Führer*'s word had long become a devalued currency as far as Churchill and Chamberlain were concerned.

By 1940, Halifax had served in a variety of government positions, had been Viceroy of India and was Foreign Secretary in some of the most difficult times that his country had faced. In other words, he was well acquainted with Rab Butler's definition of politics as 'the art of the possible'. In contrast, Churchill had been out of office for a decade during which time he had been able to see things as he thought they should be, not as they were. He had been able to dream, whilst Halifax had become accustomed to the sober chores of tailoring hope to reality. Churchill's own recollection of government had centred upon what he remembered as 'the old days, indeed the great days' of his career,[18] foremost of which was the experience of the Great War. During that conflict he had witnessed tremendous reverses, amongst them the Dardenelles of 1915 and the U-boat menace of 1917. Yet Britain had struggled on and Churchill had watched the German Army's advance in March 1918 to almost within reach of Paris be halted, pushed back and converted into outright victory for the Allies eight months later. It is not difficult to discern how these different experiences, re-enforcing natural temperaments, guided the Foreign Secretary down a path that attempted to manage his country's decline, whilst the Prime Minister believed that if the heart was willing, nothing was hopeless and everything was possible. It may have been that Halifax thought that a negotiated peace with Germany would buy time – as the 1802 Treaty of Amiens had briefly done in the protracted conflict against Napoleon. In contrast, Churchill, attuned to the reality of twentieth-century total war, saw no place for the courtly manners of nineteenth-century diplomacy.[19] May 1940 was the very worst moment to show a lack of resolve since in the existing position of weakness, admitting an intention to seek terms would fuel Hitler's appetite, ensuring that what started as an ordered diplomatic process would quickly gather the momentum of a total capitulation. According to Chamberlain's diary, Churchill made this point forcibly to Halifax, maintaining that 'we might do better without the French than with them if they tied us up to a conference with which we should enter with our case lost before hand.'[20] Nothing could be lost by fighting on since there could be nothing gained by giving up.

Although aware that approaching Mussolini would probably prove fruitless, Halifax remained adamant that it should be attempted – at the very least it would prevent the French from 'complaining'.[21] The point at issue, however, was that an approach to Mussolini was meant to start a process that would lead to an appeal to Hitler as well. This was what Churchill particularly wished to avoid. Given his precarious position in

Parliament, the Prime Minister could ill afford the Foreign Secretary's resignation and despite his own determination to fight on, he felt it necessary to reassure Halifax that he was open to reason. His tactic was to try to disentangle an approach to the Italians from an approach to the Germans and, having done so, to thereby insist that there was little to gain from appeasing the Italians. This was what he meant when he told Halifax that it was 'incredible that Hitler would consent to any terms that we could accept' but that if Britain 'could get out of this jam by giving up [to Mussolini] Malta and Gibraltar and some African colonies he [Churchill] would jump at it. But the only safe way was to convince Hitler he couldn't beat us.'[22] In effect, Churchill was maintaining that the Foreign Secretary was pursuing a pipe dream if he believed that making concessions to Italy would spare Britain the humiliation of crippling terms from Hitler.

The following day, 27 May, Halifax's position appeared to be strengthened by the news from the battle front: the Belgians were poised to surrender and it looked as if very few British soldiers could be evacuated. The Germans were within ten miles of Dunkirk, the Channel port on which the retreating British Expeditionary Force was pinning its only remaining hope of escape. If the Germans could get to Dunkirk in time, they would trap the British Army and parcel off what remained of it to a prisoner of war camp. Denuded of this force, Britain would then be at the mercy of invasion. The previous day, the War Cabinet members had been hesitant to contradict Halifax's proposal for appeasing Mussolini. Paradoxically, during the course of the discussions on 27 May their reservations mounted. On the grounds that any approach would need the all-party approval of the coalition government, Churchill had managed to get the Air Secretary, Sir Archibald Sinclair, to join the discussion in his capacity as leader of the Liberal Party. As Churchill well knew, he had Sinclair's undivided loyalty. Churchill's continued insistence that Britain's best chance of retaining her independence was by fighting on (at least for the time being) infuriated Halifax who still declared that 'he was prepared to take that risk if our independence was at stake; but if it was not at stake he would think it right to accept an offer which would save the country from avoidable disaster.' The Foreign Secretary hinted that he was on the point of resignation, confiding in his diary that he thought Churchill was talking 'rot'.[23]

In the War Cabinet, Churchill knew he could count on Attlee, Greenwood and Sinclair to back his determination to fight to the death, but a four/two split in his favour would not be enough to save the administration if Halifax and Chamberlain walked out. Churchill's fate appeared to be in the hands of the Prime Minister he had displaced. If

Chamberlain deserted him, then that was the end. He had been Prime Minister for only eighteen days.

The following morning saw a further deterioration with the news that Belgium had surrendered. Although 11,400 British troops had been successfully evacuated back to Britain from the one remaining bridgehead at Dunkirk, the position was under heavy attack and might be held for only a few more hours. Chamberlain recorded in his diary that 'terrible tales have come in through the day of ships full of troops torpedoed or bombed . . . we are told of thousands of men hiding in the dunes waiting to be taken off.'[24] A third of a million troops (200,000 British; 160,000 French) were still trapped on the wrong side of the Channel. In the War Cabinet, Halifax again raised the issue of exploring terms with Italy (and ultimately Germany). Attlee, Greenwood and Sinclair all argued against. In the discussions of the previous two days, Chamberlain had adopted a measured approach to the pros and cons of Halifax's strategy of negotiating with Italy (although in his diary he thought the attempt 'would be of no avail').[25] Whilst accepting that the situation could change, the Conservative leader now weighed in more firmly on Churchill's side, stating that whatever France might do, Britain should continue to show the utmost resolution.[26] This was vital support. Churchill was insistent that 'nations which went down fighting rose again, but those which surrendered tamely were finished.' Attlee agreed, pointing out that the country's morale to continue fighting would be shattered if its government was seen to be after a back-door peace deal.[27]

Although his will appeared to be prevailing, Churchill still had to pull out all the stops available to him, especially whilst the operation to rescue the British Expeditionary Force from Dunkirk remained in the balance. As the War Cabinet broke up, the twenty-five members of the rest of the Cabinet arrived for their meeting. Despite having spent the best part of the day in fraught bargaining with his senior colleagues, Churchill mustered every reserve of inspiration at his command to urge those around him to fight on. The new Minister for Economic Warfare, Labour's Hugh Dalton, was mesmerized by the 65-year-old Prime Minister's bravura performance, noting in his diary that 'he was quite magnificent. The man, and the only man we have, for this hour.' In front of the assembled ministers, Churchill brought the Cabinet up to date with the perilous news from France but urged that on no account should Britain sue for peace. Rather than submit to terms that would leave her a disarmed 'slave state', they should defend their island at all costs. Dalton recorded the effect of the Prime Minister's onslaught:

> 'And I am convinced,' [Churchill] concluded, 'that every man of you would rise up and tear me down from my place if I were for one moment to

contemplate parley or surrender. If this long island story of ours is to end at last, let it end only when each one of us lies choking in his own blood upon the ground.'

There were loud cries of approval all round the table, in which, I think, Amery, [Lord] Lloyd and I were the loudest.[28]

Ministers were out of their seats, clapping Churchill on the back. It was an unprecedented scene. This, more than any other time, appeared to be the moment when the Prime Minister was walking with destiny, his words of defiance reinforced by an entrenched belief that he really did intend to fight to the last round of ammunition. Having roused the fighting spirits of the Cabinet, Churchill again faced the War Cabinet later that evening with his own position now greatly strengthened (even though on the issue of defending Britain from actual invasion, Halifax and Churchill were in complete agreement). Psychologically, however, the Prime Minister had won. Wrong-footed and with Chamberlain and the other War Ministers backing Churchill, Halifax had to concede that there should be no investigation of what the good offices of Mussolini might produce. By nightfall, the news was that a further 25,000 British troops had been rescued from the Dunkirk beaches bringing the total nearer to 40,000. At 11.40 p.m., Churchill telephoned Paris. No parley would be sought. Britain would fight on.

Whilst Churchill was securing his position in Whitehall, the British 'epic' was being played out across the Channel. Hitler's decision of 24 May – to hold the Panzers back and finish off the retreating British forces with *Luftwaffe* dive-bombers instead – was a disastrous mistake, seemingly born of his fear that the Panzers had made themselves dangerously vulnerable by advancing too quickly for their infantry support to keep up.[29] By the time the Panzers were ordered to recommence the attack they had missed their opportunity to seize Dunkirk before the retreating mass of the British and French forces could fall back to it. Upon such decisions the fate of empires hinged.

With a tremendous air battle going on in the skies above, the British rescue armada – destroyers, sailing boats, pleasure craft and paddle-steamers of all shapes and sizes, anything that floated and could be laid hands upon – made trip after trip across the Channel to rescue the stranded men. Failing to dodge the bombs raining down upon them, a third of the British boats involved were sunk, including six destroyers. But with renewed pressure on the beachhead perimeter, every hour counted in which the act of deliverance could be prolonged. Lined up at the Dunkirk harbour, or plucked from the beaches, 120,000 British troops had been brought off by 30 May. Yet there were still 80,000 British troops waiting to be picked up (and many more French), their position held only by the dogged resistance of those in the rearguard, holding the ring under constant fire. It was in the forty-eight hours of 31 May and 1 June that more than 132,000 troops (most of the remaining British force plus French troops trapped with them) were rescued. When on 4 June, the last defenders were overwhelmed, more than 338,000 British and French troops had been snatched from the *Wehrmacht*'s grasp.

With the completion of the operation, Churchill faced the Commons. He confessed that 'wars are not won by evacuations': almost all the British Expeditionary Force's heavy equipment had been left behind on the beaches. But compared with the prospect of the entire force being wiped out or taken prisoner, their deliverance had taken on the quality of a miracle. Now they were back in Britain, ready to repel the imminent invasion. Even by the standards of his accompanying oratory, Churchill's peroration stood elevated as a defining declaration of the determination that he detected within the British people to see off the invader: 'We shall go on to the end. We shall fight in France, we shall fight on the seas and oceans, we shall fight with growing confidence and growing strength in the air, we shall defend our island, whatever the cost may be. We shall fight on the beaches, we shall fight on the landing grounds, we shall fight in the fields and in the streets, we shall fight in the hills; we shall never surrender.'[30] These were the words of a man who had experienced a decade of political isolation but had stayed the course. Some Labour MPs broke down in tears.

IV

The day after Churchill's great performance in the House of Commons, Reynaud tried to stiffen his government with a little of the Winston touch: Daladier was deposed from the Cabinet, and the pugnacious Charles de Gaulle brought in. The situation was desperate and, unlike Britain, France did not have a twenty-mile-wide moat in which to defend herself. The 103 French divisions that had faced the onslaught on 10 May were now reduced to 68. During 5 June, the *Wehrmacht* launched its offensive across the Somme. From there, Paris was within reach. The path was blocked by the French 10th Army, joined by the 51st Highland Division. This was soon added to with the dispatch to Normandy of fresh British and French reinforcements brought back from Dunkirk along with a Canadian division. Five days later, Italy declared war on Britain and France.

The French continued to fall back in the face of the relentless pounding from the renewed German offensive. On 12 June, the remnants of the 51st Highland Division surrendered at St Valéry, west of Dieppe. The following day, Churchill flew back to France in a desperate attempt to rally Gallic nerves. It was his fifth trip there in his month-long Premiership. There was nothing he could do – even a subsequent last-ditch offer to create an 'Anglo-French Union' was dismissed by the French defeatist element as merely a ploy for Britain to get her hands on French colonies. Jean Ybarnegaray, the Minister of State, maintained that France would be 'better a Nazi province: at least we know what that means'.[31] Such was the unhappy experience of fighting with allies. By that stage the French capital city had already been lost, the *Wehrmacht* marching unopposed into Paris on 14 June. It was the sixth capital they had captured in only nine months.[32] Having failed to keep control of his Cabinet, Reynaud resigned two days later. In his place, Marshal Pétain assumed office and France sued for peace. An armistice was agreed on 22 June, taking full effect three days later. Hitler rubbed in the humiliation by forcing the French to receive his terms in the same railway carriage in which they had dictated the armistice to the defeated German commanders in November 1918.

The remaining British forces were evacuated from Brittany with the German Panzers hot on their heels. But for the loss of 3000 troops when one of the ships involved, the *Lancastria*, took a direct hit, the operation was carried off successfully. Britain and her empire now stood alone against the combined Axis powers of Italy and the Nazi Reich; as one cockney newspaper vendor chalked up on his stand on hearing of France's collapse, Britain had made it through to playing 'in the finals'.[33] On 18 June with the last of the 136,000 British troops coming home from Cherbourg, Churchill addressed the Commons. The invasion of Britain, he informed the chamber, was imminent:

> Hitler knows that he will have to break us in this island or lose the war. If we can stand up to him, all Europe may be free, and the life of the world may move forward into broad, sunlit uplands; but if we fail, then the whole world, including the United States, and all that we have known and cared for, will sink into the abyss of a new dark age made more sinister, and perhaps more protracted, by the lights of a perverted science.
>
> Let us therefore brace ourselves to our duty and so bear ourselves that if the British Empire and its Commonwealth lasts for a thousand years men will still say, 'This was their finest hour.'[34]

When, a fortnight later, Chamberlain broadcast to the nation, Churchill's words resonated from his own lips. He even found himself repeating the phrase about fighting 'in the air and on the sea; we will fight him on the beaches' since Britain remained 'a solid and united nation, which would rather go down to ruin than admit the domination of the Nazis'.[35]

On 1 July, Chamberlain wrote in his diary, 'All reports seem to point to the invasion this week or next.'[36] In the meantime, an important issue had arisen. Under Article 8 of the Franco-German Armistice, France's warships were to be handed over to the Axis powers. Churchill argued that it was imperative that this calamity be prevented. With the full support of Chamberlain and the rest of the War Cabinet, he ordered the Royal Navy to confront the French fleet at its Algerian naval base of Mers el-Kebir near Oran. In doing so, Admiral Somerville issued repeated authorized requests to the French commanding officer, Admiral Gensoul, giving him the option of joining up to fight alongside the British fleet. If he refused, choosing instead to allow his fleet to be put at the disposal of the Germans, it was made clear to him that the Royal Navy would open fire. Determined to obey the terms Pétain had made with Germany, Gensoul refused Somerville's offer. In a matter of minutes, the result was all too clear. Somerville's ships turned their guns on the fleet of their former ally, destroying or disabling most of the ships before they could get out of harbour and killing more than 1250 French sailors.

Although he felt that he had been faced with no option, Churchill grieved at the necessity of the action at Oran. However, when he at last came to the conclusion of his account to the Commons on 4 July he was met by a far more resounding response from the Conservative benches than he had received for any of his stirring orations over the last few weeks. According to the recollection of an observer from the gallery: 'The Chief Whip, Margesson, rose to his feet. Turning towards the Tory backbenchers, he waved his Order Papers in a gesture clearly conveying that they too should rise. At his signal all the Conservatives . . . rose to a man and burst into enthusiastic cheering at the top of their voices.'[37] Dismayed and still uneasy about the action against the French fleet, Churchill was bewildered by the response. Tears welled up in his eyes. It was the first unanimous display of support that he had received in the chamber from the parliamentary Conservative Party, and the action of Margesson gave the impression that it was choreographed. If so, it was a clear sign that the forces within the party who could have toppled him had decided instead that it was time to demonstrate their loyalty. Oran had shown that he meant what he said, indeed that he could match Hitler's ruthlessness with an equal determination of his own. It impressed not only backbench Tories; it was a signal to the United States that Britain was still in the fight, all guns blazing.

V

Rousing his troops at Harfleur, Shakespeare's Henry V asserted that 'In peace there's nothing so becomes a man as modest stillness and humility: but when the blast of war blows in our ears, then imitate the action of the tiger; stiffen the sinews, summon up the blood, disguise fair nature with hard-favoured rage.' Few statements could have better described the public perception of the character of Chamberlain's peacetime ministry in comparison with the more bellicose administration led by Churchill. Writing to his sister Hilda, days after he had been deposed as Prime Minister, Chamberlain accepted the hard reality of the change, conceding that

> All my world has tumbled to bits in a moment. The national peril has so swamped all personal feelings that no bitterness remains. Indeed, I used to say to Annie [Mrs Chamberlain] before war came that, if such a thing happened, I thought I should have to hand over to someone else, for I knew what agony of mind it would mean for me to give directions that would bring death and mutilation and misery to so many. But the war was so different from what I expected that I found the strain bearable, and perhaps it was providential that the revolution which overturned me coincided with the entry of the real thing.

He sadly concluded that 'my only desire is to get out of this horrible condition of chronic misery and I frankly envy Austen's peace.'[38] It was probably a consolation that Austen, with his ill-disguised superiority complex, had not lived to see the mess into which the country's affairs had descended in the hands of his unlucky younger half-brother.

The relationship between Chamberlain and Churchill was now in the last of the many distinct phases through which it had passed. It had been professional but not warm when, as Chancellor of the Exchequer, Churchill had worked with Chamberlain on the latter's welfare reforms in the 1924–9 Conservative Government. Neither had wanted the other to succeed Baldwin as leader. From then until 1938, the two had seen little of each other and had been following their own separate agendas: until 1935, Churchill had been preoccupied with India, a subject in which Chamberlain had minimal interest. The years between 1931 and 1937 when Chamberlain presided over the Treasury were those in which Churchill's eye for economic detail was at its least penetrating. During this time, their differences on rearmament and even foreign policy were more a matter of degree than of fundamental disagreement. It was only with the approaching Czech crisis, culminating in the diplomacy of Munich, that they had become each other's principal parliamentary *bête noir*. This was the period in which Churchill stepped up his campaign to urge the bringing of the Soviet Union into a 'Grand Alliance' against

Hitler, something Chamberlain was determined to avoid. Believing that he had saved Britain and Europe from a war of annihilation, Chamberlain was angered by Churchill's unrelenting criticism of his Munich triumph; consequently he did nothing to call off the exertions of party loyalists to rid him of the turbulent priest of Epping. The declaration of war against Germany abruptly brought an end to these hostilities with Churchill's ready agreement to serve in Chamberlain's War Cabinet as First Lord of the Admiralty. From the 'Phoney War' through to the outbreak of the blitzkrieg in the west, the two men worked far better together than could have been expected. In May 1940, events forced Chamberlain out of the Premiership. This was not what he wanted, and Churchill was seemingly not his first choice as his successor. Nonetheless, when Churchill did take his place, Chamberlain chose to back his one-time rival amidst circumstances of personal disappointment which might have driven a less public spirited politician to pick over old wounds. Punctilious and businesslike, Chamberlain could not bring himself to enthuse at some of Churchill's more rambling and irrational antics, but he learned to appreciate that they were secondary to the essential greatness of a man of destiny leading his country in its moment of peril.

Churchill was conscious that his future depended upon Chamberlain's loyalty and was generous in acknowledging its presence. In July 1940, he vigorously stamped upon the so-called 'under-secretaries plot' led by Amery, Clement Davies, Harold Macmillan and others to force Chamberlain out of office. The only serious issue of difficulty that emerged between Prime Minister and ex-Prime Minister throughout this period in government together concerned the recall of another past occupant of 10 Downing Street. Keen to broaden the basis of the government further, Churchill wanted to re-enlist the services of his old boss who had led the country to victory against the Kaiser's Germany in 1918. However, Chamberlain's personal experience of working with Lloyd George during that conflict had left him with a very different impression of the latter's suitability as a colleague. For over twenty years the two had made no secret of their low opinion of one another, a fact re-enforced by Lloyd George's intervention in the Norway debate. Churchill was asking much to expect them to work side by side now. Having already raised the subject before and been rebuffed, Churchill wrote to Chamberlain on 6 June, in a further attempt to persuade him of the necessity of having Lloyd George in the government 'in this terrible hour', and assuring him that if the former war leader did not work 'fairly and honourably with you', then he would have no hesitation in having Lloyd George removed.[39] Reluctantly, Chamberlain agreed on the condition that Lloyd George was animated by a similar degree of reconciliation, confessing to his sister that 'one cannot refuse anything in times like these to the Prime Minister, who is carrying the main burden of responsibility.' Chamberlain's comment that he feared that Lloyd George was 'waiting to be the Marshal Pétain of Britain'[40] was not necessarily a base slur upon a man he despised. Unfortunately, it was a defeatist impression that the old man was giving both in public and in private. In October, Lloyd George confided to his private secretary that he would bide his time before returning to power – intending to 'wait until Winston is bust'.[41]

Chamberlain's role as Lord President of the Council – requiring him to chair committees on home affairs, attend meetings of the War Cabinet and deputize for Churchill when the Prime Minister was away from London, was an onerous one. In mid-June, his health began to give way. Although he was as mentally alert as ever, he was now in periodic pain and had to leave the capital for rest. Even whilst he was laid up, his spirit was undiminished. On 14 July, he wrote to his sister that he had 'got so tired of waiting for Hitler to begin his invasion' that he had instead joined his wife Annie in rearranging pictures. 'We must just go on fighting as hard as we can, in the belief that some time – perhaps sooner than we think – the other side will crack.'[42]

At the end of July Chamberlain underwent operations. X-rays showed he had a cancerous stricture of the bowel. In mid-August he moved to recuperate at Highfield Park, a house in Heckfield, Hampshire, which was lent to him by a non-resident aunt.

Whilst he was recuperating, the Battle of Britain was at its peak. On 8 August, the British intercepted Goering's order of the day to his units: 'Operation *Adler*. Within a short period you will wipe the British Air Force from the sky. Heil Hitler.'[43] *Adler Tag*, 'Eagle Day', commenced on 13 August, with 1485 sorties over England. The skies of the southern counties were streaked with dogfights as the Spitfires and Hurricanes of Fighter Command did battle with the numerically greater forces of the *Luftwaffe*. It was assumed that if the *Luftwaffe* succeeded in knocking out the RAF, they would use their air superiority to launch Operation *Seelöwe* – the invasion of Britain, preparations for which Hitler had ordered on 16 July.[44] On 15 August, the *Luftwaffe* launched its most important strike, its target being Fighter Command itself. Unable to stay away from the nerve centre of the action, Churchill motored up to the Command HQ at Stanmore. There he watched as the staff in the operations room charted wave after wave of enemy raiders closing in, matched by a succession of red lights flashing to indicate that successive RAF squadrons were up and in the air, ready to intercept. As the duel continued throughout the course of the day, reports periodically confirmed the all important news – the RAF was gaining the upper hand. The

Germans suffered the greatest losses of any single day in the conflict, even though their eventual number of aircraft destroyed transpired to be half what Fighter Command initially calculated. Declaring it to be 'one of the greatest days in history', Churchill suddenly remembered that Chamberlain was lying stricken and out of the picture in Hampshire. Thoughtfully, he got Colville to telephone him with the figures. Chamberlain was 'overcome with joy when he heard the news and very touched at Winston thinking of him'.[45] Later in the evening, the BBC broadcast the tally to an apprehensive nation, intently listening to their wireless sets as if to the latest 'Test Match score'.[46]

On 9 September, Chamberlain managed to make it back to 11 Downing Street. The *Luftwaffe*'s Blitz of London had began in earnest two days previously, commencing fifty-seven nights of continuous bombing. The night-time raids made it difficult for Chamberlain to sleep and on his first night back in the capital, he confided in his diary that whilst he hoped to continue to serve the government until the end of the war, he had 'to adjust myself to the new life of a partially crippled man, which is what I am. Any ideas which may have been in my mind about the possibilities of further political activity, and even a possibility of another Premiership after the war, have gone.'[47] With bombs raining down all around him, the Blitz forced Churchill to hold his evening meetings of the War Cabinet in the reinforced annexe under St James's Park. He later recalled how Chamberlain made every effort to clamber into this underground cavern: 'nothing deterred him, and he was never more spick and span or cool and determined.' That Chamberlain never grumbled about the pain he was suffering was made apparent to Churchill when he discovered from workmen who were making a special sandbagged enclosure that Chamberlain was needing 'special periodical treatment' and that 'it was embarrassing to carry this out in the shelter of No. 11, where at least twenty people were gathered during the constant raids, so a small private place was being prepared'. Concerned about the discomfort of his colleague, Churchill walked through the connecting door from Number 10 to 11 Downing Street and, finding Mrs Chamberlain, made clear that her husband 'ought not to be here in this condition', advising that she should take him away until his health returned and that he would keep him fully briefed with daily telegrams in the meantime. Consulting her husband, Mrs Chamberlain agreed and Chamberlain was carried off to Hampshire that night.[48] It was the last time Churchill saw him alive.

Back at Heckfield, Chamberlain soon realized he could not go on in office. On 22 September he offered to resign. However, Churchill suggested that he take more time to see if convalescence would lead to an improvement in his condition. Chamberlain was keen to stay on if his health allowed it, expressing in the pages of his diary the desire that 'if I could get well enough, I could give him [Churchill] more help personally, and ensure him more support politically, than anyone else.' This state of limbo did not last long. Churchill's sudden decision to reshuffle his ministers following the disastrous operation at Dakar led him to accept the Lord President's offer after all. Although surprised by the suddenness, Chamberlain claimed to be 'very much relieved'[49] at the Prime Minister's decision, which took effect on 3 October. So ended sixteen years of government service in a parliamentary career of almost twenty-two years. On 2 October Churchill offered him the Garter, but he refused. Churchill wrote to assure him that 'the help you have given me since you ceased to be my chief tided us through what may well prove to be the turning point of the war. You did all you could for peace: you did all you could for victory . . . We have been associated, as our fathers were before us, in the ups and downs of politics, now together, now apart, but I look back upon this stern year of comradeship with feelings of the deepest respect and regard for you.'[50]

Churchill was right. It was only at the end of an often strained relationship that the two of them had really appreciated the talents possessed by each other. The unity that they found in Britain's 'finest hour' contrasted with the fate of the politicians who had gone down squabbling together in the darkest moments of France's time of trial. Daladier and Reynaud were amongst those whose reward for serving their country was to be arrested and thrown into prison. Their 'Vichy' successor and sometime colleague in government, Marshal Pétain, refused to lift a finger to save them when the Germans sought to remove them to Germany. Daladier was carted off to the Buchenwald concentration camp. When the Germans came to collect him from his cell at the Fort du Portalet, Reynaud could not resist scribbling a note of defiance to Pétain: 'Marshal, At the moment when you deliver me to the enemy I say to you, Long Live France!'[51] By then, Pétain had lost all ability to distinguish between necessity and dishonour. Following their liberation, his country-men ensured that he ended his days as a convict, initially in the same prison in which he had incarcerated Reynaud.

Changing the guard in Westminster involved the nation in a less torturous convulsion. With Chamberlain's resignation, Churchill was offered the leadership of the Conservative Party. This had never been intended when he was made Prime Minister of the wartime coalition; as Chamberlain's 9 September diary entry (quoted above) made clear, once Churchill's task of presiding over the all-party coalition had reached its objective by winning the war, the old party rivalries would be renewed under the direction of the old party leaders. Churchill's assumption of the party leadership meant that the Tories would be commanded by him in peace as well as in war. His wife, <u>Clementine,</u> who had never followed his conversion from the Liberal to the Tory Party with the same degree of commitment, advised him against taking it.[52] However, the example of Lloyd George, ditched as Prime Minister by the 1922 Carlton Club meeting, made the case for maximizing personal control over the party upon which a parliamentary majority was dependent. The Assistant Government Whip, George Harvie-Watt, told Churchill that 'it would be fatal if he did not lead the Conservative Party', and dismissed his worries about the remnants of pre-war hostility towards him, assuring him that 'it was only a small section of the party that took that line and that the mass of the party was with him'.[53] This was not a statement that could have been made with any confidence only a few months earlier.

The MPs and peers of the parliamentary Conservative Party, joined by the Executive Committee members of the caucus, assembled to confirm Churchill as their leader at the Caxton Hall on <u>9 October</u>. In the chair, having reassumed the leadership of the party in the Lords, Halifax proposed Churchill in a motion which by combining approval for Churchill with praise for Chamberlain minimized the prospect of dissent. A handful of irreconcilables failed to vote, but none was prepared to vote against – it was not as if they had a choice of voting for any other candidate. This was a very changed situation to that four months earlier when senior Tories had gone out of their way to persuade Halifax to become Prime Minister. The turnaround was a testament to the growing authority and prestige that the office had given Churchill and the reticence of malcontents to force (what would be interpreted as) a second assault on a national leader within the space of those few months. Animated by the spirit of the need for unity, Halifax, the most obvious alternative candidate, made no move to press for it himself. Only after Churchill had been formally endorsed did he enter the hall and deliver a vigorous speech, admitting his past differences with the party whilst making the most of his imperialist outlook and his commitment to the national interest.

Gladstone had once been a Tory Cabinet minister but had ended up as leader of the Liberal Party. Churchill had achieved the same feat, but the other way round. The path that brought him there had twisted and turned unexpectedly. During the 1930s he had championed causes such as imperialism in India and national rearmament which appealed to the right wing of the Conservative Party. In mounting these campaigns, he had become the tribune of groups that comprised sizeable factions within the Tory Party. On this basis, Churchill had maintained that a real 'National Government' coalition should include the viewpoints for which he was spokesman. This ran counter to Baldwin's strategy which aimed at keeping his own brand of moderate Conservatism in the ascendancy by interpreting the 'National Government' more narrowly, as a coalition of the centre ground. Given the electoral dividend with which Tories had been rewarded in 1931 and 1935, it was not surprising that Baldwin was able to maintain the adherence of most of his party to this alliance with MacDonald and Simon. Chamberlain inherited this framework in 1937, but although he shared Baldwin's desire to exclude from it troublemakers like Churchill, the new Prime Minister had never generated much parliamentary affection outside the ranks of the Conservative Party. This was to be his undoing when war broke out and the opposition parties refused to serve under him. Thus coalition government held the key both to Churchill's exclusion from office in the 1930s and to his subsequent return to power. When the National Government had been narrowly drawn to reflect the political philosophy of its masters, his factional campaigns had failed to force through his own claims for office. On the other hand, when in the crisis of 1939–40 the National Government was seen to be a victim of its narrowness in being unequal to the magnitude of events, so the campaign to have it broadened swept in Churchill. From the inside he then rose to become Prime Minister (but only because Halifax refused it) and later leader of the Conservative Party (but only because Chamberlain's health had collapsed). This was the combination of political realities and unexpected twists of fate which transformed Churchill's career.

Five days after Churchill had become the Tories' leader, the Carlton Club was demolished by a German bomb. There was a certain symbolism in this destruction of the temple of the old Conservative Party. Although the building was a write-off, miraculously none of the 250 members and staff in it at the time were killed. With his aged father, Lord Hailsham, on his shoulders, Quintin Hogg emerged from the rubble, in Churchill's colourful analogy, 'as Æneas had borne Pater Anchises from the ruins of Troy'.[54] The bomb also made Margesson temporarily homeless; handed some blankets, he had to rough it in a makeshift bed in the basement of the Cabinet War Room annexe. Now loyal to his new leader, this squat was a spartan billet for the man who as Baldwin's and Chamberlain's Chief Whip had spent a decade trying to undermine Churchill and his band of supporters.

There were bad times ahead for the Conservatives. Churchill was not interested in keeping the partisan fires of party interest burning at a time when his attention was focused on the more pressing menace from Hitler. This failure to be more attentive to the requirements of the party he had come to lead proved to be a source of discontent, particularly amongst those Tories who over the past decade had given him so little reason to cherish its traditions. There was not much that they could do to reassert themselves. In December, Eden replaced Halifax at the Foreign Office (Halifax took over as Britain's Ambassador to the United States whilst retaining a seat in the War Cabinet). Eden was not a threat to the Prime Minister; Tories who grumbled about Churchill were no more disposed to replace him with the idol of the 'glamour boys' than with any of the alternative leaders from the Labour ranks. Churchill had little to fear: those who had always hated him were tamed by the reality that he was now popular and they were not.

During 1941–2, the British Empire suffered a series of reverses – Greece, Singapore, Tobruk – humiliating defeats which were only compensated by Hitler's decision to maximize his enemies by declaring war on the Soviet Union in June 1941 and on the United States that December. The entry of these great powers into the conflict vindicated the almost blind faith with which Churchill had made Britain's decision to fight on alone in June 1940. In July 1942, his parliamentary opponents badly fluffed their last chance to remove him when he decisively trounced them in a vote of no confidence that they had called on the pretext of his continuation as Minister for Defence. By then, Parliament was, in any case, no place in which to launch an attack on the Prime Minister, the majority of its members either holding government office or away serving in the armed forces. In November 1942, the British Army at last proved it could decisively beat the *Wehrmacht* when Montgomery drove Rommel back across the desert sands of El Alamein. Churchill asked for the church bells to be rung, and declared it, correctly as it transpired, to be 'the end of the beginning'.

Churchill's popularity across the nation appeared undentable. It was natural that people should respond to being led by a man who in the darkest hours of 1940 had clearly not lost confidence in them. He was also helped by the fact that his previous exclusion from office in the ten years leading up to the war meant that he could not be held responsible for the state of apparent unpreparedness which was being seen as the cause of Britain's initial poor performance in the conflict. Had he not spent his time in the wilderness calling for more rearmament and less grovelling before the European dictators? Had Chamberlain and his gang not rubbished him at the time? Similarly, the Labour Party profited from the perception that they had not been responsible for getting the country into the mess and were now playing their part in trying to get it back out. Having voted against every increase in defence spending from 1935 to 1937 and against the Defence White Paper of 1938 and conscription only months before war broke out,[55] Labour benefited from the same short memory that took hold of a nation who had cheered Chamberlain like mad on the night of his triumphant return with 'peace' from Munich. The timescale between 'hosanna' and 'crucify' was a short one. The publication in July 1940 of *Guilty Men*, a hugely successful diatribe written by 'Cato' (Peter Howard, Frank Owen and the future Labour leader, Michael Foot), became a celebrated indictment of Chamberlain's Tories, the tired old men who, Mussolini had once privately prophesied, would lose their empire. Reacting to his growing vilification in the press, Chamberlain still maintained in a letter he wrote to the King on 30 September that 'I do not feel that I have anything to reproach myself for in my attempts to avoid the present war, which might well have succeeded if they had not come up against the insatiate and inhuman ambitions of a fanatic.'[56] Nonetheless, he was hurt by the curt and often hostile attitude that the press took to his departure from public life, confiding to his diary that 'not one shows the slightest sign of sympathy for the man or even any comprehension that there may be a human tragedy somewhere in the background. However that is just what I expected.'[57]

Chamberlain broadcast to the nation for the last time on 11 October 1940, again finding the sort of sentiments which could have been spoken by Churchill himself: 'it is not conceivable that human civilisation should be permanently overcome by such evil men and evil things, and I feel proud that the British Empire, though left to fight alone, still stands across their path, unconquered and unconquerable.'[58] His last days were spent at Highfield Park, his pain relieved by visits from his son Frank (who was on army leave), from Halifax, and from the King and Queen. As a privilege, Churchill got the King's permission for Chamberlain to continue to have Cabinet papers sent to him so that he could be kept in touch with events. The situation in the war was critical, German bombs even shattered Highfield Park's windows, but Churchill continued to write to Chamberlain endeavouring to keep up his spirits, encouraged by 'the tremendous mistake' the *Luftwaffe* had made 'in concentrating on London to the relief of our factories, and in trying to intimidate a people whom they have only infuriated. I feel very hopeful about the future, and that we shall wear them down and break them up. But it will take a long time.'[59]

Chamberlain died on 9 November. Churchill later reflected that he 'was sure' that he 'wanted to die in harness'. Although cancer had denied Chamberlain this end, Churchill acknowledged that 'he met the approach of death with a steady eye. I think he died with the comfort of knowing that his country had at least turned the corner.'[60]

In his letter of condolence to Mrs Chamberlain, Churchill identified the qualities that had brought him to admire the man against whom he had at one time been pitched: 'During these long violent months of war we had come closer together than at any time in our twenty years of friendly relationship amid the ups and downs of politics. I greatly admired his fortitude and firmness of spirit. I felt when I served under him that he would never give in: and I knew when our positions were reversed that I could count upon the aid of a loyal and unflinching comrade.' Mrs Chamberlain replied, thanking Churchill and assuring him that her husband had 'felt secure in the knowledge that you too would never give in'.[61] She was in the Commons gallery on 8 May 1945 to hear Churchill announce Victory in Europe.

VI

Neville Chamberlain's funeral took place in Westminster Abbey on 14 November 1940. Churchill and his Cabinet served as his pall-bearers. On arrival, the mourners were issued with the order of service and instructions on what to do 'should it be necessary to take cover during the service'. The fear of a single bomb wiping out the entire government had necessitated such secrecy about organization and timing that the huge Abbey was not filled. The congregation 'froze as they sat beneath the shattered windows'.[62] The magnificent Henry VII chapel had also been scarred: glass had been blown out from the east window as incendiary bombs rained down around it and the Houses of Parliament. The ancient seat of sovereignty, the Coronation Chair, had been removed to a place of greater safety, leaving behind the immobile memorials of its former occupants, stoically waiting for the invasion in stone, marble and an extra layer of high-piled sandbagging.

The noon-tolling bell filled the pause following the first intonation from the choir, 'I am the resurrection and the life, saith the Lord.' The lesson was read by the canon, 'awakening deep echoes with the triumphant phrases, "O death where is thy sting? O grave where is thy victory?" There followed the familiar pledges of the first hymn 'I vow to thee, my country.'

In the second pew sat Chamberlain's indefatigable allies, Rab Butler and Sir Henry 'Chips' Channon. Moving and dignified, 'the service was long', Channon recorded, 'and the Abbey was cold, that terrible ecclesiastic cold known only to English churches.' *The Times* described the scene reverentially:

> The clear, cold midday sunshine, flooding through the open great west door, bathed the Tomb of the Unknown Warrior and its wreaths of dark-red poppies in a sudden lucid radiance. The polished slab of the Tomb gleamed in the light like a pool of clear water. At the same time, as it happened, the sunshine through the lofty clerestory windows was itself growing momentarily stronger,

and the shafts of light, sloping downwards in clusters like spears, picked out
more and more brightly the purple-lined grave of the late Prime Minister. With
his burial in the Abbey that national shrine has acquired a new memorial that
is, in some sense, as representative of Britain in this war as the Tomb of the
Unknown Warrior is of the Britain of 1914–1918.

The catafalque was lifted on to the shoulders of six purple-cassocked
bearers, joined in procession by the Prime Minister and his Cabinet to the
hymn, 'Now the labourer's task is o'er'. After the gradual advancement
down the nave, the entourage came to a halt as the small casket was
lowered into a hollow in the flooring, Mrs Chamberlain kneeling over it
momentarily to scatter chrysanthemum petals.

One Tory MP felt 'sick to see the solemn humbugging expressions on
the faces of some of those who had made his last months a hell.'[63] Lloyd
George had avoided charges of gross hypocrisy by refusing to serve as a
pall-bearer. Channon, however, was nauseated by the reality of the
Conservative Party at prayer: 'There in the Abbey, and it angered me to
see them, were all the little men who had torpedoed poor Neville's heroic
efforts to preserve peace, and made his life a misery: some seemed to be
gloating. Winston, followed by the War Cabinet, however, had the
decency to cry as he stood by the coffin.'[64]

Chamberlain had been preoccupied with efforts to minimize the
devastating effect of the destruction of the country's great industrial cities
from the skies. It had been particularly on his mind as he looked down
upon London's packed streets from his aircraft window in the plane that
had taken him to negotiate with Hitler in September 1938. As night fell
on the evening of his funeral day, the Germans launched a 500-bomber
raid upon Coventry. Chamberlain had died just in time to avoid news that
would have caused him particular distress: the massive raids of 19 to 22
November which left nearly 700 civilians dead and a further 1000
seriously injured. The *Luftwaffe*'s target on those nights was Birmingham,
the city where the Chamberlain tradition of involvement in the affairs of
the nation had first started.

Two days before the last Caesar of inter-war politics had been buried, it
had fallen to his one-time adversary and successor, Winston Churchill, to
deliver the eulogy of praise.[65] Before the assembled parliamentarians,
Churchill reflected upon the vicissitudes of political life. A dominant
theme of the account in this book, it is fitting to end with a passage from
his testament. He referred to Chamberlain's tenacity of character in peace
and war; his sense of duty and desire to 'die like his father, plain Mr
Chamberlain'. On his own dealings with his late colleague, Churchill
related how he had passed in the space of a day from being one of
Chamberlain's chief opponents to being 'one of his principal lieutenants,

and on another day of passing from serving under him to become the head of a Government of which, with perfect loyalty, he was content to be a member. Such relationships are unusual in our public life.' The 'flickering lamp' of history would 'kindle with pale gleams the passion of former days', its judgement constantly altering according to the perspective of the moment, but Churchill maintained that one truth stood out like a rock:

The only guide to a man is his conscience; the only shield to his memory is the rectitude and sincerity of his actions. It is very imprudent to walk through life without this shield, because we are so often mocked by the failure of our hopes and the upsetting of our calculations; but with this shield, however the fates may play, we march always in the ranks of honour.

It fell to Neville Chamberlain in one of the supreme crises of the world to be contradicted by events, to be disappointed in his hopes, and to be deceived and cheated by a wicked man. But what were these hopes in which he was disappointed? What were these wishes in which he was frustrated? What was that faith that was abused? They were surely among the most noble and benevolent instincts of the human heart – the love of peace, the toil for peace, the strife for peace, the pursuit of peace, even at great peril and certainly to the utter disdain of popularity or clamour. Whatever else history may or may not say about these terrible, tremendous years, we can be sure that Neville Chamberlain acted with perfect sincerity according to his lights and strove to the utmost of his capacity and authority, which were powerful, to save the world from the awful, devastating struggle in which we are now engaged. This alone will stand him in good stead as far as what is called the verdict of history is concerned.

But it is also a help to our country and to our whole Empire, and to our decent, faithful way of living that, however long the struggle may last, or however dark may be the clouds which overhang our path, no future generation of English-speaking folks – for that is the tribunal to which we appeal – will doubt that, even at a great cost to ourselves in technical preparation, we were guiltless of the bloodshed, terror and misery which have engulfed so many lands and peoples, and yet seek new victims still. Herr Hitler protests with frantic words and gestures that he has only desired peace. What do these ravings and outpourings count before the silence of Neville Chamberlain's tomb?

NOTES

Introduction, pp. 1–5

1 Maurice Cowling, *The Impact of Labour 1920–1924: The Beginning of Modern British Politics*, Cambridge 1971, pp. 5–6.

Book One

Chapter 1 Ancestral Voices: 1880–1929, pp. 9–44

1 The highest offices in question are Prime Minister, Foreign Secretary, Home Secretary and Chancellor of the Exchequer. The last father and son to have both held these offices were David Lloyd George (Prime Minister 1916–22) and Gwilym Lloyd George (Home Secretary 1954–7). In the House of Lords, the highest office is that of Lord Chancellor, a position held by Douglas Hogg (Lord Hailsham) 1928–9 and 1935–8 and his son Quintin (Lord Hailsham) 1979–87. With the first Lord Hailsham a possible contender for the Conservative leadership in 1931 and his son relinquishing his title to fight for the leadership in 1963, the Hoggs have come closest to becoming the great political dynasty of British politics this century. The third generation continued this involvement with Douglas Hogg as Agriculture Secretary in John Major's government and his wife, Sarah, head of the Prime Minister's Policy Unit.

2 Churchill's sons-in-law Duncan Sandys and Christopher Soames both held cabinet office in the 1950s–60s. Nicholas Soames (grandson of Churchill) is the only one of his blood decendants to have held office (a minister of state in John Major's Government).

3 Prime Minister: Neville Chamberlain 1937–40; Winston Churchill 1940–5, 1951–5; Chancellor of the Exchequer: Lord Randolph Churchill 1886; Austen Chamberlain 1903–5, 1919–21, Neville Chamberlain 1923–4, 1931–7; Winston Churchill 1924–9; leader of the Conservative Party: Austen Chamberlain 1921–2; Neville Chamberlain 1937–40; Winston Churchill 1940–55. Nobel Prize for Peace: Austen Chamberlain 1925; Nobel Prize for Literature: Winston Churchill 1953.

4 Peter Clarke, *A Question of Leadership: Gladstone to Thatcher*, 1992 edn, p. 67.

5 Lord Randolph Churchill to Joseph Chamberlain, 19 June 1886, quoted in Winston S. Churchill, *Lord Randolph Churchill*, 1951 edn, p. 489.

6 Robert Rhodes James, *Lord Randolph Churchill*, 1959, pp. 298–9.

7 G.R. Searle, *Country Before Party: Coalition and the Idea of 'National Government' in Modern Britain 1885–1987*, 1995, p. 41.

8 Lord Rosebery, *Lord Randolph Churchill*, 1906, p. 181.

9 Lord Randolph Churchill to his wife, 23 November 1891, in James, *Lord Randolph Churchill*, p. 353.

10 Winston S. Churchill, *My Early Life: A Roving Commission*, 1930, pp. 40, 54, 70.

11 Churchill, *My Early Life*, p. 56; Winston S. Churchill, *Great Contemporaries*, 1937, p. 64.

12 Lord Blake, *Churchill and the Conservative Party*, lecture delivered to Westminster College, Fulton, Missouri, USA, 1987, p. 2.

13 MacCullum Scott diary, 23 January 1922, quoted in Searle, p. 135.

14 9 March 1922, published in *Gleanings and Memoranda*, April 1922, quoted in R.T. McKenzie, *British Political Parties: The Distribution of Power within the Conservative and Labour Parties*, 1955, p. 93. See also Austen Chamberlain's memorandum of 6 June 1922, in David Dutton, *Austen Chamberlain: Gentleman in Politics*, 1985, p. 175.

15 Quoted in Robert Blake, *The Unknown Prime Minister: The Life and Times of Andrew Bonar Law 1858–1923*, 1955, p. 457.

16 Andrew Roberts, *The Holy Fox: A Biography of Lord Halifax*, 1991, p. 305.

17 The only other non-Oxbridge graduate who became Prime Minister gained his degree from a Scottish institution: Lord John Russell (Edinburgh University). There have, of course, been numerous Premiers who never 'benefited' from a higher education at all: including Wellington, Disraeli, Lloyd George and Winston Churchill.

18 Quoted in Peter Clarke, *A Question of Leadership*, p. 114.

19 H. Montgomery Hyde, *Neville Chamberlain*, 1976, p. 27.

20 Neville Chamberlain to Lloyd George, 29 June 1917, quoted in David Dilks, *Neville Chamberlain*, Cambridge 1984, p. 237.

21 Dilks, *Neville Chamberlain*, p. 201.

22 Neville Chamberlain diary, 17 December 1917, in Hyde, *Neville Chamberlain*, p. 28.

23 John Charmley, *Churchill: The End of Glory*, 1993, pp. 195–6.

24 Churchill to Lord Derby, 13 April 1924, quoted in Charmley, *Churchill*, p. 197.

25 Dilks, *Neville Chamberlain*, p. 398.

26 Clementine to Winston Churchill, 19 April 1924, in Martin Gilbert, *Winston S. Churchill*, companion vol. V, Part 1, p. 147.

27 P.J. Grigg, *Prejudice and Judgement*, 1948, p. 174.

28 Neville Chamberlain Diary, 1 May 1925, in Dilks, *Neville Chamberlain*, p. 431.

29 Paul Addison, *Churchill on the Home Front 1900–1955*, 1992, p. 439.

30 Dilks, *Neville Chamberlain*, p. 441.

31   Norman Rose, *Churchill: An Unruly Life*, 1994, pp. 132–3.

32   Addison, *Churchill on the Home Front*, pp. 432–41.

33   Quoted in R.A.C. Parker, *Chamberlain and Appeasement: British Policy and the Coming of the Second World War*, 1993, p. 5.

34   Quoted in Charmley, *Churchill*, p. 192.

35   *Birmingham Daily Post*, 18 January 1907, quoted in Iain Macleod, *Neville Chamberlain*, 1961, p. 50.

36   Neville Chamberlain to Baldwin, 30 August 1925, in Dilks, *Neville Chamberlain*, p. 441.

37   Neville Chamberlain to his wife, 25 January 1928, in Dilks, *Neville Chamberlain*, p. 546.

38   Neville Chamberlain diary, 19 April 1928, Neville Chamberlain Papers 2/22.

39   Neville Chamberlain diary, 1 July 1927, Neville Chamberlain Papers 2/22.

40   Neville Chamberlain to Baldwin, 30 August 1925, in Dilks, *Neville Chamberlain*, p. 441.

41   Baldwin to Lord Irwin, 15 September 1927, in Gilbert, companion vol. V, Part 1, p. 1050.

42   Neville to Hilda Chamberlain, 31 March 1928, in Macleod, p. 129.

43   Neville to Hilda Chamberlain, 5 May 1929, in Macleod, p. 130.

44   Amery to Baldwin, 11 March 1929, Baldwin Papers 26/88–92.

45   Amery diary, 27 February 1929, in John Barnes and David Nicholson (eds), *The Leo Amery Diaries 1896–1929*, 1980, p. 590.

46   Tom Jones diary, 23 February and 13 April 1929, in Keith Middlemas (ed.), *Thomas Jones Whitehall Diary*, vol. II: *1926–30*, pp. 172, 179.

47   Philip Snowden to the House of Commons, Budget debate, reported in *The Times*, 16 April 1929.

48   Chamberlain to Irwin, 12 August 1928, in Dilks, *Neville Chamberlain*, p. 559.

Chapter 2   Civil War inside the Conservative Party, pp. 45–76

1   Tom Jones diary, quoted in Martin Gilbert, *Winston S. Churchill*, vol. V: *1922–1939*, 1976, p. 328.

2   Paul Addison, *The Road to 1945: British Politics and the Second World War*, 1975, p. 28.

3   Tom Jones diary, 29 June 1929, Middlemas (ed.), p. 190.

4   Quoted in Peter Clarke, *A Question of Leadership*, p. 118.

5   Philip Williamson, 'The Doctrinal Politics of Stanley Baldwin', in Michael Bentley (ed.), *Public and Private Doctrine: Essays in British History Presented to Maurice Cowling*, Cambridge 1993, pp. 185–6; Martin J. Wiener, *English Culture and the Decline of the Industrial Spirit, 1850–1980*, Cambridge 1981, p. 100.

6   Paul Addison, 'Destiny, history and providence: the religion of Winston Churchill', in Bentley (ed.), *Public and Private Doctrine*, pp. 242–3.

7   Paul Addison, 'The Political Beliefs of Winston Churchill', in *Transactions of the Royal Historical Society*, 5: 30 (1980), 23–47; Maurice Cowling,

Religion and Public Doctrine in Modern England, vol. I, Cambridge 1980, pp. 304–12.

8   Speech to the Royal Society of St George, 6 May 1924, in Stanley Baldwin, *On England*, 1926, pp. 6–7.

9   Martin J. Wiener, *English Culture and the Decline of the Industrial Spirit, 1850–1980*, Cambridge 1981.

10   Churchill to Baldwin, 29 June 1929, Chartwell Papers 2/572(a)/51–2; Churchill to Neville Chamberlain, 5 July 1929, Neville Chamberlain Papers 7/9/30.

11   Amery diary, 17 July 1929, p. 45.

12   Peter Clarke, *The Keynesian Revolution in the Making, 1924–1936*, Oxford 1990 edn, p. 64; Tom Jones diary, 6 March 1929, pp. 175–6.

13   Beaverbrook to Sir Robert Borden (former Canadian Prime Minister), 26 March 1929, Beaverbrook Papers C/52.

14   Neville Chamberlain diary, 6 July 1931, Neville Chamberlain Papers 2/22.

15   Churchill Papers 4/113/26.

16   Neville Chamberlain to Ida Chamberlain, 28 July 1929, Neville Chamberlain Papers 18/1/663.

17   Churchill's speech to the Commons, Egyptian (proposed treaty) adjournment debate, 23 December 1929, *Hansard* 233 HC Deb. 5s., col. 2009. Churchill made out a similar case to the proprietor of the *Daily Telegraph*: Churchill to Lord Camrose, 28 July 1929, Chartwell Papers 8/225.

18   Churchill's speech to the Commons, Supply Committee – Punjab Disturbances debate, 8 July 1920, *Hansard* 131 HC Deb. 5s., col. 1730.

19   Baldwin Papers 103/161–3.

20   Churchill to Lord Lloyd, 28 July 1929; see John Charmley, *Lord Lloyd and the Decline of the British Empire*, 1987, p. 167.

21   Phillip Williamson, *National Crisis and National Government: British Politics, the Economy and Empire 1926–1932*, Cambridge 1992, p. 87.

22   Irwin to Baldwin, 8 October 1929, Baldwin Papers 103/108.

23   Lloyd George to Churchill, 16 October 1929, Chartwell Papers 2/164/54–6.

24   Davidson to Irwin, 9 November 1929, in Robert Rhodes James, *Memoirs of a Conservative: J.C.C. Davidson's Memoirs and Papers 1910–37*, 1969, pp. 309–10.

25   Lord Lytton to Lord Irwin, 20 November 1929, India Office Papers MSS.Eur.c.152.18/309.

26   Hoare to Irwin, 13 November 1929, India Office Papers MSS.Eur.c.152.18/298.

27   Tom Clarke, *My Lloyd George Diary*, 1939, p. 81.

28   Nicolson diary, 23 January 1930, in Nigel Nicolson (ed.), *Harold Nicolson: Diaries and Letters*, vol. I: *1930–1939*, 1966, p. 41.

29   During the summer, many of the City's leading banks, the Empire Congress of the Chamber of Commerce, the Federation of British Industry and the General Council of the TUC had all called for the raising of tariffs against non-empire goods. Of the 72 per cent of the Federation of British Industry's membership that expressed a preference in its September poll, under 5 per

cent supported the comprehensive maintenance of free trade. On top of the Rothermere and Beaverbrook presses, the *Daily Telegraph*, *Morning Post* and even the more moderate *Times* all abandoned opposition to the principle of a food tax.

30 See Paul Addison, 'Patriotism under Pressure: Lord Rothermere and British Foreign Policy', in Chris Cook and Gillian Peele, *The Politics of Reapprisal*, pp. 193, 204–5.

31 Rothermere interviewed in the *Daily News*, 8 February 1930.

32 Amery diary, 30 January 1930, p. 60.

33 J.C.C. Davidson to Baldwin, 26 February 1930, p. 322.

34 Quoted in Williamson, 'The doctrinal politics of Stanley Baldwin,' in Bentley (ed.), p. 182.

35 See Churchill's speech at Wanstead, 1 March 1930, in Robert Rhodes James, *Winston S. Churchill: His Complete Speeches*, vol. V, p. 4729.

36 Anne Chisholm and Michael Davie, *Beaverbrook: A Life*, 1992, p. 295.

37 Chisholm and Davie, *Beaverbrook*, p. 298.

38 Neville Chamberlain diary, 19 October 1930, Neville Chamberlain Papers 2/22.

39 A gauge of Chamberlain's insincerity regarding Churchill can easily be measured through comments in his private papers; see, for example, Neville Chamberlain Papers: letters to Walter Bridgeman, 1 and 18 November 1930, 8/10/16b (c) and (l) and diary, 6 November 1930, 2/22.

40 Neville Chamberlain to Churchill, 21 October 1930, Chartwell Papers 2/572(a)/103.

41 Churchill to Baldwin, 16 October 1930, Chartwell Papers 2/572(a)/104–5.

42 Amery diary, 14 October 1930, p. 84. Churchill's friend, Brendan Bracken, was said to be particularly loose-tongued in this respect: Tom Jones to his wife, 3 March 1930, Tom Jones diary, p. 247.

43 Churchill to Baldwin, 24 September 1930, Chartwell Papers 2/572(a)/84.

44 Churchill to Beaverbrook, 23 September 1930, Chartwell Papers 2/572(a)/79.

45 Churchill to Beaverbrook, 23 September 1930, Chartwell Papers 2/572(a)/79–80.

46 Bruce Lockhart diary in Kenneth Young (ed.), *The Diaries of Sir Robert Bruce Lockhart*, vol. I: *1915–38*, 1973, pp. 123, 132.

47 Amery diary, 28 October 1930, p. 86; Earl of Winterton, *Orders of the Day*, 1953, p. 166.

48 Austen to Neville Chamberlain, 9 October 1930, Austen Chamberlain Papers 39/2/40.

49 Keith Middlemas and John Barnes, *Baldwin: A Biography*, p. 577.

50 Stuart Ball, *Baldwin and the Conservative Party: The Crisis of 1929–31*, p. 101.

51 Rothermere to Churchill, 13 December 1930, Chartwell Papers 2/180(a)/46–8.

52 Churchill to the Commons, 26 January 1931, *Hansard* 247 HC Deb. 5s., col. 702.

53 Lane-Fox to Irwin, 28 January 1931, India Office Papers MSS.

Eur.c.152.19/221; Baldwin to the Commons, 26 January 1931, *Hansard* 247 HC Deb. 5s., cols 744, 747, 746.

54 Addison, *Churchill on the Home Front*, p. 300; Charmley, *Churchill*, p. 248; Martin Gilbert, *Churchill: A Life*, 1991, p. 499; Norman Rose, *Churchill: An Unruly Life*, 1994, p. 190.

55 Lord Templewood, *Nine Troubled Years*, 1954, p. 48.

56 Neville Chamberlain diary, 12 March 1930, Neville Chamberlain Papers 2/22; Amery diary, 24 February 1931, p. 149.

57 Churchill to Baldwin, 27 January 1931, Baldwin Papers 104/157.

58 Of the more regular attendees at the Business Committee (Baldwin, Neville Chamberlain, Churchill, Hailsham, Peel, Oliver Stanley and Sam Hoare), only Baldwin, Neville Chamberlain and Samuel Hoare were to serve in the Cabinet of August 1931. After Churchill's resignation, only a further one (Hailsham) of the seven members joined the Cabinet of November 1931. Oliver Stanley did not join the Cabinet until 1935. Lord Peel and Leo Amery (who joined in place of Churchill) would not be favoured at all by Baldwin.

59 Neville to Hilda Chamberlain, 31 January 1931, Neville Chamberlain Papers 18/1/724.

60 Churchill's speech in Epping, 23 February 1931, in James (ed.), *His Complete Speeches*, vol. V, p. 4983.

61 Austen to Ida Chamberlain, 28 February 1931, Austen Chamberlain Papers 5/1/532; Amery diary, 7 and 11 March 1931, pp. 152, 155.

62 Lane-Fox to Irwin, 21 August 1931, India Office Papers MSS.Eur.c.152.19/120.

63 Neville Chamberlain Papers, diary 2/22/8 March 1931.

64 Churchill to Rothermere, 3 February 1931, Chartwell Papers 2/120(A)/32.

65 The selection procedure for the party leader is best discussed by Vernon Bogdanor in *Conservative Century*, especially pp. 69–74, and also by McKenzie, Chapter 2. Bogdanor, in particular, argues that although the process of selection before 1965 appears at face value to have been elitist and secretive, in its desire to find a unifying figure it in fact tended to represent successfully the majority will of the parliamentary party.

66 Churchill's recollections of 1948, Churchill Papers 4/113/25 (draft copy for *The Gathering Storm*, 1948). The Deputy Secretary to the Cabinet, Tom Jones, was also amongst those who thought that Churchill was 'disliked by the [Conservative] party': Tom Jones to A.B. Houghton (former US Ambassador to Britain), Tom Jones diary, 19 June 1929, p. 189.

67 Amery diary, 30 January 1931, p. 146.

68 Nicolson diary, 28 January 1931, p. 67.

69 Neville to Hilda Chamberlain, 31 January 1931, Neville Chamberlain Papers 18/1/724.

70 John Malcolm McEwan, 'Unionist and Conservative Members of Parliament 1919–1939', unpublished Ph.D., p. 343.

71 Amery diary, 9 February 1931, p. 147; *The Times*, 4 March 1931; Amery diary, 16 March 1931, p. 156.

72 Winston to Clementine Churchill, 26 February 1931, Spencer-Churchill Papers, reproduced in Gilbert, companion vol. V, Part 2, p. 280.

73 *Daily Mail*, article: 'Mr Winston Churchill's triumphal progress', 25 February 1931; see also other glowing references to Churchill in *Daily Mail*, e.g. 27 January, 28 January and 27 March 1931.

74 Reith to Churchill, 26 February 1931, Chartwell Papers 2/183/13.

75 Lane-Fox to Irwin, 4 March 1931, India Office Papers, MSS Eur.c.152.19/ 246.

76 Dawson to Irwin, 16 February and 5 March 1931, India Office Papers, MSSEur.c.152.19/236 and 248.

77 See memoranda from Conservative Central Office in the Baldwin Papers, e.g. 48/232.

78 *Daily Telegraph*, 25 February, p. 12 and 19 March 1931.

79 ibid., 27 January 1931, 'London Day by Day' (Peterborough).

80 Ball, *Baldwin and the Conservative Party*, p. 125.

81 Rothermere to Churchill, 21 January 1931, Chartwell Papers 2/180(A)/ 52–3.

82 See Williamson, *National Crisis and National Government*, p. 177.

83 Rothermere to Churchill, 29 January 1931, Chartwell Papers 2/180(A)/50; see also his telegram of the previous day, ibid., 2/180(A)/49; Churchill to Rothermere, 3 February 1931, ibid., 2/180(A)/62.

84 Rothermere to Churchill, 31 January 1931, Chartwell Papers 2/180(A)/52.

85 Churchill to Rothermere, 3 February 1931, Chartwell Papers 2/180(A)/62.

86 Sir Richard Brooke, Vice-Chairman of Bewdley Unionist Association/ Baldwin correspondence, 1 and 2 March 1931, Baldwin Papers 104/205 and 205.

87 Amery diary, 26 February 1931, p. 150.

88 Neville to Hilda Chamberlain, 1 March 1931, Neville Chamberlain Papers 18/1/728.

89 Topping to Neville Chamberlain, confidential, 25 February 1931, Baldwin Papers 166/50–3; Neville to Hilda Chamberlain, 1 March 1931, Neville Chamberlain Papers 18/1/728.

90 Topping to Neville Chamberlain, 25 February 1931, Baldwin Papers 166/ 50–3.

91 Amery diary, 2 March 1931, p. 151.

92 Neville to Hilda Chamberlain, 1 March 1931, Neville Chamberlain Papers 18/1/728 and diary 23 February 1931; Amery diary, 5 March, p. 152.

93 Sir Martin Gilbert in his *Winston S. Churchill*, companion vol. V, Part 2, p. 294, appears to have misread Chamberlain's handwriting and incorrectly claims that Cunliffe-Lister was talking not to Horne but to Sam Hoare, transforming the context of the conversation. For the original, see Neville Chamberlain diary entry 8 March 1931, Neville Chamberlain Papers 2/22.

94 See the pro-Irwin Tory MP for Tonbridge, Col. Herbert Spender-Clay to Irwin, 5 March 1931, India Office Papers, MSS.Eur.c.152.19/251.

95 Neville Chamberlain diary entry, 30 March 1928, Neville Chamberlain Papers 2/22.

96 Neville Chamberlain diary entry, 8 March 1931, Neville Chamberlain Papers 2/22.

97 Amery diary, 7 March 1931, p.153

98 Amery diary, 5, 6 and 7 March 1931, pp. 152–3.

99 ibid., 6 March 1931, p. 152.

100 Lane-Fox to Irwin, 12 March 1931, India Office Papers, MSS.Eur.c.152.19/266; Amery diary, 12 and 13 March 1931, pp. 155–6.

101 Baldwin's speech in the Queen's Hall, 17 March 1931, in Middlemas and Barnes, *Baldwin*, p. 600.

102 Amongst those making this charge is Martin Pugh in *The Making of Modern British Politics 1867–1939*, Oxford, 1982, p. 277.

103 Churchill/Rothermere correspondence, 1 February, and letters of 3 February 1931, Chartwell Papers 2/180(A)/55, 61 and 66.

104 *Daily Mail*, 18 March 1931.

105 Of these seven members, five (Col. John Gretton, Sir Alfred Knox, Reginald Purbrick, Sir Basil Peto and Sir William Wayland) were emerging as India diehards: G. C. Webber, *The Ideology of the British Right 1918–1939*, 1986, p. 36.

106 Churchill's draft statement for his cousin, the Duke of Marlborough, in his Chairman's address to the Albert Hall meeting, Chartwell Papers 2/180/114. Full text of Churchill's speech at the Albert Hall, 18 March 1931, in James (ed.), *His Complete Speeches*, vol. V, pp. 5003–9. Both Clive Ponting and Dr Carl Bridge are incorrect in stating that Churchill spoke at this meeting 'in favour of the Beaverbrook candidate'. Clive Ponting, *Churchill*, p. 344; Carl Bridge, *Holding India to the Empire: The British Conservative Party and the 1935 Constitution*, New Delhi 1986, p. 65.

107 *Daily Mail*, 13 March 1931.

108 Young (ed.), Lockhart diary, 12 April 1931, p. 163.

109 Amery diary, 25, 26 and 27 March 1931, pp. 157–9.

Chapter 3 All Centre and No Circumference:
the National Government, pp. 77–111

1 Pugh, p. 269.

2 Official unemployment figures in *The Times*, 6 August 1931.

3 *The Times*, 1 and 30 January 1931: evidence before the Royal Commission on Unemployment Insurance.

4 Snowden's BBC Budget broadcast explanation, *The Times*, 12 September 1931.

5 *The Times*, 21 September 1931.

6 Williamson, *National Crisis and National Government*, p. 75.

7 See report of Cliveden dinner party attended by Oliver Stanley, Walter Elliot, Brendan Bracken, Harold Macmillan and Bob Boothby, in Tom Jones diary, 26 October 1931, p. 274.

8 Conversation between Macmillan and Harold Nicolson, Nicolson diary, 30 May 1931, p. 76. The Tory MP, W.E.D. Allen resigned from the Conservative Party at this time in order to join the New Party.

9 28 May 1930, *Hansard* 239 HC Deb. 5s., cols 1424–5.
10 Churchill's speech to the West Essex Conservative Association, 23 February 1931, in James (ed.), *His Complete Speeches* vol. V, p. 4984.
11 Churchill's speech to the Constitutional Club, London, 26 March 1931, ibid., p. 5010.
12 Churchill's speech in the Budget debate, 29 April 1931, *Hansard* 251 HC Deb. 5s. cols 1657–8, 1665, 1667–8.
13 Churchill's speech on the Unemployment Insurance (no. 4) Bill's second reading, 26 June 1931, *Hansard* 254 HC Deb 5s., cols 842, 843–9.
14 Nicolson diary, 23 July 1931, in Nicolson (ed.), vol. I, p. 83.
15 Clive Ponting has led the way in misunderstanding Churchill's economic views during this period and has even described Churchill's advocacy of a sub-Parliament as a 'semi-corporatist, anti-democratic alternative that would have appealed to any authoritarian state in the Mussolini mould'. Considering that the House of Commons was to retain the veto on any suggestions from the sub-Parliament, Mr Ponting must either misunderstand Churchill's proposal, or the nature of fascism, or both. Ponting, p. 351.
16 Churchill's speech to the Supply Committee, 28 May 1930, *Hansard* 239 HC Deb. 5s., cols 1424–5.
17 See Williamson, *National Crisis and National Government*, pp. 147–8.
18 Young (ed.), Lockhart diary, 10 March 1931, pp. 156–7; Robert Boothby is a case in point during this period. According to Margot Asquith, Harold Macmillan, who had been close to Churchill in the late government in formulating de-rating policy, was by this time desperately trying to disassociate himself from Churchill due to his Indian campaign. Robert Rhodes James, *Bob Boothby: A portrait*, 1991, p. 100; Lady Oxford and Asquith to Duff Cooper, quoted in John Charmley, *Duff Cooper: The Authorised Biography*, 1986, p. 65; Alistair Horne, *Harold Macmillan*, vol. I: *1894–1956*, 1988, pp. 109–10.
19 *Daily Telegraph*, 2 February 1931, 'London Day by Day' (Peterborough).
20 MacDonald diary, 9 November 1930, in David Marquand, *Ramsay MacDonald*, 1977, p. 577.
21 Marquand, *Ramsay MacDonald*, pp. 575–80; Stuart Ball, 'The Conservative Party and the Formation of the National Government: August 1931', in *Historical Journal*, 29:1 (1986), 160.
22 Neville to Ida Chamberlain, 11 July 1931; Neville to Hilda Chamberlain 18 May 1931; Neville Chamberlain diary, 6 July 1931, Neville Chamberlain Papers 2/22.
23 Churchill's speech to the Commons in the Representation of the People (no. 2) Bill debate, 2 July 1931, in James (ed.), *His Complete Speeches*, vol. V, pp. 5041, 5044.
24 Williamson, *National Crisis and National Government*, p. 245.
25 Neville Chamberlain diary, 6 July 1931, Neville Chamberlain Papers 2/22.
26 Williamson, *National Crisis and National Government*, p. 116n; Frank Owen, *Tempestuous Journey: Lloyd George, His Life and Times*, 1954, p.

717; Neville Chamberlain diary, 24 July 1931, Neville Chamberlain Papers 2/22.

27   Williamson, *National Crisis and National Government*, p. 149.

28   Nicolson diary, 20, 21 and 23 July 1931, pp. 80–3.

29   When the formation of the National Government took place with Lloyd George seriously ill and Churchill holidaying abroad, the latter flew in briefly from France for what was intended to be a secret rendezvous with the invalid Liberal. Nothing obvious emerged from it other than that both publicly endorsed the formation of the National Government – the reverse of the post-prandial conversation that had so excited Harold Nicolson in July. The position of support for the National administration continued until, with the calling of the general election in October, Churchill maintained his backing for the government whilst Lloyd George withdrew his, marginalizing himself entirely in the process and, like Mosley, finding himself marooned in the loneliness of political independence.

30   Chris Cook and John Ramsden, *By-Elections in British Politics*, 1973, p. 78.

31   Amery diary, 26 March 1931, p. 158.

32   Report in the *Yorkshire Post*, 27 March 1931, quoted in David Dutton, *Simon: A Political Life of Sir John Simon*, p. 106.

33   *The Times*, 25 August 1931.

34   *The Times*, 17 August 1931.

35   Neville to Hilda Chamberlain, 16 August 1931, Neville Chamberlain Papers 18/1/751.

36   Kingsley Wood, Cunliffe-Lister, Lord Hailsham and the Chief Whip, Eyres-Monsell.

37   Neville to Annie Chamberlain, 23 August 1931, Neville Chamberlain Papers 1/26/447.

38   Neville to Annie Chamberlain and diary entry for 23 August 1931, Neville Chamberlain Papers 1/26/447 and 2/22.

39   Neville to Annie Chamberlain, 24 August 1931, Neville Chamberlain Papers 1/26/448.

40   Keith Feiling, *The Life of Neville Chamberlain*, p. 193.

41   J.D. Fair, 'The Conservative Basis for the Formation of the National Government of 1931', in *Journal of British Studies*, 19 (1980), most clearly articulated the case for Chamberlain as the manipulator of events but this has now been ably refuted by Stuart Ball, *Historical Journal*, 29:1 (1986).

42   Ball, *Historical Journal*, 29:1 (1986), 176.

43   *The Times*, 25 August 1931.

44   Official statement of the National Government, quoted in *The Times*, 25 August 1931.

45   *The Times*, 26 August 1931.

46   Amery diary, 30 August 1931, p. 195

47   Amery diary, 29 August 1931, p. 195n.

48   Leaflet to his constituents, September 1931, Templewood Papers VII:1.

49   Hoare to Neville Chamberlain, August (?) 1931, Templewood Papers VII:1.

50   Templewood, *Nine Troubled Years*, p. 41.

51 Reported conversation between Cunliffe-Lister and Lord Bayford, 22 March 1931, in John Ramsden (ed.), *Real Old Tory Politics: The Political Diaries of Sir Robert Sanders, Lord Bayford, 1910–35*, 1984, p. 245.

52 Charmley, *Churchill*, p. 266.

53 Amery to his wife, 25 August, and Amery diary, 28 August 1931, pp. 193, 194–5.

54 Contrary to the legend, despite the fact that the miners were rioting, the soldiers, obeying Churchill's instructions, killed no one.

55 Ball, *Baldwin and the Conservative Party*, pp. 114–5, 135, 189.

56 Horne to Neville Chamberlain, 18 August 1931, Baldwin Papers 44/43.

57 Churchill to Brendan Bracken, 23 August 1931, Chartwell Papers 8/290.

58 Nicolson diary, 31 August 1931.

59 Neville to Hilda Chamberlain, 14 February 1931, Neville Chamberlain Papers 18/1/726.

60 Nicolson diary, 1 October 1931, p. 93.

61 Nicholas Mosley, *Rules of the Game: Sir Oswald and Lady Cynthia Mosley, 1896–1933*, 1982, p. 188.

62 Middlemas and Barnes, p. 175; *The Times*, 29 August 1931.

63 Amery in *The Times*, 28 August 1931

64 A.J.P. Taylor, *Beaverbrook*, p. 317.

65 Amery diary, 26 August 1931, pp. 193–4.

66 Amery diary, 28 August 1931, p. 194.

67 Churchill's speech to the Commons on the financial situation, 8 September 1931, *Hansard* 256 HC Deb. 5s., cols 44–9.

68 Young (ed.), Lockhart diary, 20 September 1930, p. 186.

69 Amery diary, 8 September 1931, p. 199.

70 Baldwin's speech, 8 September 1931, *Hansard* 256 HC Deb. 5s., cols 66–72.

71 Snowden's BBC broadcast explanation of the Budget, *The Times*, 12 September 1931.

72 Quoted in Harold Wilson, *The Labour Government 1964–1970: A Personal Record*, 1971, p. 464.

73 *The Times*, 21 September 1931.

74 Charles Loch Mowat, *Britain Between the Wars 1918–1940*, 1956 edn, p. 404.

75 Neville to Ida Chamberlain, 19 September 1931, Neville Chamberlain Papers 18/1/755.

76 *The Times*, 16 September 1931.

77 Dawson diary, 13 September 1931, quoted in Sir Evelyn Wrench, *Geoffrey Dawson and Our Times*, pp. 292–3.

78 Neville to Ida Chamberlain, 19 September 1931, Neville Chamberlain Papers 18/1/755.

79 *The Times*, 25 September 1931.

80 Amery diary, 24 September 1931, p. 204.

81 Amery diary, 23 September 1931, p. 203.

82 Amery diary, 24 September 1931, pp. 203–4.

83 Amery diary, 24 September 1931, p. 203.

84 Amery diary, 30 and 1 October 1931, p. 206.

85 Amery diary, 28 September 1931, p. 205.

86 Amery diary, 29 September 1931, p. 206.

87 Amery diary, 1 October 1931, p. 206.

88 Amery diary, 6 October 1931, p. 209.

89 Lloyd George's final message to the electorate before polling. *The Times*, 26 October 1931.

90 Quoted in Feiling, pp. 196–7.

91 Tom Stannage, *Baldwin Thwarts the Opposition: The British General Election of 1935*, 1981, pp. 22–4.

92 See James (ed.), *His Complete Speeches*, vol. V, pp. 5084–8.

93 Churchill's election address at Theydon Bois, ibid., p. 5088.

94 Churchill's election address at Wanstead, 10 October 1931, ibid., p. 5084; Bernard Wasserstein, *Herbert Samuel*, p. 331.

95 Thomas Jones to Gwendoline Davies (sister of Lord Davies), 28 October 1931, in Thomas Jones, *A Diary with Letters*, Oxford 1954, p. 20.

96 Amery diary, 27 October 1931, p. 212.

Chapter 4   The Eminence Grise, pp. 112–141

1   Churchill, *Great Contemporaries*, p. 63.

2   Neville to Hilda Chamberlain, 24 October 1931, Neville Chamberlain Papers 18/1/759.

3   Ramsay MacDonald diary, 29 October 1931, in Marquand, p. 670.

4   Amery diary, 31 October 1931, p. 217.

5   Wasserstein, p. 335.

6   Churchill to the Commons, 11 November 1931, in James (ed.) *His Complete Speeches*, vol. V, pp. 5090–7.

7   Amery diary, 11 November 1931, p. 220.

8   Churchill's speech to the Commons, 11 November 1931, in James (ed.), *His Complete Speeches*, vol. V, p. 5095.

9   Churchill's speech at Forest Hill, 23 October 1931, ibid., p. 5088.

10 Churchill's speech in Epping, 12 October 1931, ibid., p. 5086.

11 Cabinet minutes, 21 January 1932, quoted in Wasserstein, pp. 341–2.

12 Amery diary, 22 January 1932, p. 227.

13 Feiling, p. 204.

14 Hyde, *Neville Chamberlain*, pp. 72–3.

15 Chamberlain to the Commons, 4 February 1932, *Hansard* 265 HC Deb. 5s., col. 296.

16 Churchill to the Commons, 4 May 1932, *Hansard* 265 HC Deb. 5s., col. 1173.

17 Churchill to Robert Boothby, 6 February 1932, in Gilbert, companion vol. V, part 2, p. 400.

18 Speech reconstructed from Churchill notes, in Gilbert, vol. V: *1922–1939*, pp. 429–30.

19 Churchill to Sir John Reith, 28 March 1932, Chartwell Papers 2/190; Churchill's public statement, 29 June 1932, Chartwell Papers 2/190.

20 Churchill's speech on the Budget, 21 April 1932, in James (ed.), *His Complete Speeches*, p. 5137; he had already conveyed this impression to Esmond Harmsworth, 29 February 1932, in Gilbert, companion vol. V, Part 2, p. 406. For similar utterances see, for instance, Churchill's speeches to the Commons, 11 and 24 November 1931 and to the Royal Academy, 30 April 1932, in James (ed.), *His Complete Speeches*, pp. 5091, 5104–9, 5154.

21 Beaverbrook's letters to Arthur Brisbane of 6 December 1931 and to J.L. Garvin, 19 January 1932, Beaverbrook Papers C/64 and C/140.

22 Churchill's speech to the Commons on the Budget, 21 April 1932, in James (ed.), *His Complete Speeches*, vol. V, p. 5136; Churchill's speech to the Commons on the Import Duties Bill, 4 May 1932, in James (ed.), *His Complete Speeches*, vol. V, p. 5108.

23 Headlam diary, 4 May 1932, in Stuart Ball (ed.), *Parliament and Politics in the Age of Baldwin and MacDonald: The Hendlam Diary 1923–35*, 1992, p. 237.

24 Gilbert, vol. V: *1922–1939*, pp. 420–3.

25 Sidney Pollard, *The Development of the British Economy 1914–1990*, 4th edn 1992, p. 95.

26 Amery diary, 17 August 1932, p. 253.

27 Philip Snowden, *An Autobiography*, vol. II, 1934, pp. 1026–7.

28 MacDonald to Samuel, 10 September 1932, in Wasserstein, p. 357.

29 MacDonald in July 1934, in *Marquand*, p. 678.

30 Lord Lothian to Tom Jones, 9 September 1932, in Jones, *A Diary with Letters*, p. 54.

31 'Handymade' in the *Saturday Review*, 2 December 1933, quoted in Wasserstein, p. 366.

32 Quoted in Feiling, p. 216.

33 Amery diary, 22 January 1932, p. 227.

34 Wasserstein, p. 361.

35 Roy Jenkins, *The Chancellors*, 1998, pp. 366–7; David Dutton draws a quick pen-portrait in Chapter 13 of his biography, *Simon*, pp. 323–39.

36 Pollard, pp. 94–5.

37 Pollard, p. 97.

38 Pollard, p. 95; P.J. Cain and A.G. Hopkins, *British Imperialism: Crisis and Deconstruction 1914–1990*, 1993, Chapter 3.

39 It should be noted that the rest of the world also increased its share of trade with the empire during the period. It could be contended that imperial preference so stimulated the economies of the British empire that other countries found themselves drawn into its markets in order to make a decent return regardless of the higher tariffs it introduced. An alternative argument might suggest that because the empire markets were growing anyway, the mechanism of imperial preference had little to do with it, as illustrated by the growth in its trade between friend or foe alike.

40 Pollard, p. 96.

41   Peter Clarke, *Hope and Glory: Britain 1900–1990*, p. 177.

42   Carl Bridge, *Holding India to the Empire*, New Delhi 1986, p. 73.

43   Neville to Ida Chamberlain, 20 February 1932, Neville Chamberlain Papers 18/1/771.

44   Pollard, p. 89.

45   Peter Clarke, *Hope and Glory*, p. 178.

46   Neville to Hilda Chamberlain, 6 December 1931, Neville Chamberlain Papers 18/1/771.

47   Baldwin to the Cabinet, 28 November 1932, in Middlemas and Barnes, *Baldwin*, p. 690; Feiling, p. 219.

48   Pollard, p. 98; Macleod, pp. 174–5.

49   B.E.V. Sabine, *British Budgets in Peace and War 1932–1945*, 1970, pp. 52, 30; Pollard, p. 100.

50   Chamberlain to the Commons, 25 April 1933, *Hansard* 277 HC Deb. 5s., cols 60–1.

51   Sabine, p. 29.

52   Amery diary, 25 April 1933, p. 292.

53   Jenkins, p. 352.

54   Amery diary, 16 February 1933, p. 289.

55   Chamberlain to the Commons, 17 April 1934, *Hansard* 288 HC Deb. 5s., cols 905–6.

56   Chamberlain to the Commons, 15 April 1935, *Hansard* 300 HC Deb. 5s., col. 1618.

57   Pollard, pp. 120–1.

58   Ministry of Labour 1934 Report, in Mowat, p. 465.

59   Ball (ed.), Headlam diary, 15 November 1934, p. 314.

60   Harold Macmillan, *Winds of Change 1914–1939*, p. 375.

61   Ball (ed.), Headlam diary, 1 August 1934, p. 310; 3 June 1934, p. 304; 1 August 1935, p. 339.

62   Ball (ed.), Headlam diary, 18 July 1934, p. 308.

63   Ball (ed.), Headlam diary, 13 December 1934, p. 317; 8 February 1935, p. 320.

64   Churchill's statement to the Press Association, 18 January 1935, Lloyd George Papers G/141/1/1.

65   Addison, *Churchill on the Home Front*, p. 309.

66   Lloyd George, Churchill and Austen Chamberlain to J.H. Whitley (Chairman of the BBC), 23 August 1933, Lloyd George Papers G/4/5/3.

67   Churchill to Lloyd George, 24 November 1934, Lloyd George Papers G/4/5/8.

68   Neville Chamberlain diary, 28 January 1935, Neville Chamberlain Papers 2/23A.

69   Neville Chamberlain diary, 28 January and 5 February 1935, Neville Chamberlain Papers 2/23A. Lloyd George to Sir Edward Grigg, 13 January 1935, Lloyd George Papers G/141/20/1.

70   Note of conversation with Baldwin, Tom Jones diary, 17 November 1934, in Jones, *A Diary with Letters*, pp. 138–9. This did not stop Chamberlain and MacDonald retaining doubts, however, as to whether Baldwin might

not be tempted to bring him in all the same. Neville Chamberlain diary, 3 May 1935, Neville Chamberlain Papers 2/23A.

71 Lothian to Lloyd George, 20 December 1934, Lloyd George Papers G/141/28/1.

72 Rothermere to Lloyd George, 25 January 1935, Lloyd George Papers G/141/43/1.

73 Harold Macmillan to Lloyd George with copy of his press statement, 21 January 1935, Lloyd George Papers G/141/30/1 and G/141/30/40.

74 Macmillan, *Winds of Change*, p. 377.

75 Ball (ed.), Headlam diary, 15 June 1932, p. 239.

76 Neville to Hilda Chamberlain, 30 October 1932, Neville Chamberlain Papers 18/1/803.

77 Middlemas and Barnes, p. 809.

78 Maurice Cowling, *The Impact of Hitler: British Politics and British Policy 1933–1940*, Cambridge 1975, pp. 44–5.

79 Feiling, p. 240.

80 Neville to Ida Chamberlain, 26 May 1932, quoted in Maurice Cowling, *The Impact of Labour*, Cambridge 1971, p. 297.

81 Ball (ed.), Headlam diary, 19 April 1932, p. 235; 25 April 1933, p. 267.

82 Ball (ed.), Headlam diary, 23 March 1933, p. 264.

83 Parker, *Chamberlain and Appeasement*, p. 9.

Chapter 5 India: 'The Making of a First-Class Crisis', pp. 142–158

1 The 1921 census. The figure for Europeans included Armenians.

2 Figures calculated in the *Morning Post*, 29 December 1932.

3 Urmila Phadnis, *Towards the Integration of Indian States*, 1968, pp. 1–19.

4 Cain and Hopkins, pp. 181, 185.

5 Amongst the competencies were education, health and agriculture, which were now to be held by Indians nominated from new legislatures. The Indian franchise in provincial government was increased to 5 million voters. On top of these reforms at the local government level, a more democratic element was introduced into the realm of central government. Almost half the representatives of the Central Legislative Assembly were elected by its 1 million voters. Again this advance was circumscribed by the reserve power of the Viceroy to overrule it. However, the institution of this body as a forum for advice and criticism was at least a foundation stone upon which future constitutional evolution was anticipated. Wise Viceroys would not make a habit of overturning clearly expressed majority votes on the floor of the chamber.

6 Bridge, *Holding India to the Empire*, pp. 2–8, 14–15.

7 Interview between the author and Lord Deedes, 10 March 1998.

8 Hoare to Willingdon, 17 December 1931, in Bridge, *Holding India to the Empire*, p. 81.

9 Speech in Epping, 23 February 1931, James (ed.), *Complete Speeches*, p. 4985.

10 Neville to Hilda Chamberlain, 6 December 1931, Neville Chamberlain Papers 18/1/764.

11   Bridge, *Holding India to the Empire*, p. 80.

12   The Viceroy would have the power to veto the budget and have control over sterling and foreign loans; the British Government would appoint members of the Reserve Bank charged with the management of the currency.

13   Cabinet minute, 10 March 1933, Cabinet Papers 23/75, Gilbert, vol. V: *1922–1939*, pp. 470-1.

14   *Sunday Express*, 1 January 1933.

15   Hoare to Ramsay MacDonald, 1 July 1932, Templewood Papers VII:1.

16   Hoare to Willingdon, 10 February 1933, India Office Papers MSS.Eur.E.240(3)/601.

17   Hoare to Willingdon, 25 February 1933, India Office Papers MSS.Eur.E.240(3)/615.

18   Hoare to Willingdon, 5 May 1933, India Office Papers MSS.Eur.E.240(3)/693-4.

19   Hoare to Willingdon, 19 May 1933, India Office Papers MSS.Eur.E.240(3)/706.

20   Churchill to Lloyd, 22 July 1932, Chartwell Papers 2/189/94.

21   Salisbury to Churchill, 10 March 1933, Chartwell Papers 2/192/58.

22   This course of action had been particularly advocated by the India Empire Society's President and former Lord of Appeal in Ordinary, Lord Sumner. Churchill to Lord Hugh Cecil, 11 March 1933, Chartwell Papers 2/192/60; Churchill to Salisbury, 12 March 1933, Chartwell Papers 2/192/63.

23   Editorial in *The Times*, 23 February 1933.

24   In April 1933, Rab Butler had drawn up for Conservative Central Office a 'White List' of likely backbench supporters of the Indian White Paper and a 'Black List' of those likely to oppose. Central Office was advised that those on the Black List 'Mr Butler would suggest should not be recommended as speakers on India at Conservative meetings'. There were 103 names on the Black List (obvious names like Churchill's were not even mentioned) and 47 on the White List. When updated in October 1934, the White List had gone up to 56, the Black List had slipped to 60 and a new 'Grey List' of waverers had been created with 43 names (of which four were said to be White Grey, two Grey White, and one Black Grey). Butler Papers F. 73/50-3, 60-1, 68-9, 77-9, 87-8.

25   Hoare to Willingdon, 25 February 1933, India Office Papers MSS.Eur.E.240(3)/614.

26   *Indian Empire Review*, March 1933 issue, pp. 43-9.

27   Churchill/Sydenham correspondence, 2 and 7 January 1932, Chartwell Papers 2/192/1 and 2. During 1933, Churchill became more outspoken in his criticism of Baldwin's resolve 'to force the India abdication policy through at all costs and by every use of the party machinery at [his] disposal'. Churchill's press statement, 30 April 1933, Chartwell Papers 2/193/66.

28   *Indian Empire Review*, April 1933 issue, p. 18.

29   Churchill to Bracken, 29 July 1932, Chartwell Papers 2/189/95; Hoare to Willingdon, 9 September 1932, India Office Papers MSS.Eur.240.2/412.

Lord Lloyd was keen also to involve Rothermere's son, Esmond Harmsworth. See Lloyd to Churchill, 1 June 1932, Chartwell Papers 2/189/60.

30 Churchill's speech of 17 February 1933, quoted in Gilbert, vol. V: 1922–1939, p. 465, and companion vol. V, Part 2, p. 529n.

31 *The Times*, 1 March 1933.

32 Hoare to Willingdon, 3 March 1933, India Office Papers, MSS.Eur.E.240(3)/621–2.

33 ibid.

34 *Indian Empire Review*, April 1933 issue, p. 13.

35 Churchill to Margesson, 1 March 1933, Chartwell Papers 2/192/41–2.

36 Patrick Donner also recalled in his memoirs that Admiral Keynes and Lords Lymington and Wolmer were at the inception of the IDC; see Patrick Donner, *Crusade: A Life Against the Calamitous Twentieth Century*, 1984, pp. 118–19.

37 Churchill to Salisbury, 12 March 1933, Chartwell Papers 2/192/63; Churchill to Patrick Donner, 17 March 1933, Chartwell Papers 2/197/5.

38 Churchill to the Duke of Westminster, 16 April 1933, Chartwell Papers 2/197/20. Churchill's memorandum on the proposed India campaign, 16 April 1933, Chartwell Papers 2/197/21–3; Churchill's memo to Lords Ampthill, Beatty, Desborough, FitzAlan, Lloyd, Midleton and Sumner, 28 April 1933, Chartwell Papers 2/193/59.

39 Hoare to the Commons, 27 March 1933, *Hansard* 276 HC Deb. 5s., cols 713–6, 708.

40 Viscount Wolmer to the Commons, 27 March 1933, *Hansard* 276 HC Deb. 5s., cols 812, 814.

41 For instance, Lord Winterton who followed Churchill in the debate, reminding the House, in the unlikely event that it had forgotten, of Churchill's previous commitment to constitutional innovation not only in Ireland but in South Africa, and India too. Winterton to the Commons, 29 March 1933, *Hansard* 276 HC Deb. 5s., col. 1062.

42 The *Morning Post*, for example, compared the Indian safeguards to the old 'apologetic cough' in which Liberals, when pushed, used to mention the Irish Lord Lieutenant's veto, and suggested the homily that 'when a man proposes to retire, after a period of transition, and in the meantime hands over most of his power . . . the staff will look for its orders to the pushful young man with their future in his hands.' *Morning Post*, 18 March 1933.

43 John Charmley, *A History of Conservative Politics 1900–1996*, 1996, p. 89.

44 Herbert Samuel to the Commons, 27 March 1933, *Hansard* 276 HC Deb. 5s., col. 736.

45 *Indian Empire Review*, May 1933 issue, p. 20.

46 Gretton to Churchill, 30 March 1933, Chartwell Papers 2/192/131.

47 Hoare to Willingdon, 17 March 1933, India Office Papers MSS.Eur.E.240(3)/635; Hoare to Willingdon, 6 April 1933, India Office Papers MSS.Eur.E.240(3)/660.

48 Hoare to Willingdon, 31 March 1933, India Office Papers MSS.Eur.E.240(3)/655.

49 *The Times*, 30 March 1933.

50 Hoare to Willingdon, 31 March 1933, India Office Papers MSS.Eur.E.240(3)/655.

51 Churchill's speech to the Commons, 29 March 1933, *Hansard* 276 HC Deb. 5s., cols 1037, 1040, 1042, 1047–8.

52 *The Times*, 30 March 1933

53 Austen to Ida Chamberlain, 1 April 1933, Austen Chamberlain Papers 5/1/613: Edward Campbell to the Commons, 29 March 1933, *Hansard* 276 HC Deb. 5s., col. 1099.

54 Edward Campbell to the Commons, 29 March 1933, *Hansard* 276 HC Deb. 5s., col. 1099. Whilst the Duchess of Atholl rose to defend Churchill from these allegations of insincerity, and Sir Louis Stuart did his best on behalf of the Indian Empire Society to defend Churchill's words, the day had clearly reduced his esteem in the Commons. The Duchess of Atholl to the Commons, 29 March 1933, ibid., col. 1099; *Indian Empire Review*, May 1933 issue, pp. 20–2.

55 *Indian Empire Review*, May 1933 issue, p. 9.

56 Hoare to Willingdon, 31 March 1933, India Office Papers MSS.Eur.E.240(3)/655; Churchill to Page Croft, 31 March 1933, Chartwell Papers 2/192/133; Churchill to Lord Carson, 31 March 1933, Chartwell Papers 2/192/136. Victor Cazalet was also left in no doubt by Churchill that he would 'fight the White Paper to the bitter end'. See Cazalet diary, 19 April 1933, p. 154.

57 Hoare to Churchill, 31 March 1933, Chartwell Papers 2/192/135.

58 Churchill to Salisbury, 1 April 1933, Chartwell Papers 2/193/3; Churchill to Hoare, 1 April 1933, Chartwell Papers 2/193/5.

59 Gwynne also argued that Churchill's absence deprived the diehards of an able cross-examiner of witnesses and made less effective any minority report that the diehards could have produced as a viable and considered alternative to the majority report. Gwynne to Churchill, 4 April 1933, Chartwell Papers 2/193/8–9.

60 Churchill to Hoare, 5 April 1933, Chartwell Papers 2/193/11–12.

61 Lord Burnham to Churchill, 7 April 1933, Chartwell Papers 2/193/19.

62 Hoare to Willingdon, 12 April 1933, India Office Papers MSS.Eur.E.240(3)/673.

63 Hoare to Sir John Anderson, 28 April 1933, in Gilbert, *Winston S. Churchill*, companion vol. V, Part 2, p. 581.

64 See, for example, Charmley, *Churchill*, pp. 270–1; Henry Pelling, *Winston Churchill*, 2nd edn 1989, pp. 357–8; John Barnes and David Nicholson (eds), *The Empire at Bay: The Leo Amery Diaries, 1929–1945*, 1988, p. 279.

65 Page Croft to the Commons, 13 June 1934, *Hansard* 290 HC Deb. 5s., col. 1760.

66 Austen to Ida Chamberlain, 16 June 1933, Austen Chamberlain Papers 5/1/621.

67 Churchill's statement in the *Evening News*, 11 April 1933, Chartwell Papers 2/193/28.

68 Hoare to Willingdon, 6 April 1933, India Office Papers MSS.Eur.E.240(3)/ 660.

Chapter 6 'The Winstonians', pp. 159–174

1 Quoted in Stannage, p. 42.
2 Dawson to Baldwin, 6 May 1933, Baldwin Papers 106/70.
3 'The Conservative Choice', leader article in The Times, 8 June 1933.
4 Austen to Hilda Chamberlain, 28 October 1933, Austen Chamberlain Papers 5/1/637.
5 Addison, Transactions of the Royal Historical Society, 5:30 (1980), 41.
6 Baldwin's speech at Worcester, 29 April 1933, in Gilbert, vol. V: 1922–1939, p. 478.
7 The day before Baldwin's Worcester speech, the Horsham and Worthing Conservative Association of the pro-Indian reform appointee to the Joint Select Committee, Lord Winterton (who sat in the Commons), voted against the Indian White Paper by 161 to 17. Another government loyalist and junior office holder, William Ormsby-Gore, told his Stafford constituency association that 'Mr Churchill's organisation will seek to bring pressure on me through you'. Ormsby-Gore to his constituents, reported in The Times, 10 April 1933.
8 Hoare to Willingdon, 6 April 1933, India Office Papers MSS.Eur.E.240(3)/ 661.
9 Hoare to Sir John Anderson, 28 April 1933, in Gilbert, companion vol. V, Part 2, p. 582.
10 The constituencies were: Cirencester–Tewkesbury, North Islington, West Lewisham, Torquay, Hythe, Aldershot, Bath, Berwick-upon-Tweed, Dartford, East Willesden, Greenwich, Horncastle, Old Trafford, Central Wandsworth, York, Epping, Chichester, South-East Essex, Walkhampton, Westminster St George's, Bedford, Kingswinford, Nelson and Colne, Barrow-in-Furness, Ealing, Walton, Bilton, Stroud, Oldham, Burton, Gillingham, North Portsmouth, Taunton, Daventry, Kettering, Blackpool, Eastbourne, Ludlow, West Leyton, Bournemouth, Belton and Burgh Castle, Lowestoft, Farnham, Wood Green, Louth, New Forest and Christchurch, Stone, Isle of Ely, Woodbridge, Wrekin, Wells, Southsea, Canterbury, Manchester, Hampstead, King's Lynn, Newport, Cheltenham (see editions of the Indian Empire Review). It will be noted that most (though not all) of these constituencies were in essentially middle-class areas of southern England.
11 Churchill to Rothermere, 3 May 1933, Chartwell Papers 2/193/82; Churchill to Lord Beatty, 15 May 1933, Chartwell Papers 2/197/66.
12 Churchill to William Ormsby-Gore MP, 14 April 1933, Chartwell Papers 2/193/37.
13 Baldwin's speech in Worcester, 29 April 1933, in Gilbert, vol. V: 1922–1939, p. 478.
14 Churchill's press statment, 30 April 1933, Chartwell Papers 2/193/62–3.

15 Beaverbrook thought that on India Churchill was fighting out his 'farewell tour of politics' before retiring from Parliament. At any rate, thought Beaverbrook, if Churchill continued for much longer on his present course, his future might be decided by Baldwin trying to 'put a veto on him in his constituency'. Beaverbrook to the former Canadian Premier, Sir Robert Borden, 28 March and 7 January 1934, Beaverbrook Papers C/52. The India Office view reported to R.A. Butler was that Beaverbrook 'opposes Reform chiefly because of alliance with [the] *Daily Mail*, but has no sincere views'. India Office Memo 'Most Secret – To Be Destroyed', undated but clearly first half of 1933, Butler Papers F73/21.

16 Together with its favourable news coverage, the *Daily Mail* also supplemented the diehards' propaganda print-run with publications of its own. The biggest single such publication was the *Daily Mail*'s 1934 'Blue Book', 'Save India for the Empire'. Reading like a who's who of the Tory Unionism, the booklet contained a foreword by Lord Carson, a main article by Michael O'Dwyer, seven articles by Rothermere and brief statements from fourteen Tories (the Churchill line being, on this occasion, represented by Randolph rather than Winston) on why they sought to 'oppose surrender'. Thompson Papers, MSS.Eur.F.137/53/(A)/131.

17 Memorandum on the publication of the Joint Select Committee Report for J.C.C. Davidson, Davidson Papers MSS.Eng.hist.c.561/209; Davidson to R.A. Butler, 9 March 1933, Davidson Papers MSS.Eng.hist.c.561/63; Lord Camrose to Churchill, 25 October 1933, Chartwell Papers 8/326/(no subref.).

18 In November 1933 Churchill wrote to *The Times*' owner, bringing to his attention the 'petty bias and suppression' of anti-White Paper letters from leading IDL spokesmen to the paper. Churchill to J.J. Astor, 6 November 1933, Chartwell Papers 2/194/91. In fact, since the IES's foundation in 1930, *The Times* had published 'no fewer than 42 letters either from the Society as a body (10 in all) or from its individual members (Sir Michael O'Dwyer heading the list with 11, followed by Mr Wasis Ameer Ali and Lord Sydenham)'. Dawson in *The Times*, 19 January 1933. The tone of the newspaper's reporting and commentry was, however, undeniably supportive of the government's policy.

19 The BBC's willingness to do the government's bidding was already widely acknowledged and prompted the Commons debate of 22 February 1933. On 23 August, Churchill wrote a letter co-signed by Lloyd George and Austen Chamberlain to the Chairman of the BBC complaining about the Corporation's refusal to give air space to politicians who had not been nominated by their party leader or the Whips' Office. The negative reply at least gave the hope that no precedent had been created. Churchill, Lloyd George and Austen Chamberlain to J.H. Whitley, 23 August 1933, Lloyd George Papers G/4/5/3.

20 Bridge, *Holding India to the Empire*, p. 134.

21 Churchill to Rothermere, 3 May 1933, Chartwell Papers 2/193/83.

22 Churchill to Sir James Hawkey (his constituency Chairman), 30 April

1933, Chartwell Papers 2/197/35; Churchill to Salisbury, 13 May 1933, Chartwell Papers 2/197/56.

23 Rothermere to Churchill, 6 May 1933, Chartwell Papers 2/193/89.

24 Stannage, pp. 41–2.

25 The IDL was governed by a large General Council which, meeting like shareholders at a company AGM, convened annually to approve policy and elect the executive committee to manage the group's daily activities. Churchill's draft note on the India Defence League to his colleagues, undated but clearly March/April 1933, Chartwell Papers 2/197/77.

26 Sumner accepted the post of president after it had been turned down by Earl Beatty who refused on the grounds that he knew 'nothing' about the Indian reforms: Churchill/Lord Beatty correspondence, 15 and 16 May 1933, Chartwell Papers 2/197/60–4, 66–8. As the President of the Indian Empire Society, the rather more sedate organization that had disseminated opposing views to Indian reform up until that date, Sumner's appointment to the same post at the IDL symbolized the community of interest between the two organizations. Members of the IES were automatically given honorary membership of the IDL and transferred their Kensington premises to those of the IDL. The IES only had 1300 members of its own by 1933, although it retained its own programme, revenue and expenditure as well as editorial control of its journal, the *Indian Empire Review*, even after being brought under the umbrella of the IDL. *Indian Empire Review*, July 1933 issue, p. 5, and August 1933 issue, p. 19.

27 Churchill preferred not to accept the suggestion that he should sit on the IDL executive committee since this would interfere with his speaking engagements. Instead he wanted one of the vice-presidencies, a request which could not easily be refused. As Churchill wrote to the Duke of Westminster, 'Vice Presidents are ex-officio members of the Executive Committee who will really run the show, but need not attend their meetings unless they wish' – a job description that sounded ideal. Churchill to the Duke of Westminster, 24 May 1933, Chartwell Papers 2/197/78. In fact, the importance of the vice-presidency was largely determined by the character of its holder. It could certainly be supine enough. When the IDL's Chief Organizer, Vice Admiral Usborne, was seen to be inefficient at his post, he was politely given a vice-presidency instead, his organizational role being passed on to Captain Hugh Orr-Ewing. Gretton to Churchill, 21 September 1933, Chartwell Papers 2/197/81.

28 Norfolk's grandson, Lord Rankeillour, worked for the diehards on the Joint Select Committee. Donner to Churchill, 26 May 1933, Chartwell Papers 2/197/81. Sir Michael O'Dwyer was another prominent Roman Catholic on the IDL Executive. Churchill was noticeably less religious than many of his IDL colleagues. For an analysis of the correlation between the strength of religious belief and India diehardism, see Gerald Studdert-Kennedy, 'The Christian Imperialism of the Die-hard Defenders of the Raj, 1926–35', in *Journal of Imperial and Commonwealth History*, 18 (1990), 342–62.

29 The IDL executive committee was chaired by Viscount Wolmer, the future

Lord Selborne, who was Lord Salisbury's nephew and was married to
Churchill's cousin. One of the IDL vice-presidents, the Marquess of
Hartington, as heir to the Duke of Devonshire, hailed from Chatsworth,
which for generations had been the meridian of the whig world. Another
vice-president, Earl Howe, was the son of Churchill's aunt.

30 The IDL's parliamentarians were each asked to contribute £50 donations.
Donner, p. 119; Churchill to Rothermere, 6 November 1933, Chartwell
Papers 2/197/137; Churchill to Hugh Orr-Ewing (Chief Organizer, IDL),
17 November 1933, Chartwell Papers 2/197/138–9; Gretton to Gwynne, 5,
6 and 18 April 1933, in Bridge, *Holding India to the Empire*, p. 102.

31 quoted in Ball, *Baldwin and the Conservative Party*, p. 22.

32 The definition chosen here is that adopted by J.M. McEwan who has
identified eighty-two Tory MPs who persistently voted with the diehards.
The following comparisons are made with regard to this group in relation
to the 1931–5 parliamentary Conservative Party as a whole. McEwan,
unpublished Ph.D., Appendix H, pp. 498–500. McEwan, unpublished
Ph.D., pp. 350–4; Studdert-Kennedy, *Journal of Imperial and Commonwealth History*, 18 (1990), 355.

33 Just over 60 per cent of sitting Conservative MPs had been in Parliament, at
least at some stage, before the 1931 landslide. Of the 470 Tory MPs, 183
were new to the Commons, 236 had sat in the previous Parliament and a
further 51 had been MPs before 1929. Nearly 70 per cent of them had won
their constituency at the 1931 election with a sufficiently convincing
margin of victory to facilitate considerable independence of judgement
without fear of serious retribution. Of the 82 diehard MPs 57 might be
placed in this 'safe seat' category: 42 (51 per cent) had at the last election
majorities in excess of 10,000 (of which 19 – or 23 per cent – were over
20,000) whilst a further 15 (18 per cent) had been regarded as being so
secure that the opposition had not even bothered to put up candidates
against them in 1931.

34 Whilst their ranks included the names of many of the traditional great
political landed elite (interestingly these were often of whig rather than
Tory origin) the proportion was not dissimilar to that which backed the
government. Indeed, whilst Hartington, Lymington and Scone were heirs to
major estates, only about another three could be said to be primarily landed
aristocrats. This was below the average for the party as a whole. More in
line with the rest of the party, the middle classes were well represented
amongst the diehards whose number even included the working-class
member for Lanarkshire. Businessmen were reasonably represented
amongst them, supported, in part, by the nervous textiles interests of
Lancashire who had seen their market share further weakened by growing
Indian fiscal autonomy. In common with the rest of the party, half of the
diehards had been educated at major public schools (although only seven of
them were Etonians) but only just over half were university graduates.
Diehard MPs sitting for southern English constituencies were much more
likely to have had careers in the armed forces or civil service (domestic and
especially imperial) than their more business-orientated northern allies. No

less surprisingly, southern diehards were six times more likely to have gone to Oxbridge than other universities. Those in the textile belt were only marginally more likely to have attended Oxbridge than elsewhere.

35 Ten diehards represented London, fourteen represented the Home Counties, eight represented Wessex, four more the western counties and three the eastern counties. Outside the south, four represented the eastern Midlands and three the western Midlands, eleven represented Lancashire and Cheshire, five sat for Yorkshire, four for the Northern counties, seven for Scotland and six for Ulster. The university seats contributed a further three diehard MPs. See McEwan, unpublished Ph.D., p. 355n.

36 Charmley, *Churchill*, p. 272.

37 The IDL's Chief Organizer, Hugh Orr-Ewing, wrote to IDL supporters who were members of local Conservative constituency associations, asking them to forward to him the names and addresses of the officers of their associations and of the women's branches so that they could be targeted by mail. He also wrote to sympathetic chairmen of Conservative constituency associations advising them to send to the National Conference only those delegates they were sure would oppose the Indian White Paper. Copies of this correspondence were printed in a disapproving *The Times*, 29 September 1933.

38 See Stuart Papers MSS.Eng.hist.c.625/33–41, and reports in the *Indian Empire Review*, all editions, 1933–5. Two branches, Guernsey and the East India branch based in Calcutta, were, of course, outside direct parliamentary representation.

39 Of the MPs whose constituents had access to a local League branch, only twenty-two (a little over 17 per cent) voted with the diehards on the second reading of the India Bill in February 1935 and two of these were not even regular lobby division comrades of the diehards. In other words, over 80 per cent of MPs who had League branches covering their constituencies were not intimidated into voting with the diehards in Parliament. Further, doubt should be cast upon whether those MPs who did vote with the diehards did so primarily through fear of League activity in their constituencies. All but two of these twenty-two MPs had been in the Commons when at the outset of the parliamentary session's campaign, Churchill had divided the House over the second Round Table Conference on 3 December 1931. Eleven of the names could be found already voting diehard in this division, long before there was any serious talk of establishing League constituency branches. Of the remaining ten, it is not clear whether it was diehard activity close to home that was the essential encouragement in making their subsequent stand with the diehards. Some genuinely might have taken longer to formalize their views on the complicated issue of Indian constitutional reform. That League branches tended to be established in constituencies where the sitting MP was hostile should not surprise us. Diehard enthusiasts could be contented members of their local Conservative Association where the sitting MP was sympathetic for there was presumably not much energy to be expended in being reactionary when there was no one readily available to react against. Where

the League failed was in making allies out of its parliamentary targets. Graham S. Stewart, 'Winston Churchill and the Conservative Party 1929–1937', University of Cambridge unpublished Ph.D., Appendix. Using as his basis reports in the *Indian Empire Review*, Gerald Studdert-Kennedy has calculated that 60 per cent of constituency associations with sitting diehard MPs in the main urban conurbations submitted like-minded resolutions to party conferences, compared with 41 per cent of counties (excluding Greater London) south of a line from Gloucester to the Wash but only 15 per cent in the textiles area outside Liverpool and Manchester. Studdert-Kennedy, *Journal of Imperial and Commonwealth History*, 18 (1990), 346. This is not to say that those constituencies that did not submit such resolutions were in conflict with their MP on the Indian issue or that the *Indian Empire Review* list was completely comprehensive.

40 Hoare to Willingdon, 5 May 1933, India Office Papers MSS.Eur.E.240(3)/694.

41 R.A. Butler, *The Art of the Possible*, p. 51; J.C.C. Davidson to R.A. Butler, 13 March 1933, Davidson Papers MSS.Eng.hist.c.561/13.

42 UBI memorandum, undated, Thompson Papers MSS.Eur.F.137/51/37.

43 Thomspon to Lord Bingley (a UBI supporter), 24 December 1934, Thompson Papers MSS.Eur.F.137/49/365.

44 Interestingly, when the Joint Select Committee Report was finally published, since its composition and the other MPs had 'no longer any excuse for not coming out into the open [and] the Central Office, too, are now free', Thompson no longer saw a use for the continued existence of the UBI. It was Hoare and Baldwin who persuaded him to keep it going until they could get the India Bill firmly on the statute books. Thompson to Willingdon, 14 December 1934, Thompson Papers MSS.Eur.F.137/49/347.

45 Its four office-holders were more famous for their work in India than any time spent in Westminster. The former Governor of Madras and acting Viceroy for Irwin during 1929, Viscount Goschen, acted as its president despite initial misgivings about even putting his name in the newspapers for the cause (Butler, *The Art of the Possible*, p. 51). Goschen's ten-year career in the Commons had ended back in 1906, although as a peer (from 1907) he became a Joint Parliamentary Secretary for Agriculture in the 1918. Sir John Thompson, Delhi's Chief Commissioner from 1928 to 1932, chaired the organization and was supported by two vice-chairmen, Villiers and Sir Alfred Watson, the recently retired editor of India's the *Statesman*.

46 Thompson to Sir Henry Craik, 28 July 1934, Thompson Papers MSS.Eur.F.137/49/64. By September 1934, four UBI branches had been launched (London, Oxford, Guildford and North Hampshire), six more were in the process of formation and a further seven were contemplated. Owen Tweedy (UBI Secretary) to A.F. Morley (R.A. Butler's private secretary), 18 September 1934, Butler Papers F. 74/143.

47 Thompson Papers MSS.Eur.F.137/53/(B).

48 Butler, pp. 51–2.

49 Churchill to Rothermere, 6 August 1934, Chartwell Papers 2/228/21.

50 Thompson memo on UBI constituency committees, no date, Thompson Papers MSS.Eur.F.137/5.

51 In all, 326 meetings were addressed by pro-reform speakers, half of them during 1934. UBI speakers addressed 110 meetings in 1933, 158 in 1934 and 48 in 1935; Edward Villiers addressed 77 meetings and Thompson spoke at 38. Unfortunately no surviving record details the location of constituencies targeted by the UBI, although common sense would dictate that they were ones either where diehards sat or where the MP's stance was seen to be wavering. See Thompson Papers MSS.Eur.F.137/51/34–5.

52 The UBI local branches established were: Aberdeen, Alton and Petersfield (Hampshire), Bedford, Bournemouth, Bristol, Buckinghamshire, Camberley, Cambridge, Colchester, Edinburgh, Egham, Glasgow, Guildford, West Kent, London, New Forest and Christchurch, Northamptonshire, Oxford, Richmond, East Suffolk. Oxford was the first committee to be formed. Without any other surviving references to it, given the southern bias of the distribution, we must presume the Richmond branch refers not to Yorkshire but to Richmond-on-Thames. See Thompson Papers MSS.Eur.F.137/51/34.

53 Report from S.W. Swaby (northern representative of the UBI) to Owen Tweedy, 12 March 1935, Butler Papers F. 74/183–6.

54 The UBI's popularity cannot easily be discerned from its *Bulletin*'s growing print-run since it was often being sent unsolicited to groups who may, or may not, have been its happy recipient. Nevertheless, the print run of the *Bulletin* rose and fell as follows: 6263 (30 June 1934); 16,263 (30 November 1934); 11,114 (31 March 1935); 8321 (31 May 1935). See Thompson Papers MSS.Eur.F.137/51/34.

55 By August 1934 the UBI had spent only £6000, a fraction of the £30,000 that Thompson believed the IDL had spent over the same period. Thompson to Lord Brabourne, 8 August 1934, Thompson Papers MSS.Eur.F.137/49/85; Thompson to Lord Goschen, 12 August 1934, Thompson Papers MSS.Eur.F.137/49/106. By the end of 1934, however, UBI expenditure had reached 'about £11,000'. R.A. Butler to Hoare, 21 December 1934, Butler Papers F. 74/214. Unfortunately the IDL accounts have not survived.

56 As Sir Alfred Knox put it, scribbled in red chalk when returning to sender his copy of the *UBI Bulletin*, 'Where does the money come from?' Thompson to Lord Brabourne, 8 August 1934, Thompson Papers MSS.Eur.F.137/49/85.

57 Lord Goschen to *The Times*, 24 November 1933 and 19 October 1934.

58 Surviving documentation of any attempt by the UBI to raise funds is noticeable by its absence, and Thompson was perfectly relaxed about the matter, maintaining that they 'could count on such money as was necessary being forthcoming'. The leading players were closely intertwined with each other's activities and the UBI Treasurer, Lord Brabourne, was Hoare's former private secretary (and subsequently Governor of Bombay). Certainly, it is now clear that Central Office was intimately wound up in its tactics, holding meetings with the UBI and Butler throughout the period;

see documents throughout the India section of the Butler Papers, especially in F. 73 and F. 74.

59 Note of interview between Thompson, Villiers and Miss Maxse (Central Office), 27 September 1934, Thompson Papers MSS.Eur.F.137/49/203; Thompson to Lord Goschen, 12 August 1934, ibid., MSS.Eur.F.137/49/ 106. R.A. Butler to Hoare, 21 December 1934, Butler Papers F. 74/214–15.

60 House of Commons division of 31 October 1921.

61 Quoted in McKenzie, p. 86.

62 *1921 Conservative Annual Conference Report*, in McKenzie, p. 99.

63 Baldwin to the Conservative Central Council, 28 June 1933, Baldwin Papers 106/215.

64 Lord Carson to the Conservative Central Council, 28 June 1933, as reported in the *Indian Empire Review*, August 1933 issue, p. 5.

65 Hoare to Willingdon, 30 June 1933, India Office Papers MSS.Eur.E.240(3)/ 742; *The Times*, 29 June 1933; Butler, p. 52.

66 Churchill's speech to the Conservative Central Council, 28 June 1933, in James (ed.), *His Complete Speeches*, vol. V, p. 5278.

67 Ball (ed.), Headlam diary, 28 June 1933, p. 274.

68 *Indian Empire Review*, August 1933 issue, p. 6.

69 *Indian Empire Review*, November 1933 issue, p. 43.

70 *1933 Conservative Annual Conference Report*, folios 27–33.

71 Hoare to Baldwin, 5 May 1933, Baldwin Papers 106/69.

72 *Indian Empire Review*, February 1934 issue, p. 101.

73 *Indian Empire Review*, November 1934 issue, p. 467.

74 Orr-Ewing to Churchill, 20 August 1934, Chartwell Papers 2/227/13.

75 Wolmer to Churchill, 29 June 1934, Chartwell Papers 2/227/57–8.

76 *1934 Conservative Annual Conference Report*, folios 28–31.

77 Barnes and Nicholson, *The Empire at Bay*, p. 280. This point was also not lost on the liberal press: *Manchester Guardian*, 5 October 1934.

78 *1934 Conservative Annual Conference Report*, folios 28–30.

79 Page Croft to Churchill, 8 October 1934, Chartwell Papers 2/225/24.

80 Sir John Thompson (Chairman of the Union of Britain and India) to Lord Zetland, 28 November 1934, Thompson Papers MSS.Eur.F.137/49/315.

81 Report of the Council, *1935 Conservative Annual Conference Report*, folios 5–7.

82 Ball (ed.), Headlam diary, 4 December 1934, p. 316.

83 Beaverbrook to Sir Robert Borden (former Canadian Prime Minister), 22 December 1934, Beaverbrook Papers C/52.

Chapter 7 The Monstrous Monument of Shams, pp. 175–199

1 Douglas Crawford (foreign editor of the *Daily Mail*) to Churchill, 3 April 1934, Chartwell Papers 2/213/16–17.

2 Churchill to Lloyd George, 10 April 1934, Chartwell Papers 2/213/35–6.

3 Frances Stevenson's diary entry for 6 April 1934, in Gilbert, companion vol. V, Part 2, p. 743.

4 Frances Stevenson diary, in Gilbert, companion vol. V, Part 2, p. 524.

5 Note of conversation between Churchill, Brendan Bracken, Douglas Crawford, Alan Chorlton (a Manchester MP) and H.Y. Robinson (Manchester Chamber of Commerce's India Section), 8 April 1934, Chartwell Papers 2/213/27–34.

6 Salisbury to Churchill, 12 April 1934, Chartwell Papers 2/213/51–3.

7 Beaverbrook to Hoare, 19 April 1934, Templewood Papers VII: 3.

8 Hoare to Derby, 17 July 1933, in Gilbert, companion vol. V, Part 2, p. 631; Hoare to Willingdon, 20 October 1933, India Office Papers MSS.Eur.E.240(3)/846.

9 Hoare to Willingdon, 3 November 1933, India Office Papers MSS.Eur.E.240(3); further proof of Derby's improper conduct is contained in Derby to Sir Louis Kershaw, 26 July 1933; in Gilbert, companion vol. V, Part 2, p. 634.

10 Derby to Churchill, 16 April 1934, Chartwell Papers 2/213/74.

11 Manchester Chamber of Commerce's India Mission telegram, received by the Chamber of Commerce in Manchester on 23 October 1933, in Gilbert, vol. V: 1922–1939, p. 519.

12 Notes of meeting at the India Office, 26 April 1934, Gilbert, companion vol. V, Part 2, p. 776. At last with full reference to the pertinent evidence, the case against Hoare and Derby is convincingly argued by Carl Bridge, 'Churchill, Hoare, Derby and the Committee of Privileges, April to June 1934', in Historical Journal, 22, Part 1 (1979), 215–27.

13 Churchill's letters to E.A. Fitzroy (Mr Speaker), Hoare and Derby, all 15 April 1934, Chartwell Papers 2/213/66–70, 71–2, 73.

14 Hoare to Willingdon, 20 April 1934, India Office Papers MSS.Eur.E.240(4)/1044–5; Hoare to Willingdon, 27 April 1934, India Office Papers MSS.Eur.E.240(4)/1047; Hoare to Sir George Stanley, 10 May 1934, India Office Papers MSS.Eur.E.240(4)/1060. It is important to remember that Hoare was interested in encouraging Willingdon to pressurize the Indian princes into federation. He may therefore have thought that one way to do this was to paint as black a picture as possible of his own problems at Westminster in the hope that this would spur on the Viceroy to play his part in alleviating them (Hoare to Sir George Stanley, 22 May 1934, India Office Papers MSS.Eur.E.240(4)/1068). Nevertheless, it is sufficiently clear from Hoare's tone elsewhere that he felt Churchill, even if unsuccessful on the Privileges case, was bringing the government close to its knees.

15 See in particular, Robert Rhodes James, Churchill: A Study in Failure, 1970, pp. 209–11.

16 Daily Telegraph, 9 June 1934.

17 Victor Cazalet diary, 17 April 1934, p. 160; Hoare to Willingdon, 20 April 1934, India Office Papers MSS.Eur.E.240(4)/1044; Hoare to Sir George Stanley, 10 May 1934, India Office Papers MSS.Eur.E.240(4)1058.

18 J.C.C. Davidson to Lord Brabourne, 25 April 1934, Davidson Papers MSS.Eng.hist.c.561/74.

19 Willingdon to Hoare, in Gilbert, companion vol. V, Part 2, p. 771.

20 Churchill to Ramsay MacDonald, 20 April 1934, Chartwell Papers 2/213/

103–4; Clerk of the Committee of Privileges/Churchill correspondence, 25 and 26 April 1934, Chartwell Papers 2/213/151–2.

21　This said, Hoare felt that his own experience of being questioned had been 'terrible' since the committee were 'all taking their duties very seriously' and it would appear that he was not privy to its secret deliberations. Hoare to Willingdon, 3 May 1934, India Office Papers MSS.Eur.E.240(4)/1055; Hoare to Sir George Stanley, 10 and 17 May 1934, India Office Papers MSS.Eur.E.240(4)/1060, 1064.

22　Frances Stevenson diary, 11 May 1934, Countess Lloyd-George Papers, in Gilbert, companion vol. V, Part 2, p. 790.

23　Churchill's other legal adviser was, at a cost of £182, Cyril Asquith (the son of Churchill's old Liberal boss). Terence O'Connor gave his services without charge. Churchill's legal expenses are referred to in his letter to E. Roderick Dew, 30 June 1934, Chartwell Papers 2/215/20; the legal argument of Churchill's case is set out in Cyril Asquith to Churchill, 25 April 1934, Chartwell Papers 2/213/126–8.

24　Terence O'Connor to Churchill, 5 June 1934, Chartwell Papers 2/214(A)/92, 95–6; Hoare to Sir George Stanley, 15 June 1934, India Office Papers MSS.Eur.E.240(4)/1081.

25　Committee of Privileges Report, p. 17, copy in Chartwell Papers 2/223.

26　O.C. Williams (Clerk to the Committee of Privileges) to Churchill, 8 and 20 June 1934, Chartwell Papers 2/214(A)/100 and 2/214(B)/168.

27　Bridge, Holding India to the Empire, p. 131.

28　Churchill to the Commons, 13 June 1934, Hansard 290 HC Deb. 5s., cols 1733–4.

29　Amery to the Commons, 13 June 1934, Hansard 290 HC Deb. 5s., col. 1738.

30　J.P. Morris (Conservative Lancashire MP) to the Commons, 13 June 1934, Hansard 290 HC Deb. 5s., col. 1789.

31　Frances Stevenson diary, 13 June 1934, in Gilbert, companion vol. V, Part 2, p. 807; Hoare to Sir George Stanley, India Office Papers MSS.Eur.E.240(4)/1081–3; Sir Joseph Nall to Salisbury, 9 June 1934, Salisbury Papers S(4)206/91.

32　Indian Empire Review, August 1934 issue, p. 33.

33　Page Croft and the Duchess of Atholl both defended Churchill in the Commons. Amongst those who wrote sympathetically to Churchill were: Duchess of Atholl to Churchill, 16 June 1934, Chartwell Papers 2/224/118–19; Wolmer to Churchill, 13 June, Locker Lampson to Churchill, 14 June, Knox to Churchill, 19 June and O'Dwyer to Churchill, 21 June 1934, Chartwell Papers 2/214(B)/124–5, 143, 155, 172.

34　Whilst he was to take all the responsibility, Churchill did not act until he had consulted other diehards. As Hoare observed to Derby's brother, Churchill had spent the three days prior to his raising the case in the Commons with his friends preparing the offensive. All the India Defence Committee members had been telegraphed to be in the House to hear his allegations. Churchill to Edward Russell (assistant editor, Morning Post), 21 July 1934, Chartwell Papers 2/215/26; Page Croft to Churchill, 20 April

1934, Chartwell Papers 2/213/107; Hoare to Sir George Stanley, 10 May 1934, India Office Papers MSS.Eur.E.240(4)/1058.

35 Edward Russell to Patrick Donner, 18 July 1934, Chartwell Papers 2/226/92; Donner to Churchill, 19 July 1934, Chartwell Papers 2/226/91; Portsmouth IDL shared this view of Churchill's importance, at least to his face: Rear Admiral R. St P. Parry (Chairman, Portsmouth IDL) to Churchill, 3 October 1934, Chartwell Papers 2/227/40.

36 Butler, p. 54; Bridge, *Holding India to the Empire*, p. 117.

37 Austen Chamberlain to Churchill, 25 October 1934, Chartwell Papers 8/487.

38 Austen to Ida Chamberlain, 18 October 1934, and Austen to Hilda Chamberlain, 28 October 1933, Austen Chamberlain Papers 5/1/675 and 5/1/637.

39 Austen to Ida Chamberlain, 15 December 1934, Austen Chamberlain Papers 5/1/680.

40 Austen to Hilda Chamberlain, 9 March 1935, Austen Chamberlain Papers 5/1/692.

41 Salisbury to Baldwin, 20 November 1934, Baldwin Papers 106/351.

42 Hoare to Brabourne, 28 November 1934, Templewood Papers VII: 4.

43 Churchill to Ian Colvin (leader writer for the *Morning Post*), 3 November 1934, Chartwell Papers 8/486/(no sub-ref.).

44 Hoare to Willingdon, 2 November 1934, India Office Papers MSS.Eur.E.240(4)/1162.

45 Churchill to Orr-Ewing, 20 November 1934, Chartwell Papers 2/227/61.

46 Violet Pearman to M. Petherick, 29 November 1934, Chartwell Papers 2/225/93, and replies to A.C. Crossley and Richard Law, 30 November and 6 December 1934, Chartwell Papers 2/225/96, 98; Churchill duly paid up, Pearman to Petherick, Crossley and Law, 2 August 1935, Chartwell Papers 2/240(B)/180.

47 Lord Brabourne to Baldwin, 16 October 1934, Baldwin Papers 106/348.

48 Churchill to Clementine Churchill, 1 January 1935, Spencer-Churchill Papers, in Gilbert, companion vol. V, Part 2, p. 981.

49 Lord Melchett to Churchill, 22 November 1934, Chartwell Papers 2/225/75–80.

50 Baldwin said he would 'bear no malice' to anyone who voted with the diehards. Baldwin to the Commons, 12 December 1934, *Hansard* 296 HC Deb. 5s., cols 521–2.

51 Beaverbrook to Sir Robert Borden, 22 December 1934, Beaverbrook Papers C/52.

52 Austen to Ida Chamberlain, 15 December 1934, Austen Chamberlain Papers 5/1/680; Austen Chamberlain to the Commons, 12 December 1934, *Hansard* 296 HC Deb. 5s., col. 464.

53 Hoare to Willingdon, 13 December 1934, India Office Papers MSS.Eur.E.240(4)/1197.

54 See Chartwell Papers 2/225/131.

55 Winston to Clementine Churchill, 1 January 1935, Spencer-Churchill Papers, in Gilbert, companion vol. V, Part 2, p. 981.

56   Patrick Donner to Churchill, 14 December 1934, Chartwell Papers 2/227/
     85.

57   Hoare to Willingdon, 3 January 1935, India Office Papers
     MSS.Eur.E.240(5)/1208.

58   Hoare to Willingdon, 22 March 1935, India Office Papers
     MSS.Eur.E.240(5)/1266.

59   For Churchill's attempts to raise further funds to save the IDL at 'the crisis
     of its existence' see: Churchill to Rothermere, 6 August 1934, Chartwell
     Papers 2/228/20-2; Churchill to Westminster, 8 August 1934, Chartwell
     Papers 2/227/10-11; Orr-Ewing to Churchill, 16 August 1934, Chartwell
     Papers 2/227/17 and G.G.H. Du Boulay (assistant organizer of the India
     Defence League) to Violet Pearman (Churchill's secretary), Chartwell
     Papers 2/227/15; Orr-Ewing to Churchill, 30 November 1934, Chartwell
     Papers 2/227/66.

60   Churchill to Rothermere, 20 November 1934, Chartwell Papers 2/227/68.

61   Lloyd to Wolmer, 19 February 1935, Lloyd Papers 11/1. Wolmer strongly
     opposed fighting by-elections: see his 'Confidential and Secret Memoran-
     dum – The Policy of Contesting Bye-Elections' (undated but of the same
     time as Lloyd's letter), Selborne (Wolmer) Papers MSS.Eng.hist.c. 1012/71.

62   Neville Chamberlain diary, 16 March 1934, Neville Chamberlain Papers 2/
     23A.

63   Churchill to Clementine Churchill, 18 January 1935, Spencer-Churchill
     Papers, in Gilbert, companion vol. V, Part 2, p. 1034; Churchill's statement
     to the Press Association, 19 January 1935, Chartwell Papers 2/246/1.

64   Oliver Baldwin lost his seat in his father's 1931 landslide. He was returned
     to Parliament as Labour MP for Paisley in 1945 and shortly after
     succeeding to his father's earldom became Governor of the Leeward
     Islands. Middlemas and Barnes, pp. 259–60.

65   Winston to Clementine Churchill, 31 January, 21 January and 23 February
     1935, Spencer-Churchill Papers, in Gilbert, companion vol. V, Part 2, pp.
     1064, 1037, 1086–7.

66   Winston to Clementine Churchill, 21 and 31 January 1935, ibid., pp. 1038,
     1063.

67   Winston to Clementine Churchill, 21 January 1935, ibid., pp. 1038.

68   Winston to Clementine Churchill, 23 January 1935, ibid., p. 1044.

69   Churchill to the Bristol IDL, 25 January 1935, in James (ed.), *His Complete
     Speeches*, vol. V, pp. 5465–6.

70   Winston to Clementine Churchill, 31 January 1935, Spencer-Churchill
     Papers, in Gilbert, companion vol. V, Part 2, p. 1063.

71   Text of Churchill's broadcast, 30 January 1935, in Gilbert, companion vol.
     V, Part 2, pp. 1053–61.

72   Hoare to Willingdon, 31 January 1935, India Office Papers
     MSS.Eur.E.240(5)/1229.

73   Churchill to Randolph Churchill, 2 February 1935, Chartwell Papers 2/
     246.

74   *The Times*, 9 February 1935.

75   ibid.

76 Churchill to the Wavertree electors, 5 February 1935, in James (ed.), *His Complete Speeches*, vol. V, p. 5469.

77 Wolmer to Mackie, 28 December 1934, Wolmer Papers, quoted in Bridge, *Holding India to the Empire*, p. 137.

78 The precise figures were: Labour, 15,611; Conservative 13,771; Independent Conservative 10,575; Liberal 4208.

79 Winston to Clementine Churchill, 7 February 1935, in Gilbert, companion vol. V, Part 2, p. 1071. The Duke of Westminster to Churchill, 7 February 1935, Chartwell Papers 2/246/57.

80 Winston to Clementine Churchill, 7 February 1935, in Gilbert, companion vol. V, Part 2, p. 1071; Hoare to Willingdon, 7 February 1935, India Office Papers MSS.Eur.E.240(5)/1235.

81 Hoare to Willingdon, 13 February 1935, India Office Papers MSS.Eur.E.240(5).

82 Churchill to Rothermere, 20 November 1934, secret, Chartwell Papers 2/227/67–8.

83 Hoare to Willingdon, 22 February 1935, India Office Papers MSS.Eur.E.240(5)/1243.

84 Winston to Clementine Churchill, 23 February and 2 March 1935, Spencer-Churchill Papers, in Gilbert, companion vol. V, Part 2, pp. 1087, 1096–7.

85 Winston to Clementine Churchill, 2 March 1935, ibid., p. 1097.

86 Hoare to Willingdon, 1 March 1935, India Office Papers MSS.Eur.E.240(5)/1247–50.

87 ibid., MSS.Eur.E.240(5)/1248–50; Winston to Clementine Churchill, 8 March 1935, Spencer-Churchill Papers, in Gilbert, companion vol. V, Part 2, p. 1106.

88 Hoare to Lord Brabourne, 4 March 1935, Templewood Papers VII: 4; Hoare to Willingdon, 24 May 1935, India Office Papers MSS.Eur.E.240(5)/1300.

89 Violet Pearman to Capt. H. Orr-Ewing, 15 March 1935, Chartwell Papers 2/241/128.

90 Winston to Clementine Churchill, 23 February, 2 and 8 March 1935, Spencer-Churchill Papers, in Gilbert, companion vol. V, Part 2, pp. 1083, 1086, 1095–6, 1105.

91 Winston to Clementine Churchill, 10 March 1935, ibid., p. 1115.

92 Winston to Clementine Churchill, 23 February and 2 March 1935, ibid., pp. 1086, 1096.

93 Winston to Clementine Churchill, 10 March 1935, ibid., pp. 1113–4.

94 Winston to Clementine Churchill, 2 and 10 March and 13 April 1935, ibid., pp. 1097, 1115, 1139.

95 Hoare to Willingdon, 10 March 1935, India Office Papers MSS.Eur.E.240(5)

96 Thomas Jones to an unidentified person, 12 May and 2 June 1935, in Gilbert, companion vol V, Part 2, pp. 1171, 1187.

97 Winston to Clementine Churchill, 13 April 1935, ibid., p. 1140.

98 Churchill to Victor Raikes, 10 May 1935, Chartwell Papers 2/240(B)/120.

99 Churchill to Lord Salisbury, 29 May 1935, Salisbury Papers S(4)208/85. Amongst the MPs present were: Bracken, Craddock, Donner, Gretton, Knox, Lennox-Boyd, Page Croft, Purbrick, Raikes, Nairne Sandeman and Charles Taylor. The peers were: Ampthill, Carrington, Clive, FitzAlan, Lawrence, Lloyd, Midleton, Mount Temple, Phillimore, Rankeillour, Rothermere and Salisbury; the five others were: Leslie Cranfield (editor of the *Daily Mail*), H.A. Gwynne (editor of the *Observer*), Sir James Hawkey (Churchill's constituency chairman), Professor Lindemann (Churchill's friend and scientific adviser) and Capt. H. Orr-Ewing (IDL Chief Organizer).

100 Hoare to Willingdon, 31 May 1935, India Office Papers MSS.Eur.E.240(5)/1308.

101 Butler, p. 55.

102 Churchill to the Commons, 5 June 1935, *Hansard* 302 HC Deb. 5s., cols 1909, 1925.

103 Baldwin to Captain Margesson, 4 August 1935, Margesson Papers 1/3/11.

104 Hoare to Willingdon, 8 March 1935, in Gilbert, companion vol. V, Part 2, p. 1110.

105 Churchill was never right-wing enough for the extreme diehards, who could not forget his condemnation of General Dyer over Amritsar. See Sir Alfred Knox to Lord Sydenham, 24 June 1931, Stuart Papers MSS.Eng.-hist.c.620/59. Opponents on the left of the party like J.C.C. Davidson in 1969 thought that they also recalled his isolation from the right wing. James (ed.), *Memoirs of a Conservative* (Davidson memoirs), p. 384.

106 Wolmer/Salisbury correspondence, 28 February 1935, Salisbury Papers S(4)208/29–32.

107 Lloyd to Churchill, 12 June 1935, Chartwell Papers 2/240(B)/161.

108 Samuel to the Commons, 27 March 1933, *Hansard* 276 HC Deb. 5s., col. 736.

109 James, *Churchill* pp. 212–3, 215. Clive Ponting has written in a similar vein that it was Churchill's 'out-right opposition to constitutional reform in India that placed him in self-imposed exile. The longer the dissent continued and the more extreme his opposition became, the less likely he made his subsequent recall.' Ponting, p. 358.

110 Stannage, p. 47.

111 *The Times*, 18 December 1930 and 17 July 1931, Ball, *Historical Journal*, 29:1 (1986), 160–1.

112 This contradicts the case made by J.H. McEwen that the diehard campaign strengthened the cohesion of the National forces (McEwan, unpublished Ph.D., pp. 349–50). For Stonehaven's position, see Stannage, p. 48.

113 Neville Chamberlain recording a conversation with Baldwin in his diary, 11 February 1935, Neville Chamberlain Papers 2/23A.

114 Neville Chamberlain in his diary, 25 March and 29 April 1935, Neville Chamberlain Papers 2/23A.

115 Churchill to Lord Linlithgow, 8 August 1935, Chartwell Papers 2/236/155. Churchill had even more publicly made the same point on the floor of the

House of Commons. Churchill to the Commons, 5 June 1935, *Hansard* 302 HC Deb. 5s., col. 1924.

116 Churchill to Sir Robert Horne, 29 June 1935, Chartwell Papers 2/243/125–7.

Chapter 8 The Defence of the Realm, pp. 200–228

1 Hackett was up in Oxford for the day and 'willingly took part in the attempt to corner him and, if possible, remove his trousers as a mark of disrespect'. David Walter, *The Oxford Union: Playground of Power*, 1984, p. 89.

2 Quoted in Macleod, pp. 176–7.

3 Churchill to the Commons, Debate on the Address, 23 November 1932, *Hansard* 272 HC Deb. 5s., especially cols 74, 80–5 and 90–2.

4 Churchill to the Commons, Geneva Disarmament Debate, 23 March 1933, and a similar message on 13 April 1933, *Hansard* 276 HC Deb. 5s., cols 542, 545–8 and 2793–4. Churchill at Theydon Bois, 12 August 1933; and at Chingford on 13 November, quoted in Gilbert, vol. V: *1922–1939*, pp. 489, 494.

5 Geoffrey Mander to the Commons, 23 March 1933, *Hansard* 276 HC Deb. 5s., col. 583.

6 Eden to the Commons, 23 March, 23 March 1933, *Hansard* 276 HC Deb. 5s., cols 615–16.

7 Chiefs of Staff 1932 Annual Review of Imperial Defence Policy. COS 295, CAB 53/22.

8 Treasury Comments on Chiefs of Staff 1932 Review, 11 March 1932. Committee of Imperial Defence Papers 1087–B. Quoted in Michael Howard, *The Continental Commitment*, p. 98.

9 261st Meeting of the Committee of Imperial Defence, 9 November 1933. Howard, *The Continental Commitment*, p. 104.

10 Sir Bolton Eyres-Monsell to Sir Maurice Hankey, 28 February 1934, quoted in G.C. Peden, 'Sir Warren Fisher and British Rearmament against Germany', in *English Historical Review*, (January 1979), 35.

11 Cabinet Papers COS 335, CAB 52/23. Howard, p. 108.

12 Baldwin to the Commons, 30 July 1934, *Hansard* 292 HC Deb. 5s., col. 2339.

13 Simon to the Commons, 13 July 1934, *Hansard* 292 HC Deb. 5s., col. 698.

14 Macleod, p. 178.

15 Baldwin to the Commons, 10 November 1932, *Hansard* 270 HC Deb. 5s., col. 630.

16 DC(M)(32), 52nd Conclusions. 2 July 1934. Howard, p. 110.

17 Cabinet Papers CAB 27/507, meetings of 25 June and 24 July 1934, in Peden, p. 37n.

18 DC (M)(32) 12O. Quoted in Howard, p. 108.

19 Cabinet Papers 27/514, 10 July 1934.

20 Churchill to the Commons, 23 November 1932, *Hansard* 272 HC Deb. 5s., col. 92.

21 Churchill in the *Daily Mail*, 17 November 1932.

22   Amery diary, 5 October 1933, p. 304.
23   Amery diary, 27 June 1934, p. 384. Amery had first expressed the hope of
     working in tandem with Churchill on defence issues in November 1932:
     diary, 22 November 1932, p. 287.
24   The MPs were Sir Robert Horne, Frederick Guest, Leo Amery, Lord
     Winterton and Bob Boothby.
25   *1933 Conservative Annual Conference Report*, folio 24. McKenzie, pp.
     228–9.
26   *1934 Conservative Annual Conference Report*, folio 24. McKenzie, p. 229.
27   See in particular James, *Churchill*, pp. 213–5.
28   Quoted in Gilbert, vol. V: *1922–1939*, p. 553n.
29   Circular from Viscount Wolmer, Chairman of the IDL Executive Commit-
     tee, to members, 3 April 1935, Baldwin Papers 107/57–8.
30   In particular Major Desmond Morton, the head of the CID Industrial
     Intelligence Centre, and, from 1935, Clive Wigram, the head of the Foreign
     Office's Central Department.
31   Churchill to Baldwin, 24 November 1934, Baldwin Papers 1/167.
32   Cabinet Papers 27/572.
33   Cabinet Papers 27/572 and 23/80 (Cabinet Minute of 26 November 1934)
34   Frances Stevenson diary, 30 November 1934, in Gilbert, companion vol. V,
     Part 2, p. 950. Lord Winterton agreed that 'in the opinion of the House'
     Churchill had 'made an eloquent speech': Winterton to the Commons, 28
     November 1934, *Hansard* 295 HC Deb. 5s., col. 923. It should be noted,
     however, that Lloyd George's speech was also well received by Tories. In it,
     the other great 'wilderness' figure of the 1930s suggested that they might
     come to see Germany as a bulwark against Communist Russia and that a
     fresh attempt should be made to convince her that Britain and France
     would disarm with her: Lloyd George to the Commons, 28 November
     1934, *Hansard* 295 HC Deb. 5s., col. 920, and Stevenson diary, in Gilbert,
     companion vol. V, Part 2 p. 950.
35   Baldwin to the Commons, 8 March 1934, *Hansard* 286 HC Deb. 5s., col.
     2078.
36   Hoare to Willingdon, 29 November 1934, India Office Papers
     MSS.Eur.E240/1184.
37   Quoted in Gilbert, vol. V: *1922–1939*, p. 552.
38   Winston to Clementine Churchill, 5 April 1935, Spencer-Churchill Papers,
     in Gilbert, companion vol. V, Part 2, p. 1129.
39   *Daily Telegraph*, 26 April 1935.
40   Churchill to the Commons, 2 May 1935, *Hansard* 301 HC Deb. 5s., col.
     607.
41   The other National Liberals in the government were Walter Runciman,
     who continued at the Board of Trade along with Ernest Brown at the
     Ministry of Labour, and Sir Godfrey Collins at the Scottish Office. The
     National Labour flag was kept unfurled by the appointment of MacDon-
     ald's son, Malcolm, to the Colonial Office and the continuation of J.H.
     Thomas at the Dominions Office.
42   The MPs were: the Duchess of Atholl, A.J.K. Todd, Lieutenant-

Commander Astbury, Sir Joseph Nall and Linton Thorp KC. Duchess of Atholl etc., to Baldwin, 21 May 1935, Baldwin Papers 107/94.

43 Stannage, p. 119.

44 Reported in *The Times*, 5 October 1935; the Baldwin/Churchill correspondence of 6 and 7 October 1935 was equally gushing: Chartwell Papers 2/237/101 and 102.

45 Charmley, *Churchill*, p. 286.

46 Neville Chamberlain diary, 2 August 1935, Neville Chamberlain Papers 2/23A.

47 The complete figures are reprinted in Neville Thompson, *The Anti-Appeasers: Conservative Opposition to Appeasement in the 1930s*, Oxford 1971, p. 71.

48 The statements of the Labour leadership and MPs during this period provided rich pickings for Quintin Hogg in his polemic *The Left was Never Right*. See also Graham Stewart, 'The Left Wasn't Right', in *Spectator*, 10 October 1998.

49 The play on Baldwin's words is that of Tom Stoppard.

50 Cabinet Papers 22/82, Cabinet meeting of 22 July 1935.

51 Templewood Papers VIII: 1.

52 Stannage, pp. 133–4.

53 Stannage, p. 173 fn. 1. Feiling, pp. 266, 268–9; Neville Chamberlain Diary, 19 October 1935, Neville Chamberlain Papers 2/23A.

54 Neville Chamberlain diary, 2 August 1935, Neville Chamberlain Papers 2/23A.

55 Quoted in Stannage, p. 156.

56 Quoted in Macleod, p. 184.

57 Quoted in Stannage, p. 140.

58 Stannage, pp. 143, 150.

Book Two

Chapter 9 The Tangled Web of Collective Security, pp. 231–248

1 Churchill's recollections of election night (draft for *The Gathering Storm*), in Gilbert, companion vol. V, Part 2, p. 1324.

2 Different methods of classification have led various studies to produce marginally different tallies for these figures – alternative means of classification has given the combined 'National' number of MPs as between 429 and 432.

3 Oliver Locker Lampson to Churchill, 18 November 1935, Chartwell Papers 2/236/155.

4 Lady Nancy Astor to Baldwin, 17 November 1935, Baldwin Papers 47/165–6.

5 Patrick Donner to Churchill, 28 November 1935, Chartwell Papers 2/241.

6 *The Times*, 18 November 1935.

7 *The Times*, 28 November 1935.

8   Churchill's draft letter to *The Times*, 28 November 1935, Chartwell Papers 2/238/80–4.

9   Garvin to Churchill, 3 September 1935, Chartwell Papers 2/237/5.

10 Sir Eric Phipps to Hoare, 25 October, 1 and 2 November 1935, in Gilbert, companion vol. V, Part 2, p. 1309. Churchill said that the treaty was not 'at all a matter for rejoicing'. Churchill to the Commons, 11 July 1935, *Hansard* 304 HC Deb. 5s., cols 543–4, 550.

11 Nicolson diary; 21 November 1935, p. 228.

12 Baldwin to Neville Chamberlain, 5 November 1935, and Neville to Hilda Chamberlain, 9 November 1935, Neville Chamberlain Papers 18/1/938.

13 Tom Jones to Abraham Flexner, 17 November 1935, in Jones, *A Diary with Letters*, pp. 155–6.

14 As the leading historian of the 1935 general election has pointed out, in an age before detailed opinion polls, it cannot be determined for sure that the League and Abyssinia were the chief interests of the electorate. However, the exposure the issue received, both in the majority of candidates' addresses and as the first and most prominent issue in all the main parties' official manifestos, suggests that politicians certainly thought that it was the most important one for the electorate. Stannage, pp. 153–8, 171–3.

15 Sir Archibald Sinclair to Churchill, 13 October 1935, Chartwell Papers 2/237/114; Stannage, p. 133–4.

16 Richard Lamb, *The Drift to War 1922–1939*, 1989, pp. 131–40.

17 Parker, pp. 47–8.

18 Cabinet Papers, 19 June 1935, CAB 23/1/929.

19 Neville Chamberlain Papers 18/1/929.

20 Quoted in Parker, p. 50.

21 Neville to Hilda Chamberlain, 7 September 1935, Neville Chamberlain Papers 18/1/932.

22 Parker, p. 50.

23 A.J.P. Taylor, *English History 1914–1945*, p. 380.

24 Lamb, pp. 143, 146.

25 Neville Chamberlain diary, 29 November 1935, Neville Chamberlain Papers 2/23A.

26 Lamb, p. 157.

27 Bracken to Churchill, 11 December 1935, Chartwell Papers 2/238/121.

28 Baldwin to the Commons, 10 December 1935, *Hansard* 307 HC Deb. 5s., col. 856.

29 Cabinet Papers CAB 23/90B/53.

30 The Health Minister, Kingsley Wood, was 'apprehensive'; the Education Minister, Oliver Stanley, thought such a speech by Hoare would be 'disastrous'; J.H. Thomas, at the Colonial Office, thought that Hoare should resign and the Agriculture Minister, Walter Elliot, agreed. Cabinet Papers CAB 23/90B/56, 50, 57–8, 59.

31 Cabinet Papers CAB 23/90B/66.

32 Cabinet Papers CAB 23/90B/53.

33 *Hansard* 307 HC Deb. 5s., col. 2036.

34 Bracken to Churchill, 11 December 1935, Chartwell Papers 2/238/121–2.

35 Randolph to Winston Churchill, 11 and 17 December 1935, Chartwell Papers 2/238/121–2.

36 Randolph to Winston Churchill, 17 December 1935, ibid.

37 Channon diary, 17 December 1935, in Robert Rhodes James (ed.), *Chips: The Diaries of Sir Henry Channon*, 1967, pp. 62–3: J.A. Cross, *Sir Samuel Hoare: A Political Biography*, 1977, p. 252; L.S. Amery, *My Political Life*, vol. III: *The Unforgiving Years 1929–40*, 1955, p. 184.

38 Austen Chamberlain to the Commons, 19 December 1935, *Hansard* 307 HC Deb. 5s., col. 2040; Winterton diary, 19 December 1935 in Winterton, p. 210.

39 James C. Robertson, 'The Hoare-Laval Plan', in *Journal of Contemporary History*, 10, 5 (July 1975), 454–5.

40 Austen to Ida Chamberlain, 15 December, and to Neville Chamberlain, 20 December, and to Hilda Chamberlain, 22 December 1935, Austen Chamberlain Papers 5/1/717 and 718, and Neville Chamberlain Papers 1/27/124; Earl of Avon (Anthony Eden), *The Eden Memoirs: Facing the Dictators*, vol. I, p. 316; Austen to Hilda Chamberlain, 15 February 1936, Austen Chamberlain Papers 5/1/752.

41 Cowling, *The Impact of Hitler*, p. 102 fn. 35.

42 Winston to Clementine Churchill, 26 and 30 December 1935, Spencer-Churchill Papers, quoted in Gilbert, companion vol. V, Part 2, pp. 1363, 1365.

43 Eden to Churchill, 13 December 1935, Chartwell Papers 2/250.

44 Randolph to Winston Churchill, 17 December 1935, Chartwell Papers 2/238/129.

45 Report of conversation on 10 December 1935 between Randolph Churchill, Lord Beaverbrook, Count Grandi and Brendan Bracken: Randolph to Winston Churchill, 11 December 1935, Chartwell Papers 2/238/119.

46 Winston to Clementine Churchill, 26 and 30 December 1935, Spencer-Churchill Papers, quoted in Gilbert, companion vol. V, Part 2, pp. 1363, 1365.

47 Churchill, *The Gathering Storm*, p. 185.

48 Thompson, p. 78. As Dr Thompson puts it (p. 80), Churchill 'delivered strong speeches on every possible side of the question'. Churchill claimed in April 1936 that he had advised Hoare and Eden in August 1935 not to push France too far against Italy and that, given the military and international situation, he 'had strongly advised the Government not to try to take a leading part or to put themselves forward so prominently' and that Eden in particular had done the reverse. According to Hoare's notes at the time, Churchill was not prepared to act without French support, but knowing that it was unlikely to be forthcoming he was for making it clear that Britain would fight but for France's reticence, thus keeping alive the image of Britain's commitment to the League's collective security policy at the expense of Anglo-French relations. Churchill advised Hoare that 'the real

danger is Germany and nothing must be done to weaken the anti-German front. The collapse of the League will mean the destruction of the instrument that may be chiefly effective as a deterrent against German aggression.' Meanwhile, Eden told Harold Nicolson that Churchill had been 'all out for blood and thunder', an impression shared by those who listened to his dinner-table conversation at Cherkley in September 1935 (Nicolson diary, 21 August 1935, p. 211; Young (ed.), Lockhart diary, 21 September 1935, p. 330). By April 1936 with the Rhineland remilitarized and he need apparent to ally closely with France, Churchill wrote to *The Times* about the 'great sacrifices the French had made in order to endorse Britain's pro-League stance on Abyssinia': see Churchill to Lord Cranborne (Parliamentary Secretary of State for Foreign Affairs), 8 April 1936, Chartwell Papers 2/253/26–8; Hoare's note on his meeting with Churchill, 21 August 1935, Templewood Papers VIII: 1; Churchill's letter of 17 April 1936, printed in *The Times*, 20 April 1936.

49 Winston to Clementine Churchill, 8 January 1936, Spencer-Churchill Papers, quoted in Gilbert, companion vol. V, Part 3, p. 7.

50 Winston to Randolph Churchill, 26 December 1935, in Gilbert, companion vol. V, Part 2, p. 1364.

51 Neville Chamberlain diary, 21 December 1935, Neville Chamberlain Papers 2/23A.

52 Amery, *My Political Life*, vol. III, p. 143.

53 Before the crisis intensified, Lloyd had warned a seemingly receptive Neville Chamberlain of the strategic dangers to Britain if she alienated Italy. John Charmley, *Lord Lloyd and the Decline of the British Empire*, 1987, pp. 198–9.

54 These EDMs are examined in greater detail in Stewart, 'Winston Churchill and the Conservative Party 1929–37', unpublished Cambridge University Ph.D., 1995, pp. 225–7.

55 S.J. Hetherington, *Katharine Atholl 1874–1960: Against the Grain*, 1989, p. 166.

56 James (ed.), Channon diary, 24 February 1936, p. 77; Winterton diary, 19 December 1935, p. 211. Writing from the safe distance of twenty years after the event, Amery thought that had Baldwin stood firm behind Hoare; 'a score, perhaps, of Conservatives would have voted against the Government, a few more might have abstained' with common sense, Austen Chamberlain and the party Whips keeping the rest on side. Amery, *My Political Life*, vol. III, p. 185.

57 Dutton, *Austen Chamberlain*, p. 321.

58 Neville Chamberlain diary, 17 June 1936, Neville Chamberlain Papers 2/23A.

59 The book inspired the young Edward Heath. Horne, *Macmillan* pp. 106–9. Macmillan, *The Middle Way*.

60 N.J. Crowson, *Facing Fascism: The Conservative Party and the European Dictators*, pp. 72–3; Cowling, *The Impact of Hitler*, p. 141.

Chapter 10   Rocking the Boat, pp. 249–273

1   Winston to Clementine Churchill, 8 January 1936, Spencer-Churchill Papers, in Gilbert, companion vol. V, Part 3, pp. 5–6.
2   *The Times*, 16 January 1936.
3   Churchill to J.J. Astor, 2 February 1936, Chartwell Papers 2/287/28.
4   Winston to Clementine Churchill, 8, 15 and 17 January 1936, Spencer-Churchill Papers, in Gilbert, companion vol. V, Part 3, pp. 5–7, 12, 16.
5   The voting figures were National Labour (MacDonald) 8949; Labour 5967; Randolph Churchill 2427; and the Liberals 738.
6   Austen Chamberlain to the Commons, 14 February 1936, *Hansard* 308 HC Deb. 5s., cols 1360–6.
7   Sir Austen Chamberlain to Duncan Sandys, 17 February 1936, Chartwell Papers 2/251/62; Sir Austen to Hilda Chamberlain, 15 February and to Ida Chamberlain 23 February 1936, Austen Chamberlain Papers 5/1/725 and 726. Sir Austen made no secret of his support for Churchill; see Hoare to Neville Chamberlain, 23 February 1936, Templewood Papers VIII: 6.
8   Winston to Clementine Churchill, 21 February 1936, Spencer-Churchill Papers, in Gilbert companion vol. V, Part 3, p. 54.
9   Hoare to Neville Chamberlain, 23 February 1936, Templewood Papers VIII: 6.
10 Neville Chamberlain's diary, 16 February 1936, Neville Chamberlain Papers 23/a.
11 Neville Chamberlain's diary, 19 February 1936, Neville Chamberlain Papers 23/a.
12 *Daily Telegraph*, 3 March 1936.
13 Winston to Clementine Churchill, 3 March 1936, Spencer-Churchill Papers, in Gilbert, companion vol. V, Part 3, pp. 60–3.
14 Keyes to Churchill, 28 February 1936, Chartwell Papers 2/251/90.
15 The analogy was initially made by Professor Frederick Lindemann to Lord Lloyd.
16 Amery diary, 13 March 1936, p. 411.
17 Amery diary, 10 and 13 March 1936, pp. 410–11.
18 Austen to Hilda Chamberlain, 15 March 1936, Austen Chamberlain Papers 5/1/729. The government was determined to avoid fighting over the Rhineland: Harold Nicolson's report of conversation with Ramsay Mac-Donald, Nicolson diary, 10 March 1936, p. 248; Baldwin to the Cabinet, 11 March 1936, Cabinet Papers CAB 23/83/292–3.
19 Sir Maurice Hankey to Inskip recording a conversation he had with Churchill, 19 April 1936, Cabinet Papers 21/435; Gilbert, companion vol. V, Part 3, p. 107.
20 Henry Tizard to Lord Swinton, 12 June 1936, Cabinet Papers 21/426, Gilbert, companion vol. V, Part 3, p. 193.
21 Swinton to the Cabinet, 6 July 1936, Cabinet Papers 23/85; ibid., p. 235.
22 Nicolson diary, 22 April 1936, p. 258.
23 Chartwell Papers 2/251/72.
24 These MPs being: Lord Winterton, Colonel Spender-Clay, Sir Edward

Grigg, Sir Robert Horne, Churchill's cousin Freddie Guest and the Liberal National MP, George Lambert.

25 Of the deputies, only Gretton, Lambert and Spender-Clay were not Other Club members.

26 Churchill to Eden, 22 August 1936, Chartwell Papers 2/257/88; Violet Pearman to Austen Chamberlain's private secretary, 12 June 1936, Chartwell Papers 2/266(B)/211.

27 Attlee to Churchill, 21 July 1936, Chartwell Papers 2/270/4.

28 Churchill to Brig. Gen. E.L. Spears, 17 November 1936, Chartwell Papers 2/266(B)/159.

29 A third of its twenty-one members were old India diehards which, as a ratio of the parliamentary party, made it disproportionately diehard-orientated.

30 Londonderry to Churchill, 9 May 1936, Chartwell Papers 2/254/23. Churchill regarded Baldwin as 'perfectly incompetent at home' as well; Churchill to Sir Abe Bailey, 8 October 1936, Chartwell Papers 2/259/37.

31 Frederick Guest to Churchill, 19 June 1936, Chartwell Papers 2/255/38-9.

32 Reported by Neville Chamberlain to the Cabinet, 6 July 1936, Cabinet Papers 23/85, Gilbert, companion vol V, part 3, p. 233.

33 Lord Bayford to the Conference of the Association of Conservative Clubs, 23 May 1936, reported in the *Daily Telegraph*, 25 May 1936.

34 Oliver Locker Lampson to Churchill, 21 July 1936, Chartwell Papers 2/256/61.

35 Page Croft mentions besides Churchill and himself, the names of Sir Robert Horne, Austen Chamberlain, Sir Edward Grigg and Lords Winterton, Lloyd and Wolmer, making it split 50:50 between former pro- and anti-diehards: Lord Croft, *My Life of Strife*, 1948, p. 285. In fact, between 1935 and 1938, when they collaborated over Munich, Lord Lloyd and Churchill saw each other only at irregular intervals: Charmley, *Lord Lloyd and the Decline of the British Empire*, pp. 217-9. Lord Londonderry, writing to Page Croft in support of the Rothermere line of air rearmament and a preference for German rather than Communist appeasement, knew well of Croft's continuing association with Churchill from whom he did not intend to withhold views and information. Londonderry to Page Croft, 3 July 1936, Croft Papers 1/15:Lo/3/1-3.

36 Croft, p. 286.

37 *News Chronicle*, 25 May 1936, pp. 1-2; James (ed.), Channon diary, 26 May 1936, p. 80. Winterton had started corresponding with Churchill on forming a strategy for pushing the government into greater air rearmament in July 1935: Winterton/Churchill correspondence, 26 and 29 September 1935, Chartwell Papers 2/244/33 and 34-6.

38 Tom Jones' note in his diary of a conversation with Baldwin, 22 May 1936, in Gilbert, companion vol. V, Part 3, p. 166. A decade later, Page Croft backed Austen Chamberlain's protestation that the meeting was not a conspiracy against the Baldwin Government but merely a gathering of those determined to bring to parliamentary attention Britain's defence deficiencies: Croft, p. 286.

39 Winterton, pp. 216-17.

40 Austen to Ida Chamberlain, 23 February 1936, Austen Chamberlain Papers 5/1/726.

41 Austen to Hilda Chamberlain, 15 March 1936, Austen Chamberlain Papers 5/1/729.

42 Tom Jones' note of conversation with Lloyd George, 14 June 1936, in Gilbert, companion vol. V, Part 3, p. 202.

43 James (ed.), Channon diary, 28 and 15 May, pp. 80, 79.

44 See Churchill's extremely Francophile letter in *The Times*, 20 April 1936; Amery to Churchill, 20 April 1936, Chartwell Papers 2/253/79.

45 Amery diary, 30 April 1936, p. 415.

46 Churchill to Londonderry, 6 May 1936, Chartwell Papers 2/266/35.

47 Lady Violet Bonham Carter to Churchill, 19 May 1936, Chartwell Papers 2/282/59–60.

48 Amery diary, 16 July 1936, pp. 424–5.

49 ibid., 7 May and 28 July 1936, pp. 416, 426.

50 ibid., 13 February 1936, p. 407.

51 Baldwin to the Defence deputation, 29 July 1936, Premier Papers 1/193/141.

52 Cowling, *The Impact of Hitler*, p. 225.

53 Richard Griffiths, *Fellow Travellers of the Right: British Enthusiasts for Nazi Germany 1933–9*, 1980, p. 258.

54 This group consisted of Patrick Donner, Ronald Cartland, Charles Emmott, Alan Lennox-Boyd and Duncan Sandys, and it met every Thursday to consider what questions on defence to ask ministers within the Commons at Question Time. Donner, p. 191.

55 Donner joined Amery, Winterton, Colonel Ponsonby, A.A. Somerville and Duncan Sandys on a deputation to Baldwin on this issue and wrote in strong terms to the *Morning Post* on the subject on 1 May 1936. As well as those by the above, similar letters to the press making clear their opposition to appeasing Hitler in the colonies were written by the right-wing politicians Sandeman Allen, Page Croft, Charles Emmott, Alan Graham, Frederick Guest, Edward Keeling and Alan Lennox-Boyd: Patrick Donner, pp. 191–5.

56 Crowson, p. 77.

57 Imperial Policy Group policy statement signed by Lords Mansfield and Phillimore and by Alfred Wise, W. Nunn and Kenneth de Courcy, April 1936, Chartwell Papers 2/253/36.

58 Only four former India diehards (Col. Howard Clifton Brown, Lawrence Kimball, Alan Lennox-Boyd and Sir Frank Sanderson) were amongst the forty-eight names listed in the *Notices of Orders of the Day* for this right-wing motion. *Notices of Orders of the Day*, Early Day Motion for 29 June 1936, with additional names added on 30 June, 1 and 6 July 1936.

59 Churchill to Alfred Wise (Tory MP for Smethick and member of the Imperial Policy Group), 9 April 1936, Chartwell Papers 2/253/37–8.

60 Hankey to Inskip, 19 April 1936, Cabinet Papers 21/435, in Gilbert, companion vol. V, Part 3, p. 108.

61 As Churchill put it to his son, his efforts were directed towards ensuring

that 'all the Peace societies' were prepared 'to support genuine military action to resist tyranny or aggression'. Winston to Randolph Churchill, 13 November 1936, Chartwell Papers 2/283/118.

62 Churchill to Lord Robert Cecil, 9 April 1936, Chartwell Papers 2/282/9–10.

63 See Churchill to the Commons, 5 November 1936, *Hansard* 317 HC Deb. 5s., cols 318–19.

64 A.H. Richards to Churchill, 30 March and 14 April 1936; Chartwell Papers 2/282/4, 18–19; Churchill to Lord Robert Cecil, 9 April 1936, Chartwell Papers 2/282/9.

65 Churchill to the 'Focus' group, 19 May 1936, reproduced in Eugen Spier, *Focus: A Footnote to the History of the Thirties*, 1963, p. 20–2.

66 Spier contributed £9600 to 'Focus' between May 1936 and the summer of 1939: Gilbert, companion vol. V, Part 3, p. 162n; A.H. Richards (Anti-Nazi Council) to Churchill, 29 July 1936, Chartwell Papers 2/283/3. According to Dr John Charmley, who cites the research of David Irving (a controversial source), a further £25,000 was provided by Waley-Cohen: Charmley, *Churchill*, p. 315.

67 Notes of meeting held in Churchill's flat on 24 July 1936 by A.H. Richards on 29 July 1936, Chartwell Papers 2/283/4–6; Churchill also received encouragement from others to launch such a campaign: Eleanor Rathbone (Independent MP) to Churchill, 18 November 1936, Chartwell Papers 2/260/109–10.

68 Churchill to A.H. Richards, 21 October 1936, Chartwell Papers 2/283/64; Churchill to Lord Robert Cecil, 21 October 1936, Chartwell Papers 2/286/47; notes of Churchill's speech in the Savoy Hotel, 15 October 1936, Chartwell Papers 2/283/51–2.

69 Churchill to Austen Chamberlain, 17 October 1936, Chartwell Papers 2/283/43.

70 Austen Chamberlain to Lord Tyrrell, 13 February 1933, Austen Chamberlain Papers 40/22; Austen Chamberlain to Churchill, 29 November 1936, Chartwell Papers 2/286/55–6.

71 A.H. Richards to Churchill, 4 November 1936, Chartwell Papers 2/283/93. Richards had previously wanted Lloyd's inclusion: Richards to Churchill, 4 June 1936, Chartwell Papers 2/282/126. As Dr Charmley rightly observes, Lloyd was sympathetic to the Arabs and this may not have endeared him to the Jewish Anti-Nazi League members within the group: Charmley, *Churchill*, p. 316.

72 The indomitable right-winger, Lady Houston, was amongst those appalled that Churchill was now championing the League of Nations, and promised to finance him 'to run out Baldwin' if only he would drop his commitment to the League: Lady Houston to Churchill, 6 and 18 November 1936, Chartwell Papers 2/260/10, 113–4; Frederick Guest/Churchill correspondence, 23 and 27 November 1936, Chartwell Papers 2/260/158, 162.

73 Winston to Randolph Churchill, 13 November 1936, Chartwell Papers 2/283/118.

74   Churchill to Lord Robert Cecil, 2 December 1936, Chartwell Papers 2/286/65.

75   Sir Norman Angell to Lord Allen of Hurtwood, 17 November 1936, in Gilbert, companion vol. V, Part 3, p. 416.

76   Eugen Spier recalled the reluctance of most of the 'Focus' group to place Churchill at the helm of their campaign and that Sir Robert Waley-Cohen thought Churchill would drop the group's aims once he got back into the government: Spier, pp. 43, 47.

77   The parliamentary group's signatories requesting Churchill to accept the presidency included the Liberal MPs Robert Bernays, Clement Davies, Megan Lloyd George, G. le M. Mander and Labour's Josiah Wedgwood and F. Seymour Cocks. Vyvyan Adams, John P. Morris, Robert Boothby (Churchill's former PPS), E.L. Spears, Sir Patrick Hannon and J.T.C. Moore-Brabazon represented various strands of Conservative opinion. It was also signed by Lord Davies, the LNU's Vice-President and Chairman of the New Commonwealth Society.

78   Churchill to Lord Robert Cecil, 21 October 1936, Chartwell Papers 2/286/46.

79   *New Statesman*, 28 November 1936, 'A London Diary'.

80   'Winston to the Left of Us?', *Saturday Review*, 15 August 1936, quoted in Thompson, p. 127.

81   Churchill to André Corbin (French Ambassador to London), 31 July 1936, Chartwell Papers 2/256/777–8.

82   Griffiths, pp. 262–3; Parker, *Chamberlain and Appeasement*, p. 89; Page Croft to the Commons, 29 October 1936, *Hansard* 316 HC Deb. 5s., cols 72–3; Thompson, pp. 118–19.

83   Churchill to the Duchess of Atholl, 18 November and 15 December 1936, Chartwell Papers 2/260/112 and 2/261/56.

84   Ivan Maisky to Churchill, 10 November 1936, Chartwell Papers 2/260/68–70.

85   They wanted him to open their Anti-Bolshevik Exhibition scheduled for February 1937: Lord Mount Temple to Churchill, 10 November 1936, Chartwell Papers 2/260/67.

86   Sir Archibald Boyd-Carpenter to Churchill, 13 November 1936, Chartwell Papers 2/260/84; Patrick Donner to Churchill, 15 November 1936, Chartwell Papers 2/260/97.

87   Amery diary, 12 November 1936, p. 430.

88   Gilbert, companion vol. V, Part 3, pp. 384–5n.

89   Amongst the Conservatives represented were Bob Boothby, Duncan Sandys, Oliver Locker Lampson, the Duchess of Atholl and Lord Wolmer. Other Tory parliamentarians in support of the group included Ronald Cartland, Paul Emrys-Evans and John McEwan.

90   Austen Chamberlain to A.H. Richards, 12 November 1936, Chartwell Papers 2/283/99; Spier, p. 59n.

91   Reported in *The Times*, 4 December 1936.

92   *New Statesman*, 21 November 1936.

93   *Spectator*, 20 November 1936, quoted in Thompson, p. 130.

94   As later correspondence the following year suggests, the organizers of the
     'Defence of Freedom and Peace' had no intention of setting up a popular
     front as a political unit, its secretary getting extremely worried that a
     request from Churchill wondering 'what other party's support [do] you
     contemplate having, especially Labour' might be an attempt to transform
     the organization from a gathering of private citizens into one shored up by
     'parties and organisations': Violet Pearman to A.H. Richards, 22 December
     1936 and Richards to Churchill, 31 December 1936, Chartwell Papers 2/
     283/132.
95   Walter Citrine, *Men and Work*, 1964, p. 357.
96   Salisbury to Baldwin, 12 November 1936, Baldwin Papers 171/272.
97   This, at any rate, was how Churchill described his position to Lord
     Salisbury: Salisbury to Churchill, 5 December 1936, Chartwell Papers 2/
     264/103.
98   H. Montgomery Hyde, *Walter Monckton*, 1991, p. 66.
99   Churchill to Baldwin, 5 December 1936, Chartwell Papers 2/264/110.
100 Most of this information comes from private notes made by Churchill
     shortly after the abdication now available for scrutiny in the Chartwell
     Papers 2/264/6–15. The value that can be put upon their accuracy cannot
     be guaranteed but they are supported by his letters to Baldwin, 5 December
     1936, and to Lord Salisbury, 9 December 1936, Chartwell Papers 2/264/
     110, 82–4.
101 Winston to Clementine Churchill, 27 November 1936, Spencer-Churchill
     Papers, in Gilbert, companion vol. V, Part 3, pp. 438–9; A.J.P. Taylor (ed.),
     The Abdication of King Edward VIII, by Lord Beaverbrook, 1966, p. 50.
102 Lord Zetland to Lord Linlithgow, 27 November 1936, in Gilbert,
     companion vol. V, Part 3, p. 440; Sir Henry Channon had already heard
     the rumour of this via Leslie Hore-Belisha to Lady Cunard: James (ed.),
     Channon diary, 22 November 1936, p. 107.
103 Cazalet diary, recorded shortly after 7 December 1937, p. 187; Amery
     diary, 4 December 1936, p. 431; Reith diary, 6 December 1936, in Charles
     Stuart (ed.), *The Reith Diaries*, 1975, p. 191.
104 Salisbury to Churchill, 5 December 1936, Chartwell Papers 2/264/103–4.
105 Churchill to King Edward VIII, 5 December 1936, Chartwell Papers 2/264/
     100–1.
106 Amery diary, 6 December 1936, p. 432.
107 Press statement by Churchill, 5 December 1936, Chartwell Papers 2/264/
     107.
108 If this line had occurred to Churchill at the time of his article, then he
     certainly did not discuss it earlier that day in conversation with the
     constitutional lawyer, Professor J.H. Morgan. This is because Morgan
     (who had been the India diehards' chief Counsel and was 'in complete
     agreement' with Churchill on rearmament: see Morgan/Churchill corre-
     spondence, 5 June and 2 July 1935, Chartwell Papers 2/236/27–8, 92)
     wrote to Churchill the following day that this possibility had just occurred
     to him. His advice was that if the King called on Churchill to form a
     government, then the support of forty or fifty MPs would be enough to

keep him in power until a dissolution upon which 'on so grave an issue' Churchill might 'sweep the country'. Quite how Churchill's followers were to beat the combined electoral machines of the Conservative, Labour and Liberal parties in such a contest was not mentioned: Morgan to Churchill, 6 December 1936, Chartwell Papers 2/264/94. Subsequent gossip supposedly from a friend of a friend of Mrs Simpson supported the rumour of Churchill's intention to form a King's Friends' Government citing Churchill's meeting with 'an eminent constitutional lawyer' in support of this (Amery diary, 20 December 1936, p. 434). Morgan is presumably the lawyer in question here.

109 J.A. Spender to Churchill, 6 December 1936, Chartwell Papers 2/264/97; Amery diary, 7 December 1936, p. 432; Percy Loftus (Tory MP) to Churchill, 8 December 1936, Chartwell Papers 2/264/86.

110 Press statement by Churchill, 5 December 1936, Chartwell Papers 2/264/109; see also Churchill to Salisbury, 9 December 1936, Chartwell Papers 2/264/83–4.

111 Churchill to King Edward VIII, 7 December 1936, Chartwell Papers 2/264/89. This document is corroborated by what Robert Boothby told Sir Henry Channon – that Archibald Sinclair and Churchill had worked on the formula, 'As long as I am King I will never contract a marriage against the wishes of my Ministers' which, they hoped, would have defused the immediate crisis: James (ed.), Channon diary, 7 December 1936, p. 121.

112 Boothby to Churchill, 7 December 1936, Chartwell Papers 2/264/93; Winterton, p. 223.

113 Churchill mentioned his advice to his arch-critic, Geoffrey Dawson: Churchill to Dawson, 9 December 1936, Chartwell Papers 2/264/78. Channon found out what had actually been the advice from Boothby. (James (ed.), Channon diary, 7 December 1936, p. 121); Lord Winterton later claimed 'inner knowledge' proving Churchill's motives had been entirely honourable with regard to the King's abdication (Winterton, p. 223). Having dined with Churchill on 6 December, Winterton was in a good position to know Churchill's state of mind. The *New Statesman* also said it believed 'an intimate friend of Mr Churchill's' as the source for his innocence in the matter': *New Statesman*, 12 December 1936, 'A London Diary'.

114 Churchill to Baldwin, 22 December 1936, Chartwell Papers 2/264/47–8.

115 Philip Ziegler, *King Edward VIII: The Official Biography*, 1990, p. 294.

116 Since official files on the abdication crisis remain closed, Baldwin's private machinations must remain a matter of speculation, bolstered only by what is now in the public domain and the fact that there is no public evidence of a media or official attempt to question the legal grounds for the Wallis and Ernest Simpson divorce.

117 Amery diary, 7 December 1936, p. 432.

118 Winterton, p. 224.

119 Nicolson diary, 7 December 1936, and his letter to his wife (Vita Sackville-West), 9 December 1936, pp. 282, 284; Cazalet diary, p. 187; Sir Henry Channon felt that Churchill's interjection had done 'the King's cause great

harm': James (ed.), Channon diary, 7 December 1936, p. 121. After discussing it with the Liberal MP, Robert Bernays, Blanche Dugdale, the well-connected LNU Executive member and Zionist, timed Churchill's complete self-destruction down to three minutes: Blanche Dugdale's diary, 8 December 1936, in N.A. Rose (ed.), *Baffy: The Diaries of Blanche Dugdale 1936–47*, 1973, p. 34. Boothby hoped that the diminution in his authority would be only 'temporarily': Boothby to Churchill, 11 December 1936, Chartwell Papers 2/264/72.

120	Boothby to Churchill, 7 December 1936, Chartwell Papers 2/264/93; Robert Rhodes James, *Victor Cazalet: A Portrait*, 1976.

121	Henry Wickham Steed to Churchill, 7 December 1936, Chartwell Papers 2/264/88.

122	Spier, p. 47.

123	Boothby to Churchill, 11 and 7 December 1936, Chartwell Papers 2/264/71, 93.

124	Amery diary, 10 December 1936, p. 433; Dawson to Churchill, 11 December 1936, Chartwell Papers 2/264/70.

125	Rose (ed.), Dugdale diary, 15 December 1936, p. 34.

126	Young (ed.), Lockhart diary, 10 December 1936, p. 361.

127	Amery diary, 7 December 1936, p. 432.

128	Winterton diary, 12 December 1936, p. 223.

129	Young (ed.), Lockhart diary, 10 December 1936, p. 361.

130	Amery diary, 10 December 1936, p. 433.

131	Boothby to Churchill, 11 December 1936, Chartwell Papers 2/264/72. Bracken's most recent biographer has described the difference between Boothby and Bracken towards Churchill as that between 'an ordinary political ally' and 'a henchman': Charles Edward Lysaght, *Brendan Bracken*, pp. 131–2.

132	*Spectator*, 11 December 1936, Thompson, pp. 132–3.

133	Churchill to the Commons, 4 March 1937, *Hansard* 321 HC Deb. 5s., col. 578.

134	Marion L. Kenney, 'The Role of the House of Commons in British Foreign Policy during the 1937–8 Session', in *Essays in Honor of Conyers Reed*, 1953, pp. 159–60.

135	Churchill to Rothermere, in Gilbert, companion vol. V, Part 3, p. 582.

136	The voting was: Independent 7580; Conservative 3917; Independent Conservative (Lindemann) 3608.

137	Rose (ed.), Dugdale diary, 27 February 1937, p. 39.

138	Sir Maurice Hankey to Inskip and Baldwin, 1 March 1937, in Gilbert, companion vol. V, Part 3, pp. 585–6.

139	Amery diary, 5 November 1936, p. 429.

140	Garvin in the *Observer*, 21 March 1937; see also Thompson, p. 34.

141	Sir Norman Angell to Churchill, 15 March 1937, Chartwell Papers 2/311.

142	Churchill to the Duke of Windsor, 30 April 1937, Chartwell Papers 2/300.

143	James (ed.), Channon diary, 15 April 1937, p. 150.

144	James (ed.), Channon diary, 4 May 1837, p. 154.

145 Margesson to Neville Chamberlain, March 1937, Neville Chamberlain Papers 8/24/1.

146 Gwynne to Neville Chamberlain, 21 May 1937, Neville Chamberlain Papers 8/24/4.

147 Many on the left certainly grasped this point. As the *New Statesman* commented at the time of the Albert Hall meeting, 'he still talks about collective security and the League, even though Geneva is now an obvious camouflage for an alliance. Putting it that way pleases the rank and file of organizations like the League of Nations Union.' *New Statesman*, 21 November 1936, 'A London Diary'.

148 Margesson to Neville Chamberlain, March 1937, Neville Chamberlain Papers 8/24/1.

149 Quoted in R.J. Minney (ed.), *The Private Papers of Hore-Belisha*, 1960, p. 130.

Chapter 11   Mr Chamberlain's Walk with Destiny, pp. 274–318.

1 Neville to Ida Chamberlain, 8 December 1935, Neville Chamberlain Papers 18/1/941.

2 Neville to Ida Chamberlain, 21 March 1937, Neville Chamberlain Papers 18/1/999.

3 Neville Chamberlain diary, 7 October 1936, Neville Chamberlain Papers 2/23A.

4 Neville to Hilda Chamberlain, 25 April 1937, Neville Chamberlain Papers NC18/1/1003.

5 Crowson, pp. 126–9.

6 Neville Chamberlain to Cosmo Lang (Archbishop of Canterbury), 27 March 1937, in Feiling, p. 293.

7 Neville Chamberlain diary, 27 March 1937, Neville Chamberlain Papers 2/24A.

8 Feiling, p. 287.

9 Neville Chamberlain diary, 27 March 1937, Neville Chamberlain Papers 2/24A.

10 Neville Chamberlain diary, 23 March 1937, Neville Chamberlain Papers 2/24A.

11 Neville Chamberlain diary, 30 May 1937, Neville Chamberlain Papers 2/24A.

12 Neville to Hilda Chamberlain, 30 May 1937, Neville Chamberlain Papers 18/1/1006.

13 Churchill in *Colliers* magazine, 16 October 1937.

14 Robert Rhodes James (ed.), *Winston S. Churchill: His Complete Speeches 1897–1963*, vol. vi: *1935–1942*, pp. 5856–7; James (ed.), Channon diary, 31 May 1937, p. 163.

15 Feiling, p. 303.

16 Neville to Ida Chamberlain, 26 November 1937, Neville Chamberlain Papers 18/1/1030.

17 The best study of Tory attitudes to the Spanish insurrection is: Barry

Norris, 'The Conservative Party and the Spanish Civil War', unpublished Cambridge University M. Phil., 1997.

18 Eden to Chamberlain, 9 January 1938, E.L. Woodward et al (eds), *Documents on British Foreign Policy*, DBFP II, vol. 19, no. 418, p. 723.

19 Parker, *Chamberlain and Appeasement*, p. 103.

20 Neville to Hilda Chamberlain, 17 December 1937, Neville Chamberlain Papers 18/1/1032, and Neville to Hilda Chamberlain, 9 January 1938, Neville Chamberlain Papers 1/8/1034.

21 Parker, *Chamberlain and Appeasement*, p. 118.

22 Harvey diary, note to Eden, in J. Harvey (ed.), *The Diplomatic Diaries of Oliver Harvey 1937–40*, 1970, pp. 69–70.

23 Avon, *The Eden Memoirs*, vol. I, p. 563.

24 John Charmley, *Chamberlain and the Lost Peace*, 1989, pp. 47–9.

25 Neville Chamberlain diary, 19 February 1938, Neville Chamberlain Papers 2/24A; see also Neville to Hilda Chamberlain, 27 February 1938, Neville Chamberlain Papers 18/1/1040.

26 Cowling, *Impact of Hitler*, p. 176; Roberts, *The Holy Fox*, p. 84.

27 Amery diary, 21 February 1938, p. 456.

28 Amery diary, 22 February 1938, p. 458.

29 Amery diary, 24 February 1938, p. 458.

30 Harold Nicolson to his wife, 22 February 1938, Nicolson diary, p. 324.

31 David Carlton, *Anthony Eden: A Biography*, 1981, pp. 135.

32 Neville to Hilda Chamberlain, 13 March 1938, Neville Chamberlain Papers 18/1/1041.

33 The allegation is made most forcibly by Richard Howard Powers, 'Winston Churchill's Parliamentary Commentary on British Foreign Policy 1935–1938', in *Journal of Modern History*, vol. 26, 1954.

34 Neville to Hilda Chamberlain, 13 March 1938, Neville Chamberlain Papers 18/1/1041.

35 Roberts, *The Holy Fox*, p. 77.

36 FO 800/313/15, 4 April 1938 (quoted in Roberts, p. 80).

37 Neville to Hilda Chamberlain, 13 March 1938, Neville Chamberlain Papers 18/1/1041.

38 Neville to Ida Chamberlain, 20 March 1938, Neville Chamberlain Papers 18/1/1042.

39 Cabinet Papers CAB 23/92/371, Cabinet meeting of 14 March 1938.

40 Quoted in Roberts, *The Holy Fox*, pp. 102, 96.

41 Woodward et al. (eds), DBFP III, vol. 1, no. 86, 15 March 1938, pp. 55–6.

42 Cabinet Papers CAB 23/285/317.

43 Alfred Duff Cooper to his wife, Lady Diana, 13 September 1938, quoted in Charmley, *Duff Cooper*.

44 Neville Chamberlain to Halifax, 19 August 1938, Woodward et al (eds), DBFP III, vol. 2, p. 686; Patricia Meehan, *The Unnecessary War: Whitehall and the German Resistance to Hitler*, 1992, pp. 141–5. This account, in particular, opposes the line adopted by Chamberlain.

45 Henderson to Cadogan, 6 September 1938, Woodward et al. (eds), DBFP III, vol. 2, no. 793, p. 257.

46 Charmley, *Chamberlain and the Lost Peace*, p. 97.

47 Harvey diary, 10 September 1938, Harvey (ed.), p. 174.

48 Neville to Ida Chamberlain, 19 September 1938, Neville Chamberlain Papers 18/1/1069.

49 Williamson Murray, *The Change in the European Balance of Power 1938–9*, Princeton 1984, pp. 156–7.

50 Notes of conversation between Neville Chamberlain and Adolf Hitler made by Mr Kirkpatrick, Woodward et al. (eds), DBFP III, vol. 2, no. 1033, pp. 463–73.

51 Halifax to Newton, 8.20 p.m., 22 September 1938, and Halifax to Phipps, 10.10 p.m., 22 September 1938, Woodward et al. (eds), DBFP III, vol. 2, no. 1027, p. 461 and no. 1030, p. 462.

52 Halifax to Chamberlain, 10 p.m., 23 September 1938, Woodward et al. (eds), DBFP III, vol. 2, no. 1058, p. 490.

53 Halifax to UK Delegation Geneva, 1.15 p.m., 23 September 1938, no. 1043, p. 480.

54 *Documents on German Foreign Policy*, Series D, vol. 2, no. 583, quoted in Parker, p. 168.

55 Cabinet Papers CAB 23/95/180.

56 Charmley, *Chamberlain and the Lost Peace*, p. 124.

57 Quoted in Barnes and Nicholson, p. 485.

58 Roberts, *The Holy Fox*, pp. 116–18.

59 Roberts, *The Holy Fox*, p. 118.

60 Record of Anglo-French conversations, 25 September 1938, Woodward et al. (eds), DBFP III, vol. 2, no. 1093, pp. 520–35.

61 Wilson's report to the Cabinet, 27 September 1938, Cabinet Papers CAB 23/95/263–6. Notes of Wilson/Hitler conversation, 26 September 1938, DBFP III, vol. 2, no. 118, pp. 554–7; *Documents on German Foreign Policy*, Series D, vol. 2, no. 610, quoted in Parker, p. 174.

62 Parker, *Chamberlain and Appeasement*, pp. 176–7.

63 Quoted in Feiling, p. 372.

64 Cabinet Papers CAB 23/95/969.

65 Cabinet Papers CAB 23/95/273.

66 Halifax to Henderson, 6.45 p.m., 27 September 1938, Woodward et al. (eds), DBFP III, vol. 2, no. 1140, pp. 572–3.

67 Chamberlain's recollection to the Cabinet, 30 September 1938, CAB 23/95/280.

68 Copy in Cabinet Papers CAB 23/95/289.

69 Neville to Hilda Chamberlain, 2 October 1938, Neville Chamberlain Papers 18/1/1070.

70 Austen Chamberlain, *Peace in our Time*, 1928, published by Philip Allan & Co.

71 Neville to Hilda Chamberlain, 2 October 1938, Neville Chamberlain Papers 18/1/1070.

72 R. Macleod and D. Kelly (eds): *The Ironside Diaries 1937–40*, 1962, p. 62.

73 Roberts, *The Holy Fox*, pp. 95, 93; Murray, p. 217.

74 Murray, pp. 219–21.

75 Murray, pp. 231, 223, 225, 234–5.
76 Murray, pp. 221, 257, 239–41.
77 Murray, pp. 242–3.
78 Murray, pp. 238–9.
79 Murray, pp. 243–4, 257–60, 238–9.
80 General Ismay, 'Note on the Question of whether it would be to our military advantage to fight Germany now or to postpone the issue', 22 September 1938, CAB 21/544; COS 772, 27 September 1938.
81 Cabinet Papers CAB 23/95/180.
82 Murray, p. 247; Howard, pp. 122–3.
83 Howard, p. 123.
84 Murray, pp. 247–9, 251–2.
85 Murray, pp. 250–1.
86 Howard, p. 125.

Chapter 12   The Rebellion, pp. 319–344

1 Churchill to Halifax, 20 August 1939, in Gilbert, companion vol. V, Part 3, pp. 1122–3.
2 Chamberlain to Margesson, 4 September 1938, Margesson Papers, in Gilbert, vol. V: 1922–1939, p. 969.
3 Cabinet meeting of 12 September 1938, Cabinet Papers CAB 23/95.
4 Hankey diary, 2 October 1938, in Gilbert, companion vol. V, Part 3, p. 1196.
5 Churchill's statement to the press, 21 September 1938, in Gilbert, companion vol. V, Part 3, pp. 1171–2.
6 Imre Revesz to Churchill, 22 September 1938, in Gilbert, companion vol. V, Part 3, p. 1174.
7 Nicolson diary, 22 September 1938, in Nicolson (ed.), Harold Nicolson: Diaries and Letters, vol. I, pp. 363–5.
8 Other MPs who petitioned Halifax were: Robert Boothby, Anthony Crossley, Derrick Gunston, A.P. Herbert, Sir Sidney Herbert and Harold Macmillan.
9 Churchill to Sir Orme Sargent, 23 July 1947, and Halifax to Churchill, 24 July 1947, in Gilbert, companion vol. V, Part 3, pp. 1181–2.
10 Nicolson diary, 28 September 1938, p. 369.
11 Gilbert, vol. V: 1922–39, p. 987.
12 Nicolson diary, 29 September 1938, pp. 371–2.
13 Gilbert, vol. V: 1922–39, pp. 990, 992.
14 Charmley, Duff Cooper, p. 124.
15 Dugdale diaries, quoted in Rose, Churchill, p. 245.
16 Crookshank diary, 30 September 1938, Crookshank Papers MS.Eng.-Hist.d.359/217.
17 Crookshank diary, 4 September 1938, Crookshank Papers MS.Eng.-Hist.d.359/217–18.
18 Crookshank diary, 6 October 1938, Crookshank Papers MS.Eng.-Hist.d.359/218.

19 Thompson, p. 165.

20 *Manchester Guardian*, 4 October 1938, in Thompson, p. 182.

21 Duff Cooper to the Commons, 3 October 1938, *Hansard* 339 HC Deb. 5s., cols 29–40.

22 Charmley, *Duff Cooper*, p. 130.

23 Chamberlain to the Commons, 3 October 1938, *Hansard* 339 HC Deb. 5s., cols 40–50.

24 Churchill to the Commons, *Hansard* 339 HC Deb. 5s., cols 359–73.

25 The most regular participants in this grouping were: Lord Cranborne, J.P.L. Thomas, Mark Patrick, Leo Amery, Robert Bower, Ronald Cartland, Anthony Crossley, H.J. Duggan, Paul Emrys-Evans, Sir Derrick Gunston, Sir Sidney Herbert, Dudley Joel, C.G. Lancaster, Richard Law, Harold Macmillan, Harold Nicolson, Duncan Sandys, E.L. Spears, Ronald Tree and Viscount Wolmer.

26 Anthony Crossley diary, 20 September 1938, quoted in Gilbert, companion vol. V, Part 3, p. 1170; Crossley to Churchill, 28 September 1938, in Gilbert, companion vol. V, Part 3, p. 1185.

27 Amery diary, 27 September 1938, p. 519.

28 Amery diary, 26 September 1938, p. 517.

29 It is difficult to sustain Maurice Cowling's claim that 'the most significant die-hards supported Chamberlain' given that, of the three most senior diehard politicians (Churchill, Lloyd and Croft), the first two opposed Chamberlain and that Croft, whilst supporting Munich on military grounds, was an opponent of appeasement thereafter.

30 The average age of Conservative MPs elected in 1935 was fifty-one. The average age of the Munich rebels was under forty-five. Only six (Amery, Churchill, Keynes, Nicolson, Spears and Wolmer) were over fifty. Those old enough tended to have distinguished war records. Spears had reached the post of Brigadier General and Keynes had become Admiral of the Fleet. Whilst 56 per cent of Tories elected in 1935 had been to public school, for the Munich rebels this figure was over 90 per cent. Over half had been to Eton and Harrow. Whilst over 60 per cent of all post-1935 Tories had been to university, over 70 per cent of rebels had done so and all of them who had were Oxbridge graduates. Churchill, Duff Cooper, Cranborne, Duggan, Macmillan, Nicolson and Wolmer were all either born into or married to members of titled families. This group, representing around a third of the rebels, was significantly above that for the Conservative Party as a whole. Cranborne's grandfather had been Prime Minister as had Law's father; Churchill's father had been Chancellor of the Exchequer. The professions predominated over industrial career backgrounds. In terms of the constituencies represented by Munich rebels, the South predominated with a scattering in the Midlands. Those like Macmillan in Stockton manned rare outposts in the North (even rarer than the Conservative representation there).

31 Richard Law to the Commons, 3 October 1939, *Hansard* 339 HC Deb. 5s., cols 110–14.

32 Hugh Dalton, *The Fateful Years: Memoirs 1931–1945*, 1957, p. 199.

33 Crookshank diary, 4 October 1938, Crookshank Papers MS.Eng.Hist.359/217–8.

34 Churchill to Sir Sidney Herbert, 9 October 1938, in Gilbert, companion vol. V, Part 3, p. 1207.

35 Nicolson diary, 5 October 1938, p. 375; Amery diary, 5 October 1938, p. 526.

36 Amery diary, 6 October 1938, pp. 527–8; David Dutton, *Anthony Eden: A Life and Reputation*, 1997, p. 128.

37 The MPs were: Vyvyan Adams, Leo Amery, Robert Bower, Brendan Bracken, Ronald Cartland, Winston Churchill, Duff Cooper, Lord Cranborne, A.C. Crossley, H.J. Duggan, Anthony Eden, Paul Emrys-Evans, Sir Derrick Gunston, Sir Sidney Herbert, Sir Roger Keyes, Richard Law, Harold Macmillan, Duncan Sandys, E.L. Spears, J.P.L. Thomas, Harold Nicolson and Lord Wolmer.

38 Neville to Ida Chamberlain, 9 October 1938, Neville Chamberlain Papers 18/1/1071.

39 Mary Borden diary (wife of E.L. Spears), 6 October 1938, quoted in Gilbert, companion vol. V, Part 3, p. 1204.

40 Chamberlain to Churchill, 6 October 1938, Chartwell Papers 2/332.

41 Crowson, p. 107.

42 Crowson, p. 106.

43 Ida to Neville Chamberlain, 9 October 1938, and Hilda to Neville Chamberlain, 13 October 1939, Neville Chamberlain Papers 18/2/1096 and 1/15/3/159.

44 James, *Bob Boothby*, p. 186; Boothby to Churchill, 10 October 1938, Chartwell Papers 2/332.

45 James, *Bob Boothby*, p. 187.

46 Chamberlain to Margesson, 23 December 1938, Margesson Papers MARG 1/3.

47 Churchill to Page Croft, 29 October 1938, Chartwell Papers 2/332.

48 Rothermere to Churchill, 15 October 1938, Chartwell Papers 2/332.

49 Quoted in Parker, *Chamberlain and Appeasement*, p. 188.

50 James (ed.), Channon diary, 21 November 1938, p. 221.

51 Crowson, p. 108.

52 Neville to Hilda Chamberlain, 11 December 1938, Neville Chamberlain Papers 18/1/1079.

53 The poll was carried out by the British Institute of Public Opinion in November 1938. Seventy-three per cent believed it hampered the case for an understanding and 12 per cent declared themselves not up to forming an opinion. Crowson, p. 108 ftn.

54 Crowson, p. 113.

55 This is the subject of Richard Cockett's revealing work, *Twilight of Truth: Chamberlain, Appeasement and the Manipulation of the Press*, 1989.

56 Churchill's broadcast to the United States, 16 October 1938, in Gilbert, companion vol. V, Part 3, p. 1216.

57 Chamberlain to the Commons, 1 November 1938, *Hansard* 340 HC Deb. 5s., cols 73–4.

58 Chamberlain to the Commons, 17 November 1938, *Hansard* 341 HC Deb. 5s., cols 1195–6.

59 Churchill in Chingford, 9 December 1938, in Gilbert, companion vol. V, Part 3, pp. 1301–2.

60 Churchill to A.H. Richards, 12 November 1938, Chartwell Papers 2/343.

61 Hoare to Chamberlain, 5 October 1938, in Gilbert, companion vol. V, Part 3, p. 1202.

62 Hoare to Chamberlain, 5 October 1938, in Gilbert, companion vol. V, Part 3, p. 1202; Halifax to Chamberlain, 11 October 1938, PRO FO 800/328, Hal 38/28 (in Charmley, *Chamberlain and the Lost Peace*, p. 148).

63 Neville to Hilda Chamberlain, 15 October 1938, Neville Chamberlain Papers NC 18/1/1072.

64 Winston to Clementine Churchill, 29 December 1938, Chartwell Papers 1/325.

65 The other Cabinet changes were as follows: Sir John Anderson became Lord Privy Seal, Malcolm MacDonald became Dominions Secretary, de la Warr went to the Board of Education. Duff Cooper's place at the Admiralty was passed to Lord Stanhope.

66 Cowling, *The Impact of Hitler*, p. 245.

67 Nicolson was, of course, a member of the National Labour Party but the tactics to oppose him were the same. Crowson, p. 107.

68 Churchill to Sir Douglas Hacking, 18 March 1939 (unsent letter), Chartwell Papers 7/56. Gilbert, companion vol. V, Part 3, pp. 1294–6.

69 Gilbert, vol. V: 1922–39, p. 1043.

70 Thomas, *Churchill: the Member for Woodford*, p. 104.

71 Thomas, p. 109.

Chapter 13 'If they had asked nicely . . .' pp. 345–384

1 Quoted in Middlemas and Barnes, p. 1046.

2 Roberts, *The Holy Fox*, p. 124.

3 Parker, *Chamberlain and Appeasement*, p. 185.

4 Chamberlain to the Cabinet, 3 October 1938, Cabinet Papers CAB 23/95/304–5.

5 Chamberlain to the Cabinet, 31 October 1938, Cabinet Papers CAB 23/96/92.

6 Neville to Ida Chamberlain, 27 October 1938, Neville Chamberlain Papers 18/1/1074.

7 Neville to Hilda Chamberlain, 19 February 1939, Neville Chamberlain Papers 18/1/1086.

8 Chamberlain to the Cabinet, 22 November 1938, Cabinet Papers CAB 23/96/246–7.

9 Chamberlain quoted in Ian Colvin, *The Chamberlain Cabinet*, 1971, p. 262.

10 Colvin, pp. 174–5.

11 Roberts, *The Holy Fox*, pp. 128–30.

12 Quoted in Roberts, *The Holy Fox*, p. 129.

13 Roberts, *The Holy Fox*, p. 132.

14   Chamberlain to the Cabinet, 25 January 1939, Cabinet Papers CAB 23/97/
      56–7.
15   Neville Chamberlain Papers 18/1/1082, 15 January 1939.
16   Chamberlain to the Cabinet, 18 January 1939, Cabinet Papers CAB 23/97/6.
17   Chamberlain to the Cabinet, 18 January 1939, Cabinet Papers CAB 23/97/4.
18   Ciano's diary, quoted in David Dilks (ed.), *The Diaries of Sir Alexander
      Cadogan 1938–1945*, 1971, pp. 136–7.
19   Andrew Roberts has noted that it was significant that by 1939 one of the
      Cabinet ministers who was most relaxed about increasing the burden of
      rearmament was Lord Halifax who had been in India at the time of the
      crisis of August 1931. Roberts, *The Holy Fox*, pp. 134–5.
20   Cabinet 23 May 1939, Cabinet Papers CAB 23/99/244.
21   See Scott Newton, *Profits of Peace: The Political Economy of Anglo-
      German Appeasement*, Oxford 1996, pp. 87–94.
22   Newton, pp. 99–101.
23   David Stafford, *Churchill and Secret Service*, 1997, p. 156
24   Neville to Ida Chamberlain, 12 March 1939, Neville Chamberlain Papers
      18/1/1089.
25   Although the guarantee had never been formally signed, the Dominions
      Secretary, Malcolm MacDonald, had made clear to the Commons on 4
      October that 'His Majesty's Government however, feel under a moral
      obligation to Czechoslovakia to treat the guarantee as being now in force.
      In the event, therefore, of an act of unprovoked aggression against
      Czechoslovakia, His Majesty's Government would certainly feel bound to
      take all steps in their power to see that the integrity of Czechoslovakia is
      preserved.' *Hansard* 339 HC Deb. 5s., col. 303.
26   Chamberlain to the Commons, 15 March 1939, *Hansard* 345 HC Deb. 5s.
      cols 435–40.
27   Chamberlain to the Cabinet, 18 March 1939, Cabinet Papers CAB 23/98/50.
28   16 March 1939, *Hansard* 345 HC Deb. 5s., cols 613–4.
29   Eden to the Commons, 15 March 1939, *Hansard* 345 HC Deb. 5s., cols
      461–2.
30   Nicolson diary, 17 March 1939, p. 393.
31   Croft, p. 294.
32   Quoted in Parker, p. 202.
33   Chamberlain to the Cabinet, 18 March 1939, Cabinet Papers CAB 23/98/
      50.
34   Chamberlain to the Cabinet, 18 March 1939, Cabinet Papers CAB 23/98/
      62.
35   Record of conversation between Beck and Chamberlain, 4 April 1939,
      Woodward et al. (eds), DBFP III, vol. 5, no. 2, pp. 9–19; Neville to Ida
      Chamberlain, 9 April 1939, Neville Chamberlain Papers 18/1/1093; Neville
      to Ida Chamberlain, 26 March 1939, Neville Chamberlain Papers 18/1/
      1091.
36   Neville to Hilda Chamberlain, 3 April 1939, Neville Chamberlain Papers
      18/1/1092.
37   Quoted in Nicolson diary, 11 April 1939, p. 397.

38 Neville to Ida Chamberlain, 9 April 1939, Neville Chamberlain Papers 18/1/1093.

39 Chamberlain to the Cabinet, 24 April 1939, Cabinet Papers CAB 23/99/8.

40 Lloyd George to the Commons, 19 May 1939, *Hansard* 347 HC Deb. 5s., col. 1815.

41 Churchill to the Commons, 19 May 1939, *Hansard* 347 HC Deb 5s., cols 1840–9.

42 Chamberlain to the Foreign Policy Committee, Cabinet Papers CAB 27/625.

43 Dilks (ed.), Cadogan diary, 20 May 1939, p. 182.

44 On top of the pronouncements of the letter-writing class, an opinion poll conducted by Gallup in June 1939 recorded an extraordinary 84 per cent majority in favour of the three power alliance. Parker, p. 233.

45 Neville to Hilda Chamberlain, 28 May 1939, Neville Chamberlain Papers 18/1/1101.

46 Macleod and Kelly (eds), Ironside diaries, p. 77.

47 Chamberlain to the Cabinet, 19 July 1939, Cabinet Papers CAB 23/100/187.

48 Neville to Ida Chamberlain, 10 June 1939, Neville Chamberlain Papers 18/1/1102.

49 Cockett, p. 9.

50 Davidson's recollection of 1955 in James (ed.), *Memoirs of a Conservative*, p. 272.

51 Proof that Churchill's conversations were being tapped can be found in Neville to Ida Chamberlain, 9 October 1938, Neville Chamberlain Papers 18/1/1071. In having his private papers burned, Ball has managed to scupper a proper examination into (what can only be described as) his sinister activites. For what is known about his skulduggery during the 1930s see Cockett, *Twilight of Truth*, and Stafford, *Churchill and Secret Service*.

52 Neville to Hilda Chamberlain, 15 April 1939, Neville Chamberlain Papers 18/1/1094.

53 *Daily Telegraph*, 28 April 1939.

54 *The Times*, 28 April 1939.

55 The figures were 56 per cent in favour, 26 per cent against, and 17 per cent did not know. Gilbert, vol. V: 1922–39, p. 1068.

56 *Daily Telegraph*, 3 July 1939.

57 Lord Camrose's notes of his conversation with Chamberlain, in Gilbert, companion vol. V, Part 3, pp. 1544–6.

58 Hoare to Bill Astor, 11 July 1939, in Gilbert, companion vol. V, Part 3, p. 1562.

59 Neville to Ida Chamberlain, 8 July 1939, Neville Chamberlain Papers 18/1/1106. There was certainly some truth in this last charge. 'Chips' Channon found Eden's loyal accomplice, Jim Thomas, to be annoyed with Churchill for 'stealing all Anthony's thunder'. James (ed.), Channon diary, 4 July 1939, p. 252.

60 Including Brendan Bracken, Ronald Cartland, Richard Law, Harold Macmillan, Harold Nicolson and the Liberal leader, Sir Archibald Sinclair. Lloyd George also prominently opposed the measure.

61   Churchill to the Commons, 2 August 1939, *Hansard* 350 HC Deb. 5s., cols 2427–8.

62   Chamberlain to the Commons, 2 August 1939, *Hansard* 350 HC Deb. 5s., col. 2484.

63   Cartland to the Commons, 2 August 1939, *Hansard* 350 HC Deb. 5s., cols 2494–5.

64   Cartland to the Commons, 2 August 1939, *Hansard* 350 HC Deb. 5s., cols 2495.

65   Neville to Ida Chamberlain, 5 August 1939, Neville Chamberlain Papers 18/1/1111.

66   Nicolson diary, 18 July 1939, p. 406.

67   Harold Nicolson to his wife, 2 August 1939, p. 407.

68   Macleod and Kelly (eds), Ironside diaries, 27 July 1939.

69   Gilbert, vol. V: 1922–39, p. 1103 n.1.

70   Neville to Ida Chamberlain, 23 July 1939, Neville Chamberlain Papers 18/1/1108; Neville to Hilda Chamberlain, 30 July 1939, Neville Chamberlain Papers 18/1/1110.

71   Lamb, pp. 318–9; Newton, pp. 124–9.

72   Newton, pp. 122–3.

73   Halifax to the Cabinet, 2 August 1939, Cabinet Papers CAB 23/100/277.

74   See Lamb, pp. 309–16.

75   Parker, p. 244.

76   Williamson Murray has written that 'Soviet supplies of raw materials were a significant help to the German war economy and to the victory over France that destroyed the possibility of a western front until 1944.' Murray, p. 305.

77   Dilks (ed.), Cadogan diary, 28 August 1939, p. 203.

78   Charmley, *Chamberlain and the Lost Peace*, p. 205.

79   Churchill, *The Gathering Storm*, p. 317.

80   Cowling, *The Impact of Hitler*, p. 298.

81 Chamberlain to the Cabinet, 1 September 1939, Cabinet Papers CAB 23/100/443.

82   James (ed.), Channon diary, 2 September 1939, p. 262.

83   Chamberlain to the Commons, 2 September 1939, *Hansard* 351 HC Deb. 5s., col. 281.

84   James (ed.), Channon diary, 2 September 1939, p. 263.

85   Chamberlain to the Cabinet, 2 September 1939, Cabinet papers CAB 23/100/474–5.

86   ibid.

87   Chamberlain to the Commons, 3 September 1939, *Hansard* 351 HC Deb. 5s., col. 292.

Chapter 14   Assassins in the Senate, pp. 385–420

1   Quoted in Martin Gilbert, *Finest Hour: Winston S. Churchill 1931–41*, vol. VI, p. 155.

2   Recollection of Kathleen Hill, quoted in Gilbert, vol. V: 1922–39, p. 113.

3   Amery diary, 3 September 1939, p. 571.

4   Although by no means scientific by modern standards, an opinion poll in
    April 1939 had suggested that Eden, far more than Churchill or Halifax,
    was the country's preferred choice as the next Prime Minister. The opinion
    poll gave Eden 38 per cent and only 7 per cent each for Churchill and
    Halifax. Pelling, p. 397.

5   Neville to Ida Chamberlain, 10 September 1939, Neville Chamberlain
    Papers 18/1/1116.

6   Neville to Hilda Chamberlain, 15 October 1939, Neville Chamberlain
    Papers 18/1/1125.

7   Neville to Ida Chamberlain, 20 December 1939, Neville Chamberlain
    Papers 18/1/1135.

8   Neville to Ida Chamberlain, 23 July 1939, Neville Chamberlain Papers 18/
    1/1108.

9   Neville to Ida Chamberlain, 5 November 1939, Neville Chamberlain
    Papers 18/1/1129.

10 Barnes and Nicholson (eds), pp. 562–3.

11 Neville to Ida Chamberlain, 8 October 1939, Neville Chamberlain Papers
    18/1/1124.

12 Neville to Ida Chamberlain, 5 November 1939, Neville Chamberlain
    Papers 18/1/1129.

13 ibid.

14 Colville diary, 29 October 1939, p. 45.

15 Scott Newton argues that although the German negotiators were SS officers
    who in the event obeyed orders from above, they may have been acting
    sincerely in the initial stages of the communication. Newton, pp. 145–9.

16 As late as April 1940, opinion polls suggested that Chamberlain retained an
    approval rating that still approached 60 per cent. Addison, The Road to
    1945, p. 78.

17 Neville to Ida Chamberlain, 8 October 1939, Neville Chamberlain Papers
    18/1/1124.

18 Nicolson diary, 20 September 1939, p. 35.

19 Butler diary, 13 March 1940, quoted in Gilbert, Finest Hour, p. 190.

20 Gilbert, Finest Hour, p. 190.

21 Churchill to Chamberlain, 11 October 1939, and Chamberlain's response,
    Churchill Papers 19/2 (Gilbert vi., p. 60).

22 Dilks (ed.), Cadogan diary, 4 February 1940, pp. 252–3.

23 Dilks (ed.), Nicolson diary, 26 September 1939, Nicolson (ed.), Harold
    Nicolson: Diaries and Letters, vol. II, p. 37. The pro-Chamberlain 'Chips'
    Channon agreed with this assessment. James (ed.), Channon diary, 26
    September 1939, pp. 272–3.

24 (30 September 1939) Jones, p. 440.

25 Charmley, Churchill, p. 377.

26 Violet Pearman to Churchill, 28 February 1940, in Gilbert, Finest Hour, p.
    172.

27 Colville diary, 12 and 13 November 1939, in John Colville, The Fringes of
    Power: The Downing Street Diaries 1939–55, 1985, pp. 50–1.

28 Quoted in Roberts, *The Holy Fox*, p. 189.

29 Amery diary, 5 September 1939, p. 572.

30 Neville to Ida Chamberlain, 13 April 1940, Neville Chamberlain Papers 18/1/1150.

31 War Cabinet, 9 September 1939, Cabinet Papers CAB 65/1/57. Chamberlain to Churchill, 16 September 1939, Neville Chamberlain Papers 7/9/50.

32 Churchill to Chamberlain, 22 September 1939, Neville Chamberlain Papers 7/9/53.

33 Neville to Ida Chamberlain, 23 September 1939, Neville Chamberlain Papers 18/1/1122.

34 Military Coordinating Committee, 9 February 1940, in Gilbert, *Finest Hour*, p. 150.

35 James (ed.), Channon diary, 16 January 1940, pp. 282–3.

36 Churchill, *The Second World War* vol 1, p. 389

37 Colville diary, 21 November 1939, p. 52.

38 Colville, *The Fringes of Power*, pp. 36–7.

39 Colville diary, 9 and 14 November 1939, p. 50–1.

40 Neville to Ida Chamberlain, 27 January 1940, Neville Chamberlain Papers 18/1/1140.

41 Colville, *The Fringes of Power*, p. 100n.

42 Colville diary, 24 April 1940, p. 108.

43 Neville to Ida Chamberlain, 30 March 1940, Neville Chamberlain Papers 18/1/1148.

44 First Lieutenant Hubert Fox to his father, 7 February 1940, quoted in Gilbert, *Finest Hour*, p. 148.

45 War Cabinet, 22 December 1939, Cabinet Papers CAB 65/4/165, 167.

46 War Cabinet, 27 December 1939, Minute 1, Confidential Annex: Cabinet Papers 65/4/178–86.

47 War Cabinet, 2 January 1940, Confidential Annex: Cabinet Papers CAB 65/11/9, 13–17.

48 War Cabinet, 12 January 1940, Cabinet Papers CAB 65/11/115.

49 War Cabinet, 12 March 1940, Cabinet Papers CAB 65/12/109, 111.

50 War Cabinet, 29 February 1940, Cabinet Papers CAB 65/5/274–5.

51 Colville diary, 15 February 1940, p. 84.

52 Dilks (eds), Cadogan diary, 11 March 1940, p. 261.

53 Neville to Ida Chamberlain, 16 March 1940, Neville Chamberlain Papers 18/1/1147. Anglo-French intervention in the Scandanavian war theatre is analysed by David Dilks, 'Great Britain and Scandinavia in the "Phoney War"', in *Scandinavian Journal of History*, 2 (1977), 29–51, and R.A.C. Parker, 'Britain, France and Scandinavia 1939–40', in *History*, 61, 203 (October 1976), 369–87.

54 War Cabinet, 14 March 1940, Cabinet Papers CAB 65/12/124.

55 Dilks, *Scandinavian Journal*, 2 (1977), pp. 48–9.

56 Colville diary, 6 April 1940, pp. 96–7.

57 Roberts, *The Holy Fox*, p. 193.

58 Neville to Hilda Chamberlain, 20 April 1940, Neville Chamberlain Papers 18/1/1151.

59 Military Coordinating Committee, 26 April 1940, in Gilbert, *Finest Hour*, p. 269.
60 *Documents on German Foreign Policy*, series D, vol. IX, pp. 104–5, 108, quoted in Dilks, *Scandinavian Journal*, 2 (1977), 51.
61 Colville diary, 23 April 1940, p. 107.
62 Colville diary, 25 April 1940, p. 108.
63 Colville diary, 3 May 1940, p. 116.
64 Colville diary, 25 April 1940, p. 108.
65 Reith diary, 3 May 1940, in Stuart (ed.), *The Reith Diaries*, p. 249.
66 Chamberlain to the Commons, 7 May 1940, *Hansard* 360 HC Deb. 5s., cols 1084–5.
67 Neville to Ida Chamberlain, 27 April 1940, Neville Chamberlain Papers 18/1/1152.
68 Nicolson diary, 30 April 1940, p. 74.
69 *Evening Standard*, 6 May 1940 (Barnes and Nicholson (eds), p. 567).
70 *Daily Mail*, 6 May 1940 (Barnes and Nicholson (eds), p. 567).
71 Nicolson diary, 4 May 1940, p. 75.
72 Nicolson diary, 4 May 1940, p. 75.
73 Nicolson diary, 30 April 1940, p. 74. Similar fears were reported in his diary on 1 May 1940, pp. 74–5.
74 Hatfield Papers A1, in Andrew Roberts, *Eminent Churchillians*, pp. 148–9.
75 Nicolson diary, 7 May 1940, p. 76.
76 Chamberlain to the Commons, 7 May 1940, *Hansard* 360 HC Deb 5s., cols 1073–86.
77 Keyes to the Commons, 7 May 1940, *Hansard* 360 HC Deb. 5s., cols 1125–30.
78 Amery to the Commons, 7 May 1940, *Hansard* 360 HC Deb. 5s., cols 1141–50.
79 Chamberlain to the Commons, 8 May 1940, *Hansard* 360 HC Deb. 5s., cols 1265–6.
80 Lloyd George to the Commons, 8 May 1940, *Hansard* 360 HC Deb. 5s., cols 1277–83.
81 Colville diary, 8 May 1940, p. 119.
82 James (eds), Channon diary, 8 May 1940, p. 301.
83 Amery diary, 8 May 1940, p. 610.
84 Churchill to the Commons, 8 May 1940, *Hansard* 360 HC Deb. 5s., cols 1348–62.
85 James (eds), Channon diary, 8 May 1940, p. 302.
86 James (eds), Channon diary, 8 May 1940, p. 302.
87 Waterhouse diary, 9 May 1940, in Roberts, *Eminent Churchillians*, p. 145.
88 Nicolson diary, 8 May 1940, pp. 78–9.
89 Colville diary, 8 May 1940, p. 119.
90 Amery diary, 8 May 1940, pp. 610–11. Dunglass's intervention was similarly noted by Harold Nicolson: Nicolson diary, 8 May 1940, p. 79.
91 Of the forty-one rebel MPs, thirty-three were Conservatives, four were

Liberal Nationals, two were National Labour and two Independent Nationals.

92 One analysis puts the number of abstentions at thirty-six: Jorgen S. Rasmussen, 'Party Discipline in War-Time: The Downfall of the Chamberlain Government', in *Journal of Politics*, 32 (1970).

93 Nicolson diary, 8 May 1940, p. 79; Amery, *My Political Life*, pp. 368–9.

94 James (eds), Channon diary, 8 May 1940, p. 303.

95 As Chamberlain put it to his sister: 'A number of those who voted against the Government have since either told me or written to me to say that they had nothing against me except that I had the wrong people in my team.' Neville to Ida Chamberlain, 11 May 1940, Neville Chamberlain Papers 18/1/1155. Gretton abstained, primarily, he claimed to Waterhouse, to get rid of Simon, Hoare and Leslie Burgin. Roberts, *Eminent Churchillians*, p. 158.

96 Neville to Ida Chamberlain, 11 May 1940, Neville Chamberlain Papers 18/1/1155.

97 Amery diary, 9 May 1940, p. 612.

98 ibid.

99 Jim Thomas thought that Halifax was the 'favourite at the moment but I heard the usual rumour that he won't think of it'. Roberts, *Eminent Churchillians*, p. 140.

100 Blake, *Churchill*, p. 265.

101 Halifax Papers, quoted in Roberts, *The Holy Fox*, p. 199.

102 Dalton diary, Ben Pimlott (ed.), *The Political Diary of Hugh Dalton*, 1986, p. 344.

103 Roberts, *Holy Fox*, pp. 201–3.

104 Halifax diary, 9 May 1940, quoted in Robert Blake, 'How Churchill Became Prime Minister', in Blake and Louis (eds), *Churchill*, Oxford 1993, p. 265.

105 Halifax Papers, quoted in Roberts, *The Holy Fox*, p. 199.

106 Blake, *Churchill*, p. 266.

107 Halifax diary, 9 May 1940, quoted in Robert Blake, 'How Churchill Became Prime Minister', in Blake and Louis (eds), *Churchill*, Oxford 1993, p. 265.

108 Roberts, *The Holy Fox*, p. 203.

109 Halifax diary, 9 May 1940, in Roberts, *The Holy Fox*, p. 205.

110 Amery diary, 9 May 1940, p. 611–12.

111 Lord Avon, *The Eden Memoirs*, vol. II: *The Reckoning*, 1965, pp. 96–7.

112 Moran diary, 7 December 1947, in Lord Moran, *Winston Churchill: The Struggle for Survival 1940–1965*, 1966, p. 323.

113 Simon diary, 9 May 1940, in Dutton, *Simon*, p. 293.

114 Halifax diary, 9 May 1940, quoted in Blake, 'How Churchill Became Prime Minister', in Blake and Louis (eds), p. 266.

115 Colville, *The Fringes of Power*, p. 123.

116 Halifax diary, 9 May 1940, in Blake, 'How Churchill Became Prime Minister', in Blake and Louis (eds), p. 266.

117 Neville to Ida Chamberlain, 11 May 1940, Neville Chamberlain Papers 18/
     1/1155.
118 Dalton diary, in Pimlott (ed.), p. 343.
119 Neville to Ida Chamberlain, 11 May 1940, Neville Chamberlain Papers 18/
     1/1155.
120 Quoted in John W. Wheeler-Bennett, *King George VI, His Life and Reign*,
     1958, pp. 443–4.
121 Winston S. Churchill, *The Second World War*, vol. I, 1948, p. 527.

Epilogue Burying Caesar, pp. 421–448

1   Churchill to Chamberlain, 10 May 1940, Neville Chamberlain Papers 7/9/
    80
2   Neville to Hilda Chamberlain, 17 May 1940, Neville Chamberlain Papers
    18/1/1156.
3   Winston S. Churchill, *The Second World War*, vol. II: *Their Finest Hour*,
    1949, p. 29.
4   Amery diary, 13 May 1940, p. 617.
5   Roberts, *Eminent Churchillians*, p. 154.
6   A.J.P. Taylor (ed.), *Off the Record*, 1973, p. 175.
7   Neville to Ida Chamberlain, 11 May 1940, Neville Chamberlain Papers 18/
    1/1155.
8   Churchill to Chamberlain, 16 May 1940, Neville Chamberlain Papers.
9   Neville to Hilda Chamberlain, 17 May 1940, Neville Chamberlain Papers
    18/1/1156.
10 Colville diary, 10 May 1940, p. 122.
11 Nancy to Tom Dugdale, 18 June 1940, quoted in Roberts, *Eminent
    Churchillians*, p. 164. Other negative reactions to Churchill's appointments
    are chronicled in Sheila Lawlor, *Churchill and the Politics of War,
    1940–1941*, Cambridge 1994, pp. 36–41.
12 Roberts, *Eminent Churchillians*, p. 144.
13 John Wheeler-Bennett (ed.), *Action This Day: Working with Churchill*,
    1968, pp. 48–9.
14 Quoted in Roberts, *Eminent Churchillians*, p. 142.
15 Quoted in Roberts, *Eminent Churchillians*, p. 161.
16 Churchill, *Their Finest Hour*, p. 52.
17 Chamberlain diary, 26 May 1940, Neville Chamberlain Papers 2/24A.
18 Churchill to Ivy Chamberlain, 18 March 1937, in Gilbert, companion vol.
    V, Part 3, p. 626.
19 This particular analogy is well brought out in Roberts, *The Holy Fox*, pp.
    214–16, 226.
20 Neville Chamberlain diary, 26 May 1940, Neville Chamberlain Papers 2/
    24A.
21 Halifax diary, 26 May 1940, in Roberts, *The Holy Fox*, p. 217.
22 Neville Chamberlain diary, 26 May 1940, Neville Chamberlain Papers 2/
    24A.
23 Halifax diary, 27 May 1940, in Roberts, *The Holy Fox*, p. 220.

24 Neville Chamberlain diary, 28 May 1940, Neville Chamberlain Papers 2/24A.

25 Neville Chamberlain diary, 26 May 1940, Neville Chamberlain Papers 2/24A.

26 Phrased in more defeatist and less spirited terms, Chamberlain's reasons for wanting to fight on were similar to those of Churchill. In his diary entry of 19 May 1940, Chamberlain had written that he expected Hitler's ultimatum would soon be made, 'though the terms will probably be such as to force us to fight on, we should be fighting only for better terms, not for victory. Our only hope, it seems to me, lies in Roosevelt in the USA. But unfortunately they are so unready themselves that they can do little to help us now.' Neville Chamberlain Papers 2/24A.

27 War Cabinet meeting no. 145, 28 May 1940, Cabinet Papers 65/13.

28 Dalton diary, 28 May 1940, in Dalton, *The Fateful Years*, pp. 335–6.

29 It is possible that delaying the advance of the Panzers was the result of a miscued political calculation by Hitler. The evidence, however, points to his belief, backed up by others in his command, that the Panzers were overexposed and would not operate effectively in the Flanders marsh. Consequently he accepted Goering's boast that the *Luftwaffe* could do the job. See B.H. Liddell Hart, *History of the Second World War*, 1970, pp. 76, 80–1.

30 Churchill to the Commons, 4 June 1940, *Hansard*, 361 HC Deb. 5s., cols. 787–796.

31 Britain's last-ditch scheme to keep France in the war is described by Avi Shlaim, 'Prelude to Downfall: the British offer of Union to France, June 1940,' in *Journal of Contemporary History*, 9, 5 (July 1974).

32 Warsaw – September 1939; Copenhagen and Oslo – April 1940; The Hague and Brussels – May 1940; Paris – June 1940. Gilbert, *Finest Hour*, p. 543.

33 Alistair Horne, *To Lose a Battle: France 1940*, 1969, p. 511.

34 Churchill to the Commons, 18 June 1940, *Hansard*, 362 HC Deb 5s., cols. 52–61.

35 Chamberlain's broadcast of 30 June 1940, Feiling, p. 449.

36 Chamberlain diary, 1 July 1940, Neville Chamberlain Papers 2/24A.

37 Paul Einzig, *In the Centre of Things*, 1960, p. 221.

38 Neville to Hilda Chamberlain, 17 May 1940, Neville Chamberlain Papers 18/1/1156.

39 Churchill/Chamberlain correspondence, 6 June 1940, Neville Chamberlain Papers 7/9/86–7.

40 Chamberlain diary, 18 June 1940, Neville Chamberlain Papers 2/24A.

41 3 October 1940, Colin Cross (ed.), *Life with Lloyd George: The Diary of A.J. Sylvester*, 1975, p. 281.

42 Neville to Hilda Chamberlain, 14 July 1940, Neville Chamberlain Papers 18/1/1165.

43 Quoted in John Terraine, *The Right of the Line: The Royal Air Force in the European War 1939–1945*, 1939–1945, 1985, p. 186.

44 Although it was assumed by the British at the time to be the prelude to

invasion, the air assault has alternatively been viewed as Hitler's attempt to get Britain to sue for peace without his having to implement the risky operation of a seaborne invasion.

45 Colville diary, 15 August 1940, pp. 223–4.

46 Terraine, p. 187.

47 Chamberlain diary, 9 September 1940, Neville Chamberlain Papers 2/24A.

48 Churchill, *Their Finest Hour*, p. 283–4.

49 Chamberlain diary, 30 September 1940, Neville Chamberlain Papers 2/24A, Chamberlain to Lord Stanhope, 1 October 1940, quoted in Feiling, p. 453.

50 Churchill to Chamberlain, 2 October 1940, Neville Chamberlain Papers 7/9/104.

51 Herbert R. Lottman, *Pétain: Hero or Traitor?*, 1985, p. 293.

52 Mary Soames, *Clementine Churchill*, 1979, pp. 299–300.

53 Sir George Harvie-Watt, *Most of My Life*, 1980, pp. 38–9.

54 Churchill, *Their Finest Hour*, p. 285.

55 Stewart, 'The Left Wasn't Right', in *Spectator*, 10 October 1998, pp. 16–18.

56 Chamberlain to King George VI, 30 September 1940, quoted in Feiling, p. 452.

57 Chamberlain diary, 4 October 1940, Neville Chamberlain Papers 2/24A.

58 Chamberlain's broadcast of 11 October 1940, quoted in Feiling, p. 454.

59 Churchill to Chamberlain, 20 October 1940, Neville Chamberlain Papers 2/24A.

60 Churchill, *Their Finest Hour*, pp. 284, 437.

61 Annie Chamberlain/Churchill correspondence, 11 November 1940, Neville Chamberlain Papers 7/9/107, 109.

62 Colville diary, 14 November 1940, p. 294.

63 Charles Waterhouse, quoted in Roberts, *Eminent Churchillians*, p. 193.

64 James (eds), Channon diary, 14 November 1940, p. 338.

65 Churchill to the Commons (meeting in Church House) 12 November 1940, *Hansard* 365 HC Deb 5s., cols. 1617–1619.

BIBLIOGRAPHY

Private Papers

Baldwin Papers (Cambridge University Library)
Beaverbrook Papers (House of Lords Record Office)
Butler Papers (Trinity College, Cambridge)
Austen Chamberlain Papers (Birmingham University Library)
Neville Chamberlain Papers (Birmingham University Library)
Chartwell (Churchill) Papers (Churchill College, Cambridge)
Crookshank Papers (Bodleian Library, Oxford)
Davidson Papers (Bodleian Library, Oxford)
Lloyd Papers (Churchill College, Cambridge)
Lloyd George Papers (House of Lords Record Office)
Margesson Papers (Churchill College, Cambridge)
Salisbury Papers (Hatfield House)
Stuart Papers (Bodleian Library, Oxford)
Templewood Papers (Cambridge University Library)
Thompson Papers (India Office Library, British Library)

Cabinet Papers (Public Record Office, Kew)
India Office Papers (India Office Library, British Library)
Conservative Party Archives (Bodleian Library, Oxford)

Published Primary Sources

Parliamentary Debates (Hansard), 5th Series
Notices of Orders of the Day (House of Lords Record Office)
Martin Gilbert, *Winston S. Churchill*, companion vol. V, Part 1 (1979).
Martin Gilbert, *Winston S. Churchill*, companion vol. V, Part 2 (1981).
Martin Gilbert, *Winston S. Churchill*, companion vol. V, Part 3 (1982).
Robert Rhodes James (ed.), *Winston S. Churchill: His Complete Speeches 1897–1963*, vol. IV (New York 1974).
Robert Rhodes James (ed.), *Winston S. Churchill: His Complete Speeches 1897–1963*, vol. V (New York 1974).
Robert Rhodes James (ed.), *Winston S. Churchill: His Complete Speeches 1897–1963*, vol. VI: *1935–1942* (New York 1974).

E.L. Woodward et al. (eds), *Documents on British Foreign Policy 1919–39*, third series (1946–54)

Newspapers and Journals

Daily Mail
Daily News
Daily Telegraph
Indian Empire Review
Morning Post
New Statesman
News Chronicle
Sunday Express
The Times
UBI Bulletin

Diaries

Stuart Ball (ed.), *Parliament and Politics in the Age of Baldwin and MacDonald: The Headlam Diary 1923–35* (1992).

John Barnes and David Nicholson (eds), *The Empire at Bay: The Leo Amery Diaries 1929–55* (1988).

John Colville, *The Fringes of Power: The Downing Street Diaries 1939–55* (1985).

David Dilks (ed.), *The Diaries of Sir Alexander Cadogan 1938–45* (1971).

John Harvey (ed.), *The Diplomatic Diaries of Oliver Harvey 1937–40* (1970).

Robert Rhodes James (ed.), *Chips: The Diaries of Sir Henry Channon* (1967).

Robert Rhodes James (ed.), *Memoirs of a Conservative: J.C.C. Davidson's Memoirs and Papers 1910–37* (1969).

R. Macleod and D. Kelly (eds), *The Ironside Diaries 1937–40* (1962).

Keith Middlemas (ed.), *Thomas Jones Whitehall Diary*, vol. II: *1926–30* (Oxford 1969).

R.J. Minney (ed.), *The Private Papers of Hore-Belisha* (1960),

Nigel Nicolson (ed.), *Harold Nicolson: Diaries and Letters*, vol. I: *1930–39* (1966).

Nigel Nicolson (ed.), *Harold Nicolson: Diaries and Letters*, vol. II: *1939–45* (1967).

Hugh Pimlott (ed.), *The Political Diary of Hugh Dalton* (1986).

John Ramsden (ed.), *Real Old Tory Politics: The Political Diaries of Sir Robert Sanders, Lord Bayford, 1910–35* (1984).

Norman Rose (ed.), *Baffy: The Diaries of Blanche Dugdale 1936–47* (1973).

Charles Stuart (ed.), *The Reith Diaries* (1975).

Kenneth Young (ed.), *The Diaries of Sir Robert Bruce Lockhart*, vol. I: *1915–38* (1973).

Memoirs

L.S. Amery, *My Political Life*, vol. III: *The Unforgiving Years 1929–40* (1955).

Earl of Avon (Anthony Eden), *The Eden Memoirs*, vol. I: *Facing the Dictators* (1962).

Earl of Avon (Anthony Eden), *The Eden Memoirs*, vol. II: *The Reckoning* (1965).

Lord (R.A.) Butler, *The Art of the Possible* (1971).

Winston S. Churchill, *My Early Life: A Roving Commission* (1930).

Winston S. Churchill, *The Gathering Storm* (1948).

Walter Citrine, *Men and Work* (1964).

Tom Clarke, *My Lloyd George Diary* (1939).

Lord Croft (Sir Henry Page Croft), *My Life of Strife* (1948).

Hugh Dalton, *The Fateful Years: Memoirs 1931–1945* (1957).

Patrick Donner, *Crusade: A Life against the Calamitous Twentieth Century* (1984).

P.J. Grigg, *Prejudice and Judgement* (1948).

Thomas Jones, *A Diary with Letters 1931–1950* (Oxford 1954).

Philip Snowden, *An Autobiography*, vol. II (1934).

Eugen Spier, *Focus: A Footnote to the History of the Thirties* (1963).

Lord Templewood (Sir Samuel Hoare), *Nine Troubled Years* (1954).

Lord Winterton, *Orders of the Day* (1953).

Secondary Sources

Paul Addison, *The Road to 1945: British Politics and the Second World War* (1975).

Paul Addison, *Churchill on the Home Front 1900–1955* (1992).

Stanley Baldwin, *On England* (1926).

Stuart Ball, *Baldwin and the Conservative Party: The Crisis of 1929–31* (Yale 1988).

Michael Bentley (ed.), *Public and Private Doctrine: Essays in British History Presented to Maurice Cowling* (Cambridge 1993).

Robert Blake, *The Unknown Prime Minister: The Life and Times of Andrew Bonar Law 1858–1923* (1955).

Robert Blake, *Churchill and the Conservative Party* (Fulton, Missouri 1987).

Robert Blake and Wm. Roger Louis (eds), *Churchill* (Oxford 1993).

Carl Bridge, *Holding India to the Empire: The British Conservative Party and the 1935 Constitution* (New Delhi 1986).

P.J. Cain and A.G. Hopkins, *British Imperialism: Crisis and Deconstruction 1914–1990* (1993).

John Campbell, *F.E. Smith, First Lord Birkenhead* (1984).

David Carlton, *Anthony Eden: A Biography* (1981).

Austen Chamberlain, *Peace in our Time* (1928).

John Charmley, *Duff Cooper: The Authorised Biography* (1986).

John Charmley, *Lord Lloyd and the Decline of the British Empire* (1987).

John Charmley, *Chamberlain and the Lost Peace* (1989).

John Charmley, *Churchill: The End of Glory* (1993).

John Charmley, *A History of Conservative Politics 1900–1996* (1996).

Anne Chisholm and Michael Davie, *Beaverbrook: A Life* (1992).

Winston S. Churchill, *Lord Randolph Churchill* (1906; 1959 edn).

Winston S. Churchill, *Great Contemporaries* (1937).

Peter Clarke, *The Keynesian Revolution in the Making, 1924–1936* (Oxford 1990 edn).

Peter Clarke, *A Question of Leadership: Gladstone to Thatcher* (1992 edn).

Peter Clarke, *Hope and Glory: Britain 1900–1990* (1996).

Richard Cockett, *Twilight of Truth: Chamberlain, Appeasement and the Manipulation of the Press* (1989).

Ian Colvin, *The Chamberlain Cabinet* (1971).

Chris Cook and Gillian Peele, *The Politics of Reapprisal 1918–39* (1975).

Chris Cook and John Ramsden, *By-Elections in British Politics* (1973).

Maurice Cowling, *The Impact of Hitler: British Politics and British Policy 1933–1940* (Cambridge 1975).

Maurice Cowling, *Religion and Public Doctrine in Modern England*, vol. I (Cambridge 1980).

J.A. Cross, *Sir Samuel Hoare: A Political Biography* (1977).

N.J. Crowson, *Facing Fascism: The Conservative Party and the European Dictators 1935–1940* (1997).

David Dilks, *Neville Chamberlain*, vol. I: *Pioneering and Reform 1869–1929* (Cambridge 1984).

David Dutton, *Austen Chamberlain: Gentleman in Politics* (1985).

David Dutton, *Simon: A Political Life of Sir John Simon* (1992).

David Dutton, *Anthony Eden: A Life and Reputation* (1997).

Keith Feiling, *The Life of Neville Chamberlain* (1946).

Martin Gilbert, *Winston S. Churchill*, vol. V: *1922–39* (1976).

Martin Gilbert, *Finest Hour: Winston S. Churchill 1939–41*, vol. VI (1983).

Richard Griffiths, *Fellow-Travellers of the Right: British Enthusiasts for Nazi Germany 1933–9* (1975).

S.J. Hetherington, *Katharine Atholl 1874–1960: Against the Grain* (Aberdeen 1989).

Alistair Horne, *Harold Macmillan*, vol. I: *1894–1957* (1988).

Michael Howard, *The Continental Commitment* (1972).

H. Montgomery Hyde, *Neville Chamberlain* (1976).

H. Montgomery Hyde, *Walter Monckton* (1991).

Robert Rhodes James, *Lord Randolph Churchill* (1959).

Robert Rhodes James, *Churchill: A Study in Failure* (1970).

Robert Rhodes James, *Victor Cazalet: A Portrait* (1976).

Robert Rhodes James, *Bob Boothby: A Portrait* (1991).

Richard Lamb, *The Drift to War 1922–1939* (1989).

Charles Edward Lysaght, *Brendan Bracken* (1979).

R.T. McKenzie, *British Political Parties: The Distribution of Power within the Conservative and Labour Parties* (1955).

Iain Macleod, *Neville Chamberlain* (1961).

Harold Macmillan, *The Middle Way* (1938).

Harold Macmillan, *Winds of Change 1914–1939* (1966).

David Marquand, *Ramsay MacDonald* (1977).

Patricia Meehan, *The Unnecessary War: Whitehall and the German Resistance to Hitler* (1992).

Keith Middlemas and John Barnes, *Baldwin: A Biography* (1969).

Lord Moran, *Winston Churchill: The Struggle for Survival 1940–65* (1966).

Nicholas Mosley, *Rules of the Game: Sir Oswald and Lady Cynthia Mosley, 1896–1933* (1982).

Charles Loch Mowat, *Britain Between the Wars 1918–1940* (1955).

Williamson Murray, *The Change in the European Balance of Power 1938–9* (Princeton 1984).

Scott Newton, *Profits of Peace: The Political Economy of Anglo-German Appeasement* (Oxford 1996).

Frank Owen, *Tempestuous Journey: Lloyd George, His Life and Times* (1954).

R.A.C. Parker, *Chamberlain and Appeasement: British Policy and the Coming of the Second World War* (1993).

Henry Pelling, *Winston Churchill* (1974; 2nd edn 1989).

Urmila Phadnis, *Towards the Integration of Indian States* (1968).

Sidney Pollard, *The Development of the British Economy 1914–1990*, 4th edn (1992).

Clive Ponting, *Churchill* (1994).

Martin Pugh, *The Making of Modern British Politics 1867–1939* (Oxford 1982).

Andrew Roberts, *The Holy Fox: A Biography of Lord Halifax* (1991).

Andrew Roberts, *Eminent Churchillians* (1994).

Norman Rose, *Churchill: An Unruly Life* (1994).

B.E.V. Sabine, *British Budgets in Peace and War 1932–1945* (1970).

G.R. Searle, *Country Before Party: Coalition and the Idea of 'National Government' in Modern Britain 1885–1987* (1995).

Anthony Seldon and Stuart Ball (eds), *Conservative Century: The Conservative Party since 1900* (Oxford 1994).

Tom Stannage, *Baldwin Thwarts the Opposition: The British General Election of 1935* (1980).

A.J.P. Taylor, *English History 1914–1945* (Oxford 1965).

A.J.P. Taylor, *Beaverbrook* (1972).

A.J.P. Taylor (ed.), *The Abdication of King Edward VIII, by Lord Beaverbrook* (1966). David A. Thomas, *Churchill: The Member for Woodford* (Ilford, Essex 1995).

Neville Thompson, *The Anti-Appeasers: Conservative Opposition to Appeasement in the 1930s* (Oxford 1971).

David Walter, *The Oxford Union: Playground of Power* (1984).

Bernard Wasserstein, *Herbert Samuel* (Oxford 1992).

G.C. Webber, *The Ideology of the British Right 1918–1939* (1986).

John W. Wheeler-Bennett, *King George VI, His Life and Reign* (1958).

Martin J. Wiener, *English Culture and the Decline of the Industrial Spirit, 1850–1980* (Cambridge 1981).

Philip Williamson, *National Crisis and National Government: British Politics, the Economy and Empire 1926–1932* (Cambridge 1992).

Sir Evelyn Wrench, *Geoffrey Dawson and Our Times* (1955).

Philip Ziegler, *King Edward VIII: The Official Biography* (1990).

Articles

Paul Addison, 'The Political Beliefs of Winston Churchill', in *Transactions of the Royal Historical Society*, 5:30 (1980), 23–47.

Stuart Ball, 'The Conservative Party and the Formation of the National Government: August 1931', in *Historical Journal*, 29:1 (1986), 160–76.

Stuart Ball, 'Failure of an Opposition? The Conservative Party in Parliament 1929–31', in *Parliamentary History* (1985).

Carl Bridge, 'Churchill, Hoare, Derby and the Committee of Privileges, April to June 1934', in *Historical Journal*, 22/1 (1979), 215–27.

J.D. Fair, 'The Conservative Basis for the Formation of the National Government of 1931', in *Journal of British Studies*, 1:29 (1986).

Marion L. Kenney, 'The Role of the House of Commons in British Foreign Policy during the 1937–8 Session', in *Essays in Honor of Conyers Reed* (1953).

R.A.C. Parker, 'Economics, Rearmament and Foreign Policy: The United Kingdom before 1939 – a Preliminary Study', in *Journal of Contemporary History* (1975).

G.C. Peden, 'The Burden of Imperial Defence and the Continental Commitment Reconsidered', in *Historical Journal* (1984).

G.C. Peden, 'Sir Warren Fisher and British Rearmament against Germany', in *English Historical Review*, (January 1979), 35.

Jorgen S. Rasmussen, 'Party Discipline in War-Time: The Downfall of the Chamberlain Government', in *Journal of Politics*, 32 (1970).

James C. Robertson, 'The Hoare–Laval Plan', in *Journal of Contemporary History*, 10, 5 (July 1975), 454–5.

Gerald Studdert-Kennedy, 'The Christian Imperialism of the Die-hard Defenders of the Raj, 1929–35', in *Journal of Imperial and Commonwealth History*, 18 (1990), 342–62.

Unpublished Theses

John Malcolm McEwan, 'Unionist and Conservative Members of Parliament 1919–1939', London University Ph.D. (1959).

Barry Norris, 'The Conservative Party and the Spanish Civil War', Cambridge University M. Phil. (1997).

Graham S. Stewart, 'Winston Churchill and the Conservative Party 1929–37', Cambridge University Ph.D. (1995).

INDEX

Note. The following have been abbreviated throughout: Winston Churchill to WSC, Neville Chamberlain to NC, Prime Minister to PM, National Government to NG.